In Their Own Words

In Their Own Words

Criminals on Crime: An Anthology

PAUL CROMWELL
University of South Florida

MICHAEL L. BIRZER
Wichita State University

SIXTH EDITION

New York   Oxford

OXFORD UNIVERSITY PRESS

Oxford University Press is a department of the University of Oxford.
It furthers the University's objective of excellence in research, scholarship,
and education by publishing worldwide.

Oxford New York
Auckland   Cape Town   Dar es Salaam   Hong Kong   Karachi
Kuala Lumpur   Madrid   Melbourne   Mexico City   Nairobi
New Delhi   Shanghai   Taipei   Toronto

With offices in
Argentina   Austria   Brazil   Chile   Czech Republic   France   Greece
Guatemala   Hungary   Italy   Japan   Poland   Portugal   Singapore
South Korea   Switzerland   Thailand   Turkey   Ukraine   Vietnam

For titles covered by Section 112 of the US Higher Education
Opportunity Act, please visit www.oup.com/us/he for the latest
information about pricing and alternate formats.

Published by Oxford University Press
198 Madison Avenue, New York, NY 10016
www.oup.com

Oxford is a registered trademark of Oxford University Press

Library of Congress Cataloging-in-Publication Data
In their own words : criminals on crime : an anthology / by Paul Cromwell,
Michael L. Birzer.—Sixth Edition.
   pages cm
   ISBN 978-0-19-992005-1 (alk. paper)
 1. Criminology—Fieldwork.   2. Crime—Research.   3. Criminals—Research.
I. Cromwell, Paul F. editor of compilation.   II. Birzer, Michael L., 1960– editor of
compilation.
   HV6030.I488 2013
   364—dc23   2012033668

Printing number: 9 8 7 6 5 4 3 2 1

Printed in the United States of America
on acid-free paper

To my incredibly wonderful wife and best friend for the past 36 years.

Paul Cromwell

For my loving wife Gwynne and my wonderful son, Michael, Jr.

Michael L. Birzer

CONTENTS

PREFACE

⤴

This new edition of *In Their Own Words* includes the addition of a new co-editor. Dr. Michael Birzer, my long-time friend and colleague, has agreed to join me in compiling this and future editions. Michael is a highly skilled and respected qualitative methods professor who brings his expertise and energies to bear toward making the book a more valuable resource for students and other readers.

This anthology provides the reader with an opportunity to view the world from the perspective of criminal offenders. *In Their Own Words*, Sixth Edition, is a collection of field studies of crime and criminals derived from a long tradition of field research in criminology. In this new edition, which contains 11 new chapters, students will encounter a diverse array of criminals, including new studies of auto thieves, shoplifters, armed robbers, murderers, gang members, methamphetamine producers, and drug abusers and dealers—all of whom discuss their motives, perceptions, strategies, and rationalizations of crime. Readers will note that the Methods section of each chapter that appeared in the original has been redacted for brevity. Instead, a brief note in the Introduction to the chapter describes the study's methods and respondents. Readers are encouraged to go to the original source of the material for a fuller and more complete methodology.

METHODS OF FIELD RESEARCH

Field research is not a single research methodology. Also called *ethnography*, field research provides a way of looking at the complex contexts in which any research problem exists. Good field research results in what Glassner and Carpenter (1985) call *thick description*—access to the often conflicting and detailed views of the social world held by the subjects being studied.

According to Maxfield and Babbie (1995), field research "encompasses two different methods of obtaining data: direct observation and asking questions." *Asking questions* involves in-depth interviews (also called ethnographic interviews) with research subjects. Field study interviews are much less structured than survey research interviews. At one level, field interviews may be likened to conversations (Maxfield & Babbie, 1995). At a more structured level, researchers ask open-ended questions in which a specific response is elicited but the respondent is allowed and encouraged to explain more completely and clarify responses. The question is simply a guide that structures but does not limit the interviewee's responses.

Observation takes several forms in field research. These techniques may be categorized on a continuum according to the role played by the researcher (Gold, 1969; Maxfield & Babbie, 1995). At one degree of involvement, the researcher observes an activity or individuals without their knowledge. A researcher watching shoplifters through a one-way mirror in a department store is an example of this technique. Gold (1969) labels this method *the complete observer*.

At a more involved level of interaction, the researcher is identified as a researcher and interacts with the participants in the course of their activities but does not actually become a participant (Maxfield & Babbie, 1995). Gold (1969) identifies this technique the *observer-as-participant*.

The *participant-as-observer* (Gold, 1969) technique involves participating with the group under study while making the purpose of the research clear. Wilson Palacios and Melissa Fenwick use a version of this technique in their study of the Ecstasy club scene in southern Florida (Chapter 22of this book).

The most complete involvement of researcher with subject is the complete participant. Gold (1969, p. 33) describes this role as follows:

> The true identity and purpose of the complete participant in field research are not known to those he observes. He interacts with them as naturally as possible in whatever areas of their living interest him and are acceptable to him in situations in which he can play or learn to play requisite day-to-day roles successfully.

A number of ethical, legal, and personal risk considerations are involved in the complete participant role, and the researcher must tread carefully to avoid pitfalls. Because of these problems, complete participation is seldom possible in criminological research.

USE OF FIELD RESEARCH IN CRIMINAL JUSTICE AND CRIMINOLOGY

Field studies are particularly well suited to investigating several important issues in criminology and criminal justice. Only through field research can we observe the everyday activities of offenders: how they interact with others, how they perceive the objects and events in their everyday lives, and how they perceive the sanction threat of the criminal justice system. By understanding offenders' perspectives, decision-making processes, and motivations, field research may inform crime prevention and control strategies. Wright and Decker (1994) point out that criminal justice policymaking is predicated on assumptions about the perceptions of criminals: "The traditional policy of deterrence rests squarely on the notion that offenders are utilitarian persons who carefully weigh the potential costs and rewards of their illegal actions."

However, the studies in this collection offer strong arguments for other, perhaps equally compelling motivations for many crimes, including so-called economic crimes. Even robbery and burglary, crimes assumed to be driven almost entirely by instrumental (economic) motivations, may have expressive roots as well. Burglars report that excitement, thrills, and a "rush" often accompany the criminal act. Some burglars report having occasionally committed a burglary out of revenge or anger against the victim (see Shover and Honaker's article in Chapter 3 in this volume). By contrast, gang membership, which traditionally has been perceived as turf oriented and centered on conflict, is shown to be increasingly about money—drugs and drug sales. Thus, effective crime control strategies must take into account the various factors that drive crime. Field research that allows offenders to "speak for themselves" is ideally suited to these issues.

Field studies such as those in this book also have great value in educating criminal justice and criminology students. The field has sometimes suffered from a distance between student and subject of the study. Would anyone argue that it is possible to train a physician without contact with sick people? The essence of medical training is of course the experience of diagnosing and treating the sick. Yet, in our combined 30 years as criminal justice practitioners and administrators, and our 35 years as criminal justice and criminology educators, we have been troubled by the realization that most graduates never encounter an actual criminal during the course of their education. Some universities provide internships or practicums or arrange field trips to prisons or other correctional facilities. Despite these efforts, however, few students ever experience a "real criminal" during their education. By viewing the criminal event from the perspective of the participants, these studies can come to understand an individual's decision to engage in crime on a personal level and supplement the statistical data from other research.

In Their Own Words enriches the reader's understanding of criminal typologies, criminal decision-making processes, criminological theories, and criminal subcultures and lifestyles. The studies in this book vary in terms of their settings, the crimes being studied, and the researcher's involvement and role in the environment. In every case, however, the story is told from the perspective of, and in the words of, the offender. In each case, the researcher places the offender's words in a theoretical context and provides analyses and conclusions.

NEW TO THIS EDITION

- Section 1, "Strategies for Field Research," has been added.
- Eleven new chapters have been added covering topics including burglars, female auto thieves, shoplifters, armed robbers, lethal and sublethal violence, drugged druggists, middle-class drug dealers, barrio gangs, meth cooks, illegal steroids, and female street offenders' efforts to desist from crime.

- The number of cited studies featuring research on female offenders has been increased.
- Coverage of emerging crimes, including meth production, steroid dealing, and pharmaceutical drug addiction and use among pharmacists, has been increased.

REFERENCES

Glassner, B., & Carpenter, C. (1985). *The feasibility of an ethnographic study of property offenders: A report prepared for the National Institute of Justice.* Washington, DC: NIJ Mimeo.

Gold, R. (1969). Roles in sociological field observation. In G. J. McCall &J. L. Simmons (Eds.), *Issues in participant observation.* Reading, MA: Addison-Wesley.

Maxfield, M. G., & Babbie, E. (1995). *Research methods for criminal justice and criminology.* Belmont, CA: Wadsworth.

Wright, R. T., & Decker, S. H. (1994). *Burglars on the job: Streetlife and residential break-Ins.* Boston: Northeastern University Press.

ACKNOWLEDGMENTS

O ver the life span of this book, several colleague have contributed in important ways, not only by allowing me to use the fruits of their scholarly labors, but also by serving as consultants and advisors as I attempted to organize the materials and locate new qualitative studies. Among those individuals who have assisted me in many ways since the first edition in 1996 and who should rightly share the editorship are Neal Shover at the University of Tennessee at Knoxville, Scott Decker at Arizona State University, Richard Wright at the University of Missouri–St. Louis, Bruce Jacobs at the University of Texas–Dallas, John Heith Copes at the University of Alabama–Birmingham, Dean Dabney at Georgia State University, and Andy Hochstetler at Iowa State University. All have become valuable contributors and helpful colleagues in developing and identifying new material for the book.

It is again important to express deep appreciation for the researchers and authors of the studies that are presented here. The credit for an anthology such as this goes to these individuals. Our task was simply to select the best exemplars of contemporary field research in crime and criminal behavior and attempt to bring them together in an integrated and effective manner. We gratefully acknowledge the scholarly efforts of these researchers. It is truly their book.

In the process of preparing this new edition, we have also benefited from the numerous reviewers who commented on the selections, the organization and integration of materials, and the general worth of the project. Special appreciation is extended to Sarah Becker, Louisiana State University; Kathryn A. Branch, University of Tampa; Arina Gertseva, Washington State University; Jessie L. Krienert, Illinois State University; Lois Presser, University of Tennessee; and Karen Weiss, West Virginia University.

Of special note in developing the Sixth Edition, we must acknowledge the constant attention and assistance from our editor at Oxford, Sarah Calabi, and her assistant, Richard Beck. We must also express our continued appreciation to Jimmie Cromwell, who, with Oxford's Richard Beck, labored over the complex and newly expensive process of gaining reprint permissions.

ABOUT THE CONTRIBUTORS

Patricia Adler is Professor of Sociology at the University of Colorado.

Kristin L. Anderson is Professor of Sociology at Western Washington University.

Jana S. Benson is a doctoral student at Arizona State University.

Michael L. Benson is Professor of Criminal Justice at the University of Cincinnati.

Fiona Brookman is Head of Criminology at the University of Glamorgan.

John J. Brent is a doctoral student at the University of Delaware.

Charles R. Bussard is employed by the Kentucky Department of Juvenile Justice.

Michael Cherbonneau is a doctoral candidate and lecturer at the University of Missouri–St. Louis.

Glenn S. Coffey is Assistant Professor at the L. Douglas Wilder School of Public Affairs at Virginia Commonwealth University.

Heith Copes is Associate Professor of Criminology and Criminal Justice at the University of Alabama at Birmingham.

Paul Cromwell is Professor of Criminal Justice at the University of South Florida.

Dean Dabney is Associate Professor of Criminal Justice at Georgia State University.

Scott H. Decker is Chairperson and Foundation Professor of Criminal Justice at Arizona State University.

Melissa E. Fenwick is Instructor of Criminal Justice at Western Connecticut State University.

Dick Hobbs is Head and Professor of Sociology at the London School of Economics.

Andy Hochstetler is Associate Professor of Sociology at Iowa State University.

Richard Hollinger is Professor of Criminology at the University of Florida.

David Honaker is deceased. He was formerly employed by the University of Tennessee at Knoxville.

Bruce A. Jacobs is Professor of Crime and Justice Studies in the School of Economic, Political, and Policy Sciences at the University of Texas at Dallas.

Robert Jenkot is Associate Professor at Coastal Carolina University.

Peter B. Kraska is Professor of Criminal Justice at Eastern Kentucky University.

Jody Miller is Professor of Criminal Justice and Criminology at Rutgers University.

Christopher Mullins is Associate Professor of Criminology and Criminal Justice at Southern Illinois University at Carbondale.

James N. Olson is Professor of Psychology at the University of Texas–Permian Basin.

Wilson R. Palacios is Associate Professor of Criminology at the University of South Florida.

Mark R. Pogrebin is Professor of Criminal Justice at the University of Colorado at Denver.

Edwardo L. Portillos is Assistant Professor of Sociology at the University of Colorado, Colorado Springs.

Kim Romenesko is a Senior Administrative Specialist at the University of Wisconsin–Milwaukee.

Neal Shover is Professor Emeritus of Sociology at the University of Tennessee–Knoxville.

Paul B. Stretesky is Associate Professor of Sociology at Colorado State University.

Quint Thurman is Professor of Criminal Justice and Provost and Vice President of Academic Affairs at Sul Ross State University in Alpine texas.

Debra Umberson is Professor of Sociology at the University of Texas at Austin.

Lynne Vieraitis is Associate Professor of Crime and Justice Studies in the School of Economic, Political, and Policy Sciences at the University of Texas at Dallas.

Richard T. Wright is Curators Professor in the Department of Criminology and Criminal Justice at the University of Missouri–St. Louis.

Marjorie Zatz is Professor of Justice and Social Inquiry in the School of Social Transformation at the University of Arizona.

SECTION I

꙳

Doing Fieldwork with Offenders

Ethnographic fieldwork with active offenders presents a host of challenges. These challenges include but are not limited to developing gatekeepers or key informants, gaining access to research informants, establishing rapport, and identifying personal safety risks to the researcher(s). In spite of these challenges, criminological ethnographies have the potential to provide rich and informative data. Ethnographic accounts of active offenders can provide a great deal of information about offenders themselves, as well as backstage accounts of their criminal activities that we would never be able to attain through other methods. Consequently, ethnographic data can be used to develop or enhance theory, and to help shape crime policy.

In the preface of this book, we discuss the issue of distance between students and the object(s) of their study. Most criminology or criminal justice students (and many of their professors) never come into contact with a criminal, except perhaps during a jail or prison tour. One could hardly image a physician going through training without ever making contact with a sick person. Doesn't it make sense that researchers and students of crime and criminals would have contact with the very persons they study?

In this section, we present two approaches to ethnographic research. One position argues that we should focus on studying the criminal in his or her natural environment—the streets. The leading proponent of this position has been Ned Polsky (1967, pp. 122–123), who states:

> We are always going to be in this spot—always slowly fitting together a jigsaw puzzle that is decades out of date and never even knowing if we have all the pieces, or the right pieces—unless we change our research methods.
>
> This means—there is no getting away from it—the study of career criminals *au naturel*, in the field, the study of such criminals as they normally go about their work and play, the study of "uncaught" criminals and the study of others who in the past have been caught but are *not* caught at the time you study them.

The first article in this section, Bruce A. Jacobs' "Researching Crack Dealers: Dilemmas and Contradictions," repeats Polsky's call for criminologists to reach beyond the comfort of their office and the convenience of interviewing offenders in contrived situations and get into the field to work with criminals in their true environment. It is only in the field that the criminologist will see firsthand what these people do and how they do it.

Jacobs takes us on a journey into the world of street-level crack dealers. This article serves as a sobering reminder of the dangers of such studies, recounting Jacobs' own experience of being held and robbed at gunpoint by one of his participants. The article advances the thesis that "the importance of a strong indigenous tie to the research setting at the beginning of field relations...cannot be overstated." Jacobs informs us of the importance of balancing the conflicting agendas of the ethnographic audience, which can range from offenders to social control agents such as the police. Maintaining balance and safety is important. But how does the field researcher effectively maintain balance while uncovering the rich context of backstage criminology? Jacobs' article sheds light on this very question, which hopefully will inform other researchers in similar field situations.

Maintaining balance requires that researchers remain aware of the consequences that can evolve from their fieldwork and create serious problems as the study progresses. These consequences include problems from not only the offenders under study, but also the police. The very nature of criminological field research will in some cases attract police attention and scrutiny. Many researchers have had to negotiate with the police as their field research evolves. There have been numerous instances in which researchers have been arrested or harassed by the police while collecting data in the field (Humphreys, 1970; Leo, 1995; Scarce, 1994). As Jacobs' study illuminates, as interaction with field participants increases, a researcher is increasingly confronted with the need to compromise (Georges & Jones, 1980). In the end, Jacobs' article provides crucial information on how researchers can maintain balance in collecting field data while effectively negotiating social distance.

In Chapter 2, Heith Copes and Andy Hochstetler provide an alternative approach to the study of criminals in their natural environment. They argue that criminals can and do provide accurate accounts of their behavior when interviewed in prison and investigate why inmates are willing to participate in prison research. Some criminologists argue that when interviews are conducted in prison and jail environments, offenders provide only the information that the criminologist wants to hear, which may result in exaggerated accounts of their criminality. However, Copes and Hochstetler point out that offenders behind bars have offered open and frank accounts of their lives and crimes during interviews. Because researchers usually do not directly observe the criminal event, data about this event depend on the offender's ability to reflectively discern and communicate aspects of his or her offending. Thus, in the interview, the researcher becomes the data collection instrument, facilitating, guiding, and interpreting the criminological construction of the criminal event as told by the inmate.

It is hard to make an argument against direct engagement with those offenders who can provide reflexive descriptions of their criminal experiences and how they make sense of those experiences. However, what would make an offender want to talk to a researcher? More specifically, Copes and Hochstetler ask, "What would make someone who has been incarcerated for behavior that society has defined as immoral and illegal disregard the potential risks and inconveniences to sit down and openly discuss their lives and misdeeds?" In their study, they asked this question of 73 individuals incarcerated in one of two medium-security prisons in Alabama and Louisiana. Their research informs us that incarcerated inmates participate in prison interviews for numerous reasons. These include the desire to satisfy immediate material needs, such as lack of money ($20 goes a long way in prison), and even the altruistic desire to help out a trusted confederate. Inmates also participate to fulfill emotional and psychological needs, and to give back to others.

An interesting centerpiece of this article that is particularly relevant for qualitative researchers is the discussion of the study's implications for institutional review boards (IRBs). If you have done ethnographic work or used another qualitative approach in your studies of offenders, you have likely experienced the huge challenge of getting past the IRB in order to do your research. Getting research approved by an IRB can be an arduous, frustrating process. Copes and Hochstetler offer some advice here. They argue that crafting the language of the IRB application to demonstrate the direct benefits of having inmates tell their stories may go a long way toward ensuring a smoother approval process. Copes and Hochstetler argue that the process of telling their stories and reflecting on their crimes can have emotional impacts on inmates, which can potentially culminate in therapeutic effects. The article presents the idea that understanding how the research process can benefit those directly involved can make the IRB process much easier to negotiate, allowing researchers to go about their important work of studying and making sense of the meaning that offenders ascribe to their criminality. In all, the article represents an important contribution to our understanding of the motivations that underlie an offender's willingness to talk frankly and honestly about their crimes with researchers.

REFERENCES

Georges, R. A., & Jones, M.O. (1980). *People studying people: The human element in fieldwork*. Berkeley: University of California Press.

Humphreys, L. (1970). *Tearoom trade: Impersonal sex in public places*. New York: Aldine.

Leo, R. A. (1995). Trial and tribulation: Courts, ethnography, and the need for evidentiary privilege for academic researchers. *American Sociologist, 26*, 86–112.

Polsky, N. (1967). *Hustlers, beats, and others*. New Brunswick: Aldine.

Scarce, R. (1994). (NO) trial (But) tribulations: When courts and ethnography conflict. *Journal of Contemporary Ethnography, 23*, 123–149.

CHAPTER 1

Researching Crack Dealers: Dilemmas and Contradictions

Bruce A. Jacobs

Jacobs discusses the difficulties and dangers associated with studying criminals in the field

"Yo, Bruce, come on down the set [neighborhood]. Meet where we usually do," Luther said, and hung up the phone. A trusted contact for an ongoing study of street-level crack dealers and a crack dealer himself, I had no reason to question him. "Just another interview," I thought. Notebooks and file folders in hand, I went to the bank, withdrew $50 for subject payments, and drove 15 minutes to the dope set I was coming to know so well.

Luther flagged me down as I turned the corner. The 17-year-old high school drop-out opened the door and jumped in. "Swerve over there." He pointed to a parking space behind the dilapidated three-story apartment building he called home. "Stop the car—turn it off." Nothing out of the ordinary; over the previous three months, we often would sit and talk for a while before actually going to an interview. This time, though, there was an urgency in his voice I should have detected but did not. He produced a pistol from under a baggy white T-shirt. "Gimme all your fuckin' money or I'll blow your motherfuckin' head off!"

"What the fuck's your problem?" I said, astonished that someone I trusted had suddenly turned on me. The gun was large, a six-shooter, probably a long-barrel .45. It was ugly and old looking. Most of its chrome had been scratched off. Its black handle was pockmarked from years of abuse. Why was he doing this? How did I get myself into this situation? It was the kind of thing you hear about on the evening news but don't expect to confront, even though I knew studying active offenders risked such a possibility.

Source: Adapted from Jacobs, B. A. (1998). Researching crack dealers: Dilemmas and contradictions. In J. Ferrell & M. S. Hamm (Eds.), *Ethnography at the edge: Crime, deviance and field research* (160–177). Boston: Northeastern University Press.

I frantically pondered a course of action as Luther's tone became more and more hostile. He was sweating. "Just calm down, Luther, just calm down—everything's cool," I trembled. "Don't shoot—I'll give you what you want." "Gimme all your fuckin' money!" he repeated. "I ain't fuckin' around—I'll waste you right here!" I reached in my left-hand pocket for the $50 and handed it over. As I did so, I cupped my right hand precariously an inch from the muzzle of his gun, which was pointing directly into my abdomen. I can survive a gunshot, I thought to myself, as long as I slow the bullet down. He snatched the five crisp $10 bills and made a quick search of the vehicle's storage areas to see if I was holding out. "OK," he said, satisfied there were no more funds. "Now turn your head around." I gazed at him inquisitively. "Turn your motherfuckin' head around!" For all I knew, he was going to shoot and run; his right hand was poised on the door handle, his left on the trigger. "Just take your money, man, I'm not gonna do anything." "Turn the fuck around!" he snapped. "OK," I implored, "I won't look, just lemme put my hand over my eyes." I left small openings between my fingers to see what he was really going to do. If he were truly going to fire, which he appeared to be intent on doing—the gun was being raised from the down-low position in which it had been during the entire encounter to right below head level—I would smack the gun upward, jump out of the car, and run a half block to the relative safety of a commercial street.

As I pondered escape routes, he jammed the gun into his pants as quickly as he had drawn it, flung open the door, and disappeared behind the tenements. I hit the ignition and drove slowly and methodically from the scene, grateful to have escaped injury, but awestruck by his brazen violation of trust. All I could do was look back and wonder why.

If this were the end of the story, things would have normalized, I would have learned a lesson about field research, and I would have gone about my business. But Luther was not through. Over the next six weeks, he called my apartment five to 10 times a day, five days a week, harassing, taunting, irritating, baiting me. Perhaps twice over that six-week period, I actually picked up the phone—only to find out it was him and hang up. Luther would call right back and let the phone ring incessantly, knowing I was there and letting the answering machine do the dirty work. On several occasions, it became so bad that I had to disconnect the line and leave the apartment for several hours.

I'd arrive home to see the answering machine lit up with messages. "I can smell the mousse in your hair—huh, huh, huh," his sinister laugh echoing through the apartment. "I know you're there, pick it up." More often than not, I would hear annoying dial tones. One message, however, caught my undivided attention: "897 Longacre—huh, huh, huh," he laughed as I heard him flipping through the phone book pages and identifying my address. "We'll [he and his homeboys] be over tomorrow." I didn't sleep well that night or for the next six weeks.

What was I to do—report the robbery, and go to court and testify to stop what had become tele-stalking? Some researchers contend that when crimes against fieldworkers occur, staff are to "report them to the police to indicate that such violations will have consequences" (Williams et al., 1992, p. 365). I did not feel I had this option. Calling the authorities, no matter how much I wanted to, not only would have endangered future research with Luther's set and those connected to it, but would also have risked retaliation—because Luther's homies knew where I lived and worked.

So I called the phone company and got caller ID, call return, and call block. These devices succeeded in providing his phone number and residence name, which I used to trace his actual address, but I could still do nothing to stop him. Changing my number was the last thing I wanted to do, because those who smell fear often attack. As other researchers have noted, concern about "violence may cause ethnographers to appear afraid or react inappropriately to common street situations and dangers....Fearful behavior is easily inferred by violent persons" and may often lead to violence itself (Williams et al., 1992, p. 350). Thus, Berk and Adams stress the importance of maintaining one's cool when threatened: "The investigator will be constantly watched and tested by the very people he is studying. This is especially true [with] delinquents who...value poise in the face of danger" (Berk & Adams, 1970, p. 110). Danger, it must be remembered, is "inherent" in fieldwork with active offenders, "if for no other reason than there is always the possibility of dangerous cultural misunderstandings arising between researchers and subjects" (Sluka, 1990, p. 114). This is especially true of research among active street-corner crack sellers, who routinely use violence or threats of violence to gain complicity (Williams et al., 1992, p. 347).

After enduring six weeks of this postrobbery harassment, and with no end in sight, I had to do something. I called the police and told them the story. An officer came out and listened to messages I had saved. As he listened, the telephone rang, and Luther's number displayed on the caller ID. "Do you want me to talk to him?" the officer asked sternly. "No," I replied, feeling more confident with a cop three feet away. "Lemme see if I can work things out." I picked up the phone and started talking.

"What do you want?"

"Why do you keep hangin' up on me? All I want is to talk."

"What do you expect me to do, *like* you? [sardonically, on the verge of losing it]. You fuckin' robbed me and I trusted you and now you call me and leave these fuckin' messages and you want me to *talk* to you [incredulous]?"

"I only did that 'cause you fucked me over. I only ganked [robbed] you 'cause you *fucked me*."

"What are you talking about?"

He proceeded to explain that without him, none of the 40 interviews I obtained would have been possible. True, Luther was the first field contact to believe that I was a researcher, not a cop. He was my first respondent, and he was responsible for starting a snowball of referrals on his word that I was "cool" (Biernacki & Waldorf, 1981). But after he could no longer provide referrals, I moved on, using his contacts to find new ones and eliminating him from the chain. My newfound independence was inexplicable to him and a slap in the face. He wanted vengeance; the robbery and taunting were exactly that (see Garfinckel, 1956).

ETHNOGRAPHY AND SOCIAL DISTANCE?

Such are the risks ethnographers take when studying dangerous, unstable offenders. Although "robbery, burglary, and theft from field staff are uncommon, [they] do occur. In fact, many crack distributors are frequent and proficient robbers, burglars, and thieves" (Williams et al., 1992, p. 364). Not so ironically, someone I had trusted and considered a "protector" (Williams et al., 1992, p. 350) had become someone to be protected from. Such flip-flops are entirely possible in the world of active offenders, who themselves often admit an inability to control or understand their behavior.

All of this merely underscores the changeable, unpredictable nature of fieldwork relations, especially with active offenders. Johnson notes that "it is incumbent on the investigator to assess the influences of these changes" (1983, p. 205). The important point is for researchers to put themselves in a position where they can do this. Unfortunately, the very nature of criminological fieldwork may work against this.

Much of the problem revolves around the dilemma between social distance and immersion in fieldwork, and the difficulty researchers have in resolving it. The notion of "social distance" is thought to be in some ways foreign to the ethnographic enterprise. Wolff, for example, contends that successful fieldwork inevitably requires surrender—psychological, social, and otherwise—to the setting, culture, and respondents one is studying. It requires "total involvement, suspension of received notions, pertinence of everything, identification, and risk of being hurt" (1964, p. 237). Ethnographers are advised to immerse themselves in the native scene (Lowies, 1937, p. 232), to become a member of what they are studying (Powdermaker, 1966, p. 19). They are told to become an actual physical and moral part of the setting (Evans-Pritchard, 1964, pp. 77–79). As Berk and Adams put it, "The greater the social distance between the participant observer and the subjects, the greater the difficulty in establishing and maintaining rapport" (1970, p. 103).

Building rapport with active offenders typically becomes more difficult, though, as the "deviantness" of the population one studies increases (Berk & Adams 1970). With any offender population, trying to become "one of them" too quickly can be downright harmful. Some contend that the most egregious error a fieldworker can make is to assume that the fieldworker can gain the immediate favor of his or her hosts by telling them that he or she wants to "'become one of them' or by implying, by word or act, that the fact that they tolerate his [or her] presence means that he [or she] is one of them" (Wax, 1983, p. 197. Similarly, Polsky warns:

> You damned well better not pretend to be "one of them," because they will test this claim out and one of two things will happen. Either the researcher will get drawn into participating in actions one would otherwise not engage in, or the researcher could be exposed as a result of not doing so, the latter having perhaps even greater negative repercussions. (1967, p. 124)

The more attached the researcher gets too early in the process, the more vulnerable she or he may be to exploitation. The researcher is still a researcher, no matter how close the researcher thinks she or he is getting. Subjects know this and may also know there will be few if any serious repercussions if they try to pull something, especially at the beginning of research when the fieldworker tends to be the most desperate for acceptance. Problems are only compounded by the fact that researchers tend to be far more streetwise by the end of fieldwork than they are at the beginning. Perhaps the least important time to be streetwise is at the end; both the number and seriousness of threats tend to decline with time. Where threats are often highest—at the beginning, when the researcher may be labeled a narc, a spy, or simply a suspicious character—the researcher may also be least capable of handling them. This only makes the threats that do materialize more threatening.

Researchers who are victimized at this early stage may often be barred from reporting it; doing so threatens to breach promises of confidentiality and anonymity made to subjects. The practical matter of being labeled a narc who "sold someone out" is a separate issue and potentially more problematic: snitching violates a sacred norm of street etiquette, even if the person being snitched on is in the wrong. At best, snitching will terminate future chains of respondents. At worst, it will label the researcher a "rat" and subject him or her to street justice. Both outcomes are of course undesirable and will likely bring an end to one's research.

Being immersed while remaining to some degree objective is the key. Some researchers stress the importance of using "interactional devices and strategies that allow the fieldworker to stay on the edges of unfolding social scenes rather than being drawn into their midst as a central actor" (Emerson, 1983, p. 179). Others recommend engaging in a paradoxical and "peculiar combination of engrossment and distance" (Karp & Kendall, 1982, p. 261). Like the Simmelian stranger, researchers are told to be familiar yet not too familiar, involved yet not too involved, all the while making the balance seem natural (Simmel, 1908). Some modicum of social distance is thus critical to the ethnographic enterprise—"as a corrective to bias and overrapport brought on by too strong an identification with those studied" (Emerson, 1983, p. 179).

In some sense, then, social distance between the researcher and the active offenders she or he studies can be beneficial. As Wright and Decker observe, "The secrecy inherent in criminal work means that offenders have few opportunities to discuss their activities with anyone besides associates, a matter which many find frustrating" (1994, p. 26). By definition, criminal respondents will often have "certain knowledge and skills that the researcher does not have" (Berk & Adams, 1970, p. 107). This asymmetry may empower them to open up or to open up sooner than they otherwise would. Offenders may enjoy speaking about their criminal experiences with someone who is "straight." Perhaps it is a satisfaction gained from teaching someone supposedly smarter than they are, at least in terms of academic degrees. The fact that respondents may see something in the research that benefits them, or an opportunity to correct faulty impressions of what it is they actually do (see Polsky, 1967), only facilitates these dynamics.

All of it may come down to dramaturgy. Yet, the very nature of criminological fieldwork dictates that the researcher either can't or won't "act" in certain ways at certain times. Acting inappropriately can compromise the research itself, the field-worker's ability to remain in the setting, or the ability to remain there safely. The moral and practical conundrum between social distance, immersion, and "partici-pant" observation in criminological fieldwork may, in many ways, be unresolvable.

My failure to manage the distance–immersion dialectic with Luther appeared to have more to do with a practical shortfall in managing informant relations—a myopia if you will—than with going native. Clearly, I had lost objectivity in the process of "handling" Luther. Whether this was a function of over-immersion is open to question, but it undoubtedly played some role. Whether it was avoidable is also open to question, particularly when one considers the practical and method-ological paradoxes involved in fieldwork with active offenders. Although myopic (mis)management led to my exploitation by Luther, without putting myself in such a position, I would never have been able to collect the data I did. In many ways, the "shortfall" was necessary and, at some level, advantageous.

The bottom line is that no matter how deft the fieldworker is at managing relations, he or she ultimately never gains total control. Criminological fieldwork-ers exist in a dependent relationship with their subjects (Manning, 1972). This makes one wonder who is indeed the "subject" and what he or she can be "subject to" at any given moment. Some contend that the hierarchical relationship between interviewer and subject in social research is "morally indefensible" (Oakley, 1981, p. 41) and should be thrown out. Perhaps the hierarchy may be jettisoned as a mat-ter of course, by the very nature of the fieldworker–active offender relationship. Luther's actions toward me stand as an exemplary case.[2]

STUDYING ACTIVE OFFENDERS

Studying active drug dealers is problematic precisely because their activity is crim-inal. Active offenders are generally "hard to locate because they find it necessary to lead clandestine lives. Once located, they are reluctant, for similar reasons, to give accurate and truthful information about themselves" (Irwin, 1972, p. 117). "Outsiders" are often perceived as narcs seeking to obtain damaging evidence for juridical purposes (see Goode, 1971). Indeed, the most common suspicion that subjects have about fieldworkers is that they are spies of some sort. As Sluka notes, "It is difficult to find an [ethnographer] who has done fieldwork who has not encountered this suspicion" (1990, p. 115).

Collecting data from drug dealers, particularly from active ones, is likely to be difficult and dangerous unless one can construct friendships within a dealing community (see Adler, 1985). Because of this difficulty, some researchers target institutional settings (Scully, 1990). Such settings afford the chance of obtaining data without the risk of physical harm associated with "street" interviews (Agar, 1973). Unfortunately, collecting valid and reliable data in such settings may not be entirely possible, as criminologists have "long suspected that offenders do not behave naturally" in them (Wright & Decker, 1994, p. 5). Sutherland and Cressey argue that "those who have had intimate contacts with criminals 'in the open' know that criminals are not 'natural' in police stations, courts, and prisons and that they must be studied in their everyday life outside of institutions if they are to be understood" (1970, p. 68). Polsky is more emphatic, commenting,

> We can no longer afford the convenient fiction that in studying criminals in their natural habitat, we...discover nothing really important that [cannot] be discovered from criminals behind bars. What is true for studying the gorilla of zoology is likely to be even truer for studying the gorilla of criminology. (1967, p. 123)

There are fundamental qualitative differences between the two types of offenders. Institutionalized drug dealers, for example, may represent those not sophisticated or skilled enough to prevent apprehension, or those who simply do not care about getting caught and who sell to anyone with money. Studies of incarcerated offenders are thus open to the charge of being based on "unsuccessful criminals, on the supposition that successful criminals are not apprehended or are at least able to avoid incarceration." This weakness is "the most central bogeyman in the criminologist's demonology" (McCall, 1978, p. 27).

Knowing this, I entered the field and began frequenting a district near a major university that is both prestigious and expensive, yet which borders a dilapidated neighborhood with a concentrated African American population and heavy crack sales. A lively commercial district, with restaurants, quaint cafes, bars, theaters, and stores, splits the two. The area is known for racial and ethnic diversity, making it relatively easy for most anyone to blend in. Over a nine-month period, I frequented the area and made myself familiar to the regular crowd of hangers-out in the dividing commercial district. Some of these individuals were marginally homeless and spent entire days in the district smoking, drinking, playing music, and begging. Although not crack dealers themselves, they knew who the dealers were and where they worked. After gaining their trust, I was shown the dealers' congregation spots and quickly took to the area.

At first, I would simply walk by, not explicitly acknowledging that anything was going on. Sometimes I would be escorted by one of the "vagabonds," but most of the time I went alone. My objective was simply to let dealers see me. Over the days and weeks, I walked or drove through slowly to gain recognition, trying to capitalize on what Goffman has called second seeings: "Under some circumstances if he and they see each other seeing each other, they can use this fact as an excuse for an acquaintanceship greeting upon next seeing" (1971, p. 323). Unfortunately, this did not go as easily as Goffman suggests, as dealers openly yelled "SCAT!"—a term for the police undercover unit—at me.[3] Jump-starting participation was clearly the toughest part of the research because dealers suspected I was the police. Ironically, it was the police who gave me my biggest credibility boost.

POLICE AND CREDIBILITY

Ferrell notes that "a researcher's strict conformity to legal codes can be reconceptualized as less a sign of professional success than a possible portent of methodological failure.... A willingness to break the law," by contrast, "[opens] a variety of methodological possibilities" (Ferrell & Hamm, 1998) , p.26

Hanging with offenders on street corners, driving them around in my car, and visiting their homes must have been a curious sight. My appearance is somewhat akin to that of a college student. Shorts, T-shirts, cross-trainers, and ball caps with rounded brims, "just like SCAT wear 'em" (as one respondent put it), make up my typical attire. Further, I am white, clean-cut, and affect a middle-class appearance, traits the relatively poor, African American respondents associated with the police. These traits appeared to make them even more leery that I was SCAT, or that I worked for SCAT in some capacity.

To offenders who hadn't gotten to know me well, or to those waiting to pass judgment, I was on a deep-cover assignment designed to unearth their secrets and put them in jail. To cops on the beat, I was just another college boy driving down to crackville with a user in tow to buy for me. Such relations are commonplace in the street-level drug scene and have generalized subcultural currency: users serve as go-betweens and funnel unfamiliar customers to dealers for a finder's fee, usually in drugs and without the customer's consent, but generally with his or her tacit permission. When cops see a relatively nicely dressed, clean-shaven white boy driving a late-model car (with out-of-state plates, I might add) and a black street person in the passenger seat, they lick their chops.

Several police stops of me in a one-month period lent some credibility to this proposition. I had not obtained, as Wright and Decker had, a "prior agreement with the police" (1994, p. 28) whereby the police knew what I was doing and pledged not to interfere. I chose not to; the last thing I wanted was to let police know what I was doing. As Polsky explains:

> Most of the danger for the fieldworker comes not from the cannibals and head-hunters but from the colonial officials. The criminologist studying uncaught criminals in the open finds sooner or later that law enforcers try to put him on the spot—because, unless he is a complete fool, he uncovers information that law enforcers would like to know. (1967, p. 147)

Because my grant was not a federal one, I could not protect the identity of my respondents with a certificate of confidentiality (which theoretically bars police from obtaining data as it pertains to one's subjects). My work was undercover in a sense and eminently discreditable. However, contrary to admonitions by some to avoid contact with the police while doing research with dangerous populations (see Sluka, 1990), my run-ins with police turned out to be the most essential tool for establishing my credibility.

My first run-in came two weeks after making initial contact with offenders. I was driving Luther through a crack-filled neighborhood—a neighborhood which also happened to have the highest murder rate in a city which itself had the fourth-highest murder rate in the nation (Federal Bureau of Investigation, 1995). We were approaching a group of 10 mid-teen youths and were about to stop when a St. Louis city patrol car pulled behind. Should I stop, as I planned on doing, and get out and talk with these youths (some of whom Luther marginally knew), or would that place them in imminent danger of arrest? Or should I continue on as if nothing was really going on, even though I had been driving stop and go, under 10 miles an hour, prior to and during the now slow-speed pursuit? I opted for the latter, accelerating slowly in a vain attempt to reassert a "normal appearance" (Goffman, 1963).

Sirens went on. I pulled over and reassured Luther there was nothing to worry about since neither of us had contraband (I hoped). As officers approached, I thought about what to tell them. Should I say I was a university professor doing field research on crack dealers (a part I clearly didn't look), lie, or say nothing at all? "Whatcha doin' down here?" one of the officers snapped. "Exit the vehicle, intertwine your fingers behind your heads, and kneel with your ankles crossed," he commanded. The searing June sidewalk was not conducive to clear thinking, but I rattled something off: "We used to work together at _____. I waited tables, he bussed, and we been friends since. I'm a sociology major up at _____ and he said he'd show me around the neighborhood sometime. Here I am." "Yeah right," the cop snapped again while searching for the crack he thought we already had purchased. Three other police cars arrived, as the cop baited Luther and me as to how we really knew each other, what each other's real names were (which neither of us knew at the time), and what we were doing here. Dissatisfied with my answers, a sergeant took over, lecturing me on the evils of crack and how it would destroy a life others in this very neighborhood wished they had. I found no fault with the argument, listened attentively, and said nothing. After a final strip search in the late afternoon sun revealed nothing, they said I was lucky, vowed to take me in if I ever showed my face again, and let us go.

On a second occasion, Luther and his homie Frisco were in my car when we pulled up to a local liquor store. The two became nervous upon seeing two suits in a "tec" (detective) car parked at the phone booth. I told Luther and Frisco to wait, and I went into the store. As I exited, the two men approached and showed their badges. "What you doin' with these guys—do you know 'em?" "Yes," I said, deciding to tell them who I really was and what I was doing. "Mind if we search your car?" one asked. "No problem," I replied. "Go right ahead." As one searched my car (for crack, guns, or whatever else he thought he'd find), his partner cuffed both Luther and Frisco and ran warrants. As I soon learned, both detectives knew the two as repeat violent offenders with long rap sheets. They took Frisco in on an outstanding warrant and let Luther go with me. "I respect what you're doing," the searching officer said as he finished and approached, "but you don't know who you're dealing with. These guys are no good." I told him thanks and promptly left with Luther, feeling remorseful about Frisco being taken in only because he was with me.

On a third occasion, I was sitting on my car making small talk with four or five dealers when a patrol car rolled by. The officers inside gave a stern look and told us to break it up. "All right," I said, not going anywhere. We continued to talk for a few minutes when the officers, clearly agitated, rolled by again and demanded in no uncertain terms, "Break it up and we mean now." I hopped in my car, drove four or five blocks, made a left, and heard sirens. "Here we go again." This time, I was not nearly as nervous as I had been on the other occasions, ready to dispense my professor line, show my consent forms and faculty ID, and see their shocked reaction. "Get out of the car and put your hands on the trunk," the driver predictably ordered as I began my explanation. They searched me anyway, perhaps thinking it was just another mendacious story, but I kept conversing in a relaxed, erudite tone. Cops are known to have perceptual shorthands to render quick and accurate typifications of those with whom they're interacting (Van Maanen, 1978), and I could tell my conversational style was creating a good impression. I told them that I was doing interviews, that I was paying respondents for their time, and that the research was part of a university grant designed to better understand the everyday lives of urban youth. This was, of course, specious. The study's true purpose was to identify how crack dealers avoid arrest, something I dared not admit, for obvious reasons. "You can do what you want," one of them said, satisfied after a thorough search revealed no contraband, "but if I were you, I'd be real careful. You don't want to mess around with these punks." His words rang all too true several weeks later when Luther pointed the gun at my abdomen.

I did not realize it at the time, but my treatment by police was absolutely essential to my research. Police provided the "vital test" (Goffman, 1974) I desperately needed to pass if my study were to be successful. The differential enforcement practices of these police officers (and many others around the country)—in which young, minority males are singled out as "symbolic assailants" and "suspicious characters" deserving of attention (see Skolnick, 1980)—benefited *me* immensely. Police detained *me* because I was with "them." Driving alone in these same areas at the same time, though suspicious, would not likely have attracted nearly as much attention. I was "guilty by association" and "deserving" of the scrutiny young black males in many urban locales receive consistently. For my research, at least, this differential enforcement was anything but negative.

As Douglas (1972) notes, it is often necessary for researchers to convince offenders they are studying that the researchers do not represent the authorities. Sluka adds that subjects "are going to define whose side they think you are on. They will act towards you on the basis of this definition, regardless of your professions" (1990, p. 123). Words may be futile in convincing offenders who or what one really is. Ultimately, "actions speak louder than words.... The researcher will have to demonstrate by...actions that he is on the side of the deviants, or at least, not on the side of the officials" (Douglas, 1972, p. 12). The police had treated me like just another user, and had done so with offenders present. This treatment provided the "actions" for me, the picture that spoke a thousand words.

Offenders' accounts of my treatment spread rapidly through the grapevine, solidifying my credibility for the remainder of the project and setting up the snowball sampling procedure I would use to recruit additional respondents. Without the actions of *police* I may not have been accepted by *offenders* as readily as I was or, perhaps, never accepted at all. A skillful researcher can use the police—indirectly and without their knowledge or, as in my case, without even the researcher's own intent—to demonstrate to offenders that the researcher is indeed legitimate and not an undercover police officer. Often thought to be a critical barrier to entry, the police may be the key to access. Of course, undercover officers themselves can manipulate this very dynamic to gain credibility with those they target—something savvy law enforcement administrators may exploit by setting up fake arrests in plain view. Such tactics may make a researcher's identity even more precarious; in my case, though, this did not occur.

Why police never attempted to confiscate my notes during these pull-overs I'll never know. Perhaps it was because the notes appeared to be chicken scratch and were indecipherable by anyone but me. Perhaps it was because my notes didn't reveal anything the cops did not already know, or at least thought they knew. Regardless, the law is clearly against ethnographers, who can be held in contempt and sent to jail for protecting sources and withholding information (Soloway & Walters, 1977, pp. 175–176). As Carey points out, "There is no privileged relationship between the…researcher and his subject similar to that enjoyed by the lawyer and client or psychiatrist and patient" (1972, p. 77). This, of course, says nothing about issues of guilty knowledge or guilty observation (Adler, 1985, p. 24). Being aware of dealing operations and watching transactions take place makes one an accessory to their commission, a felony whether one participates or not. Fieldworkers are co-conspirators by definition, no matter their motive or intent. As Polsky concludes, "If one is effectively to study adult criminals in their natural settings, he must make the moral decision that in some ways he will break the law himself" (1967, pp. 133–134).

RESEARCHING ACTIVE CRACK SELLERS: IN PERSPECTIVE

By definition, criminological fieldworkers regularly intrude into the lives of individuals engaged in felonies—felonies for which these individuals can receive hard time. The more illegal the behavior, the more offenders as research subjects have to lose if found out. Obviously, this makes it tougher—and more risky—for researchers to gain access.

Street-level crack selling is thus a paradox of sorts: there is perhaps no other behavior so openly visible and so negatively sanctioned by law as crack selling. It must be this way for sellers to be available to their customers. This is particularly true in a declining drug market such as St. Louis (Gollub, Hakeem, & Johnson, 1996) where demand is finite and dwindling, while the number of sellers has remained constant or increased. To compete in such conditions, sellers will often stand out longer and in more difficult conditions than they previously would, in greater numbers, and in greater numbers together. Individual sellers also may rush to customers to steal sales from competitors, drawing even more attention. This situation creates ideal conditions for police—or researchers—to identify open-air sellers and infiltrate them.

Access notwithstanding, the importance of a strong indigenous tie to the research setting at the beginning of field relations—as a way of vouching for the researcher—cannot be overstated. Access and safe access are two wholly different notions. In my case, this tie was Luther—or at least so I thought. More generally, it is an indigenous offender or ex-offender turned fieldworker who acts as gate-keeper and protector. Yet, in a twist of sorts, field research with active offenders often requires strong ties in order to generate weak ones—that is, to initiate the methodological snowball. Micro-structurally and methodologically, this is unique; multiple weak ties rather than one or two strong ones are thought to be indispensable for social-network creation (Granovetter, 1973). Indeed, one or two strong ties may actually cut off an actor from an entire social network.

In field research, developing strong ties with the wrong person or persons can, at a minimum, bias the sample or, worse, generate no sample at all.[4] Researchers may gain entry, but it may be with the wrong person. As my encounter with Luther attests, the outcome can be far more threatening than obtaining a biased sample or no sample. Perhaps the larger point here is that, no matter how strong or safe one's ties, danger is inherent in fieldwork with active offenders. Nowhere is this more true than among street-corner crack sellers. Although many dangers can be addressed through planning and preparation, more often than not, danger management hinges on a creative process of "trial and blunder" (see Karp & Kendall, 1982) and results from a combination of skill and luck (Ellen, 1984, p. 97). As Sluka notes, "Good luck can sometimes help overcome a lack of skill, and well-developed skills can go far to help overcome the effects of bad luck. But sometimes no amount of skill will save one from a gross portion of bad luck" (1990, p. 124). Inevitably, criminological fieldwork is unpredictable and less subject to rational planning than we want it to be. How researchers handle this problem ultimately is a personal choice.

Researching active offenders requires one to balance conflicting agendas. Such agendas emanate from specific audiences—whether police or criminals—each with their own biases toward the ethnographic enterprise. Simply taking sides or currying favor with one audience over the other is not the issue, though this may be done at some point. Research strategies must be weighed carefully because their consequences are inevitably dialectical: police can get you "in" with offenders, but offenders can get you "in trouble" with police. Personal security is dependent on offender acceptance, yet security can be compromised by dependency. Police can be researchers' last bastion of hope against volatile offenders, but reliance on authorities may undermine the very purpose for being in the field. Caught among these contradictions stands the researcher, a true one-person "island in the street" (Sanchez-Jankowski, 1991). In this lonely position, the researcher must decide when to shade the truth and when to be forthright, when to offer and when to omit, when to induce and when to lie back. Such judgments are subjective and context specific, as any ethnographer will tell you. They must be made with the audience in mind, whether that audience is legal or illegal, academic or social. Each choice affects the kinds of data obtained and revealed. And how far an ethnographer is willing to go to get such data intertwines with the results that ethnographer hopes ultimately to obtain—as my encounter with Luther attests.

NOTES

1. All names are pseudonyms to protect identities.
2. Luther's stalking came to an end only because police picked him up on two unrelated counts of armed robbery and armed criminal action. He is now serving 10 years in a Missouri state penitentiary. With the help of colleagues, I moved. My phone number is now unlisted and unpublished, something I recommend to other ethnographers researching active offenders.
3. SCAT is an acronym for "street corner apprehension team." This 15-man undercover team is charged with curbing street-level drug sales by apprehending dealers immediately after sales to one of their "buy" officers. Hiding nearby in unmarked cars, personnel "swoop" down on offenders in an attempt to catch them with marked money just given them by buy officers. This money either has traceable dye or serial numbers previously recorded that link dealers to undercover transactions. SCAT units were highly feared because they were reportedly merciless in their arrest procedures (i.e., they conducted strip searches).
4. Douglas's research on nudist beach goers, for example, was jeopardized because of his early bond with a marginal and generally disliked participant (something Douglas did not know until later)—a participant with whom he was able to bond precisely because of that person's marginality; see Douglas (1972).

REFERENCES

Adler, P. (1985). *Wheeling and dealing: An ethnography of an upper-level drug dealing and smuggling community.* New York: Columbia University Press.

Agar, M. (1973). *Ripping and running: A formal ethnography of urban heroin addicts.* New York: Seminar.

Berk, R. A., & Adams, J. M. (1970). Establishing rapport with deviant groups. *Social Problems, 18,* 102–117.

Biernacki, P., & Waldorf, D. (1981). Snowball sampling. *Sociological Methods and Research, 10,* 141–163.

Carey, J. T. (1972). Problems of access and risk in observing drug scenes. In J. D. Douglas (Ed.), *Research on deviance* (pp. 71–92). New York: Random House.

Douglas, J. D. (1972). Observing deviance. In J. D. Douglas (Ed.), *Research on deviance* (pp. 3–34). New York: Random House.

Ellen, R. F. (1984). *Ethnographic research: A guide to general conduct.* London: Academic.

Emerson, R. M. (Ed.). (1983). *Contemporary field research.* Prospect Heights, IL: Waveland.

Evans-Pritchard, E. E. (1964). *Social anthropology and other essays.* New York: Free Press.

Federal Bureau of Investigation. (1995). *Crime in the United States.* Washington, DC: Government Printing Office.

Ferrell, J., & Hamm, M. S. (1998). *Ethnography at the edge: Crime, deviance and field research.* Boston: Northeastern University Press.

Garfinkel, H. (1956). Conditions of successful degradation ceremonies. *American Journal of Sociology, 61,* 420–424.

Goffman, E. (1963). *Stigma: Notes on the management of spoiled identity.* Englewood Cliffs, NJ: Prentice Hall.

———. (1971). *Relations in public: Micro studies of the public order.* New York: Basic.

———. (1974). *Frame analysis: An essay on the organization of experience.* Cambridge, MA: Harvard University Press.

Gollub, A., Hakeem, F., & Johnson, B. D. (1996). Monitoring the decline in the crack epidemic with data from the Drug Use Forecasting Program. Unpublished manuscript.

Goode, E. (1970). *The marijuana smokers.* New York: Basic.

Granovetter, M. (1973). The strength of weak ties. *American Journal of Sociology, 78,* 1360–1380.

Irwin, J. (1972). Participant observation of criminals. In J. D. Douglas (Ed.), *Research on Deviance* (pp. 117–138). New York: Random House.

Johnson, J. M. (1983). Trust and personal involvements in fieldwork. In R. M. Emerson (Ed.), *Contemporary field research* (pp. 203–215). Prospect Heights, IL: Waveland.

Karp, I., & Kendall, M. B. (1982). Reflexivity in field work. In P. F. Secord (Ed.), *Explaining human behavior: Consciousness, human action, and social structure* (pp. 249–273). Beverly Hills, CA: Sage.

Lowies, R. H. (1937). *The history of ethnological theory.* New York: Farrar and Rinehart.

Manning, P. K. (1972). Observing the police: deviance, respectables, and the law. In J. D. Douglas (Ed.), *Research on deviance* (pp. 213–268). New York: Random House.

McCall, G. (1978). *Observing the law.* New York: Free Press.

Oakley, A. (1981). Interviewing women: A contradiction in terms. In H. Roberts (Ed.), *Doing feminist research* (pp. 30–61). London: Routledge and Kegan Paul.

Polsky, N. (1967). *Hustlers, beats, and others.* Chicago: Aldine.

Powdermaker, H. (1966). *Stranger and friend: The way of an anthropologist.* New York: Norton.

Sanchez-Jankowski, M. (1991). *Islands in the street: Gangs in American urban society.* Berkeley: University of California Press.

Scully, D. (1990). *Understanding sexual violence.* Boston: Unwin Inman.

Simmel, G. (1908). The stranger. In D. Levine (Ed.), *Georg Simmel* (pp. 143–149). Chicago: University of Chicago Press.

Skolnick, J. (1980). A sketch of the policeman's "working personality." In G. F. Cole (Ed.), *Criminal justice: Law and politics* (pp. 118–137). North Scituate, MA: Duxbury.

Sluka, J. A. (1990). Participant observation in violent social contexts. *Human Organization, 49,* 114–126.

Soloway, I., & Walters, J. (1977). Workin' the corner: The ethics and legality of fieldwork among active heroin addicts. In R. S. Weppner (Ed.), *Street ethnography* (pp. 159–178). Beverly Hills, CA: Sage.

Sutherland, E., & Cressey, D. (1970). *Criminology* (8th ed.). Philadelphia: Lippincott.

Van Maanen, J. (1978). The asshole. In P. K. Manning and J. Van Maanen (Eds.), *Policing: A View from the Streets* (pp. 221–238). Santa Monica, CA: Goodyear.

Wax, R. H. (1983). The ambiguities of fieldwork. In R. M. Emerson (Ed.), *Contemporary field research* (pp. 191–202). Prospect Heights, IL: Waveland.

Williams, T., Dunlap, E., Johnson, B. D., & Hamid, A. (1992). Personal safety in dangerous places. *Journal of Contemporary Ethnography, 21,* 343–374.

Wolff, K. H. (1964). Surrender and community study: The study of Loma. In A. J. Vidich, J. Bensman, & M. R. Stein (Eds.), *Reflections on community studies* (pp. 233–263). New York: Wiley.

Wright, R. T., & Decker, S. H. (1994). *Burglars on the job: Streetlife and residential break-ins.* Boston: Northeastern University Press.

⅏

CHAPTER 2

Consenting to Talk: Why Inmates Participate in Prison Research

Heith Copes and Andy Hochstetler

The authors discuss the various motivations of prisoners' willingness to discuss their past criminal activities. They reveal that prisoners may talk about their crimes due to the financial rewards offered by the researchers, their desire to "teach" researchers and others about crime, to reduce boredom, and curiosity, as well as for certain psychological benefits to self.

Criminologists have a long history of interviewing inmates to gain insights into the nature of crime and criminality. By posing questions to inmates, researchers offer the incarcerated an opportunity to explain their histories, offenses, and lifestyles from their own perspectives. This task is important, because those who have engaged in criminal and deviant activities are in the "unique position of being able to describe, in their own words, the motivations and causes of crime, the level and nature of crime calculus, and the perceived effectiveness of crime control activities in deterring crime" (Miethe & McCorkle, 2001, p. 17). When the voices of those who have engaged in illegal activity are coupled with researchers' analyses, academics and criminal justice professionals can get a more realistic glimpse into the world of offenders, move closer toward theoretical explanations of criminal lifestyles and decisions, and better design effective crime control policy.

Clearly, posing questions to offenders is an important step in developing a full understanding of crime and criminality. But if criminologists are to garner the benefits of the offender's perspective, it is necessary that they both locate these individuals and convince them to talk about their misdeeds. Finding people who have direct experience with criminal behavior can be difficult, as these individuals often desire to remain hidden, especially from those outside their social worlds, but finding them is in no way impossible. While there are many places that ethnographers can go to locate offenders (e.g., street corners, bars, shelters, rehabilitation

Source: Written especially for this volume. Used with permission of the authors.

meetings, jails, prisons), here we will focus on those offenders confined to prisons and jails.

Undoubtedly, it is easier to locate people who have engaged in criminal behaviors in prisons than on the streets. After all, they are captive populations. Even if criminologists do seek out incarcerated offenders, they must still confront the task of convincing them to share their stories. Ethnographic research requires that we intrude into people's lives and ask them to reveal personal information that they may not have shared with others before—information that could possibly have negative consequences for them. Despite the inconveniences and potential risks of talking to researchers, inmates are often quite willing to discuss their lives and criminal careers in great detail. Many novice interviewers assume inaccurately that inmates will not discuss certain topics with them. They mistakenly believe that they will be met with "hostility and a lack of co-operation" from those whom they wish to interview (Shover, 1985, p. 154). Fortunately, as Berg (2001, p. 95) notes, "Once subjects have been persuaded to participate in an interview, they often tell far more details than the interviewers would ever want to know." This willingness to talk has been documented by numerous researchers (Akerstrom, 1985; Girshick, 1999; Shover, 1985; Shover, 1996). We too have been astounded by inmates' openness and frankness in their descriptions of their lives and crimes.

What would make someone who has been incarcerated for behavior that society has defined as immoral and illegal disregard the potential risks and inconveniences to sit down and openly discuss their lives and misdeeds? Answers to this question have important implications for qualitative researchers engaged in recruiting inmates and interpreting their finished work. The motives that inmates have for participating in research ultimately affect the nature of the stories they relay and the type of information they withhold. It was for these reasons that during two separate research projects we posed the question, "Why did you agree to talk to us?" In total, we asked this question of 73 individuals. All were incarcerated in medium-security prisons at the time of the interviews. The first project involved inmates in Louisiana who had committed at least one carjacking ($n = 33$). The other project involved inmates in Alabama who were discussing their perceptions of parole revocation ($n = 40$). In what follows, we discuss the various motives that inmates expressed for consenting to an interview. We found much diversity in their answers. The reasons that inmates gave for consenting to the interview included: to satisfy immediate material needs, to benefit emotionally and psychologically, and to give back to others. In a few cases, inmates agreed as a result of misunderstanding the benefits that we were capable of providing.

IMMEDIATE REWARDS

Many inmates agreed to be interviewed for altruistic reasons, such as doing their part to keep the next generation from making similar mistakes or helping out a trusted confederate (Shover, 1985). A smaller number of inmates consented to interviews for more self-serving and mundane reasons. Inmates said that they were willing to tell their stories to us because they could use the money that we offered, they wanted to have a conversation with someone from the outside, they were eager to get a change of scenery, or they were curious to see what it was like to be interviewed.

Financial Incentives

Researchers who rely on survey and interview methods often provide small monetary incentives to participants to encourage them to either complete a questionnaire or consent to an interview. Financial incentives can be powerful motivators. This is especially true among populations that have little means of earning money, such as those confined in an institution. Even those who are interviewed in the streets, who could conceivably make more money through hustling than researchers can offer, are attracted to the prospect of making quick cash (Wright & Decker, 1994). While researchers face some ethical dilemmas when deciding how much money to offer, most agree that it is appropriate to compensate study participants for their time and knowledge. A survey of ethnographic studies appearing in the top criminology and criminal justice journals showed that over 20% offered financial inducements to participants, with the average amount offered being $41.25 (Copes, Brown, & Tewksbury, 2011). We offered the inmates in Louisiana $20 and those in Alabama $15 to encourage them to sit down and talk with us.

Undoubtedly, our financial incentive did encourage participation; however, it was uncommon for inmates to state that their primary reason for participating in the research was the money. Statements such as, "$20 about the only thing good you know. That's about it. That's about the only thing good [about doing this]," or "I needed [the money], you know what I'm saying. I needed it. It helped," were uncommon. In fact only a handful of inmates claimed that money was the sole driving force behind their participation. Doubtless, easy money does intrigue offenders and whet other motives for participating.

It was more common for inmates to acknowledge that money helped, but that other reasons for their cooperation were more important. As such, financial compensation was seen as a nice bonus. Gerald stated, "I'm gonna be blessed with $20, and hopefully I can help you with your study, your career, or whatever you are doing." Echoing this, Francis answered:

> To be honest with you, broke. Needed some money. But no, then again, it was a chance to see what's really up, different aspects on what someone thinks and the like. [Maybe] I could get some pointers on trying to classify my life.... The money was good, but the interview and session was pretty good too.

While participants mentioned money as a benefit, they underplayed its importance by suggesting that altruism or personal growth were the "real" reasons for participating (Fry & Dwyer, 2001). Regardless of the priority of money as a motivator, it is clear that even small financial gestures helped to generate compliance.

Conversations with Outsiders

The secrecy inherent in criminal participation means that offenders have few opportunities to relate their exploits to those who are not associates. Offenders often find this inability to share their "war stories" frustrating (Letkemann, 1973). This is especially the case when surrounded by audiences who are familiar with and largely uninterested in such stories as something other than diversionary banter. Such frustration is possibly even greater among captive populations, because deep reflection on or analysis of one's mistakes is discouraged in most informal contexts of the prison. For example, Derrick claimed he wanted to participate because "just to talk to a stranger for thirty minutes is cool with me, cause I'm getting tired of talking to them [other inmates]." Incarcerated individuals have few opportunities to have meaningful conversations with those who are not incarcerated or are not criminal justice personnel. They have little opportunity to share their stories with people who do not judge them or assume they are being deceptive or hyperbolic. In the words of Bryan, "It's good [talking to you]. It ain't too often that we get to converse with someone ... on an intelligent level, you know what I'm saying. [With someone] that's already overcome certain obstacles and is already success-ful." Similarly, Michael explained, "I ain't never got a visit since I been up here. I haven't seen nobody from the streets in seven years. Ain't had a visit, you know. It was just cool talking to you." When a person is cut off from the conventional and ordinary world, any taste of it can be rewarding or at least provide a relief from routine. Inmates welcomed the chance to talk to someone who was not in some way connected to the institution (Athens, 1997, p. 103).

Additionally, some offenders were motivated by the desire to teach those with formal educations something about life in the streets. Many ethnographers have fostered respondents' teaching role in order to generate their cooperation (Berk & Adams, 1970). As Miller (2001, p. 30) points out, "Providing respondents with the opportunity to act as teachers can afford them with a sense of meaning and importance." Because marginalized individuals seldom have the chance to lend their voice to social discourse, the opportunity to do so acts as a lure for their par-ticipation. The value of simple conversation with a person whom they need not impress, with whom they have no official or emotional tie, and with whom they can share their expertise cannot be overestimated as a motive for offenders inside and outside of prison walls to participate in ethnographic interviews.

Change of Setting/Pass Time

To effectively manage prison populations, it is necessary for prison staff to struc-ture the daily activities of inmates. This creates a predictable, monotonous routine for prisoners, which can make time creep and the days run together. To disrupt this routine, inmates often seek out activities in the hopes of making time go a little faster. Many inmates enroll in church services, educational programs, and self-help classes not out of a desire to change their ways, but in order to change their setting. As Rufus stated, "What are we doing in the dorm? Nothing. This right here, this is passing my time." This desire to break the routine of prison life is a motivating factor for many of those who participate in research, as an interview "provides a break from the boredom and monotony of prison life" (Matthews, 2002, p. 10). Several inmates stated that they simply enjoyed the pleasure of "getting away and getting out for a while." In responding to our question about why they came to talk to us, participants gave statements such as Michaels's "I just want a little walk, you know what I'm saying" and Millicent's "You stay in the dorm. You be cooped up in there 24 hours a day. Ain't nothing else to do back in the dorm except playing cards or something." Warren expressed the sentiment most bluntly:

> A dude told me about it and I said, shoot, I gotta get up there 'cause there ain't nothing to do around here. Absolutely nothing! We don't have nothing but running, exercising, reading, and writing. That's it! I just wanted to get out, to be honest with you.... I would have sure done it for free.

Certainly, when people spend most of their time in a confined area, any opportunity to travel beyond its borders is welcomed. Doubtless, this motivation increases in bleak settings. The novelty of speaking to a person who is not part of an offender's past or institutional life makes the break from monotony all the more enjoyable.

Curiosity

Many of those who are confined in state institutions share the common human interest in experiencing the unknown. This trait drove several of the participants to consent to the interview (Matthews, 2002). Robbie exemplified this curiosity in his response to our question: "Well, I wanted to see what it was really about. You know, curiosity. Curiosity killed the cat. I just wanted to see what's happening up here, you know. I decided to come down and see."

Several other individuals also made direct references to wanting to "come up here and see what it was like." Part of "seeing what it was like" was to discern whether something was amiss and to exude confidence in the face of what could be a deception. Showing confidence in chaotic or unknown situations is a trait highly valued by many serious street offenders (Katz, 1988). Investigators often get the impression when doing research on the streets and in jails and prisons that some of the first people they interview see themselves as scouts who can speak with authority to others about whether the situation is "cool." If investigators press these individuals for names, dates, or other sorts of information that could lead to trouble, early participants generally caution friends and associates against interacting with the interviewer.

In our study, developing a good rapport with early interviewees did encourage others to participate. Referring to a former interviewee, Sidney said, "The guy that I was talking to about it, me and him are cool, and he say, 'Do you want to do the interview?' I said, yeah, that's cool."

PSYCHOLOGICAL BENEFITS TO SELF

Many offenders decided to participate in the interviews because they had begun to reassess their crimes and related mistakes. Either they had already become engaged in a new way of life or they were exploring the possibility of a new approach. In fact, the interview was often viewed as part of a therapeutic process or as evidence of recovery. Many expressed the belief that talking to professionals, even if they were criminologists and not psychiatrists, might "help them come to terms with their personal problems" (Wright & Decker, 1997, p. 25). Thus, sharing their stories acts as a catharsis for inmates and as evidence that they are on the right path to recovery.

Catharsis

Talking to interviewers allows offenders to "let it all out" without being perceived as weak or vulnerable. For people who have engaged in illegal behavior, the simple act of talking about their misdeeds makes them feel better about what they have done and may aid in the important process of making sense of and contextualizing past mistakes (Maruna, 2001). Several of those with whom we spoke thanked us for allowing them to talk and acknowledged that they felt better about themselves because of the experience (see Shover, 1985). When asked if anything good came from the experience, Melvin answered, "The therapeutic value of being able to discuss as many details of my life and to remain honest in those assessments." Similarly, Shawn said:

> It makes me feel better by talking about [my past]. I mean, it's like looking back over all the devious shit that I've done and got away with, I figure, you know, if I can come sit down here and talk to you about half the shit I done did then I can sleep better.

Interviewing offenders not only benefits social science, but also allows those directly involved in the behavior to explain away, to both others and themselves, the guilt caused by criminal participation. Indeed, for many research participants, the interview was a genuine, emotional experience.

The Right Track

The interview is a reflective setting. Offenders get the message that they are supposed to be assessing what went wrong for them. Some think that an assessment of their prospects for reform should immediately follow the telling of their unfortunate story. After the interview, two participants said they were going to go "straight" and do what they could to get back in school (see Wright & Decker, 1997, p. 25). In fact, one of the participants later contacted us about how to apply for school. We are unaware of whether he followed through with our advice or actually went "straight." More important for present purposes, many inmates express such statements of conventional goals and assessments of prospects at the conclusion of their interviews, even when they are not requested to do so.

Additionally, participating in research requires that the offender adapt or respond to a conventional stance. They are forced to explain errors and crimes in a way that might be understood by strangers to the street criminal's world (Maruna

& Copes, 2005). Offenders, especially those on the slippery path to reform, are likely to portray crime as an aberration and, as such, as something interesting and worth exploring. From this perspective, criminal acts say nothing about who the offenders are deep inside or who they want to be. Loosely structured interviews aid this interpretation and narrative, if only by the implicit assumptions that the causes of crime are complex and the choice to offend is worthy of reflection (Presser, 2010; Sandberg, 2010).

Offenders experience few settings in which an honest recounting of their stories might be interpreted as evidence of noble aims. In an ethnographic interview, however, their honesty is more important than an accounting that balances their criminal records and other failures against their accomplishments. Interviews, therefore, fit neatly into offenders' self-improvement projects and help them to refine and construct their stories as honest, struggling citizens. Many have only had such conversations with themselves and are eager to voice these stories in a setting where they will not be viewed as overly sentimental or a con game. Their enthusiasm for relating their stories of change should also be interpreted in light of treatment program designs that emphasize the acts of claiming one's mistakes, confessing, and sharing tales of struggle and redemption. Many offenders have participated in such programs and all are aware of them. Being given a chance to tell their story, or testify, represents an opportunity to take a step, however small, in the right direction. For this reason, inmates in our studies commonly responded to questions about participation with answers that were much more profound and ambitious than one might initially expect. Charles commented, "I don't know it's like even though I consider myself halfway, I am getting my mind right." Philip reflected on his motives: "I'm just trying to get right, you know. I want to go out there and do the right thing and make my mom proud. Settle down, have a little family. I'm tired of coming in here. Selling drugs ain't going to take you nowhere." Participation in the research process indicates to both the inmates themselves and outsiders that they are indeed on the right path to getting their lives in order.

SOCIAL BENEFITS TO OTHERS

Many participants choose to take part in research to help others—either specific people (like us) or more abstract ones. In some cases, this is part of their project to do the right thing and make amends for past misdeeds. When this is the case, they often want to teach the moral lessons of their stories to an imagined audience of people confronting situations similar to the ones that led them astray. In their mind, this goal can be met when someone's life is directly affected, as is hopefully the case when offenders speak to student groups. Most offenders recognize that they are more likely to reach their target audience indirectly. They therefore intend to help a researcher understand criminal acts in a way that might indirectly benefit those at risk of engaging in crime or help others recognize the social problems that might have contributed to their acts.

Helping Abstract Others

Many of those who agreed to talk to us did so because they recognized that they had acted improperly and hoped that their testimonies could help deter young people from making similar bad choices. The altruistic intentions of offenders have shaped qualitative criminology since its earliest days. As far back as 1938, the five Martin boys interviewed by Shaw and colleagues claimed that they agreed to give their life histories in the "genuine hope that the documents might be useful in preventing other boys from becoming involved in delinquency and crime" (Shaw, McKay, & McDonald, 1938, p. 143). Today, any qualitative researcher is likely to hear statements such as Anthony's:

> Maybe it might help somebody. Help some young person. Hopefully, they haven't really gotten into [violent crime] yet. Maybe, they might be stealing cars or something like that, you know. Maybe, I might be able to help them or you might be able to help them by hearing what I have to say.

Similarly, Omar expressed the sentiment, "I just hope whatever I said could help. Like I said, it's too late for me. My day is right around the corner. I hope the information could get help to others...and help the next person." Kenneth said he hoped that his words could "inspire somebody else not to end up in this place."

In a similar vein, some participants identify a desire to improve community understanding and recognition of some of the external sources of crime as the main reason for participating. As Thomas explained:

> I was cool about it because I really want to let people know why people do it. That's the only reason why I participated. You know, just so they can have understanding that it's more than what society would think. Society put a label on them and put them in jail for the rest of their lives. [People should] try to learn something about this person and why he or she did these things. Then, you understand. I mean [understand] why you want to rob, why you want to kill, why you want to jack this or jack that. If you got a good understanding of their background and environment, then you have a better understanding of why people do these things.

Kelvin echoed this optimism:

> If the analysis would help somebody else, man if it would give y'all some kind of idea about how to help people from coming back like this. If me being one of the tools to help guide y'all toward getting a solution for this, then man, that's the reason I really did it....I don't wanna see nobody coming here, so if it help one person, it's a plus.

Participants with this motivation believe that "their life history [can] make an entertaining and perhaps useful contribution to understanding crime and those who commit it" (Shover, 1996, p. 190).

Helping the Researcher

These varieties of altruism are common, but participation in a research project can also help other people who are more proximate and more certain to benefit from this aid. Researchers are often impressed at how many participants decide to participate in a project primarily because it will help the researcher. This decision often stems from a practical recognition that completion of a research project will benefit an academic career. Although participants often have little understanding of how academic careers advance, they do understand that they are being asked to help and are in a position to aid someone in a conventional pursuit. When asked why he agreed to talk to us, Bryan responded: "Oh, you alright. I just heard you was at school. If it can help you out, by me being in here, I mean by me giving you this... I just hope something comes out of this. Maybe, you can get something out of this."

In keeping with the reflective tone of many interviews, in addition to express-ing the desire to help a researcher's academic or professional advancement, offenders often identify failure in the workplace and educational environment as the reason that they went astray. Derrick lamented, "This is helping you, you know.... At least you are doing what you should be doing. I should be in college right now." Offenders also frequently want to help students. As "experts" on crime, they wish to give their expertise to those who study it. The fact that students of crime typically are attached to a university gives the offender a way to tap into, if only temporarily and loosely, this prestigious world and put their experience to good use.

As a result of this desire to help us, several participants refused to take money for the interview, because they believed this money was coming directly from our pockets. Shover (1985) observed a similar reaction from those with whom he spoke. Like Shover, we insisted that these individuals accept the money.

MISUNDERSTANDING

Ethical guidelines require researchers to disclose the nature and possible dangers of their research to participants. When doing research in a prison setting, it is important to inform inmates that their participation is completely voluntary and will have no effect, either positive or negative, on their status as an inmate. That is, inmates are informed in advance that participation will not affect parole, admit-tance into work or social programs, or their relations with prison staff. Despite these acknowledgements, many inmates are motivated to volunteer because they believe that they will somehow benefit from cooperation.

Even though we took special care to let inmates know that we neither worked for nor were affiliated with the prison or the department of corrections, several inmates believed that we could help them with their criminal justice status in some indirect manner. The few who thought this way believed that the study was one of the many programs that the prison implemented to help ex-cons get back on their feet. For example, George acknowledged that he agreed to participate because "the prison has a lot of programs that are going on. You don't know what you get-ting yourself into. It could be something good, you know what I'm saying." Upon further probing, it became clear that he believed that our research was part of a program set up by the prison to help inmates. He agreed to talk to us because he thought it was a prerequisite for acceptance into the program. Fortunately, we were able to clarify this misunderstanding, and the inmate left the interview with the concluding remark, "Well, if nothing else, at least I got out of the dorms."

Millicent, who also misinterpreted our solicitation, agreed to come and meet with us because, "I didn't know I was coming in here for an interview. I thought I was coming here to sign some papers to go home." After we explained the intent of the interviews, she consented to participate. It is possible that inmates participating in such research are under the impression that the interaction is a chance for them to tell stories that might help them with their case. This belief often stems from their perception that interviewers are informants or are operating at the behest of criminal justice officials. However, none of our interviewees expressed this idea explicitly. We found that inmates who were participating for this reason were easy to identify by their reluctance to address many questions and their apparent deceptions. Researchers are able to detect such deceptions by comparing inmates' words with official records. Based on our experiences, however, this motivation is exceedingly rare.

DISCUSSION

Like researchers, offenders have a project when they come to an interview (Presser, 2004). To some extent, their narratives are predetermined and independent of the questions that are asked. Offenders' constructions of their stories may have as much to do with the reasons they consent to the interview as with the prompts and probing questions from the researcher. Stories of struggle or reform are, for example, fairly consistent across offenders and appear as a limited number of types. These narratives rear their heads in much of what offenders say about a variety of topics. Interviewers become familiar with certain scripts, such as the addiction tales of heroin users, the born-again stories of penitents, and the hard-knock stories of early life on the streets of large housing projects. The ubiquity of these storylines does not deny that the stories are true or diminish the value of what offenders say for understanding crime. These accounts are part of human and lived experience. Nevertheless, offenders' motivations for sharing and the constructions of their accounts should not be overlooked by qualitative researchers or their readers. One reason is that these motivations introduce an angle into the account that might otherwise be missed if researchers do not pay attention to what offenders are attempting to accomplish in interviews. Furthermore, they raise some potential methodological biases.

Participation in almost all research projects and data collection efforts is voluntary. Beyond checking to make sure that individuals who decline to participate do not differ on potentially important variables from those who do, little can be done about selection biases introduced by volunteering. Students of crime must accept that they generally only know the stories of those who choose to tell them and as they choose to tell them. Participating inmates are likely to adopt certain postures. At some times and in some settings, these may be very different than the identities and images they adopt when committing crimes. Offenders may be insightful and careful where they know that such a stance is appropriate and their every word will be analyzed. Conversely, some will choose to play the role of the criminal in the hope that researchers will not be disappointed with their stories. This assumed persona may resemble the over-the-top identities and cool poses that are characteristic of street-corner environments and the decision to offend. In any case, the proportional distribution of accounts is influenced by an offender's decision to participate in a study, the interview setting, the story that is most viable in that setting, and the motives of participants.

Qualitative researchers themselves introduce another source of potential bias. Articulate and interesting respondents are more likely to influence findings at every stage of analysis. These interviews last longer and researchers draw from them more heavily. To prove this point, one need only recognize how articulate and insightful many participants are whose statements find their way into print. It is the hope of every researcher that his or her article will be interesting, and it is tempting to select colorful statements for inclusion. Participants, especially those on whom interviews heavily rely, probably are more reflective, intelligent, and well spoken than the typical street offender. The bright, self-reflective, and verbose may be more likely to volunteer in the first place because they either believe that they have something interesting and worthwhile to say or suspect that they are capable of saying it well. Their narratives follow a logical plotline and are easy to organize and understand. Despite the selection bias toward articulate volunteers, every qualitative researcher of street crime learns that a good interview that provides insight on more than a few simple points is highly valuable. Readers should not forget that the ramblings of intellectually challenged, hopelessly intoxicated, and mentally ill respondents will seldom make it into a paper, as the data from these interviews are often useless (see Miller, 1986, p. 187). Such omissions are justifiable, but these shortcomings certainly speak to some of the origins and lived experience of crime.

The Value of Talk

For many years, qualitative research was seen as the most appropriate way to gauge criminal motives. Apart from recognizing that reasonable offenders would hide a few details and bend the truth on occasion, the offender was viewed as an impartial narrator of events. This is, of course, not the way that any of us act when reconstructing our motives or answering difficult questions (Presser, 2010; Sandberg, 2010). Wider academic interest in the formation of accounts and narratives of complex events has directed attention to this fact. For example, those of us who chose to go to college probably cannot accurately explain the decision-making processes or events that led us to that conclusion, although we do have a story available should anyone ask. Many questions asked of offenders by qualitative researchers require similar narrative construction. Variation in these constructions may be important over and above the facts relayed. In fact, there is an increasing awareness among criminologists that the way that offenders understand and depict their lives may have significant effects on their prospects for rehabilitation. The story that offenders tell and how they tell it may indicate their progress toward ending their criminal career (Maruna, 2001).

Similarly, the decision to participate in a study and the reason given for this decision might also be relevant and important. Some offenders see their participation in a study as a reaffirming or generative exercise. This decision and its motivations represent the front board of the stories they will relate. For some, this participation is a small gesture of restitution. For others, it is an attempt to elicit some understanding from an impartial and attentive outsider. A few see the decision as yet another sign that they are on the right track or as a chance to explore their motives publicly. Some participants are simply raconteurs or curiosity seekers who want to see what kind of reaction their stories will elicit or what a research effort is about. For many others, there is nothing better to do and nothing to hide. Unfortunately, a few use the unusual venue to fictitiously portray themselves as unremorseful hard men or criminal insiders who occupy a strange and exciting world. Almost none of these individuals are as interesting or exceptional as they think, and their insights are familiar, predictable, and fairly easy to tune out. Occasionally, a good qualitative researcher can turn an interview that has this tone or is otherwise unproductive around. This ability to transition might occur because an offender's motives shift over the course of an interview or because he or she strikes on something unexpected and decides to explore it. But if offenders are really there only for the money or to show off, the good that will come of talking to them is reduced (Jacques & Wright, 2008).

Implications for Institutional Review Boards

The current findings and discussion of why offenders consent to interviews has important implications for how researchers complete institutional review board (IRB) reports. The IRB is designed to ensure that researchers treat human participants in a way that is consistent with ethical guidelines. When determining if a certain research project using human subjects is ethical, the researcher must demonstrate that the benefits of the study outweigh potential harm to participants. Those who engage in ethnographic research typically point to the abstract benefits of the research, such as how the study can inform criminal justice personnel on how best to thwart the actions of offenders. Thus, the general public benefits from the words of offenders, but little is said about the actual participants. The current research suggests that offenders can experience direct benefits from telling their stories to researchers. Interviews can have real emotional impacts. An understanding of how the research process can benefit those directly involved in it can go a long way toward facilitating the IRB process, thereby making it easier for ethnographic researchers to leave their offices and speak with thieves, hustlers, and heavy drug users, both inside prisons and out in the free world.

CONCLUSIONS

Like offenders' words themselves, offenders' motives for participating in a study are of interest for voyeuristic, theoretical, and practical reasons. Numerous patterns and subtexts appear in narratives depending on the narrator's purpose and understanding of what is appropriate. These patterns form a significant part of the story and color how the facts are related. The same is true for participants in qualitative criminological research. Their motives tell something about where the offenders have been, where they are, and where they are going.

It is clear that criminologists have much to gain from interviewing inmates. The accounts of offenders have allowed us to understand the meanings they associate with crime, criminal decision-making processes, and the most effective crime control strategies (Decker, 2005). What has been less clear is what these participants have to gain in this research. We have provided a list of many, but certainly not all, of the reasons that offenders have for talking with interviewers. It is important to point out that we elicited the cooperation of individuals who were incarcerated for either violent crimes or parole revocations at the time of the interview. Inmates may have different motives than active offenders for agreeing to be a part of academic research. Those who are living outside prison walls obviously do not participate in research to get a look at new scenery, although they may be looking for a novel activity. Nevertheless, we believe that the reasons these incarcerated individuals gave for their participation are likely similar to the reasons that nonincarcerated individuals give. That is, participants on both sides of prison walls are likely curious, desire the financial compensation, see the experience as therapeutic, or simply want to help others by relaying their lived experiences.

In addition, one's position in the social structure may affect interpretation of the research event and motivations for being a part of a study. Those who are approaching the end of their criminal careers surely have different reasons for participating than those just embracing crime or those in the midst of their careers. Similarly, those who engage in especially egregious criminal acts, like murder and rape, may not have the same motivations as those whose crimes are more mundane. White-collar offenders are likely to devote a great deal of effort in interviews to defending their character. Penitents are rare among this group. But once again, we contend that differences among types of offenders are merely in the relative frequency of motives for participation and not in distinct motives. The desire to help others, to get on the right track, or to just share their lives with others are certainly not unique to those in prisons, those considering giving up crime, or those who engage in violent street crimes (see Wright & Decker, 1994; Wright & Decker, 1997).

REFERENCES

Akerstrom, M. (1985). *Crooks and squares: Lifestyles of thieves and addicts in comparison to conventional people.* New Brunswick, NJ: Transaction.

Athens, L. (1997). *Violent criminal acts and actors revisited.* Urbana: University of Illinois Press.

Berg, B. L. (2001). *Qualitative research methods for the social sciences* (4th ed.). Needham Heights, MA: Allyn and Bacon.

Berk, R., & Adams, J. M. (1970). Establishing rapport with deviant groups. *Social Problems, 18,* 102–117.

Copes, H., Brown, A., & Tewksbury, R. (2011). A content analysis of ethnographic research published in top criminology and criminal justice journals from 2000–2009. *Journal of Criminal Justice Education, 22,* 341–359.

Decker, S. (2005). *Using offender interviews to inform police problem solving* (Problem-Solving Tools Series, Guide No. 3). Washington, DC: U.S. Department of Justice.

Fry, C., & Dwyer, R. (2001). For love or money? An exploratory study of why injecting drug users participate in research. *Addiction, 9,* 1319–1325.

Girshick, L. (1999). *No safe haven: Stories of women in prison.* Boston: Northeastern University Press.

Jacques, S., & Wright, R. (2008). Intimacy with outlaws: The role of relational distance in recruiting, paying, and interviewing underworld research participants. *Journal of Research in Crime and Delinquency, 46,* 22–38.

Katz, J. (1988). *Seductions of crime: The moral and sensual attractions of doing evil.* New York: Basic.

Letkemann, P. (1973). *Crime as work.* Englewood Cliffs, NJ: Prentice-Hall.

Maruna, S. (2001). *Making good: How ex-convicts reform and rebuild their lives.* Washington, DC: American Psychological Association.

Maruna, S., & Copes, H. (2005). Excuses, excuses: What have we learned from five decades of neutralization research? *Crime and Justice: An Annual Review of Research, 32.* 1–100.

Matthews, R. (2002). *Armed robbery.* Portland, OR: Willan.

Miethe, T. D., & McCorkle, R. C. (2001). *Crime profiles: The anatomy of dangerous persons, places and situations.* Los Angeles: Roxbury.

Miller, E. M. (1986). *Street women.* Philadelphia: Temple University Press.

Miller, J. (2001). *One of the guys: Girls, gangs, and gender.* Oxford: Oxford University Press.

Presser, L. (2004). Violent offenders, moral selves: Constructing identities and accounts in the research interview. *Social Problems, 51,* 82–102.

———. (2010). Collecting and analyzing the stories of offenders. *Journal of Criminal Justice Education, 21,* 431–446.

Sandberg, S. (2010). What can "lies" tell us about life? Notes towards a framework of narrative criminology. *Journal of Criminal Justice Education, 21,* 447–465.

Shaw, C. R., McKay, H. D., & McDonald, J. F. (1938). *Brothers in crime.* Chicago: University of Chicago Press.

Shover, N. (1985). *Aging criminals.* Beverly Hills, CA: Sage.

———. (1996). *Great pretenders: Pursuits and careers of persistent thieves.* Boulder, CO: Westview.

Wright, R. T., & Decker, S. (1994). *Burglars on the job: Streetlife and residential break-ins.* Boston: Northeastern University Press.

———. (1997). *Armed robbers in action: Stickups and street culture.* Boston: Northeastern University Press.

SECTION II

✯

Criminal Lifestyles and Decision Making

The chapters in Section II explore the lifestyles and decision-making strategies of criminals. These articles are primarily concerned with offenders' views and attitudes about both criminal and conventional activities and their perceptions of the risks and benefits associated with a criminal lifestyle. Furthermore, we examine how those perceptions are formed and how they change over time. We also consider issues centering on how offenders process their environment and the factors that may influence their criminal decision making. Because a criminal lifestyle is largely hidden from public view and open only to the initiated, criminologists continue to investigate this important issue in order to understand it better. These studies represent a step forward in understanding the dynamics of criminal lifestyles and criminal decision making in that context.

In Chapter 3, "The Socially Bounded Decision Making of Persistent Property Offenders," Neal Shover and David Honaker argue that an adequate understanding of the decision-making processes of property offenders can be gained only through exploring how these offenders' decisions are influenced by their lifestyles. They contend that offenders' risk assessments can best be understood by exploring the personal and social contexts in which decisions are made. They examine how the lifestyles of persistent property offenders affect their assessment of the risks and benefits of crime. Shover and Honaker's research focuses on the decision to commit a crime and emphasizes how closely that decision fits into the rational-choice model, in which decisions are based on an "assessment of potential returns from alternative courses of action and the risk of legal sanctions."

In Chapter 4, "Deciding to Commit a Burglary," Richard T. Wright and Scott H. Decker examine the dynamics underlying the decision to commit a burglary. The authors interviewed 105 active residential burglars by taking them to the scenes of their past crimes and asking them to reconstruct the burglary in extensive detail. In this chapter, they examine the factors that motivated the crime—that is, "Why burglary?" The participants of the study tended to be misfits in a world that values punctuality, schedules, and discipline. Crime appealed to some precisely because it allowed them to flaunt their independence from the routine imposed by the world of work. Their crimes were committed primarily because of their perception of an immediate need for money. This need for money largely stemmed from offenders' desire to maintain their lifestyle, which the authors describe as "high living" and "life as party," although some offenders committed burglaries for licit activities such as food, clothing, and shelter and others committed burglaries for revenge, thrills, and other noneconomic reasons.

In Chapter 5, "Opportunities and Decisions: Interactional Dynamics in Robbery and Burglary Groups," Andy Hochstetler analyzes the decision-making processes of criminals working in groups. He argues that although the role of co-offenders has been recognized for decades, it has not been adequately studied. He finds that interaction among groups of offenders can "reduce the appeal of law abidance" and make criminal opportunities appear to be more attractive. Although the role and influence of co-offenders varies widely, participants mutually influence each other in terms of decisions to offend, target selection, and evaluation of the risk–gain calculus.

CHAPTER 3

৵

The Socially Bounded Decision Making of Persistent Property Offenders

Neal Shover and David Honaker

In the following selection, the authors argue that the risk assessments of offenders are best understood by exploring the personal and social contexts in which decisions are made. They examine the lifestyles of persistent property offenders relative to the influence of these lifestyles on how criminals assess the risks and benefits of crime. The focus of the research is on the decision to commit a crime, with emphasis on how closely that decision fits the rational-choice model.

The study population includes a sample of 60 recidivist property offenders incarcerated in Tennessee state prisons, but who were nearing their release date. Subjects ranged in age from 23 to 70 years of age, with an average age of 34.1 years. Each member of the sample was interviewed approximately one month before his release from prison. Seven to 10 months after release, the authors traced, contacted, and interviewed 46 of the original sample of 60 men. The data used in this study were collected in the postrelease interviews.

INTRODUCTION

The 1970s were marked by the eclipse of labeling theory as the dominant individual-level criminological theory and by the reappearance of interest in approaches originally advanced by classical theorists. Economists and cognitive psychologists, along with many in the criminological mainstream, advanced an interpretation of crime as *choice*, offering models of criminal decision making grounded in the assumption that the decision to commit a criminal act springs from the offender's assessment of its anticipated net utilities (e.g., Becker, 1968; Heineke, 1978; Carroll,

Source: Shover, N., & Honaker, D. (1992). The socially bounded decision making of persistent property offenders. *Howard Journal of Criminal Justice, 31*, 276–293. Used with permission of Blackwell Publishers, Ltd.

1978; Reynolds, 1985). This movement in favor of rational-choice approaches to crime spurred empirical investigation of problems that heretofore were limited primarily to studies of the death penalty and its impact on the homicide rate.

Early investigations of a rational-choice interpretation of crime reported a weak but persistent relationship between the certainty of punishment and the rates of serious property crimes (Blumstein, Cohen, & Nagin, 1978). It was recognized, however, that an understanding of criminal decision making also requires knowledge about individual perceptions and beliefs about legal threats and other constraints on decision making (e.g., Manski, 1978). Investigators moved on two main fronts to meet this need. Some used survey methods to explore differential involvement in minor forms of deviance in samples of restricted age ranges, typically high school and college students (e.g., Waldo & Chiricos, 1972). Alternatively, they examined the link between risk assessments and criminal participation in samples more representative of the general population. Serious shortcomings of these studies are that most either ignore the potential rewards of crime entirely or fail to examine its emotional and interpersonal utilities. Still other investigators turned attention to serious criminal offenders and began expanding the narrow existing knowledge base (e.g., Claster, 1967), chiefly through the use of cross-sectional research designs and survey methods.

For more than a decade now, investigators have studied offenders' attitudes toward legitimate and criminal pursuits, their perceptions of and beliefs about the risks of criminal behavior, and their estimates of the payoffs from conventional and criminal pursuits (e.g., Petersilia, Greenwood, & Lavin, 1978; Peterson & Braiker, 1980). These studies raise serious questions about the fit between offenders' calculus and a priori assumptions about their utilities and criminal decision making. One investigation of 589 incarcerated property offenders concluded, for example, that the subjects apparently do not utilize "a sensible cost-benefit analysis" when weighing the utilities of crime (Figgie International, 1988, p. 25). They substantially underestimate the risk of arrest for most crimes, routinely overestimate the monetary benefit they expect, and seem to have "grossly inaccurate perceptions of the costs and benefits associated with property crime" (Figgie International, 1988, p. 81). Unfortunately, both design and conceptual problems undermine confidence in the findings of this and similar studies. Cross-sectional survey methods, for example, are poorly suited for examining dynamic decision-making processes. Most such studies also fail to examine offenders' estimates of the likely payoffs from noncriminal alternatives or their nonmonetary utilities, such as emotional satisfaction (Katz, 1998).

As newer, empirically based models of criminal decision making have been developed (e.g., Clarke & Cornish, 1985; Cornish & Clarke, 1986), a growing number of investigators are using ethnographic methods to examine the offender's criminal calculus, often in real or simulated natural settings (e.g., Carroll, 1982; Carroll & Weaver, 1986). The research reported here continues this line of ethnographic inquiry by using retrospective interviews to examine criminal decision making by serious and persistent property offenders. The focus of our attention is the decision to commit a crime rather than the target-selection decision that has received substantial attention elsewhere (e.g., Scarr, 1973; Repetto, 1974; Maguire, 1982; Bennett & Wright, 1984a; Rengert & Wasilchick, 1985; Cromwell, Olson, & Avary, 1991). The first objective is to examine how closely the decision to commit a crime conforms to a classical rational-choice model in which it is assumed that decisions are based largely on an assessment of potential returns from alternative courses of action and the risk of legal sanctions. A second objective is to examine the influence of the lifestyle pursued by many persistent property offenders on the salience of their utilities and the risks they assess in criminal decision making.

FINDINGS

Analysis reveals that the most striking aspect of the subjects' decision making for the crimes they described is that a majority gave little or no thought to the possibility of arrest and confinement. Of 34 subjects who were asked specifically whether they considered the risk of arrest or who spontaneously indicated whether they did so, 21 (62%) said they did not. The comments of two subjects are typical:

Q: Did you think about…getting caught?

A: No.

Q: How did you manage to put that out of your mind?

A: It never did come into it.

Q: Never did come into it?

A: Never did, you know. It didn't bother me.

Q: Were you thinking about bad things that might happen to you?

A: None whatsoever.

Q: No?

A: I wasn't worried about getting caught or anything, you know. I was a positive thinker through everything, you know. I didn't have no negative thoughts about it whatsoever.

The 13 remaining subjects (38%) acknowledged that they gave some thought to the possibility of arrest, but most said they managed to dismiss it easily and to carry through with their plans:

Q: Did you worry much about getting caught? On a scale of one to 10, how would you rank your degree of worry that day?

A: The worry was probably a one. You know what I mean? The worry was probably one. I didn't think about the consequences, you know. I know its stupidity, but it didn't that I might go to jail, I mean it crossed my mind but it didn't make much difference.

Q: As you thought about doing that [armed robbery], were there things that you were worried about?

A: Well, the only thing that I was worried about was…getting arrested didn't even cross my mind, just worrying about getting killed is the only thing, you know, getting shot. That's the only thing…but, you know, you'd have to be really be crazy not to think about that…you could possibly get in trouble. It crossed my mind, but I didn't worry about it all that much.

Some members of our sample said they managed deliberately and consciously to put out of mind all thoughts of possible arrest:

When I went out to steal, I didn't think about the negative things. 'Cause if you think negative, negative things are going to happen. And that's the way I looked at it.…I done it just like it was a job or something. Go out and do it, don't think about getting caught, 'cause that would make you jumpy, edgy, nervous. If you looked like you were doing something wrong, then something wrong is gonna happen to you.…You just, you just put [the thought of arrest] out of your mind, you know.

Q: Did you think about [the possibility of getting caught] very much that night?
A: I didn't think about it that much, you know.…It comes but, you know, you can wipe it away.
Q: How do you wipe it away?
A: You just blank it out. You blank it out.

Another subject said simply that "I try to put that [thought of arrest] the farthest thing from my mind that I can."

Many subjects attribute their ability to ignore or to dismiss all thought of possible arrest to a state of intoxication or drug-altered consciousness:

Q: You didn't think about going to prison?
A: Never did. I guess it was all that alcohol and stuff, and drugs.…The day I pulled that robbery? No. I was so high I didn't think about nothing.

Another subject told us that he had been drinking the entire day that he committed the crime and, by the time it occurred, he was in "nightlight city."

Although it is clear that the formal risks of crime were not considered carefully by most members of the sample, equally striking is the finding that very few thought about or assessed legitimate alternatives before opting to commit a criminal act. Of 22 subjects who were asked specifically whether they had done so, 16 indicated they gave no thought whatsoever to legitimate alternatives. The six subjects who did either ignored or quickly dismissed them as inapplicable, given their immediate circumstances.

We recognize the methodological shortcomings of the descriptions of criminal decision making and behavior used as data for this study. Because the subjects were questioned in detail only about specific offenses they could remember well, the sample of descriptions may not be representative of the range of crimes they committed. By definition, they are memorable ones. Moreover, the recall period for these crimes ranged from one to 15 years, raising the possibility of errors caused by selective recall. Whether or not this could have produced systematic bias in the data is unknown. We cannot rule out the possibility that past crimes are remembered as being less rational than they actually were at the time of commission. Such a tendency could account in part for our interpretation of the data and our description of their style of decision making. The fact that we limited the sample to recidivists means also that we cannot determine how much their behavior may reflect either innate differences (Gottfredson & Hirschi, 1990) or experiential effects, that is, the effects of past success in committing crime and avoiding arrest (Nagin & Paternoster, 1991). It could be argued that the behavior of our subjects, precisely because they had demonstrated a willingness to commit property crimes and had done so in the past, limits the external validity of their reports. Given sample selection criteria and these potential data problems, generalizations beyond the study population must be made with caution.

This said, we believe that the remarkable similarity between our findings and the picture of criminal decision making reported by others who have studied serious property offenders strengthens their credibility significantly. A study of 83 imprisoned burglars revealed that 49% did not think about the chances of getting caught for any particular offense during their last period of offending. Although 37% of them did think about it, most thought there was little or no chance it would happen (Bennett & Wright, 1984a). Interviews with 113 men convicted of robbery or an offense related to robbery revealed that "over 60%...said they had not even thought about getting caught." Another 17% said that they had thought about the possibility but "did not believe it to be a problem" (Feeney, 1986, pp. 59–60). Analysis of prison interviews with 77 robbers and 45 burglars likewise revealed their "general obliviousness toward the consequences [of their crimes] and no thought of being caught" (Walsh, 1986, p. 157). In summation, our findings along with the findings from other studies suggest strongly that many serious property offenders seem to be remarkably casual in weighing the formal risks of criminal participation. As one of our subjects put it, "You think about going to prison about like you think about dying, you know." The impact of alcohol and drug use in diminishing concern with possible penalties also has been reported by many others (e.g., Bennett & Wright, 1984b; Cromwell, Olson, & Avary, 1991).

If the potential legal consequences of crime do not figure prominently in crime commission decision making by persistent thieves, what do they think about when choosing to commit crime? Walsh (1980; 1986) shows that typically they focus their thoughts on the money that committing a crime may yield and the good times they expect to have with it when the crime is behind them. Carroll's data (1982) likewise indicate that the amount of gain offenders expect to receive is "the most important dimension" in their decision making, whereas the certainty of punishment is the least important of the four dimensions on which his subjects assessed crime opportunities. Our findings are consistent with these reports; our subjects said that they focused on the expected gains from their crimes:

> I didn't think about nothing but what I was going to do when I got that money, how I was going to spend it, what I was going to do with it, you know.

See, you're not thinking about those things [possibility of being arrested]. You're thinking about that big pay check at the end of 30 to 45 minutes worth of work.

At the time [that you commit crime], you throw all your instincts out the window.... Because you're just thinking about money, and money only. That's all that's on your mind, because you want that money. And you throw, you block everything off until you get the money.

Although confidence in our findings is bolstered by the number of points on which they are similar to reports by others who have explored crime commission decision making, they do paint a picture of decision making that is different from what is known about the way at least some of them make target selection decisions. Investigators (e.g., Cromwell, Olson, & Avary, 1991) have shown that target decisions approximate simple commonsense conceptions of rational behavior (Shover, 1991). A resolution of the problem presented by these contradictory findings is suggested by others (Cromwell, Olson, & Avary, 1991) and also apparent in our data: criminal participation often results from a *sequence* of experientially and analytically discrete decisions, all of potentially varying degrees of intentional rationality. Therefore, once a *motivational* crime commission decision has been made, offenders may move quickly to selecting, or to exploiting an apparently suitable target. At this stage of the criminal participation process, offenders are preoccupied with the *technical* challenge of avoiding failure at what now is seen as a *practical* task. As one subject put it, "You don't think about getting caught, you think about how in hell you're going to do it *not* to get caught, you know." His comments were echoed by another man: "The only thing you're thinking about is looking and acting and trying *not* to get caught." Last, consider the comments of a third subject: "I wasn't afraid of getting caught, but I was cautious, you know. Like I said, I was thinking only in the way to prevent me from getting caught." Just as bricklayers do not visualize graphically or deliberate over the bodily carnage that could follow from a collapsed scaffold once there is a job to be done, many thieves apparently do not dwell at length on the likelihood of arrest or on the pains of imprisonment when proceeding to search out or exploit suitable criminal opportunities.

The accumulated evidence on crime commission decision making by persistent offenders is substantial and persuasive: the rationality they employ is limited or bounded severely (e.g., Carroll, 1982; Cromwell, Olson, & Avary, 1991). Although unsuccessful persistent offenders may calculate potential benefits and costs before committing criminal acts, they apparently do so differently or weigh utilities differently than as sketched in a priori decision-making models. As Walsh (1980, p. 141) suggests, offenders' "definitions of costs and rewards seem to be at variance with society's estimates of them." This does not mean that their decision making is *irrational*, but it does point to the difficulties of understanding it and then refining theoretical models of the process. Our objective in the remainder of this chapter is an improved understanding of criminal decision making based on analysis of the socially anchored purposes, utilities, and risks of the acts that offenders commit. Put differently, we explore the contextual origins of their bounded rationality.

Lifestyle, Utilities, and Risk

It is instructive to examine the decision making of persistent property offenders in context of the lifestyle that is characteristic of many in their ranks: life as party. The hallmark of *life as party* is the enjoyment of "good times" with minimal concern for obligations and commitments that are external to the person's immediate social setting. It is a lifestyle distinguished in many cases by two repetitively cyclical phases and correspondingly distinctive approaches to crime. When offenders' efforts to maintain the lifestyle (i.e., their party pursuits) are largely successful, crimes are committed in order to sustain circumstances or a pattern of activities they experience as pleasurable. As Walsh (1986, p. 15) puts it, crimes committed under these circumstances are "part of a continuing satisfactory way of life." By contrast, when offenders are less successful at party pursuits, their crimes are committed in order to forestall or avoid circumstances experienced as threatening, unpleasant, or precarious. Corresponding to each of these two phases of party pursuits is a distinctive set of utilities and stance toward legal risk.

Life as Party

Survey and ethnographic studies alike show that persistent property offenders spend much of their criminal gains on alcohol and other drugs (Petersilia, Greenwood, & Lavin, 1978; Maguire, 1982; Gibbs & Shelley, 1982; Figgie International, 1988; Cromwell, Olson, & Avary, 1991). The proceeds of their crimes, as Walsh has noted (1986, p. 72), "typically [are] used for personal, nonessential consumption (e.g., 'nights out'), rather than, for example, to be given to family or used for basic needs." Thieves spend much of their leisure hours enjoying good times. Our subjects were no different in this regard. For example:

> I smoked an ounce of pot in a day, a day and a half. Every other day I had to go buy a bag of pot, at the least. And sometimes I've went two or three days in a row....And there was never a day went by that I didn't [drink] a case, case and a half of beer. And [I] did a 'script of pills every two days.

Although much of their money is consumed by the high cost of drugs, a portion may be used for ostentatious enjoyment and display of luxury items and activities that probably would be unattainable on the returns from blue-collar employment:

> It was all just, it was all just a big money thing to me at the time, you know. Really, what it was impressing everybody, you know. "Here Floyd is, and he's never had nothing in his life, and now look at him: he's driving new cars, and wearing jewelry," you know.

Life as party is enjoyed in the company of others. Typically it includes shared consumption of alcohol or other drugs in bars and lounges, on street corners, or while cruising in automobiles. In these venues, party pursuers celebrate and affirm values of spontaneity, autonomy, independence, and resourcefulness. Spontaneity means that rationality and long-range planning are eschewed in favor of enjoying the moment and permitting the day's activities and pleasures to develop in an unconstrained fashion. This may mean, for example, getting up late, usually after a night of partying, and then setting out to contact and enjoy the company of friends and associates who are known to be predisposed to partying:

A: I got up around about 8:30 that morning....

Q: Eight-thirty? Was that the usual time that you got up?

A: Yeah, if I didn't have a hangover from the night before....

Q: What kind of drugs were you doing then?

A: I was doing...Percadans, Dilauds, taking Valiums, drinking....Anyway, I got up that morning about 8:30, took me a bath, put on some clothes and...decided to walk [over to his mother's home]. This particular day,...my nephew was over [there]....He was just sitting in the yard and talking and drinking beer, you know....It was me, him and my sister. We was sitting out there in the yard talking. And this guy that we know, he came up, he pulled up. So my nephew got in the car with him and they left. So, you know, I was sitting there talking to my sister....And then, in the meantime, while we was talking, they come back, about 30 minutes later with a case of beer, some marijuana and everything, and there was another one of my nephews in the car with them. So me, two of my sisters, and two of my nephews, we got in the car with this guy here and we just went riding. So we went to Hadley Park and...we stayed out there. There were so many people out there, they were parked on the grass and things, and the vice squad come and run everybody away. So when they done that, we left....So we went back out [toward his mother's home] but instead of going over to my mother's house we went to this little joint [tavern]. Now we're steady drinking and smoking weed all during this day. So when we get there, we park and get out and see a few friends. We [were] talking and getting high, you know, blowing each other a shotgun [sharing marijuana].

Enjoyment of party pursuits in group context is enhanced through the collective emphasis on personal autonomy. Because it is understood by all that participants are free to leave if they no longer enjoy or do not support group activities, the continuing presence of each participant affirms for the remainder the pleasures of the lifestyle. Uncoerced participation thus reinforces the shared assumption that group activities are appropriate and enjoyable. The behavioral result of the emphasis on autonomy is acceptance of or acquiescence in group decisions and activities.

Party pursuits also appeal to offenders because they permit conspicuous display of independence (Persson, 1981). This generally means avoidance of the world of routine work and freedom from being "under someone's thumb." It also may include being free to avoid or to escape from restrictive routines:

I just wanted to be doing something. Instead of being at home, or something like that. I wanted to be running, I wanted to be going to clubs, and picking up women and shooting pool. And I liked to go to [a nearby resort community] and just drive around over there. A lot of things like that....I was drinking two pints or more a day....I was doing Valiums and I was doing Demerol....I didn't want to work.

The proper pursuit and enjoyment of life as party is expensive, largely because of the costs of drugs. As one of our subjects remarked: "We was doing a lot of cocaine, so cash didn't last long, you know. If we made $3,000, $2,000 of it almost instantly went for cocaine." Some party pursuers must meet other expenses as well if the lifestyle is to be maintained:

A: Believe it or not, I was spending [$700] a day.
Q: On what?
A: Pot, alcohol, women, gas, motel rooms, food.
Q: You were living in hotels, motels?
A: Yeah, a lot of times, I was. I'd take a woman to a motel. I bought a lot of clothes. I used to like to dress pretty nicely, I'd buy suits.

Party pursuits require continuous infusions of money and no single method of generating funds allows enjoyment of it for more than a few days. Consequently, the emphasis on spontaneity, autonomy, and independence is matched by the importance attached to financial resourcefulness. This is evidenced by the ability to sustain the lifestyle over a period of time. Doing so earns for offenders a measure of respect from peers for their demonstrated ability to "get over." It translates into "self-esteem...as a folk hero beating the bureaucratic system of routinized dependence" (Walsh, 1986, p. 16). The value of and respect for those who demonstrate resourcefulness means that criminal acts, as a means of sustaining life as party, generally are not condemned by the offender's peers.

The risks of employing criminal solutions to the need for funds are approached blithely but confidently in the same spontaneous and playful manner as are the rewards of life as party. In fact, avoidance of careful and detailed planning is a way of demonstrating possession of valued personal qualities and commitment to the lifestyle. Combined with the twin assumptions that peers have chosen freely and that one should not interfere with their autonomy, avoidance of rational planning finds expression in a reluctance to suggest that peers should weigh carefully the possible consequences of whatever they choose to do. Therefore, the interaction that precedes criminal incidents is distinguished by circumspection and the use of linguistic devices that relegate risk and fear to the background of attention. The act of stealing, for example, is referred to obliquely but knowingly as "doing something" or as "making money":

A: [After a day of partying,] I [got] to talking about making some money, because I didn't have no money. This guy that we were riding with, he had all the money....So me and him and my nephew, we get together, talking about making some money. This guy tells me, he said, "Man, I know where there's a good place at."

Q: Okay, so you suggested you all go somewhere and rob?

A: Yeah, "make some," well, we called it "making money."

Q: Okay. So, then you and this fellow met up in the bar.... Tell me about the conversation?

A: Well, there wasn't much of a conversation to it, really.... I asked him if he was ready to go, if he wanted to go do something, you know. And he knew what I meant. He wanted to go make some money somehow, any way it took.

To the external observer, inattention to risk at the moment when it would seem most appropriate may seem to border on irrationality. For the offender engaged in party pursuits, however, it is but one aspect of behaviors that are rational in other respects. It opens up opportunities to enjoy life as party and to demonstrate commitment to values shared by peers. Resourcefulness and disdain for conventional rationality affirm individual character and style, both of which are important in the world of party pursuits (Goffman, 1967).

Party Pursuits and Eroding Resources

Paradoxically, the pursuit of life as party can be appreciated and enjoyed to the fullest extent only if participants moderate their involvement in it while maintaining identities and routines in the straight world. Doing so maintains its "escape value," but it also requires an uncommon measure of discipline and forbearance. The fact is that extended and enthusiastic enjoyment of life as party threatens constantly to deplete irrevocably the resources needed to sustain enjoyment of its pleasures. Three aspects of the life-as-party lifestyle can contribute to this end.

First, some offenders become ensnared increasingly by the chemical substances and drug-using routines that are common there. In doing so, the meaning of drug consumption changes:

> See, I was doing drugs every day. It just wasn't every other day, it was to the point that, after the first few months doing drugs, I would have to do "X amount" of drugs, say, just for instance, just to feel like I do now. Which is normal.

Once the party pursuer's physical or psychological tolerance increases significantly, drugs are consumed not for the high they once produced but instead to maintain a sense of normality by avoiding sickness or withdrawal.

Second, party pursuits erode legitimate fiscal and social capital. They cannot be sustained by legitimate employment and they may in fact undermine both one's ability and inclination to hold a job. Even if offenders are willing to work at the kinds of employment available to them, and evidence suggests that many are not (Cromwell, Olson, & Avary, 1991), the time schedules of work and party pursuits conflict. The best times of the day for committing many property crimes are also the times the offender would be at work, and it is nearly impossible to do both consistently and well. For those who pursue life as a party, legitimate employment often is foregone or sacrificed (Rengert & Wasilchick, 1985). The absence of income from noncriminal sources thus reinforces the need to find other sources of money.

Determined pursuit of life as party also may affect participants' relationships with legitimate significant others. Many offenders manage to enjoy the lifestyle successfully only by exploiting the concern and largesse of family and friends. This may take the form of repeated requests for and receipt of personal loans that go unreturned, occasional thefts, or other forms of exploitation:

> I lived well for awhile. I lived well...until I started shooting cocaine real bad, intravenously.... [A]nd then everything, you know, went up in smoke, you know. Up my arm. The watches, the rings...the car, you know. I used to have a girl, man, and her daddy had two horses. I put them in my arm. You know what I mean? I made her sell them horses. My clothes and all that stuff, a lot of it, they went up in smoke when I started messing with that cocaine.

Eventually, friends and even family members may come to believe that they have been exploited or that continued assistance will only prolong a process that must be terminated. As one subject told us, "Oh, I tried to borrow money, and borrow money and, you know, nobody would loan it to me. Because they knew what I was doing." After first refusing further assistance, acquaintances, friends, and even family members may avoid social contacts with the party pursuer or sever ties altogether. This dialogue occurred between the interviewer and one of our subjects:

> Q: Besides doing something wrong, did you think of anything else that you could do to get money?...Borrow it?
> A: No, I'd done run that in the ground. See, you burn that up. That's burned up, right there, borrowing, you know.... Once I borrow, you know, I might get $10 from you today and, see, I'll be expecting to be getting $10 tomorrow, if I could. And then, when I see you [and] you see me coming, you say, "No, I don't have none." As the guys in the penitentiary say, "You absorb all of your remedies," you see. And that's what I did: I burned my remedies up, you know.

Last, when party pursuits are not going well, feelings of shame and self-disgust are not uncommon (Frazier & Meisenhelder, 1985). Unsuccessful party pursuers as a result may take steps to reduce these feelings by distancing themselves voluntarily from conventional others:

> Q: You were married to your wife at that time?
> A: Yeah, I was married.
> Q: Where was she living then?
> A: I finally forced her to go home, you know....I made her go home, you know. And it caused an argument, for her to go home to her mother's. I felt like that was the best thing I did for her, you know. She hated me...for it at the time, didn't understand none of it. But, really, I intentionally made her

go. I really spared her the misery that we were going to have. And it came. It came in bundles.

When party pursuers sustain severe losses of legitimate income and social resources, regardless of how it occurs, they grow increasingly isolated from conventional significant others. The obvious consequence is that this reduces interpersonal constraints on their behavior.

As their pursuit of life as party increasingly assumes qualities of difficulty and struggle, offenders' utilities and risk perceptions also change. Increasingly, crimes are committed not to enhance or sustain the lifestyle so much as to forestall unpleasant circumstances. Those addicted to alcohol or other drugs, for example, must devote increasing time and energy to the quest for monies to purchase their chemicals of choice. Both their drug consumption and the frequency of their criminal acts increase (Ball, Shaffer, & Nurco, 1983; Johnson et al., 1985). For them, as for others, inability to draw on legitimate or low-risk resources eventually may precipitate a crisis. One of our respondents retold how, facing a court appearance on a burglary charge, he needed funds to hire an attorney:

> I needed some money bad or if I didn't, if I went to court the following day, I was going to be locked up. The judge was going to lock me up. Because I didn't have no lawyer. And I had went and talked to several lawyers and they told me...they wanted $1,000, that if I couldn't come up with no $1,000, they couldn't come to court with me....So I went to my sister. I asked my sister, I said, "Look here, what about letting me have $700 or $800 dollars," which I knowed she had the money because she...had been in a wreck and she had gotten some money out of a suit. And she said, "Well, if I give you the money you won't do the right thing with it." And I was telling her, "No, no, I need a lawyer." But I couldn't convince her to let me have the money. So I left....I said, shit, I'm fixin' to go back to jail....So as I left her house and was walking, I was going to catch the bus, the [convenience store] and bus stop was right there by each other. So, I said I'm going to buy me some gum....And in the process of me buying the chewing gum, I seen two ladies, they was counting money. So I figured sooner or later one of them was going to come out with the money....I waited on them until...one came out with the money, and I got it.

Confronted by crisis and preoccupied increasingly with relieving immediate distress, the offender eventually may experience and define himself as propelled by forces beyond his control. Behavioral options become dichotomized into those that hold out some possibility of relief, however risky, and those that promise little but continued pain. Legitimate options are few and are seen as unlikely solutions. A criminal act may offer some hope of relief, however temporary. The offender may imbue the criminal option with almost magical prospects for ending or reversing the state of discomfort:

> I said, well, look at it like this: if I don't do it, then tomorrow morning I've got the same [problems] that I've got right now. I could be hungry. I'm going to want food more. I'm going to want cigarettes more. I'm going to want everything more. But, if I do it, and if I make it, then I've got all I want.

Acts that once were the result of blithe unconcern with risk can over time come to be based on a personal determination to master or reverse what is experienced as desperately unpleasant circumstances. As a result, inattention to risk in the offender's decision making may give way to the perception that he has nothing to lose:

> It…gets to the point that you get into such a desperation. You're not working, you can't work. You're drunk as hell, been that way two or three weeks. You're no good to yourself, and you're no good to anybody else. Self-esteem is gone [and you are] spiritually, mentally, physically, financially bankrupt. You ain't got *nothing to lose*.

Desperate to maintain or reestablish a sense of normality, the offender pursues emotional relief with a decision to act decisively, albeit in the face of legal odds recognized as narrowing. By acting boldly and resolutely to make the best of a grim situation, one gains a measure of respect, if not from others, then at least from oneself.

> I think, when you're doing drugs like I was doing, I don't think you tend to rationalize much at all. I think it's just a decision you make. You don't weigh the consequences, the pros and the cons. You just do it.
>
> You know, all kinds of things started running through my mind. If I get caught, then there, there I am with another charge. Then I said, well if I don't do something, I'm going to be in jail. And I just said, "I'm going to do it."

The fact that sustained party pursuits often cause offenders to increase the number of offenses they commit and to exploit criminal opportunities that formerly were seen as risky should not be interpreted as meaning they believe they can continue committing crime with impunity. The opposite is true. Many offenders engaged in crimes intended to halt or reverse eroding fortunes are aware that eventually they will be arrested if they continue doing so:

> Q: How did you manage not to think about, you know, that you could go to prison?
> A: Well, you think about it afterwards. You think, "Wow, boy, I got away with it again." But you know, sooner or later, the law of averages is gonna catch up with you. You just can't do it [commit crime] forever and ever and ever. And don't think you're not gonna get caught, cause you will.

Bennett and Wright (1984a) likewise show that a majority of persistent offenders endorse the statement that they will be caught "eventually." The cyclical transformations of party pursuits from pleasant and enjoyable to desperate and tenuous is one reason they are able to commit crimes despite awareness of inevitable and potentially severe legal penalties.

The threat posed by possible arrest and imprisonment, however, may not seem severe to some desperate offenders. As compared to their marginal and precarious existence, it may be seen as offering a form of relief:

[When I was straight], I'd think about [getting caught]: I could get this, and that [penalties]....[A]nd then I would think, well, I know this is going to end one day, you know. But, you know, you get so far out there, and get so far off into it that it really don't matter, you know. But you think about that....I knew, eventually, I would get caught, you know....I was off into drugs and I just didn't care if I got caught or not.

When I [got] caught and they caught me right at the house it's kind of like, you feel good, because you're glad it's over, you know. I mean, a weight being lifted off your head. And you say, well, I don't have to worry about this shit no more, because they've caught me. And it's over, you know.

In sum, because of offenders' eroding access to legitimately secured funds, their diminishing contact with and support from conventional significant others, and their efforts to maintain drug consumption habits, crimes that once were committed for recreational purposes increasingly become desperate attempts to forestall or reverse uncomfortable or frustrating situations. Pursuing the short-term goal of maximizing enjoyment of life, legal threats can appear to the offender either as remote and improbable contingencies when party pursuits fulfill their recreational purposes or as an acceptable risk in the face of continued isolation, penury, and desperation.

We analyzed the descriptions of crime provided by our subjects, and their activities on the day the crime occurred. We focused specifically on: (1) the primary purpose of their crimes, that is, whether they planned to use the proceeds of crime for pleasure or to cope with unpleasant contingencies, and (2) the extent and subjective meaning of their drug use at the time they decided to commit the crime in question. On the basis of the analysis, we classified the crimes of 15 subjects as behaviors committed in the enjoyment of life as a party and 13 as behaviors committed to enhance or restore enjoyment of this lifestyle. The 12 remaining offenders could not be classified because of insufficient information in the crime descriptions or because they committed isolated criminal acts that do not represent a specific lifestyle. Two subjects, for example, described crimes that were acts of vengeance directed at the property of individuals who had treated them or their relatives improperly. One of the men related how he decided to burglarize a home for reasons of revenge:

I was mad....When I was in the penitentiary, my wife went to his house for a party and he give her a bunch of cocaine....It happened, I think, about a week before I got out....I just had it in my mind what I wanted to do: I wanted to hurt him like I was hurt....I was pretty drunk, when I went by [his home], and I saw there wasn't no car there. So, I just pulled my car in.

The other subject told how an acquaintance had stolen drugs and other possessions from his automobile. In response the subject "staked out the places where he would be for several days before I caught him, at gun point, [and] made him take me to his home, [which] I ransacked, and found some of the narcotics that he had stolen from me." Although neither of these crimes was committed in pursuit of life as party, other crimes committed by both these subjects during their criminal careers did occur as part of that lifestyle. Other investigators have similarly reported that revenge is the dominant motive in a minority of property offenses (e.g., Cromwell, Olson, & Avary, 1991, p. 22).

Implications

We have suggested that daily routines characteristic of the partying lifestyle of persistent and unsuccessful offenders may modify both the salience of their various decision utilities and their perceptions of legal risk in the process of their crime commission decisions. This is not to say that these decisions are irrational, only that they do not conform to decision making as sketched by rational-choice theories. Our objective was not to falsify the rational-choice approach to criminal decision making, for we know of no way this could be accomplished. Whatever it is, moreover, rationality is not a dichotomous variable. Indeed, offenders' target selection decision making appears more rational in the conventional sense than do crime commission decisions.

The lesson here for theories of criminal decision making is that although utilities and risk assessment may be properties of individuals, they also are shaped by the social and personal contexts in which decisions are made. Whether their pursuit of life as party is interpreted theoretically as the product of structural strain, choice, or even happenstance is of limited importance to an understanding of persistent offenders' discrete criminal forays. What is important is that their lifestyle places them in situations that may facilitate important transformations in the utilities of prospective actions. If nothing else, this means that some situations more than others make it possible to discount or ignore risk. We are not the first to call attention to this phenomenon:

> [The] situational nature of sanction properties has escaped the scales and indicators employed in official record and self-report survey research. In this body of research an arrest and a year in prison are generally assumed to have the same meaning for all persons and across all situations. The situational grounding of sanction properties suggests, [however,] that we look beyond official definitions of sanctions and the attitudinal structure of individuals to the properties of situations. (Ekland-Olson, Lieb, & Zurcher, 1984, p. 174)

Along the same line, a longitudinal survey of adult offenders concludes:

> [Decision making] may be conditioned by elements within the immediate situation confronting the individual... [such that] perceptions of the opportunity, returns, and support for crime within a given situation may influence... perceptions of risks and the extent to which those risks are discounted. (Piliavin, Gartner, & Matsueda, 1986, p. 115)

The same interpretation has been suggested by Shover and Thompson (1992) for their failure to find an expected positive relationship between risk estimates and crime desistance among former prison inmates.

In light of the sample and data limitations of this study, we cannot and have not argued that the lifestyle we described generates or produces the characteristic decision-making behaviors of persistent property offenders. The evidence does not permit such interpretive liberties. It does seem reasonable to suggest, however, that the focal concerns and shared perspectives of those who pursue life as party may function to sustain offenders' free-wheeling, but purposeful, decision-making style. Without question there is a close correspondence between the two. Our ability to explain and predict decision making requires that we gain a better understanding of how utilities and risk perceptions are constrained by the properties of situations encountered typically by persons in their daily rounds. In other words, we must learn more about the daily worlds that comprise the immediate contexts of criminal decision-making behavior.

REFERENCES

Ball, J. C., Shaffer, J. W., & Nurco, D. N. (1983). The day-to-day criminality of heroin addicts in Baltimore: A study in the continuity of offense rates. *Drug and Alcohol Dependence, 12*, 119–142.

Becker, G. (1968). Crime and punishment: An economic approach. *Journal of Political Economy, 76*, 169–217.

Bennett, T., & Wright, R. (1984a). *Burglars on burglary.* Hampshire, U.K.: Gower.

———. (1984b). The relationship between alcohol use and burglary. *British Journal of Addiction, 79*, 431–37.

Blumstein, A., Cohen, J., & Nagin, D. (Eds.). (1978). *Deterrence and incapacitation: Estimating the effects of criminal sanctions on crime rates.* Washington, DC: National Academy of Sciences.

Carroll, J. S. (1978). A psychological approach to deterrence: The evaluation of crime opportunities. *Journal of Personality and Social Psychology, 36*, 1512–1520.

———. (1982). Committing a crime: The offender's decision. In V. J. Konecni & E. B. Ebbesen (Eds.), *The criminal justice system: A social-psychological analysis* (pp. 49–68). New York: Freeman

Carroll, J. S., & Weaver, F. (1986). Shoplifters' perceptions of crime opportunities: A process-tracing study. In D. B. Cornish & R. V. Clarke (Eds.), *The reasoning criminal: Rational choice perspectives on offending* (pp. 19–38). New York: Springer-Verlag.

Clarke, R. V., & Cornish, D. B. (1985). Modeling offenders' decisions: A framework for research and policy. In M. Tonry & N. Morris (Eds.), *Crime and justice: A review of research* (Vol. 4, pp. 147–185). Chicago: University of Chicago Press.

Claster, D. S. (1967). Comparison of risk perception between delinquents and nondelinquents. *Journal of Criminal Law, Criminology, and Police Science, 58*, 80–86.

Cornish, D. B. & Clarke, R. V. (Eds.). (1986). *The reasoning criminal: Rational choice perspectives on offending.* New York: Springer-Verlag.

Cromwell, P. F., Olson, J. N., & Avary, D. W. (1991). *Breaking and entering: An ethnographic analysis of burglary.* Newbury Park, CA: Sage.

Ekland-Olson, S., Lieb, J., & Zurcher, L. (1984). The paradoxical impact of criminal sanctions: Some microstructural findings. *Law and Society Review, 18*, 159–178.

Feeney, F. (1986). Robbers as decision-makers. In D. B. Cornish & R. V. Clarke (Eds.), *The reasoning criminal: Rational choice perspectives on offending.* New York: Springer-Verlag, 53–71

Figgie International. (1988). *The Figgie report part VI: The business of crime: The criminal perspective.* Richmond, VA: Figgie International Inc.

Frazier, C. E., & Meisenhelder, T. (1985). Criminality and emotional ambivalence: Exploratory notes on an overlooked dimension. *Qualitative Sociology, 8,* 266–284.

Gibbs, J. J., & Shelley, P. L. (1982). Life in the fast lane: A retrospective view by commercial thieves. *Journal of Research in Crime and Delinquency, 19,* 299–330.

Goffman, E. (1967). *Interaction ritual.* Garden City, NY: Anchor.

Gottfredson, M. R., & Hirschi, T. (1990). *A general theory of crime.* Stanford, CA: Stanford University Press.

Heineke, J. M. (Ed.). (1978). *Economic models of criminal behavior.* Amsterdam: North-Holland.

Johnson, B. D., Goldstein, P. J., Preble, E., Schmeidler, J., Lipton, D. D., Spunt, B., et al. (1985). *Taking care of business: The economics of crime by heroin addicts.* Lexington, MA: D.C. Heath.

Katz, J. (1998). *Seductions of crime.* New York: Basic.

Maguire, M., in collaboration with Bennett, T. (1982). *Burglary in a dwelling.* London: Heinemann.

Manski, C. F. (1978). Prospects for inference on deterrence through empirical analysis of individual criminal behavior. In A. Blumstein, J. Cohen, & D. Nagin (Eds.), *Deterrence and incapacitation: Estimating the effects of criminal sanctions on crime rates.* Washington, DC: National Academy of Sciences.

Nagin, D. S., & Paternoster, R. (1991). On the relationship of past to future participation in delinquency. *Criminology, 29,* 163–189.

Persson, M. (1981). Time-perspectives amongst criminals. *Acta Sociologica, 24,* 149–165.

Petersilia, J., Greenwood, P. W., & Lavin, M. (1978). *Criminal careers of habitual felons.* Washington, DC: U.S. Department of Justice, National Institute of Law Enforcement and Criminal Justice.

Peterson, M. A., & Braiker, H. B. (1980). *Doing crime: A survey of California prison inmates.* Santa Monica, CA: Rand Corporation.

Piliavin, I., Gartner, R., & Matsueda, R. (1986). Crime, deterrence, and rational choice. *American Sociological Review, 51,* 101–119.

Rengert, G. F., & Wasilchick, J. (1985). *Suburban burglary.* Springfield, IL: Charles C. Thomas.

Repetto, T. A. (1974). *Residential crime.* Cambridge, MA: Ballinger.

Reynolds, M. O. (1985). *Crime by choice: An economic analysis.* Dallas: Fisher Institute.

Scarr, H. A. (1973). *Patterns of burglary* (2nd ed.). Washington, DC: U.S. Department of Justice, National Institute of Law Enforcement and Criminal Justice.

Shover, N. (1991). Burglary. In M. Tonry (Ed.), *Crime and justice: An annual review of research* (Vol. 14: pp.73–113). Chicago: University of Chicago Press.

Shover, N., & Thompson, C. Y. (1992). Age, differential expectations, and crime desistance. *Criminology, 30,* 89–104.

Waldo, G. P., & Chiricos, T. G. (1972). Perceived penal sanction and self-reported criminality: A neglected approach to deterrence research. *Social Problems, 19,* 522–540.

Walsh, D. (1980). *Break-ins: Burglary from private houses.* London: Constable.

———. (1986). *Heavy business.* London: Routledge and Kegan Paul.

CHAPTER 4

⤸

Deciding to Commit a Burglary

Richard T. Wright and Scott H. Decker

Why burglary? Based on their study of residential burglary in St. Louis, Wright and Decker discuss the dynamics underlying the decision to commit a burglary. The authors interviewed 105 active residential burglars, taking them to the scenes of their past crimes and asked them to reconstruct the burglary in extensive detail. In this chapter they examine the factors which motivated the crime—that is, "why burglary?" The subjects in their study tended to be misfits in a world that values punctuality, schedules and discipline. Crime appealed to some of the subjects precisely because it allowed them to flaunt their independence from the routine imposed by the world of work (See Shover and Honaker, 1992 and, 1993 in this volume). Their crimes were committed primarily based on their perception of an immediate need for money. Their need for money revolved primarily about maintaining their lifestyle, which the authors described as 'high living" and which Shover, 1992 (in this volume) termed "life as party," although some committed burglaries for licit activities such as food, clothing and shelter and others had committed burglaries for revenge, thrills and other non-economic reasons.

The demographic characteristics of residential burglars have been well documented. As Shover (1991) has observed, such offenders are, among other things, disproportionately young, male, and poor. These characteristics serve to identify a segment of the population more prone than others to resort to breaking in to dwellings, but they offer little insight into the actual causes of residential burglary. Many poor, young males, after all, never commit any sort of serious offense, let alone a burglary. And even those who carry out such crimes are not offending most of the time. This is not, by and large, a continually motivated group of criminals; the motivation for them to offend is closely tied to their assessment of current circumstances and prospects. The direct cause of residential burglary is a percep-

Source: Excerpted from Richard T. Wright and Scott H. Decker, *Burglars on the Job: Streetlife and Residential Break-ins*. Boston: Northeastern University Press. 1994. pp. 35–61.

tual process through which the offense comes to be seen as a means of meeting an immediate need, that is, through which a motive for the crime is formed.

Walker (1984: viii) has pointed out that, in order to develop a convincing explanation for criminal behavior, we must begin by "distinguishing the states of mind in which offenders commit, or contemplate the commission of, their offenses." Similarly, Katz (1988:4), arguing for increased research into what he calls the foreground of criminality, has noted that all of the demographic information on criminals in the world cannot answer the following question: "Why are people who were not determined to commit a crime one moment determined to do so the next?" This is the question to which the present chapter is addressed. The aim is to explore the extent to which the decision to commit a residential burglary is the result of a process of careful calculation and deliberation.

In the overwhelming majority of cases, the decision to commit a residential burglary arises in the face of what offenders perceive to be a pressing need for cash. Previous research consistently has shown this to be so (Bennett and Wright, 1984; Cromwell et al. 1991) and the results of the present study bear out this point. More than nine out of ten of the offenders in our sample—95 of 102—reported that they broke into dwellings primarily when they needed money.

> Well, it's like, the way it clicks into your head is like, you'll be thinking about something and, you know, it's a problem. Then it, like, all relates. "Hey, I need some money! Then how am I going to get money? Well, how do you know how to get money quick and easy?" Then there it is. Next thing you know, you are watching [a house] or calling to see if [the occupants] are home. (Wild Will— No. 010)
>
> Usually when I get in my car and drive around I'm thinking, I don't have any money, so what is my means for gettin' money? All of a sudden I'll just take a glance and say, "There it is! There's the house"...Then I get this feelin', that right moment, I'm movin' then. (Larry William—No. 017)

These offenders were not motivated by a desire for money for its own sake. By and large, they were not accumulating the capital needed to achieve a long-range goal. Rather, they regarded money as providing them with the means to solve an immediate problem. In their view, burglary was a matter of day-to-day survival.

> I didn't have the luxury of laying back in no damn pin-striped [suit]. I'm poor and I'm raggedy and I need some food and I need some shoes ... So I got to have some money some kind of way. If it's got to be the wrong way, then so be it. (Mark Smith—No. 030)
>
> When I first started out, when I was younger, [burglary] was excitement or a high. But now it's to get by, you know, to survive. I don't ask my father for anything. My mother is not able to help. (Larry Harris—No. 035)

Given this view, it is unsurprising that the frequency with which the offenders committed burglaries was governed largely by the amount of money in their pockets. Many of them would not offend so long as they had sufficient cash to meet current expenses.

> Usually what I'll do is a burglary, maybe two or three if I have to, and then this will help me get over the rough spot until I can get my skit straightened out. Once I get it straightened out, I just go with the flow until I hit that rough spot where I need the money again. And then I hit it...the only time I would go and commit a burglary is if I needed the money at that point in time. That would be strictly to pay light bill, gas bill, rent. (Dan Whiting—No. 102)
>
> Long as I got some money, I'm cool. If I ain't got no money and I want to get high, then I go for it. (Janet Wilson—No. 060)
>
> You know how they say stretch a dollar? I'll stretch it from here to the parking lot. But I can only stretch it so far and then it breaks. Then I say, "Well, I guess I got to go put on my black clothes. Go on out there like a thief in the night." (Ralph Jones—No. 018)

A few of the offenders sometimes committed a burglary even though they had sufficient cash for their immediate needs. These subjects were not purposely saving money, but they were unwilling to pass up opportunities to make more. They attributed their behavior to having become "greedy" or "addicted" to money.

> I have done it out of greed, per se. Just to be doing it and to have more money, you know? Say, for instance, I have two hundred dollars in my pocket now. If I had two more hundreds, then that's four hundred dollars. Go out there and do a burglary. Then I say, "If I have four hundred dollars, then I can have a thousand." Go out there and do a burglary. (No. 018)
>
> It's like when you smoke a cigarette, you know, you want more and more from the nicotine. Well, from my experience, you can get bigger and better stuff the more times that you do it and you can make more money. I'm addicted to money, I love money. So I just keep doing [burglaries]. (Robert Jones—No. 103)

Typically, the offenders did not save the money that they de-rived through burglary. Instead, they spent it for one or more of the following purposes: (I) to "keep the party going"; (2) to keep up appearances; or (3) to keep themselves and their families fed, clothed, and sheltered.

Keeping the Party Going

Although the offenders often stated that they committed residential burglaries to "survive," there is a danger in taking this claim at face value. When asked how they spent the proceeds of their burglaries, nearly three-quarters of them—68 of 95—said they used the money for various forms of (for want of a better term) high-living. Most commonly, this involved the use of illicit drugs. Fifty-nine of the 68 offenders who spent the money obtained from burglary on pleasure-seeking pursuits specifically mentioned the purchase of drugs. For many of these respondents, the decision to break into a dwelling of-ten arose as a result of a heavy session of drug use. The objective was to get the money to keep the party going (Shover and Honaker, 1990). The drug most frequently implicated in these situations was "crack" cocaine.

> [Y]ou ever had an urge before? Maybe a cigarette urge or a food urge, where you eat that and you got to have more and more? That's how that crack is. You smoke

it and it hits you [in the back of the throat] and you got to have more. I'll smoke that sixteenth up and get through, it's like I never had none. I got to have more. Therefore, I gots to go do another burglary and gets some more money. (Richard Jackson—No. 009)

It's usually, say we'll be doing some coke and then you really want more, so we'll go and do [a burglary] and get some money. (Sasha Williams—No. 094)

I might find somebody with some good crack...while I'm high I say, "Damn, I want me some more of this shit!" Go knock a place off, make some more money, go buy some more dope. (Die Leo—No. 079)

Lemert [1953:304] has labeled situations like these "dialectical, self-enclosed systems of behavior" in that they have an internal logic or "false structure" which calls for more of the same. Once locked into such events, he asserts, participants experience considerable pressure to continue, even if this involves breaking the law.

> A man away from home who falls in with a group of persons who have embarked upon a two or three-day or even a week's period of drinking and carousing... tends to have the impetus to continue the pattern which gets mutually reinforced by [the] interaction of the participants, and [the pattern] tends to have an accelerated beginning, a climax and a terminus. If midway through a spree a participant runs out of money, the pressures immediately become critical to take such measures as are necessary to preserve the behavior sequence. A similar behavior sequence is [evident] in that of the alcoholic who reaches a "high point" in his drinking and runs out of money. He might go home and get clothes to pawn or go and borrow money from a friend or even apply for public relief, but these alternatives become irrelevant be-cause of the immediacy of his need for alcohol. (Lemert, 1953:303)

Implicit in this explanation is an image of actors who become involved in offending without significant calculation; having embarked voluntarily on one course of action (e.g., crack smoking), they suddenly find themselves being drawn into an unanticipated activity (e.g., residential burglary) as a means of sustaining that action. Their offending is not the result of a thoughtful, carefully reasoned process. Instead, it emerges as part of the natural flow of events, seemingly coming out of nowhere. In other words, it is not so much that these actors consciously choose to commit crimes as that they elect to get involved in situations that drive them toward law breaking (Kennedy and Baron, 1993)·

Other subjects, though they claimed that a perceived need for drugs typically triggered their decision to do a burglary, were not under the influence of drugs when the decision was reached. Their aim was to get high rather than to stay high. They regarded themselves as having a drug "habit" which compelled them to crime; the urge for drugs seemed beyond their ability to control and had to be satisfied by whatever means necessary. Although some in this group were addicted to narcotics such as heroin, this was not always the case.

> See, sometimes I wake up and don't have no [marijuana]. I have to go do my [burglary] and get me some money and get me some. (Carl Jackson—No. 022)

Getting and using drugs were major preoccupations for a majority of the offenders, not just a small cadre of addicts. Many of them reported committing burglaries *solely* for the purpose of obtaining money to buy drugs. But even some of those who did burglaries for other reasons ended up spending a portion of the profits on drugs.

> Lot of times when I commit burglary I use some of the money to get drugs, but I don't do the burglaries for that purpose. (Larry Washington—No. 013)

For these offenders, indulgence in drug use represented a crucial aspect of their street identity as "hip"; the street corner culture from which most of them— black and white, male and female—were drawn is oriented largely toward getting high (Anderson, 1990). In the past, this almost exclusively involved the drinking of beer or cheap wine. While drinking remains a feature of street culture— 14 offenders, 21 percent of those who spent their money on high-living, mentioned the purchase of alcohol—it is increasingly being accompanied by illicit drug use. The money required to support such use is substantial and this ensured that the offenders were almost perpetually in need of cash (Shover and Honaker, 1992).

Beyond the purchase of illicit drugs and, to a lesser extent, alcohol, 10 of the 68 offenders—15 percent— also used the proceeds from their residential burglaries to pursue sexual conquests. All of these offenders were male. Some liked to flash money about, believing that this was the way to attract women.

> I guess I like to flash [money] a lot, impress the girls and stuff. Go out and spend some money, you know? (Wayne Jones—No. 055)
>
> [I commit burglaries to] splurge money with the women, you know, that's they kick, that's what they like to do. (Jon Monroe—No. 011)
>
> [I use the burglary money for] gifts for young ladies — flowers or negligee or somethin'. Some shoes, "Put them shoes on, them pumps." [Then] watch 'em nude. (Jack Daniel—No. 054)

Like getting high, sexual conquest was a much-prized symbol of hipness through which the male subjects in our sample could accrue status among their peers on the street. The greatest prestige was accorded to those who were granted sexual favors solely on the basis of smooth talk and careful impression management. Nevertheless, a few of the offenders took a more direct approach to obtaining sex by paying a street corner prostitute (sometimes referred to as a "duck") for it. While this was regarded as less hip than the more subtle approach described above, it had the advantage of being easy and uncomplicated. As such, it appealed to offenders who were wrapped up in partying and therefore reluctant to devote more effort than was necessary to satisfy their immediate sexual desires.

> I spend [the money] on something to drink,…then get me some [marijuana]. Then I'm gonna find me a duck. (Ricky Davis—No. 105)

It would be misleading to suggest that any of the offenders we spoke to committed burglaries *specifically* to get money for sex, but a number of them often directed a portion of their earnings toward this goal.

In short, among the major purposes for which the offenders used the money derived from burglary was the maintenance of a lifestyle centered on illicit drugs, but frequently incorporating alcohol and sexual conquests as well. This lifestyle reflects the values of the street culture, a culture characterized by openness to "illicit action" (Katz, 1988:209–15), to which most of our subjects were strongly committed. Viewed from the perspective of the offenders, then, the oft-heard claim that they broke into dwellings to survive does not seem quite so farfetched. The majority of them saw their fate as inextricably linked to an ability to fulfill the imperatives of life on the street.

Keeping Up Appearances

Of the 95 offenders who committed residential burglaries primarily for financial reasons, 43 reported that they used the cash to purchase various "status" items. The most popular item was clothing; 39 of the 43 said that they bought clothes with the proceeds of their crimes. At one level, of course, clothing must be regarded as necessary for survival. The responses of most of the offenders, however, left little doubt that they were not buying clothes to protect themselves from the elements, but rather to project a certain image; they were drawn to styles and brand names regarded as chic on the streets.

> See, I go steal money and go buy me some clothes. See, I likes to look good. I likes to dress. All I wear is Stacy Adams, that's all I wear. [I own] only one pair of blue jeans cause I likes to dress. (No. 011)
>
> I buy fashionable clothes or whatever, you know, just spend [the money]. (Mike West—No. 049)
>
> [I] buy Stacy Adams clothes, sweaters. When I grew up, I always had the basic shit. [My parents] were wealthy and I always got [cheap] shoes and shit and I was always in competition with other kids and [my parents] never understood that. So I would go out and buy me Nikes. I'd buy three brand new sixty-dollar pairs of shoes and clothes. (Joe Wilson—No. 099)
>
> A lot of times I'll buy clothes or tennis shoes or some jogging outfits, something like that. Some type of jacket or buy a hat. (Maurice Ross—No. 040)

Wearing appropriate clothing is an important aspect of fitting into any social situation. This is no less true for street culture, which has its own "dress code." As Anderson (1990) has observed, dressing in the latest status symbol clothing is virtually mandatory for those who want to be seen as hip on the street. The subjects in our sample were responding to this fact by using the money that they made from burglary to purchase fashionable outfits.

After clothes, cars and car accessories were the next most popular status items bought by the offenders. Seven of the 43 reported spending at least some of the money they got from burglaries on their cars.

> I spent [the money] on stuff for my car. Like I said, I put a lot of money into my car...I had a '79 Grand Prix, you know, a nice car. (Matt Detteman—No. 072)

The attributes of a high-status vehicle varied. Not all of these offenders, for example, would have regarded a 1979 Grand Prix as conferring much prestige on its owner. Nevertheless, they were agreed that driving a fancy or customized car, like wearing fashionable clothing, was an effective way of enhancing one's street status.

A sizable portion of the offenders therefore used the profits from their offenses to acquire the material trappings of success. In doing so, they sought to create an impression of affluence and hipness so that they would be admired by their peers on the street and by others. A British burglar interviewed by Bennett and Wright (1984:139) made explicit reference to the desire of offenders to be seen as a "better class of person."

> I don't know if you've ever thought about it, but I think every crook likes the life of thieving and then going and being somebody better. Really, you are deceiving people; letting them think that you are well off... You've got a nice car, you can go about and do this and do that. It takes money to buy that kind of life.

Shover and Honaker (1990:11) have suggested that the concern of offenders with outward appearances, as with their notorious high-living, grows out of what is typically a strong attachment to the values of street culture; values which place great emphasis on the "ostentatious enjoyment and display of luxury items." In a related vein, Katz (1988) has argued that for those who are committed to street life, the reckless spending of cash on luxury goods is an end in itself, demonstrating their disdain for the ordinary citizen's pursuit of financial security. Seen through the eyes of the offenders, therefore, money spent on such goods has not been "blown," but rather represents a cost of raising or maintaining one's status on the street.

Keeping Things Together

While most of the offenders spent much of the money they earned through residential burglary on drugs and clothes, a substantial number also used some of it for daily living expenses. Of the 95 who committed burglaries to raise money, 50 claimed that they needed the cash for subsistence.

> I do [burglaries] to keep myself together, keep myself up. (James Brown—No. 025)

Necessities mentioned most frequently were food, shelter, and clothing for the children. Thirty-eight of the 50 offenders (76 percent) reported using money from their burglaries to pay for one or all of these needs. Some of them used the money *solely* for such expenses.

> [I spend the money from my burglaries for] needs, not wants, needs—roof over my head, food in my mouth and things for my kids. (Lynn—No. 095)

The majority, however, paid for their immediate subsistence needs and spent the remaining cash on status-enhancing items and high-living.

> [I use burglary money to buy] food, clothing, drugs — in that order. And a place to stay, that's gon come automatic cause I'm an always find a place to stay. (No. 035)

Quite a few of the offenders—13 of 50—said that they paid bills with the money derived from burglary. Here again, however, there is a danger of being misled by such claims. To be sure, these offenders did use some of their burglary money to take care of bills. Often, though, the bills were badly delinquent because the offenders avoided paying them for as long as possible—even when they had the cash—in favor of buying, most typically, drugs. It was not until the threat of serious repercussions created unbearable pressure for the offenders that they relented and settled their accounts.

> [Sometimes I commit burglaries when] things pressuring me, you know? I got to do somethin' about these bills. Bills. I might let it pass that mornin'. Then I start trippin' on it at night and, next thing you know, it's wakin' me up. Yeah, that's when I got to get out and go do a burglary. *I got* to pay this electric bill off, this gas bill, you know? (No. 009)

Similarly, several of the subjects in our sample reported doing burglaries to pay parking or traffic tickets they had long ignored, having preferred to use their money for high-living.

> I started getting tickets and it was, like, I got four tickets for improper registration plates. Then it was like, "Hey, I need some money, this stuff is calculating up." I [needed] some money and I [didn't] want to run and ask Mom. So I just did [a burglary]. (No. 010)

Spontaneity is a prominent feature of street culture (Shover and Honaker, 1992); it is not surprising that many of the offenders displayed a marked tendency to live for the moment. Often they would give every indication of intending to take care of their obligations, financial or otherwise, only to be distracted by more immediate temptations. For instance, a woman in our sample, after being paid for an interview, asked us to drive her to a place where she could buy a pizza for her children's lunch. On the way to the restaurant, however, she changed her mind and asked to be dropped off at a crack house instead. In another case, we persuaded a male subject to allow three consultants on our research to come along on a visit to the scene of his most recent residential burglary in exchange for a larger than usual participation fee. At the agreed time and place, we arrived to find him sitting with friends in a car in an incoherent state; he had used the promised research payment as a means of obtaining cocaine on credit and was in the process of consuming it despite his scheduled meeting with us!

Katz (1988:216) has suggested that, through irresponsible spending, persistent offenders seek to construct "an environment of pressures that guide[s] them back toward crime." Whether offenders spend money in a conscious attempt to create such pressures is arguable; the subjects in our sample gave no indication of doing so, appearing simply to be financially irresponsible. One offender, for example, told us that he never hesitated to spend money, adding, "Why should I? I can always get some more." However, the inclination of offenders to free-spending leaves them with few alternatives but to continue committing crimes. Their next financial crisis is never far around the corner.

The high-living of the offenders, thus, calls into question the extent to which they are driven to crime by genuine financial hardship. At the same time, though, their spendthrift ways ensure that the crimes they commit will be economically motivated (Katz, 1988). The offenders perceive them-selves as needing money, and their offenses typically are a response to this perception. Objectively, however, few are doing burglaries to escape impoverishment.

Why Burglary?

The decision to commit a residential burglary, then, is usually prompted by a perceived need for cash. Burglary, however, is not the only means by which offenders could get some money. Why do they choose burglary over legitimate work? Why do they elect to carry out a burglary rather than borrow the money from a friend or relative? Additionally, why do they select burglary rather than some other crime?

Given the streetcorner context in which most burglary decisions were made, legitimate work did not represent a viable solution for most of the offenders in our sample. These subjects, with few exceptions, wanted money there and then and, in such circumstances, even day labor was irrelevant because it did not respond to the immediacy of their desire for cash (Lemert, 1953). Moreover, the jobs available to most of the of-fenders were poorly-paid and could not sustain their desired lifestyles. It is notable that 17 of the 95 offenders who did burglaries primarily to raise money *were* legitimately employed.

> [I have a job, but] I got tired of waiting on that money. I can get money like that. I got talent, I can do me a burg, man, and get me five or six hundred dollars in less than a hour. Working eight hours a day and waiting for a whole week for a check and it ain't even about shit. (No. 022)
>
> [E]ven if I had a job, I betcha I couldn't find a job payin' me over minimum wage. Then they probably want to pay me every two weeks, so I would have to supplement that week that I wouldn't get paid with somethin'. (Mike Jackson—No. 046)

Beyond this, a few of the offenders expressed a strong aversion to legitimate employment, saying that a job would impinge upon their way of life.

> I ain't workin' and too lazy to work and just all that. I like it to where I can just run around. I don't got to get up at no certain time, just whenever I wake up. I ain't gotta go to bed a certain time to get up at a certain time. Go to bed around one o'clock or when I want, get up when I want. Ain't got to go to work and work eight hours. Just go in and do a five minute job, get that money, that's just basically it. (Tony Scott —No.085)
>
> I done got lazy...I don't even want to work eight hours. I figure I can do maybe only one hour and get paid as much as I would if I worked a full day. (Kip Harris—No. 069)

These subjects closely matched the "high-level thieves" described by Shover (1991:92): "Misfits in a world that values precise schedules, punctuality, and disciplined subordination to authority, high-level thieves value the autonomy to structure life and work as they wish." Indeed, crime appealed to some of the subjects precisely because it allowed them to flaunt their independence from the routine imposed by the world of work (Shover and Honaker, 1992). Not taking orders from anyone—be it a girlfriend, a wife, or an employer—is a bedrock value on which male streetcorner culture rests; to be regarded as hip one must always do as he pleases. Accordingly, those who defined themselves most strongly in terms of their street reputation found the idea of getting a job to be distasteful because legitimate employment would require them to do as they were told by the boss.

> I guess [burglary is] in my blood. I don't too much want to work with a job and listen to no boss. But I can, like, do two or three burglaries and take money home to my kids. (Roger Brown—No. 058)

Nevertheless, a majority of the offenders reported that they wanted lawful employment; 43 of the 78 unemployed subjects who said that they did burglaries mostly for the money claimed they would stop committing offenses if someone gave them a "good" job.

> I'm definitely going to give it up as soon as I get me a good job. I don't mean making fifteen dollars an hour. Give me a job making five-fifty and I'm happy with it. I don't got to burglarize no more. I'm not doing it because I like doing it, I'm doing it because I need some [drugs]. (No. 079)
>
> Anything like five dollars an hour might slow me down, stop me completely. And the people at the job ain't buggin' me. I'll stay there the rest of my life if the people don't bother me cause I don't take nothing from 'em and therefore I would've went off on one of 'em or either beat 'em up. They don't bother me and I won't bother them and that five dollars is standin' strong. And wouldn't have to steal nothin' cause I'd have my money there. And I might cut down off my drugs—mainly you do drugs cause there's nothing to do. (No. 009)

While such claims may or may not be sincere — some of these subjects had held reasonably high-paying jobs in the past, but lost them owing to dishonesty or drug and alcohol problems — it is unlikely that they will ever be challenged. Decent employment opportunities are limited for inner-city residents (Wilson, 1987) and the offenders, who by and large are poorly educated, unskilled, and heavy illicit drug or alcohol users, are not well placed to compete for the few good jobs available. Most of them realized this and were resigned to being out of work. In their eyes, burglary represented a more realistic means of "earning" some money.

> Look, [there] ain't no job! I been out here lookin' for work, can't find no work. So I do what I do best. (Leroy Robison—No. 045)

Instead of committing burglaries, of course, the offenders perhaps could have borrowed some cash from a friend or relative. But they did not view this as a feasible alternative. Some of them were unwilling to ask for money because they felt that this would damage their status.

> I like to stand on my own two feet as a man, you know what I'm sayin'? I like to pay my way and I don't like to ask no-body for nothin'. Don't want nobody talkin' about me like I won't pay my way. I ain't freeloadin' off nobody. I'm a man, so I take care of myself. (Jeffery Moore—No. 006)

Others had borrowed money in the past, but were reluctant to ask for more.

> I can't keep askin' my wife, my brothers and sister and my mother. They'll tell me the same thing, "You a grown man, go out there and get you a job!" Or [they'll hand me some money and say], "Here, don't come back too soon." You know, you can only do that for so long. (No. 018)

And still others simply found that it was impossible to borrow money.

> After you ask for a few dollars from people—your loved ones or your grand-mother—and they tell you what they ain't got, you lay back down and try to go to sleep. You don't have no cigarettes, no beer, no nothing. Yeah, it builds up, animosity builds up inside you. Seems like that old devil just push you on out the door [to do a burglary]. (No. 069)

In any case, borrowing money offers only a short-term solution to financial needs. There usually is an expectation that loans will be repaid and this can provide the impetus for carrying out a burglary. Indeed, Katz (1988:217) has gone so far as to suggest that this obligation is a major source of the monetary troubles that drive offenders to crime: "Economic pressures toward crime emerge, not as the direct result of particular substantive needs as much as through the pressure of obligations accumulated in social networks. Borrowing and credit relations among offenders form a subtle, elaborate institution." In the course of our interviews we were told of burglaries that had been carried out because the offender owed money or wanted to reclaim a pawned article. We even encountered an offender who recently had broken into the residence of a fellow burglar in order to collect on a bad debt.

When faced with an immediate need for cash, then, the offenders in our sample perceived themselves as having little hope of getting money both quickly *and* legally. Many of the most efficient solutions to financial troubles are against the law (Lofland, 1969). However, this does not explain why the subjects decided specifically on the crime of residential burglary. After all, most of them admitted committing other sorts of offenses in the past, and some still were doing so. Why should they choose burglary?

For some subjects, this question held little relevance because they regarded residential burglary as their "main line" and alternative offenses were seldom considered when the need for money arose.

> I guess the reason why I stick to burglary is because it makes me a lot of money...I guess you could say why I just do [burglary] is because I've been doing it for a while and I'm kind of stuck with it. (Carl Watson—No. 032)
>
> [I do burglary] because it's easy and because I know it. It's kind of getting a specialty or a career. If you're in one line, or one field, and you know it real well,

then you don't have any qualms about doing it. But if you try something new, you could really mess up…At this point, I've gotten away with so much [that] I just don't want to risk it—it's too much to risk at this point. I feel like I have a good pattern, clean; go in the house, come back out, under two minutes every time. (Darlene White—No. 100)

[Burglary is] easy for me. People have armed robberies and sell crack or whatever; I do burglaries. That's the easiest thing I do…I'm just saying that's what best suits me. (Karl Alverez —No. 08)

I don't know [why I decided on burglary]. I guess I'm good at it…I just like burglary, that's it. (No. 013)

When these subjects did commit another kind of offense, it typically was triggered by the chance discovery of a vulnerable target. As noted in the first chapter, most of the burglars we interviewed identified themselves as hustlers, people who were always looking to "get over" by making some fast cash; it would have been out of character for them to pass up any kind of presented opportunity to do so.

If I see another hustle, then I'll do it, but burglary is my pet. (Larry Smith— No. 065)

Burglars usually just stick to burglary. There's only one time that I was in the process of doing a burglary and I did a robbery. I was gettin' ready to do a burglary and a guy walked up and had a money sack. So I forgot all about the burglary and got the money sack. (No. 055)

The immediacy of their need for money, however, drove most of the offenders to look actively for any illicit opportunity to obtain cash rapidly, and they were open to crimes other than residential burglary. As one put it: "When you need money, you're going to do what you have to." These offenders chose to break into a dwelling when that act represented what they perceived to be the "most proximate and performable" (Lofland, 1969:61) crime available to them. Both their subjective state and the objective characteristics of the situation played a part in shaping this perception. For such offenders, making the decision to commit a residential burglary instead of another type of offense involved more than a cool assessment of the potential costs and benefits associated with the various alternatives; emotion, mood, and intuition also had a powerful influence on this process (Scheff, 1992).

[S]ometimes you feel better about one thing than you do another and sometimes you know where the money is at. It depends on what's there at the time, whether there is transportation or you are in the area. It's just what looks good at the time. What's more comfortable for you to do, what feels better. (Earl Martin—No. 083)

[W]hen you high on crack, you want some more crack and you don't want to wait, so you got to do a robbery. Now a burglary, you might be high at three in the morning, now whose house can you go in at three in the morning and they ain't gonna be there? (Diamond Craig—No. 027)

A few offenders typically did not themselves choose to commit residential burglaries, but went along with offenses suggested by someone else. In need of cash, these subjects were especially receptive to presented criminal opportunities, even if they were not particularly enamored of burglary.

> I got a friend that do burglaries with me. He usually the one that sets them up. If he ain't got one set up, then I might go off into somethin' else. (Larry Brown—No. 052)

Some of these offenders seemed, when on their own, to lack the stomach for any sort of serious wrongdoing. Others had a preference for a different type of crime, but were tempted to do an occasional burglary when asked to lend a hand. One subject told us that he usually stayed away from burglary in favor of drug selling, explaining that he regarded the former as morally worse than the latter because "the victim comes to you in drug selling, [while] in burglary you go to the victim." Nevertheless, he admitted being willing to commit a break-in when presented with a good opportunity by one of his associates.

The range of moneymaking crimes from which the majority of the offenders could choose was fairly limited. By and large, they did not hold jobs that would allow them to violate even a low-level position of financial trust (Cressey, 1953). Similarly, few had the technical expertise required to disarm the sophisticated security systems protecting lucrative commercial targets or the interpersonal skills needed to commit frauds. It is not surprising, therefore, that, besides residential burglary, almost all of them stuck to a limited number of crimes requiring little skill, such as theft (mostly shoplifting), stealing cars, streetcorner drug selling and robbery.

For many of the offenders, the few profitable criminal opportunities objectively available to them were restricted still further by their belief that certain crimes were too risky or were morally unacceptable. A number of them, for instance, had curtailed or severely limited their participation in drug selling because they felt that the risks of apprehension and punishment were too great.

> It's hard right now, man…I can go back to selling drugs which I could lose my ass. A burg, I could get away with four years [imprisonment]. If I get caught on burglary, I know I'm guaranteed four years. I get caught with drugs, I'm a do thirty [years]. So see, I got away from drugs and fell with the number one [offense, burglary]. (Charlie—No. 024)
>
> See, right now they harder on druggies than a burglar or auto thief. They tryin' to save the younger generation now. They sayin' drugs is the cause of the crimes now. (Joe Outlaw—No. 056)

Likewise, some regarded robbery, especially armed robbery, as carrying too much risk.

> See, if you rob a person, they can identify you cause you lookin' right at 'em, you know? They lookin' right at you and they can identify you. And armed robbery is what? Five to ten [years]? Or ten to fifteen [years]? (No. 006)
>
> [T]hey givin' too much time for robbin'. After my eight years for robbery, I told myself then I'll never do another robbery because I was locked up with so many guys that was doin' twenty-five to thirty years for robbery and I think that's

what made me stick to burglaries, because I had learned that a crime committed with a weapon will get you a lot of time. (No. 013)

One offender decided against committing robberies because he was afraid of being hurt by the victim or witnesses.

> I'm not going to try no strong robberies cause these people could possibly see me out there in the street and I might be full of some alcohol or something and they could get me. They could shoot me or stab me or anything and I wouldn't know. (No. 040)

A couple of the burglars we worked with believed that it was wrong to threaten or to use violence to get money and there-fore were reluctant to do robberies. Although the offender quoted below does not say that he avoided robbery for moral reasons, the tone of his voice left no doubt that this was the case.

> I'd never personally rob a human being, like walk up to them and say, "Give me you wallet and give me your purse!" No way. (No. 079)

Even those who were willing to do robberies, however, sometimes were unable to do so because they did not have the "facilitating hardware" (Lofland, 1969:69–72), namely, a firearm.

> Well, lately I haven't did any [robberies]. But when I was doin' it, I robbed every Friday ... I ain't got no pistol, that's the only reason [I haven't been doing them], ... I swear. (No. 011)

Handguns are in great demand on the street. One of the subjects in our sample claimed that he would rather have a pistol than cash because "a gun is money with a trigger." Offenders who are in need of immediate cash often are tempted to sell their weapon instead of resorting to a difficult or risky crime. The result of this is that they do not always have a pistol at their disposal. In such circumstances residential burglary, which typically requires nothing more than readily available objects (e.g., a screwdriver, hammer, or small crowbar) for its commission, becomes correspondingly more attractive.

The Seductions of Residential Burglary

For some offenders, the perceived benefits of residential bur-glary may transcend the amelioration of financial need. A few of the subjects we interviewed—7 of 102 —said that they did not typically commit burglaries as much for the money as for the psychic rewards. These offenders reported breaking into dwellings prima-rily because they enjoyed doing so. Most of them did not enjoy burglary per se, but rather the risks and challenges inherent in the crime.

> [I]t's really because I like [burglaries]. I know that if I get caught I'm a do more time than the average person, but still, it's the risk. I like doin' them. (No. 013)
>   I think [burglary is] fun. It's a challenge. You don't know whether you're getting caught or not and I like challenges. If I can get a challenging [burglary, I] like that. It's more of the risk that you got to take, you know, to see how good you can really be. (No. 103)

These subjects seemingly viewed the successful completion of an offense as "a thrilling demonstration of personal competence" (Katz, 1988:9). Given this, it is not surprising that the catalyst for their crimes often was a mixture of boredom and an acute sense of frustration born of failure at legitimate activities such as work or school.

> [Burglary] just be something to do. I might not be workin' or not going to school—not doing anything. So I just decide to do a burglary. (No. 017)

The offense provided these offenders with more than some-thing exciting to do; it also offered them the chance to "be somebody" by successfully completing a dangerous act. Similarly, Shover and Honaker (1992:288) have noted that, through crime, offenders seek to demonstrate a sense of control or mastery over their lives and thereby to gain "a measure of respect, if not from others, at least from [themselves]."

The purest example of the psychic rewards of residential burglary was provided by a probationer who, because he denied being currently active, was not included in our sample. Nevertheless, we spoke to him at great length. This man described, with obvious glee, breaking in to places, rearranging the furniture and leaving, often without taking anything. He portrayed himself as a prankster, explaining that he got a great charge out of picturing the victims trying to make a credible-sounding police report. That his motivations were more sinister, however, was suggested when he commented: "I know that [the victims] are still wondering what I took. And I didn't take a thing!" Though the offenses had occurred months earlier, this individual still appeared to derive satisfaction from having desecrated the living space of his victims; he clearly was pleased by the prospect that his actions continued to unsettle their lives. Katz (1988:69) noted a phenomenon closely akin to this among the offenders he surveyed, concluding that nonacquisitive burglaries were experienced as a "black sacrament," a quasi-religious act of defilement through which criminals attempted "to project something negative into the victim's world."

> While only a small number of the subjects in our sample said that they were motivated *primarily* by the psychic rewards of burglary, many of them perceived such rewards as a secondary benefit of the offense. Sixteen of the 95 offenders who did burglaries to raise cash also said that they found the crime to be "exciting" or "thrilling."
>
> Burglary is excitin'. [I do it] mostly for the money, but a lot of times it arouses my suspicion and curiosity. (No. 046)
>
> [Beyond money], it's the thrill. If you get out [of the house], you smile and stand on it, breathe out. (No. 045)
>
> It's just a thrill going in undetected and walking out with all they shit. Man, that shit fucks me up. (No. 022)

Several of those who were motivated predominantly by financial pressures claimed that the offense represented "a challenge" or "an adventure" as well.

It wasn't just gettin' money…it was just the thing of doing it, the thrill out of going in [the house] and doing it. I guess it was a challenge. (No. 055)

[Burglary] is a challenge…like going on a treasure hunt. (Billy Kelly—No. 048)

[After the money, burglary] is adventure to me. (Rodney Price—No. 057)

And a number of the subjects who reported committing burglaries mostly as a way of making money added that breaking into dwellings was "fun" too.

[I do burglaries] for the money. Sometimes it is kind of fun. (Ed Alverez—No. 082)

Finally, one of the offenders who did burglaries chiefly for monetary reasons alluded to the fact that the crime also provided him with a valued identity.

My main reason [for committing burglaries] is because of the money…and knowin' that you can hustle, knowin' that you a hustler. (No. 054)

Beyond all of this, quite a few of the offenders who *usually* resorted to burglary out of financial need occasionally committed the offense to get even with someone for a real or imagined wrong. A number of then mentioned doing burglaries from time to time for "revenge." In the case below, for example, a black offender broke into the home of a young white man who had called him "a nigger" during an altercation over a scratched car door.

I was driving my mother's car and [I pulled into the parking lot of a convenience store]. When I opened my door, I hit this guy's car — a gray Cutlass—and he wanted to fight about it … So we were going to [settle it there], but the police broke it up. So I was thinking about gettin' even … I followed him [home] … I just kept him in sight till I seen what house he was staying in…It was Wednesday and, uh, I was plannin' on doing it Friday, but I had to learn their routine first. I watched a little bit the rest of Wednesday and then I came back and watched it a little bit Thursday, but, uh, I had to move quick cause I wanted to get even…That was a grudge there, a pay back, so it wasn't too much for the money. I broke up more stuff in there than I stole…Normally when I break in a house, it's so that I can get me a high, cause I be having the urge to smoke a little coke. But this particular day, they just pissed me off. I just wanted to get even. I just wanted to hit 'em where it hurts—in they pocket — and I think I did pretty good. (John Black—No. 008)

Other offenders described break-ins designed to punish an ex-lover, collect on a bad debt, or "pay back" an unscrupulous drug dealer. Black (1983:34) has suggested that crimes such as these are essentially moralistic and involve "the pursuit of justice." Indeed, he has gone so far as to argue that many burglaries are best thought of as a form of self-help or "secret social control" (Black, 1983:37). This may be overstating the matter, but it is clear that, on occasion, some offenders find burglary an appealing means of righting a perceived wrong. For instance, several burglars in our sample who often worked together reported targeting the homes of homosexuals who were buying up and renovating property on the periphery of their own neighborhood. These offenders explained that they did not like gays and broke into their dwellings as a means of forcing them to move out of the area. From their perspective, such crimes were justifiable in the circumstances; they represented an attempt to keep the neighborhood from being overrun by outsiders whose way of life was different and threatening.

SUMMARY

Offenders typically decided to commit a residential burglary in response to a perceived need. In most cases, this need was financial, calling for the immediate acquisition of money. However, it sometimes involved what was interpreted as a need to repel an attack on the status, identity, or self-esteem of the offenders. Whatever its character, the need almost invariably was regarded by the offenders as pressing, that is, as something that had to be dealt with immediately. Lofland (1969:50) has observed that most people, when under pressure, have a tendency to become fixated on removing the perceived cause of that pressure "as quickly as possible." Those in our sample were no exception. In such a state, the offenders were not predisposed to consider unfamiliar, complicated, or long-term solutions (see Lofland, 1969:50) and instead fell back on residential burglary, which they knew well. This often seemed to happen almost automatically, the crime occurring with minimal calculation as part of a more general path of action (e.g., partying). To the extent that the offense ameliorated their distress, it nurtured a tendency for them to view burglary as a reliable means of dealing with similar pressures in the future. In this way, a foundation was laid for the continuation of their present lifestyle which, by and large, revolves around the street culture. The sell-indulgent activities supported by this culture, in turn, precipitated new pressures; and thus a vicious cycle developed.

That the offenders, at the time of actually contemplating offenses, typically perceived themselves to be in a situation of immediate need has at least two important implications. First, it suggests a mind-set in which they were seeking less to maximize their gains than to deal with a present crisis. Second, it indicates an element of desperation which might have weakened the influence of threatened sanctions and neutralized any misgivings about the morality of breaking into dwellings (see Shover and Honaker, 1992). We will return to these issues at various points throughout the book.

REFERENCES

Anderson, E. (1990), *Street Wise: Race, Class, and Change in an Urban Community,* Chicago: University of Chicago Press.

Bennett, T., and Wright, R. (1983), "Offenders' Perception of Targets," *Home Office Research Bulletin* 15:18–20, London: Home Office Research and Planning Unit.

Black, D. (1983), "Crime as Social Control," *American Sociological Review* 48:34–45.

Cressey, D. (1953), *Other People's Money,* Glencoe, IL: Free Press.

Cromwell, P., Olson, J., and Avary, D. (1991), *Breaking and Entering: An Ethnographic Analysis of Burglary*, Newbury Park, CA: Sage.

Katz, J. *(1988), Seductions of Crime: Moral and Sensual Attractions in Doing Evil*, New York: Basic Books.

Kennedy, L., and Baron, S. *(1993)*, "Routine Activities and a Sub-culture of Violence," *Journal of Research in Crime and Delinquency 30:88–r 12*.

Lemert, E. *(1953)*, "An Isolation and Closure Theory of Naive Check Forgery," *Journal of Criminal Law, Criminology, and Police Science 44:296–307*.

Lofland, J. (1969), *Deviance and Identity*, Englewood Cliffs, NJ: Prentice-Hall.

Scheff, T. (1992), "Rationality and Emotion: Homage To Norbert Elias." In Coleman, J., and Fararo, T., *Rational Choice Theory: Advocacy and Critique*, pp. 101–19, Newbury Park, A: Sage.

Shover, N. (1991), "Burglary." In Tonry, M., *Crime and Justice: A Review of Research, vol. 14*, pp. 73–113, Chicago: University of Chicago Press.

Shover, N., and Honaker, D. (1990), "The Criminal Calculus of Persistent Property Offenders: A Review of Evidence." Paper presented at the Forty-second Annual Meeting of the American Society of Criminology, Baltimore, November.

———. (1992), "The Socially Bounded Decision Making of Persistent Property Offenders," *Howard Journal of Criminal Justice 31, no. 4:276–93*.

Walker, N. (1984), Foreword. In Bennett, T., and Wright, R., *Burglars on Burglary: Prevention and the Offender*, pp. *viii–ix*, Aldershot: Gower.

Wilson, W. (1987), *The Truly Disadvantaged: The Inner City, the Underclass, and Public Policy*, Chicago: University of Chicago Press.

CHAPTER 5

ᕁ

Opportunities and Decisions: Interactional Dynamics in Robbery and Burglary Groups

Andy Hochstetler

Street offenders more often than not are co-offenders. The theoretical importance of understanding how co-offending shapes conduct has been recognized for decades but is often ignored by investigators. Drawing from interviews with 50 male robbers and burglars who committed their crimes with others, this paper examines how interactional dynamics modify both the perception of criminal opportunities and criminal decision making. Offenders construct opportunity by improvising situational interpretations, communicating expectations, and negotiating shared meanings. As opposed to many prevailing notions of criminal decision making, decisions in groups are incremental, contextually situated, and affected significantly by variation in members' influence. The findings therefore highlight shortcomings of decision-making investigations that obscure marked variation in choice by focusing narrowly on individual assessments of risks and utilities.

Criminologists generally focus their research either on the correlates of crime in offenders' backgrounds or else on characteristics of situations and environments where crime is likely to occur. The immediate social context in which offenders construct criminal decisions is a rich and largely unexplored area. Only a few investigators focus on mental processes, action, and interactions that link offenders' backgrounds to immediate environments and discrete criminal choices (Short, 1998, p. 25).

This empirical neglect results in understandings of crime that emphasize offender characteristics and situational correlates of offending without considering

Source: Hochstetler, A. (2001). Opportunities and decisions: Interactional dynamics in robbery and burglary groups. *Criminology, 39*, 737–763. Used with permission of the American Society of Criminology.

the processes and events through which these correlates and characteristics result in criminal agency. It is well known, for example, that most street offenders in the United States choose crime in the presence of co-offenders (Bureau of Justice Statistics, 1999; Reiss, 1988; Zimring, 1981). However, little research into the potential influence of co-offenders on construction of criminal opportunity or on how criminal groups negotiate meaning and align action to offend exists.

The theoretical importance of understanding how co-offending shapes conduct is recognized in many of criminology's classics. However, investigators generally assume that co-offending influences choice without analysis of the interpersonal interactions that create group effects (McCarthy, Hagan, & Cohen, 1998; Reiss, 1988; Reiss & Farrington, 1991; Tremblay, 1993; Warr, 1996). In this paper, I apply an interactionist approach to investigating the processes by which offenders subjectively interpret and define situations in choosing to commit crime (Athens, 1997; Groves & Lynch, 1990; Katz, 1988; Katz, 1991). I draw on interviews with 50 robbers and burglars who committed their crimes with others. Analysis of these interviews reveals some common patterns of interpersonal dynamics, rooted in street activities, which contribute to situational construction of criminal opportunity. By incrementally signaling to communicate their emerging preferences, by referring to target characteristics, and by referencing identities and expectations attributed to co-offenders, group thieves negotiate a shared sense of opportunity. Interaction can reduce the appeal of law abidance to group participants and make developing criminal opportunity difficult to refuse. In addition, co-offender interaction can act as a catalyst for crime by increasing access to illicit pathways and easing the pursuit of criminal objectives.

BACKGROUND

Revival of interest in deterrence and control interpretations of crime in the closing decades of the twentieth century gave new impetus to investigations of criminal decision making. The resulting corpus of research reveals two recurrent approaches to examining the decision-making process. One depicts criminal decisions as the outcome of a straightforward cognitive process in which offenders weigh rewards against costs. Investigators informed by this approach typically require subjects to imagine themselves in hypothetical settings and to evaluate the potential rewards and risks of choosing crime (Carroll & Weaver, 1986; Cornish & Clarke, 1986; Nagin & Paternoster, 1993; Piliavin et al., 1986; Piquero & Rengert, 1999; Taylor & Nee, 1988; Wright, Logie, & Decker, 1996). The vignettes presented to subjects typically contain a small number of variables. Investigators consistently find that expected risks and rewards are significant considerations in offending decisions and target selection. However, research designs that utilize artificial criminal scenarios obscure motivational and contextual factors that potentially complicate offenders' opportunity assessments. Moreover, investigators usually proceed as if criminal decisions are made by lone offenders and fail to consider that interactional dynamics produce decision-making contexts that potential offenders cannot fully anticipate through advance calculation of risk and benefits.

The second approach to criminal choice situates offending decisions in the context of offenders' larger lives and lifestyles (Ekland-Olson, Lieb, & Zurcher, 1984; Gibbs & Shelley, 1982; Jacobs & Wright, 1999; McCarthy, Hagan, & Cohen, 1998; Shover, 1996; Tunnell, 1992; Wright & Decker, 1994; Wright & Decker, 1997). Investigators informed by this approach typically draw from interviews conducted with active or inactive thieves. Their findings show that criminal decisions are embedded in offenders' chaotic lifestyles. The lifestyles and routines of street life place offenders in situations that impede careful choice and that evoke motivations and cultural outlooks that make crime attractive. One observer, for example, notes that "contexts populated almost exclusively by young, drug-using males simply are not the kind in which decision makers pay close attention to threat and virtue" (Shover, 1996, p. 170). However, investigators of criminal decision making and context typically slight the role of situations immediately antecedent to crime and favor analysis of offenders' more entrenched habits and routines (Fleisher, 1995; Jacobs & Wright, 1999; Tunnell, 1992; Wright & Decker, 1994; Wright & Decker, 1997). This led Hagan and McCarthy (1992, p. 556) to conclude that although the context of street life produces delinquency, "exactly what aspects of life on the street cause delinquency" remain unclear. Although many investigators note that offenders share a style of living and often socialize with other offenders, researchers rarely examine how co-offending affects the decision to commit a particular crime (Cordilia, 1986).

Decision making in criminal groups is seldom a focus of investigation, but acceptance of group effects on individual criminal motivation is widespread. Many investigators note that participation and interaction with co-offenders may moderate individuals' fear of punishment and increase chances of offending (Cloward & Ohlin, 1960; Ekland-Olson, Lieb, & Zurcher, 1984; Erikson & Jensen, 1977; Short & Strodtbeck, 1965; Shover & Henderson, 1995). There also is reason to suspect that some participants play a much greater part in encouraging criminal decisions in groups than do others. Results of self-report surveys of youthful offenders document reported variation in individual influence on group decisions to commit crime (McCarthy, Hagan, & Cohen, 1998; Warr, 1996). Even experienced thieves often contend that they "got involved primarily because of partners" (Feeney, 1986, p. 58; see also Bennett & Wright, 1984). Despite widespread acceptance of group effects on choice, some observers find evidence for the effects of interpersonal dynamics on crime choice unconvincing. Gottfredson and Hirschi (1990, p. 158) acknowledge that criminal cooperation eases individual effort required to offend, but are skeptical of imprecise assertions that interpersonal dynamics heavily influence offending decisions. Nevertheless, denying the presence of significant group effects is premature given the substantial evidence that interaction significantly affects choice in other types of small groups.

In classic sociological experiments, investigators found that subjects provided with simple estimating tasks modified their estimates to comply with the estimates of copresent others (Asch, 1951; Sherif, 1936). These early experiments on group conformity inspired scores of scholars in diverse disciplines to investigate interaction and decisions in small groups. In studies ranging from experiments on shifts in individual preferences resulting from accommodation of other group members' preferences to *post hoc* interpretations of foreign policy, investigators find that dynamics of small-group interaction affect choice (Hart, Stern, & Sundelius, 1997; Turner, Wetherall, & Hogg, 1989). One explanation for individual conformity to group preferences is that some participants persuade others to conform, but individuals modify their preferences and behavior to suit expectations even in the absence of communication with other group participants (Kameda & Davis, 1990; Maas, West, & Cialdini, 1987; Shelley, 1998; Turner, Weatherall, & Hogg, 1989; Wright & Ayton, 1994). Group effects result not only from communication, but also from individual participants' expectations and attempts to gauge preferences of others in their group. Group participants predict the group's likely course and adjust their actions to suit their expectations.

Failure to examine choice processes in crime groups potentially is a significant oversight. This article contributes to our understanding of criminal choice in three ways. First, it bridges an empirical gap in the literature between offenders' abstract motivations and lifestyles and their choice of a target. Second, it examines how interaction between co-offenders influences assessments of criminal opportunity and subsequently offending decisions. Offenders construct their sense of opportunity incrementally and in accord with expectations derived from the situational context and the actions of others. The discussion emphasizes that offenders do not respond passively to situational opportunity; they create it by selecting and transforming the situations they confront. Third, and relatedly, findings reinforce the importance of continued investigation of the varied processes and interpersonal interactions that contribute to the construction of criminal opportunity and criminal decisions.

STREET ACTIVITIES AS CONTEXT

Street thieves' descriptions of decision making contrast with depictions of crime choice that cast it as calculating and purposeful. Many thieves report that they do not plan their crimes or spend only a few minutes planning (Cromwell, Olson, & Avary, 1991, p. 61; Feeney, 1986; Short, 1998, p. 10; Tracy, 1987). As other investigators have found, thieves often ignore and can put out of mind consequences of being caught while considering a crime (Cromwell, Olson, & Avary, 1991; Shover & Honaker, 1992). In this study, several subjects exhibited an extreme lack of concern with consequences by choosing to commit crimes in which they were sure to be suspects. Some pawned goods using accurate identification, loitered or aimlessly drove their cars near the scene of recently completed robberies, robbed victims they knew, or indifferently allowed themselves to be photographed during an offense. To reconcile offenders' descriptions of criminal deliberation with assumptions of calculating actors, decision making is best understood as "socially bounded" (Shover & Honaker, 1992). Offenders construct decisions in accord with conduct norms and during the activities of street life (Feeney, 1986; Jacobs & Wright, 1999; Shover, 1996; Tunnell, 1992; Wright & Decker, 1994; Wright & Decker, 1997).

The hallmark of street life, as a style of living, is pursuit of pleasure and status through conspicuous leisure and consumption "with minimal concern for obligations and commitments that are external to the immediate social setting" (Shover & Honaker, 1992, p. 283). Street offenders live for the moment (Fleisher, 1995, pp. 213–214). A burglar explains that his attitude prevented due attention to consequences:

> You just don't care, you know. You get the attitude that, hey, whatever happens happens. I'm not gonna worry about that [consequences] until it happens, and that's...the frame of mind you are in [when stealing].

Commitment to street life and crime coincides with periods of drug use and related family and economic crises. Many offenders explain that they had temporarily given up on conventional living and devoted themselves fully to partying. Investigators find that a host of problems accompany theft and that it is much more common during offenders' heaviest periods of overindulgence in drugs and drink (Deschenes, Anglin, & Speckhart, 1991; Faupel, 1987; Horney, Osgood, & Marshall, 1995). A burglar recalls that a lengthy period of intoxication and reckless living made stealing a sensible option:

> Things were crazy anyway. I was worried and paranoid all the time. We sat around the apartment and listened to a police scanner, for Christsakes. Our apartment was full of stolen stuff and crank, and we were living off of hot credit cards [purchased from other thieves and hotel bartenders]. If you're like that anyway, why not do a crime so you got something to really worry about.

Thieves share their chaotic lifestyles and parties with compatible friends and a loose network of associates who live similarly (Cordilia, 1986; Katz, 1988, p. 212; McCarthy, Hagan, & Cohen, 1998). Expensive drug and alcohol habits, fighting, shoplifting, writing bad checks, and amassing debt to drug dealers, lawyers, and other creditors are normal in their circles of friends. Street offenders often sleep in cheap motels or on associates' couches or move from party to party with little idea of where they will rest next (Wright & Decker, 1997, p. 38). Curtis, a heroin addict, explains that a continuous and mobile party allowed him to maintain his drug habit by reciprocal sharing with others. His lifestyle made locating criminal opportunities effortless and led him to his robbery co-offender, a man that he scarcely knew. When I asked Curtis, "Were you partying with Willie?" he responded:

> To an extent, you know, because you go from one place to another place. I'd been like that for some time. You have a car, or he has a car and that's the situation. Then this turns into a better situation, and then you get high some more. It's kind of a balance, who's going to do something [crime] last. Who is doing things

just kind of shift back and forth....I guess most people who have been doing it understand.

During the activities of street life, offenders encounter audiences who admire risk-taking, fearlessness, and the ability to provide money and drugs for the party (Katz, 1988; Miller, 1998; Shover, 1996). As one burglar notes, "You never know how many friends you've got until you got a pocket full of pills." Criminal events provide money and drugs for conspicuous consumption and are ideal venues for displaying courage and familiarity with dangerous situations (Katz, 1988, p. 148). Offenders often purport that one goal of their crimes is "showing off" courage or ability by exhibiting lack of hesitation, willingness to take risks, or exaggerated calm in the face of danger (Katz, 1988, p. 304; Matza, 1964; Shover, 1996, p. 110). Crime is a form of "edgework" or voluntary chance-taking that contains "a serious threat to one's physical or mental well-being or one's sense of an ordered existence" (Lyng, 1990, p. 857). Part of the enjoyment of edgework is that it sets capable risk-takers who can "maintain control over a situation that borders on chaos" apart from others (Lyng, 1990, p. 859; Shover, 1996). A middle-aged thief proudly recalls his group's management of challenging criminal events: "It's bad to say, but we was good at what we done."

All group participants define a range of appropriate action from a broad understanding of the situation and how they expect copresent others to act in it (Fine, 1979). Street crime originates in "permissive environs allowing the performance of various respectable and non-respectable activities" (Luckenbill, 1977, p. 178). Small groups of friends intent on "partying," a word unambiguously meaning drug consumption and action-seeking to offenders, comprise most theft groups (Giordano, Cernkovich, & Pugh, 1986; Katz, 1988, p. 198; Shover, 1996). In this sample, 44 subjects were drinking or under the influence of controlled substances during their crime. Levels of consumption on the day of the crime were extreme even by the standards of men who construct their lives around drug use and drinking. A robber reports: "I drank a lot. After my divorce, I drank a lot. But, on that day I drank more. We was drinking a *whole lot* on that day!" A robber currently serving his third sentence for the crime describes the occasion preceding his last offense:

> Well, it more or less started out like most of them do: getting high with my buddy there and riding around drinking. Stopped off to get a few Valiums, and we was just riding around here and there. You know, stopped at a buddy's here. It was an all day thing, drinking and driving, driving and drinking....I was in and out [of consciousness]. I would get so drunk he would drive, and then he would get so drunk I would drive while he was sleeping. And just more or less the whole day went on like that.

Offenders encounter many people during their extended parties. As a result, the composition of a group often changes as it proceeds toward crime. Some participants excuse themselves from company suspected to be on a criminal course, whereas others are quick to volunteer. A persistent robber remembers the outcome of his group's plan to rob a gas station: "The other guys backed out, didn't show…just me and the guy that worked at the station, we carried out the plan." Continued participation in a scene already construed by others as potentially criminal conveys approval of a criminal course. Restraining influences on a group diminish as those wary of crime and less committed to the party depart. A burglar recalls recognizing the apparent criminal potential in his companions:

> We were at a party and everyone else goes to bed. They go to sleep. We just sittin' around doing nothing. Now, when you have got a bunch of crank heads sitting around at four in the morning with nothing to do, they are scheming. There is nothing to do but scheme.

Experienced offenders are adept at sizing up trustworthiness and criminal willingness in associates (Gould et al., 1974, pp. 45–46; McCarthy, Hagan, & Cohen, 1998, p. 174). Of course, many street offenders are so committed to street life that they can safely assume that those around them are open to criminal proposals. When I asked Greg, a burglar whose most recent conviction contained 32 counts, what happens when his associates refuse to accompany him for a burglary, he answered: "I never had that problem. If they have hit a lick before, they know you can make pretty good money….Everybody needs more money."

INTERACTIONAL DYNAMICS

Antecedent events and copresent others open group participants' eyes to opportunity, but interaction begins enactment of a criminal course and the more intentional stages of decision making. All interactions are temporally embedded and contextual. Offenders' forward-looking opportunity appraisals are based on the sense they make of situations using contextually relevant precedent and experience (Vaughan, 1998), but actors do not simply apply lessons from experience to static situations. They "continuously engage patterns and repertoires from the past, project hypothetical pathways forward in time and adjust their actions to the exigencies of emerging situations" (Emirbayer & Mische, 1998, p. 1012). How do group offenders interact with each other and their environments to reach a criminal decision?

Subjects described three general styles of interaction that made illicit opportunity apparent and readily accessible. Most crime groups made criminal sense of a scene by referencing group identities, improvisational communicative signals, or conspicuously attractive targets. These styles of decision making are fluid and overlapping; all three considerations play a part in the decisions of many groups. However, qualitative differences in group decisions are apparent. The relative importance of the three recurring considerations in criminal choice is contingent on a group's shared criminal experience and on the experience and motivation of individual participants. Participants in groups with extensive experience frame their situations and opportunities using this experience; groups without shared experience improvise and rely on situational and interactional cues.

Incremental Signaling

In many cases, small decisions and incremental actions made more or less intentionally and by multiple participants alter situations and perceptions until criminal choice is attractive, what I term *incremental signaling*. Offenders without shared experience or on the periphery of street life are especially likely to approach crime gradually using incremental gestural or verbal moves. When offenders are unsure of others' objectives, they use signals to negotiate shared definitions. One offender makes a move toward crime, and then checks others' responses to find out if they see similar potential and are receptive to the directive (Cromwell, Olson, & Avary, 1991, p. 67).

Shared contexts and immediate precipitating experiences turn actors' attention to similar reference signals and solutions to mutual problems; signaling articulates these anticipatory courses of action (Hilton & Slugowski, 1998; Wade, 1994). A burglar explains that his partners easily interpreted his otherwise oblique suggestion because their recently incurred obligations made criminal potential apparent:

> I guess I figured they owed me. I mean I wouldn't have cared a bit, the thought would have never crossed my mind if I had went out and bought $100 worth of pot and smoked every bit. I wouldn't have thought [that] they owed me anything. But, I bought $300 worth of rock, and it was gone in like two hours. . . . He shared it (burglary profit) with me because he better have. Bubba was telling Tommy, "We have to get some more money." I had spent my whole paycheck on them. So I told them, "Look, I got no more money! All my money was left back in Memphis, it's about time y'all come up with something."

Deliberation begins ambiguously, but escalates quickly. Typically, someone in the group mentions an apparent need for money. The context makes it clear that a suggestion is being made that the group has the potential for acquiring money illegally. Next, a participant mentions a specific type of crime or target. This statement of intent is similar conceptually to a *keynote*, a term familiar to collective behavior scholars. Keynotes are exploratory directives that resonate with those thinking along similar lines, but who are still turning over multiple interpretations of a situation (Turner & Killian, 1987, p. 59). In consequential and urgent situations, keynotes inspire action. Urgent situations are sufficiently ambivalent to encourage actors to turn to others for guidance but convey a finite set of appropriate preferences (Fine, 1979; Kohn & Williams, 1956, p. 173; McPhail, 1991; Turner & Killian, 1987, p. 53). Two robbers recall definitive progressions in verbal deliberation:

> Yeah, it went, "We need some damn money" and then here he sat and told us all. Well, we were all sittin' there, and he was telling us about robberies or whatever, and he told us how to do it.
>
> We was riding around gettin' high, and I was telling them that I needed to make some money for Christmas. They kinda looked at each other and started laughin'. They pretty much said, "You need some easy money, you're with the

right people." I said, "That's what I'm talking about." When they said fast and easy, I didn't know they meant armed robbery.

Decisions are based on the style of presentation provided for alternatives as well as on the objective situation (Kuehberger, 1996). Offenders often build confidence using optimistic conversation referred to as "talking it up" or "gassing each other up" (Cromwell, Olson, & Avary, 1991, p. 69; Shover, 1996; Tunnell, 1992). Several subjects in this study noted that what is most significant about the optimistic talk preceding crime is what participants do not say. They contend that selective omission of information by some participants reduced fear for others. For example, two burglars reported that the homes they targeted belonged to a co-offender's family members. This information was withheld, however, and the subjects were surprised when their partners were suspected and arrested immediately.

Because conversations are short and criminal consent is often unspoken, many participants are not sure that a crime really will be committed until the last minute (Katz, 1988, p. 225; Matza, 1964, p. 54). A heroin addict engaged in a payroll dispute with his employer approached an older man in his neighborhood with a reputation as a competent thief. He explains how the incremental banter and actions before their robbery allowed the group to work toward a crime and postpone consideration of the risks:

> It is not like you approach him and say "Hey, look here, I have this problem." It's more like you are getting high and everything like that. You talkin' about "this son of a bitch who did this to you" and "that son of a bitch that did that to you" and then I said, "I ought to go over there and take my money! Et cetera, et cetera, et cetera." One guy goes, "Yeah, yeah, yeah, I ought to!" I ought to do this, and I ought to do that. And one thing leads to another, and basically I find myself in a situation where like I'm laying on the side of a hill saying, "What the hell am I doing this for?"

Criminal proposals are provisional but are often made by those participants who have established a relatively firm definition of a situation. One thief reported that his drug habit did not allow him to be selective about criminal opportunity. When conversations turn to crime, he immediately directs the group toward action with a challenge: "Let's go then...if they are for real, if they really want to do something, then they will do it right then cuz there ain't no sense talking about it." Because criminal conversations often begin with ambiguous or exploratory statements, the influence of people who speak tersely and forcefully during decision making is substantial, particularly if other participants do not openly oppose their position (DeGrada et al., 1999; Turner & Killian, 1987, p. 85). An offender remembers how an outspoken participant influenced his group's decision making:

> He wanted them how he wanted them, and he was the main one who hollered at people to get things done. He said, "Let's go do this!" And I tell you, he had a way of talking you into it. He had this way, "Oh come on, pussy" and this and that and the other. There was one that was real dominant. It was almost like, how do I want

to word this? It was almost manipulation as far as getting us to do something that we didn't want to. Like, I'm not saying that any of us didn't want to do what we did; it's like we are skeptical and he would manipulate us into going on into it.

Unchecked assertive directives result in a situation in which "each thinks others are committed" to offending (Matza, 1964, p. 54). Therefore, conversations can rapidly evolve past the point where participants begin to see statements that discourage crime as evidence of cowardice or the speaker's inability to meet the demands of a situation.

Target Convergence

Some groups reach criminal decisions when participants mutually and instantaneously recognize an appealing target, what I term *target convergence*. These groups seemingly converge on a target with only the slightest communication between offenders. The eight subjects whose groups clearly reached their decisions in this manner had participants with extensive criminal experience and exposure to street life. However, none of these groups had committed a robbery or burglary together previously. The groups did not discuss crime because they did not set out to commit one, but when an opportunity appeared, talk was not necessary. Appealing targets trigger a group's partially formed and contingent criminal frame of a situation. Targets stand out against a recently constructed backdrop of illicit potential.

Many spontaneous robbers find conspicuous contrast between their situational understandings and ignorant victims who, without realizing the danger, "flash their money around" or "play [the robbers] for punks" or who simply are "somewhere they don't belong." In these situations, deliberative communication with robbery partners is limited to abrupt gestures, nods, or a few words. A robber recalls that his crime began when an older group of men challenged his friends to a fight. When the younger men did not balk, the groups made a frail peace by mentioning mutual associates and sharing a bottle. The newfound allies, apparently on edge from the averted fight, assaulted a stranger who entered the scene minutes later:

> We were just sitting there chillin', and I asked one of the guys do he got a cigarette....About this time, he says "Nah," and he says "but I bet you this dude got one coming down the street." So, I went over there and, you know, asked the dude for a cigarette. One of them dudes comes runnin' across the parking lot and hit him—just Boom! So, when he hit him, [he] hit the ground, and just immediately we started kicking him. While we was beating him, others was going in his pockets gettin' everything he got.

Target convergence typifies mugging and robbery during drug deals, but burglars also can become instantly aware of opportunity. A burglar explains how an encounter with an inviting target during an interstate drug run aligned action in his group:

> I was all high and stuff and seeing tracers and blown away. A big snow come up, and we pulled into this cul-de-sac to stop. There was this hunting lodge or a big

house, like an A-frame, and I was sure there was nobody in there. I don't think nothing was even said. I don't know if he said something or I did. We were high and just talking gibberish, like in rhymes. We just ran up there and busted in a window.

Establishing Identity

Criminality can be a group identity or a mental device shared by participants for organizing events and predicting group action (Cromwell, Olson, & Avary, 1991; Short & Strodtbeck, 1965). Participants' knowledge of others in the group, whether gained in firsthand experience or by reputation, frames how a group sees its potential. The characters inhabiting street scenes often have reputations for criminal capability that precede them. These reputations play a significant part in turning group participants' heads toward illicit opportunity. James, a habitual burglar, reported that a young accomplice probably knew how their group would fund a spontaneous beach vacation: "This is what I do. I am a burglar. He knows that and he knows that if he is with me, we are going to steal." Another experienced burglar reflects on why an accomplice who had never committed a burglary volunteered for their crime: "I am sure he looked at me as someone who could give him an alternative."

Most group offenders have firsthand knowledge of co-offenders' criminal potential. Interaction in these experienced groups retains some of its improvisational character. However, subjects from experienced groups report that their group interaction began and proceeded with the potential for crime in participants' minds. Shared criminal experiences are especially salient in ascribing criminal potential to a group (Wood et al., 1997; Wright & Decker, 1994, p. 37). Several subjects knew others in their group for years before committing a felony together, but stole every time they were together after the first offense. Although individual criminal careers are usually diverse, crime groups often specialize in method and target selection. This shared specialization suggests that participants associate assembly of the practiced group with particular opportunity (Warr, 1996). An offender with several years' experience installing burglar alarms and with some expertise in burglary reports that after he revealed his skills to younger relatives during a spontaneous theft: "They come to get me to get high about every night. I would have been stealing some, but not near as much."

A modicum of success enthuses some crime groups. A young man remembers the discussion that followed his first burglary: "We sat and joked about it, we was talking about how easy it was ... hey, we can do this every day."

After many successful crimes, stealing with a group becomes a routine that provides offenders with a sense of security. Confidence in partners and in the group's criminal ability and good fortune reinforces the group's criminal identity. One addict recalls that he regularly met with co-offenders and that theft plans needed no discussion in his group: "We were beginning to use stealing as a job; we got up of a morning; we did us a pill and then we were out and in the process and looking for something to steal."

INFLUENCE AND SCENE SETTING

To this point, I have described how offenders cooperatively negotiate shared recognition of criminal opportunity. Indeed, most subjects took care to assert that crime participants mutually influence each other and that each offender exercises considerable agency in crime choice. Nevertheless, as the preceding discussion of interactional dynamics implies, some participants have more influence on a group's behavior than do others (Warr, 1996). Almost all subjects readily identified the most influential person(s) in their group's decision. Nine interviewees identified themselves as leaders and several more viewed themselves as instigators in their last offense. A self-proclaimed instigator describes a burglary in which he stole a van from a residential garage:

> I don't know him that well. I had the idea of gettin' the van, you know. Whenever I had the idea of getting the van, he went along with it. We were coming from a friend's house. He was just following me. He was ten years younger.

Directives made to a group have the greatest influence when participants attribute relevant expertise or experience to the speaker (Berger et al., 1977; Foddy & Smithson, 1996; Levine & Russo, 1987; Maas, West, & Cialdino, 1987; Shelley, 1998; Warr, 1996). Offenders sometimes ascribe expertise to partners with a paucity of information, however. Subjects cite co-offenders' age, toughness, confident demeanor, and criminal reputations as sources of influence. Partners' presumed and proven criminal abilities not only lead others to look toward criminal opportunity, but also define power relations in the group. A novice burglar explains that a co-offender's past exploits increased his influence over the group:

> Whether we wanted to do it or not, we would, cuz we figured he was right. I mean, it was like we knew he had been around more than we had. I mean, just getting around into things; like just getting high or stealing or whatever. He wasn't scared of nothin'.

Groups ascribe influence to some participants. In turn, these participants enact their influence. Suspecting that present company and surroundings approximate opportunity, actors adjust the situation to fit their preferred perspective for understanding events (Best, 1982; Goffman, 1969; Heise, 1979).

With motives of helping friends, showing off, and benefiting from task cooperation, some offenders maneuver so that others make criminal sense of a scene. Actors accomplish scene setting by "moving about to confirm that all the parts of a scene are present,... or assembling required paraphernalia or mustering human participants,... or locomoting to a setting where a required situation exists intact" (Heise, 1979, p. 39).

In some groups, offenders provide drugs and alcohol to reduce fear of criminal participation (Cromwell, Olson, & Avary, 1991, p. 64). A severe alcoholic reports that when he refused a criminal proposal, his partner bought more liquor in an attempt to "get me drunk...to where I didn't give a damn." Collecting and displaying weapons or other facilitating hardware also elicits criminal ideas and shapes the behavior of others (Carlson, Marcus-Newhall, & Miller, 1990; Lofland, 1969, pp. 69–72). A young man recalls his surprise when his partners suddenly presented tools needed to stage a robbery: "The guns was theirs; they had them and some ski masks already in the car." A habitual burglar explains why it may seem to some offenders that tools suddenly appear in a potentially criminal scene: "Burglary tools, always did have them with me. You never know when you are going to run up on something." A young burglar describes using a set of keys in his effort to recruit accomplices for a burglary:

> Sometimes it just happens to be luck—like one time a store. One day I was in front of the store, it was closed and I walked to the store and tried to open the doors. It was locked. It was closed, and when I was walking away from the store I happened to look at the ground and seen a set of keys. So . . . I pick up the keys, and I go to the lock and open the door. I lock it back up, go home and tell about two or three friends. We was just livin' across the street from the store. Four of us come back, . . . took all kind of stuff out that store.

Most subjects reported that at least one group participant contemplated or made some preparation for their crime before the group assembled. The consistent finding that many thieves keep a store of potential targets in mind until they need them or an opportune situation arises supports their claim (Maguire, 1982; Wright & Decker, 1994, p. 63; Wright & Decker, 1997). Six subjects said that before discussing specific criminal plans their group arrived at a target that was preselected by another participant. A home invasion robber contends that until he saw the target, he thought his group's plan was to intimidate a nonpaying drug customer as his partners had implied:

> I mean, as soon as we pulled up—and they had gone in and come out to get me—and when I got inside, that's when I first knew. I mean, they didn't tell me outside before I went in; that's the part I couldn't understand about it. All I knew is that the people in there [a wealthy attorney's home] wouldn't mess with these two guys.

Offenders who are the most hesitant or uninformed often become acutely aware of the influence of others on their actions in the instant before they offend. When confronting a target, they realize that their previous decisions and the actions of co-offenders constrain their options. The most motivated offenders in a group often turn from subtle to overt means of influence in an attempt to overcome this late hesitation. When confronting a target, a decisive move finally "brings into relief" criminal definitions and polarizes options (Katz, 1988, p. 305). A burglar reports that his presumed consent placed him in a situation that compelled him to respond:

> [By the] time he got the one [partner] and put him through the window, I mean, what am I gonna do, you know? I didn't want to look like a punk and leave. I wouldn't leave them standing there and me a punk. Then, if they got away from it, then I would be a punk for leaving. That's how I was. I mean, I thought I was in a little gang or whatever.

A robber remembers that he was disgusted with his partners' failure to follow through on the group's quickly formulated plan. He explains that frustration led to his decision to take the initiative:

> We pulled into a couple of places, and nobody would do it. It was driving me crazy. I can't take that. They were findin' every little thing that could go wrong. I finally said, "All right, by God, pull in the next place you see." I went in and said, "I have a gun" and robbed it.

DISCUSSION

Understanding why people who are not determined to commit a crime one minute become so the next requires attention to the immediate situations that link street life and criminal decisions (Jacobs & Wright, 1999, p. 150; Katz, 1988, p. 3; Short, 1998). This paper shows that interaction with other people in distinctive compositional settings and organizing activities conditions criminal choice. Findings support portrayals of criminal decision making as complex, bounded by the desperate circumstances of offenders' lives, and framed by the pursuit of an escapist party. Moreover, findings suggest that examining offenders' fallible perceptions of costs and benefits or their commitment to conduct norms of street life only begins to capture complexity in criminal decision making.

Inadequate attention to the many sources of extrasituational, situational, and interactional variation in individual offenders' considerations in choosing crime, particularly in studies of target selection, structures research findings and creates an overly rational and simplistic understanding of choice (Bennett & Wright, 1984; Rankin & Wells, 1982; Tunnell, 1992). Burglars obviously scan for signs of occupancy, witnesses, and escape routes in the instant before stealing (Bennett & Wright, 1984). This utilitarian rationality is commensurable with extended, less deliberate, and complex routes to offending. When given freedom to describe events, offenders depict improvisational, contextual, and variable processes leading to their choice. To varying degrees, incremental signaling, target convergence, constraining and enabling actions by others, and the situational dynamics of the criminal setting shape their decisions.

The abstract context of crime is a style of living that creates need for disposable cash and provides few feasible approaches for getting it (Jacobs & Wright, 1999; Wright & Decker, 1994, p. 39). In the immediate context of criminal events, motivation often results from collaboratively constructed perceptions of opportunity. The most insightful and self-reflective thieves refer to both lasting and situational contexts when they report that a learned approach to crime avoidance is "staying out of trouble" or "off the streets." For them, the law-abiding path seems narrow and crime results from inaction and failure to take precautions by avoiding street life, its activities, and potential crime partners.

Many investigators portray criminal motivation either as an enduring predisposition or else as an attraction to offending that remains dormant until an encounter with a target (Jacobs & Wright, 1999, p. 164). Criminological theories suggest models of overdetermined individuals who are driven to crime and waiting for a chance to satisfy their preferences. However, conceptual distinctions between opportunity and motivation blur when ethnographers and situational analysts examine decisions and interaction preceding crime (Athens, 1997; Short & Strodtbeck, 1965; Wolfgang, 1958). Burglars and robbers construct criminal opportunity by comparing recently formulated understandings with developing events and adjusting situations to make events and understanding correspond. Criminal choice "blends indiscriminately into the flow of practical activity" as offenders improvise action and expectations to suit ever-shifting circumstances in informal situations (Emirbayer & Mische, 1998). Some crime groups are more goal directed than are others, but only a few pursue determined and consistent ends known equally to all; more typically, the rational path mutates as options open and close and as participants interact to make sequential choices. Participants in this study contend that the immediate allure of crime is incomprehensible without considering preparation, cajoling, encouragement, and other enabling and constraining action by others.

Findings from investigations of the situational complexities of choice have significant implications for future research. On the one hand, offending results when offenders stumble into developing crime. Therefore, social and geographic proximity to crime groups and situations that precipitate thoughts of crime have causal significance (Fagan, Piper, & Cheng, 1987, p. 588). Those without experience in street life are unlikely to find themselves in the presence of men considering a burglary, but theft groups are difficult for many impoverished young men to avoid. On the other hand, this study reveals that purposive, but contingent, action by some actors often precedes even unplanned crime. Dangerous places, alcohol and drug use, appropriate victims, tools, and supportive co-offenders are correlates of criminal situations, but these elements do not converge in scenes spontaneously (see Sampson & Lauritsen, 1994, p. 39). Actors assemble the elements of criminal situations to direct action, play with danger, and create opportunity.

The complexity of situations and variability in offenders' situational skills and constructions of opportunity receives little empirical attention (Birkbeck & LaFree, 1993). Therefore, the intersections between offenders' lives and the effects of these encounters on variation in their decision making are largely unexplored. For example, many robbers are motivated sufficiently to wait in the car while partners rob a store, but contend that they would never serve as gunmen. Others may never attempt a burglary unless in the presence of people who they assume burglarize routinely. In an event, one offender can be an experienced thief who displays unusual forethought in scouting out a target, whereas his co-offenders are drunken young men who join the decision in its last stages.

Qualitative and interactionist studies of crime have great potential. This paper, however, is not a call for a particular methodology, but for empirical attention to the "immediate background and context of offenders' action" (Katz, 1991). Examining event characteristics may support well-worn theories and improve specification of established models. For example, offenders without biographical characteristics correlated with street crime may offend when their lives take a short-term turn for the worse or when they are in the company of those who clearly are at risk of offending. Reducing the accessibility of targets may deter groups without experience. Groups that have committed many crimes may be willing to take on greater risks or only be displaced by a challenging target. In methodologies that examine crime as an outcome of individual offenders' characteristics, potential sources of variation escape notice. Group crimes are an intersection of participants' pathways in which characters and their characteristics meld and interact with environments to shape events.

REFERENCES

Asch, S. E. (1951). Effects of group pressure upon the modification and distortion of judgment. In H. Guetzkow (Ed.), *Groups, leadership and men* (pp. 177–190). Pittsburgh: Carnegie Press.

Athens, L. H. (1997). *Violent criminal acts and actors revisited*. Chicago: University of Chicago Press.

Bennett, T., & Wright, R. T. (1984). *Burglars on burglary: Prevention and the offender*. Aldershot, UK: Bower.

Berger, J., Fisek, M. H., Norman, R. Z., & Zelditch, M. J. (1977). *Status characteristics and social interaction: An expectation-states theory*. New York: Elsevier.

Best, J. (1982). Crime as strategic interaction. *Urban Life, 11*, 107–128.

Birkbeck, C. B., & LaFree, G. (1993). The situational analysis of crime and deviance. *Annual Review of Sociology, 19*, 133–137.

Bureau of Justice Statistics. (1999). *Criminal victimization in the United States*. Washington, DC: Department of Justice.

Carlson, M., Marcus-Newhall, A., & Miller, N. (1990). Effects of situational aggression cues: A quantitative review. *Journal of Personality and Social Psychology, 58*, 622–633.

Carroll, F. M., & Weaver, J. S. (1986). Crime perceptions in a natural setting by expert and novice shoplifters. *Social Psychology Quarterly, 48*, 349–359.

Cloward, R. A., & Ohlin, L. E. (1960). *Delinquency and opportunity*. New York: Free Press.

Cordilia, A. T. (1986). Robbery arising out of a group drinking context. In A. Campbell & J. J. Gibbs (Eds.), *Violent transactions*. New York: Blackwell.

Cornish, D. B., & Clarke, R. V. (1986). *The reasoning criminal: Rational choice perspectives on offending*. New York: Springer-Verlag.

Cromwell, P. F., Olson, J. N., & Avary, D. W. (1991). *Breaking and entering: An ethnographic analysis of burglary*. Newbury Park, CA: Sage.

DeGrada, E., Kruglanski, A. W., Mannetti, L., & Pierro, A. (1999). Motivated cognition and group interaction: Need for closure affects the contents and processes of collective negotiations. *Journal of Experimental Social Psychology, 35*, 346–365.

Deschenes, E. P., Anglin, M. D., & Speckhart, G. (1991). Narcotics addiction: Related criminal careers, social and economic costs. *Journal of Drug Issues, 21*, 405–434.

Ekland-Olson, S., Lieb, J., & Zurcher, L. (1984). The paradoxical impact of criminal sanctions: Some microstructural findings. *Law and Society Review, 18*, 159–178.

Emirbayer, M., & Mische, A. (1998). What is agency? *American Journal of Sociology, 103*, 962–1023.

Erikson, M. L., & Jensen, G. F. (1977). Delinquency is still group behavior: Toward revitalizing the group premise in the sociology of deviance. *Journal of Criminal Law and Criminology, 70,* 102–116.

Fagan, J., Piper, E., & Cheng, Y. (1987). Contribution of victimization to delinquency in inner cities. *Journal of Criminal Law and Criminology, 78,* 586–613.

Faupel, C. E. (1987). Drugs-crime connections: Elaborations from the life of hard-core heroin addicts. *Social Problems, 34,* 54–68.

Feeney, F. (1986). Robbers as decision-makers. In D. B. Cornish & R. V. Clarke (Eds.), *The reasoning criminal: Rational choice perspectives on offending.* New York: Springer-Verlag, 52–71.

Fine, G. (1979). Rethinking subculture: An interactionist analysis. *American Journal of Sociology, 85,* 1–20.

Fleisher, M. S. (1995). *Beggars and thieves: Lives of urban street criminals.* Madison: University of Wisconsin Press.

Foddy, M., & Smithson, M. (1996). Relative ability, paths of relevance, and influence in task oriented groups. *Social Psychology Quarterly, 59,* 40–53.

Gibbs, J. J., & Shelley, P. L. (1982). Life in the fast lane: A retrospective view by commercial thieves. *Journal of Research in Crime and Delinquency, 19,* 299–330.

Giordano, P. C., Cernkovich, S. A., & Pugh, M. D. (1986). Friendship and delinquency. *American Journal of Sociology, 91,* 1170–1202.

Goffman, E. (1969). *Where the action is.* London: Allen Lane.

Gottfredson, M. R., & Hirschi, T. (1990). *A general theory of crime.* Stanford, CA: Stanford University Press.

Gould, L., Walker, A. L., Crane, L. E., & Lidz, C. W. (1974). *Connections: Notes from the heroin world.* New Haven, CT: Yale University Press.

Groves, W. B., & Lynch, M. J. (1990). Reconciling structural and subjective approaches to the study of crime. *Journal of Research in Crime and Delinquency, 27,* 348–375.

Hagan, J., & McCarthy, B. (1992). Street life and delinquency. *British Journal of Sociology, 43,* 533–561.

Hart, P. T., Stern, E. K., & Sundelius, B. (1997). *Beyond groupthink: Political group dynamics and policy-making.* Ann Arbor: University of Michigan Press.

Heise, D. (1979). *Understanding events: Affect and the construction of social action.* New York: Cambridge University Press.

Hilton, D. J., & Slugowski, B. R. (1998). Judgment and decisionmaking in social context: Discourse processes and rational inference. In T. Connoly & H. R. Arkes (Eds.), *Judgment and decisionmaking: An interdisciplinary reader* (2nd ed.). New York: Cambridge University Press 651–676.

Horney, J., Osgood, D. W., & Marshall, I. H. (1995). Criminal careers in the short term: Intra-individual variability in crime and relation to local life circumstances. *American Sociological Review, 60,* 655–673.

Jacobs, B. A., & Wright, R. T. (1999). Stick-up, street culture, and offender motivation. *Criminology, 37,* 149–174.

Kameda, T., & Davis, J. H. (1990). The function of reference point in individual and group risk decision making. *Organizational Behavior and Human Decision Processes, 46,* 55–76.

Katz, J. (1988). *The seductions of crime: Moral and sensual attractions in doing evil.* New York: Basic.

————. (1991). The motivation of persistent robbers. In M. Tonry (Ed.), *Crime and justice: An annual review of research* (Vol. 14, pp. 277–306). Chicago: University of Chicago Press.

Kohn, M. L., & Williams, R. M. (1956). Situational patterning in intergroup relations. *American Sociological Review, 21,* 164–174.

Kuehberger, A. (1996). The influence of framing on risky decisions: A meta-analysis. *Organizational Behavior and Human Decision Processes, 75,* 23–55.

Levine, J. M., & Russo, E. M. (1987). Majority and minority influence. In C. Hendrick (Ed.), *Group processes.* Newbury Park, CA: Sage, Vol. 8, 13–54.

Lofland, J. (1969). *Deviance and identity.* Englewood Cliffs, NJ: Prentice-Hall.

Luckenbill, D. F. (1977). Criminal homicide as situated transaction. *Social Problems, 25,* 176–186.

Lyng, S. (1990). Edgework: A social-psychological analysis of voluntary risk-taking. *American Journal of Sociology, 95,* 851–886.

Maas, A., West, S. G., & Cialdini, R. B. (1987). Minority influence and conversion. In C. Hendrick (Ed.), *Group processes.* Newbery Park, CA: Sage, Vol. 8, 55–79., Maguire, M. (1982). *Burglary in a dwelling.* London: Heinemann.

Matza, D. (1964). *Delinquency and drift.* New York: John Wiley.

McCarthy, B., Hagan, J., & Cohen, L. E. (1998). Uncertainty, cooperation and crime: Understanding the decision to co-offend. *Social Forces, 77,* 155–176.

McPhail, C. (1991). *The myth of the madding crowd.* New York: Aldine de Gruyter.

Miller, J. (1998). Up it up: Gender and accomplishment of street robbery. *Criminology, 36,* 37–66.

Nagin, D., & Paternoster, R. (1993). Enduring individual differences and rational choice theories of crime. *Law and Society Review, 27,* 467–496.

Piliavin, I. M., Gartner, R., Thorton, C., & Matsueda, R. L. (1986). Crime, deterrence and rational choice. *American Sociological Review, 51,* 101–119.

Piquero, A., & Rengert, G. F. (1999). Specifying deterrence with active residential burglars. *Justice Quarterly, 16,* 450–480.

Rankin, J. H., & Wells, L. E. (1982). The social context of deterrence. *Sociology and Social Research, 67,* 18–39.

Reiss, A. J., Jr. (1988). Co-offending and criminal careers. In M. Tonry & N. Morris (Eds.), *Crime and justice: A review of research* (Vol. 10, 117–170). Chicago: University of Chicago Press.

Reiss, A. J., Jr., & Farrington, D. (1991). Advancing knowledge about co-offending: Results from a prospective longitudinal survey of London males. *Journal of Criminal Law and Criminology, 82,* 360–95.

Sampson, R., & Lauritsen, J. L. (1994). Violent victimization and offending: Individual-, situational-, and community-level risk factors. In A. J. Reiss & J. A. Roth (Eds.), *Understanding and preventing violence* (Vol. 3,1–114). Washington, DC: National Academy Press.

Shelley, R. K. (1998). Some developments in expectation states theory: Graduated expectations? In John Skvoretz & Jacek Czmatka (Eds.) *Advances in group processes* (Vol. 15). Stamford, CT: JAI Press.

Sherif, M. (1936). *The psychology of social norms.* New York: Harper & Row.

Short, J. F. (1998). The level of explanation problem revisited. *Criminology, 36,* 1–36.

Short, J. F., & Strodtbeck, F. (1965). *Group process and gang delinquency.* Chicago: University of Chicago Press.

Shover, N. (1996). *Great pretenders: Pursuits and careers of persistent thieves.* Boulder, CO: Westview.

Shover, N., & Henderson, B. (1995). Repressive crime control and male persistent thieves. In H. D. Barlow (Ed.), *Crime and public policy: Putting theory to work.* Boulder, CO: Westview, 227–246.

Shover, N., & Honaker, D. (1992). The socially bounded decision making of persistent property offenders. *Howard Journal of Criminal Justice, 31,* 276–290.

Taylor, M., & Nee, C. (1988). The role of cues in simulated residential burglary. *British Journal of Criminology, 28,* 396–401.

Tracy, P. E., Jr. (1987). Race and class differences in self-reported delinquency. In M. E. Wolfgang & T. P. Thornberry (Eds.), *From boy to man, from delinquency to crime.* Chicago: University of Chicago Press, 87–121.

Tremblay, P. (1993). Searching for suitable co-offenders. In R. V. Clarke & M. Felson (Eds.), *Advances in criminological theory: Routine activity and rational choice* (Vol. 5, 17–36.). New York: Transaction.

Tunnell, K. D. (1992). *Choosing crime: The criminal calculus of property offenders.* Chicago: Nelson Hall.

Turner, R. H., & Killian, L. (1987). *Collective behavior* (3rd ed.). Englewood Cliffs, NJ: Prentice Hall.

Turner, J. C., Wetherall, M. S., & Hogg, M. A. (1989). Referent informational influence and group polarization. *British Journal of Social Psychology, 28,* 135–147.

Vaughan, D. (1998). Rational choice, situated action, and the social control of organizations. *Law and Society Review, 32,* 501–538.

Wade, A. L. (1994). Social processes in the act of juvenile vandalism. In M. B. Clinard, R. Quinney, & J. Wildeman (Eds.), *Criminal behavior systems: A typology* (3rd ed.). New York: Anderson.

Warr, M. (1996). Organization and instigation in delinquent groups. *Criminology, 34,* 11–37.

Wolfgang, M. E. (1958). *Patterns in criminal homicide.* Philadelphia: University of Pennsylvania Press.

Wood, P. B., Gove, W. R., Wilson, J. A., & Cochran, J. K. (1997). Nonsocial reinforcement and habitual criminal conduct: An extension of learning theory. *Criminology, 35,* 335–366.

Wright, G., & Ayton, P. (1994). *Subjective probability.* Chichester, UK: John Wiley.

Wright, R. T., & Decker, S. (1994). *Burglars on the job: Streetlife and residential break-ins.* Boston: Northeastern University Press.

———. (1997). *Armed robbers in action.* Boston: Northeastern University Press.

Wright, R. T., Logie, R. H., & Decker, S. (1996). Criminal expertise and offender decision making: An experimental study of the target selection process in residential burglary. *Journal of Research in Crime and Delinquency, 29,* 148–161.

Zimring, F. E. (1981). Kids, groups and crime: Some implications of a well-known secret. *Journal of Criminal Law and Criminology, 72,* 867–885.

SECTION III

✛

Property Crimes

If you turn on the television news or open the daily paper, you might conclude that violent crime—muggings, robberies, and assaults—is rampant. It's easy to come to this conclusion: violent crime is what makes news. In reality, property crime and not violent crime make up the vast majority of crimes reported to the police authorities in the United States. According to the FBI's Uniform Crime Reporting Program (UCR), property crime includes the offenses of burglary, larceny-theft, motor vehicle theft, and arson. Larceny and theft are the most common property offenses reported to police authorities. While the incidence of property crime remains high, it has steadily decreased over the past decade.

The articles featured in this section explore motor vehicle theft, shoplifting, and identity theft. Motor vehicle theft, or auto theft, as it sometimes called, is the unlawful taking of a self-propelled road vehicle that is owned by another, with the intent to deprive the owner of it permanently. In 2009, there were nearly 800,000 motor vehicle thefts reported to the police nationwide (Federal Bureau of Investigation, 2010).

Shoplifting falls under the broad category of larceny-theft. Larceny-theft is simply the unlawful taking of property from another person out of his or her presence. Shoplifting is often considered a "folk crime" because of the high percentage of persons who have committed the offense at least once in their lives. It is perhaps the most widely distributed crime in the United States, with an estimated one in 15 persons having shoplifted in their lifetime.

Burglary is the unlawful or forcible entry or attempted entry of a residence with the intent to commit a crime. It may or may not involve a forcible entry. In 2010, there were an estimated 2,159,879 burglaries—a number down slightly from the previous year (Federal Bureau of Investigation, 2010).

Identify theft is one of the fastest-growing crimes in the United States. In 2005, over 6 million households reported that at least one member in the home had experienced some form of identity theft (Baum, 2007). Generally, identity theft entails an offender gaining access to the personal information of the victim and then using that information to defraud him or her. Offenders may obtain personal information in a number of ways, including collecting personal information that has been discarded in the trash, intercepting mail, acquiring subscription lists and credit card carbons, using phony telemarketers, and conducting Internet searches (Berghel, 2000). In some cases, the offender acquires a personal item from the victim such as a driver's license number or Social Security card and in turn uses that information to commit a fraud.

In Chapter 6, "Establishing Connections: Gender, Motor Vehicle Theft, and Disposal Networks," Christopher W. Mullins and Michael G. Cherbonneau describe the role that gender plays in motor vehicle theft, and specifically initiation into motor vehicle theft. They argue that while motor vehicle theft is a largely male-dominated offense, women are increasingly participating in this kind of criminal activity. The authors fill an important gap in the literature by examining the gendered nature of motor vehicle theft through direct comparison of qualitative data obtained from 35 juvenile and adult men and women actively involved in auto theft in St. Louis. The authors take an enlightening look at the convergences and divergences of men's and women's experiences in this area of crime.

In Chapter 7, the discussion turns to shoplifters. Paul Cromwell and Quint Thurman ("'The Devil Made Me Do It': Use of Neutralizations by Shoplifters") look at the techniques that shoplifters use to neutralize their crimes. Findings from interviews with 137 apprehended shoplifters reveal a widespread use of techniques of neutralization. The authors identify two new neutralizations, which they term *justification by comparison* and *postponement*. They argue that while earlier formulations of neutralization theory contend that deviants neutralize moral prescriptions prior to committing a crime, research is incapable of determining whether a stated neutralization occurs before or after the fact, and that neutralization more typically follows rather than precedes deviance. This claim parallels Hirschi's (1969) thesis that (1) an after-the-fact rationalization in one instance may be a causal neutralization in another instance, and (2) the assumption that delinquent acts come before justifying beliefs is the more plausible causal ordering.

In Chapter 8 ("Identity Theft: Assessing Offenders' Motivations and Strategies"), Heith Copes and Lynne Vieraitis examine the social, technical, intuitive, and system skills associated with the offense of identity theft. Through interviews with 59 identity thieves incarcerated in the federal prison system, the authors found that identity thieves represent a diverse group and largely come from working-class and middle-class backgrounds. About half of those interviewed had lifestyles similar to those of persistent street offenders, and about half used the proceeds of their crimes to live relatively middle-class lives. Offenders' most frequent way of acquiring information was to buy it from others, steal it from mailboxes or trashcans, or obtain it from persons they knew.

REFERENCES

Baum, K. (2007). *Identity theft, 2005* (NCJ 219411). Washington, DC: Bureau of Justice Statistics, National Crime Victimization Survey, November 2007.

Berghel, H. (2000). Identify theft, social security numbers, and the web. *Communications of the ACM, 43*(2), 17–21.

Federal Bureau of Investigation. (2010). *Crime in the United States.* Retrieved March 6, 2012, from http://www2.fbi.gov/ucr/cius2009/index.html.

Hirschi, T. (1969). *Causes of delinquency.* Berkeley: University of California Press.

✌

CHAPTER 6

Establishing Connections: Gender, Motor Vehicle Theft, and Disposal Networks

Christopher W. Mullins and Michael G. Cherbonneau

As with most other serious street crimes, motor vehicle theft is a male-dominated offense. Nevertheless, women do engage in motor vehicle theft, albeit at a reduced rate of participation. Here we examine the gendered nature of motor vehicle theft through direct comparison of qualitative data obtained from 35 juvenile and adult men and women actively involved in auto theft in St. Louis, Missouri. By tracing similarities and differences between men's and women's pathways of initial involvement, enactment strategies, and post-theft acts, we provide a contextual analysis of offenders' perceptions and behavior. Such an approach allows a more precise discussion of gender's influence (or lack of influence) on motor vehicle theft. Analysis shows that initiation into auto theft and property disposal networks are governed by male gatekeepers, and this leads to some key similarities in techniques between men and women. The ways in which women negotiate male-dominated networks is also discussed, with particular emphasis on the innovative strategies they draw upon to accomplish their crimes within these landscapes and when opportunities are constrained by male gatekeepers.

The past 15 years has witnessed the emergence of a rich body of literature devoted to understanding how gender structures the accomplishment of specific crimes. The preeminent research in this vein uncovers gender similarities and differences through direct comparison of male and female accounts of their participation in street crime (Miller, 2002). The general consensus within comparative work on gender is that while some overlap in men's and women's experiences

Source: Adapted from Mullins, C. W., & Cherbonneau, M. G. (2010). Establishing connections: Gender, motor vehicle theft and disposal networks. *Justice Quarterly, 28*(2), 278–281, 286–302. Used with permission of the publisher.

with street crime exist—for example, motives and (to a lesser extent) enactment strategies—there is also significant divergence—for example, pathways into crime, initiation experiences, criminal network ties, and so-called "hypothetical desistance" (Brookman et al., 2007; Mullins & Wright, 2003; Mullins, Wright, & Jacobs, 2004; Miller, 1998).

The list of crimes examined to come to these conclusions include male and female gang members (Campbell, 1993; Miller, 2001), residential burglars (Decker et al., 1993; Mullins & Wright, 2003), strong-arm and armed robbers (Brookman et al., 2007; Campbell, 1993; Miller, 1998), and persons involved in retaliatory and assaultive violence (Mullins, Wright, & Jacobs, 2004). Noticeably absent from these gendered comparisons of specific crimes is motor vehicle theft. This is surprising given that "cars have long served as objects for men to position themselves in terms of masculinity, enabling an elaborated performance of the masculine" (Best, 2006, p. 89). In fact, the masculine nature of car culture in general and car theft in particular is assumed to be masculine in nature. Yet, women *do* steal cars as well. An understanding of auto theft participation by females can contribute to existing debates about their role in common street crime and the ways in which they negotiate the many layers of male-dominated space within the criminal underworld. It can also shine light on various interactional dynamics that shape motor vehicle theft experiences.

In the pages that follow, we examine the gendered nature of motor vehicle theft through direct comparison of qualitative data obtained from 35 individuals actively involved in auto theft in St. Louis, Missouri. By tracing similarities and differences between men's and women's pathways of initial involvement, enactment procedures, and methods for selling stolen vehicles and vehicle parts, we provide a contextual analysis of offenders' perceptions and behavior. Such an approach allows for a more precise discussion of gender's influence (or lack of influence) on motor vehicle theft.

CONCEPTUAL CONTEXT

Motor vehicle theft is a serious property crime that accounted for 11% of all property offenses reported in 2007, with nearly 1.1 million stolen vehicles—one out of every 232 registered nationwide—reported stolen in 2007 (Federal Bureau of Investigation [FBI], 2008; Federal Highway Administration, 2008). Like most other serious crimes, it is also profoundly gendered in its commission. Among the 12.6% of auto thefts cleared by arrest in 2007, the ratio of male to female arrestees was 4.6 to 1 (FBI, 2008). While imprecise, the gendered division of motor vehicle theft in measures of apprehended individuals is corroborated by other data sources such as "Monitoring the Future" (see *Sourcebook of Criminal Justice Statistics*, 2003, table 3.44) and also seems to hold in other industrialized nations (Graham & Bowling, 1995, tables C1, C2; Henderson, 1994; O'Connor & Kelly, 2006; Roe & Ashe, 2008, table 2.1; Walker, Butland, & Connell, 2000; Yates, 2003/4). Despite its commonality, motor vehicle theft is less studied than other property offenses (Clarke & Harris, 1992). This pattern of neglect has begun to change owing to the score or so of studies published within the past two decades that explore the offense in detail and at varying units of analysis (Cherbonneau & Wright, 2009). Yet, the majority deal directly with offender perceptions, mostly examining offenders from outside the United States (e.g., Australia, Canada, and the United Kingdom). Further, the offender-based literature is dominated by male perspectives (e.g., Copes, 2003).

To date, most work on gender and car theft has focused on the ubiquitous use of stolen cars by young men for so-called "joyriding," attributing these actions to masculinity enactment (Henderson, 1994; Walker, Butland, & Connell, 2000; Williams, 2005). Due to this assumption of masculinity, little prior research has directly compared male and female experiences. To date, only one study situates men and women's experiences in motor vehicle theft within the purview of gender. Drawing from interviews with 17 young people (five women and 12 men) under correctional supervision in Eastern Ontario, O'Connor and Kelly (2006, p. 263) explored the relationship between gender and car stealing, concluding that "the most salient point to understand about young people's participation in auto theft is that it involves an intersection of masculinities, femininities and car culture."

While insightful, O'Connor and Kelly (2006) treated motor vehicle theft as a gendered crime in its own right and framed male and female accounts around the symbolic meanings of car culture and thus did not demonstrate conclusively the impact of gender on auto theft participation. In accordance with a majority of offender-based research on auto theft (Kilpatrick, 1997), the O'Connor and Kelly sample was based on young offenders recruited through criminal justice channels in Canada, and their responses may not be representative of currently active offenders elsewhere. The youthfulness of their sample is also problematic, as perceptions and decision making of auto thieves have been linked to age and experience (Light, Nee, & Ingham, 1993; Slobodian & Browne, 1997; Spencer, 1992; Stephen & Squires, 2003).

Like burglary, auto theft appears to be a "social crime" (see Mullins & Wright, 2003), or at least begins as such; few thieves begin careers stealing cars on their own (Dawes, 2002; Kilpatrick, 1997; Light, Nee, & Ingham, 1993; Spencer, 1992; Stephen & Squires, 2003). Instead, initiation into auto theft is facilitated through interaction with neighborhood peers, usually older and more experienced males. Novices learn from these "technical advisors" (Fleming, Brantingham, & Brantingham, 1994) the skill set needed to steal cars through a role best described as an "apprenticeship" (Light, Nee, & Ingham, 1993; Spencer, 1992). Group status is stratified by skill (but see Stephen & Squires, 2003). Initially, novices typically are relegated to the role of "lookout" and passenger, although in many cases thieves move quickly from apprentices to co-offenders (Light, Nee, & Ingham, 1993; Fleming, 2003). Those who persist may eventually offend independently or form their own crews. Dawes (2002, p. 203) summed it up best stating "the peer group is central in providing the catalyst for [young offenders'] introduction and continuation to car theft and joyriding behavior. [It] provides a structure for the advancement in status for young joyriders to learn the skills of car theft and to graduate to the status of leader of a joyriding crew."

As car theft and disposal are group activities lodged within social networks, the nature and composition of those networks will influence car thieves' lived experiences. The "graduation" Dawes (2002) speaks of will be mediated by the nature of the networks individuals have exposure to and experiences within. Underworld street networks are male dominated, with gatekeepers drawing upon rigid, sexist assumptions about the personalities and abilities of women vis-à-vis criminal action. Thus, women often have difficulty gaining access to street-based criminal networks (Messerschmidt, 1997; Steffensmeier, 1983; Steffensmeier & Terry, 1986). Where women have gained access to these networks, it is often through male relatives or romantic partners who can vouch for their skills and steadfastness (Mullins & Wright, 2003). Thus, these "apprenticeship" experiences should have a situational gendered element to them.

Little is known about tactics and the network experiences of female car thieves, and even less is known about potential interactions of gender with these actions. Recent comparative work has demonstrated that motivation and sometimes enactment strategies can be more similar than different among male and female offenders (Miller, 1998; Mullins & Wright, 2003; Mullins, Wright, & Jacobs, 2004). And while convergence is as important as divergence in establishing the extent that any given behavior is strongly gendered, Miller (2002) cautions about the overapplication of a gendered lens in qualitative analysis as well as reinforcing the need to carefully contextualize social actors' perceptions within both broader and narrower environments. Even though aggregate data suggest that there are clear gender differences in offense participation (which appears to be the case with auto theft), careful exploration of perceptions and experiences of both men and women involved in diverse forms of crime are needed. This idea is the starting point of the analyses presented here. Our goal is to examine female auto thieves' perceptions of their offending in an explicitly comparative fashion by directly comparing women's accounts with those of men involved in motor vehicle theft.

DATA AND METHODS

Data for this study were derived from open-ended qualitative interviews with active auto thieves recruited from the streets of St. Louis, Missouri. The St. Louis Metropolitan Area (which extends into Illinois) has a population of just over 2.8 million, but St. Louis City itself is much smaller, having only about 354,000 residents. St. Louis City is beset by high rates of criminal offending.... We recruited and interviewed 35 active auto thieves. Thirty of the interviews were conducted during 2006. The remaining five were done the following year to clarify and amplify empirical issues raised by the earlier interviews.

The auto thieves ranged in age from 17 to 49, with a mean age of 27 years. Twenty-seven were male and eight were female. All of the respondents were African-American. The sample, on average, had completed 11 years of education, with two entering the twelfth grade at the time of the interview. Twelve of our subjects were high school dropouts, typically leaving school by the tenth grade, while the majority had at least a high school education, with 15 who completed high school or a GED and another six who completed a vocational program or some college. Only eight of our subjects held a legitimate job at the time of the interview, despite the high number with high school or higher education. Although some respondents said they were actively looking for work, most were committed to an admixture of illegal endeavors for their main source of income, with drug sales and auto theft being the most common mentioned activities toward this end. The average age at which respondents committed their first auto theft was 15, though many had been in or around stolen cars prior to this.

INITIATION INTO AUTO THEFT

Acquiring the necessary skills to commit a crime begins with the process of being exposed to the crime itself. Almost invariably, the men and women we interviewed were initially exposed to auto theft within the context of joyriding. Everyone mentioned riding in stolen cars in their early teens, and doing so with some frequency. Simply, the neighborhoods they grew up in were flush with opportunities to observe and interact with individuals bearing both the requisite attitudes and knowledge to initiate an individual into motor vehicle theft.

As with other street crime, auto theft requires a basic set of skills. An individual's introduction to stealing cars coincides with their acquiring this necessary technical expertise. While brute force can be used to gain entry into the vehicle, some dexterity and basic technical skills are required to defeat the vehicle's ignition. Complex knowledge is not compulsory, although a familiarity with certain vehicle parts and their operation is essential. As expected, almost everyone in our sample—32 out of 35 respondents—discussed a period of learning how to steal a car; particularly "breaking down" the steering wheel column and/or tampering with ignitions. Thirty-one of the 32 thieves who were coached by others received instruction from neighborhood peers or family members whose source of criminal tutelage was likewise acquired from others in a social context.

Asked how they became involved in auto theft, Goldie's comments were typical, regardless of gender: "Well, hanging out with [a] couple older guys, you know, they showed me the ropes.... [W]hat cars to target and what cars you can't steal.... That's how I got into it.... Just hanging with older guys, they showed me." About half of the sample—both men and women—discussed being taken along on their first theft as a lookout while an older co-offender would physically steal the car. Typically, this role was taken for a few weeks or months before the initiate would be the one responsible for most of the "theft work." Some of the men and women traced a majority of their learning to the time spent riding in cars stolen by peers and observed them start and stop vehicles until they figured out how to replicate the basic procedure. For others, the learning experiences were more structured. Offenders were shown how to effect entry and bypass the ignition, but also informed of the types of cars to target, those that require different techniques, how to check for alarms, and presuppositions about the efforts by police to recover stolen vehicles such as search patterns, "hot sheets," and the length of time in which vehicles can be "safely" displayed in public. Formal learning was common among those who began as lookouts and was especially the case among those affiliated with tight-knit crews. J's initiation into "vehicle-taking" was typical among predominantly male crews:

> When I was doing it my first time it was one person with me.... He made sure I did it right and shit.... You got to do it real quick so he made sure I get it done and shit.... It was sort of like an initiation type of thing...once you steal your first car, you know they ain't worried about you stealing your second 'cause...you know how to do it and shit. So, I knew they knew I knew how to do it, so that was like my initiation.

Once the basic proficiencies of car stealing were honed, men and women alike tended to pass on this knowledge. One such person was Killa, who, at the time of the interview, was serving as "technical advisor" (Fleming, Brantingham, & Brantingham, 1994) to younger males in his neighborhood:

> KILLA: I'm like switching roles from learning to now teaching.
> INTERVIEWER: Are they the lookout or do they have a more hands-on role during the theft?
> KILLA: Yeah, they'll lookout. Some lookout, some know how to break it down, some know how to just do it all themselves. It's all in how they learn.... You gotta learn from someone, yeah, it's a cycle.... It's not that easy.... It takes a little finesse.

Comparing experiences reported by the men and women at the time of their first direct participation[1] in taking a vehicle produced some noteworthy themes related to the onset of offending and tutelage. All of the men began offending in sexually homogeneous groups. Overwhelmingly, they were initiated by same-sex peers or same-sex members of their family (again, with one exception). Twenty-six of the 27 males also discussed being taught by other men, either a peer ($n = 22$) or family member ($n = 4$). In all likelihood, this is a reflection of two general social facts. First, criminal networks are largely male in nature. Second, these experiences typically occur in late adolescence—a period where interactional networks display strong gender segregation (especially where illicit activity is a prominent component of the network).

In contrast to the men, direct auto theft participation by women occurred in the company of opposite sex peers. Four of the women first offended within mix-sex groups (Lavanda, Lil' Bunny, Lil' Bit, and The Beast); Jewells Santana was the only woman in an otherwise all-male group. Two of the women first offended with a single partner, not in a large group; one was with her brother (Tonya James) and one with a romantic partner (Jasmine King). Even Chocolate, the only female to commit her first theft solely in the company of women, admitted, "Someone did teach us how to do it because on another incident a guy was with us and showed us how to do it." The following exchange with Lil' Bit illustrates how, even for a woman who currently worked with a group of women, and was initiated by a mixed-sex group, the technical knowledge necessary to take a car without the proper keys was tied to her interactions with a man.

> INTERVIEWER: These women you got involved with. At first, were you just jumping in cars and driving off in them?
>
> LIL' BIT: Yeah.
>
> INTERVIEWER: Is that because you guys [female friends] didn't know how to steal them?
>
> LIL' BIT: Basically, yeah.
>
> INTERVIEWER: Did these other girls you were hanging with, did they know how?
>
> LIL' BIT: no.
>
> INTERVIEWER: And how did you guys eventually learn how to break down a car?
>
> LIL' BIT: A boy showed me that used to go steal cars....He was older than me....At first I just used to ride around with them in stolen cars and then I got tired of just riding around [with] boys so I asked him and he told me. Well he showed me and then he told me.

Thus, even though her current preference was for working with women, Lil' Bit needed to draw on masculine expertise to acquire the needed technical skills to successfully engage in motor vehicle theft.

Early experiences riding in stolen cars were ubiquitous in the interviews for both men and women. Thus, the opportunity to observe an experienced thief at work, as well as have the fundamental techniques explained, was a fairly universal experience. The contextual nature of joyriding and car theft then produced a situation where women did not experience the same sort of gendered barriers to initiation seen with other crimes (i.e., burglary, see Decker et al., 1993; Mullins & Wright, 2003). Some of our female interviewees then circulated these skills and learnt from men within female networks in very much the same way that many men did or were currently doing (such as in the case of Killa, depicted above) among themselves.

ENACTMENT

Unless one purposely targets idling vehicles unattended or otherwise obtains the proper keys, defeating door locks and vehicle ignitions requires a degree of mechanical expertise that surpasses common sense (Copes & Cherbonneau, 2006). The modal enactment method in the sample—discussed equally by men and women—was using a flathead screwdriver to pry off the ignition covering around the keyhole to expose the ignition switch.[2] To start the vehicle, one simply inserts the screwdriver into the exposed ignition and turns clockwise. This constitutes the basics of what men and women learned during their initiation experiences.[3]

Although a growing number of newer (and mostly high-end) cars have built-in safeguards to limit ignition tampering, all 27 males and five of the females described using this approach (or a variant of the general script) in a recent theft. However, some of the discourse from these five women suggests that even though they learned how to bypass keyed ignitions from someone else (as discussed previously, typically a male), their knowledge of what was working or why was comparatively limited. For example, Jasmine King recounted her most recent theft of an unlocked Ford Taurus this way:

> I got in there and I had a screwdriver and I took the screwdriver and stuck it in the—you know, where the ignition thing go....Once I stuck it in there...some wires fell down, and I just messed with the wire. I never know which wire it is—I guess I just be that nervous....It be about four or five wires—different wires....I cut all of them at the same time, you know, and then after I cut them I just be flicking them together to see which ones work to start it.

Seldom did the men we interview describe this sort of fumbling guesswork in their thefts.[4] Even when asked about general auto theft techniques or prodded about specific enactment strategies, men were able to articulate a more convincing account of their aptitude. Young G's explanation of how to steal a 2000 Dodge Intrepid illustrates this distinction:

> First, you got to get the flathead head in the ignition. Once you get the flathead up in the ignition, you hit it a couple of times before you can get it kind of one-way....It's gonna be loose....You put [the screwdriver] on the other side. Bang it in some more [to] get it loose on that side...where you can just stick your hand in it and pull it [ignition cover] out. Once you do that...you stick the flathead up in...where the key ignition was...and start it up.

While tampering vehicle ignitions was the modal method discussed for starting a standstill engine, both males and females went after targets that required less effort to obtain. These offenders seized vehicles left idling and unattended by careless owners, thereby eschewing technical effort in favor of patient observation. Jewels Santana, who accomplished her most recent auto theft using this method, explained the general technique:

> I see somebody leave their car running or something with the keys in it...I might hop in and just drive off....That's just how easy it is. Just wait until somebody park their car, they'll leave the A/C on or something, run in the store real quick or pay for their gas or something. Just hop in the car and leave.

Taking advantage of momentarily unattended vehicles is an especially common practice when the spontaneity and late-night partying of street-life participation leaves offenders stranded far from home with no means of getting back (Copes, 2003; Copes & Cherbonneau, 2006). In such situations, offenders often lack proper tools to enter vehicles and manipulate ignitions. Poorly equipped for the task at hand, targeting vehicles left running emerges as the "most proximate and performable" (Lofland, 1969, p. 61) way to overcome their current predicaments (c.f., Wright & Decker, 1994, p. 200). Poo#2's description of stealing a Monte Carlo for transportation after he was stranded at a party was exemplary of the circumstances underpinning this style of enactment: I went there, they all [my ride] got drunk and left, and I got drunk and dozed off....I don't feel much like staying at other people's houses that I ain't comfortable, you know, so I jumped up, got up. It was hopeless and I was looking for anything." Poo#2 proceeded to walk to a nearby familiar gas station where "there's a lot of dudes be going to that filling station, getting out of their cars and going in there to talk" and simply waited until somebody let down their guard. In his words:

> Dude was at the gas station in a Monte Carlo....He's putting gas in there and I just jumped in the shit and drive off....I just needed a ride home....With a young dude in a Monte Carlo, easiest thing in the world. Like taking candy from a baby.

The presentation of "found" opportunities (see Copes & Cherbonneau, 2006) does more than pique the "larceny sense" (Sutherland, 1937) of the casual observer, but, as Poo#2 made clear, these opportunities are tailor-made for would-be thieves seeking to reverse immediate situational misfortunes. The important contrast between men and women who exploited found opportunities is that men were more likely to do so because of some situational (dis)advantage, whereas women were more likely to actively seek them out over more outwardly difficult targets requiring "mechanical" means of enactment.

While pulling away in unattended vehicles is, in some respects, riskier than stealing unoccupied cars (as the owner is almost always assumed to be nearby and to also immediately report the theft to authorities), it nevertheless constitutes a form of theft that requires less technical knowledge. The Beast highlighted how a lack of mechanical finesse could steer one toward different enactment styles. After explaining that she knew how to break down ignitions from working with a male friend, she went on to say that when they were working together she always deferred the task of breaking down targets to him as "he knows more than me," and admitted that doing it on her own took "about 45 minutes to an hour." In a similar vein, Lil' Bit said, "We knew how to break them down but sometimes we don't want to....Breaking it down will take a little longer than just pulling off."

While both men and women either sought out or took advantage of opportunities created by careless car owners, five females (Chocolate, Lavanda, Lil' Bit, Lil' Bunny, The Beast) reported stealing vehicles in ways that men did not. Although the exact techniques varied from one theft to the next, the common thread among enactment procedures described by men was that face-to-face interaction with victims was always avoided, thereby keeping intact the stealth-like quality of the offense (see Donahue, McLaughlin, & Damm, 1994). Women, on the other hand, described thefts in which prior interaction with the victim was an important ruse toward accomplishing the theft. Not surprisingly, men were the targets in all such thefts. Chocolate conned men into leaving their vehicles overnight at a confederate's automotive garage and would return later to steal the vehicle. If confronted by the owner, she claimed ignorance. Chocolate explained the hustle she did "a lot of times" this way:

> You leave the car with me so I can tint it up and dazz[le] it up for you…at an auto tint place.…I get the word of mouth out. Like a lotta little dudes I know that got nice cars and they're ballin' now.…I be bringing by the cars that we had stole [and fixed up at the auto shop] and I let them look at the cars that we got, the spokes, the rims, and the tint all looking good, and they like be like, "Damn whose motherfucking car is that?" I'll be like, "It's mine, I just bought it"; kind of flo-show. "Where'd you get all that shit from?" "[I got it] at such and such place. Come down and leave your car.…When you get it back it will look like this." They be like, "They be doing that shit?" I was just like, "Well then leave it," and shit like that. So they leave it and I'd steal their car and shit, and don't fuck with them no more and acting like I don't be knowing what happened.

Chocolate further explained that it is an easy scam for females to pull "versus [males, who] just go out, pick a person, and say 'Yeah you, come over here.' You know a dude gonna talk to a girl long. If she got ass and titties, they gonna talk. There's a lot of males around that want it."

Three females—Lil' Bit, Lil' Bunny, and The Beast—stole vehicles from unknown men who approached them in public settings as they went about their day-to-day activities and solicited their company. Lil' Bunny described one such instance while waiting at a bus stop:

> LIL' BUNNY: Like this one man, wanted to take me for a ride and shit. Wanted to go get some drinks.…I just met him waiting on the bus stop. He riding up, "Where you going, little mama?" "Over my friend house." "You wanna go get some drinks?" "Yeah."…[I get in his car and he asked] "What you drinking?" "Absolut and cranberry, you hear me?" He get out the car, leave his keys in the car, I'm gone. I don't want to be with you. You only want one thing: you want to fuck, so I'm gone.…
>
> INTERVIEWER: So you kind of set him up?
>
> LIL' BUNNY: He set himself up. Mm-hmm.
>
> INTERVIEWER: Do you usually do it that way?
>
> LIL' BUNNY: Yeah, especially if I ain't stealing them [by breaking down the ignition]. I don't know you. Why am I trying to drink with you? You doing things to me. So I use your ride, I'm gone.…I don't know you. You think I'm fixing to drink with you? Hell nah, my pussy ain't free either [laughing].

Chocolate and Lavanda also described situations where they intentionally targeted specific men so that they could create an opportunity to make off with their vehicles. As with Maher's street-level sex workers (1997), the women interviewed here exploited a typical male blind spot—seeing women as little else than sex objects—to accomplish an offense (see also Contreras, 2009; Miller, 1998; Mullins & Wright, 2003).

All in all, most offenders used a narrow range of techniques to steal cars, which they learned from others during their initiation experiences. Of course, a patient thief could steal a car without these skills, though there is a tradeoff in the level of risk incurred while doing so. For example, the women who set up or otherwise took advantage of men entered into more provocative and dangerous situations. While rare, it is telling that the most recent auto thefts described by half of the females we interviewed were accomplished by enactment methods that resulted in obtaining the proper keys. In essence, women's lack of technical expertise led to what appear to be riskier forms of enactment.

DISPOSAL

Nearly all of our interviewees discussed having some relationship or connection to a chop shop of some sort where they would dispose of a stolen car and get paid. Many of these locales were repair garages that did a side business in buying stolen cars to strip down for parts. Interviewees also discussed selling parts to friends, family members, or people on the streets as well. However, in most of these cases, car thieves seemed to take the most valuable portable accessories off the car before taking it to the shop (i.e., radios, speakers, rims).

Three women specifically mentioned that they did not know of a chop shop or garage. Lil' Bunny simply drove the car for recreational use and then abandoned it when she thought it might be on the police "hot sheet" (Topalli & Wright, 2004). Likewise, Lil' Bit drove vehicles for a couple of days but then "after I'm through with the car...I sell whatever in the car that could be sold." Asked why she did not sell to chop shops, Lil' Bit replied, "I don't know where no chop shop at. I don't know where no one at. I know they say there's one on the East Side but I never been to it so I don't know where it's at." The third, Tonya James, had a longer history of car theft (compared to Lil' Bunny and Lil' Bit) and used chop shops earlier in her career. When asked about her current use of them, she replied, "I don't know any chop shops....They [the police] caught up with them and they're closed down, that was seven or eight years ago. But man, I don't know none today....I wish I did." With no connections, she stripped valuable accessories off of the cars she stole to sell on the streets (see below). No men specifically mentioned not knowing a chop shop as a personal barrier to disposal; in fact, most discussed how essential it was to have those connections.

Men, however, were likely to dismantle stolen vehicles themselves and sell off specific parts of high value (or those easily sold) on the streets. Only one female mentioned this tactic. In these street disposal approaches, men mentioned specific orders from associates, simply knowing people, or generally trying to sell parts on the streets. JD explained how he sold parts on the street:

> You see a person in a real car you can ask 'em, you know, "I can get you such and such."...You gotta ask people. You won't tell him [how] you get it, but you know, [tell them] "I can get it."...If I feel like I can't trust you, why ask you? If I feel like it's a problem, I'm not gonna say nothing to you....I approach people I know.

Only one female, Lil' Bit, adopted this disposal technique. Recall, she was one of the females who did not know of any locally run chop shops. Without knowledge of this common outlet, she resorted to selling on the streets, but with a somewhat different approach than JD. Whereas he sought out potential buyers directly, Lil' Bit informed others about the property she had available, who, for the promise of a "finder's fee," helped her locate interested buyers. Asked how she finds people that buy stolen goods, Lil' Bit said:

> I mean 'cause people tell. Like some of the dudes, that's their white [crack-cocaine]. They know that I got some parts and they'll tell who[ever], they'll just go around. If they see somebody they know that like rims and stuff like that then they ask them do they wanna buy a radio, rims, or whatever, and if they do, they'll come and tell me. They'll bring the person who want to buy it to me, and I give them a little money for, you know what I'm saying, bringing them to me.... I give them like $30 [on a $100 sale].

It is here that social networks were of upmost importance. In order to be successful, people needed to know where chop shops were and how to approach the operators. They needed to know who would buy stolen auto parts and how best to deal them on their own. This knowledge was typically acquired through other, often more experienced criminal associates. Young G described how he gained entry into these networks:

> I know the owner [through my brother]....My brother was actually the one that...will take the car to the shop and I will just come along 'cause he knew the owner well, better than everybody else [in our crew], so that's why he was the ringleader, 'cause all the money, you know what I'm saying, to get the money in the first place it would have to go through him, so that's why he would get paid the most money. 'Cause without him, we wouldn't even be getting paid no ways.... [The owner] know my brother since birth, so he got a lot of trust in him. That's really what it's all about, trust.

Jasmine King described having to develop this trust over time. "They [the men who ran the chop shop] was cool because they knew who I was. They knew I wasn't no snitch. They knew I wasn't trying to get them in trouble or nothing. They knew I was just wanting some money." She went on to explain that at first she was introduced to the chop shop through her boyfriend at the time, and, once connected, she explained that "I got cool with them and they got to trust you." However, she did reveal that once on her own (having since split up with her boyfriend), the shop owner paid her appreciably less than he did her boyfriend, as illustrated in the following exchange:

> INTERVIEWER: How much did the guy [boyfriend] get that you used to work with?
> JASMINE KING: He was getting more.
> INTERVIEWER: Why is that?
> JASMINE KING: I don't know, maybe he was better at it than I was, I don't know. Maybe he didn't have to break 'em down like I did, but I done seen him

drive the cars before with a screwdriver in it, you know what I'm saying, so I don't know. I don't know.... I have said something to him [chop shop contact] before like, "Come on now, you know it's worth more than that. You're gonna get more."... [And he says,] "That's the best I can do right now."

INTERVIEWER: Do you have access to any other people like that where you could sell cars?

JASMINE KING: No. He the only person I know.

INTERVIEWER: Do you think he knows that?

JASMINE KING: Yeah.

Without these contacts the ability to profit from auto theft was significantly curtailed. The next profitable source for those who lacked access to these higher outlets was to sell vehicle parts and accessories on the streets. Recall how Tonya James was forced to sell on the streets since she did not know of any chop shops that were currently operating. Yet, even those who sold parts on the street relied upon social networks to either move parts or become aware of customers. The following exchange with Chocolate emphasized the importance of informal network connections:

INTERVIEWER: It seems you got your people setup pretty much—you got your girls...and you got people you know you can sell the stuff to.

CHOCOLATE: Yeah. Yeah, exactly.

INTERVIEWER: Do you ever try to look for more connections?

CHOCOLATE: I got more connections now, I just ain't gonna fixing to reveal them. They all good.

INTERVIEWER: But are you always out looking for connections?

CHOCOLATE: Yeah, always looking for something different. If you find something different, you find more money.

We should also note that Chocolate was not dependent on these networks to make car theft profitable; her uncle owned a garage, giving her ready access to a disposal source.

Westside provided a rich description of exactly how these networks can work and how trust is central to their functioning. He described his current involvement in the world of car theft in St. Louis as "an overseer":

WESTSIDE: Me personally,...I oversee it now: "Handle that. Get that. We take this."...I mean I got the connect[ion to the chop shop]. [If] the youngsters want to eat how we wanted to eat, they know if they get this certain type of car, they know they can get a certain amount of dollar from it, so they get it, come to me, and I take 'em to where they need to go....I take them to my dude....He sees what he can salvage from them, see if he can strip it down, see what else he...can do. Like if this car has rims on it, he'll strip it down and pull all the accessories out, TVs, whatever the case, and just strip it for salvage....Yeah, that's what we do pretty much....We've been working together for damn near seven years, eight years damn near....

INTERVIEWER: I was wondering what's to stop him from... *Westside* [inter-rupting]: From my little partners going to him? Because nah, we don't do it like that....It's in stone that my guy don't trust nobody but me. For all he know, these little cats could be bringing them folks up in here with them because they get caught up on the jam....You're in a situ-ation where you feel like they probably don't know how to hold they own. You put them in an interrogation room, goddamn they singing and telling every motherfucking thing that need not be told....I remember my dude ain't want to fuck with me back in the day because I was a, you know, he had to just see how I moved. You know what I mean? And you can tell, you can tell who's real and who ain't—pressure bust pipes and bitches too!

Trust is central in establishing connections for criminal disposal of goods, yet these informal social connections in the criminal underworld are often gate-kept by men. This has strong consequences for women's ability to make and maintain these relationships. Steffensmeier (1983) and Steffensmeier and Terry (1986) iden-tified men's negative attitudes toward women as a key barrier to women's inclu-sion in offending and disposal networks (see also Maher, 1997; Mullins & Wright, 2003). Compared to prior work on the topic, we found much more diversity within men's attitudes toward women in the data.

Over half of the men asked said they did not know any women car thieves, and moreover would not work with them if they did. Typically, they provided a stereotypical explanation that crime in general, and car theft in particular, was a male activity, and that women were "too soft" to be successful criminals. For example, Young G dismissed female offenders by saying that "little chicks just be scared....They just too girly to do something like that....They just don't got what it takes for real." Others suggested that women could not stand up to police ques-tioning and would thus snitch. Killa straightforwardly said, "They [women] can just be broken easily." Thus, if a female associate were caught, she would reveal everything to the police. E#2 agreed saying that women, "They'll do a switch on you...put police in front of them, man, it's over. Yeah, they'll cry."

Others discussed the issue in a more pragmatic fashion. These men did not deny the abilities of women to engage in criminal behavior, but thought that women did not have the exact skill set needed for car theft. J discussed refusing to teach one of his female peers how to steal cars, emphasizing that "I ain't got the time....They [women] don't learn so fast." End Dog made a similar statement, explaining he had worked with a women on a theft once, but "she moved too slow, so no, she was way slow, slower than normal...too slow for me. Not going to get caught." Poo#2 combined these themes, saying:

It's a man thing....It's just not appropriate to take a woman with you to do some-thing like that....It's not safe....It's a dangerous risk....She can't run as fast as you can. If you have to ask her to outrun the police she's gonna get caught, and nine times out of 10, she's gonna tell who you is.

Of those who *knew* female car thieves, all but one said they had no problem working with women. Capone, who had previously worked with Chocolate, insisted that:

CAPONE: The women I mess with ain't gonna tell—they solid. Just like her [Chocolate],[5] she's solid.

INTERVIEWER: Do you ever work with her [Chocolate]?

CAPONE: Couple times. She's cool. She's cool.

T-Raw said, "I've worked with some women [who] know more shit than men. A lot of the women stronger than men, you know what I'm saying....A lot of the women they some soldiers, gotta give it to 'em."

This degree of open-mindedness was not just limited to men who had worked with women. Asked if a female could have joined the all-male crew that introduced him to auto theft, Tye said, "Yeah, if she wanted to get down, it was up to her. It's her decision....A female never tried to get with us...but I've heard of females that...do get down, that's real smooth with it." Thus, there is limited support within criminal networks for working with women, and it is no doubt through these pathways that the women we interviewed gained access to offender and disposal networks.

Taken as a whole, our examination of the data has uncovered several core themes of gender-neutral and gender-specific perspectives and experiences. In general, the motivation and enactment techniques of men and women were very similar. Where women had access to vehicle or parts disposal networks, their experiences tended to be very similar to men's. In the context of the types of groups responsible for offenders' initiation into auto theft and subsequently their access to networks (especially for disposal), strong gender differences emerged.

DISCUSSION

Throughout our analysis we have relied on a tried and true method for exploring both the divergences and convergences in the perspectives and experiences of men and women involved in street crime (see Miller & Mullins, 2006). Car theft requires slightly more specialized knowledge to enact than most other street crimes. This information is typically disseminated and acquired in social networks. Car theft also requires knowledge of underground disposal networks to be profitable (though, unlike other forms of theft, there is a utilitarian value to a car in and of itself). Prior work has suggested that women have a social capital disadvantage due to sexist attitudes held by the male gatekeepers of these networks (Messerschmidt, 1997; Mullins & Wright, 2003; Steffensmeier, 1983; Steffensmeier & Terry, 1986). Here we found that this is indeed the case on the streets of St. Louis. Almost universally, individuals learned the basic techniques of car theft and were initiated into social networks that facilitated disposal through male peers or family members. However, unlike prior work, we did find a larger subset of males who were tolerant of women offenders as long as their expertise was similar to males.

Thus, for our male interviewees, their introduction to auto theft occurred within gender-homogenous networks and interaction experiences. The females, however, experienced initiation and socialization into auto theft and disposal networks typically through opposite-sex interactions. While men and women did not describe radical differences in the content of what was learned or how they were treated by others, such initiatory experiences did have gendered ramifications later in the offenders' car theft careers.

As with Mullins and Wright's (2003) work on residential burglary, we found few differences in offense enactment. This is, in all likelihood, a function of the fact that there are only so many ways to take control of a car to steal it. As with most tasks, once an effective technique is found for completion, it is repeated. Auto theft seems to be no different. Men and women alike described the tactic of popping out the ignition and using a screwdriver to start the vehicle. They mentioned learning this technique from others and replicating it due to ease and functionality. As an interesting area of departure, women were the only ones who described specifically seeking out a vehicle left running. Men did rely on these methods, however, both situationally (i.e., they were stranded and/or lacked the necessary tools) and opportunistically (i.e., they chanced upon a vehicle left running and perceived the opportunity too enticing to pass up). It is worth noting that the same females who relied on these techniques most often were also the least integrated into criminal networks. They were the women who mentioned not knowing chop shops and generally not having access to male-dominated networks; thus, their primary use of stolen vehicles was either expressive (i.e., joyriding) or utilitarian (i.e., using them for personal transport)—any profits were serendipitous (i.e., found money or drugs while rummaging a vehicles' interior) or by chance (i.e., a member of their neighborhood network inquired about and offered a small sum for a vehicle stolen for some other purpose). Their lived gendered experiences narrowed the disposal options available and thus constrained opportunities. As we explored previously, this in turn influenced disposal patterns and women's ability to profit from motor vehicle theft, and profit well.

As with many other studies on street life, we also found women taking advantage of men's sexual objectification of them to enact a crime, in this case car theft (see Contreras, 2009; Maher, 1997; Miller, 1998; Mullins & Wright, 2003). This well-confirmed aspect of offender agency highlights how power relationships shape situational interactional contexts, forcing social actors to modify behaviors and adopt innovative interactional strategies for goal accomplishment. Five of our eight female interviewees drew upon this tactic on occasion; it was not resorted to only when the offender lacked other options. As explored previously, those females who had little technical expertise with breaking steering columns down tended to target vehicles left running at convenience stores and gas stations. A general lack of technical expertise lead women to engage in riskier thefts, which also tended to produce less gain.

The issue of similarities and differences are not a zero-sum experience. Women's experiences here were varied. Some were deeply embedded in criminal networks; their interactional experiences provided opportunities to get to be known and trusted by male gatekeepers in the St. Louis underworld. Once established, they were able to engage in and profit from motor vehicle theft; thus, their experiences, techniques, and knowledge overlapped strongly with the men who were interviewed. Two of the women described past exposure to these networks. While some avenues of profitability were no longer open to them, as these earlier connections had since dried up, they still drew upon the skills acquired while attached to active criminal networks. Two of the females interviewed here had no real access to active crime groups; their techniques of commission and disposal reflected this dual lack of technical and social capital, as did their use of the vehicle once stolen (i.e., utilitarian usage versus selling for profit). Further, two others only had access to disposal networks through males. As a group, women's experiences were far more diverse in nature than men's experiences. We conclude that this is a product, in part, of what social ties and connections they were able to establish and maintain throughout their criminal careers.

CONCLUSION

This paper has examined the convergences and divergences of men's and women's experiences in motor vehicle theft, adding to the qualitative literature on street-life subculture, street crime, and the experiences of gender within each and at the intersection of both domains. As other recent work has shown (Brookman et al., 2007; Miller, 1998; Miller, 2002; Mullins & Wright, 2003; Mullins, Wright, & Jacobs, 2004), men and women share many motivational drives and enactment techniques for committing crime. Such findings speak directly to broader theorizations of crime that either postulate gender-specific motivations for criminal involvement or suggest that there is a more universal criminal experience. In terms of initiation into car crimes, our data here highlight the generally criminogenic nature of certain neighborhood situations and experiences and show them influencing both women and men in similar fashion (at least the women interviewed in this project).

Yet, despite similarities of early crime experiences, our findings support prior work that establishes a strong set of misogynistic attitudes toward women that shapes female experiences with offending and within offender networks (and more generally of life lived within neighborhoods inhabited by offenders—see Miller, 2008). We do not doubt these attitudes preclude some women from getting involved at all in criminal activities (thus contributing to the wide gender gap in motor vehicle theft) and that those women who do become involved are frequently presented with negative social stimuli that push some toward (if not outright into) criminal desistance. Yet, unlike other work, our findings highlight some diversity of men's opinions of female peers, with a minority judging potential women co-offenders by skill set and not by sex category. This is an area which requires more investigation. Much of the early (and even recent) work establishing pervasive misogyny on the streets is grounded in data which are older (i.e., Mullins & Wright's 2003 data were collected in 1989 and 1990). There is no reason to believe that attitudes in street-life social networks remain static over time. They should exhibit the same dynamic characteristics that mainstream norms do. Thus, to a small degree, attitudes toward female offenders may be changing. More work is needed to explore how individuals respond to initially negative experiences with these gendered barriers then decide to either seek entry into networks anyway or who decide to either forgo crime in general or crimes with gatekeepers (i.e., burglary, drug selling, and auto theft).

An immutable limitation of the data presented here is undoubtedly sample size, particularly in the number of female participants. Moreover, due to the nature of nonprobabilistic sampling using "snowball" and chain-referral methods, we gained the views of a number of women within one established street-life network. We cannot make broad generalizations of our findings here beyond the data themselves. Be that as it may, the current findings confirm themes and experiences reported in other criminological research using qualitative methods—be they gender-specific or mixed-gender offender-based examinations of street crime in general. Further, Guest, Bunce, and Johnson (2006) establishes experimentally that most major themes in qualitative interviewing tend to be uncovered and saturated early during data collection—especially with regard to the types of meta-themes dealt with here. With the experimental work of Guest and co-authors (2006) in mind, we are confident in the validity of the information we uncovered in the female narratives. Hopefully more work on female experiences in crime in general and car crime specifically will provide further insight into our findings.

Our uncovering of a high diversity of female experiences within criminal social networks contributes to the current debates within feminist criminology concerning the divergence and convergence of male and female experiences of street life. As described by both male and female interviewees, in some social groups femininity is not necessarily the barrier to entry and cooperation that some work has suggested. However, women are still not universally respected on the streets and there is still a strong culture of misogyny held and perpetuated by criminally involved men of all ages (Miller, 1998; Miller & Mullins, 2006; Mullins, 2006). As discussed, such negative perceptions and experiences were prominent in the data explored here. Our understanding of the conditional nature of these attitudes and what factors shape men's attitudes toward women in criminal social networks would benefit from a closer look at these variant contexts and experiences.

Such contexts and experiences are of the utmost importance to understand as criminology continues to explore both the prominent gender gap in offending and the manner in which experiences within criminal networks influence criminal career trajectory. Opportunity structures on the streets clearly frame both of these issues. Offender decision making is situated within the context of street-life social networks. If and how gender shapes such networks will feed back into decision-making events. Gendered perceptions, knowledge, and opportunities will shape if, and if so how, individuals offend. Such forces will also affect how offenders negotiate post-offense actions, especially transforming ill-gotten goods into money or other desired goods. Hopefully future research will continue to explore how gender at the macro and meso levels intersects with micro-level offending decisions and actions.

NOTES

1. By direct participation, we mean the first time where the interviewee took an active role in the stealing of a car. This includes being a lookout. Due to our interviewees' wide exposure to stolen cars before they began to steal cars themselves, we found it necessary to make this distinction.
2. While the exact technique varies from one vehicle make to the next, this one reportedly worked well on newer vehicle makes (and models) including, among others, Chrysler-Dodge (Charger, Intrepid, Neon, Stratus), Chrysler-Plymouth (Sebring), General Motors–Buick (LeSabre, Regal), and General Motors–Pontiac (Grand Am, Bonneville, Sunfire). For older vehicles manufactured in the 1980s and early to mid-1990s (General Motors–Chevrolet: Caprice, Blazer/Suburban, Malibu, Monte Carlo; General Motors–Buick: Regal, Riviera; General Motors–Oldsmobile: Cutlass; General Motors–Pontiac: Grand Prix), thieves took advantage of their weak tilt-steering column design, which, when broken, provides access to the ignition switch, which can be easily manipulated by pulling a lever or "horseshoe" and then depressing a coiled spring screw to start up the engine.
3. Car thieves do engage in a semirational process of target selection. When assessing prospective targets, offenders' primary perceptual filter at work concerns its "stealability" (i.e., one that they can take successfully based on their ability and available on-hand hardware). This filter is grounded in their personal perception of their own skills. As we examine here, those skill sets are gendered, and thus the target selection process drawn upon by our informants is gendered as well.
4. This could easily be an artifact of the interview process. Due to the general demands of hegemonic masculinity, the men may have felt a need to present a veneer of competency. Especially when being interviewed by a male, they no doubt carefully constructed their presentation of self. Women would experience less social pressure to do so, especially in a realm typically viewed as masculine (see Mullins, 2006, for more discussion of masculine self-presentation in interview situations).
5. Capone was interviewed on the same day and immediately after Chocolate, who at the time of Capone's interview was waiting with the recruiter outside the interview room. Capone also described working with his 19-year-old niece "a couple of times" owing to the fact that she was a competent auto thief. He was also proud to report that much like himself, "she hood. She be high-speeding [eluding police] and everything—she get away."

REFERENCES

Best, A. L. (2006). *Fast cars, cool rides: The accelerating world of youth and their cars.* New York: New York University Press.

Brookman, F., Mullins, C. W., Bennett, T., & Wright, R. (2007). Gender, motivation and the accomplishment of street robbery. *British Journal of Criminology, 47,* 861–884.

Campbell, A. (1993). *Men, women, and aggression.* New York: Basic.

Cherbonneau, M., & Wright, R. (2009). Auto theft. In M. Tonry (Ed.), *The Oxford handbook of crime and public policy* (pp. 191–222). New York: Oxford University Press.

Clarke, R. V., & Harris, P. (1992). Auto theft and its prevention. In M. Tonry (Ed.), *Crime and justice: A review of research* (vol. 16, pp. 1–54). Chicago: University of Chicago Press.

Contreras, R. (2009). "Damn, yo—who's that girl?": An ethnographic analysis of masculinity in drug robberies. *Journal of Contemporary Ethnography, 38,* 465–492.

Copes, H. (2003). Streetlife and the rewards of auto theft. *Deviant Behavior, 24,* 309–332.

Copes, H., & Cherbonneau, M. (2006). The key to auto theft: Emerging methods of auto theft from the offenders' perspective. *British Journal of Criminology, 46,* 917–934.

Dawes, G. (2002). Figure eights, spin outs and power slides: Aboriginal and Torres Strait Islander youth and the culture of joyriding. *Journal of Youth Studies, 5,* 195–208.

Decker, S., Wright, R., Redfern, A., & Smith, D. (1993). A woman's place is in the home: Females and residential burglary. *Justice Quarterly, 10,* 143–162.

Donahue, M., McLaughlin, V., & Damm, L. 1994. Accounting for carjacking: An analysis of police records in a southeastern city. *American Journal of Police, 13*(4), 91–111.

Federal Bureau of Investigation (FBI). (2008). *Uniform crime report: Crime in the United States, 2007.* Washington, DC: U.S. Department of Justice.

Federal Highway Administration. (2008). *Highway statistics, 2007.* Washington, DC: U.S. Department of Transportation.

Fleming, Z. (2003). "The thrill of it all": Youthful offenders and auto theft. In P. Cromwell (Ed.), *In their own words: Criminals on crime* (3rd ed., pp. 99–107). Los Angeles: Roxbury.

Fleming, Z., Brantingham, P., & Brantingham, P. (1994). Exploring auto theft in British Columbia. In R. V. Clarke (Ed.), *Crime prevention studies* (Vol. 3, pp. 47–90). Monsey, NY: Criminal Justice Press.

Graham, J., & Bowling, B. (1995). *Young people and crime.* Home Office Research Study, 145. London: Home Office.

Guest, G., Bunce, A., & Johnson, L. (2006). How many interviews are enough? An experiment with data saturation and variability. *Field Methods, 18*(1), 59–82.

Henderson, J. (1994). Masculinity and crime: The implications of a gender-conscious approach to working with young men involved in "joyriding." *Social Action, 2*(2),19–26.

Kilpatrick, R. (1997). Joy-riding: An addictive behaviour. In J. E. Hodge, M. McMurran, & C. Hollin (Eds.), *Addicted to crime?* (pp. 165–190). New York: John Wiley & Sons.

Light, R., Nee, C., & Ingham, H. (1993). *Car theft: The offender's perspective.* Home Office Research Study 130. London: Home Office.

Lofland, J. (1969). *Deviance and identity.* Englewood Cliffs, NJ: Prentice-Hall.

Maher, L. (1997). *Sexed work: Gender, race and resistance in a Brooklyn drug market.* Oxford: Oxford University Press.

Messerschmidt, J. W. (1997). *Crime as structured action: Gender, race, class, and crime in the making.* Thousand Oaks, CA: Sage.

Miller, J. (1998). Up it up: Gender and the accomplishment of street robbery. *Criminology, 36*(1), 37–66.

———. (2001). *One of the guys: Girls, gangs and gender.* New York: Oxford University Press.

———. (2002). The strengths and limits of "doing gender" for understanding street crime. *Theoretical Criminology, 6,* 433–60.

———. (2008). *Getting played: African American girls, urban inequality and gendered violence.* New York: New York University Press.

Miller, J., & Mullins, C. W. (2006). The status of feminist theories in criminology. In F. T. Cullen, J. P. Wright, & K. R. Blevins (Eds.), *Taking stock: The status of criminological theory, advances in criminological theory* (vol. 15, pp. 217–249). New Brunswick, NJ: Transaction Publishers.

Mullins, C. W. (2006). *Holding your square: Masculinities, streetlife and violence.* Cullompton, Devon, UK: Willan.

Mullins, C. W., & Wright, R. T. (2003). Gender, social networks, and residential burglary. *Criminology, 41*(3), 813–840.

Mullins, C. W., Wright, R. T., & Jacobs, B. A. (2004). Gender, streetlife, and criminal retaliation. *Criminology, 42*(4), 911–940.

O'Connor, C., & Kelly, K. (2006). Auto theft and youth culture: A nexus of masculinities, femininities and car culture. *Journal of Youth Studies, 9,* 247–267.

Roe, S., & Ashe, J. (2008). *Young people and crime: Findings from the 2006 Offending, Crime and Justice Survey.* London: Home Office.

Slobodian, P., & Browne, K. (1997). Car crime as a developmental career: An analysis of young offenders in Coventry. *Psychology, Crime and Law, 3,* 275–286.

Sourcebook of Criminal Justice Statistics. 2003. High school seniors reporting involvement in selected delinquent activities in last 12 months. Retrieved June 4, 2012, from http://www.albany.edu/sourcebook/pdf/t344.pdf.

Spencer, E. (1992). *Car crime and young people on a Sunderland housing estate.* Crime Prevention Unit Series paper no. 40. London: Home Office.

Steffensmeier, D. (1983). Organization properties and sex-segregation in the underworld: Building a sociological theory of sex differences in crime. *Social Forces, 61,* 1010–1032.

Steffensmeier, D., & Terry, R. (1986). Institutional sexism in the underworld: A view from the inside. *Sociological Inquiry, 56,* 304–323.

Stephen, D., & Squires, P. (2003). "Adults don't realize how sheltered they are." A contribution to the debate on youth transitions from some voices on the margins. *Journal of Youth Studies, 6,* 145–164.

Topalli, V., & Wright, R. (2004). Dubs and dees, beats and rims: Carjackers and urban violence. In D. Dabney (Ed.), *Crime types: A text reader* (pp. 149–169). Belmont, CA: Wadsworth.

Walker, L., Butland, D., & Connell, R. W. (2000). Boys on the road: Masculinity, car culture and road safety education. *Journal of Men's Studies, 8*(2), 153–169.

Williams, C. (2005). *Stealing a car to be a man: The importance of cars and driving in the gender identity of adolescent males.* Unpublished Ph.D. diss., Queensland University of Technology, School of Psychology and Centre for Counseling.

Wright, R. T., & Decker, S. H. (1994). *Burglars on the job: Streetlife and residential break-ins.* Boston: Northeastern University Press.

Yates, J. (2003/4). Adolescent males: Masculinity and offending. *IUC Journal of Social Work Theory and Practice, 8,* 13 pages.

CHAPTER 7

✦

"The Devil Made Me Do It": Use of Neutralizations by Shoplifters

Paul Cromwell and Quint Thurman

This study is based on 137 interviews with shoplifters obtained over a period of 12 months in 1997–1998 in a midwestern city of approximately 360,000. The authors obtained access to a court-ordered diversion program ostensibly for adult "first offenders" (although few were actually first offenders) charged with theft. Of these, most were charged with misdemeanor shoplifting and required to attend an eight-hour therapeutic/education program as a condition of having their record expunged. The average group size was 18 to 20 participants. The participants were encouraged to discuss with the group the offense that brought them to the diversion program, why they did what they did, and how they felt about it. A series of educational exercises and role-playing activities completed each session's activities. The authors participated in the sessions as observers, recording their stories and experiences and occasionally asking questions. The participants were told that we were researchers studying shoplifting. At the conclusion of each daily session, participants were approached and asked if they would agree to a one-on-one interview. Interviews were obtained with 137 subjects. The mean age of the sample was 26. The age range was 18 to 66 years of age. Forty-eight were male and 49 were female. Seventy-eight (78) were non-Hispanic white, 17 were Hispanic, and 42 were African-American.

> You know that cartoon where the guy has a little devil sitting on one shoulder and a little angel on the other? And one is telling him "Go ahead on, do it," and the angel is saying "No, don't do it." You know?...Sometimes when I'm thinking about boosting something, my angel don't show up.
>
> —30-YEAR-OLD MALE SHOPLIFTER

Source: Cromwell, P., & Thurman, Q. (2003). "The devil made me do it": Use of neutralizations by shoplifters. *Deviant Behavior, 24,* 535–550. Used with permission of the publisher.

114

Nearly five decades ago Gresham Sykes and David Matza (1957) introduced neutralization theory as an explanation for juvenile delinquency. At that time, delinquency theory was the central attraction of criminology, with theorists such as Albert Cohen, Walter Miller, Edwin Sutherland, Richard Cloward and Lloyd Ohlin, and Sheldon and Eleanor Glueck establishing a foundation upon which subsequent theorists would build. The challenge then, as it still exists today, was to explain the unconventional behavior of juveniles. This paper examines Sykes and Matza's theory as it might apply to a specific form of criminal activity that is highly popular among juveniles and young adults. Here we look at offenders who shoplift and explore the justifications that they say they rely upon to excuse behavior they also acknowledge as morally wrong.

THE PROBLEM

Shoplifting may be the most serious crime with which the most people have some personal familiarity. Research has shown that one in every 10 to 15 persons who shops has shoplifted at one time or another (Lo, 1994; Russell, 1973; Turner & Cashdan, 1988). Further, losses attributable to shoplifting are considerable, with estimates ranging from 12 to 30 billion dollars lost annually (Klemke, 1982; Nimick, 1990; Griffin, 1988). Shoplifting also represents one of the most prevalent forms of larceny, accounting for approximately 15% of all larcenies according to data maintained by the Federal Bureau of Investigation (Freeh, 1996).

Unlike many other forms of crime, people who shoplift do not ordinarily require any special expertise or tools to engage in this crime. Consequently, those persons who shoplift do not necessarily conform to most people's perception of what a criminal offender is like. Instead, shoplifters tend to be demographically similar to the "average person." In a large study of nondelinquents, Klemke (1982) reported that as many as 63% of those persons he interviewed had shoplifted at some point in their lives. Students, housewives, business and professional persons, as well as professional thieves constitute the population of shoplifters. Loss prevention experts routinely counsel retail merchants that there is no particular profile of a potential shoplifter. Turner and Cashdan (1988) conclude, "While clearly a criminal activity, shoplifting borders on what might be considered a 'folk crime.'" In her classic study, Mary Cameron (1964) wrote:

> Most people have been tempted to steal from stores, and many have been guilty (at least as children) of "snitching" an item or two from counter tops. With merchandise so attractively displayed in department stores and supermarkets, and much of it apparently there for the taking, one may ask why everyone isn't a thief. (p. xi)

Because of its somewhat normative nature, shoplifting provides an excellent forum for criminologists to study various theories for explaining why some people commit crime and others do not since it appears to cross racial, ethnic, gender, and class lines and is frequently committed by "otherwise noncriminal" persons.

Furthermore, since shoplifting is a crime that is widely distributed across the general population by people whose values are thought to be generally consistent with the conventional moral code, it also represents an excellent choice for testing the merits of one theory in particular, that is, the theory of neutralization.

Neutralization theory argues that "ordinary" individuals who engage in deviant or criminal behavior may use techniques that permit them to recognize extenuating circumstances that enable them to explain away delinquent behavior. Without worrying about guilty feelings that would stand in their way of committing a criminal act, the theory asserts that those persons are free to participate in delinquent acts that they would otherwise believe to be wrong.

THEORETICAL CONSIDERATIONS

American criminology in the 1950s focused on whether or not juvenile delinquents in particular shared a common American culture or somehow belonged to another culture or had in fact formed their own subculture. Did they belong to the underclass culture that William Julius Wilson (1987) would identify some years later in *The Truly Disadvantaged* or had they somehow made a poor adaptation to a conventional culture that they did not fit, and thus, become their own youth subculture or counterculture as Howard Becker (1963) suggested in *Outsiders*?

Sykes and Matza's theory is an elaboration of Edwin Sutherland's proposition that individuals can learn criminal techniques, and the "motives, drives, rationalizations and attitudes favorable to violations of the law." Sykes and Matza argued that these justifications or rationalizations protect the individual from self-blame and the blame of others. Thus, the individual may remain committed to the value system of the dominant culture while committing criminal acts without experiencing the cognitive dissonance that might be otherwise expected. He or she deflects or "neutralizes" guilt in advance, clearing the way to blame-free crime. These neutralizations also protect the individual from any residual guilt following the crime. It is this ability to use neutralizations that differentiates delinquents from nondelinquents (Thurman, 1984).

While Sykes and Matza do not specifically maintain that only offenders who are committed to the dominant value system make use of these techniques of neutralizations, they appear to contend that delinquents maintain a commitment to the moral order and are able to drift into delinquency through the use of "techniques of neutralization." This approach assumes that should delinquents fail to internalize conventional morality, neutralization would be unnecessary, since there would be no guilt to neutralize. However, Hirschi (1969) argued that there is wide variation in the commitment to the conventional moral order. Furthermore, subsequent research implies that both delinquents and nondelinquents make use of neutralization strategies (Austin, 1977; Mannle & Lewis, 1979).

Thurman (1984) contends that commitment to conventional values and neutralization is empirically and conceptually distinct. Using this line of reasoning, individuals at any point on the committed/noncommitted continuum might utilize neutralization strategies. The specific purpose of the neutralization could be to reduce cognitive dissonance arising from guilt, to maintain self-image in the face of condemnation by others, to establish a defense against possible prosecution, or to facilitate subsequent offenses. Mannle and Lewis (1979) and Austin (1977) found that unconventional boys are most likely to neutralize, suggesting that neutralization is inversely related to moral commitment. Thurman (1984) supplies a logical rationale to this contradictory finding. He suggests that when "moral commitment is high, the level of guilt operates as a formidable obstacle to deviance which neutralizations cannot effectively reduce. Conversely, when commitment is low, guilt exists at levels susceptible to neutralization strategies" (p. 295).

One issue that has not been satisfactorily settled is when neutralization occurs. Sykes and Matza (1957) and social learning theory (Akers, 1985) contend that deviants must neutralize moral prescriptions prior to committing a crime. However, most research is incapable of determining whether the stated neutralization is a before-the-fact neutralization or an after-the-fact rationalization. As Hirschi (1969) surmises, an after-the-fact rationalization in one instance may be a causal neutralization in another instance. He states, "The assumption that delinquent acts come before justifying beliefs is the more plausible causal ordering" (p. 208).

While Sykes and Matza's work referred to juvenile offenders, subsequent research has found that adult offenders also make use of neutralization techniques (Nettler, 1974; Geis & Meier, 1977; Zeitz, 1981; Thurman, 1984; Coleman, 1985; Benson, 1985; Jesilow, Pontell, & Geis, 1993; Dabney, 1995; Gauthier, 2001). This appears to be particularly true for white-collar offenders whose otherwise conventional lifestyles and value systems would not countenance criminal involvement.

TECHNIQUES OF NEUTRALIZATION

Sykes and Matza (1957) identified five techniques of neutralization commonly offered to justify deviant behavior: *denial of responsibility, denial of the victim, denial of injury, condemning the condemners,* and *appeal to higher loyalties.*

Five additional neutralization techniques have since been identified. These include *defense of necessity* (Klockars, 1974), *metaphor of the ledger* (Minor, 1981), *denial of the necessity of the law, the claim that everybody else is doing it,* and *the claim of entitlement* (Coleman, 1994).

The purpose of this study is to determine the extent to which adult shoplifters use techniques of neutralizations and to analyze the various neutralizations available to them.

FINDINGS

The informants appeared to readily use neutralization techniques. We identified nine categories of neutralizations; the five Sykes and Matza categories, the *defense of necessity* and *everybody does it* neutralizations identified by Coleman (1994) and two additional neutralizations that we labeled *justification by comparison* and *postponement.* Only five of the 137 informants failed to express a rationalization or neutralization when asked how they felt about their illegal behavior. All but one stated that they felt that stealing was morally wrong. In many cases, the respondent offered more than one neutralization for the same offense. For example, one female respondent stated, "I don't know what comes over me. It's like, you know, is somebody else doing it, not me" (denial of responsibility). "I'm really a good person. I wouldn't ever do something like that, stealing, you know, but I have to take things sometimes for my kids. They need stuff and I don't have any money to get it" (defense of necessity). They frequently responded with a motivation ("I wanted the item and could not afford it") followed by a neutralization ("Stores charge too much for stuff. They could sell things for half what they do and still make a profit. They're just too greedy"). Thus, in many cases, the motivation was linked to the excuse in such a way as to make the excuse a part of the motivation. The subjects were in effect explaining the reason the deviant act occurred and justifying it at the same time. The following section illustrates the neutralizations we discovered in use by the informants.

Denial of Responsibility (I Didn't Mean It)

Denial of responsibility frees the subject from experiencing culpability for deviance by allowing him or her to perceive themselves as victims of their environment. The offender views him or herself as being acted upon rather than acting. Thus, attributing behavior to poor parenting, bad companions, or internal forces ("the devil made me do it") allows the offender to avoid disapproval of self or others, which in turn diminishes those influences as mechanisms of social control. Sykes and Matza (1957) describe the individual resorting to this neutralization as having a "billiard ball conception of himself in which he see himself as helplessly propelled into new situations" (p. 666).

> I admit that I lift. I do. But, you know, it's not really me—I mean, I don't believe in stealing. I'm a churchgoing person. It's just that sometimes something takes over me and I can't seem to not do it. Its like those TV shows where the person is dying and he goes out of his body and watches them trying to save him. That's sorta how I feel sometimes when I'm lifting. (26-year-old female)
>
> I wasn't raised right. You know what I mean? Wasn't nobody to teach me right from wrong. I just ran with a bad group and my mamma didn't ever say nothin' about it. That's how I turned out this way—stealin' and stuff. (22-year-old female)
>
> If I wasn't for the bunch I ran with at school, I never would have started taking things. We used to go the mall after school and everybody would have to steal something. If you didn't get anything, everybody called you names—chicken-shit and stuff like that. (20-year-old male)

Many of the shoplifter informants neutralized their activities citing loss of self-control due to alcohol or drug use. This is a common form of denial of responsibility. If not for the loss of inhibition due to drug or alcohol use, they argue, they would not commit criminal acts.

I was drinking with my buddies and we decided to go across the street to the [convenience store] and steal some beer. I was pretty wasted or I wouldn't done it. (19-year-old white male)

I never boost when I'm straight. It's the pills, you know? (30-year-old white female)

Denial of Injury (I Didn't Really Hurt Anybody)

Denial of injury allows the offender to perceive his or her behavior as having no direct harmful consequences to the victim. The victim may be seen as easily able to afford the loss (big store, insurance company, and wealthy person), or the crime may be semantically recast, as when auto theft is referred to as joyriding, or vandalism as a prank.

> They [stores] big. Make lotsa money. They don't even miss the little bit I get. (19-year-old male)
>
> They write it off their taxes. Probably make a profit off it. So, nobody gets hurt. I get what I need and they come out O.K. too. (28-year-old male)
>
> Them stores make billions. Did you ever hear of Sears going out of business from boosters? (34-year-old female)

Denial of the Victim (They Had It Coming)

Denial of the victim facilitates deviance when it can be justified as retaliation upon a deserving victim. In the present study, informants frequently reported that the large stores from which they stole were deserving victims because of high prices and the perception that they made excessive profits at the expense of ordinary people. The shoplifters frequently asserted that the business establishments from which they stole overcharged consumers and thus deserved the payback from shoplifting losses.

> Stores deserve it. It don't matter if I boost $10,000 from one, they've made ten thousand times that much ripping off people. You could never steal enough to get even. . . . I don't really think I'm doing anything wrong. Just getting my share. (48-year-old female)
>
> Dillons [food store chain] are totally bogus. A little plastic bag of groceries is $30, $25. Probably cost them $5. . . . Whatta they care about me? Why should I care about them? I take what I want. Don't feel guilty a bit. No, sir. Not a bit. (29-year-old female)
>
> I have a lot of anger about stores and the way they rip people off. Sometimes I think the consumer has to take things into their own hands. (49-year-old female)

Condemning the Condemners (The System Is Corrupt)

Condemning the condemners projects blame on lawmakers and law-enforcers. It shifts the focus from the offender to those who disapprove of his or her acts. This neutralization views the "system" as crooked and thus unable to justify making and enforcing rules it does not itself live by. Those who condemn their behavior are viewed as hypocritical since many of them engage in deviant behavior themselves.

> I've heard of cops and lawyers and judges and all kind of rich dudes boosting. They no better than me. You know what I'm saying. (18-year-old male)
>
> Big stores like J.C. Penney—when they catch me with something—like two pairs of pants, they tell the police you had like five pairs of pants and two shirts or something like that. You know what I'm saying? What they do with the other three pairs of pants and shirts? Insurance company pays them off and they get richer—they's bigger crooks than me. (35-year-old female)
>
> They thieves too. Just take it a different way. They may be smarter than me—use a computer or something like that—but they just as much a thief as me. Fuck 'em. Cops too. They all thieves. Least I'm honest about it. (22-year-old male)

Appeal to Higher Loyalties (I Didn't Do It for Myself)

Appeal to higher loyalties functions to legitimize deviant behavior when a nonconventional social bond creates more immediate and pressing demands than one consistent with conventional society. The most common use of this technique among the shoplifters was pressure from delinquent peers to shoplift and the perceived needs of one's family for items that the informant could not afford to buy. This was especially common with mothers shoplifting for items for their children.

> I never do it 'cept when I'm with my friends. Everybody be taking stuff and so I do too. You know—to be part of the group. Not to seem like I'm too good for 'em. (17-year-old female)
>
> I like to get nice stuff for my kids, you know. I know it's not O.K., you know what I mean? But, I want my kids to dress nice and stuff (28-year-old female)

The Defense of Necessity

The defense of necessity (Coleman, 1998) serves to reduce guilt through the argument that the offender had no choice under the circumstances but to engage in a criminal act. In the case of shoplifting, the defense of necessity is most often used when the offender states that the crime was necessary to help one's family.

> I had to take care of three children without help. I'd be willing to steal it to give them what they wanted. (32-year-old female)
>
> I got laid off at Boeing last year and got behind on all my bills and couldn't get credit anywhere. My kids needed school clothes and money for supplies and stuff. We didn't have anything and I don't believe in going on welfare, you know. The first time I took some lunch meat at Dillons (grocery chain) so we'd have supper one night. After that I just started to take whatever we needed that day. I knew it was wrong, but I just didn't have any other choice. My family comes first. (42-year-old male)

Everybody Does It

Here the individual attempts to reduce his or her guilt feelings by arguing that the behavior in question is common (Coleman, 1998). A better label for this neutralization might be "diffusion of guilt." The behavior is justified or the guilt is diffused because of widespread similar acts.

> Everybody I know do it. All my friends. My mother and her boyfriend are boosters and my sister is a big-time booster. (19-year-old female)
> All my friends do it. When I'm with them it seems crazy not to take something too. (17-year-old male)
> I bet you done did it too...when you was coming up. Like 12, 13 years old. Everybody boosts. (35-year-old female)

Justification by Comparison (If I Wasn't Shoplifting, I Would Be Doing Something More Serious)

This newly identified neutralization involves the offender justifying his/her actions by comparing his/her crimes to more serious offenses. While it might be argued that justification by comparison is not a neutralization in the strict Sykes and Matza sense, in that these offenders are not committed to conventional norms, they are nonetheless attempting to maintain their sense of self-worth by arguing that they could be worse or are not as bad as some others. Even persons with deviant lifestyles may experience guilt over their behavior and/or feel the necessity to justify their actions to others. The gist of the argument is that "I may be bad, but I could be worse."

> I gotta have $200 every day—day in and day out. I gotta boost $1000, $1500 worth to get it. I just do what I gotta do....Do I feel bad about what I do? Not really. If I wasn't boosting, I'd be robbing people and maybe somebody would get hurt or killed. (40-year-old male)
> Looka here. Shoplifting be a little thing. Not a crime really. I do it 'stead of robbing folks or breaking in they house. [Society] oughta be glad I boost, stead of them other things. (37-year-old male)
> It's no thing. Not like its "jacking" people or something. It's just a little lifting. (19-year-old male)

Postponement

In a previous study, one of the present authors (Thurman, 1984) suggested that further research should consider the excuse strategy of postponement, by which the offender suppresses his or her guilt feelings—momentarily putting them out of mind to be dealt with at a later time. We found this strategy to be a common occurrence among our informants. They made frequent statements that indicated that they simply put the incident out of their mind. Some stated that they would deal with it later when they were not under so much stress.

> I just don't think about it. I mean, if you think about it, it seems wrong, but you can ignore that feeling sometimes. Put it aside and go on about what you gotta do. (18-year-old male)
> Dude, I just don't deal with those kinda things when I'm boosting. I might feel bad about it later, you know, but by then it's already over and I can't do anything about it then, you know? (18-year-old male)
> I worry about things like that later. (30-year-old female)

DISCUSSION AND CONCLUSION

We found widespread use of neutralizations among the shoplifters in our study. Even those who did not appear to be committed to the conventional moral order used neutralizations to justify or excuse their behavior. Their use of neutralizations was not so much to assuage guilt but to provide them with the necessary justifications for their acts to others. Simply because one is not committed to conventional norms does not preclude their understanding that most members of society do accept those values and expect others to do so as well. They may also use neutralizations and rationalizations to provide them with a convincing defense for their crimes that they can tell to more conventionally oriented others if the need arises.

As stated earlier, our research approach could not determine whether the informants neutralized before committing the crime or rationalized afterwards. We suggest, however, that Hirschi (1969) was correct in stating that a postcrime rationalization may serve as a precrime neutralization the next time a crime is contemplated. Whether neutralization allows the offender to mitigate guilt feelings before the crime is committed or afterwards, the process still occurs. Once an actor has reduced his or her guilt feelings through the use of techniques of neutralization, he or she can continue to offend, assuaging guilt feelings and cognitive dissonance both before and after each offense. It would follow that continued utilization of neutralization and rationalization habitually over time might serve to weaken the social bond, reducing the need to neutralize at all.

Our exploratory study of shoplifters' use of neutralization techniques also suggests that neutralization (theory) may not be so much a theory of crime but rather a description of a process that represents an adaptation to morality that leads to criminal persistence. Neutralization focuses on how crime is possible, rather than why people might choose to engage in it in the first place. In a sense, neutralization serves as a form of situational morality. While the offender knows an act is morally wrong (either in his or her eyes or in the eyes of society), he or she makes an adaptation to convention that permits deviation under certain circumstances (the various neutralizations discussed). Whether the adaptation is truly neutralizing (before the act) or rationalizing (after the act) the result is the same—crime without guilt.

REFERENCES

Akers, R. (1985). *Deviant behavior: A social learning approach.* Belmont, CA: Wadsworth.

Austin, R. L. (1977). Commitment, neutralization and delinquency. In T. N. Ferdinand (Ed.), *Juvenile delinquency: Little brother grows up* (pp. 121–137). Newbury Park, CA: Sage.

Becker, H. S. (1963). *Outsiders: Studies in the sociology of deviance.* New York: Free Press.

Benson, M. (1985). Denying the guilty mind: Accounting for involvement in white-collar crime. *Criminology, 23*(4), 589–599.

Cameron, M. (1964). *The booster and the snitch.* New York: Free Press.

Coleman, J. W. (1985). *The criminal elite: The sociology of white collar crime*. New York: St. Martin's.

———. (1994). Neutralization theory: An empirical application and assessment. Ph.D. diss., Oklahoma State University.

———. (1998). *Criminal elite: Understanding white collar crime*. New York: St. Martin's.

Dabney, D. (1995). Neutralization and deviance in the workplace: Theft of supplies and medicines by hospital nurses. *Deviant Behavior, 116*, 312–321.

Freeh, L. (1996). *Crime in the United States—1995*. Washington, DC: U.S. Department of Justice.

Gauthier, D. K. (2001). Professional lapses: Occupational deviance and neutralization techniques in veterinary medical practice. *Deviant Behavior, 21*, 467–490.

Geis, G., & Meier, R. (1977). *White collar crime*. New York: Free Press. Griffin, R. (1988). *Annual report: Shoplifting in supermarkets*. Van Nuys, CA: Commercial Service Systems.

Hirschi, T. (1969). *Causes of delinquency*. Berkeley: University of Californian Press.

Jesilow, P., Pontell, H. M., & Geis, G. (1993). *Prescriptions for profit: How doctors defraud Medicaid*. Berkeley, CA: University of California Press.

Klemke, L. W. (1992). *The sociology of shoplifting: Boosters and snitches today*. Westport, CT: Praeger.

Klockars, C. B. (1974). *The professional fence*. New York: Free Press.

Lo, L. (1994). Exploring teenage shoplifting behavior. *Environment and Behavior, 26*(5), 613–639.

Mannle, H. W., & Lewis, P. W. (1979). Control theory reexamined: Race and the use of neutralizations among institutionalized delinquents. *Criminology, 17*(1), 58–74.

Minor, W. W. (1981). Techniques of neutralization: A reconceptualization and empirical examination. *Journal of Research in Crime and Delinquency, 18*, 295–318.

Nettler, G. (1974). Embezzlement without problems. *British Journal of Criminology, 14*, 70–77.

Nimick, E. (1990). Juvenile court property cases. In U.S. Department of Justice (Ed.), *OJJDP Update on Statistics* (pp. 1–5). Washington, DC: U.S. Department of Justice.

Russell, D. H. Emotional aspects of shoplifting. Psychiatric Annals, 1973, 3, 77–79.

Sykes, G. M., & Matza, D. (1957). Techniques of neutralization: A theory of delinquency. *American Sociological Review, 22*(6), 664–670.

Thurman, Q. C. (1984). Deviance and neutralization of moral commitment: An empirical analysis. *Deviant Behavior, 5*, 291–304.

Turner, C. T., & Cashdan, S. (1988). Perceptions of college students' motivations for shoplifting. *Psychological Reports, 62*, 855–862.

Wilson, W. J. (1987). *The truly disadvantaged*. Chicago: University of Chicago Press. Zeitz, D. (1981). *Women who embezzle or defraud: A study of convicted felons*. New York: Praeger.

CHAPTER 8

⚶

Identity Theft: Assessing Offenders' Motivations and Strategies

Heith Copes and Lynne Vieraitis

Despite rates of identity theft, little is known about those who engage in this crime. The current study is exploratory in nature and is designed to shed light on the offenders' perspectives. To do this, we interviewed 59 identity thieves incarcerated in federal prisons. Results show that identity thieves are a diverse group, hailing from both working-class and middle-class backgrounds. Nearly half of those we interviewed led lifestyles similar to those of persistent street offenders. The rest used the proceeds of their crimes to live "respectable" middle-class lives. Regardless of their chosen lifestyle, offenders were primarily motivated by the quick need for cash and saw identity theft as an easy, relatively risk-free way to get it. They employed a variety of methods to both acquire information and convert it to cash. The most common methods of acquiring information were to buy it from others, steal it from mailboxes or trashcans, or obtain it from people they knew. Identity thieves developed a set of skills to enable them to be successful at their crimes. These skills included social skills, technical skills, intuitive skills, and system knowledge. By developing these skills they thought they could commit identity theft with impunity.

Over the past several years, the United States has enjoyed a significant decline in rates of serious street crime. However, crimes of fraud continue to increase and with emerging opportunities for economic crime this trend is expected to continue (Shover & Hochstetler, 2006). In the last 10 years, one form of fraud, identity theft, has garnered America's attention as it became one of the most

Source: Excerpted and adapted from Copes, H., & Vieraitis, L. (2007). *Identity theft: Assessing offenders' strategies and perceptions of risk*. Project funded by the National Institute of Justice, Grant # 2005-IJ-CX-0012. For a complete version of the study, go to http://www.ncjrs.gov/App/Publications/Abstract.aspx?ID=240910. Used with permission of the authors.

common economic crimes in the nation (Bernstein, 2004; Perl, 2003). According to recent data from the Federal Trade Commission, 685,000 complaints of fraud were reported in 2005. Thirty-seven percent of these complaints (255,565) were for identity theft, making it the most prevalent form of fraud in the United States (Federal Trade Commission [FTC], 2006).

To combat these rising rates, Congress passed the Identity Theft and Assumption Deterrence Act (ITADA) in 1998. According to ITADA, it is unlawful if a person:

> knowingly transfers or uses, without lawful authority, a means of identification of another person with the intent to commit, or to aid or abet, any unlawful activity that constitutes a violation of Federal law, or that constitutes a felony under any applicable State or local law.

This law made identity theft a separate crime against the person whose identity was stolen, broadened the scope of the offense to include the misuse of information and documents, and provided punishment of up to 15 years of imprisonment and a maximum fine of $250,000. Under U.S. Sentencing Commission guidelines a sentence of 10 to 16 months incarceration can be imposed even if there is no monetary loss and the perpetrator has no prior criminal convictions (U.S. General Accounting Office, 2002).[1]

Identity theft occurs when a criminal appropriates an individual's personal information such as name, address, date of birth, or Social Security number to assume that person's identity to commit theft or multiple types of fraud. Identity thieves utilize a variety of methods to acquire victims' identities, most of which are "low-tech" (Newman & McNally, 2005). These methods include stealing wallets or purses, dumpster diving, stealing mail from residential and business mailboxes, and buying information on the street or from employees with access to personal information. More sophisticated methods or "high-tech" methods include hacking into corporate computers and stealing customer and/or employee databases, skimming, and using the Internet to purchase information from websites or trick consumers into divulging account information (Newman & McNally, 2005).

By exploiting personal and financial information, an identity thief can obtain a person's credit history; access existing financial accounts; file false tax returns; open new credit accounts, bank accounts, charge accounts, and utility accounts; enter into a residential lease; and even obtain additional false identification documents such as a duplicate driver's license, birth certificate, or passport. Identity theft also occurs when an offender commits crimes in the victim's name and gives that person a criminal record. Identity thieves may use the victim's personal information "to evade legal sanctions and criminal records (thus leaving the victim with a wrongful criminal or other legal record)" (Perl, 2003).

Although estimates of the costs vary, identity theft is one of the most expensive financial crimes in America, costing consumers an estimated $5 billion and businesses $48 billion each year. The FTC Identity Theft Clearinghouse estimates the total financial cost of identity theft to be over $50 billion a year, with the average loss to businesses being $4,800 per incident and an average of $500 to the victim whose identity is misused (FTC, 2006).

Despite the fact that identity theft is one of the fastest growing economic crimes in the United States, researchers have devoted little attention to understanding those who engage in this offense. To date, no one has conducted a systematic examination of a sample of offenders to ascertain a reliable or comprehensive picture of identity theft and how it can be controlled more effectively (for an exception, see Allison, Schuck, & Lersch, 2005). The goal of the current research is to explore the offenders' perspectives. Through semi-structured interviews with 59 identity thieves incarcerated in federal prisons, we examine their life experiences and criminal careers, the apparent rewards and risks of identity theft, and measures employed to carry out their crime. Because so little is known about those who commit identity theft, the current study is exploratory and is designed to act as a springboard for future research on identity theft.

DESCRIPTIVE STATISTICS

The common perception of identity thieves is that they are more akin to white-collar fraudsters than they are to street-level property offenders. That is, they hail disproportionately from the middle classes, they are college educated, and they have stable family lives. To determine if identity thieves, at least the ones we interviewed, resemble other fraudsters, we collected various demographic characteristics, including age, race, gender, employment status, and educational achievement. We also asked offenders about their socioeconomic status, family status, and criminal history, including prior arrests, convictions, and drug use. Overall, we found identity theft to be quite democratic, with participants from all walks of life. In fact, they were just as likely to resemble persistent street offenders as they were middle-class fraudsters.

Gender, Race/ethnicity, and Age

Our final sample of 59 inmates included 23 men and 36 women. This discrepancy in gender is likely a result of our sampling strategy and the higher response rate from female inmates rather than the actual proportion of identity theft offenders. In addition, more males were unavailable for interviews because of disciplinary problems and/or prison lockdowns. Offenders in our sample ranged in age from 23 to 60 years, with a mean age of 38 years. They included 18 white females, 16 black females, two Asian females, eight white males, and 15 black males.

MOTIVATIONS FOR IDENTITY THEFT

Numerous studies of street-level property offenders and fraudsters find that the primary motivation for instigating these events is the need for money (Shover, 1996; Shover, Coffey, & Sanders, 2004; Wright & Decker, 1994). When asked what prompted their criminal involvement, the overwhelming response was money.

Lawrence[2] probably best reflects this belief: "It's all about the money. That's all it's about. It's all about the money. If there ain't no money, it don't make sense." Indeed, identity theft is financially rewarding. Gladys estimated that she could make "$2000 in three days." Lawrence made even larger claims: "I'll put it to you like this, forging checks, counterfeiting checks…in an hour, depending on the proximity of the banks—the banks that you're working—I have made $7000 in one hour." These estimates were consistent with those given by other offenders in the sample and with previous estimates (Bureau of Justice Statistics, 2006).

Although estimates on how much they made from their crimes varied widely among respondents, most brought in incomes greater than they could have earned with the types of legitimate work they were qualified for or from other illegal enterprises. In fact, several of them described how they gave up other criminal endeavors for identity theft because they could make more money. When asked why she stopped selling drugs, Bridgette answered, "[Selling drugs is] not the answer. That's not where the money is." Dale switched from burglaries to identity theft arguing, "[Identity theft] is easier and you keep the money, you know. You keep a lot of money."

But how did they spend the money gained through their illegal enterprises? Ethnographic studies of street offenders indicate that few "mentioned needing money for subsistence" (Wright, Brookman, & Bennett, 2006, p. 6). This was also true for the majority of those with whom we spoke. Jacob said that he spent most of his money on "a lot of nice clothes." When asked what he did with the money, Lawrence replied, "Partying. Females. I gave a lot of money away. I bought a lot of things." Finally Carlos said, "We're spending it pretty much as fast as we can get it, you know?" The majority of them spent the money on luxury items, drugs, and partying.

But not all identity thieves were so frivolous with their proceeds. In fact, many of them claimed that they spent money on everyday items. When asked what he did with the money, Jake answered, "Nothing more than living off it, putting it away, saving it.…Nothing flashy. Just living off it." Similarly, Bonnie responded, "Just having extra money to do things with…but nothing extravagant or anything like that." Oscar simply stated, "Just pay bills, you know."

Identity thieves used the proceeds of their crimes to fund their chosen life-styles. Much has been written describing the self-indulgent lifestyles of persistent street offenders. Of the 54 for which we had information about their lifestyle, 23 led lifestyles similar to persistent street offenders. Like their street offender counterparts, these individuals led a "life of party." Proceeds were more likely to be spent maintaining partying lifestyles filled with drug use and fast living than putting money aside for long-term plans. Bridgette explained succinctly why she committed identity theft: "Getting money and getting high." This lifestyle was described by Lawrence:

> I made a lot of money and lost a lot of money. It comes in and you throw it out.…A lot of people put things in their names.…Back and forth to Miami, to Atlanta. I mean it's a party.…Just to party, go to clubs, strip clubs and stuff. Just to party.

The ease with which money was made and spent is reflected in the words of Sheila:

> I was eating great food, buying clothes, going shopping, getting my hair done, you know, wasting it. I wish I would have bought a house or something like that, but it probably would have got taken away anyways.

However, not all indulged in such a lifestyle. In fact, some showed restraint in their spending. Nearly half of those we had lifestyle information on used the money they gained from identity theft to support what could be considered conventional lives ($n = 24$). In addition, seven others could be classified as drifting between a party lifestyle and a more conventional one. These offenders made efforts to conceal their misdeeds from their friends and family and to present a law-abiding front to outsiders. They used the proceeds of identity theft to finance comfortable middle-class lives, including paying rent or mortgages, buying expensive vehicles, and splurging on the latest technological gadgets. Bruce engaged in identity theft "to maintain an upper-class lifestyle. To be able to ride in first class, the best hotels, the best everything." Their lifestyles were in line with the telemarketers interviewed by Shover, Coffey, and Sanders (2004). This is not to say that they did not indulge in the trappings of drugs and partying. Many did. As Denise explains, "I didn't do a lot of partying. I bought a lot of weed, paid out a lot, kept insurance going and the car note, put stereos in my car." Nevertheless, they put forth an image of middle-class respectability.

Offenders have a variety of options when seeking means to fund their chosen lifestyles. Regardless of their lifestyle, offenders are often confronted with a perceived need for quick cash. This was certainly true for the identity thieves we spoke with, regardless of their lifestyle. These self-defined desperate situations included drug habits, gambling debts, family crises, and loss of jobs. Shover's (1996, p. 100) description is applicable here: "Confronted by crisis and preoccupied increasingly with relieving immediate distress, the offender may experience and define himself as propelled by forces beyond his control." Edgar succinctly described why he engaged in identity theft: "Poverty. Poverty makes you do things." When asked how she got involved in identity theft, Sherry explained, "Well, let's see. I had been laid off at work, my son was in trouble, about to go to jail. I needed money for a lawyer." Sylvia described the situations that led her to start her crimes:

> I had a mortgage company that went under. My partner embezzled a bunch of money. Certain events happened and you find yourself out there almost to be homeless, and I knew people that did this, but they never went to jail. And back then they didn't go to jail, so it was a calculated risk I took.

In the face of mounting financial problems, she, like other identity thieves, thought identity theft could offer hope of relief, even if only temporarily.

For those who were addicted to alcohol or other drugs ($n = 22$), their addictions led them to devote increasing time and energy to the quest for monies to fund their habits. For identity thieves, as for other offenders, the inability to draw on legitimate or low-risk resources eventually may precipitate a crisis that they believe can only be relieved through crime. Penni explained, "I started smoking meth and then when I started smoking meth, I stopped working, and then I started doing this for money." In explaining how she and her husband relapsed into drug use, Sherry said, "My husband had lost his job at [an airline] and I was working at a doctor's office, and then I lost my job. So we were both on unemployment." The loss of both sources of income set them onto a path of drug use and identity theft. Finally, Heidi claimed that her relapse precipitated her crimes. In her words, "I was clean for three and a half years before I relapsed on methamphetamines, and that's what brought me back into this."

In addition to the financial rewards of identity theft, there are also intrinsic ones. Criminologists should not forget that crime can be fun and exciting (Katz, 1988). Eleven interviewees mentioned that they found identity theft "fun" or "exciting." These offenders said that they enjoyed the "adrenaline rush" provided by entering banks and stores and by "getting over" on people. Bruce describes what it was like going into banks, "It was fairly exciting to...I mean, every time you went to a retail establishment and you gave them the credit card, you don't know what's going to happen." Similarly, Cori described, "It's just, it was, it was like a rush....At first it was kind of fun. The lifestyle is addicting, you know." Bridgette described what it was like: "It was like a high....It's all about getting over." When asked to describe the rush he felt from engaging in identity theft, Lawrence replied:

> It's money. It's knowing I'm getting over on them. Knowing I can manipulate the things and the person I got going in there. It's everything. It wasn't just...I guess you can say it is a little fear, but it's not fear for me, though. It's fear for the person I got going in there. I don't know. It's kind of weird. I don't know how to explain it....But it's the rush. Knowing that I created this thing to manipulate these banks, you know what I'm saying? They're going to pay me for it and I'm going to manipulate this dude out of the money when they cashing those checks.

Dustin attributed his continuance with identity theft to the thrill:

> I like to go out with money. But eventually it got to the point where I didn't need money. I was just doing it for the high. But that is basically what it was. The rush of standing there in her face and lying. [Laughter.] That's what it was. I'm being honest. I didn't need the money. I had plenty.

But even for these individuals, except Dustin, the thrill factor of identity theft was a secondary motivation to the money. Thrills alone did not instigate or propel identity theft. It is possible, however, that offenders persisted with identity theft because of the excitement of these crimes.

Previous reports on identity theft have pointed out that some of these crimes are precipitated by the desire to hide from the law or to get utilities or phone service activated (Newman, 2004). Only three people with whom we spoke mentioned such reasons. Jolyn told us that she had a warrant out so she used another's identity to get a telephone. Although her crimes started as a means to get telephone services, she eventually used this information to garner Social Security benefits. Additionally, Jamie said, "I needed my utilities on. [I did it] for that reason. I've never used it as far as applying for a credit card, though, because I knew that was a no."

METHODS AND TECHNIQUES OF IDENTITY THEFT

Acquiring Information

Offenders in our sample utilized a variety of methods to procure information and then convert this information into cash and/or goods. In fact, most did not specialize in a single method; instead, they preferred to use a variety of strategies. Although some offenders in our sample acquired identities from their place of employment (35%), mainly mortgage companies, the most common method of obtaining a victim's information was to buy it ($n = 13$). Offenders in our sample bought identities from employees of various businesses and state agencies who had access to personal information such as name, address, date of birth, and Social Security number ($n = 5$). Information was purchased from employees of banks, credit agencies, a state law enforcement agency, mortgage companies, state departments of motor vehicles, hospitals, doctor's offices, a university, car dealerships, and furniture stores. Those buying information said that it was easy to find someone willing to sell them what they wanted. According to Gladys, "It's so easy to get information, and everybody has a price." Penni said:

> People that work at a lot of places, they give you a lot of stuff...hospitals, DMV, like Wal-Mart, a lot of places, like [local phone company]. People fill out applications. A lot of stuff like that, and you get it from a lot of people. There's a lot of tweekers [drug addicts] out there, and everybody's trying to make a dollar and always trading something for something.

When describing how she obtained information from a bank employee, Kristin said:

> She was willing to make some money too, so she had the good information. She would have the information that would allow me to have a copy of the signature card, passwords, work address, everything, everything that's legit.

Eight offenders who purchased information did so from persons they knew or who they were acquainted with "on the streets." Lawrence explained, "[People on the streets] knew what I was buying. I mean any city, there's always somebody buying some information." The identity thieves bought information from other offenders who obtained it from burglaries, thefts from motor vehicles, prostitution, and pick-pocketing. One offender purchased information from boyfriends or girlfriends of the victims. For the most part, those with whom we spoke did not know nor care where their sellers obtained their information. As long as the information was good they asked no questions.

Five individuals obtained information by using the mailbox method, and another two got information by searching trashcans. Those offenders typically stole mail from small businesses such as insurance companies or from residential mailboxes in front of homes or apartments. Some offenders simply drove through residential areas and pulled mail out, often taking steps to appear to be legitimate, that is, they placed flyers advertising a business in mailboxes. Mailboxes and trashcans for businesses that send out mail with personal information (account numbers, Social Security numbers, and date of birth) such as insurance companies were also popular targets.

Although most of the offenders we interviewed did not know their victims, of those who did six said that the victim willingly gave them the information in exchange for a cut of the profits. In these cases, the "victim" gave the offender information to commit the identity theft and then reported that their identity had been stolen. According to Lawrence, "What I did was I had got this guy's personal information, he actually willingly gave it to me." Five offenders used family members' information without their knowledge, and in one case the information was on family members who were deceased. Another five stole from friends or acquaintances without their knowledge.

Other methods of acquiring victims' information included various thefts (house and car burglary, purse-snatching) ($n = 3$) and socially engineering people to get their information ($n = 2$). One individual set up a fake employment site to get information from job applicants. Another used the birth announcements in newspapers to get the names of new parents and, posing as an insurance representative, called the parents to get information for "billing purposes." Interestingly, the offender made the phone calls from the waiting room of the hospitals where the infants were born so that the name of the hospital would appear on the victims' caller ID if they had it. Another offender used rogue Internet sites to run background checks and order credit reports on potential victims. In addition, nine individuals claimed to work in a group where others obtained information. These thieves chose not to ask where the information came from.

Converting Information

After they obtain a victim's information the offender must convert that information to cash or goods. Most commonly, offenders used the information to acquire or produce additional identity-related documents such as driver's licenses or state identification cards. Some offenders created the cards themselves with software and materials, for example, paper and ink, purchased at office supply stores or given to them by an employee of a state department of motor vehicles. Other offenders knew someone or had someone working for them who produced IDs. Identification cards were needed to withdraw cash from the victim's existing bank account or to open a new account.

Offenders used a variety of methods to profit from the stolen identities. The most common strategies were applying for credit cards in the victims' names (including major credit cards and department store credit cards), opening new bank accounts and depositing counterfeit checks, withdrawing money from existing bank accounts, applying for loans, and applying for public assistance programs. Identity thieves often used more than one technique when cashing in on their crimes.

The most common strategy for converting stolen identities into cash was by applying for credit cards. Twenty-three offenders used the information to order new credit cards. In a few cases, the information was used to get the credit card agency to issue a duplicate card on an existing account. They used credit cards to buy merchandise for their own personal use, to resell the merchandise to friends and/or acquaintances, or to return the merchandise for cash. Offenders also used the checks that are routinely sent to credit card holders to deposit in the victim's account and then withdraw cash or to open new accounts. Offenders also applied for store credit cards at places such as department stores and home improvement stores. According to Emma:

> [I would] go to different department stores, or most often it was Lowes or Home Depot, go in, fill out an application with all the information, and then receive instant credit in the amount from say $1,500 to $7,500. Every store is different. Every individual is different. And then at that time, I would purchase as much as that balance that I could at one time. So if it was $2,500, I would buy $2,500 worth of merchandise.

Another common strategy is to produce counterfeit checks. Sixteen offenders either made fraudulent checks on their own or knew someone who would produce these checks for them. Although most offenders who counterfeited checks made personal checks, others made insurance checks or payroll checks. They cashed these checks at grocery stores, purchased merchandise, and paid bills such as utilities or cell phones.

Sometimes identity thieves would use the stolen identities to either open new bank accounts as a way to deposit fraudulent checks or to withdraw money from an existing account. Sixteen of the people we interviewed used this approach. Using this strategy required the offender to have information about the victims' bank account.

Another method of conversion included applying for and receiving loans. Fourteen individuals used this strategy. The majority of those who applied for loans engaged in some type of mortgage fraud. These types of scams often involved using victims' information to purchase homes for themselves. In one case, the offenders were buying houses and then renting them for a profit. Others applied for various auto loans, home equity loans, or personal loans.

SKILL SETS

As with any behavior, skills improve with experience. With practice, persistent burglars learn to assess the risks and value of homes almost instantaneously, crack dealers and prostitutes learn to discern undercover officers, and hustlers learn to recognize potential marks. Identity thieves have also developed a skill set to successfully accomplish their crimes. Four broad categories of skills emerged in our analysis of the interviews: (1) social skills, (2) intuitive skills, (3) technical skills, and (4) system knowledge.

Good social skills are perhaps the most important skills that identity thieves claim to possess. Social skills are the ability to manipulate the social situation through verbal and nonverbal communication. To be successful, an identity thief must possess the ability to "pass" as a regular customer in stores and banks and "be" the person they claim to be. This ability allows identity thieves to construct a larcenous situation as real and remove any doubts about the legitimacy of the situation. Identity thieves accomplish this through dress, mannerisms, and speech. When questioned as to what skills make a "good" identity thief, Gladys responded:

> I mean I can go into a place.... Knowing how to look the part in certain situations...you go up to a place and you look in there and get the feeling about how a person would look, and I'd take off a ring or something, put on a ring, take off some of your make-up, or go put on a hat or a scarf, put some glasses on.

Bridgette also made sure that whomever she sent into the bank was dressed to appear to be the person he/she claimed to be.

> I always made them dress accordingly, if you're going in to cash an insurance check, I want to dress nice and casual. If you were cashing a payroll check, you got to wear a uniform. I always try to find a uniform that match whatever company we were using. With the lab tech, we went right to the uniform shop and got it, the little nurse scrub sets and everything.

Tameka also "dressed" the part, "I might have on a nurse uniform, a lot of these they had me on I had on a nurse uniform." In describing what it was like interacting with bank and store employees, Bruce, an experienced thief, said:

> You definitely have to be adaptable. It's not even being pleasant with people. It's just having authority. You have to have authority of whatever situation you are in. And if you have that authority, people will not go any further than to peripherally question you. That's about it.

Emma explained:

> I would just act as if I were that person and I would go in and I'd be talking to the person processing the application and, say if it were at Home Depot, I would be saying, "Oh, we're doing some remodeling of our home" or something like that, and I'd engage the people.

The ability to socially engineer people and situations is especially important when things go wrong. When describing how she would conduct herself in a bank when questioned by employees, Tameka said:

> If it was a tricky question, you should be able to talk to the bank manager, cause there were times when I asked to speak to the manager if I was withdrawing a large sum of money. In essence, you had to become these people.

A second skill that identity thieves develop is intuitive skills, which can be defined as "an acute sensitization to and awareness of one's external surrounding" (Faupel, 1986). Some offenders superstitiously believed they have developed the ability to sense trouble, believing that if they do not "feel bad" about a crime, then they are safe. April replied, "You kind of get, I don't know, almost like you dreaded walking into it." The ability to recognize criminal opportunity, sense danger, and know when to call off a criminal plan has been referred to as "larceny sense," "grift sense," and "intuitive sense" (Faupel, 1986; Maurer, 1951; Sutherland, 1937). When asked how he got better at identity theft, Bruce responded:

> Sensing...sensing what was going on within a situation, like at a bank, like I could sense what was going on with tellers. I could tell how they were looking at the screen, how long they were looking at it, and I could sense whether something had been written or if I was cashing too many checks. Just a sense of how people react in situations and then also just the situations themselves. As many as they presented themselves, I would find a way around them. So I guess just honing the thinking on your feet...in the situations that came up.

Several offenders in this study believed they would not have been caught if they had paid attention to their premonitions. For instance, Kimi described the moments before she was arrested:

> I knew the detectives were watching. I knew that and I had the feeling and I told [my co-defendant], but he was trying to kick heroin that day. And this stupid fool was shooting, and I'm all surrounded by heroin addicts. So one person, up all night, she was smoking meth and smoking weed, but everyone else was shooting heroin, and I'm surrounded by them. And I told him, I said, we got to leave. I have this freaking feeling something's going to go wrong.

Whether or not repeat offenders have a heightened ability to sense danger is less important than the fact that many believe they do.

A third type of skill identity thieves develop are technical skills. This refers to the technical knowledge needed to produce fraudulent documents such as identification, checks, and credit applications. Making these documents look real is an increasingly difficult task. For example, determining the right types of paper to print checks on, how to replicate watermarks, and matching the colors on driver's licenses are necessary skills that must be learned. Lawrence described:

> I use a different type of paper. I use a regular document. The paper always came straight from the bank. A lot of people, they would get paper out of like Target or Office Max or places like that. That kind of paper right there, it's not always efficient. Nine times out of 10, the bank may stop it. They want to check the company payroll.

Although many identity thieves contract out for their documents, a sizable number learn these tricks through experimentation and practice. Kimi described her process:

We studied IDs, then I went to the stamp shop, the paint shop, got the logos right, and I know the [bank] was one of the hardest banks for us to get money out, but when I found out about the logos, when I passed it through the black light, it became real easy.... I went to the stamp shop and bought a stamp and sat there for hours and hours with the colors, and I made like seven different IDs before it come through under the black light.

The final skill discussed by identity thieves is system knowledge. This includes knowing how banks and credit agencies operate and knowing which stores require identification when cashing checks. Sherry said:

> You have to have an idea of how banks work. At some point in your life, live a nor-mal life and understand how credit is extended and things like that. (Sherry)
>
> I was a bank teller. I knew how to approach a person. I knew the insights, you know, what they would look for, how much I could get, when to go out. (Sheila)

The development of these various skills plays an important role in crime per-sistence. By developing these skills, identity thieves increase their chances of being successful at crime; that is, these skills allow them to avoid the formal sanctions associated with identity theft. Those who commit crime with impunity have overly optimistic views of their crimes (Cusson, 1993; Paternoster et al., 1982), which was the case for many of those we interviewed. Offenders came to believe that they could continue offending because they could rely on their skills to evade sanc-tions, thereby nullifying the deterrent effects of criminal sanctions.

CONCLUSION

Our interviews with 59 offenders incarcerated in federal prisons revealed information about their motivations for identity theft and the methods they employ to acquire information and convert it into cash and/or goods. Results show that identity thieves are a diverse group. Offenders are primarily motivated by the quick need for cash and see identity theft as an easy, relatively risk-free way to get it. They employ a variety of methods to both acquire information and convert it to cash and have developed a set of skills to enable them to do so successfully.

NOTES

1. In 2004, the Identity Theft Penalty Enhancement Act established a new federal crime, aggravated identity theft. Aggravated identity theft prohibits the knowing and unlawful transfer, possession, or use of a means of identification of another person during and in relation to any of more than 100 felony offenses, including mail, bank, and wire fraud; immigration and passport fraud; and any unlawful use of a Social Security number. The law mandates a minimum two years in prison consecutive to the sentence for the under-lying felony. In addition, if the offense is committed during and in relation to one of the

more than 40 federal terrorism-related felonies, the penalty is a minimum mandatory five years in prison consecutive to the sentence for the underlying felony.
2. Offenders' names have been changed.

REFERENCES

Allison, S. F. H., Schuck, A. M., & Lersch, K. M. (2005). Exploring the crime of identity theft: Prevalence, clearance rates, and victim/offender characteristics. *Journal of Criminal Justice, 33,* 19–29.

Bernstein, S, E. (2004). New privacy concern for employee benefit plans: Combating identity theft. *Compensation and Benefits Review, 36,* 65–68.

Bureau of Justice Statistics. (2006). *Identity theft, 2004* (NCJ 212213). Washington, DC: U.S. Department of Justice.

Cusson, M. (1993). Situational deterrence: Fear during the criminal event. In R. Clarke (Ed.), *Crime prevention studies* (Vol. 1, pp. 55–68). Monsey, NY: Willow Tree.

Faupel, C. E. (1986). Heroin use, street crime, and the "main hustle": Implications for the validity of official crime data. *Deviant Behavior, 7,* 31–45.

Federal Trade Commission (FTC). (2006). *Consumer fraud and identity theft complaint data: January–December 2005.* Retrieved December 9, 2008, from http://www.consumer.gov/sentinel/pubs/Top10Fraud2005.pdf.

Katz, J. (1988). *Seductions of crime.* New York: Basic.

Maurer, D. W. (1951). *Whiz mob: A correlation of the technical argot of pickpockets with their behavior patterns.* Gainesville, FL: American Dialect Society.

Newman, G. R. (2004). *Identity theft.* Washington, DC: U.S. Department of Justice.

Newman, G. R., & McNally, M. M. (2005). *Identity theft literature review.* Presented at the National Institute of Justice Focus Group Meeting. Retrieved December 9, 2008, from http://www.ncjrs.gov/pdffiles1/nij/grants/210459.pdf.

Paternoster, R., Saltzman, L., Chiricos, T., & Waldo, G. (1982). Perceived risk and deterrence: Methodological artifacts in perceptual deterrence research. *Journal of Criminal Law and Criminology, 73,* 1238–1258.

Perl, M. W. (2003). It's not always about the money: Why the state identity theft laws fail to address criminal record identity theft. *Journal of Criminal Law and Criminology, 94,* 169–208.

Shover, N. (1996). *Great pretenders: Pursuits and careers of persistent thieves.* Boulder, CO: Westview.

Shover, N., Coffey, G., & Sanders, C. (2004). Dialing for dollars: Opportunities, justifications and telemarketing fraud. *Qualitative Sociology, 27,* 59–75.

Shover, N., & Hochstetler, A. (2006). *Choosing white-collar crime.* Cambridge, UK: Cambridge University Press.

Sutherland, E. (1937). *The professional thief.* Chicago: University of Chicago Press.

U.S. General Accounting Office. (2002). *Identity theft: Prevalence and cost appear to be growing.* GAO 02–363. Washington, DC: Author.

Wright, R. T., Brookman, F., & Bennett, T. (2006). The foreground dynamics of street robbery in Britain. *British Journal of Criminology, 46,* 1–15.

Wright, R., & Decker, S. (1994). *Burglars on the job.* Boston: Northeastern University Press.

SECTION IV

꙳

Violent Crime

While the last section examined property crimes, Section IV takes a look at violent crime. According to the FBI's Uniform Crime Reporting Program, violent crime is composed of four offenses: murder and nonnegligent manslaughter, forcible rape, robbery, and aggravated assault. Violent crimes such as robbery, assault, and murder have profoundly affected the way we live and have clearly altered our lifestyles. In 2010, over 1.2 million violent crimes were reported to police nationwide. While even one violent crime is too many, it is encouraging to note that violent crime is trending downward even faster than the rates for property crime. This actually represents a 6% reduction when compared with 2009 numbers. For example, the 2010 estimated violent crime totals were about 13% below the 2006 level and 13% below the 2001 level. In all, there were an estimated 403 violent crimes per 100,000 citizens in 2010 (Federal Bureau of Investigation, 2010).

While the decrease in violent crimes is grounds for optimism, the fact remains that they continue to be a serious problem in the United States. Violent crime is often considered less rationally conceived than property crime. Violent behavior is often expressed in the "heat of passion," during periods of great emotional turmoil. The violent act is thought to be more expressive than instrumental, having no real functional purpose or acceptable rationale. However, as the three studies featured in this section demonstrate, violent crime has both expressive and instrumental roots. These chapters discuss the motives for offenders' behavior, strategies they use to accomplish their crimes, and rationalizations used to avoid responsibility for their acts.

The first article in this section, Kristin L. Anderson and Debra Umberson's "Gendering Violence: Masculinity and Power in Men's Accounts of Domestic Violence," looks at domestic violence. Domestic violence has long been problematic. Prior to the passage of legislation mandating that police authorities follow certain protocols in the investigation of domestic violence, including mandatory arrests, domestic violence received a less than effective response from the criminal justice system. In many cases, the police deemed domestic violence an issue that should be handled within the family. Consequently, these cases were "resolved" by having one of the parties leave for the evening until "things cooled down." Approaches such as these were ineffective and provided only short-term resolutions. In essence, the manner in which the criminal justice system handled domestic violence was at times devastating and occasionally fatal for victims.

Academic treatments of domestic violence have devoted a great deal of attention to its victims. While this is an important step in developing an understanding of the crime from the victim's perspective, it is also critical that researchers construct an understanding of the offender's perspective. Anderson and Umberson's article does just that, examining the construction of gender in men's accounts of domestic violence. This postmodern treatment of domestic violence discusses both masculinity and power in men's accounts of domestic violence. The authors interviewed 33 heterosexual male domestic violence offenders and found that that these batterers blamed their female partners for the violence in their relationship. These men identified themselves as victims of a biased criminal justice system. According to the study, "the men excused, justified, rationalized, and minimized their violence against their female partners." These offenders constructed their battering as an appropriate response to "extreme provocation, loss of control, or an incident blown out of proportion." This is similar to one other study that examined court files from 1,873 protection from abuse orders in domestic violence cases and found that abusers overwhelmingly used neutralizations to justify their actions (Etter & Birzer, 2007). Anderson and Umberson have made a substantial contribution to the domestic violence literature. Moreover, their research provides an alarming glimpse into male batterers' constructions of their own offending.

In Chapter 10 ("Serendipity in Robbery Target Selection"), Bruce A. Jacobs argues that rational-choice theory downplays the phenomenological forces that undermine reasoned calculation. Rational-choice theory proposes that offenders make conscious decisions to commit crimes based on a calculated weighing of risks and benefits. According to this theory, if the benefits outweigh the risks involved in committing the crime, the offender will carry out the crime. Jacobs argues that this is a "sterile view" of criminal offending. Using data collected from interviews of unincarcerated robbery offenders who specialize in carjacking and drug robbery, he finds that in many cases, victims became victims after crossing paths with offenders at the right or wrong time, or converging along "an axis of serendipity." Thus, serendipity speaks to the nondeterministic nature of the offender's decision making, and that opportunity is often unpredictable and must be appraised. Jacobs is on to something salient here. If we were to ask those who regularly interact with offenders (i.e., police and probation or parole authorities), those persons that see firsthand what Katz (1988) refers to as "the seductions of crime," it's possible that they would inform us that offenders' calculations to commit a crime would involve more than a simple weighing of risks and benefits. It would seem that there are indeed many phenomenological factors that may confound the risk and benefit calculation.

In Chapter 11, Fiona S. Brookman ("Accounting for Homicide and Sublethal Violence") analyzes the excuses and justifications employed by offenders in acts of lethal and sublethal violence. The data reported in this study were the result of interviews of 30 violent offenders (24 men and six women) in the United Kingdom. Some of these offenders had been convicted of murder and manslaughter, while others had been convicted of assault or other forms of violence coupled with armed robbery. Brookman discovered that although some offenders acknowledged their crimes as wrong, they also provided accounts in which they made use of neutralizations and deemed themselves not blameworthy of their crimes. There were also those offenders who did not accept that their crimes of violence were wrong or provided accounts that were similar to the expectations of street codes. The author advances the thesis that offenders' accounts of their offending do not occur within a social or narrative vacuum. She also points out that violent offenders may actually share much in common with nonviolent offenders, and "that they adopt more than one kind of language or discourse" to rationalize or neutralize their crimes.

REFERENCES

Etter, G. W., & Birzer, M. L. (2007). Domestic violence abusers: A descriptive study of the characteristics of defenders in protection from abuse orders in Sedgwick County, Kansas. *Journal of Family Violence, 22,* 113–119.

Federal Bureau of Investigation. (2010). *Crime in the United States.* Retrieved March 8, 2012, from http://www2.fbi.gov/ucr/cius2009/index.html.

Katz, J. (1988). *Seductions of crime: Moral and sensual attractions in doing evil.* New York: Basic.

CHAPTER 9

Gendering Violence: Masculinity
and Power in Men's Accounts
of Domestic Violence

Kristin L. Anderson and Debra Umberson

This chapter examines the construction of gender within men's accounts of domestic violence. The analyzed data was gathered through in-depth interviews conducted with 33 domestically violent heterosexual men recruited through the Family Violence Diversion Network, a nonprofit organization located in a mid-sized southwestern city. The analysis indicated that these batterers used diverse strategies to present themselves as nonviolent, capable, and rational men. They claimed that female partners were responsible for the violence in their relationships and constructed men as victims of a biased criminal justice system. The men excused, justified, rationalized, and minimized their violence against their female partners, constructing their violence as a rational response to extreme provocation, loss of control, or an incident blown out of proportion. This study suggests that violence against female partners is a means by which batterers reproduce a binary framework of gender.

In the 1970s, feminist activists and scholars brought wife abuse to the forefront of public consciousness. Published in the academic and popular press, the words and images of survivors made one aspect of patriarchy visible: male dominance was displayed on women's bruised and battered bodies (Dobash & Dobash, 1979; Martin, 1976). Early research contributed to feminist analyses of battery as part of a larger pattern of male domination and control of women (Pence & Paymar, 1993; Yllo, 1993). Research in the 1980s and 1990s has expanded theoretical understandings of men's violence against women through emphases on women's agency and

Source: Anderson, K. L., & Umberson, D. (2001). Gendering violence: Masculinity and power in men's accounts of domestic violence. *Gender & Society, 15,* 358–380. © 2001 Sociologists for Women in Society. Used with permission of the publisher.

resistance to male control (Bowker, 1983; Kirkwood, 1993); the intersection of physical, structural, and emotional forces that sustain men's control over female partners (Kirkwood, 1993; Pence & Paymar, 1993); and the different constraints faced by women and men of diverse nations, racial ethnic identities, and sexualities who experience violence at the hands of intimate partners (Eaton, 1994; Island & Letellier, 1991; Jang, Lee, & Morello-Frosch, 1998; Renzetti, 1992). This work demonstrates ways in which the gender order facilitates victimization of disenfranchised groups.

Comparatively less work has examined the ways in which gender influences male perpetrators' experiences of domestic violence (Yllo, 1993). However, a growing body of qualitative research critically examines batterers' descriptions of violence within their relationships. Dobash and Dobash (1998), Hearn (1998), and Ptacek (1990) focus on the excuses, justifications, and rationalizations that batterers use to account for their violence. These authors suggest that batterers' accounts of violence are texts through which they attempt to deny responsibility for violence and to present nonviolent self-identities.

Dobash and Dobash (1998) identify ways in which gender, as a system that structures the authority and responsibilities assigned to women and men within intimate relationships, supports battery. They find that men use violence to punish female partners who fail to meet their unspoken physical, sexual, or emotional needs. Lundgren (1998) examines batterers' use of gendered religious ideologies to justify their violence against female partners. Hearn (1998, p. 37) proposes that violence is a "resource for demonstrating and showing a person is a man." These studies find that masculine identities are constructed through acts of violence and through batterers' ability to control partners as a result of their violence.

This article examines the construction of gender within men's accounts of domestic violence. Guided by theoretical work that characterizes gender as performance (Butler, 1990; Butler, 1993; West & Fenstermaker, 1995), we contend that batterers attempt to construct masculine identities through the practice of violence and the discourse about violence that they provide. We examine these performances of gender as "routine, methodical, and ongoing accomplishment[s]" that create and sustain notions of natural differences between women and men (West & Fenstermaker, 1995, p. 9). Butler's concept of performativity extends this idea by suggesting that it is through performance that gendered subjectivities are constructed: "Gender proves to be performative—that is, constituting the identity it is purported to be. In this sense, gender is always a doing, though not a doing by a subject who may be said to preexist the deed" (1990, p. 25). For Butler, gender performances demonstrate the instability of masculine subjectivity; a "masculine identity" exists only as the actions of individuals who stylize their bodies and their actions in accordance with a normative binary framework of gender.

In addition, the performance of gender makes male power and privilege appear natural and normal rather than socially produced and structured. Butler (1990) argues that gender is part of a system of relations that sustains heterosexual male privilege through the denigration or erasure of alternative (feminine/gay/lesbian/bisexual) identities. West and Fenstermaker (1995) contend that cultural beliefs about underlying and essential differences between women and men, and social structures that constitute and are constituted by these beliefs are reproduced by the accomplishment of gender. In examining the accounts offered by domestically violent men, we focus on identifying ways in which the practice of domestic violence helps men to accomplish gender. We also focus on the contradictions within these accounts to explore the instability of masculine subjectivities and challenges to the performance of gender.

FINDINGS

How do batterers talk about the violence in their relationships? They excuse, rationalize, justify, and minimize their violence against female partners. Like the batterers studied by previous researchers, the men in this study constructed their violence as a rational response to extreme provocation, a loss of control, or a minor incident that was blown out of proportion. Through such accounts, batterers deny responsibility for their violence and save face when recounting behavior that has elicited social sanctions (Dobash & Dobash, 1998; Ptacek, 1990).

However, these accounts are also about the performance of gender. That is, through their speech acts, respondents presented themselves as rational, competent, masculine actors. We examine several ways in which domestic violence is gendered in these accounts. First, according to respondents' reports, violence is gendered in its practice. Although it was in their interests to minimize and deny their violence, participants reported engaging in more serious, frequent, and injurious violence than that committed by their female partners. Second, respondents gendered violence through their depictions and interpretations of violence. They talked about women's violence in a qualitatively different fashion than they talked about their own violence, and their language reflected hegemonic notions of femininity and masculinity. Third, the research participants constructed gender by interpreting the violent conflicts in ways that suggested that their female partners were responsible for the participants' behavior. Finally, respondents gendered violence by claiming that they are victimized by a criminal justice system that constructs all men as villains and all women as victims.

Gendered Practice

Men perpetrate the majority of violence against women and against other men in the United States (Bachman & Saltzman, 1995). Although some scholars argue that women perpetrate domestic violence at rates similar to men (Straus, 1993), feminist scholars have pointed out that research findings of "sexual symmetry" in domestic violence are based on survey questions that fail to account for sex differences in physical strength and size and in motivations for violence (Dobash et al., 1992; Straton, 1994). Moreover, recent evidence from a large national survey suggests that women experience higher rates of victimization at the hands of partners than men, and that African American and Latina women experience higher rates of victimization than European American women (Bachman & Saltzman, 1995).

Although the majority of respondents described scenarios in which both they and their partners perpetrated violent acts, they reported that their violence was more frequent and severe than the violence perpetrated by their female partners. Eleven respondents (33%) described attacking a partner who did not physically resist, and only two respondents (6%) reported that they were victimized by their partners but did not themselves perpetrate violence. The 20 cases (61%) in which the participants reported "mutual" violence support feminist critiques of "sexual symmetry":

> We started pushing each other. And the thing is that I threw her on the floor. I told her that I'm going to leave. She took my car keys, and I wanted my car keys, so I went and grabbed her arm, pulled it, and took the car keys away from her. She—she comes back and tries to kick me in the back. So I just pushed her back and threw her on the floor again. (Juan)

Moreover, the respondents did not describe scenarios in which they perceived themselves to be at risk from their partners' violence. The worst injury reportedly sustained was a split lip, and only five men (15%) reported sustaining any injury. Female partners reportedly sustained injuries in 14 cases (42%). Although the majority of the injuries reportedly inflicted on female partners consisted of bruises and scratches, a few women were hospitalized, and two women sustained broken ribs. These findings corroborate previous studies showing that women suffer more injuries from domestic violence than men (Langhinrichsen-Rohling, Neidig, & Thorn, 1995). Moreover, because past studies suggest that male batterers underreport their perpetration of violence (Dobash & Dobash, 1998), it is likely that respondents engaged in more violence than they described in these in-depth interviews.

Domestic violence is gendered through social and cultural practices that advantage men in violent conflicts with women. Young men often learn to view themselves as capable perpetrators of violence through rough play and contact sports, to exhibit fearlessness in the face of physical confrontations, and to accept the harm and injury associated with violence as "natural" (Dobash & Dobash, 1998; Messner, 1992). Men are further advantaged by cultural norms suggesting that women should pair with men who are larger and stronger than themselves (Goffman, 1977). Women's less pervasive and less effective use of violence reflects fewer social opportunities to learn violent techniques, a lack of encouragement for female violence within society, and women's size disadvantage in relation to male partners (Fagot et al., 1985; McCaughey, 1998). In a culture that defines aggression as unfeminine, few women learn to use violence effectively.

Gendered Depictions and Interpretations

Participants reported that they engaged in more frequent and serious violence than their partners, but they also reported that their violence was different from that of their partners. They depicted their violence as rational, effective, and explosive, whereas women's violence was represented as hysterical, trivial, and ineffectual. Of the 22 participants who described violence perpetrated by their partners, 12

(55%) suggested that their partner's violence was ridiculous or ineffectual. These respondents minimized their partners' violence by explaining that it was of little concern to them:

> I came out of the kitchen, and then I got in her face, and I shoved her. She shoved, she tried to push me a little bit, but it didn't matter much. (Adam)
>
> I was seeing this girl, and then a friend of mine saw me with this girl and he went back and told my wife, and when I got home that night, that's when she tried to hit me, to fight me. I just pushed her out of the way and left. (Shad)

This minimizing discourse also characterizes descriptions of cases in which female partners successfully made contact and injured the respondent, as in the following account:

> I was on my way to go to the restroom. And she was just cussing and swearing, and she wouldn't let me pass. So, I nudged her. I didn't push her or shove her, I just kind of, you know, just made my way to the restroom. And, when I done that she hit me, and she drew blood. She hit me in the lip, and she drew blood....I go in the bathroom and I started laughing, you know. And I was still half lit that morning, you know. And I was laughing because I think it maybe shocked me more than anything that she had done this, you know. (Ed)

Although his partner "drew blood," Ed minimized her violence by describing it as amusing, uncharacteristic, and shocking.

Even in the case of extreme danger, such as when threatened with a weapon, respondents denied the possibility that their partners' violence was a threat. During a fight described by Steve, his partner locked herself in the bathroom with his gun:

> We were battering each other at that point, and that's when she was in the bathroom. This is—it's like 45 minutes into this whole argument now. She's in the bathroom, messing with my [gun]. And I had no idea. So I kicked the door in—in the bathroom, and she's sitting there trying to load this thing, trying to get this clip in, and luckily she couldn't figure it out. Why, I don't—you know, well, because she was drunk. So, luckily she didn't. The situation could have been a whole lot worse, you know, it could have been a whole lot worse than it was. I thank God that she didn't figure it out. When I think about it, you know, she was lucky to come out of it with just a cut in her head. You know, she could have blown her brains out or done something really stupid.

This account contains interesting contradictions. Steve stated that he had "no idea" that his partner had a gun, but he responded by kicking down the door to reach her. He then suggested that he was concerned about his partner's safety and that he kicked in the door to save her from doing "something really stupid" to herself. Similarly, Alejandro minimized the threat in his account of an incident in which his partner picked up a weapon:

> So, she got angry and got a knife, came up at me, and I kick her. [*And then what happened?*] Well, I kick her about four times because she—I kick her, and I say

"Just stop, stay there!" and she stand up and come again and I had to kick her again. Somebody called the police, somebody called the police. I guess we were making a lot of noise. And I couldn't go out, I couldn't leave home, because I was not dressed properly to go out. And so I couldn't go, so the only alternative I had at this moment was to defend myself from the knife. So I had to kick her.

Alejandro suggested that his partner's attack with a knife was not enough of a threat to warrant his leaving the house when he was "not dressed properly to go out."

In addition to emphasizing their partners' incompetence in the practice of violence, some respondents depicted the violence perpetrated by their partners as irrational:

She has got no control. She sees something and she don't like it, she'll go and pull my hair, scratch me, and [act] paranoid, crazy, screaming loud, make everybody look at her, and call the police, you know. Just nuts. (Andrew)

She came back and started hitting me with her purse again so I knocked the purse out of her hand, and then she started screaming at me to get out. I went back to the room, and she came running down the hall saying she was going to throw all my stuff out and I'd just had enough, so I went and grabbed her, pulled her back. And grabbed her back to the bed and threw her on the bed and sat on her—told her I wasn't going to let her up until she came to her senses.... She came back up again, and I just grabbed her and threw her down. After that, she promised—she finally said that she had come to her senses and everything. I went into the other room, and she went out to clean up the mess she had made in the living room, and then she just started just crying all night long, or for a while. (Phil)

Phil and Andrew described their partners' acts as irrational and hysterical. Such depictions helped respondents to justify their own violence and to present themselves as calm, cool, rational men. Phil described his own behavior of throwing his partner down as a nonviolent, controlled response to his partner's outrageous behavior. Moreover, he suggests that he used this incident to demonstrate his sense of superior rationality to his partner. Phil later reported that a doctor became "very upset" about the marks on his wife's neck two days after this incident, suggesting that he was not the rational actor represented in his account.

In eight other cases (36%), respondents did not depict their partner's violence as trivial or ineffectual. Rather, they described their partner's behavior in matter-of-fact terms:

Then she starts jumping at me or hitting me, or tell[ing] me "Leave the house, I don't want you, I don't love you" and stuff like that. And I say, "Don't touch me, don't touch me." And I just push her back. She keeps coming and hit me, hit me. I keep pushing back, she starts scratch me, so I push hard to stop her from hurting me. (Mario)

Other respondents depicted their partner's violence in factual terms but emphasized that they perceived their own violence as the greater danger. Ray took his partner seriously when he stated that "she was willing to fight, to defend herself," yet he also mentioned his fears that his own violence would be lethal: "The worst time is when she threw an iron at me. And I'm gonna tell you, I think that was the worst time, because, in defense, in retaliation, I pulled her hair, and I thought maybe I broke her neck." Only two respondents—Alan and Jim—consistently identified as victims:

> One of the worst times was realizing that she was drunk and belligerent. I realized that I needed to take her home in her car and she was not capable of driving. And she was physically abusive the whole way home. And before I could get out of the door or get out of the way, she came at me with a knife. And stupidly, I defended myself—kicked her hand to get the knife out. And I bruised her hand enough to where she felt justified enough to call the police with stories that I was horribly abusing. (Jim)

Jim reported that his partner has hit him, stabbed him, and thrown things at him. However, he also noted that he was arrested following several of these incidents, suggesting that his accounts tell us only part of the story. Moreover, like Steve and Alejandro, he did not describe feelings of fear or apprehension about his partner's use of a knife.

Although female partners were represented as dangerous only to themselves, the participants depicted their own violence as primal, explosive, and damaging to others:

> I explode for everything. This time it was trying to help my daughter with her homework; it was a Sunday, and she was not paying any attention, and I get angry with my daughter, and so I kick the TV....I guess I broke the TV, and then I kick a bookshelf. My daughter tried to get into the middle, so I pushed her away from me and I kicked another thing. So, she [his partner] called the police. I am glad she called the police because something really awful could have happened. (Alejandro)
>
> She said something, and then I just lost control. I choked her, picked her up off her feet, and lifted her up like this, and she was kind of kicking back and forth, and I really felt like I really wanted to kill her this time. (Adam)
>
> I feel that if there had been a gun in the house, I would have used it. That's one reason also why I refuse to have a gun. Because I know I have a terrible temper and I'm afraid that I will do something stupid like that. (Fred)

In contrast to their reported fearlessness when confronted by women wielding weapons, respondents constructed their own capacity for violence as something that should engender fear. These interpretations are consistent with cultural constructions of male violence as volcanic—natural, lethal, and impossible to stop until it has run its course.

Respondents' interpretations of ineffectual female violence and lethal male violence reflect actual violent practices in a culture that grants men more access to violence, but they also gender violence. By denying a threat from women's violence, participants performed masculinity and reinforced notions of gender difference. Women were constructed as incompetent in the practice of violence, and their successes were trivialized. For example, it is unlikely that Ed would have responded with laughter had his lip been split by the punch of another man (Dobash & Dobash, 1998). Moreover, respondents ignored their partners' motivations for violence and their active efforts to exert change within their relationships.

In her examination of Irigaray's writings on the representation of women within the masculine economy, Butler (1993, p. 36) writes that "the economy that claims to include the feminine as the subordinate term in a binary opposition of masculine/feminine excludes the feminine—produces the feminine as that which must be excluded for that economy to operate." The binary representation of ineffectual, hysterical female behavior and rational, lethal male violence within these accounts erases the feminine; violence perpetrated by women and female subjectivity are effaced in order that the respondents can construct masculinities. These representations mask the power relations that determine what acts will qualify as "violence" and thus naturalize the notion that violence is the exclusive province of men.

Gendering Blame

The research participants also gendered violence by suggesting that their female partners were responsible for the violence within their relationships. Some respondents did this by claiming that they did not hit women with whom they were involved in the past:

> I've never hit another woman in my life besides the one that I'm with. She just has a knack for bringing out the worst in me. (Tom)
>
> You know, I never hit my first wife. I'm married for five years—I never hit her. I never struck her, not once. (Mitchell)

Respondents also shifted blame onto female partners by detailing faults in their partners' behaviors and personalities. They criticized their partners' parenting styles, interaction styles, and choices. However, the most typically reported criticism was that female partners were controlling. Ten of the 33 respondents (30%) characterized their partners as controlling, demanding, or dominating:

> She's real organized and critiquing about things. She wanna—she has to get it like—she like to have her way all the time, you know. In control of things, even when she's at work in the evenings, she has to have control of everything that's going on in the house. And—but—you know, try to get, to control everything there. You know, what's going on, and me and myself. (Adam)
>
> You know, you're here with this person, you're here for five years, and yet they turn out to be aggressive, what is aggressive, too educated, you know. It's the reason they feel like they want to control you. (Mitchell)

In a few cases, respondents claimed that they felt emasculated by what they interpreted as their partners' efforts to control them:

> She's kind of—I don't want to say dominating. She's a good mother, she's a great housekeeper, she's an excellent cook. But as far as our relationship goes, the old

traditional "man wears the pants in the family," it's a shared responsibility. There's no way that you could say that I wear the pants in the family. She's dominating in that sense. (Ted)

    You ask the guy sitting next door to me, the guy that's down the hall. For years they all say, "Bill, man, reach down and grab your eggs. She wears the pants." Or maybe like, "Hey man, we're going to go—Oh, Bill can't go. He's got to ask his boss first." And they were right. (Bill)

These representations of female partners as dominating enabled men to position themselves as victims of masculinized female partners. The relational construction of masculinity is visible in these accounts; women who "wear the pants" disrupt the binary opposition of masculinity/femininity. Bill's account reveals that "one is one's gender to the extent that one is not the other gender" (Butler 1990, p. 22); he is unable to perform masculinity to the satisfaction of his friends when mirrored by a partner who is perceived as dominating.

Moreover, respondents appeared to feel emasculated by unspecified forces. Unlike female survivors who describe concrete practices that male partners utilize to exert control (Kirkwood, 1993; Walker, 1984), participants were vague about what they meant by control and the ways in which their partners exerted control:

I don't think she's satisfied unless she has absolute control, and she's not in a position to control anyway, um, mentally.... [*When you said that, um, that she wasn't really in a position to control, what did you mean by that?*] Well, she's not in a position to control, in the fact that she's not, the control that she wants, is pretty much control over me. I'm pretty much the only person that she sees every day. She wants to control every aspect of what I do, and while in the same turn, she really can't. (George)

Respondents who claimed that their partners are controlling offered nebulous explanations for these feelings, suggesting that these claims may be indicative of these men's fears about being controlled by a woman rather than the actual practices of their partners.

Finally, respondents gendered violence through their efforts to convince female partners to shoulder at least part of the blame for their violence. The following comments reflect respondents' interpretations of their partners' feelings after the argument was over:

Finally, for once in her life, I got her to accept 50/50 blame for the reason why she actually got hit. You know, used to be a time where she could say there was never a time. But, she accepts 50/50 blame for this. (Tom)

    She has a sense that she is probably 80 to 90% guilty of my anger. (Alejandro)

Contemporary constructions of gender hold women responsible for men's aggression (Gray, Palileo, & Johnson, 1993). Sexual violence is often blamed on women, who are perceived as tempting men who are powerless in the face of their primal sexual desires (Scully, 1990). Although interviewees expressed remorse for their violent behavior, they also implied that it was justified in light of their partners' controlling behavior. Moreover, their violence was rewarded by their partners' feelings of guilt, suggesting that violence is simultaneously a performance of masculinity and a means by which respondents encouraged the performance of femininity by female partners.

"The Law Is for Women": Claiming Gender Bias

Participants sometimes rationalized their violence by claiming that the legal system overreacted to a minor incident. Eight of the 33 interviewees (24%) depicted themselves as victims of gender politics or the media attention surrounding the trial of O. J. Simpson:

> I think my punishment was wrong. And it was like my attorney told me—I'm suffering because of O. J. Simpson. Mine was the crime of the year. That is, you know, it's the hot issue of the year because of O. J. Two years ago they would have gone "Don't do that again." (Bill)
>
> I'm going to jail for something I haven't even done because the woman is always the victim and the guy is always the bad guy. And O. J., I think, has made it even worse—that mentality. I know that there's a lot of bad, ignorant, violent guys out there that probably think that it's wonderful to batter their wife on a regular basis, but I think there's a lot of reverse mentality going on right now. (Jim)
>
> I don't necessarily agree with the jail system, which I know has nothing to do with you guys, but you have to sign a form saying that you'll come to counseling before you've ever been convicted of a crime. And, like I said, here I am now with this [inaudible] that I have to come to for 21 weeks in a row—for what could amount to some girl calling—hurting herself and saying her boyfriend or husband did it. (Tom)

These claims of gender bias were sometimes directly contradicted by respondents' descriptions of events following the arrival of the police. Four participants (12%) reported that the police wanted to arrest their female partner along with or instead of themselves—stories that challenged their claims of bias in the system. A few of these respondents reported that they lied to the police about the source of their injuries to prevent the arrest of their partners. Ed, the respondent who sustained a split lip from his partner's punch, claimed that he "took the fall" for his partner:

> They wanted to arrest her, because I was the one who had the little split lip. And I told them that—I said, "No, man, she's seven months pregnant." I told the officer, you know, "How can you take her to jail? She's seven months pregnant!" And I said, "Look, I came in here—I started it, I pushed her. And she hit me." You know, I told them that I had shoved her. And after that they said, "Okay, well, we have to remove, move you out of this—out of this situation here." Something about the law. So, I said, "Well, you know. I started it." I told them I had started it, you know. And, they said, "Okay, well, we'll take you then." So I went to jail. (Ed)

When the police arrived, these respondents were in a double bind. They wanted to deny their own violence to avoid arrest, but they also wanted to deny victimization at the hands of a woman. "Protecting" their female partners from arrest allowed them a way out of this bind. By volunteering to be arrested despite their alleged innocence, they became chivalrous defenders of their partners. They were also, paradoxically, able to claim that "gender bias" led to their arrest and participation in the Family Violence Diversion Network (FVDN) program. When Ed argued that the criminal justice system is biased toward women, we confronted him about this contradiction:

> ED: I am totally against, you know,—ever since I stepped foot in this program and I've only been to the orientation— [that] it speaks of gender, okay, and everything that—it seems like every statement that is made is directed toward men, toward the male party.... As I stated earlier, the law is for women. In my opinion, it—
>
> INTERVIEWER: Although, they would have arrested her if you hadn't intervened.
>
> ED: They would, that's right. That's another thing. That's right, that's right. They would have arrested her. But, you know even, even with her statement saying, look this is what, this is what happened, I'm not pressing charges. The state picked up those charges, and, they just took it upon themselves, you know, to inconvenience my life, is what they did.
>
> INTERVIEWER: Okay. And the other alternative would have been that she would have been going through this process instead of you.
>
> ED: Well, no, the other alternative, that was, that was, that would come out of this, is [that] I would have spent 30 days in jail.

Ed repeatedly dismissed the notion that the legal system would hold his partner accountable for her actions, despite his own words to the contrary. His construction of men as victimized by an interfering justice system allowed him to avoid the seemingly unacceptable conclusion that either he or his partner was a victim of violence.

Another respondent, Jim, reportedly prevented his partner's arrest because he felt it to be in his best interests:

> She was drunk and behind the wheel and driving erratically while backhanding me. And a cop pulled us over because he saw her hit me. And I realized that she was gonna get a DWI [driving while intoxicated], which would have been her second and a major expense to me, besides, you know, I think that there's a thin line between protecting somebody and possessing somebody. But I protect her, I do. I find myself sacrificing myself for her and lying for her constantly. And I told the cops that I hit her just because they saw her hit me and I figured that if I told them that I hit her, rather than her get a DWI, that we would both go to jail over an assault thing. Which is what happened. (Jim)

When batterers "protect" their partners from arrest, their oppressor becomes a powerful criminal justice system rather than a woman. Although even the loser gains status through participation in a fight with another man, a man does not gain prestige from being beaten by a woman (Dobash & Dobash, 1998). In addition, respondents who stepped in to prevent their partners from being arrested ensured that their partners remained under their control, as Jim suggested when he described "the thin line between being protected by somebody and possessing somebody." By volunteering to be arrested along with his partner, Jim ensured that she was not "taken into possession" (e.g., taken into custody) by the police.

By focusing the interviews on "gender bias" in the system, respondents deflected attention from their own perpetration and victimization. Constructions of a bias gave them an explanation for their arrest that was consistent with their self-presentation as rational, strong, and nonviolent actors. Claims of "reverse mentality" also enabled participants to position themselves as victims of gender politics. Several interviewees made use of men's rights rhetoric or alluded to changes wrought by feminism to suggest that they are increasingly oppressed by a society in which women have achieved greater rights:

> I really get upset when I watch TV shows as far as, like, they got shows or a TV station called Lifetime and there are many phrases "TV for women." And that kind of made me upset. Why is it TV for women? You know, it should be TV for everyone, not just women. You don't hear someone else at a different TV station saying, "TV for men." ... As far as the law goes, changing some of the laws goes too, some of the laws that guys are pulled away from their children. I kind of felt sorry for the guys. (Kenny)

A number of recent studies have examined the increasingly angry and antifeminist discourse offered by some men who are struggling to construct masculine identities within patriarchies disrupted by feminism and movements for gay/lesbian and civil rights (Fine et al., 1997; Messner, 1998; Savran, 1998). Some branches of the contemporary "men's movement" have articulated a defensive and antifeminist rhetoric of "men's rights" that suggests that men have become the victims of feminism (Messner, 1998; Savran, 1998). Although none of our interviewees reported participation in any of the organized men's movements, their allusions to the discourse of victimized manhood suggest that the rhetoric of these movements has become an influential resource for the performance of gender among some men. Like the angry men's rights activists studied by Messner, some respondents positioned themselves as the victims of feminism, which they believe has co-opted the criminal justice system and the media by creating "myths" of male domination. The interviews suggest that respondents feel disempowered and that they identify women—both the women whom they batter and women who lead movements to criminalize domestic violence—as the "Other" who has "stolen their presumed privilege" (Fine et al., 1997, p. 54): "Now girls are starting to act like men, or try and be like men. Like if you hit me, I'll call the cops, or if you don't do it, I'll do this, or stuff like that" (Juan). Juan contends that by challenging men's "privilege" to hit their female partners without fear of repercussions, women have become "like men." This suggests that the construction of masculine subjectivities is tied to a position of dominance, and that women have threatened the binary and hierarchical gender framework through their resistance to male violence.

DISCUSSION: SOCIAL LOCATIONS
AND DISCOURSES OF VIOLENCE

Respondents' descriptions of conflicts with female partners were similar across racial, ethnic, and class locations. Participants of diverse socioeconomic standings and racial ethnic backgrounds minimized the violence perpetrated by their partners, claimed that the criminal justice system is biased against men, and attempted to place responsibility for their violence on female partners. However, we identified some ways in which social class influenced respondents' self-presentations.

Respondents of higher socioeconomic status emphasized their careers and the material items that they provided for their families throughout the interviews:

> We built two houses together and they are nice. You know, we like to see a nice environment for our family to live in. We want to see our children receive a good education. (Ted)
>
> That woman now sits in a 2,700-square-foot house: She drives a Volvo. She has everything. A brand-new refrigerator, a brand-new washer and dryer. (Bill)

Seven respondents fit these criteria. We define disenfranchised respondents as those who report personal earnings of less than $15,000 per year and who have not completed a two-year college program. Nine respondents fit these criteria.

Conversely, economically disenfranchised men volunteered stories about their prowess in fights with other men. These interviewees reported that they engaged in violent conflicts with other men as a means of gaining respect:

> Everybody in my neighborhood respected me a lot, you know. I used to be kind of violent. I used to like to fight and stuff like that, but I'm not like that anymore. She—I don't think she liked me because I liked to fight a lot, but she liked me because people respected me, because they knew that they would have to fight if they disrespected me. You know, I think that's one thing that turned her on about me; I don't let people mess around. (Tony)
>
> My stepson's friend was there, and he start to push me too. So I started to say, "Hey, you know, this is my house, and you don't tell me nothing in my house." So I start fighting, you know, I was gonna fight him. (Mario)

The use of violence to achieve respect is a central theme in research on the construction of masculinities among disenfranchised men (Messerschmidt, 1993; Messner, 1992). Although men of diverse socioeconomic standings valorize fistfights between men (Campbell, 1993; Dobash & Dobash, 1998), the extent to which they participate in these confrontations varies by social context. Privileged young men are more often able to avoid participation in social situations that require physical violence against other men than are men who reside in poor neighborhoods (Messner, 1992).

We find some evidence that cultural differences influence accounts of domestic violence. Two respondents who identified themselves as immigrants from Latin America (Alejandro and Juan) reported that they experienced conflicts with female partners about the shifting meanings of gender in the United States:

She has a different attitude than mine. She has an attitude that comes from Mexico—be a man, like, you have to do it. And it's like me here, it's 50/50, it's another thing, you know, it's like "I don't have to do it." . . . I told her the wrong things she was doing, and I told her, "It's not going to be that way because we're not in Mexico, we're in the United States." (Juan)

Juan's story suggests that unstable meanings about what it means to be a woman or a man are a source of conflict within his relationship, and that he and his partner draw on divergent gender ideologies to buttress their positions. Although many of the respondents expressed uncertainty about appropriate gender performances in the 1990s, those who migrated to the United States may find these "crisis tendencies of the gender order" (Connell, 1992, p. 736) to be particularly unsettling. Interestingly, Juan depicts his partner as clinging to traditional gender norms, while he embraces the notion of gender egalitarianism. However, we are hesitant to draw conclusions about this finding due to the small number of interviews that we conducted with immigrants.

Race or ethnicity, class, and gender matter in the context of the interview setting. As white, middle-class, female researchers, we were often questioning men who resided in different social worlds. Like other female researchers who have interviewed men with histories of sexual violence, we found that the interviewees were usually friendly, polite, and appeared relatively comfortable in the interview setting (Scully, 1990). Unlike Ptacek, a male researcher who interviewed batterers, we did not experience a "subtext of resistance and jockeying for power beneath the otherwise friendly manner these individuals displayed in our initial phone conversations" (1990, p. 140). However, respondents may have offered more deterministic accounts of gender and assumed more shared experiences with the interviewer had they been interviewed by men rather than women (Williams & Heikes, 1993). For example, whereas Ptacek (1990) found that 78% of the batterers that he interviewed justified their violence by complaining that their wives did not fulfill the obligations of a good wife, participants in this study rarely used language that explicitly emphasized "wifely duties."

Previous studies also suggest that when white, middle-class researchers interview working-class people or people of color, they may encounter problems with establishing rapport and interpreting the accounts of respondents (Edwards, 1990). Riessman (1987) found that white researchers feel more comfortable with the narrative styles of white and middle-class respondents and may misinterpret the central themes raised by respondents of color. These findings suggest that shared meanings may have been less easily achieved in our interviews conducted with Latino, Native American, and African American men. For example, there is some evidence that we attempted to impose a linear narrative structure on our interviews with some respondents who may have preferred an episodic style (see Riessman, 1987):

We just started arguing more in the house. And she scratched me, and I push her away. Because I got bleeding on my neck and everything, and I push her away.

And she called the police and I run away so they don't catch me there. There's a lot of worse times we argued. She tried to get me with the knife one time, trying to blame me that I did it. And the next time I told her I was going to leave her, and she tried to commit suicide by drinking like a whole bunch of bottles of Tylenol pill. And I had to rush her to the hospital, you know. That's about it. [*So, in this worst fight, she scratched you and you pushed her. She called the police?*] A few times she kicked me and scratched me on my neck and everything, and my arms. (Andrew)

Andrew, who identifies as Latino, recounts several episodes that are salient to his understanding of the problems within his relationship. The interviewer, however, steers him toward a sequential recounting of one particular incident rather than probing for elaboration of Andrew's perceptions of these multiple events.

In contrast, racial ethnic locations can shape what interviewers and interviewees reveal. One way in which this dynamic may have influenced the interviews was suggested by Tom, who identified as African American:

I've never dated a black woman before. Not me. That was my choice—that's a choice I made a long time ago....I tend to find that black women, in general, don't have any get-up-and-go, don't work. I can't say—it's just down players. But I just don't see the desire to succeed in life.

Tom introduced the issue of interracial dating without prompting and went on to invoke a variety of controlling images to represent black women (Collins, 1991). It is difficult to imagine that Tom would have shared these details if he had been interviewed by an African American woman or perhaps even a white man. Given the middle-class bias of our sample and our own social locations, future research ought to compare accounts received by differently located interviewers and a wider class and racial ethnic range of respondents.

CONCLUSIONS

Many scholars have suggested that domestic violence is a means by which men construct masculinities (Dobash & Dobash, 1998; Gondolf & Hannekin, 1987; Hearn, 1998). However, few studies have explored the specific practices that domestically violent men use to present themselves as masculine actors. The respondents in this study used diverse and contradictory strategies to gender violence, and they shifted their positions as they talked about violence. Respondents sometimes positioned themselves as masculine actors by highlighting their strength, power, and rationality compared with the "irrationality" and vulnerability of female partners. At other times, when describing the criminal justice system or "controlling" female partners, they positioned themselves as vulnerable and powerless. These shifting representations evidence the relational construction of gender and the instability of masculine subjectivities (Butler, 1990).

Recently, performativity theories have been criticized for privileging agency, undertheorizing structural and cultural constraints, and facilitating essentialist readings of gender behavior: "Lacking an analysis of structural and cultural context, performances of gender can all too easily be interpreted as free agents acting out the inevitable surface manifestations of a natural inner sex difference" (Messner, 2000, p. 770). Findings from our study show that each of these criticisms is not necessarily valid.

First, although the batterers described here demonstrate agency by shifting positions, they do so by calling on cultural discourses (of unstoppable masculine aggression, of feminine weakness, and of men's rights). Their performance is shaped by cultural options.

Second, batterers' performances are also shaped by structural changes in the gender order. Some of the batterers interviewed for this study expressed anger and confusion about a world with "TV for women" and female partners who are "too educated." Their arrest signaled a world askew—a place where "the law is for women" and where men have become the victims of discrimination. Although these accounts are ironic in light of the research documenting the continuing reluctance of the legal system to treat domestic violence as a criminal act (Dobash & Dobash, 1979), they demonstrate the ways in which legal and structural reforms in the area of domestic violence influence gender performances. By focusing attention on the "bias" in the system, respondents deflected attention from their own perpetration and victimization and sustained their constructions of rational masculinity. Therefore, theories of gender performativity push us toward analyses of the cultural and structural contexts that form the settings for the acts.

Finally, when viewed through the lens of performativity, our findings challenge the notion that violence is an essential or natural expression of masculinity. Rather, they suggest that violence represents an effort to reconstruct a contested and unstable masculinity. Respondents' references to men's rights movement discourse, their claims of "reverse discrimination," and their complaints that female partners are controlling indicate a disruption in masculine subjectivities. Viewing domestic violence as a gender performance counters the essentialist readings of men's violence against women that dominate U.S. popular culture. What one performs is not necessarily what one "is."

Disturbingly, however, this study suggests that violence is (at least temporarily) an effective means by which batterers reconstruct men as masculine and women as feminine. Participants reported that they were able to control their partners through exertions of physical dominance and through their interpretive efforts to hold partners responsible for the violence in their relationships. By gendering violence, these batterers not only performed masculinity but reproduced gender as dominance. Thus, they naturalized a binary and hierarchical gender system.

REFERENCES

Bachman, R., & Saltzman, L. E. (1995). *Violence against women: Estimates from the redesigned survey, August 1995* (NCJ-154348 Special Report). Washington, DC: Bureau of Justice Statistics.

Bowker, L. H. (1983). *Beating wife-beating.* Lexington, MA: Lexington Books.

Butler, J. (1990). *Gender trouble: Feminism and the subversion of identity.* New York: Routledge.

———. (1993). *Bodies that matter: On the discursive limits of sex.* New York: Routledge.

Campbell, A. (1993). *Men, women, and aggression.* New York: Basic.

Collins, P. H. (1991). *Black feminist thought: Knowledge, consciousness, and the politics of empowerment.* New York: Routledge.

Connell, R. W. (1992). A very straight gay: Masculinity, homosexual experience, and the dynamics of gender. *American Sociological Review, 57,* 735–751.

Dobash, R. E., & Dobash, R. P. (1979). *Violence against wives: A case against the patriarchy.* New York: Free Press.

Dobash, R. E., & Dobash, R. P. (1998). Violent men and violent contexts. In R. E. Dobash & R. P. Dobash (Eds.), *Rethinking violence against women.* Thousand Oaks, CA: Sage, 358–380

Dobash, R. P., Dobash, R. E., Wilson, M., & Daly, M. (1992). The myth of sexual symmetry in marital violence. *Social Problems, 39,* 71–91.

Eaton, M. (1994). Abuse by any other name: Feminism, difference, and intralesbian violence. In M. A. Fineman & R. Mykitiuk (Eds.), *The public nature of private violence: The discovery of domestic abuse.* New York: Routledge, 199–215.

Edwards, R. (1990). Connecting method and epistemology: A white woman interviewing black women. *Women's Studies International Forum, 13*(5), 477–490.

Fagot, B., Hagan, R., Leinbach, M. B., & Kronsberg, S. (1985). Differential reactions to assertive and communicative acts of toddler boys and girls. *Child Development, 56,* 1499–1505.

Fine, M., Weis, L., Addelston, J., & Marusza, J. (1997). (In)secure times: Constructing white working-class masculinities in the late 20th century. *Gender & Society, 11,* 52–68.

Goffman, E. (1977). The arrangement between the sexes. *Theory & Society, 4*(3), 301–331.

Gondolf, E. W., & Hannekin, J. (1987). The gender warrior: Reformed batterers on abuse, treatment, and change. *Journal of Family Violence, 2,* 177–191.

Gray, N. B., Palileo, G. J., & Johnson, G. D. (1993). Explaining rape victim blame: A test of attribution theory. *Sociological Spectrum, 13,* 377–392.

Hearn, J. (1998). *The violences of men: How men talk about and how agencies respond to men's violence against women.* Thousand Oaks, CA: Sage.

Island, D., & Letellier, P. (1991). *Men who beat the men who love them: Battered gay men and domestic violence.* New York: Harrington Park.

Jang, D., Lee, D., & Morello-Frosch, R. (1998). Domestic violence in the immigrant and refugee community: Responding to the needs of immigrant women. In S. J. Ferguson (Ed.), *Shifting the center: Understanding contemporary families.* Mountain View, CA: Mayfield, 481–491.

Kirkwood, C. (1993). *Leaving abusive partners: From the scars of survival to the wisdom for change.* Newbury Park, CA: Sage.

Langhinrichsen-Rohling, J., Neidig, P., & Thorn, G. (1995). Violent marriages: Gender differences in levels of current violence and past abuse. *Journal of Family Violence, 10,* 159–176.

Lundgren, E. (1998). The hand that strikes and comforts: Gender construction and the tension between body and symbol. In R. E. Dobash & R. P. Dobash (Eds.), *Rethinking violence against women.* Thousand Oaks, CA: Sage,141–168.

Martin, D. (1976). *Battered wives.* New York: Pocket Books.

McCaughey, M. (1998). The fighting spirit: Women's self-defense training and the discourse of sexed embodiment. *Gender & Society, 12*, 277–300.

Messerschmidt, J. (1993). *Masculinities and crime: A critique and reconceptualization of theory.* Lanham, MD: Rowman & Littlefield.

Messner, M. A. (1992). *Power at play: Sports and the problem of masculinity.* Boston, MA: Beacon.

———. (1998). The limits of the "male sex role": An analysis of the men's liberation and men's rights movements' discourse. *Gender & Society, 12*, 255–276.

———. (2000). Barbie girls versus sea monsters: Children constructing gender. *Gender & Society, 14*, 765–784.

Pence, E., & Paymar, M. (1993). *Education groups for men who batter: The Duluth model.* New York: Springer.

Ptacek, J. (1990). Why do men batter their wives? In K. Yllo & M. Bograd (Eds.), *Feminist perspectives on wife abuse.* Newbury Park, CA: Sage, 133–157

Renzetti, C. M. (1992). *Violent betrayal: Partner abuse in lesbian relationships.* Newbury Park, CA: Sage.

Riessman, C. K. (1987). When gender is not enough: Women interviewing women. *Gender & Society, 1*, 172–207.

Savran, D. (1998). *Taking it like a man: White masculinity, masochism, and contemporary American culture.* Princeton, NJ: Princeton University Press.

Scully, D. (1990). *Understanding sexual violence: A study of convicted rapists.* Boston, MA: Unwin Hyman.

Straton, J. C. (1994). The myth of the "battered husband syndrome." *Masculinities, 2*, 79–82.

Straus, M. A. (1993). Physical assaults by wives: A major social problem. In R. J. Gelles & D. R. Loseke (Eds.), *Current controversies on family violence.* Newbury Park, CA: Sage, 55–77.

Walker, L. (1984). *The battered woman syndrome.* New York: Springer.

West, C., & Fenstermaker, S. (1995). Doing difference. *Gender & Society, 9*, 8–37.

Williams, C. L., & Heikes, E. J. (1993). The importance of researcher's gender in the in-depth interview: Evidence from two case studies of male nurses. *Gender & Society, 7*, 280–291.

Yllo, K. (1993). Through a feminist lens: Gender, power, and violence. In R. J. Gelles & D. R. Loseke (Eds.), *Current controversies on family violence.* Newbury Park, CA: Sage., 35–54.

CHAPTER 10

⁂

Serendipity in Robbery Target Selection

Bruce A. Jacobs

Drawing from interviews with 57 unincarcerated robbery offenders, most of whom specialized in either carjacking or drug robbery, this chapter explores the role of serendipity in the robbery target selection process. Serendipity is defined as the art of finding something valuable while engrossed in something different (Roberts, 1989). On average, the robber subjects were in their 20s. The majority had no high school degree. Most were unmarried. Although respondents typically were involved with drugs and committed a wide variety of offenses, they were recruited specifically because of their prior experience with drug robbery and carjacking.

Criminologists long have argued that the selection of predatory robbery targets is guided by rational choice. Offenders weigh the costs and benefits of contemplated conduct and proceed when the latter exceed the former (see, e.g., Carroll & Weaver, 1986; Cornish & Clarke, 1986). This relatively sterile view of offender decision making downplays the phenomenological forces that undermine reasoned calculation. Time pressure, uncertainty, emotion, and needs of various kinds can "bound" rationality and give rise to choices that are more or less spontaneous (Bennett & Wright, 1984). The dynamic tension between reflexive action and reasoned calculation comes into particular relief when opportunity and motivation converge along an axis of serendipity—chance circumstances that align to energize predatory conduct. It is this convergence and its implications for offender decision making that concern the present paper.

TARGET SELECTION

Any crime requires the intersection of suitable targets and motivated offenders (Felson, 1998), and robbery is no exception. Which targets are perceived to be

Source: Adapted from B. A. Jacobs. (2010). Serendipity of robbery target selection. *British Journal of Criminology, 50*(3), 514–529. Used with permission of the publisher.

suitable, when, and under what circumstances varies across situations and even within them. Contextual factors are labile and subjectively perceived.

As a criminological construct, target selection implies that something is being selected and someone is doing the selecting. Both presume agency. Understandably, the offender is the locus of much of this inquiry (see, e.g., Cornish & Clarke, 1986). Offenders' target selection strategies vary in their sophistication, calculation, focus, and degree of planning. Planning is of particular concern to criminologists because of assumptions of offender rationality and, more specifically, the belief that target selection hinges on offenders' objective information-processing capabilities. As Hochstetler (2002, p. 46) observes, "Decision-making investigators focus on offenders' agency and perceptual construction of situations as illicit opportunity. These investigators view crime as the outcome of purposeful action resulting from assessments of risk and reward."

That being said, a growing body of research in the offender decision-making tradition shows how the selection of predatory robbery targets is awash in ambiguity (Wright & Decker, 1997). Phenomenological forces like emotion and impulsivity destabilize choice and give rise to miscalculations of risk and reward. Offenders may not think about the prospects of sanctions, may think about the prospects but dismiss them, may inflate anticipated rewards, or may focus on anticipated rewards to the exclusion of risks (Bennett & Wright, 1984). All of these possibilities are consistent with a general lack of planning. Indeed, "street robbery is characterized as a spontaneous, impulsive [affair] more often than it involves real [preparation]" (Alarid, Burton, & Hochstetler, 2009, p. 7). Offenders typically "do not plan their crimes or spend only a few minutes planning" (Hochstetler 2001, p. 744; see also Feeney, 1986; Wright, Brookman, & Bennett, 2006).

Target selection can be an artifact of opportunity, but the lens through which opportunities are perceived is no doubt influenced by need. Prior researchers (Bennett & Wright, 1984; Topalli & Wright, 2004) have offered the terms "alert" and "motivated" opportunism to encapsulate the dynamic interplay between need and opportunity. Alert opportunism describes offenders who face needs that are present but not necessarily pressing. Offenders are not desperate, "but they anticipate need in the near term and become increasingly open to opportunities that may present themselves during the course of their day-to-day activities" (Topalli & Wright, 2004, pp. 156–157). By contrast, motivated opportunism is characterized by needs that are, or soon will be, acute. "Attention and openness to possibilities expands [sic] to allow offenders to tolerate more risk. Situations that previously seemed unsuitable start to look better" (Topalli & Wright, 2004, p. 157).

The distinction between alert and motivated opportunism is murky in street culture. Street culture promotes anomic, cash-intensive living that creates an endless supply of deficits and an equally endless need to extend surpluses so that they don't become deficits (Jacobs & Wright, 1999). The confluence of need and inducement gives rise to perpetual searches for scores big and small. Thus, alert and motivated opportunism presuppose a conceptual distinction between offenders who have to make something happen and offenders who face situations that simply "happen." In so doing, the two constructs fail to specify the role of serendipity in alert opportunism and downplay its potential relevance to motivated opportunism. Serendipity, for example, can be manufactured in probabilistic ways, and this manufacturing process need not flow from desperation or truncated rationality (as motivated opportunism implies). By the same token, alert opportunism can involve considerable time pressure if prevailing circumstances are "right" but fleeting. The role of serendipity in mediating these processes is of considerable interest.

SERENDIPITY

Traditionally, serendipity has been interpreted as the art of finding something valuable while engrossed in something different (Roberts, 1989). The discovery is unanticipated, unexpected, and anomalous (Merton & Barber, 2006). The challenge of serendipity is to recognize the inherent value of the unexpected discovery lest it be perceived as just another failed experiment or finding of residual but apparent insignificance. Horace Walpole, credited for coining the word serendipity, refers to this ability as "sagacity" (Roberts, 1989, p. 244). Serendipity promises success from setbacks but only for those wise enough to recognize that in setbacks there are opportunities.

Many of science and industry's most important discoveries have been products of serendipity. These include penicillin, X- rays, vulcanized rubber, and infrared radiation (Roberts, 1989). Serendipity also has been implicated in numerous product developments that arguably have become indispensable to Western popular culture—everything from Post-it Notes and NutraSweet to Ivory Soap and Velcro. Chance is implicated in these discoveries, but chance lies at the confluence of effort and preparation. As Louis Pasteur was once quoted as saying, "Chance favors only the prepared mind" (in Van Andel, 1994, p. 635). The fact that serendipity is deemed a faculty suggests that it is a skill that can be cultivated, exercised, and harnessed for positive ends. Serendipity and luck are not necessarily the same thing, though they are related. Luck is perceptual and "constructed" in the sense that emergent outcomes, be they positive or negative, are ascribed to good or bad luck. Luck implies fatalism—the belief that one's destiny is beyond his or her control (Miller, 1958). Yet some people are more lucky than others, and these people may be doing things that enhance their opportunity structure for luck. They may have a unique ability to recognize chance opportunities when they arise. Or, they have access to networks that convey relevant information, are more open to new experiences than others, and have a better-developed intuitive capacity. Lucky people also tend to be optimistic in the sense that expectations of good fortune often produce good fortune. When bad fortune comes instead of good fortune, optimists reframe the experience in positive ways (Wiseman, 2003).

In street culture, serendipity's meaning is more nuanced. Certainly, serendipity is an artifact of finding something valuable when looking for something unrelated. But serendipity also is about how offenders transform unfavorable developments into valued outcomes. Analysts may call this luck, but some settings are "more lucky" than others, and, not infrequently, this will be determined by the position in which offenders place themselves and how they react once they are there. In other social settings, serendipity affords a built-in temporal cushion between discovery, recognition, and action. In street culture, such phases are more or less coterminous. Targets of predatory robbery are there one moment and gone the next, requiring decisive action. The alternative is to "manufacture" serendipity, adopting targeting strategies that are sensitive to time and space in order to *make* things happen. Not infrequently, the decision to do this will be energized by negative situations that offenders realize they can transform into positive ones. The extent to which robbery targets emerge spontaneously (pure serendipity) or through some degree of manipulation (manufactured serendipity) offers a window into the offender decision-making process that in turn sheds light on the conceptual interface between perception, need, opportunity, and rational choice. Two forms of robbery—carjacking and drug robbery—provide a medium to explore this interface.

Pure Serendipity

One of the most striking findings to emerge from the interviews is the extent to which targets of predatory robbery materialized almost magically in time and space. Victims "became" victims after crossing paths with offenders at the right— or wrong (depending on one's perspective)—time. In a number of cases, serendipity made the target selection process appear to be almost effortless.

Driving around one afternoon, one respondent was approached by a young man who broached the idea of a drug sale. Although the respondent did need drugs and also had a firearm on his person, his explicit intention was not to commit a robbery (at the time, he was driving to his girlfriend's house and attempting to meet a friend there). When the would-be victim introduced the idea of a drug transaction, the respondent realized that he could simply take what he would otherwise have had to buy and secure more than he could have purchased in the process. Robbery was the inevitable result:

> Well one of these young guys come up to my car asking me if I wanted to buy some drugs....I had wanted me some drugs that day and I didn't have enough money and I happened to see the little guy on the street, so he had me just pull over. I was going to see a friend of mine....I needed to go to a friend of mine and get something....So he [the friend] wasn't at home, so I saw him [the victim] and he happened to run up to my car. So I said yes, I would like to buy some. So he got in the car with me, he wasn't aware that I had a gun in the car. So I told him, "You know what time it is, this is a robbery." So I stuck my gun up in his face to let him know that I wasn't playing. So he gave me $450 cash, he gave me five grams of Boy [heroin]...and four-tenths and about 20 pills. (Blackwell)

Another respondent described a strikingly similar encounter, also unfolding as the respondent roamed the streets in unrelated pursuits. The eventual victim approached the respondent and his brother's vehicle at a red light, soliciting a drug sale. This simple interrogatory transformed the offenders' decision-making calculus, implanted the robbery idea, and unleashed the offense:

> No, we [were not looking to rob anybody]. We just out riding and then we stopped at a red light and he [the eventual victim] walked up on us talking about did you want to buy something, so he [my brother] pulled out a gun.... He didn't say nothing, he just pulled it [the gun] out.... And then when he pulled the gun on him, then he told me to get out of the car and take his little stuff.... I think he [my brother] really thought he had rocks or something, but he only had like six packs of weed... [and] like $600 something.... Just took his stuff and we just pulled off. (V-O)

As Roberts (1989, p. 244) points out, persons attuned to the prospects of serendipity will observe a phenomenon that is unexpected and take note of it "rather than dismiss it as trivial or annoying." This faculty is particularly valuable in carjacking, the other modality of robbery explored in this paper. By its nature, carjacking is less dependent on the mobility of the offender than of the victim (Jacobs, Topalli, & Wright, 2003). For perpetrators, the trick is to have the "sagacity" (Roberts, 1989) to recognize opportunities when they appear. As Joseph Henry once remarked, "The seeds of great discovery are constantly floating around us, but they only take root in minds well prepared to receive them" (in Roberts, 1989, p. 65). Edwin Sutherland (1937) famously called this the "larceny sense" (see also Copes & Cherbonneau, 2006). Little Tye illustrates it emphatically below:

> My partner, he wanted him some rims. He had just bought this little Malibu and he just wanted rims. I needed a radio and some speakers, so it all came down like, they were goin' over there. We saw this little cat over there by a little liquor store... with his gal over there, pumping his beats, riding his rims, goddamn, me and my partner got on [it].... It's just something we wanted to do. [We had money but] we'd rather go take it than spend the money in our pockets.... That's what I'm saying, we don't need no money. We have money. We're selling dope, we got money. We stay in the projects, we got money. It's just something, we steal cars, I mean that's what we want. We don't want it, we go sell it. I mean we don't give it away, we go sell it to get more money.... You know what happens, when you see, like, a baby when they see someone, they get surprised and so happy. When they see something they want, they're gonna cry for it, they want it. [That's like us.] That's how we live, I mean.... You can never have enough of money.

Unlike other forms of street robbery that emerge by chance, carjacking puts a particular premium on spontaneity. A "regular" robbery victim might be banked in a perceptual reservoir for future consideration (see, e.g., Hochstetler 2001; Wright & Decker, 1994; Wright & Decker, 1997), but a desirable car is there one minute and gone the next. Acting decisively can mean the difference between hitting a "lick," as offenders refer to it, or going home empty-handed. Carjacking is rapid and simple, and the reward doubles as an escape mechanism:

I was coming from the club and I was drunk and high...you know, everybody go to the East Side to go see girls and stuff, you know, meet girls....We was coming back to [town]. We was leaving [one place and] coming back in to [town]. We seen him [the eventual victim] on our way to [town]. We had seen him at a stoplight....It was like at night, real late at night, about 2:00 in the morning....He was just riding through and he stopped at a stoplight....I was like, man, I like that car, man, and I love [the color] red....It [the idea to carjack]...come in my head once I see the car. I say I want that and I'm gonna go get that....He [the victim] looked like a punk. I wanted to take the car from him, you know, so we went over there and took it....I already got what I need, a gun...ran up to him and put the gun to his head, "Get out of the car." He got out of the car and we was up on him, we skirted off. (C-Ball)

Manufacturing Serendipity

The foregoing accounts reveal the fluidity and open-endedness of target selection when serendipity is more or less "pure." While it is an overstatement to suggest that targets select themselves in such cases, their situated vulnerability moves offenders from an indifferent state to one in which they are determined to act (c.f. Topalli & Wright, 2004). Although happenstance certainly produces moments of pure serendipity, more typically, effort is required to convert opportunities into scores. Effort requires knowledge of when, where, and under what circumstances strategies for manipulating time and space will produce favorable outcomes. To outsiders uninitiated in the ways of the street, the process can be difficult to master. To offenders accustomed to street-level dynamics, it can become almost second nature.

At the most basic level, manufacturing serendipity requires that offenders have a reasonably well-developed "perceptual shorthand" (Skolnick, 1966) to identify the likely emergence of predatory targets based on time, place, and circumstance. Palpable to the offenders who exercise it but difficult for many to articulate, it is a shorthand that maximizes the efficiency of effort relative to expected rewards.

By manufacturing serendipity, I mean fashioning circumstances that create fortuitous accidents. Manufacturing serendipity requires that offenders manipulate activity patterns in ways that produce temporal and spatial convergence with would-be crime targets. The convergence is anticipatory because it is based on probabilistic assessments of likely target-rich times and places (see also Brantingham & Brantingham, 1978; Copes & Cherbonneau, 2006; Topalli, 2005). The convergence is historical in the sense that it draws from experiential knowledge of the perceived suitability of such venues. Offenders are passive-aggressive "foragers" who move with purpose and logic (Bernasco & Block, 2009, p. 95) even as their activity appears random. Offenders rely on emergent and difficult-to-predict circumstances while manipulating activity patterns in ways that permit exploitation of the targets that do emerge. This curious mix of agency and constraint can result in substantial bounties:

I cruise around neighborhoods mostly every day like that to find out where the dope dealers are you know....When I left out of [one area], I'm coming up from [street] going towards [street]. I make a left on [street]. See, first I started in [one area] looking. Couldn't find nobody in [that area], so I go over on [street]. See I know these little cats on [street], they usually be out. I didn't see them. So I say, ok, it was about 12:00. I'm gonna find somebody, you know. I go up on [street] and [street], that dude standing out flagging you know.... So he flagged me down. He said, "Hey brother, what's up, you looking?" I told him, "Yeah, I'm looking." He said, "What you looking for?" Told him, "I'm looking for some Boy [heroin] and some rock." He said, "All right, look, check this here out. You don't mind if I get in your car?" I told him, "No, come on, get on in there." He said, "Drive around the corner." I take him around the corner, instead of going right around the corner, go right around the corner, jump right on [street], jump on [the Interstate.... He said], "Hey, brother, what's up, what's up?" "You know what's up, you know what's up now. You can't get out of the car. Say, what's up. You gonna get out of the car when we doing 65 miles an hour on the highway, can't get out of the car, you know what's up, you know." So he say, "Don't kill me, man, don't kill me." "I'm not gonna kill you, I just want your dope and your money, man, that's all I want and be kind enough to take you back down on [street] and drop you off by the highway." That's how I got him. (Do-dirty)[1]

Whereas the above respondent discusses the importance of circulating generally within a target-rich environment, other offenders applied a more direct approach. Manufacturing serendipity could be quite purposive in this regard. The logic that drives the selection process is the same—putting oneself in a position to capitalize on emergent opportunities that are uncertain but possible and drawing from experiential knowledge to do so—but the selection process itself is less random. Thus, one respondent, Goldie, received information about the possible emergence of a carjacking target. Although the information was not precise, it was sufficiently specific to get him to lurk. Pure serendipity may be about finding something fortuitous while looking for something different, but manufactured serendipity creates an opportunity structure for fortuity by merging luck with preparation. As Roberts (1989, p. 119) notes, "Discoveries have been made, not only 'by really trying,' but also by clever design or *conception*."[2] Goldie illustrates this logic as it relates to his hunch about a carjacking target:

I'm standing across the street like I'm waiting on a bus or something sitting at this stoplight.... I got the drop that he [a car] usually come through this certain place, [street] and [street] around this time. I was standing at the bus stop waiting on him, you know.... I'm standing there hoping, and if he don't come, you know, but he did.... Just chilling and he pulled up, you know, and the [stop]light changed just in time. I ran up over there, put the gun to his head, asked him if he was going to get out or die, you know what I'm saying, either one, you going to get out this motherfucker or die?... First night [waiting for him]. First night got his ass.... [Lucky.] Yeah.

Manufacturing serendipity can be particularly important when predatory robberies flow from moralistic concerns. Criminologists have long recognized that robbery and assault serve as social control devices for offenders who are wronged by others (Black, 1983). The need to manufacture serendipity for moralistic reasons can on occasion be quite reflexive—a product of provocative target behavior at a discrete moment in time. Although in purely serendipitous incidents, would-be victims also play a role in their own selection, in those incidents, being at the right place results less from victim precipitation than bad timing. In a moralistically energized incident, the target behaves in a way that creates a specific imbalance in need of rectification. The offender transforms the imbalance into an opportunity for gain. Being aggrieved certainly is not invited or appreciated by respondents (which the notion of serendipity can, at times, imply), but the affront does permit offenders to turn something unwelcome into something propitious, and that lies at the core of serendipity as a situational process. J Rock thus explains what he did to a drug dealer who "disrespected" him:

> Like I ask them [for drugs] for something and they don't give it to me, I'll tell 'em, "I'm coming back for your ass," and I come back. You think I'm bullshitting, I'll rob his ass. Come right back.... [Put the gun in their face] "Give me all your dope and all your money now. I asked for something and you wouldn't give me nothing, so now I want it all."....Don't fuck with me, nobody, nobody, nobody.

Although objective financial need certainly primes the selection process (as the above respondent implies), manufacturing serendipity requires a perceptual trigger to generate awareness of debasement (Tittle, 1995). In street culture, sensitivity is high, so such triggers are in ample supply. This is especially true of carjacking because imbalances are frequently created by mobile displays of wealth perceived by would-be offenders to be insulting. Flossing, as it is sometimes called, constitutes both a putdown and a provocation (Jacobs, Topalli, & Wright, 2003) and creates an imbalance that cries out for rectification. The provocation may not be welcome, but the opportunity to make something fortuitous come out of it is:

> We were tired of seeing them just coming through, always trying to floss as they went past...always wanting to go somewhere and stare, or always showing off, talking a lot....Me and my partner, we saw him pull up to the lot [while we were sitting in a park next door]....He [the victim] went into the [gas station], and he was pumping the gas. His partner was listening to the news....It was late, round about 2, 2:30....Boy I knew he had some money....People drive around like that....From his pockets, we took about five Gs....You floss it too much, you get robbed....He tried to floss, man. (Snake)

DISCUSSION

The methods and motives of robbery are well understood. Less clear are the situational factors that give rise to perceptions of opportunity irrespective of method or motive. The objective of this paper has been to refocus attention on this situated convergence through the concept of serendipity.

Robberies have long been described as "low-level, desperate, and impulsive exploits" that rarely involve advance planning (Alarid, Burton, & Hochstetler, 2009, p. 2; see also Feeney, 1986). Although prior research emphasizes the role of opportunity in triggering such events, only recently have studies begun in earnest to identify the situated manner in which opportunity is constructed (see, e.g., Hochstetler, 2001). The present paper has sought to expand this line of inquiry by sensitizing readers to the notion of serendipity.

Serendipity requires that offenders both make, and let, things happen. The latter is especially consequential given the frequency with which moments of pure serendipity arise. The transition from relative indifference to committed action is rapid, and the capacity for motivation to "flex" in this way has not been examined in any great detail by prior etiological studies of crime. Likely, this is because criminologists view offender motivation through static risk factors. Risk factors create predispositions to crime, but they neither cause nor shape crime in the offending moment. The offending moment is the magical instant by which indifference transforms into committed action. The speed of this transformation can be torrid, as this paper has demonstrated.

Spontaneity may imply irrationality, but the spontaneity that drives serendipity is firmly rooted in reasoned calculation, a process long associated with rational choice. Over two centuries ago, this tradition embarked with two seminal treatises in utilitarian theory—Beccaria's 240-year-old *An Essay on Crimes and Punishment* and Bentham's comparably historic *An Introduction to the Principles of Morals and Legislation*. By focusing on sanction threats and how would-be offenders react to them, Beccaria (1764/1963) presumed that offenders ponder what they are going to do and how they are going to do it before they do it. Bentham (1789) similarly opined that would-be offenders exercise a "quantum of sensibility" in how they construct, define, and respond to criminogenic circumstances.

Over the years, rational-choice theorists have refined the focus by adding concepts like decision frames (Tversky & Kahneman, 1981), editing/evaluation (Kahneman & Tversky, 1979) and noncompensatory strategizing (Johnson & Payne, 1986). Decision frames come from "prospect theory" (Lattimore & Witte, 1986), an approach that explores how offenders discern among various conduct options based on the discrete outcome probabilities of each. Editing/evaluation is a more complicated process in which offenders code, combine, segregate, cancel, simplify, and detect dominance in relation to some anticipated action. This analytic process requires that offenders be sensitive to things such as decision weights, value functions, and risk perceptions as each relates to outcome probabilities (Lattimore & Witte, 1986).

Noncompensatory strategizing, the third approach, is simpler and more relevant to serendipity. It holds that offender rationality is limited, and that offenders weigh but a few aspects of a few alternatives and ignore the rest (Johnson & Payne, 1986, p. 173). Noncompensatory strategizing promotes "standing decisions" (Cook, 1980) that offenders cultivate over time and which they invoke on command. Steeped in "iterative agency" (Emirbayer & Mische, 1998), standing decisions sensitize offenders to patterns and practices and permit efficient reaction to emergent cues (Emirbayer & Mische, 1998). Offenders learn "which discriminative cues are associated with 'good' targets," and these cues "then serve as a 'template'" applied in subsequent actions (Cromwell & Olsen, 2004, p. 19). Expertise may play a role in this process (Topalli, 2005), although the nature of expertise's role is unclear. Novice offenders, for example, may be less constrained by biases and more apt to "go with the flow," which can expand choice and the universe of would-be crime opportunities to recognize.

Despite its centrality to offender decision making, theorists have largely ignored serendipity's function in the noncompensatory strategic toolkit. Certainly, opportunities arise, but opportunities mean nothing unless or until they are perceived, recognized, and acted upon by offenders. Serendipity bridges the gap between the emergence of opportunity and opportunity's exploitation because it is a faculty that offenders exercise.

Prior research mistakes serendipity for opportunity and fails to grasp the distinction between the two. Opportunity is inherent; serendipity is referential. Opportunity is situation-focused; serendipity nests offenders in those situations. Opportunity is fixed; serendipity is adaptable. Opportunity is an event; serendipity is a capacity. Even when prior research explores opportunity, it does so almost exclusively through the lens of need (see, e.g., Hochstetler 2001; Topalli & Wright, 2004). Thus, studies repeatedly emphasize how intense pressures energize offending decisions and distort the manner in which offenders reach these decisions. Wright and Decker (1994, pp. 200–201) found that all but a few of their offenders typically "began to contemplate the commission of their [offenses] while under intense emotional pressure to obtain money as quickly as possible." This required them to develop a repository of crime targets they could tap when desperation inevitably set in. Only one person in Wright and Decker's sample of over 100 offenders qualified as purely opportunistic (i.e., serendipitously minded)—someone who "'just happen[ed] upon' a vulnerable target and, as a result, commit[ted] an offense on the spur of the moment" (1994, p. 99). Moreover, nearly 90% of their sample had a *specific target* in mind before setting out to offend (Wright & Decker, 1994, p. 63). In an earlier study of British offenders, Bennett and Wright (1984) found similarly that only 7% of their sample fit the "opportunist" category—equivalent to someone who responded reflexively to unexpected but favorable situational cues, that is, someone who responded serendipitously. It is precisely because desperate offenders cannot predict when and under what circumstances opportunities will arise that serendipity was a residual category in these studies.

The robbery literature is afflicted similarly by its disproportionate focus on need and how opportunity passively works through it (see Wright & Decker, 1997). The robbery literature is peppered with descriptions of desperate offenders trolling the streets seeking to attack the first suitable target into which they run. Thus, Jacobs' robbers were "very much spinning out of control" (2000, pp. 42–43). Wright and Decker's (1997) robbers lurched from one crisis to the next. Topalli and Wright's (2004) carjackers sacrificed prudence for immediacy. Feeney's (1986) robbers, at times, careened into crimes.

None of these studies explore serendipity as an empirical process or meaningfully link it to the construction of criminal opportunity *in situ*. Part of the problem is that studies on criminality in general, and on offender decision making in particular, conflate desperation with impulsivity and imply that the latter and former are one and the same. Concomitantly, these studies presume that desperation so limits rationality that serendipity, as a faculty, cannot meaningfully be exercised. The renowned lack of planning on the part of many robbery offenders is thought to be *prima facie* evidence of their recklessness. Certainly, the present study does not wish to disabuse readers of the urgency that frequently imbues robbery offenders' actions. It does, however, wish to sensitize readers to the distinction between impulsivity and recklessness so that serendipity's conceptual import can better be grasped.

Impulsivity lies at the heart of street crime, and robbery tends to be no exception. Impulsive people want things the easy way; they are risk seeking, attracted to thrills, and unable to defer gratification (Gottfredson & Hirschi, 1990). Numerous scholars (see, e.g., Nagin & Pogarsky, 2003) have noted how present orientation interferes with the ability to process potential setbacks, setbacks being critical to understanding how serendipity operates as a faculty. In particular, impulsivity subsumes a "here and now" worldview and the "commensurate tendency to devalue or discount delayed consequences" (Pogarsky & Piquero, 2004, p. 374).

> By seeking immediate gratification, those [with high levels of impulsivity] are relatively unmoved by the potential pains of punishment that are both uncertain and removed in the future. As such, the "emotional force" of present desires overwhelms the apprehension of pain in the future. (Wright et al., 2004, p. 182).

But the present orientation that guides the serendipitous exploitation of crime targets underscores a sensitivity to future consequences, not an ignorance of them. Indeed, the longer-term outlook that mediates serendipitous conduct arguably is risk averse, not risk seeking. Not only have choice theorists failed to appreciate this wrinkle in offender decision making, they have emphasized just the opposite:

> In decision making parlance, the criminal opportunity presents a choice between a sure thing (restraint from the criminal act), and a gamble that arises because the contemplated conduct can produce a gain with some probability and a loss with complementary probability. Individuals who tend more toward the safety of a sure thing rather than risk a loss are considered risk-averse. In contrast, individuals with the opposite propensity, namely, to risk a loss for even the slightest chance of reward, are considered risk-seeking. (Nagin & Pogarsky, 2001, p. 885)

Offenders who act serendipitously, and particularly those who do not face pressing needs at the time, capitalize on a "sure thing" *and* make moot the uncertainty of the crime target's reemergence. By forestalling the emergence of desperation that ultimately will *require* them to act, offenders reveal the forward-thinking potential of impulsive action.

Impulsivity can also affect the manner in which serendipity is enacted. Conventional criminological wisdom holds that offenders living in and for the moment will be hard pressed to focus on anything but that moment (Gottfredson & Hirschi, 1990). Conventional wisdom also holds that "bounded rationality" is especially problematic in high-velocity, uncertain environments imbued with desperation (such as street culture). On their face, such conditions would seem to restrict the functional expression of serendipity because they compromise choice. The present study brings this into question and is supported by research in cognitive psychology, which suggests that bounded rationality may improve rather than undermine the perceptual clarity upon which serendipity relies to operate. Actors who face strict limits on the factors they can realistically attend to can discern emergent cues more efficiently. When information loads lighten, decision-makers are better able to ignore irrelevant data and focus on cues of real substance (see, e.g., Khatri & Ng, 2000). Bounds on rationality may thereby encourage offenders to lock into discrete moments and discern them resourcefully and creatively, sharpening serendipity's edge and the strategic vision necessary to invoke it.

That being said, two essential links in offender decision making must be addressed if analysts ever are to understand why offenders perceive things the way they do and how they act once the perception is made (Piquero & Pogarsky, 2002). The first is the manner by which information known to an actor becomes a judgment. The second is the manner by which such judgments influence actual behavior (Piquero & Pogarsky, 2002, p. 154). Research on offender decision making has left these processes largely untapped. When it does explore them, the bulk of the focus is on person-based traits as opposed to situations (see, e.g., Nagin & Pogarsky, 2003). Because serendipity explores persons nested in situations, the oversight is problematic.

A cursory review of the data presented in the current paper reveals the prominence of situational factors. A number of factors were relevant, but the role of weapon availability and co-offenders was especially germane. Firearms routinely transformed indifference into committed action, irrespective of objective needs. Firearms obviously inflict serious injury, they can do it from a distance, and everyone knows that firearms have these attributes, which makes for a highly effective contingent threat (Cook, 1982) and a rapid way to convert nascent motives into action. Co-offenders were equally powerful in catalyzing the process, which is understandable given that decision-makers in group settings "do not respond passively to situational opportunity; they create it by selecting and transforming the situations they confront" (Hochstetler, 2001, p. 740). In particular, co-offenders encourage accomplices to take risks. They embolden behavior, diffuse responsibility, and enhance perceptions of dominance—all of which entice decision-makers to seek out opportunity with greater vigor and manufacture it with more intense resolve. Co-offenders, finally, quicken the pace by which actual decisions are made, which can reveal serendipitous circumstances more readily or encourage offenders to act on them with less regret. Certainly, the cases of V-O, Little Tye, and C-Ball highlight this powerful process of "social exchange" (McCluskey & Wardle, 1999; see also Alarid, Burton, & Hochstetler, 2009).

Because serendipity is a faculty that involves the situated capacity to turn setbacks into opportunities, the manner in which "setback experiences" influence serendipity's structure and process warrants empirical attention. Deterrence theorists have made analogous arguments regarding the relationship between prior punishment experiences and future criminality (see, e.g., Paternoster & Piquero, 1995): punishment experiences can influence the manner in which offenders contemplate additional crime (see Minor & Harry, 1982, on the "experiential effect") by promoting more nuanced decisions that carry a lower risk of detection. Setback experiences may similarly sensitize offenders in the realm of opportunity perception and perhaps promote greater efficacy in serendipity's exercise. We know this happens in the "real world." Research on entrepreneurship, for example, shows a direct correlation between prior failures and innovation potential (Minniti & Bygrave, 2001). The most prolific entrepreneurs the world over typically experience setback after setback before tasting success, and only taste success because failure is pedagogical (Roberts, 1989). Street offenders are widely perceived to be failures in almost every sense of the word. Maybe it is failure that makes serendipity possible and real.

Experiential effects highlight this "accretive" potential (Zimring & Hawkins, 1973) of serendipity. Accretion is important because it implies dynamic interplay and/or conditional interaction between different forms of serendipity, both of which ultimately influence how or when serendipity is expressed. For example, having a crime target fall onto one's lap doesn't mean that serendipity won't be manufactured a moment later if a previously established target emerges or if some affront moves offenders from a neutral state to one in which they are determined to act. Crime targets may also emerge one after another in a purely serendipitous manner, which can alter the trajectory of serendipity-based decision making: a series of purely serendipitous encounters can make offenders "resistant" to incidents that might otherwise require serendipity to be manufactured (e.g., in response to an affront). Conversely, frustration tolerances may rise after a spate of good but unexpected fortune, permitting offenders to develop greater cognitive clarity in how they exercise serendipity: a series of positive outcomes can liberate the psyche from worry and allow offenders to devote energy to cultivating chance encounters that bear yet more fruit. At the same time, bad fortune can also make offenders more attuned to their environment, more sensitive to affronts, and more apt to manufacture serendipity from negative events. Whether hypersensitivity "primes" reactions in general, or makes offenders more discerning of crime targets in particular, is unclear and merits additional research attention.

In the final analysis, serendipity speaks to the nondeterministic nature of offender decision making. Although opportunity may, in some cases, "make the thief" (as the nineteenth-century French saying holds; see Fattah, 1993, p. 246), opportunity is unpredictable and must be appraised. Appraisals are based on the sense that offenders "make of situations using contextually relevant precedent and experience." Indeed, offenders "construct criminal opportunity by comparing recently formulated understandings [against] developing events and adjusting situations to make events and understanding correspond" (Hochstetler, 2001, pp. 747, 756). By definition, uncertain events rarely occur in predictable frequencies, but emergent cues can be recognized, processed, and manipulated for productive ends. Serendipity hinges on this curious combination of agency and constraint.

When action and receptivity interact in such a way, favorable outcomes result from unexpected and even negative events.

NOTES

1. Bennett and Wright's (1984) "searchers" acted in a reasonably similar manner, but unlike the offenders explored here, their offenders waited before exploiting targets. Offenders who manufacture serendipity act more or less contemporaneously after spotting the target.
2. This is why building contractors occasionally hire archaeologists to be on site during certain excavations. The frequency with which artifacts of one sort or another are unearthed while digging makes the occurrence predictable. Such a practice betrays the inherent recognition of a likely serendipitous find simply by preparing for it (Roberts, 1989, p. 106).

REFERENCES

Alarid, L. F., Burton, V. S., & Hochstetler, A. L. (2009). Group and solo robberies: Do accomplices shape criminal form? *Journal of Criminal Justice, 37*, 1–9.

Beccaria, C. (1764/1963). *On crimes and punishments.* Trans. H. Paolucci. Indianapolis: Bobbs-Merrill.

Bennett, T., & Wright, R. (1984). *Burglars on burglary: Prevention and the offender.* Aldershot: Gower.

Bentham, J. (1789). *An introduction to the principles of morals and legislation.* London: Hafner.

Bernasco, W., & Block, R. (2009). Where offenders choose to attack: A discrete choice model of robberies in Chicago. *Criminology, 47*, 93–130.

Black, D. (1983). Crime as social control. *American Sociological Review, 48*, 34–45.

Brantingham, P. J., & Brantingham, P. L. (1978). A theoretical model of crime site selection. In M. D. Krohn & R. X. Akers (Eds.), *Crime, law and sanctions* (pp.105–118). Beverly Hills, CA: Sage.

Carroll, J., & Weaver, F. (1986). Shoplifters' perceptions of crime opportunities: A process-tracing study. In D. B. Cornish & R. V. G. Clarke (Eds.), *The reasoning criminal: Rational choice perspectives on offending.* New York: Springer-Verlag, 19–37.

Cook, P. J. (1980). Research in criminal deterrence: Laying the groundwork for the second decade. In M. Tonry and N. Morris (Eds.), *Crime and justice: An annual review of research* (Vol. 2). Chicago: University of Chicago Press, 211–268.

———. (1982). The role of firearms in violent crimes: An interpretative review of the literature, with some new findings and suggestions for further research. In M. E. Wolfgang & N. A. Weiner, *Criminal violence* (pp. 236–291). Beverly Hills, CA: Sage.

Copes, H., & Cherbonneau, M. (2006). The key to auto theft: Emerging methods of auto theft from the offenders' perspective. *British Journal of Criminology, 46*, 917–934.

Cornish, D. B, & Clarke, R. V. (1986). *The reasoning criminal: Rational choice perspectives on offending.* New York: Springer-Verlag.

Cromwell, P., & Olson, J. N. (2004). *Breaking and entering: Burglars on burglary.* Belmont, CA: Wadsworth.

Emirbayer, M., & Mische, A. (1998). What is agency? *American Journal of Sociology, 103*, 962–1023.

Fattah, E. A. (1993). The rational choice/opportunity perspectives as a vehicle for integrating criminological and victimological theories. In R. V. Clarke & M. Felson (Eds.), *Routine activity and rational choice: Advances in criminological theory* (pp. 225–258). New Brunswick, NJ: Transaction.

Feeney, F. (1986). Robbers as decision-makers. In D. Cornish & R. Clarke (Eds.), *The reasoning criminal: Rational choice perspectives on offending* (pp. 53–71). New York: Springer-Verlag.

Felson, M. (1998). *Crime and everyday life* (2nd ed.). Thousand Oaks, CA: Pine Forge.

Gottfredson, M., & Hirschi, T. (1990). *A general theory of crime.* Palo Alto, CA: Stanford University Press.

Hochstetler, A. (2001). Opportunities and decisions: Interactional dynamics in robbery and burglary groups. *Criminology, 39,* 737–764.

———. (2002). Sprees and runs: The construction of opportunity in criminal episodes. *Deviant Behavior, 23,* 45–74.

Jacobs, B. A., Topalli, V., & Wright, R. (2003). Carjacking, street life, and offender motivation. *British Journal of Criminology, 43,* 673–688.

Jacobs, Bruce A. (2000). *Robbing drug dealers: Violence beyond the law.* New York: Aldine de Gruyter.

Jacobs, B. A., & Wright, R. (1999). Stick-up, street culture, and offender motivation. *Criminology, 37,* 149–173.

Johnson, E., & Payne, J. (1986). The decision to commit a crime: An information-processing analysis. In D. B. Cornish & R. V. Clarke (Eds.), *The reasoning criminal* (pp. 170–185). New York: Springer-Verlag.

Kahneman, D., & Tversky, A. (1979). Prospect theory: An analysis of decisions under risk. *Econometrica, 47,* 313–327.

Khatri, N., & Ng, H. A. (2000). The role of intuition in strategic decisionmaking. *Human Relations, 53,* 57–86.

Lattimore, P., & Witte, A. (1986). Models of decision making under uncertainty: The criminal choice. In D. B. Cornish & R. V. Clarke (Eds.), *The reasoning* (pp. 130–155.. New York: Springer-Verlag.

McCluskey, K., & Wardle, S. (1999). The social structure of robbery. In D. Canter & L. Alison (Eds.), *The social psychology of crime: Groups, teams, and networks* (pp. 247–285). Aldershot, UK: Ashgate/Dartmouth.

Merton, R. K., & Barber, E. (2006). *The travels and adventures of serendipity: A study in sociological semantics and the sociology of science.* Princeton, NJ: Princeton University Press.

Miller, W. (1958). Lower class culture as a generating milieu of gang delinquency. *Journal of Social Issues, 14,* 5–19.

Minniti, M., & Bygrave, W. (2001). A dynamic model of entrepreneurial learning. *Entrepreneurship Theory and Practice, 25,* 5–16.

Minor, W. W., & Harry, J. (1982). Deterrent and experiential effects in perceptual deterrence research: A replication and extension. *Journal of Research in Crime and Delinquency, 19,* 190–203.

Nagin, D. S., & Pogarsky, G. (2001). Integrating celerity, impulsivity, and extralegal sanction threats into a model of general deterrence: Theory and evidence. *Criminology, 39,* 865–889.

———. (2003). An experimental investigation of deterrence: Cheating, self-serving bias, and impulsivity. *Criminology, 41,* 167–191.

Paternoster, R., & Piquero, A. R. (1995). Reconceptualizing deterrence: An empirical test of personal and vicarious experiences. *Journal of Research in Crime and Delinquency, 32,* 251–286.

Pogarsky, G., & Piquero, A. R. (2004). Studying the reach of deterrence: Can deterrence theory help explain police misconduct? *Journal of Criminal Justice, 32,* 371–386.

Roberts, R. M. (1989). *Serendipity: accidental discoveries in science.* New York: John Wiley & Sons.

Skolnick, J. H. (1966). *Justice without trial: Law enforcement in democratic society.* New York: Wiley.

Sutherland, E. H. (1937). *The professional thief.* Chicago: University of Chicago Press.

Tittle, C. R. (1995). *Control balance.* Boulder, CO: Westview.

Topalli, V. (2005). Criminal expertise and offender decision-making: An experimental analysis of how offenders and non-offenders differentially perceive social stimuli. *British Journal of Criminology, 45,* 269–295.

Topalli, V., & Wright, R. (2004). Dubs, dees, beats, and rims: Carjacking and urban violence. In D. Dabney (Ed.), *Crime Types: A text reader.* Belmont CA: Wadsworth, 149–169.

Tversky, A., & Kahneman, D. (1981). The framing of decisions and the psychology of choice. *Science, 211,* 453–458.

Van Andel, P. (1994). Anatomy of the unsought finding: Serendipity: Origin, history, domains, traditions, appearances, patterns and programmability. *British Journal for the Philosophy of Science, 45,* 631–648.

Wiseman, R. (2003). *The luck factor.* London, UK: Random House.

Wright, R., Brookman, F., & Bennett, T. (2006). The foreground dynamics of street robbery in Britain. *British Journal of Criminology, 46,* 1–15.

Wright, B. R. E., Caspi, A., Moffitt, T. E., & Paternoster, R. (2004). Does the perceived risk of punishment deter criminally prone individuals? Rational choice, self-control, and crime. *Journal of Research in Crime and Delinquency, 41,* 180–213.

Wright, R., & Decker, S. H. (1994). *Burglars on the job.* Boston: Northeastern University Press.

———. (1997). *Armed robbers in action: Stickups and street culture.* Boston: Northeastern University Press.

Zimring, F. E., & Hawkins, G. J. (1973). *Deterrence: The legal threats in crime control.* Chicago: University of Chicago Press.

✍

CHAPTER 11

Accounting for Homicide and Sublethal Violence

Fiona S. Brookman

In this chapter, the author analyzes the excuses and justifications employed by men and women in the United Kingdom when discussing acts of lethal and sublethal violence. The themes discussed in this chapter draw upon data elicited from in-depth semi-structured interviews with 30 violent offenders (24 men and 6 women). Just under a third of these individuals had been convicted of murder or manslaughter. The remainder had been convicted of grievous or actual bodily harm and various forms of violence coupled with armed or street robbery. In exploring the accounts provided by these offenders, the author identifies a diverse range of justifications and excuses for violence and considers how these offender narratives are both linked to and emerge from the underlying tenets and narratives of mainstream society or a violent subculture.

INTRODUCTION AND BACKGROUND

I intended just to beat him up, I certainly didn't intend to kill him, and I certainly didn't think I'd gone that far, you know. I'd punched him and pushed him and he fell over, and then he grabbed hold of my trouser leg and I just shook it, shook that off, and just kicked him a couple of times in the face, and I actually thought that, you know, when he let go I actually thought that was it and walked away, and I thought he'd be okay. The damage was he died of actual inhalation of blood, drowned in his own blood, through the injuries, which were broken cheek bone, broken jaw bone. I think he'd lost a couple of teeth and broke the bridge of his nose; I think, you know, that just caused the bleeding inside his mouth, and I think he choked on that. He threw the first punch. (Steve)

Steve offers an account of the murder of another young man. Within it he makes a number of justifications that draw upon culturally embedded mitigations (such as the lack of intention to harm). He is, in Goffman's terms, undertaking "remedial

Source: Written especially for this volume.

work"—that is, "transforming what could be seen as offensive into what could be seen as acceptable" (Goffman, 1971, p. 139). There are a multitude of ways in which people "manage" their accounts of wrongdoing that are closely linked to the construction and management of social identity. This chapter is concerned with unraveling some of these different linguistic techniques by focusing upon the accounts of men and women who have committed acts of homicide and sublethal violence. First, however, it is necessary to consider some background literature.

In 1968, Scott and Lyman suggested the need to develop the "sociology of talk" and more closely scrutinize the giving and receiving of accounts. They defined an account as "a linguistic device employed whenever an action is subjected to valuative inquiry. . . . A statement made by a social actor to explain unanticipated or untoward behavior." Over the years, there has been a good deal of work by various scholars probing the meanings of offender accounts in relation to a diverse range of crimes, including handling or purchasing stolen goods (Henry, 1976; Henry, 1978), stealing office supplies (Hollinger, 1991), rape (Scully & Marolla, 1984; Scully & Marolla, 2006), murder (Ray & Simons, 1987), violent gun offenses (Progrebin, 2006), shoplifting (Cromwell & Thurman, 2003), snitching (Topalli, 2005), and economic crime by the upper-middle class (Willott, Griffin, & Torrance, 2001).

It has been acknowledged that there are various linguistic techniques that offenders can adopt in accounting for their behavior, and that there are some important and, at times, subtle differences between them. For example, Scott and Lyman (1968) make the distinction between excuses and justifications. Excuses are "accounts in which one admits that the act in question is bad, wrong or inappropriate but denies full responsibility" (p. 47). Justifications, by contrast, are "accounts in which one accepts responsibility for the act in question, but denies the pejorative quality associated with it" (p. 47; see also Henry, 1976, p. 46). Sykes and Matza (1957) draw a distinction between rationalizations and neutralizations, stating: "Justifications are commonly described as rationalizations. They are viewed as following deviant behavior and of protecting the individual from self-blame and the blame of others after the act." In contrast, techniques of neutralization (another form of justification) precede deviant behavior and allow offenders who are otherwise wedded to conventional society to resolve their anticipated law-breaking and avoid anticipated guilt. As they put it, neutralizations "precede deviant behavior and make deviant behavior possible" (Sykes & Matza, 1957, p. 666; see also Mills, 1940).[1]

It has been suggested that whether offenders adopt justifications or excuses depends upon the deviant act in which they are engaged. For example, there is some evidence that violent offenders tend to provide justifications whereas property offenders more often employ excuses (see Maruna & Copes, 2005, p. 19). Other research has suggested that justifications for violence are more often used amongst peers, while excuses are used more often when presenting one's story to outsiders or strangers (Harvey, Weber, & Orbuch, 1990; Toch, 1993).

Academics have questioned the extent to which one can really know or measure whether the accounts provided by offenders are preemptive self-talk motivations (i.e., neutralizations) or after-the-fact rationalizations (Cromwell & Thurman, 2003; Maruna & Copes, 2005). Interestingly, Scott and Lyman (1968) adopted the term neutralization but did *not* take it to mean preemptive self-talk motivation for offending—rather, they used it to mean after-the-fact justification. In fact, recent research suggests that both mechanisms may be operating. That is, offenders may draw upon cultural norms to both account for their behavior retrospectively and inform it in the first instance. For example, Jimerson and Oware (2006, p. 26) point out that street codes[2] may be both prescripts and accounts for behavior. In this chapter, I will not be focusing on this important distinction. Rather, the aim here is simply to present the accounts of violent men and women and consider the different ways in which they excuse and justify their actions. These accounts will then be considered in terms of whether and how they connect to and emerge from the underlying tenets and narratives of mainstream society or a violent subculture.

EXCUSING LETHAL AND SUBLETHAL VIOLENCE

Violent offenders who excused their behavior accepted that it was wrong but nevertheless did not accept full responsibility. These accounts fell into four subgroups: (1) "raised the violent way," (2) "under the influence of alcohol or drugs," (3)" the lesser of two evils," and "it wasn't the 'real' me I elaborate on each of these below.

"Raised the Violent Way": Upbringing and Lifestyle

One way in which offenders can partially excuse their acts of violence is to mark them as symptomatic of an unfortunate background or circumstance. When reflecting upon their recourse to violence, many interviewees made direct links to both their upbringing and a social and cultural background that actively instilled aggressive and violent norms in them. The family and neighborhood in particular were identified as having exposed them to violence. In this way, the men and women located their own violent acts as part of "normal" behavior, while simultaneously recognizing that those from a nonviolent background might not agree. Both Dan and Wilf singled out their fathers as having been instrumental in encouraging them to be violent men:

> Me old man was in the army. It goes right back to my grandparents, all my family have been in the military, strict—'cos you're in the military, it was alright to be aggressive...there's no two ways about it. As I say, all me family have been like it, and unfortunately, my old man, oh, he was an obnoxious git. He used to hit all the family...me especially. He wanted me to be aggressive, obviously he wanted me to be in the army. I think it's through where you grown up, and the area and that. (Dan)

Wilf provided a similar account, suggesting that violence was "drummed into" him while also pointing to the effects of alcohol in removing his fear of violence:

> I was brought up in a sort of a rough background, yeah, it was a rough back-
> ground, and I used the rough pubs, and that was the only life I knew, and it was
> drummed into me from an early age. Now in the beginning, I didn't like violence,
> I used to be very fearful of violence, but alcohol took that away as well, and, um,
> you know, growing up in an area and my father used to say, "If anybody wants to
> get violent with you, or you think there's gonna be violence, put your back against
> the wall and box your ears off" [laughs]. Yeah, I've got a few things to say to me
> dad when I see him. (Wilf)

Simon similarly emphasized the normality of violence in his background and
social environment. In this account, he at least partially shifts responsibility for
his actions from an individual to a subcultural level. Moreover, he makes a clear
distinction between those who may be repulsed by violence as a result of their lack
of socialization within such an environment and those whose lives are embedded
within it. He also alludes to social situations that simply necessitate violence if one
is to survive.

> I think it all depends on what sort of lifestyle you're living from a start. I mean,
> if I lived from when I was born and I never wanted for anything and I was sent
> to proper educated schools, I wouldn't be exposed to violence, so my idea of vio-
> lence would be repulsive, maybe. If I seen someone fighting in the pub, I'd be the
> sort of person to think, "Oh, that's disgusting," but I think that because of the
> kind of life I've lived, I've been exposed to violence anyway, so it's second nature
> to me, it's the norm, violence to me isn't anything that's repulsive, to me it's a nor-
> mal thing. I mean, if you've got someone being aggressive to you, it's no good you
> saying, oh let's sit down and talk about it when the guy's got a knife to your throat
> or something. (Simon)

Several of the women interviewed also called attention to the expectations of violence inherent in the reputational demands of embedded criminality:

> In the area I grew up, my family had quite a reputation for being violent and...I
> felt I had to live up to that and I had something to prove....I had to live up to the
> reputation I built myself. Couldn't let myself be walked over....I couldn't back
> down. (Jane)

Whereas some offenders pointed to living within a culture that condoned and
encouraged violence, others who had not shared such experiences pointed instead
to being drawn into violent crimes by errant peers (who were themselves part of
a violent subculture). Paul made sense of his armed robbery of a shop in these
terms:

> I'd just finished a five-year sentence, like five months and eight days before this
> happened. I had all sorts running through my head at the time, I was well aware
> that I'd, that I would've not have done this on my own sort of back as such. I was
> still working, even though I had developed quite a big habit; all my family were
> aware of my relapse and that I was existing without, without crime, basically, I
> was on some medical intervention from the doctor as well, so I was ticking over,
> but I was very aware that I had been [sighs] coerced. I suppose that I felt very
> angry about allowing myself to be coerced, allowing myself to have my buttons

pushed. I was very silly to say the least, I think stupid's a little bit more accurate. I had all this running through my head when we were driving off from the location, at which point I phoned my mother and informed her that I would probably be going back to prison very soon. (Paul Mika)

In various ways, each of these accounts points to external causes. The men and women see themselves as victims of circumstance and a product of their environment, over which they have had little control. In Goffman's (1961) terms, these men and women adopt "sad tales" of their past to explain their lack of responsibility for their present circumstances. Sandberg (2009) uses the phrase "oppression discourse" to describe how street drug dealers in Oslo justify their criminal behavior (e.g., lack of employment opportunities, racism, and ethnic discrimination). In short, offenders who point to external forces and causes view themselves as being acted upon rather than acting (Cromwell & Thurman, 2003).

"Under the Influence": The Role of Alcohol and Drugs

Another way in which violent offenders commonly deny full responsibly for their actions is to suggest that they were not fully in control of themselves as a result of their use of or addiction to alcohol or drugs. McAndrew and Egerton (1969) suggest that raising people to believe that they are not themselves when drunk allows them to conceive their behavior as an episodic happening, not part of their real identity (cited in Henry, 1976, p. 92). Some offenders linked their violence to impairment from having consumed excess alcohol or drugs or as a result of the physiological effects of withdrawal.

> Fuelled by drink, I suppose. Because I know I would never have done it if I was sober. I know I wouldn't have. I wouldn't. If I was sober it wouldn't have happened. (Paddy)

Paddy mitigates responsibility for committing a violent robbery on the basis of intoxication. In Scott and Lyman's (1968, p. 48) terms, he offers an "appeal to defeasibility" by claiming that his full mental capacity was temporarily voided.

Other inmates linked their violence (typically street robbery) to their need to fund an expensive drug habit.

> Well, drugs, like all my violence all revolved around drugs, like, that's how it become, like, it's only petty; well, I beat him up, you know, chucked him about a little bit, like, and he went to the police and had me for it. . . . I'm not a violent person, no. I don't go round looking for it, you know. (David)
>
> I had a big habit, a really big habit; I would smoke, I could go through like £150 a day, I was bad. I am going to sound really awful, but I am not a bad person, honestly. (Tallulah)

In summary, linking violent offending to intoxication or withdrawal allows offenders to suggest that they were at best partially responsible for their actions, as their "true" self was temporarily suspended. This storyline is one that is sufficiently embedded in mainstream culture to be explicable (if not wholly acceptable) as an excuse.

The Lesser of Two Evils

Some of the interviewees minimized the "badness" of their violence by juxtaposing their particular form of violent offending with other forms that they considered more morally reprehensible. Paul Mika, for example, reasoned that the armed robbery of commercial premises was a more acceptable and "honest" way of securing money than either burglary or street robbery:

> Really, it's the, it's the only crime I've had any major long-term involvement with. It might sound a little bit strange, but I don't think burglary is something I could ever do, because I mean, personally, I would hate to have my stuff rummaged through. It may sound a little twisted logic, but for me, holding somewhere up is almost a little more honest in a strange sort of way, it's, really, that's what I've always done to fund my habit from a certain time onwards. I'm not particularly good at it, it's not a particularly smart thing to do—I should know better, to be perfectly honest, but when push comes to shove and you need the money there and then, that is what I've always resorted to. I know that you can't justify any of it, but in my own head, it's not morally as wrong to go to a place or a shop or a post office and do that than to specifically target an individual on the street. I'm well aware that there's consequences for the people who work in there, and they will feel just as bad as if you'd robbed them on the street. But in my own twisted little way, I suppose it's, it's more justifiable in my head to do it to a business.

He later added:

> I would feel extremely guilty about targeting a specific person or individual and taking what's *theirs,* I suppose. When you do it from a business, it's faceless. Granted, there's a face behind the counter, but you don't actually feel as if you're taking from them. Whereas from a person, it's the other way round, it's specific target of that person....I do know people in here who do that kind of thing, almost as a specialty, they're known as street robbers, they'll sort of prowl little bits of a nearest city to here and just target anybody that looks vulnerable, regardless of whether they look affluent or not. It's not for me, really not my kind of thing at all.

Cromwell and Thurman (2003, p. 546) have observed that shoplifters adopt what they term "justification by comparison" when neutralizing their offending. These shoplifters reason that if they weren't shoplifting, they would be doing something more serious instead: "The gist of the argument is that I may be bad, but I could be worse." Violent offenders adopt a similar excuse by drawing fine distinctions between different kinds of violent crimes and suggesting that some are more serious or damaging than others.

It Wasn't the "Real" Me

Some interviewees explained their violent offending by distancing themselves almost completely from the person "back then." They effectively claimed a new social identity—the person "back then" was simply not the real person either prior to the violent episode or presently (i.e., the person sitting "today" with the researcher). As Henry (1976, p. 92) points out, one can preserve one's self-identity through a process of "normalization"—that is, "describing one's identity as different from that which committed the crime."

Nichola exemplifies this normalization process when discussing her involvement in six armed robberies:

> NICHOLA: Because it was in England, I felt it wasn't real. I would never have dreamed of doing it in Scotland because it would have been real and I would have had family around me....It wasn't real life. It was like I had taken on a role and character and I was playing it out.
>
> INTERVIEWER: When did you start taking on the role?
>
> NICHOLA: When I first met them. I was drinking a lot and out my face, and I had split up with my girlfriend, and I was acting like I was cool, but I wasn't. It was very much his influence. I am my own person and I can't say I didn't enjoy it in the beginning, but now...I can't believe it. I can't believe I was capable for doing these things, but I look back and it's not real—but obviously it is real, and I done it.

Nichola further distances herself from the violent acts by pointing to the negative influence of those with whom she was associating at the time.

Tracey violently assaulted a man who had "grassed"[3] her to the police for theft. At the time she perceived no other options but to pay him back for such disrespect. However, she conceded that the levels of violence she used were unnecessary (he was beaten with a metal bar and kicked in the head for a sustained period until he fell unconscious). She talked about the "monster" in her taking over and later linked her uncontrollable rage to head injuries that she had sustained in a motor vehicle accident. In this way, she distanced her "true" self from the person who committed the vicious assault:

> TRACEY:When you're in the midst of it all, you just, you just, I see red, d'ya know what I mean? I just turn into this monster, this horrible thing, ya know what I mean?
>
> INTERVIEWER: Right, ok, was there any other way that you could sort of pay him back for grassing, rather than beating him up?
>
> TRACEY: Are we talking about now or then?
>
> INTERVIEWER: Back then. Were there any other options?
>
> TRACEY: Well, you don't go round doing stuff like that, but back then, I just, I didn't think like that. I didn't want to think like that. He done something wrong to me, and I weren't letting that lie, do you know what I mean? Not a chance, back then...and I was just ruthless, do you know what I mean?
>
> INTERVIEWER: What would you do now?
>
> TRACEY: I wouldn't go round and do something like that. It scares me now the thought of what I did do, know what I mean—what I done in the past and that. But I had a lot of...that car crash that I were in, I mean, it smashed all my face up and its all metal now, and I were in hospital for an absolute time, and I died loads of times and they had to bring me back on life support machine, and I were lucky I didn't have brain damage, and for months

and months after they were always doing CT scans and whatnot and saying that I were alright, but my mum and everybody noticed a change in me, do you know what I mean, that I had this temper that I couldn't control and everything, do you know what I mean?

INTERVIEWER: You think it changed you?

TRACEY: Yeah. I can't tell you why or how or what, d'ya know what I mean, I don't know, all I know is that I mean, I am that bubbly person again now.

Tracey's story is particularly interesting and layered. On the one hand, she draws upon subculturally approved norms and codes in explaining her recourse to violence to seek revenge. However, in contrasting her former and present self, she seeks to further sanitize her violence by suggesting that injuries sustained during a road traffic accident had changed her (temporarily) into an uncontrolled person—a "monster."

JUSTIFYING HOMICIDE AND SUBLETHAL VIOLENCE

Violent offenders who justified their behavior accepted that they were responsible but denied that their actions were wrong. These accounts fell into five subgroups: (1) self-defense, (2) for the greater good, (3) the deserving victim, (4) violence is all around us, and (5) for the sake of the criminal business. I elaborate on each of these below.

"It Was Him or Me": Self-Defense

One of the ways that violent offenders, particularly those who have taken a life, rationalize the event is to draw upon standard legal mitigation. As Matza (1964, p. 61) states: "The criminal law, more than any other comparable system of norms, acknowledges and states the principled grounds under which any actor may claim exemption." In the United Kingdom, as in many other jurisdictions, the law attempts to distinguish between different categories of homicide according to their apparent seriousness or gravity. For example, a conviction for murder may be reduced to manslaughter if the killing stems from provocation or the killer was suffering from diminished responsibility. Having been embroiled in the legal system, offenders are aware of such mitigations, and many gave accounts that aligned with standard, culturally understood legal defenses. Gavin, for example, drew upon the defense of self-defense:

> The situation that I was in . . . it was either me or him, he pulled a knife out on me, and it was either he stabbed me or, you know . . .

Steve (who we met in the opening quotation) drew upon fairly standard mitigation when recounting the events that led him to murder another man. Specifically, he emphasized his lack of intent, his belief that the injuries were not severe, the fact that he was not the initial aggressor, and his fear for his own safety:

I intended just to beat him up, I certainly didn't intend to kill him, and I certainly didn't think I'd gone that far, you know.... He threw the first punch. He tried to stop me intervening, I tried to push past him, he threw the first punch, and then I, you know, I beat him up. I think we'd all had a lot to drink, and we'd been in the pub for a couple of hours, we'd all had a lot to drink.... Yeah, I think I would have reacted differently if I was sober, I think you're more amicable when you, you know, when you're sober, you're straight-headed. I landed one punch and I think it was several kicks to the face—that was it? I think the whole thing lasted, maybe, I don't know, I'd be surprised if it lasted over a minute. Yeah, I was very, I was very frightened, you know, I had lost my temper and was, you know, did intend on giving him a good hiding, but the chances were that it could have turned the other way, it could have been, you know, it could have been me who got hurt, you know, I was well aware of that. And I think, you know, I mean that in that back of my mind just mentally, you know, just fight a bit harder, you know, to make sure that it wasn't me that was gonna get hurt. I'm quite positive that, well, quite sure in my own mind, that had it have been me on the floor, it would have been me getting kicked and not him, I'm quite certain about that. I thought, you know, as we walked away, he'd probably get up and walk into his house and, you know, wash his face off, swill his face, you know? I really didn't believe that he was that badly injured.

Drawing upon these well-known culturally understood mitigations allows violent offenders to realign themselves with conventional society and, partially at least, remove the stigma associated with damaging labels such as "murderer."

For the Greater Good

Some offenders suggested that their violent acts were excusable because they served an important function that could otherwise not be achieved. In Sykes and Matza's (1957) terms, they "appealed to higher loyalties."

Paul was serving a four-year prison sentence for possession of a firearm. He had used the handgun to threaten five youths in his hometown who he claimed were trying to sell heroin to young children (his own included) in the area.

I just said, don't come around this area trying and sell heroin to kids; you know what I mean, I wasn't just sticking up for my children, I was sticking up for a number of children. To be honest with you, I didn't stop and think and look at the circumstances.... I have done all that now, I could have generated alternative solutions and things like that, you know what I mean, I could have phoned the police, I could have just chased them off with something else other than a gun, but I felt that they still would have still continued. But since I have been locked up, not one, not one of these lads have been around the area offering drugs, so, who am I—I shouldn't have done it, I fully understand it, you know, I shouldn't, what I done was idiotic and stupid, but I helped a lot of kids, do you understand me, I helped a lot of families, basically. I had 150 statements, 150 signatures on a piece of paper when I went to court saying "Look what this man has done, he has stopped heroin coming into our area by these so-called five lads who keep trying to supply kids," you know what I mean?

Paul was of the view that the police were neither willing nor able to deal with the problem, and that ultimately he had successfully resolved a local drug-related problem. Violence was, on this occasion, a necessity, and Paul presented an image of himself as the local hero or savior.

The Deserving Victim

A number of interviewees portrayed their violent offences as less distasteful by painting a picture of the victim as in some way deserving of attack. In this way, they moved away from focusing upon the act to focusing upon the status of the victim. For example, Laura, when discussing her selection of targets to rob, distinguished between elderly innocent victims who ought to be avoided and younger males who flashed their wealth and were therefore "fair game":

> LAURA: There was a garage what we was always looking at, but we never did the garage.
> INTERVIEWER: Why not?
> LAURA: Because the man who runs the garage was really old, could have a heart attack. I think about things like that. I don't think it's fair robbing on old people, but people that walk around with a lot of gold, and quite young, about twenties...

Later in the interview Laura suggested that her preference was to rob men (she had, however, robbed both men and women). What she revealed, nevertheless, was that her choice of target was driven not simply by issues of "deserving" and "undeserving" victims, but also by detection of the offence:

> LAURA: Cause they won't be able to go to the police and say, "Some girl's just robbed me." Especially if they've got a bit of street cred or something. Cause the way he was, the way he dressed, the way he walked, the way he talked. If I was a man and some little girl come up to me and robbed me, I'd be ashamed to go to the police. See what I mean?
> INTERVIEWER: What do you mean by the way he talked, the way he walked?
> LAURA: He walked like a thug and he talked like a thug.... He was probably some kind of drug dealer or something.

Casting the victim as a drug dealer and "thug" rendered this man a deserving victim. In much the same way as Scully and Marolla (2006) found that some rapists would justify their acts by suggesting that "nice girls don't get raped," Laura suggested that decent people do not get violently robbed on the street. Ironically, Laura placed the victim firmly within her own subculture—that is, as a person who is not an innocent member of more conventional society. That she could make such a judgment is perhaps a testament to her connections to both cultures.

Another prominent kind of deserving victim is one who either initiates the recourse to violence (so that the offender feels that he or she is defending him or herself) and/or one who continues to abuse the offender. Vandel reasoned that the levels of violence he enacted upon his victim were justified by the fact that the victim, even once down on the floor and beaten (literally and symbolically), failed to be quiet and continued to issue threats:

> I don't wanna hurt him, I don't, I don't wanna cause him no pain, I don't wanna put him in the hospital, you know what I mean? I just wanted to just, for him, after them three punches, yeah, he should have gone in the lift, yeah? And he should have gone home, and he should have gone to bed, yeah? Or gone to the hospital and got his jaw fixed, but he carried on, he carried on shouting his mouth off saying… "I'm gonna break your jaw, I'm gonna do this, I'm gonna do that." Bearing in mind he's on the floor, man, you know what I mean? He's got blood running down his face and that, he's already lost and he ain't gonna win, you know what I mean? But… he kept coming back, he keep saying… "This, that, the other," you know what I mean? And I just thought, well, if he's gonna be like this, then I'm just gonna deal with it, man, and I did what I did, but I wouldn't do that to every man, you know what I mean?

In various ways, Laura and Vandel adopted the "denial of victim" neutralization (Sykes & Matza, 1957), in that they lessen the impact of their acts of violence by virtue of the characteristics or behavior of the victim.

Violence Is All Around Us

For many of the offenders, their acts of violence could and should not be distinguished from violence that occurred in mainstream society. To condemn their acts would be to condemn governments and others in authority for similar transgressions. Moreover, these men and women were firmly of the view that the violence enacted within mainstream culture was effective and necessary, and that, by extension, so was their own. Clint, for example, articulated this sentiment when comparing his violence to that enacted in the creation of the British Empire:

> Well how was this country built, know what I mean, it was built on robbing the rest of the world, wasn't it? We went over, battering the country, killing them off and then, like, bringing back the wealth to this country. It's the same for every human being, you've got to fight for whatever you believe in. (Clint)

Jeff similarly pointed to aggressive government strategies employed by superpowers to subdue other nation-states (no doubt making comparisons with more recent events in Afghanistan and Libya).

> Look at India with the nuclear bombs and that, I mean, they've been threatened by the Americans and the English all grouping together, sanctions and all of that, and if they don't pull their socks up, then you know we'll act with aggression.

A related justification espoused by some interviewees was that violence was a technique used by those put in place to uphold law and order (e.g., police or prison officers):

> You get a lot in prison as well, where its prison officers attacking you or you attacking them. Why do they attack you? It's the same scenario. They're sat in the office in the segregation unit and you're being a bit funny by saying, "I ain't

> getting out of bed," you know, and the door opens and a blue one's stood there and said, "Get out of your fucking bed now," but unknown, well, you know, really, there's 10 round the corner, and you say, "Ain't getting out of bed," "Get him," SMACK, give you a good hiding, belt you up, throw you in the strip cell. They use the violence the same way. (Jim)

The very people put in place to punish and condemn the violent offenders were themselves seen to be equally guilty of misusing violence. In this way, some of the violent offenders "condemned the condemners" (Cromwell & Thurman, 2003, p. 544).

Other interviewees suggested that the law surrounding violence was flawed in that it apportioned blame to some individuals or circumstances when it ought not to. Luciano had violently assaulted a man who had made "a pass" at his girlfriend and felt at least partially justified in his actions. For him, the moral bind of the law on this issue was, at best, partial.

> I don't go along with the law entirely in saying that, you know, somebody can do that to your girlfriend and, you know,... it's like, you know, one of the lads here now, his house got burgled and he actually caught the burglar in his house like, and he ended up giving the guy an hiding, like, and he come to prison for it.... That's, in my eyes, totally wrong, like so, so that's it, that's what the law says, you know, if you take it into your own hands, then.

By drawing upon the story of another inmate, Luciano further marked his position of opposition to the law.

For the Sake of the (Criminal) Business

Some of the violence enacted by the men and women interviewees occurred within the context of other illegal activities, such as drug dealing. Many of these offenders suggested that violence was a necessary aspect of their business if they were to be successful. Prior research has clearly illustrated the powerful pulls toward violence within such settings. For example, Topalli, Wright, and Fornango (2002, p. 341) identified the need for drug dealers to maintain a "menacing and capable" street reputation in St. Louis, noting, "As drug dealers conduct their trade outside the limits of legal protection, a reputation for formidability represents one of the only mechanisms available to them for deterring victimization." Dan and Paul told similar stories about their involvement in violence connected to middle- to high-level drug dealing:

> Well, like I say, I was into the drugs, only cannabis, but because I was doing cannabis, obviously I was going to meet everyone else doing everything else. And they are not necessarily people that I would want to meet, they're tough people and it is a business to them, big money, and they are tough and they will sort their problems out. You have to act tough to a certain extent, then, so they wouldn't come and give you grief. They'll sit and say, "Well, yeah, he's alright, he knows what he's doing, he can look after himself, fine, the type of man we can do business with." (Dan)

If I had a choice, I would not be using violence. If I could walk away and keep my position, I would. You have to do it. If you don't, what is going to happen to you? At the end of the day, the people I'm connected to, it takes years to get where I am at the top. So I have to do it. I'm ashamed of it, but this is the way it is. I don't force people to take the piss—they choose, they know the score. They have the option. (Paul)

Both Dan and Paul projected self-images of "tough guys" who had succeeded in illegitimate business as a direct result of their willingness and preparedness to adopt violence. They drew upon standard subcultural justifications that are understandable even to those who are not immersed within that subculture.

Accounts that Don't "Fit"

Many of the accounts offered by offenders to explain their violent actions fitted well into the preexisting categories of either excuse or justification (though on occasion, accounts contained elements of both). However, some accounts defied such logical placement. For example, Jane (who had committed an extremely violent and prolonged assault upon a young female with several accomplices) clearly accepted that her actions were wrong, yet offered relatively little in the way of excuses, as the following account illustrates:

JANE: From the beginning, I remember when I hit her, and her eye really came up bad, I just thought, "I have gone too far."

INTERVIEWER: Why didn't you stop then?

JANE: I was frightened she would go to the police. My intention then was to kill her. Do you know what I mean? I just thought, when I hit her and it come out huge, I thought "I'm gonna go back to jail," and I thought, "Right, you can't go now." You know what I mean, "I can't let you go." Punched her in the eye first of all, but then it went on for hours. Do you know what I mean? Shaved her hair off and broke her ribs with a hammer; made her drink bleach. It was quite a big case, do you know what I mean? Yeah. It just went from bad to worse.... We were out of control. I just don't know. I don't know. Obviously she owed me money, but I would never have...things just got out of hand. I think people were showing off in front of people, and she lost her sense of being a person like. I just went overboard. The four of us were, yeah, bigging ourselves up. Loads of things. Shaved her hair off.

INTERVIEWER: Whose idea was that?

JANE: All of ours—it all got mixed up. Made her sniff glue and drink bleach, and my friend hit her with a hammer. My friends had to go a couple of hours later, it was just me and her. They went and I was on my own with her. She was sitting in the chair, and I said just go and get out, and she ran out the back door like.

INTERVIEWER: Why did you then let her go?

JANE: I was on a comedown, like, do you know what I mean? I was left on my own and my baby was upstairs, and I wanted it to end. . . . I had sobered a bit and come down off the drugs, do you know what I mean?

Within this account, Jane clearly takes responsibility for her actions. She identifies herself as the ringleader and provides explanations for her actions that in no way seem to present her in a positive light. For example, she states that she intended to kill the victim in an effort at self-preservation (i.e., to avoid being identified for the assault and imprisoned). She suggests that her actions were unwarranted, and she states that she and her co-offenders went overboard and were showing off and, in detail, describes the violence inflicted on the young victim. There are perhaps a few glimmers of excuse-making. For example, her reference to "coming down" indicates that she was under the influence of alcohol and drugs during the assault, but she never specifically implicates intoxication in the attack.

In short, there will be some violent offenders who neither excuse nor justify their actions. They accept responsibility for acts that they acknowledge are wrong or bad (and for which they may or may not harbor feelings of remorse or guilt). Essentially, these offenders admit that they are guilty as charged.[4]

CONCLUSION

Throughout this paper, I have considered the various ways in which violent offenders in the United Kingdom account for their behavior. In keeping with previous research in this area, a range of justifications and excuses have been identified. At one end of the spectrum are offenders who accept that their violent acts were "wrong" or "bad" but nevertheless offer up accounts that render them somehow only partially blameworthy or responsible. At the other end are those who do not accept that their acts of violence were wrong. Finally, there are some offenders who accept responsibility for both their violent acts and the pejorative nature of those acts.

Accounts do not occur within a social or narrative vacuum. Rather, offenders naturally draw upon accredited subcultural "formula stories" (see Loseke, 2007). Hence, as Scott and Lyman (1968, p. 46) observed: "Accounts are 'situated' according to the statuses of the interactants, and are standardized within cultures so that certain accounts are terminologically stabilized and routinely expected when activity falls outside the domain of expectations." Some of the men and women in this study provided accounts that fitted with the expectations of street codes. Brookman, Copes, & Hochstetler (2011) discovered that violent offenders portray themselves as respectable by situating their past violence within the prescripts of the code of the street. By referencing a larger category, offenders can locate their actions within subculturally approved beliefs and norms and link themselves to histories that transcend individual action. Others excuse their violence by drawing upon mainstream legal discourses such as self-defense.

Whether violent offenders view their own behavior as wrong or offensive depends upon the extent to which they are committed (partially or fully) to mainstream society, from where the majority of judgments about right and wrong, good and bad, emanate. Recently, Topalli (2005) made an important contribution to neutralization theory when he identified how persistent violent street offenders neutralize "being good" rather than "being bad." Topalli's offenders were so committed to a subcultural code that they felt no need to neutralize their law-breaking behavior.

Interestingly, the offenders considered here gave accounts that were informed by both mainstream culture (with its propagation of essentially nonviolent norms[5]) and street or subcultures that approved of, sanctioned, and at times actively encouraged violence as the standard operating procedure. Hence, many of the men and women were, at one and the same time, drawing upon conventional mainstream cultural norms or rules as well as subcultural norms or codes to explain away their actions. This is particularly evident in interviewees' comparisons of their past self (as part of a violent subculture) to their present self (while incarcerated for their deeds). For example, Tracey talked about having no option "back then" but to resort to retaliatory violence in response to disrespect and pointed to her "vicious" former identity. She contrasted that identity to her current self, stating, "Well, you don't go round doing stuff like that.... It scares me now, the thought of what I did do".

The violent offenders depicted in this chapter share much in common with Sandberg's street drug dealers in Oslo in that they adopt more than one kind of language or discourse to rationalize their crimes. Sandberg (2009) described the street drug dealers in his study as "bilingual," in that they drifted between an "oppression" and "gangster" discourse when accounting for their crimes. Through oppression discourse, they justified their offending as a necessity that resulted from their inability to find paid work, as well as racism and discrimination. By contrast, through gangster discourse, they provided presentations of themselves as tough, good fighters who never "snitched"—that is, these men were telling "the code of the street" (Jimerson & Oware, 2006).

This chapter has not made any attempt to compare the accounts of the violent individuals. However, there are likely to be important differences in the ways that offenders within the broad category of "violent offender" make sense of and justify their actions. For example, one's identity is inextricably bound up with one's sociodemographic status (i.e., along dimensions such as gender, age, race, and social class). For example, Willott, Griffin, & Torrance (2001, p. 453) found that upper-middle-class economic offenders described themselves as being "trapped" into certain expectations associated with their high social standing (e.g., responsibilities to family, employees, and the profession). In a similar though reversed manner, many of the violent offenders in the current study essentially described themselves as trapped within a subculture with embedded expectations of violence when affronted or challenged (Anderson, 1999). Future research might pay particular attention to these sorts of differences.

On a related note, one might expect some criminal labels to be much more damaging than others (e.g., sex offender or "dangerous" offender; see Green, South, & Smith, 2006). If this is true, might different categories of offender adopt different kinds of excuses or justifications? Of course, the extent to which any label is damaging depends upon one's acceptance of the moral bind of the law in the first instance. These issues merit further exploration.

Finally, longitudinal follow-up research with offenders may help to further our understanding of the contingent nature of accounts and identity as we revisit individuals through their life course and document their evolving identities and narratives. When, how, and why might these individuals change?

I end with the thoughts of Lee, an armed robber who also had convictions for assaulting police officers and street fights. Lee's comments, made toward the end of the interview, present a picture of violent crime as somehow positive in terms of helping society to evolve:

> Y'know, if you didn't have crime, you wouldn't have police forces, you wouldn't have prisons—y'know, it's bizarre, really, if you think about it. Suppose the only way the universe evolves sometimes is when something bad has happened. (Lee)

Lee's position is not dissimilar to Durkheim's (1985) sentiments in his classic work on the functions of crime. For Durkheim, crime is "bound up with the fundamental conditions of all social life and by that very fact it is useful, because these conditions of which it is a part are themselves indispensable to the normal evolution of morality and law" (Durkheim, 1985, p. 70).

What better way to rationalize crime than to understand it as serving a (positive) function within society?

NOTES

1. Sykes and Matza (1957) describe five "techniques of neutralization": denial of responsibility, denial of injury, denial of victims, condemnation of condemners, and appeal to higher loyalties. Since then, additional neutralization techniques have been identified by other researchers, such as the defence of necessity (Klockars, 1974; Minor, 1981; Coleman, 1988), justification by comparison (Cromwell & Thurman, 2003), and techniques of risk denial (Peretti-Watel, 2003).

2. As described in Anderson's (1999, 33) study of violence in Philadelphia, street codes are "a set of informal rules governing interpersonal public behavior, particularly violence. The rules prescribe both proper comportment and the proper way to respond if challenged. They regulate the use of violence and so supply a rationale allowing those inclined to aggression to precipitate violent encounters in an approved way." Anderson (1999) contends that the code of the street evolved from street culture, and that it rests on assumptions about respect and deference and to whom one should grant it. The major requirements of street codes are that people challenge disrespect and that some affronts require substantial and decisive violence.

3. "Grassing" is a term used in the United Kingdom to refer to passing information to the police about others' criminal activities. It is synonymous with the terms "snitching" and "ratting" that are more often used in the United States.

4. Thanks to Pete Gregory for initially pointing out that some of the offenders in this study were simply stating that they did it, that it was wrong, and "that was that" (i.e., they felt no need to offer any kind of exculpatory account or justify their acts). There is a potential fourth category of account in which offenders deny responsibility (I didn't do it) and also deny that the offense in question is wrong (if I had done this, it wouldn't be wrong). There were no such cases of this account in the current sample.

5. The socially constructed nature of violence is such that certain categories of violence (notably corporate and state violence) are not perceived or punished as "real crimes," despite the greater harm that is often caused by such actions. For example, the International Labour Organization estimated that, at a bare minimum, 2.2 million workers die across the globe each year through work-related "accidents" and diseases (International Labour Organization, 2005, p. 1). This translates to more than 5,000 work-related deaths every day and comprises the greatest proportion of global violence-related deaths (see World Health Organization, 2002; Brookman & Robinson, forthcoming).

REFERENCES

Anderson, E. (1999). *Code of the street: Decency, violence, and the moral life of the inner city.* New York: W. W. Norton.

Brookman, F., Copes, H., & Hochstetler, A. (2011). Street codes as formula stories: How inmates recount violence. *Journal of Contemporary Ethnography, 40*(4), **397–424.**

Brookman, F., & Robinson, A. (forthcoming). Violent crime. In M. Maguire, R. M. Morgan, & R. Reiner (Eds.), *The Oxford handbook of criminology,* (5th ed.). Oxford: Oxford University Press.

Coleman, J. W. (1988). *Criminal elite: Understanding white collar crime.* New York: St. Martin's Press.

Cromwell, P., & Thurman, Q. (2003). "The devil made me do it": Use of neutralizations by shoplifters. *Deviant Behavior, 24,* 535–550.

Durkheim, E. (1985). *The rules of sociological method,* trans. S. A. Solovay & J. H. Mueller, ed. G. E. G. Caitlin. New York: Free Press.

Goffman, E. (1961). *Asylums: Essays on the social situation of mental patients and other inmates.* London: Pelican.

——. (1971). *Relations in public.* Harmondsworth: Penguin.

Green, G., South, N., & Smith, R. (2006). "They say that you are a danger but you are not": Representations and construction of the moral self in narratives of "dangerous individuals." *Deviant Behavior, 27,* 299–328.

Harvey, J. H., Weber, A. L., & Orbuch, T. L. (1990). *Interpersonal accounts: A social psychological perspective.* Cambridge: Blackwell.

Henry, S. (1976). Fencing with accounts: The language of moral bridging. *British Journal of Law and Society, 3,* 91–100.

——. (1978). *The hidden economy.* Oxford: Martin Robertson.

Hollinger, R. (1991). Neutralizing in the workplace: An empirical analysis of property theft and production deviance. *Deviant Behavior, 12,* 169–202.

International Labour Organization. (2005). *World day for safety and health at work 2005: A background paper.* Geneva: International Labour Office.

Jimerson, J. B., & Oware, M. K. (2006). Telling the code: An ethnomethodological ethnography. *Journal of Contemporary Ethnography, 35,* 24–50.

Klockars, C. B. (1974). *The professional fence.* New York: Free Press.

Loseke, D. (2007). The study of identity as cultural, institutional, organizational, and personal narratives: Theoretical and empirical integrations. *Sociological Quarterly, 48,* 661–688.

McAndrew, C., & Egerton, R. (1969). *Drunken comportment: A social explanation.* Chicago: Aldine.

Maruna, S., & Copes, H. (2005). What have we learned from five decades of neutralization research? *Crime and Justice: A Review of Research, 32,* 221–320.

Matza, D. (1964). *Delinquency and drift.* New York: Wiley.

Mills, C. W. (1940). Situated actions and vocabularies of motive. *American Sociological Review, 5,* 904–913.

Minor, W. T. (1981). Techniques of neutralization: A reconceptualization and empirical examination. *Journal of Research in Crime and Delinquency, 18,* 295–318.

Peretti-Watel, P. (2003). Neutralization theory and the denial of risk: Some evidence from cannabis use among French adolescents. *British Journal of Sociology, 54*(1), 21–42.

Progrebin, M. (2006). Retrospective accounts of violent events by gun offenders. *Deviant Behavior, 27*(4), 479–501.

Ray, M. C., & Simons, R. L. (1987). Convicted murderers' accounts of their crimes: A study of homicide in small communities. *Symbolic Interaction, 10*(1), 57–70.

Sandberg, S. (2009). Gangster, victim or both? The interdiscursive construction of sameness and difference in self-presentations. *British Journal of Sociology, 60*(3), 523–542.

Scott, M. B., & Lyman, S. M. (1968). Accounts. *American Sociological Review, 33,* 46–61.

Scully, D., & Marolla, J. (1984). Rape and psychiatric vocabularies of motive: Alternative perspectives. In A. W. Burgess (Ed.), *Handbook on rape and sexual assault.* New York: Garland Press, 150–158.

———. (1999). Convicted rapists' vocabulary of motive: Excuses and justifications. In P. Cromwell (Ed.), *In their own words: Criminals on crime.* Los Angeles: Roxbury, 137–146.

Sykes, G., & Matza, D. (1957). Techniques of neutralization: A theory of delinquency. *American Sociological Review, 22,* 664–670.

Toch, H. (1993). Good violence and bad violence: Self-presentations of aggressors through accounts and war stories. In R. B. Felson & J. T. Tedeschi (Eds.), *Aggression and violence: Social interactionist perspectives.* Washington, DC: American Psychological Association.

Topalli, V. (2005). When being good is bad: An expansion of neutralization theory. *Criminology, 43*(3), 797–835.

Topalli, V., Wright, R., & Fornango, R. (2002). Drug dealers, robbery and retaliation. *British Journal of Criminology, 42,* 337–351.

Willott, S., Griffin, C., & Torrance, M. (2001). Snakes and ladders: Upper middle class male offenders talk about economic crime. *Criminology, 39,* 441–467.

World Health Organization. (2002). *World report on violence and health.* Geneva: Author.

SECTION V

⤳

Occupational
White-Collar Crime

Section V examines occupational/white-collar crime. The term *occupational crime* refers to crimes committed through opportunities created in the course of a legal occupation. In the past, the label *white-collar crime* almost always connoted crimes committed by the rich and powerful. Today, most criminologists have broadened the term to refer to crimes committed by persons in a wide range of situations. The focus today is on the nature of the crime and not the person committing it, thus the term *occupational crime*.

Recall the recent headlines in newspapers everywhere that read something like this: "Madoff Sentenced to 150 Years in Federal Prison for Investment Scandal." Bernard Madoff, founder of the Bernard L. Madoff Investment Securities, Inc., a Wall Street–affiliated investment firm, was recently sentenced to federal prison for one of the largest investment scandals in recent history. He pled guilty to numerous charges that stemmed from an investment fraud that prosecutors estimate to be over $50 billion.

Occupational/white-collar crimes are not victimless crimes. Not every white-collar crime results in the incredible dollar loss of the Madoff scandal, but nevertheless, victims suffer both financially and emotionally. These crimes arguably result in more harm in terms of dollar loss and emotional turmoil than street crime, which almost always receives the bulk of media attention. White-collar offenders can skillfully carry out crimes with the potential to destroy companies and devastate families. A single white-collar criminal can wipe out a victim's life savings or cost investors billions of dollars. Fraud schemes represent some of the most sophisticated of these crimes. While white-collar crime is nonviolent, the effects of these financially motivated crimes can be just as devastating.

Much of the research reported in this book tends to support the idea that many offenders accept responsibility for their crimes. However, the most consistent theme in the following articles on occupational crime is that these offenders concoct elaborate justifications, excuses, and rationalizations to avoid accepting responsibility for their criminal behavior. Perhaps that is because the primary identity of most of these offenders is noncriminal. They are health care workers, lawyers, bankers, stockbrokers, and so on. For these people to conceive of themselves as criminals is difficult, if not impossible.

In Chapter 12, "Crime on the Line: Telemarketing and the Changing Nature of Professional Crime," Neal Shover, Glenn S. Coffey, and Dick Hobbs examine the world of telemarketing fraud. In perhaps one of the most insightful studies of telemarketing offenders to date, Shover and his associates interviewed 47 criminal telemarketers. The authors found that unlike their fellow thieves, telemarketing criminals are disproportionately drawn from the middle class. They are drawn to the business of telemarketing crime because they find the work attractive and rewarding. They are also drawn to the lifestyle and the income it provides. The authors note that their subjects, like those who engage in "street crimes," pursue a hedonistic lifestyle featuring alcohol, drugs, and conspicuous consumption.

In Chapter 13, "Drugged Druggists: The Convergence of Two Criminal Career Trajectories," Dean A. Dabney and Richard C. Hollinger take a fascinating look at the paths of entry into prescription drug abuse by pharmacists. They conducted interviews with 50 recovering drug-addicted pharmacists in order to describe and construct meaning for their onset of and progression into illicit pharmaceutical drug abuse. The authors discovered that pharmacists had two distinct paths of entry into drug use. One group, which they named "recreational abusers," began using prescription drugs for their euphoric effects. The other group, identified as "therapeutic self-medicators," began using prescription drugs much later in their careers for primarily medicinal reasons. What is especially salient in Dabney and Hollinger's study is that once both groups became addicted, the distinguishing characteristics between the two groups disappeared. This, according to the authors, reveals a "dynamic convergence into a single pattern for the mature deviant." Thus, the authors argue that their findings suggest that previous scholarship in this area may have falsely assumed the discovery of multiple static types of offenders, when it may have been that they were really observing a single criminal career at different points along its dynamic trajectory.

In Chapter 14, "Denying the Guilty Mind: Accounting for Involvement in White-Collar Crime," Michael L. Benson explains how individuals convicted of occupationally related crimes attempt to avoid the stigma of criminality by denying criminal intent. His study is based on interviews of 30 convicted white-collar offenders. The offenders included those who had been convicted of securities and exchange fraud, antitrust violations, embezzlement, false claims, and tax evasion. Benson's research identifies a process that is perceived by white-collar offenders as "a long and drawn-out degradation ceremony." In this ceremonial process, the prosecutor serves as the chief denouncer who in turn calls on the offender's family, friends, and associates to serve as witnesses. Consequently, the offender attempts to diminish the impact of the degradation ceremony and thus prevent becoming a "publicly valid label." Benson's research goes a long way toward adding meaning to how white-collar criminals construct their criminality, and, perhaps more importantly, how they attempt to neutralize and resolve the degradation ceremony that transforms their reputations from respected citizen to criminal.

The studies presented in this section are somewhat unusual in that ethnographic research of crime "in the suites" is much more difficult to accomplish than studies of crime "in the streets." Potential subjects are less likely to talk with researchers and are not as easily approached. Thus, the pool of field studies of so-called white-collar crime is small; however, the papers included here are excellent examples of what can be accomplished with a difficult population.

CHAPTER 12

⚡

Crime on the Line: Telemarketing and the Changing Nature of Professional Crime

Neal Shover, Glenn S. Coffey, and Dick Hobbs

Although it has become an important part of the legitimate economy, criminals also have been quick to exploit the opportunities presented by telemarketing. Although it was nearly unheard of until recent decades, few adults today are unfamiliar with telemarketing fraud. There are countless variations on the basic scheme, but typically a consumer receives a phone call from a high-pressure salesperson who solicits funds or sells products based on untrue assertions or enticing claims. Callers offer an enormous variety of products and services and often use names that sound similar to bona fide charities or reputable organizations. Goods or services either are not delivered at all, or else they are substantially inferior to what was promised. Telemarketing fraud touches the lives of many citizens, but the criminological consequences of this development are poorly charted. In this chapter, the authors examine offenders who have stepped forward to exploit these new opportunities. Drawing from interviews with 47 criminal telemarketers, the authors present a picture and interpretation of them, their pursuits, and their lifestyles. As vocational predators, they share several important characteristics with the professional thieves sketched by earlier generations of investigators. Like the latter, they pursue a hedonistic lifestyle featuring illicit drugs and conspicuous consumption and acquire and employ an ideology of legitimation and defense that insulates them from moral rejection. Unlike professional thieves, however, telemarketing criminals disproportionately are drawn from middle-class, entrepreneurial backgrounds. They are markedly individualistic in their dealings with one another and with law enforcement. Finally, their work organizations are more permanent and conventional in outward appearance than the criminal organizations created by blue-collar offenders, which were grounded in the culture of the industrial proletariat.

Source: Shover, N., Coffey, G. S., & Hobbs, D. (2003). Crime on the line: Telemarketing and the changing nature of professional crime. *British Journal of Criminology, 43*(3), 489–505.

The findings show how the backgrounds and pursuits of vocational predators reflect the qualities and challenges of contemporary lucrative criminal opportunities. Like the markets that they seek to manipulate and plunder, the enacted environments of professional criminals embrace infinite variations and are largely indistinguishable from the arenas that capacitate legitimate entrepreneurial pursuits.

W riting at the dawn of the twentieth century, E. A. Ross (1907, p. 3) was one of the first sociologists to call attention to the fact that crime "changes its quality as society develops." Ross focused specifically on growing social and economic interdependence and the variety of ways this permits both exploitation of trust and the commission of crime at a distance from victims. The transformative social and economic changes he noted only gained speed as the century progressed. In the United States and other Western nations, the middle decades of the century saw the emergence or the expansion of state policies and corporate practices with enormous criminological significance. These included a fundamental shift in the state's public welfare functions, which had the effect of expanding programs and subsidies for citizens across the income spectrum. One measure of this is the fact that by 1992, 51.7% of American families received some form of federal payments, ranging from Social Security, Medicare, and military retirement benefits to agricultural subsidies (Samuelson, 1995, p. 158).

In addition, the years following World War II witnessed a rapid growth of the domestic economy, which made available goods that either were unknown or were unattainable by most citizens just a decade earlier. Houses, automobiles, refrigerators, television sets, and a host of other commodities now were within the reach of a growing segment of the population. The disposable income available to the new owners of these commodities allowed them also to purchase the new comprehensive insurance policies offered by insurance underwriters. Increasingly, the middle-class family now was insured against not only major hazards to life, home, and business, but also loss of or damage to household items (Clarke, 1990).

As the century drew to a close, there were fundamental changes also in the structure and dynamics of economic relationships and in communications technology (Adler, 1992; Lash & Urry, 1994). Most important, widespread use of telecommunications (Batty & Barr, 1994; Turkle, 1995), electronic financial transactions, and consumer credit (Tickell, 1996) presaged a depersonalized, cashless economy. Electronic financial transfers among banks and businesses, automatic teller machines (Hirschhorn, 1985), and home banking increasingly are used across the globe (Silverstone, 1991). In the new world of personal computers and virtual identities, individuals and organizations conduct business with remote others whose credentials and intentions cannot be easily determined.

The net result of these political and economic developments is a cornucopia of new criminal opportunities (Grabosky, Smith, & Dempsey, 2001; Taylor, 1999). Federally funded health care programs, for example, have given physicians and hospitals access to new pools of tax revenue for which oversight is so weak that it has been called a "license to steal" (Sparrow, 1996). The growth of health insurance fraud, therefore, can be seen as "emblematic of the emerging forms of...crime that reflect the changing economy of the late twentieth century" (Tillman, 1998, p. 197). The new criminal opportunities extend far beyond health care, however.

The changing landscape of criminal opportunities is strikingly apparent in crimes of fraud. Fraud is committed when misrepresentation or deception is used to secure unfair or unlawful gain, typically by perpetrators who create and exploit the appearance of a routine transaction. Fraud violates trust, it is nonconfrontational, and it can be carried out over long distances. In organizational complexity and reach, it ranges from itinerant vinyl siding scamsters to international banking crimes that can destabilize national economies. The number of Americans victimized by it is large and substantially exceeds the number victimized by serious street crime (Rebovich et al., 2000; Titus, 2001). A 1991 survey of U.S. households found that compared to crimes of burglary, robbery, assault, and theft, fraud "appears to be very common" (Titus, Heinzelmann, & Boyle, 1995, p. 65). Although a number of methodological shortcomings limit confidence in the findings of previous studies of fraud victimization, there seems little doubt that it is an increasingly commonplace crime.

TELEMARKETING AND FRAUD

The rapid growth of telemarketing is one of several consequential changes in the nature of economic relationships in recent decades. In 2000, telemarketing sales accounted for $611.7 billion in revenue in the United States, an increase of 167% over comparable sales for 1995. Total annual sales from telephone marketing are expected to reach $939.5 billion by the year 2005 (Direct Marketing Association, 2001). The reasons for the growth of telemarketing are understood easily in context of the "general acceleration of everyday life, characterized by increasingly complicated personal and domestic timetables" (Taylor, 1999, p. 45). The daily schedule no longer permits either the pace or the style of shopping that were commonplace a few decades ago, and the need to coordinate personal schedules and to economize on time now drives many household activities. In the search for convenience, telemarketing sales have gained in popularity.

But although it has become an important part of the legitimate economy, criminals also have been quick to exploit the opportunities presented by telemarketing. Although it was nearly unheard of until recent decades, few adults today are unfamiliar with telemarketing fraud. There are countless variations on the basic scheme, but typically a consumer receives a phone call from a high-pressure salesperson who solicits funds or sells products based on untrue assertions or enticing claims. Callers offer an enormous variety of products and services, and often they use names that sound similar to bona fide charities or reputable organizations (U.S. Senate, 1993). Goods or services either are not delivered at all, or they are substantially inferior to what was promised. Telemarketing fraud touches the lives of many citizens. A 1992 poll of a national sample of Americans showed that 2% of respondents had been victimized in the preceding six months (Harris, 1992).

FINDINGS

Of all who begin employment in criminal telemarketing, some quickly discover it is not their cup of tea; they dislike it or they do not perform well. Others find the work attractive and rewarding but see it only as a means to other life and career goals. Most, therefore, pursue it only temporarily. Others, however, discover they are good at fraudulent telephone sales, and they are drawn to the income and the lifestyle it can provide. On average, the members of our interview sample were employed in these endeavors for 8.25 years. Their ages when interviewed range from 26 to 69, with a mean of 42.4 years. Their ranks include 38 white males, 3 African American males, and 6 white females. Nearly all have been married at least once, and most have children.

Organization and Routine

Like its legitimate forms, criminal telemarketing is a productive enterprise that requires the coordinated efforts of two or more individuals. To work in it, therefore, is to work in an organizational setting (Francis, 1988; Schulte, 1995; Stevenson, 2000). The size of criminal telemarketing organizations can vary substantially. Some are very small, consisting of only two or three persons, but others are considerably larger (see, e.g., *Atlanta Journal-Constitution*, 2000). Their permanence and mobility vary also, ranging from those that operate and remain in one locale for a year or more to others that may set up and operate for only a few weeks before moving on. These "rip and tear" operators count on the fact that up to six months' time may pass before law enforcement agencies become aware of and target them. "Boiler rooms," operations featuring extensive telephone banks and large numbers of sales agents, have become less common in the United States in recent years, largely because of the law-enforcement interest they attract. There is reason to believe, however, that criminal telemarketers increasingly are locating them in countries with weak laws and oversight and operating across international borders (see, e.g., Australian Broadcasting Corporation, 2001).

Larger telemarketing operations commonly take on the characteristics and dynamics of formal organizations; they are hierarchical, with a division of labor, graduated pay, and advancement opportunities. Established by individuals with previous experience in fraudulent sales, they generally employ commissioned sales agents to call potential customers, to make the initial pitch, and to weed out the cautious and the steadfastly disinterested. We took steps to ensure that our offender interview sample included persons who formerly held a variety of positions in criminal telemarketing firms. It includes 22 owners, eight managers, and 17 sales agents.

Experienced telemarketers generally do not call individuals randomly but work instead from "lead lists" (also known as "mooch lists"). These are purchased from any of dozens of businesses that compile and sell information on consumer behavior and expressed preferences. Individuals whose names appear on lead lists typically are distinguished by past demonstrated interest or participation in promotions of one kind or another. When a person is contacted by telephone, the sales agent generally works from a script. Scripts are written materials that lay out both successful sales approaches and responses to whatever reception sales agents meet with from those they reach by phone. Promising contacts are turned over to a "closer" a more experienced and better paid sales agent. "Freeloaders" are the most effective closers; much like account executives in legitimate businesses, they maintain contacts with individuals who previously sent money to the company (i.e., "purchased" from it) in hopes of persuading them to send more. As one subject told us:

> I had it so perfected that I could get these customers to buy again....I made sure they were happy so I could sell them again. It didn't do me—I didn't want the one time, I didn't want the two-timer. I wanted to sell these people 10 times.

The organization of larger telemarketing firms and the routine employees follow when handling promising calls explains why those who "buy" from them typically report contact with multiple "salespersons" (American Association of Retired Persons, 1996).

The products and services offered by criminal telemarketers span a wide gamut. In one scam, subjects identified and located unaware owners of vacant property, led them to believe that buyers for the property could be found easily, and then charged high fees to advertise it. Other schemes we encountered included collection for charities, drug education programs, and sale of "private" stocks. One subject sold inexpensive gemstones with fraudulent certificates of grossly inflated value and authenticity. The stones were sealed in display cases such that purchasers would have difficulty getting them appraised, particularly since they were told that if they broke the seal, the value of the stones would decrease and the certificate of authenticity would become invalid. "Private stocks" by definition are not listed or traded on a stock exchange, but telemarketers are able to entice investors with smooth talk and promising prospectives. Dependent on their salesmen for market reports, those who purchase soon discover that the nonexistent stocks take a nosedive, and they lose their investments. A high proportion of the companies represented by our interview subjects promised that those who purchased products from them were odds-on winners of a prize soon to be awarded once other matters were settled. Typically, this required the customers to pay fees of one kind or another. Some of our subjects solicited money for nonexistent charities or legitimate organizations they did not represent. In the products they sell, criminal telemarketers clearly are limited only by the human imagination.

Backgrounds and Careers

A substantial body of research into the lives and careers of street criminals has shown that many are products of disadvantaged and disorderly parental homes.

We were interested in determining if the homes in which our subjects were reared reveal similar or functionally equivalent criminogenic characteristics. They do not. Overwhelmingly, the members of our sample describe their parents as conventional and hardworking and family financial circumstances as secure, if not comfortable. Their parental families were traditional in nature, with the father providing the main source of income. Nevertheless, one-half of the mothers also were employed outside the home. Although the fathers' reported occupations ranged from machinist to owner of a chain of retail stores, 32 were business owners or held managerial positions. A substantial proportion of our subjects was exposed to and acquired entrepreneurial perspectives and skills while young. Business ownership appealed to many of them:

> You're always pursuing more money, most of us are. We're raised that way, we are in this country. And that's the way I was raised. But I also wanted to do my own thing. I wanted to be in business for myself, I wanted the freedom that came with that.

Clearly, telemarketing criminals are not drawn from the demographic pools or locales that stock and replenish the ranks of street criminals. Although we questioned them at length about their early and adolescent years, their responses reveal little that distinguishes them from others of similar age and class background. Certainly, the disadvantages and pathologies commonplace in the early lives of most street criminals are in scant evidence here.

If our subjects' early years reveal few clues to their later criminality, there also are few signs that they distinguished themselves in conventional ways. Their educational careers, for example, are unremarkable; eight dropped out of high school, although most graduated. Twenty-one attended college, but on average they invested only two years in the quest for a degree. Five claimed a baccalaureate degree. When invited to reflect on how they differ from their siblings or peers, many reported they were aware of an interest in money from an early age. One subject told us:

> I had certain goals when I was a teenager, you know. And I had a picture of a Mercedes convertible on my bedroom mirror for years. You know, I do have a major addiction, and I don't think I'll ever lose it. And I don't think there's any classes [treatment] for it. And it's money, it's Ben Franklin.

He and others like him were aware also that there are ways of earning a good income that do not require hard work and subordination to others.

Another subject said:

> You know, I was, I've never been a firm believer [that] you got to work for a company for 30 years and get a retirement. Like my dad thinks. I'm all about going out [and] making that million and doing it, doing it very easily. And there's a lot of ways to do it.

Typically, they began working for pay while young and maintained employment throughout their adolescent years.

None of our subjects said that as children they aspired to a career in telemarketing, either legitimate or criminal. Some had previous sales experience before beginning the work, but most did not. Their introduction to it was both fortuitous and fateful; while still in high school or, more commonly, while in college, they either responded to attractive ads in the newspaper or were recruited by friends or acquaintances who boasted about the amount of money they were making.

> [A former acquaintance]...looked me up, found me and said, "You gotta come out here....We're gonna make a ton of money." I went out for three weeks—left my wife back home. And I got on the phones, and I was making a thousand dollars a week. I'm like, "Oh, my God, Jenni, pack the stuff, we're going to Arizona."...He was like, "Man, you're, you're a pro at this shit." And I just, I don't know what it was. I was number one....I don't know, I loved it.

The influence of others is remarkably similar to what is known about the criminal careers of street criminals, particularly those who go on to pursue crime with a high degree of skill and success (Hobbs, 1995, ch. 2; Winlow, 2001, pp. 66–86).

For our subjects, many of whom were foundering on conventional paths, criminal telemarketing was a godsend; it came along at a time when they needed to show that they could make something of themselves. In the words of one of them, it was "a salvation to me as a means of income. And being able to actually accomplish something without an education." Criminal telemarketing was the reason some reported for dropping out of college:

> [It] was just something I picked up as a part time job, when I was 16....When I was in college, my second year in college, [fellow students] were talking about finishing their four years of college and making $28,000 or $30,000 a year. And I was making $1,000 a week part time, you know....And I just couldn't see doing it. I mean, I wound up, after the end of my second year of college, I never went back. I was making too much money. It just seemed so easy.

New recruits generally start as sales agents, although most of our subjects later worked also as closers and reloaders. Employment mobility is common; individuals move from one firm to another, with some eventually taking managerial positions (Doocy et al., 2001).

After gaining experience, former managers told us, they were confident they knew enough about the business to strike out on their own. They did so expecting to increase their income substantially. As one put it:

> In my mind I believed I was smarter than the owners of these other companies that were making millions of dollars. And I just said, "I can do this on my own."

Typically, defectors lure productive personnel from their current employer with promises of more money, and on the way out, they are not above plundering the business's files and lead lists:

> I downloaded every lead in his file. I took it all. I opened up...my own office, took all those people, and said, "Now, watch me."

Based in part on the widely shared assumption that the market is never saturated, they generally open a company based on similar products and sales approaches.

What about the criminal histories of fraudulent telemarketers? Information elicited in the interviews and a review of information contained in presentence investigation reports shows that 13 of our subjects had previous criminal records, seven for minor offenses (e.g., petty theft and possession of marijuana) and six for felonies. Of the latter, three were convicted previously of telemarketing offenses. Clearly, many of our subjects are not one-time or accidental violators; they have histories of multiple arrests and convictions. Others have reported similar findings. Thirty percent of 162 sales agents employed by a California-based fraudulent telemarketing firm, for example, had records of at least one criminal offense, and another 16.4% had records of alcohol or drug offenses (Doocy et al., 2001). For members of our sample who have previous arrests, the age of onset for criminal activity is considerably higher than for street criminals. Our data do show persuasively, however, that many appear to have recurrent trouble with the law, and, like street criminals, they are persistent users of alcohol and other drugs. This picture is confirmed also by information contained in their presentence reports.

Attractions and Lifestyles

Overwhelmingly, our subjects told us they got into and persisted at telemarketing for "the money." How well does it pay? Only one subject reported earning less than $1,000 weekly, and most said their annual earnings were in the range of $100,000 to $250,000. Five told us their annual earnings exceeded $1 million. The fact that they can make money quickly and do so without incurring restrictive responsibilities adds to the attractiveness of the work. They find appealing both the flexible hours and the fact that it requires neither extensive training nor advanced education. Few employers impose rigid rules or strictures; generally, there are neither dress codes nor uniforms. The work can be done in shorts and a tee shirt (Doocy et al., 2001).

As important as the income it yields and the casual approach to employment it permits, criminal telemarketing appeals to many who persist at it for reasons of career and identity. Despite class and parental expectations, most of our subjects had not previously settled upon promising or rewarding occupations. Asked what he "liked about telemarketing" one subject's reply was typical: "Well, obviously, it was the money." Immediately, however, he added, "It gave me a career, [and] to me it was my salvation." As with him, criminal telemarketing enables others to own their own business despite their unimpressive educational background, their limited credentials, and the absence of venture capital. As president of their own corporation, telemarketing provides both outward respectability and an income sufficient to maintain the good life.

Other aspects of the work are attractive as well. Its interpersonal and psychological challenge, for example,

[It] has strong appeal to many salespersons. The ability to impose one's will upon another person—and to achieve a measurable financial reward for doing so—is highlighted in many of the reports of illegal telemarketing practices.... Enforcement officials told us that sellers often have mirrors in the cubicles in which they work. They are told to look into the mirror and see the face of a hot shot salesperson. Sometimes there will be a motto on the wall, such as: "Each No gets me closer to the Yes I want." Boiler room owners and managers...may put large bills on a bulletin board and say that the next sale or the highest total for the day will qualify for this extra reward. Often the sales people have to stand up when they consummate a transaction, so that the boss can note them and they can take pleasure in the achievement. (Doocy et al., 2001, p. 17)

Characteristically, our subjects believe they are outstanding salespersons; they are supremely confident of their ability to sell over the telephone despite resistance from those they contact. Doing so successfully is a high. One subject told us:

You could be selling a $10,000 ticket, you could be selling a $49.95 ticket. And it's the same principle, it's the same rules. It's the same game. I like to win. I like to win in all the games I play, you know. And the money is a reason to be there, and a reason to have that job. But winning is what I want to do. I want to beat everybody else in the office. I want to beat that person I am talking to on the phone.

His remarks were echoed by others:

[I] sold the first person I ever talked to on the phone. And it was just like that first shot of heroin, you know. I'm not a heroin addict....I've only done heroin a couple of times. But it was amazing. It was like, "I can't believe I just did this!" It was incredible. It was never about the money after that....Yeah, it was about the money initially, but when I realized that I could do this every day, it was no longer about the money. It was about the competition, you know. I wanted to be the best salesman, and I want to make the most money that day. And then it became just the sale. It wasn't the money. I didn't even add the figures in my head anymore. It was just whether or not I can turn this person around, you know, walk him down that mutual path of agreement, you know. That was exciting to me. It was power, you know; I can make people do what I wanted them to do. And they would do it.

It was the money, but it was [also] the ability to control people, to be able to say over the phone, "John, go pick up your pen and write this down." And you write it down! You do exactly like a robot—they would do exactly what they were told to do. And they would do it pleasingly, they would do it without hesitation, because, again, they had enough confidence and faith in you to believe that you were gonna do the right thing about it.

Another subject said simply that the work "gives you power. It gives you power." The importance of this dimension of the payoff from fraud has been commented on by others as well (e.g., Duffield & Grabosky, 2001).

Criminal telemarketers generally distinguish between working hard and "working smart." When asked, therefore, how he viewed those who work hard for modest wages, one replied, "I guess somebody's gotta do it." By contrast, work weeks of 20 to 30 hours are common for them, and even for owners and managers, the need for close oversight of operations decreases substantially once things are up and running. The short work week and their ample income provide considerable latitude in the use of leisure time and in consumption patterns.

The lifestyles of telemarketing participants vary by age and the aspects of the work that employees find most appealing, but ostentatious consumption is common to all. The young, and those attracted to the work and leisure it permits, live life as party (Shover, 1996). Use of cocaine and other illicit drugs is common among this segment of the criminal telemarketing workforce.

> The hours were good. You'd work, sometimes, from about 9:00 to 2:00, 9:00 to 3:00, sometimes from 12:00 to 4:00. Basically, we set our own hours. It was freedom. The money was fantastic.... You got the best of the girls. For me, it wasn't really about the job, it was a way of life....I had an alcohol problem at a young age, and to be able to support the alcohol and drug habit with the kind of money that we were making seems to go hand in hand. And then you've got the fast lifestyle...up all night, sleep all day, you know. So, everything kinda coincided with that fast lifestyle, that addictive lifestyle.

Asked how he spent the money he made, another subject responded saying:

> Houses, girls, just going out to nightclubs. And a lot of blow [cocaine]....Lots and lots of blow, enormous amounts. And other than that, you know, I look back, I get sick when I think about how much we spent, where the hell I put it all. I'm making all this money [but] I don't have a whole hell of a lot to show for it, you know. That lifestyle didn't allow you to save.

Heavy gambling is commonplace. One subject said that they "would go out to the casinos and blow two, three, four, five thousand dollars a night. That was nothing—to go spend five grand, you know, every weekend. And wake up broke!" Commenting on one of his employees, a subject who owned a telemarketing firm when he was arrested said that the man

> had a Porsche Speedster after he sold his Porsche 911. He had a Dodge Viper, he had a Ferrari 348, he had a Lexus LS400, he had a BMW 850i, he had a Jeep Grand Cherokee. He liked his cars. Now, he didn't have all these at one time, but he ran through them, you know. He traded the Dodge Viper...in for the Ferrari. He always had a Porsche.

What we learned about the lifestyles and spending habits of criminal telemarketers differs little from what is known about street criminals and other vocational predators. It also confirms what has been learned about the relationship between easy, unearned income and profligacy: "The way money is acquired is a powerful determinant of how it is defined, husbanded, and spent" (Shover, 1996, p. 104).

The lifestyles of telemarketers change somewhat as they get older and take on more conventional responsibilities:

I started to realize that, as I was getting older in the industry, it was affecting my children and my relationship with my wife. To the point that it wasn't what I wanted. I wanted more of a home-type of family, where I got home at 6:00 and have dinner and spend time with my wife and children. And with that industry, it doesn't really do that. My lifestyle? Play golf, go to the lake, you know. I had a family, but...I was also, you know, making good money. And I wanted to party and that kind of thing. So, I did that a lot. We got together and partied a lot and went here and there and went to, you know—nightlife, go out to clubs occasionally, But, when you're married and have kids, it's limited. It changes. It changed a lot over those years.

For older and more experienced telemarketers, the lifestyle centers around home and family and impressing others with signs of their apparent success:

I played some golf. [In the summer] water skiing, fishing. I'm real heavy into bass fishing, me and my dad and my brothers. Hunting. Doing things with my wife and kids. I spent a lot of time with them. Evenings, maybe just walking the golf course, or whatever. Watching the sunset.

Another subject told us that after he moved up in the telemarketing ranks, "My partner and I played, we played a lot of golf. The office was right down from the golf course. We'd go to the golf course and play two or three times a week." Save for the unrestrained hedonism of their lives when young and neophytes at criminal telemarketing, the broad outlines of their occupational careers, particularly for those who went on to form their own businesses, resemble the work careers of more conventional citizens.

Legitimation and Defense

Doocy et at. (2001, p. 18) remark that the telemarketing offender they interviewed "conveyed the assured appearance of a most respectable entrepreneur" and "conveyed no hint that what he was doing might not be altogether legitimate." Our subjects are no different. Notwithstanding the fact that all were convicted felons, most reject the labels *criminal* and *crime* as fitting descriptions of them and their activities. They instead employ a range of mitigating explanations and excuses for their offenses, although claims of ignorance figure in most (Scott & Lyman, 1968; Sykes & Matza, 1957). Some former business owners told us, for example, that they set out to maintain a legitimate operation, emulated the operations of their previous employers, and assumed, therefore, that their activities violated no laws. Others said they are guilty only of expanding their business so rapidly that they could not properly oversee day-to-day operations. Some said that indulgence in alcohol and illicit drugs caused them to become neglectful of or indifferent toward their businesses. Most claimed that the allure of money caused them to "look the other way." Those who owned or managed firms are prone also to blame rogue sales agents for any fraudulent or deceptive activities. As one put it: "The owners are trying to do the right thing. They're just attracting the wrong people. It's the salesmen." Another subject likewise suggested: "I guess I let the business get too big and couldn't watch over all of the agents to prevent what they were doing." For their part, sales agents charge that their owners and managers kept them in the dark about the business and its criminal nature.

Fraud offenders typically derive moral justification for their activities from the fact that their crimes cannot succeed without acquiescence or cooperation from their victims; unlike victims of burglary and robbery, those who fall prey to fraud usually are willing, if halting or confused, participants in their own victimization (Goffman, 1952). Chief among the legitimating and defensive tenets of telemarketing criminals is the belief that "the mooch is going to send his money to someone, so it might as well be me" (Sanger, 1999, p. 9). In other words, "customers" are thought to be so greedy, ignorant, or incapable that it is only a matter of time before they throw away their money on something impossible. The tendency of fraud offenders to see their victims as deserving of what befalls them was noted by Maurer (1940) more than six decades ago, and it remains true of contemporary telemarketing criminals. One of our subjects told us, "They know what they're doing. They're bargaining for something, and when they lose, they realize that they were at fault." There is neither concern nor sympathy for them. Another subject said:

> If these people can't read, so be it. Screw them, you know. It [doesn't say] everybody's gonna get the diamond and sapphire tennis bracelet. They're dumb enough not to read, dumb enough to send me the money, I really don't care, you know. I'm doing what I have to do to stay out of jail. They're doing what they have to do to fix their fix. They're promo junkies, and we're gonna find them and get them, and we're gonna keep getting them. And they're gonna keep buying. And, you know what I used to say, "They're gonna blow their money in Vegas, they're gonna spend it somewhere. I want to be the one to get it."

Telemarketing criminals selectively seize on aspects of their victims' behavior and point to these as a justification or excuse for their crimes. They maintain that they were not victimizing their customers but engaging in a routine sales transaction, no different than a retail establishment selling a shirt that is marked up 1,000%. Telemarketing fraud is therefore construed by its practitioners as perfectly in tune with mainstream commercial interactions: a "subculture of business" (Ditton, 1977, p. 173).

Ensconced in their outwardly respectable and self-indulgent lifestyles, our subjects professed belief that, so far as the law was concerned, they were risking nothing more severe than a fine, an adverse civil judgment, or a requirement they make restitution. They claim the entire problem more appropriately was a "civil matter" and "should not be in criminal court." As one put it: "If you have people that are not satisfied, we would be happy to give their money back."

INTERPRETATION

Our description of telemarketing crime and criminals is noteworthy for several reasons, but principally for what it reveals about the relationship between social change and the changing character of lucrative professional theft (Taylor, 1999). Defined by cultural criteria rather than legal yardsticks (see Sykes, 1978, p. 109), the concept of professional crime has become infused with contradiction and ambiguity by the evolution of this new kind of "respectable" predator.

Sociological debate over the descriptive validity of professional theft has been carried out largely as a dialogue with the tradition of Sutherland (1937), who located a behavior system of criminal specialists featuring technical skill, consensus via a shared ideology, differential association, status and, most important, informal organization grounded in a shared cultural identity. Subsequently, scholars presented alternative perspectives regarding crimes other than theft (Einstadter, 1969; Lemert, 1958). However, Shover (1973) perhaps came closest to Sutherland's original conception by locating the social organization of burglary based on highly instrumental and constantly evolving networks of dependency as the key variable. In his view, these networks continue to evolve due to innovative strategies in policing, security, and technology, and telemarketing fraudsters resemble Shover's professional burglar in their adaptive pragmatic organization.

Telemarketers also share many core characteristics with "hustlers" (President's Commission on Law Enforcement and Administration of Justice, 1966; Shover, 1996), or "rounders" (Letkemann, 1973), offenders whose lack of commonality or consensus contradicts the notion of a cohesive, tightly knit behavior system (see also Holzman, 1983; Polsky, 1964; Roebuck & Johnson, 1962). Yet Letkemann (1973) suggests that explicit commitment to criminal activity as a means of making a living is the best criterion for differentiating between professional and non-professional criminals, which also echoes Sutherland's classic work, and offers some support for the notion of an occupational group defined by members' commitment to illegal economic activities (Becker, 1960).

Although the investigation of professional thieves and their pursuits has a long history in criminology, the canon is replete with portraits of offenders who have passed from the scene. However, for contemporary observers, "fraud masters" (Jackson, 1994) deservedly command more attention than "cut purses" (Tobias, 1967), "cannons" (Maurer, 1964), and "good burglars" (Shover, 1973). Economic and social change inevitably transform the worlds in which offenders entertain options and organize for pursuit of criminal income (Hobbs, 1997; McIntosh, 1975; Shover, 1983). The classic criminal subcultures of shared practices and beliefs as the basis of criminal community have met the same fate as blue-collar communities based on traditional industries (Soja, 1989). The new entrepreneurial milieu is an enabling environment for a great range and variety of money-making schemes (Ruggiero & South, 1997), and the perceptual templates of contemporary professional criminals feature cues that are geared to success in a sphere emptied out of anachronistic practice (Wright & Decker, 1994).

Automobile theft and "chop shops" were not found in nineteenth century society, for the obvious reason that there were no automobiles to steal or sell. The shift to a postindustrial order inevitably changed selectively the human qualities and social capital requisite for successful exploitation of criminal opportunities.

Traditional professional thieves hailed from locations in the class and social structure where the young generally do not acquire the human capital requisite to success in the world of well-paid and respectable work. The blue-collar skills of an
industrial society, however, are not equal to the challenge of exploiting contemporary, increasingly white-collar criminal opportunities. The postindustrial service-
oriented economy instead places a premium on entrepreneurial, interpersonal,
communicative and organizational skills, and it is the children of the middle class
who are most likely to be exposed to and acquire these.

The knowledge and skills needed to exploit criminal opportunities vocation-
ally and successfully do not differ greatly from those required for success in the
legitimate world. Like the professional thief, the new and increasingly white-collar
vocational predators commit planned violations of the law for profit (Van Duyne,
1996), but they do so in the style of the middle class. They take on and publicly
espouse a belief system that defends against moral condemnation from outsiders,
and they are dismissive of both the world of hourly employment and the lives of
those confined to it. But although the professional thieves of an earlier era publicly
endorsed and were expected to adhere to norms of loyalty and integrity in dealings with one another (Cohen & Taylor, 1972; Irwin, 1970; Irwin & Cressey, 1962;
Mason, 1994; Maurer, 1964; McVicar, 1982; Shover, 1973; Taylor, 1984), criminal
telemarketers by contrast are extremely individualistic and self-centered in their
contacts with criminal justice officials and agencies. Whether this is because of
their privileged backgrounds or because the nature of criminal relationships has
been "transformed by the advent of a market culture," their illicit pursuits manifest
qualities not only of entrepreneurial creativity but also independence and "posses-
sive individualism" (Taylor, 1999).

Professional thieves of earlier eras found a measure of success in crime
despite their humble beginnings, and much about what they made of themselves
is understandable in the light of their blue-collar roots. The lives they constructed
emphasized freedom to live "life as party" (Shover & Honaker, 1991) by "earning and burning money" (Katz, 1988, p. 215), to roam without restraint, and to
celebrate these achievements with others of similar perspective. The class origins
of contemporary garden-variety white-collar criminals are more advantaged,
but they live their lives in substantially similar fashion. Unlike the "foot pads" of
Elizabethan England, they generally do not gravitate to a criminal netherworld
or a self-contained criminal fraternity. Nor do they confine their leisure pursuits
to others of similar work. The proletarian underworld was an essential network
for exchanging, controlling, and disseminating information (Hobbs, 1995, pp.
21–23; McIntosh, 1971), but the telemarketing fraudster depends on networks of
information that are largely indistinguishable from those that underpin the noncriminal sector.

What Benney (1981, p. 263) called "the fabulous underworld of bourgeois
invention" ironically has been decimated by the embourgeoisement of crime.
Criminals now emerge from the economic mainstream and engage both socially
and pragmatically with derivations of normative economic activity. The acquisitive

entrepreneurial ethic that underpins both legal and illegal performances within the postindustrial marketplace thrives upon "new technical, social, psychological and existential skills" (Bauman, 1992, p. 98), which in turn are bordered by new configurations of cultural and technological capital.

Although the old underworld was safely ensconced in the locales, occupational practices, leisure cultures, and oppositional strategies of the industrial proletariat (Hobbs, 1997; Samuel, 1981), it is the bourgeois who have emerged with the education and ideological flexibility to engage with lucrative contemporary professional crime, which is located not within a proletarian outpost of traditional transgression, but within rhetorics that legitimate and enable the entire "spectrum of legitimacy" (Albanese, 1989, p. 101).

Telemarketing fraudsters should be seen as "fluid sets of mobile marauders in the urban landscape, alert to institutional weakness in both legitimate and illegitimate spheres" (Block, 1983, p. 245). These spheres are pliant and not territorially embedded (Chaney, 1994, p. 149). Detached from an "underworld" (Haller, 1990, pp. 228–29), contemporary professional crime has mutated from an overworld in which the bourgeoisie rather than blue-collar culture is sovereign. This helps explain why telemarketing fraudsters, unlike the professional thieves of previous generations, are likely to spend their weekends on the lake, playing golf, or having friends over for a barbeque. Still, they blow their earnings on drugs, gambling, fast living, and conspicuous consumption. They earn a reasonably good return from crime, but like "box men" of yore, few spend appreciable time in jails and prisons.

REFERENCES

Adler, P. S. (1992). *Technology and the future of work*. New York: Oxford University Press.

Albanese, J. (1989). *Organized crime in America*. Cincinnati, OH: Anderson.

American Association of Retired Persons. (1996). *Telemarketing fraud and older Americans: An AARP survey*. New York: Author.

Atlanta Journal-Constitution. (2000). Alleged scam on elderly by telemarketers is revealed. September 6, B3.

Australian Broadcasting Corporation. (2001). *Beyond the boiler room*. Ruetrieved September 24, 2003, from www.abc.net.au/4corners/.

Batty, M., & Barr, B. (1994). The electronic frontier: Exploring and mapping cyberspace. *Futures, 26*(7), 699–712.

Bauman, Z. (1992). *Intimidations of modernity*. London: Routledge.

Becker, H. (1960). Notes on the concept of commitment. *American Journal of Sociology, 66*, 32–40.

Benney, M. (1981). *Low company*. Sussex, UK: Caliban.

Block, A. (1983). *East side–west side: Organizing crime in New York, 1930–1950*. Newark, NJ: Transaction.

Chaney, D. (1994). *The cultural turn*. London: Routledge.

Clarke, M. (1990). Control of insurance fraud: A comparative view. *British Journal of Criminology, 30*, 1–3.

Cohen, S., & Taylor, L. (1972). *Psychological survival*. Harmondsworth: Penguin.

Direct Marketing Association. (2001). Retrieved June 5, 2012, from http://www.the-dma.org.

Ditton, J. (1977). *Part time crime.* London: Macmillan.

Doocy, J., Schichor, D., Sechrest, D., & Geis, G. (2001). Telemarketing fraud: Who are the tricksters and what makes them trick? *Securities Journal, 14,* 7–26.

Duffield, G., & Grabosky, P. (2001). The psychology of fraud. Paper 199. Griffith, Canberra: Australian Institute of Criminology.

Einstadter, W. J. (1969). The social organization of armed robbery. *Social Problems, 17,* 54–83.

Francis, D. (1988). *Contrepreneurs.* Toronto: Macmillan.

Grabosky, P. N., Smith, R. G., & Dempsey, G. (2001). *Electronic theft: Unlawful acquisition in cyberspace.* New York: Cambridge University Press.

Goffman, E. (1952) On cooling the mark out: Some aspects of adaptation to failure. *Psychiatry, 15,* 451–463.

Haller, M. (1990). Illegal enterprise: A theoretical and historical interpretation. *Criminology, 28*(2), 207–235.

L Harris and Associates, Inc. (1992). *Telemarketing fraud.* Charlotte: University of North Carolina, Institute for Research in Social Science.

Hirschhorn, L. (1985). Information technology and the new services game. In M. Castells (Ed.), *High technology, space, and society* (pp. 172–190). Beverly Hills, CA: Sage.

Hobbs, R. (1995). *Bad business: Professional crime in contemporary Britain.* Oxford: Oxford University Press.

———. (1997). Professional crime: Change, continuity, and the enduring myth of the under-world. *Sociology, 31,* 57–72.

Holzman, H. (1983). The serious habitual property offender as moonlighter: An empirical study of labor force participation among robbers and burglars. *Journal of Criminal Justice Law and Criminology, 73,* 1774–1792.

Irwin, J. (1970). *The felon.* Upper Saddle River, NJ: Prentice Hall.

Irwin, J., & Cressey, D. (1962). Thieves, convicts and the inmate culture. *Social Problems, 10,* 142–55.

Jackson, J. (1994). Fraud masters: Professional credit card offenders and crime. *Criminal Justice Review, 19,* 24–55.

Katz, J. (1988). *Seductions of crime.* New York: Basic.

Lash, S., & Urry, J. (1994). *Economies of signs and space.* London: Sage.

Lemert, E. (1958). The behavior of the systematic check forger. *Social Problems, 6,* 141–149.

Letkemann, P. (1973). *Crime as work.* Upper Saddle River, NJ: Prentice Hall.

Mason, E. (1994). *Inside story.* London: Pan.

Maurer, D. W. (1940). *The big con.* Indianapolis, IN: Bobbs-Merrill.

———. (1964). *Whiz mob.* New Haven, CT: College and University Press.

McIntosh, M. (1971). Changes in the organization of thieving. In S. Cohen (Ed.), *Images of deviance.* Harmondsworth: Penguin.

———. (1975). *The organization of crime.* New York: Macmillan.

McVicar, J. (1982). Violence in prisons. In P. Marsh & A. Campbell (Eds.), *Aggression and violence.* Oxford: Blackwell.

Polsky, N. (1964). The hustler. *Social Problems, 12,* 3–15.

President's Commission on Law Enforcement and Administration of Justice. (1966). Professional crime. In *Task force report* (ch. 7). Washington, DC: US Government Printing Office.

Rebovich, D., Layne, J., Jiandani, J., & Hage, S. (2000). *The national public survey on white collar crime*. Glen Allen, VA: National White Collar Crime Center.

Roebuck, J., & Johnson, R. (1962). The jack of all trades offender. *Crime & Delinquency, 8*, 172–181.

Ross, E. A. (1907). *Sin and society: An analysis of latter-day iniquity*. Boston: Houghton Mifflin.

Ruggiero, V., & South, N. (1997). The late modern city as a bazaar. *British Journal of Sociology, 48*, 54–70.

Samuel, R. (1981). *East End underworld: The life and times of Arthur Harding*. London: Routledge and Kegan Paul.

Samuelson, R. J. (1995). *The good life and its discontents*. New York: Random House.

Sanger, D. (1999). Confessions of a phone-scam artist. *Saturday Night, 114*, 86–98.

Schulte, F. (1995). *Fleeced! Telemarketing rip-offs and how to avoid them*. Essex, UK: Prometheus.

Scott, M. B., & Lyman, M. L. (1968). Accounts. *American Sociological Review, 33*, 46–62.

Shover, N. (1973). The social organization of burglary. *Social Problems, 20*, 499–514.

———. (1983). Professional crime: Major offender. In S. H. Kadish (Ed.), *Encyclopedia of crime and justice* (pp. 1263–1271). New York: Macmillan.

———. (1996). *Great pretenders: Pursuits and careers of persistent thieves*. Boulder, CO: Westview.

Shover, N., & Honaker, D. (1991). The socially bounded decision making of persistent property offenders. *Howard Journal, 31*, 276–293.

Silverstone, R. (1991). *Beneath the bottom line: Households and information and communication technologies in the age of the consumer*. London: Brunel University Centre for Research on Innovation, Culture, and Technology.

Soja, E. (1989). *Postmodern geographies*. London: Verso.

Sparrow, M. K. (1996). *License to steal: Why fraud plagues America's health care system*. Boulder, CO: Westview.

Stevenson, R. J. (2000). *The boiler room and other telephone sales scams*. Urbana: University of Illinois Press.

Sutherland, E. H. (1937). *The professional thief*. Chicago, IL: University of Chicago Press.

Sykes, G. (1978). *Criminology*. New York: Harcourt Brace Jovanovitch.

Sykes, G., & Matza, D. (1957). Techniques of neutralization: A theory of delinquency. *American Sociological Review, 22*, 667–670.

Taylor, L. (1984). *In the underworld*. Oxford: Blackwell.

Taylor, I. (1999). *Crime in context: A critical criminology of market societies*. Boulder, CO: Westview.

Tickell, A. (1996). Taking the initiative: Leeds' Financial Centre. In G. Haughton & C. Williams (Eds.), *Corporate city? Partnerships, participation in urban development in Leeds*. Aldershot, UK: Avebury.

Tillman, R. (1998). *Broken promises: Fraud by small business health insurers*. Boston: Northeastern University Press.

Titus, R. (2001). Personal fraud and its victims. In N. Shover & J. P. Wright (Eds.), *Crimes of privilege: Readings in white collar crime* (pp. 57–67). New York: Oxford University Press.

Titus, R. M., Heinzelmann, F., & Boyle, J. M. (1995). Victimization of persons by fraud. *Crime & Delinquency, 41*, 54–72.

Tobias, J. J. (1967). *Crime and industrial society in the 19th century*. London: Batsford.

Turkle, S. (1995). *Life on the screen: Identity in the age of the Internet.* New York: Simon and Schuster.

U.S. Senate. (1993). *Telemarketing fraud and section 568, The Telemarketing and Consumer Fraud and Abuse Protection Act.* Hearing before the Subcommittee on Consumer of the Committee on Commerce, Science, and Transportation. 103d Cong.

Van Duyne, P. (1996). The phantom and threat of organized crime. *Crime, Law, and Social Change, 21,* 241–277.

Winlow, S. (2001). *Badfellas.* Oxford, UK: Berg.

Wright, R., & Decker, S. (1994). *Burglars on the job: Streetlife and residential break-ins.* Boston: Northeastern University Press.

✦

CHAPTER 13

Drugged Druggists: The Convergence of Two Criminal Career Trajectories

Dean A. Dabney and Richard C. Hollinger

Structured personal interviews were used to examine the individual life histories of a group of pharmacists, all of whom previously had been in treatment and were now in recovery for past illicit prescription drug abuse. In-depth interviews with 50 recovering drug-addicted pharmacists are utilized to help understand both the onset and progression into illicit prescription pharmaceutical drug abuse. Thematic content analysis reveals two distinct paths of entry into drug use. Nearly half (23) of the pharmacists engaged in the use of street and/or prescription drugs before entering their professional careers. This first group, which we call "recreational abusers," began using prescription drugs principally for their euphoric effects, exploiting their newly discovered access to and knowledge about pharmaceuticals. The remaining 27 pharmacists, termed "therapeutic self-medicators," began using prescription drugs much later in their careers and primarily for medicinal reasons. These two distinct modes of entry eventually converged into a single, common criminal career trajectory. Once addicted, the distinguishing characteristics between the two groups begin to disappear and common themes emerged, indicating dynamic convergence into a single pattern for the mature deviant. We conclude that early differentiation followed by subsequent convergence of behaviors and motivations suggests that some theorists and practitioners alike have erroneously concluded that they have discovered multiple static types of crime and criminals when in some cases they are examining a single criminal/deviant career at different points along its dynamic trajectory.

INTRODUCTION

Self-report studies reveal that between 40 and 65% of all practicing pharmacists engage in some form of illicit drug use at least once during their professional careers. Approximately 20% of pharmacists in earlier studies report using drugs

Source: Dabney, D. A., & Hollinger, R. C. (2002). Drugged druggists: The convergence of two criminal career trajectories. *Justice Quarterly, 19,* 182–213.

regularly enough that they experienced negative life consequences, such as missing work, blackouts, health problems, or difficulties with interpersonal relationships. Interestingly, only 5% to 10% of these "regular" users consider themselves to be "drug abusers" (Dabney, 1997; Dabney, 2001; McAuliffe et al., 1987; Normack et al., 1985).

Although scholars generally agree about the high incidence and prevalence, substantial knowledge gaps prevent us from fully understanding the complex causal etiology of criminal drug use among this particular category of health care professionals. Most vexing is the limited understanding of how these individuals come to initially use and then abuse the prescription substances that they are entrusted to dispense. The present study is an attempt to fill this current knowledge void by identifying the underlying causes of illicit prescription drug use among practicing pharmacists.

This is the first empirical inquiry designed to systematically identify the reasons why pharmacists begin, and subsequently continue to use unauthorized prescription medicines. Our substantive objectives are two-fold. We begin by exploring the ways in which criminal/deviant roles and associations develop and evolve within the personal and professional worlds of these addicts. Specifically, we draw upon the personal experiences of 50 recovering drug-impaired pharmacists using lengthy, face-to-face interviews in order to map out the criminal career trajectory of pharmacists who become addicted to prescription medicines. The lessons learned from these data will then be applied to contemporary theory on criminal careers in an effort to expand conceptual understanding of this phenomenon.

Drug-Addicted Pharmacist Literature

Various explanations have been offered to explain illicit drug use among pharmacists. For example, existing drug abuse hypotheses include inadequate professional socialization, occupational role conflicts, low risk of detection, minimal negative consequences, and a professionwide atmosphere of denial (Bissell, Haberman, & Williams, 1989; Dabney & Hollinger, 1999; Gallegos et al., 1988; Hankes & Bissell, 1992; McAuliffe, 1984; Penna & Williams, 1985;Quinney, 1963 Sheffield, 1988). Still, uncertainty exists regarding (1) what factors are most influential in explaining pharmacists' initial entry into theft and addiction and (2) what stimuli facilitate an ongoing pattern of drug theft and abuse that eventually results in addiction.

The explanations most commonly found in the scholarly literature regarding medical professionals' drug abuse can be divided into two generic conceptual categories, "recreational abuse" and "therapeutic self-medication." Some of the first studies of the phenomenon of illicit prescription drug abuse suggested that health care professionals engage in prescription drug theft and use primarily for recreational reasons, exacerbated by nearly unlimited access to prescription medications and combined with a perceived invincibility to drug addiction (McAuliffe, 1984; McAuliffe et al., 1987). However, the momentum has turned away from "recreational abuser" explanations, and instead, a less judgmental model has come to flourish. Today, most scholars and practitioners alike assume that the vast majority of health care professionals steal and use prescription drugs principally for therapeutic reasons (Bissell, Haberman, & Williams, 1989; Chi, 1983; Gallegos et al., 1988; Normack et al., 1985; Sheffield, O'Neill, & Fisher, 1992; Winick, 1961). In the case of the pharmacist, factors such as work-related stress, heightened access to drugs, and the physical and emotional demands of pharmacy practice are thought to be the impetus for early forays into illegal drug use. Driven by pitfalls of drug tolerance, levels of use escalate and the pharmacist draws upon his/her vast clinical knowledge as a means of regulating his/her use and convincing him/herself that he/she is in control of an ever-growing drug habit (Dabney & Hollinger, 1999; Hankes & Bissell, 1992).

The principal objective of this research was to ascertain which of these two competing models, recreational or therapeutic, is the most accurate in explaining the illicit prescription drug use careers of practicing pharmacists. Despite the pervasiveness of both explanations in the literature, we quickly recognized that perhaps neither was entirely correct. In fact, we ultimately realized that both models were partially accurate. As we shall see, one can readily identify two very different paths of entry among drug using pharmacists. However, as drug theft and use gives way to drug abuse and eventually uncontrollable addiction, these two deviant career trajectories converge and we see that the motivational and behavioral patterns of mature deviants appear very much the same.

Criminal Career Literature

We turn to the broader criminological literature for conceptual clarification. Analogous to an occupational career, it has become increasingly popular to use the term "career" in speaking about various forms of criminal or deviant behavior that occur over a period of time (Becker, 1963; Nettler, 1982). Our current understanding of this concept can be traced to scores of scholarly efforts wherein academics have repeatedly shown patterned aspects to how offenders enter into and then proceed through their deviant or criminal routines (see Greenberg, 1996, for a sampling). We note that these career-based inquiries have often targeted samples of drug offenders (Adler, 1993; Becker, 1953; Blackwell, 1983; Coombs, 1981; Faupel, 1987; Faupel, 1991; Rubington, 1967; Smith & Smith, 1984; Waldorf, 1983). For example, Adler (1993) and others (Hafley & Tewksbury, 1996) have written at length about the various "career" stages (i.e., entry, escalation, and exit) that go along with using and dealing marijuana. Similarly, Faupel and Klockars (1987) identified a four-step career progression that was observed in a sample of hard-core heroin users. We have learned a lot from these offender-based studies. Namely, we have learned that not all heroin or marijuana users think or act the same. At the same time, we have come to identify shared ideals, motivations, and behaviors that serve to reinforce our stereotypical images of a given type of criminal subculture.

These latter realizations have given way to several more generic efforts at theorizing. Scholars such as Best and Luckenbill (1994) and, more recently, Tittle and Paternoster (2000) provide us with conceptual models of "criminal/deviant careers." These works seek to summarize the lessons that we have learned from past research efforts and thus crystallize our understanding of this important dimension of the criminological enterprise. In the tradition of deductive reasoning, these scholars begin by identifying and defining a set of core components (i.e., fundamental motivational and behavioral dimensions) that they see as being common to all crimes. This underlying framework is then used to funnel seemingly different criminal acts and actors into a series of abstract conceptual categories. As an abbreviated example, Tittle and Paternoster (2000) argue that there are nine underlying dimensions to criminal behavior: sociality, pervasiveness, communication, differentiation, culture, self-identity, philosophical integration, self-control from within group, and recruitment. While they recognize that each criminal and crime type possesses its own unique combination of these nine factors, they contend that all criminal behavior can be organized along a three-point continuum. This continuum places "individualized deviance" is at one end, "subcultural deviance" in the center, and "fully organized deviance" at the other end. The authors list suicide and serial murder as examples of individualized deviance, the deviant behaviors of recreational drug users and street gang members as examples of subcultural deviance, and racketeering and collective terrorism as examples of fully organized forms of deviance.

Several years earlier, Best and Luckenbill (1994) also introduced a conceptual framework that seeks to organize both deviant individuals and their deviant behaviors within a career-based context. Deviant acts, or what they term "transactions," are said to manifest themselves in one of three forms: individualized deviance, deviant exchanges, or deviant exploitation. Secrecy and solitude are the hallmarks of individualized deviance. Collectivity and cooperation are central to deviant exchanges. And deviant exploitation takes on a coercive quality, as when an unsuspecting victim is surreptitiously targeted by a stealthy offender.

Best and Luckenbill (1994) also outline a series of generic motivational categories that go along with their behavioral scheme. The authors theorize that different types of generic motives (defensive, adventurous, and mental calculations) should be present in different types of deviant transactions and thus coin the term "sociology of deviance" to describe the patterned forms of behavior and motivation that are indigenous to a given type of crime or deviance.

Once they have finished describing the behavioral and motivational elements of deviant acts, Best and Luckenbill (1994) shift the unit of analysis to the individual. The authors' discussion of deviant actors, or what they term the "sociology of deviants," applies the abovementioned framework and thus seeks to demonstrate the way that an individual's behaviors are patterned and interconnected within "a network of social relations" (Best & Luckenbill, 1994, p. 5). The term "social organization" speaks to the way that one's motives, associations, and transactions dictate the types of dynamic roles that are experienced while engaging in both deviant and non-deviant activities. This line of reasoning leads Best and Luckenbill to conclude that different types of deviant activities will produce different roles and associations for those who choose to engage in them. They go so far as to categorize deviant actors and relationships within a five-category typology. These categories are placed on a continuum delineated by differing levels of sophistication in social organization. Moving from the least sophisticated level of social organization to the most, this list includes (1) loners, (2) colleagues, (3) peers, (4) teams, and (5) formal organizations. Best and Luckenbill (1994) see the deviant or criminal career as the synthesized reality in which actors and their actions come to be patterned and regimented over time. In short, the nature of the behavior interacts with the social organization of the perpetrators (i.e., their deviant roles and associations) to produce somewhat predictable career paths.

The conceptual models provided to us by Best and Luckenbill (1994) and Tittle and Paternoster (2000) occupy an important place in our understanding of criminal careers, especially those involving drug users. First and foremost, these discussions elevate the empirical lessons that we have learned from street ethnographies of drug users to a higher level of abstraction. In doing so, they allow us to group similar offenders and offenses into categories. In turn, these categories provide direction about the types of behaviors and motivations that one might encounter when seeking to enforce or prevent specific or general categories of acts or actors. One must be careful, however, not to lose sight of the fact that these categories are theoretical abstractions that will not always fare so well when superimposed onto complex social realities. Best and Luckenbill (1994) emphasize this point when they speak of the fluid nature of deviant careers and how circumstances might lead to an individual or individuals experiencing noticeable vertical or lateral shifts across their criminal career trajectory. Tittle and Paternoster (2000) make scant mention of career fluidity and relativity.

The existing literature provides little hard evidence on if and how the notions of career fluidity and relativity might manifest themselves in real-life situations. Given that our inquiry uncovered a clear instance of career fluidity and relativity in action, we were left with the task of filling in the conceptual space on our own. What follows is an effort to clarify and extend the implied conceptual flexibility of the criminal career hypothesis. Namely, we use the details of criminal career trajectories observed in 50 drug-recovering pharmacists to elucidate the strengths and weaknesses of the career-based notion of drug abuse and thus provide valuable evidence of the types of shifts and fluidity that exist therein.

STUDY GROUP DEMOGRAPHICS

The pharmacists that were interviewed represented a variety of social and demographic backgrounds. For example, 78% were men and 22% were women. The vast majority (48) of interviewees were white, with the exception of one Hispanic and one African American individual. A broad age range was present, with 8% being under the age of 30, 38% in their 30s, 36% in their 40s, 12% in their 50s, and 6% over the age of 60.

Table 13.1 Defining Characteristics of Pharmacists' Illicit Prescription Drug Use Motivation and Behaviors

SIGNIFICANT CHARACTERISTICS	TYPE I (N = 23) RECREATIONAL ABUSERS	TYPE II (N = 27) THERAPEUTIC SELF-MEDICATORS
(1) Nature of drug use	Recreational	Therapeutic/medicinal
(2) Onset of drug use	Prior to or during Rx school—early in pharmacy careers	Post Rx school—well into pharmacy careers
(3) General trajectory of drug use	Rapid, steep trajectory	Slow, progressive trajectory
(4) Principal mode of rationalization	"Better living through chemistry—live your work"	"I know enough to monitor and control my self-medication"
(5) Scope of the drug use	Indiscriminate experimentation	Selective drug types/schedules
(6) Social organization of deviant transactions	Deviant exchanges turning into individual deviance	Individual deviance
(7) Underlying motive for drug use	Adventurous motives based in permissive drug use ideals followed by defensive motives aimed at survival	Defensive motives aimed first at job-related pain or stress relief, then survival
(8) Social organization of deviants	Peers → colleagues → loners	Loners

Turning to issues of professional status, we note that 86% held bachelor's degrees in pharmacy, while 16% held some advanced pharmacy degree. While many of the pharmacists moved from job to job and crossed over different practice settings, they categorized their "primary practice setting" as follows: 36% hospital pharmacy, 28% independent retail pharmacy, 26% chain retail pharmacy, 4% home infusion pharmacy, 4% nursing homes, and 2% employed as temporary contract pharmacists. These demographic characteristics closely resemble the descriptive elements that were revealed in a 1992 nationwide study of 179,445 of the 194,570 pharmacists who were licensed to practice at the time (Martin, 1993).

TWO PATHS OF ENTRY INTO A DEVIANT CAREER

Given our specific interest in the various career aspects of deviant behavior, a significant portion of each interview was focused on the pharmacist's entry into illicit drug use. After examining the transcripts of the interviews, it quickly became apparent that their initial deviant drug use took on two distinct forms. Nearly one half of the pharmacists began using prescription drugs recreationally to "get high." These individuals usually had a history of "street" drug use prior to their even beginning the formal pharmacy education process. Alternatively, the other half of the pharmacists interviewed described how they began using prescription drugs much later for therapeutic purposes when confronted with some physical malady while on the job.

Recreational Abusers

Of the 50 pharmacists interviewed, nearly half (23, or 46%) could be classified as "recreational abusers." One of the defining characteristics of these individuals is that they all began experimenting with street drugs during their teenage years. They each described their early drug use experiences as being "recreational" in nature. These respondents commonly experimented with "street" drugs such as marijuana, cocaine, alcohol, and various psychedelics while in high school and during their early college years. The motivation behind this use was quite simple; they were adventurous and wanted to experience the euphoric, mind-altering effects that the drugs offered. Due to procurement problems, these individuals reported that they engaged in little, if any, prescription drug use before entering pharmacy school.

Initial Prescription Drug Use

For the recreational abuser, the onset of the illicit prescription drug use career usually began shortly after entering pharmacy training. These respondents were quick to point to the recreational motivations behind their early prescription drug use. As one 42-year-old male pharmacist stated, "I just wanted the effect, I really just wanted the effect. I know what alcohol is. But what if you take a Quaalude and drink with it? What happens then?" Similarly, a 36-year-old male pharmacist said:

> It was very recreational at first, yeah. It was more curiosity...experimental. I had read about all these drugs. Then I discovered I had a lot of things going on with me at that time and that these [drugs] solved the problem for me instantly. I had a lot of self-exploration issues going on at that time.

Trends in the data indicate that pharmacy school provided these individuals with the requisite access to prescription drugs. They recalled how they exploited their newly found access to prescription drugs in an effort to expand or surpass the euphoric effects that they received from weaker street drugs. For example, a 27-year-old male pharmacist said:

> It was a blast. It was fun.... It was experimentation. We smoked a little pot. And then in the "model pharmacy" [a training facility in college], there was stuff [prescription drugs] all over the place. "Hey this is nice...that is pretty nice." If it was a controlled substance, then I tried it. I had my favorites, but when that supply was exhausted, I'd move on to something else. I was a "garbage head"! It was the euphoria.... I used to watch Cheech and Chong [movies]. That's what it was like. I wasn't enslaved by them [or so I thought]. They made the world go round.

Pharmacy as a Drug Access Career Choice

It is important to note that the majority of the recreational abusers claimed that they specifically chose a career in pharmacy because it would offer them an opportunity to expand their drug use behaviors. For example, a 37-year-old male pharmacist said: "That's one of main reasons I went to pharmacy school, because I'd have access to medications if I needed them." Further evidence of this reasoning can be seen in the comments of a 41-year-old male pharmacist:

> A lot of my friends after high school said, "Oh great, you're going into pharmacy school. You can wake up on uppers and go to bed on downers," all that stuff. At first, [I said] no. The first time I ever [used prescription drugs], I thought, "No, that's not why I'm doing it [enrolling in pharmacy school]. No, I'm doing it for the noble reasons." But then after a while I thought, well, maybe they had a point there after all. I [had to] change my major. So I [based my choice] on nothing more than: "Well, it looks like fun and gee, all the pharmacy majors had drugs." The [pharmacy students] that I knew...every weekend when they came back from home, they would unpack their bags, and bags of pills would roll out. I thought, "Whoa, I got to figure out how to do this." [I would ask:] "How much did you pay for this?" [They would respond:] "I haven't paid a thing, I just stole them. Stealing is okay. I get shit wages so I got to make it up somehow. So we just steal the shit." Well, I thought, "This is it; I want to be a pharmacist." So I went into pharmacy school.

This trend was observed over and over again among recreational abusers. Namely, access to prescription drugs was a critical factor in their career choice.

Learning by Experimentation

Once in pharmacy school, the recreational abusers consistently described how they adopted an applied approach to their studies. For example, if they read about a particularly interesting type of drug in pharmacy school, they often would indicate that they wanted to try it. Or, if they were clerking or interning in a pharmacy, which offered access to prescription medicines, they would describe how they stole drugs just to try them. If a teacher or employer told them about the unusual effects of a new drug, interviewees would state that this piqued their interest. This pattern of application-oriented learning is exemplified in the comments of a 49-year-old male pharmacist:

> I began using [prescription drugs] to give myself the whole realm of healing experience...to control my body, to control the ups and the downs....I thought I could chemically feel, do, and think whatever I wanted to if I learned enough about these drugs and used them. Actually, I sat in classes with a couple of classmates where they would be going through a group of drugs, like, say, a certain class of muscle relaxants, skeletal muscle relaxants, and they would talk about the mechanism of pharmacology and then they would start mentioning different side effects, like drowsiness, sedation, and some patients report euphoria, and at a high enough dose, hallucinations and everything. Well, hell, that got highlighted in yellow. And then that night, one of us would take some [from the pharmacy], and then we would meet in a bar at 10:00 or in somebody's house and we would do it together.

The above quote stands as an example of how recreational abusers often superimposed an educational motive onto their progressive experimentation with prescription drugs in pharmacy school. They explained that they wanted to experience the drug effects that they read about in their pharmacy textbooks. These individuals adeptly incorporated their scientific training and professional socialization in such a way that allowed them to excuse and redefine their recreational drug use. Many went as far as to convince themselves that their experimental drug use was actually beneficial to their future patients. This adaptation strategy is illustrated in the comments of a 59-year-old male recreational abuser:

> In a lot of ways, [college drug use] was pretty scientific. [I was] seeing how these things affected me in certain situations... [just] testing the waters. I thought that I'll be able to counsel my patients better the more I know about the side effects of these drugs. I'll be my own rat. I'll be my own lab rat. I can tell [patients] about the shakes and chills and the scratchy groin and your skin sloughing off. I can tell you all about that stuff.

Socially Acceptable Recreational Drug Use in Pharmacy School

The recreational abusers unanimously agreed that there was no shortage of socially acceptable experimental drug use while in pharmacy school. They recalled liberal use of alcohol and street drugs among many of their fellow pharmacy students. Moreover, all 23 claimed that it was not uncommon for students to use amphetamines to get through all-night study sessions once or twice each semester. Many of the recreational abusers recalled that they were not satisfied with this type of controlled drug use. They were more interested in expanding their usage. One 48-year-old male pharmacist described the make-up of his pharmacy school cohort as follows:

> There were a third of the pharmacy students in school because Mom and Dad or Grandfather or Uncle Bill were pharmacists. They looked up to them and wanted to be one [too]. A [second] third had been in the [Vietnam] war. They were a pharmacy tech in the war or had worked in a pharmacy. They had the experiential effect of what pharmacy is and found a love for it or a desire to want it. Then you had the other third... and we were just drug addicts. We didn't know what the practice was all about, but we did know that we got letters after our names, guaranteed income if we didn't lose our letters. And we had access to anything [prescription drugs] we needed.

Many of the recreational abusers claimed that they specifically sought out fellow pharmacy students who were willing to use prescription drugs. The most common locus of these peer associations was in pharmacy-specific fraternities. The interviewees said that there was usually ample drug use going on in these organizations, allowing them the opportunity to cautiously search out and identify other drug users. Once they were connected with other drug users, the prescription drug use of all involved parties increased. This type of small group drug use allowed for access to an expanded variety of drugs, a broader pharmacological knowledge base, and even larger quantities of drugs. However, numerous respondents were quite clear about the fact that these drug-based associations were tenuous and temporary in nature. Over time, as the intensity of their drug use increased, the recreational abusers described how they became more reclusive. They became more guarded and selective with their relationships, fearing that their heightened prescription drug use would come to be defined as problematic by fellow pharmacy students. One 43-year-old male pharmacist said:

> You get the sense pretty quickly that you are operating [using] on a different level. Those of us that were busily stealing [prescription drugs] from our internship sites began to tighten our social circle. We might party a little bit with the others, but when it came to heavy use, we kept it hush, hush.

Unlike other pharmacy students who were genuinely experimenting with drugs on a short-term basis, these recreational abusers observed that there was an added intensity associated with their own prescription drug use. While most of these recreational abusers entered pharmacy school with some prior experiences in recreational street drug use, their precollege prescription drug use was usually not extensive. As such, it was not until they got into pharmacy school that they began to develop more pronounced street and prescription drug use habits. A 38-year-old female pharmacist discusses this transition into increased usage in the following interview excerpt:

> I went off to pharmacy school. That was a three-year program. I had tried a few things [before that], but I would back off because it was shaming for me not to get straight As. The descent to hell started when I got to pharmacy school. There were just so many things [prescription drugs] available and so many things that I thought I just had to try. It might be a different high; it might be a different feeling, anything to alter the way that I just felt. I was pretty much using on a daily basis by the time I got to my last year.

Pharmacy Practice Yields Even More Drug Access and Use
Pharmacy school was just the beginning of the steep career trajectory for the recreational abusers. School was followed by pharmacy practice that offered even greater access to prescription medicines. Daily work experiences meant exposure to more new drugs. Introduction to a newly developed compound was followed by some quick research on the effects of the drug and then almost immediate experimentation. This is well illustrated by a 37-year-old male pharmacist describing his early work experience:

> In '82, I remember I came down here and applied for a job...in May of '82. I remember even then, I went out to the satellite [pharmacy facility] and I heard about this one drug, Placidyl. As soon as I got to the interview, they were showing me around. A friend took me around...and I saw a Placidyl on the shelf there....I took a chance, kind of wandering around, and I went back and took some off the shelf. So even then, I was [stealing and misusing]. You know, why would you do that in the middle of interviewing for a job? I took it even then. I just jumped at the chance.

Once recreational abusers got into a permanent practice setting, most described how they quickly realized that they had free rein over the pharmacy stock. At first, these individuals relied upon other more experienced pharmacists for guidance in gaining access to (or in using) newly available prescription drugs. Later, their nearly unrestricted access meant that they could now try any drugs that they pleased. And most did. More importantly, increased access allowed the pharmacists-in-training to secretly use the drugs that they most liked. No longer did they have to worry about others looking over their shoulders. Not surprisingly, the level of their drug use usually skyrocketed shortly after entering pharmacy practice. This trend is demonstrated in the comments of a 41-year-old male pharmacist:

> By the time I got to pharmacy school in 1971, I was smoking dope [marijuana] probably every day or every other day, and drinking with the same frequency, but not to the point of passing out kind of stuff. Then, in 1971, that was also the year that I discovered barbs [barbiturates]. I had never had barbs up until I got to pharmacy school. So it was like '75 or '76 [when I got out of pharmacy school], I was using heavy Seconals and Quaaludes and Ambutols [all barbiturates]. I withdrew and it [the heavy abuse] just took off.

At the start, the recreational abusers' drug use was openly displayed and took on an air of excitement, much like others' experimentation with street or prescription drugs. However, as it intensified over time, the majority described how they slowly shielded their use from others. They thought it important to appear as though they still had the situation under control. As physical tolerance and psychological dependence increasingly progressed, these individuals began to lose control. Virtually all of the recreational abusers eventually developed serious prescription drug use habits. Using large quantities and sometimes even multiple drug types, their prescription drug use careers were usually marked by a steep downward spiral. This trend was clearly evidenced in the hand-sketched timeline that was drawn by each respondent. What started out as manageable social drug experimentation persistently progressed to increasingly more secretive drug abuse. In almost all of the cases, it took several years for the drug use to reach its peak addictive state. The intense physical and psychological effects of the drug use meant that the recreational abuser's criminal/deviant career was punctuated by a very "low bottom." Commonly identified signs of "bottoming out" included life-threatening health problems, repeated dismissal from work, having action taken against their pharmacy license, habitual lying, extensive cover-ups, divorce, and suicide attempts. By all accounts, the personal and professional lives of these recreational abusers suffered heavily from their drug abuse. In the end, most were reclusive and paranoid—what started out as collective experimentation ended in a painful existence of solitary addiction.

Therapeutic Self-Medicators

The criminal/deviant career paths of the remaining 27 (54%) interviewees fit a different substantive theme. To differentiate these individuals from the recreational abusers, we call this latter group of pharmacists "therapeutic self-medicators." One of the defining characteristics of this group was that they had little or no experience with street or prescription drug use prior to entering pharmacy school. In fact, many of these individuals did not even use alcohol. What little drug involvement they did report was usually occasional experimentation with marijuana. If they had ever used prescription drugs, it was done legitimately under the supervision of a physician. Members of this group did not begin their illicit prescription drug use until they were well into their formal pharmacy careers.

The onset of the therapeutic self-medicators' drug use was invariably attributed to a problematic life situation, accident, medical condition, or occupationally related pain. When faced with such problems, these pharmacists turned to familiar prescription medicines for immediate relief. Rather than reporting a recreational, hedonistic, or pleasure motivation, these pharmacists had simply decided to use readily available prescription drugs to treat their own medical maladies.

Therapeutic Motives for Prescription Drug Use

The therapeutic self-medicators unanimously insisted that their drug use was never recreational. They never used drugs just for the euphoric effects. Instead, their drug use was focused on specific therapeutic goals. This is illustrated in the comments of a 33-year-old male pharmacist:

> There was no recreation involved. I just wanted to press a button and be able to sleep during the day. I was really having a tough time with this sleeping during the day. I would say by the end of that week I was already on the road [to dependency]. The race had started.

Other pharmacists described how their drug use began as a way of treating insomnia, physical trauma (e.g., a car accident, sports injury, or a broken bone), or some chronic occupationally induced health problem (e.g., arthritis, migraine headaches, leg cramps, or back pain).

It is important to point out that during the earliest stages of their drug use, these individuals appeared to be "model pharmacists." Most claimed to have excelled in pharmacy school. Moreover, occupational and career success usually continued after they entered full-time pharmacy practice. Personal appraisals, as well as annual supervisory evaluations, routinely described these individuals as hardworking and knowledgeable professionals.

Since they were usually treating the physical pain that resulted from the rigors of pharmacy work, all of the therapeutic self-medicators described how their early prescription drug use began under seemingly innocent, even honorable, circumstances. Instead of taking time off from work to see a physician, they chose to simply self-medicate their own ailments. Many felt that they could not afford to take the time off to get a prescription from a doctor who often knew less about the medications than they did. A 50-year-old male pharmacist described this situation as follows:

> When I got to [a job at a major pharmacy chain], the pace there was stressful. We were filling 300 to 400 scripts a day with minimal support staff and working

12- to 13-hour days. The physical part bothered me a lot. My feet and my back hurt. So, I just kept medicating myself until it got to the point where I was up to six to eight capsules of Fiorinol-3 [narcotic analgesic] a day.

Peer Introductions

Without exception, the therapeutic self-medicator pharmacists described how there was always a solitary, secretive dimension to their drug use. While they usually kept their drug use to themselves, it was not at all uncommon for the pharmacists to claim that their initial drug use was shaped by their interactions with co-workers. Many interviewees described how they got the idea to begin self-medicating from watching a co-worker do so. Others claimed that they merely followed the suggestion of a concerned senior pharmacist who was helping them remedy a physical malady, such as a hangover, anxiety, or physical pain. For example, a 38-year-old male pharmacist described an incident that occurred soon after being introduced to his hospital pharmacy supervisor:

> I remember saying one time that I had a headache. [He said,] "Go take some Tylenol with codeine elixir [narcotic analgesic]." I would never have done that on my own. He was my supervisor at the time, and I said to myself, "If you think I should?" He said, "That's what I would do." I guess that started the ball rolling a little bit mentally.

Members of the therapeutic self-medicator group took notice of the drug-related behaviors and suggestions of their peers but never acted upon them in the company of others. Instead, they maintained a public front condemning illicit prescription drug use but quietly followed through on the suggestive behaviors when in private.

Perceived Benefits of Self-Medication

The recreational abusers used drugs to get high. Conversely, the therapeutic self-medicators saw the drug use as a means to a different end. Even as their drug use intensified, they were able to convince themselves that the drugs were actually having a positive, rather than negative, effect on their work performance. This belief was not altogether inaccurate, since they began using the drugs to remedy a health problem that was detracting from their work efficiency.

Some therapeutic self-medicators looked to their notion of professional obligation to justify their illegal drug use. For example, in describing his daily use of Talwin, a Schedule II narcotic analgesic, a 43-year-old male pharmacist maintained: "I thought I could work better. I thought I could talk better with the nurses and patients. I thought I could socialize better with it."

A Slippery Slope

At first, these pharmacists reported that their secretive and occasional therapeutic self-medication seemed to work well. The drugs remedied the problematic situation (i.e., pain, insomnia, etc.) and thus allowed them to return to normal functioning. However, over time, they invariably began to develop a drug tolerance.

This meant that they had to take larger quantities to achieve the same level of relief. In the end, each had to face the fact that the regular use of a seemingly harmless therapeutic medicine had resulted in a serious and addictive drug abuse habit. The following interview excerpt from a 50-year-old male pharmacist offers a good overview of the life history of a therapeutic self-medicator:

> Well, I didn't have a big problem with that [early occasional self-medication behavior]. I wasn't taking that much. It was very much medicinal use. It was not an everyday thing. It really was used at that point for physical pain. But that's when I started tampering with other things and started trying other things. I would have trouble sleeping, so I would think, "You know, let's see what the Dalmane [benzodiazepine] is like?" When I was having weight problems ... "Let's give this Tenuate [amphetamine] a try." And I just started going down the line treating the things that I wanted to treat. And none of it got out of hand. It wasn't until I came down here [to Texas] ... that things really started to go wild.

It generally took between five and 10 years for these pharmacists to progress into the later stages of drug abuse. Such a timeframe suggests that the therapeutic self-medicators were able to prevent their drug abuse from interfering with their personal or professional lives for a considerable time. For example, consider the exchange that occurred between the interviewer (I) and a 42-year-old male pharmacist (P):

> P: Every time I drink even two martinis, I throw up. I get diarrhea and I puke and I'm sick. So I took some Zantac [antacid]. I tried to cure my hangovers a little bit.
>
> I: These were just for medicinal purposes?
>
> P: Yeah, medicinal. Zantac [antacid], I mean, how can that hurt? And I go to work, but I'm sick and I don't want to go smelling like alcohol. Now I am deeply trying to just make it by. So now I begin to take pills to cure being sick so I can go to work. First I'm taking things strictly to cure hangovers, which began happening with practically drinking nothing and it's scaring me to death....So I start working and I start to take a few pills. I feel a little better. Now the [mood-altering] meds start to happen. I take a couple V's [Valium, a benzodiazepine] now and then. I'm taking a few Xanax [benzodiazepine]. Next, I'm taking some Vicodin [narcotic analgesic]. It took years [for the usage pattern] to go anywhere. Then somebody comes in with drugs and says, "These are my mother-in-law's prescriptions, she passed away, she had cancer. " I look at it, and it's all morphine. She says, "I don't know what to do. Will you please take it for me?" [The respondent replies, laughing], "We'll destroy the drugs, don't worry."

With the exception of their unauthorized self-medication, most individuals continued to serve the role of the "model pharmacist." Despite their progressive drug use, they usually continued to garner the respect and admiration of their peers and employers alike. It was not uncommon for them to be promoted into senior management positions, even after their prescription drug use became a daily occurrence. The bulk of the self-medicator group experienced a slow, progressive transition from occasional therapeutic drug use to a schedule of repeated daily dosage intake. In retrospect, they attributed their increased usage to the body's tendency to develop a chemical tolerance to the medications. This situation necessitated larger and more frequent dosage units to achieve the desired therapeutic effects.

A handful of therapeutic self-medicators were not so lucky. For them, there was less time between the onset of their use and manifestation of drug addiction. Their abuse progression was much faster. This is illustrated by the comments of a 49-year-old male pharmacist:

> About two or three years after I had my store, I was working long, long hours. Like 8:00 to 8:00 Monday through Saturday and some hours on Sunday. And my back hurt one day. It was really killing me....I started out with two Empirin-3 [narcotic analgesic]. Just for the back pain. I mean, I hurt, my back hurt, my head hurt. I don't know why, but I just reached for that bottle, and I knew it was against the law to do that, but I did it anyway. Man, I felt good. I was off and running. This was eureka. This was it. It progressed. I started taking more and more.

The key to a self-medicator's fast-paced progressive drug use seemed to lie in the given individual's perceived need to treat a wider and growing array of physical ailments. In fact, it got to the point that many "drug-thirsty" pharmacists now recognized that they were actively inventing ailments to treat. As a 40-year-old female pharmacist put it, "I had a symptom for everything I took."

There were 27 pharmacists who could be classified as therapeutic self-medicators. These pharmacists entered their pharmacy careers admittedly as extremely naive about drug abuse. They were either counseled or had convinced themselves that there was no harm in the occasional therapeutic use of prescription medicines. In short, the normative and behavioral advances in their criminal and deviant behavior were largely the result of a well-intentioned exploitation of their professional position and knowledge. The justifications for their drug use were firmly entrenched in a desire to excel in their jobs while always efficiently caring for their patients. The therapeutic self-medicators always used their drugs in private, carefully disguising their addiction from others around them. Over time, their false confidence and self-denial allowed their drug use to progress significantly into addiction. Once their façade was broken, these pharmacists awoke to the stark reality that they were now chemically dependent on one or more of the drugs that they so confidently had been "prescribing" for themselves.

COMMON COGNITIVE AND BEHAVIORAL THEMES

We found clear evidence of two very different modes of entry among the respondents, namely recreational abusers and therapeutic self-medicators. However, it is important to note that these were *not* mutually exclusive categories of offenders. In other words, these two categories were not completely dichotomous. As is usually the case, real life seldom fits cleanly into nice, neat categories. In fact, we were able to identify a number of cognitive and behavioral themes that were common to almost all of the drug-using pharmacists interviewed. These themes were expressed by nearly all of the drug-abusing pharmacists that we interviewed, regardless of how the individual initially began their illicit drug abuse career. The existence of these common themes suggests that pharmacy-specific occupational contingencies play a central role in the onset and progression of illicit use of prescription medicines. Let us examine the three most common of these cognitive and behavioral themes in more detail.

I. I'm a Pharmacist, So I Know What I Am Doing

Intuitively, it should not be surprising that pharmacists would steal prescription medicines as a way of treating their own physical ailments. After all, they have been exposed to years of pharmacy training that emphasized the beneficial, therapeutic potential of prescription medicines. Each pharmacist has dispensed medicines to hundreds of patients and then watched the drugs usually produce the predicted beneficial results. They all have read the literature detailing the drug's chemical composition and studied the often times dramatic beneficial, curative effects of these chemical substances. Pharmacists, more so than any other member of society, are keenly aware of how and why drugs work. There was strong evidence to suggest that both the therapeutic self-medicators and the recreational abusers actively utilize the years of pharmacological knowledge that they had acquired. So, when health or emotional problems occurred, it makes perfect sense that they should put their knowledge to work on themselves. This personal application of pharmaceutical information can be seen clearly in the comments of a 40-year-old female self-medicator:

> So, in 1986, I was sent to the psychologist. That was when I was forced to recognize that I had an alcohol problem. And I recognized that I had to do something. And in my brilliant analysis, I made a decision that since alcohol was a central nervous system depressant, the solution for me was to use a central nervous system stimulant. That would solve my alcohol problem. So I chose the best stimulant that I had access to, and that was [pharmaceutical-grade] cocaine. I started using cocaine in 1986. I never thought that it would progress. I never thought it was going to get worse. I thought, "I'm just going to use it occasionally."

Similar trends were observed among the recreational abuser group, only here, the applied use of drugs was based upon more recreational motives.

Virtually all of the therapeutic self-medicators and the recreational abusers described how they became masters at quickly diagnosing their own ailments or emotional needs, then identifying the appropriate pharmacological agent that would remedy the problem. Moreover, as professionals, they were quite confident that they would be able to limit or self-regulate their drug intake as to never become addicted. All of the respondents drew upon their social status as pharmacists to convince themselves that their drug use would not progress into dependency. As a 40-year-old female self-medicator put it, "I'm a pharmacist, I know what I am doing." To a person, the interviewees agreed that a well-trained, professional pharmacist could not possibly fall prey to drug addiction. They recall being even more adamant in their view that personally they were immune from such problems, believing that only stupid, naive people became addicted to drugs. This distinct form of denial is illustrated in the remarks of a 35-year-old male recreational abuser:

> Yeah, I thought, "It [addiction] can't happen to me because I know too much." We somehow think that knowledge is going to prevent it from happening to us when [we know that] knowledge has nothing to do with it. It's like heart disease or anything else. Its like, "Well, I know about this so it can't happen to me." [In fact,]...now I teach pharmacy. I developed a chemical dependency curriculum at our pharmacy school. I do a clerkship in it and I don't think there is one in the country, except for mine, that deals with some of that. Maybe they [the students] can personalize [pharmacists' drug abuse] a little bit.

One 39-year-old male self-medicator went so far as to say: "I mean, we know more [about the effect of drugs] than doctors. We have all the package inserts. We have the knowledge. We know a lot about the drugs, so what's the big deal?" Interviewees did not understand why they should use personal sick leave to go to a doctor and pay money to acquire a written prescription to dispense a drug that was on the shelves right behind them. This just did not make any sense, since they firmly believed that pharmacists knew more about dispensing medicines than most doctors. Elsewhere (Dabney & Hollinger, 1999), we refer to this denial mechanism as a "paradox of familiarity," arguing that familiarity can breed consent, not contempt toward prescription drug use.

II. No Cautionary Tales or Warnings

Remarkably, the vast majority of both the recreational abusers and therapeutic self-medicators claimed that they never had been warned about the dangers of drug addiction. Rather, they insisted that their formal training had only stressed the beneficial side of prescription medicines. For example, a 48-year-old male recreational abuser stated:

> I never had anybody come right out and tell me that [prescription drug abuse] was probably unethical and illegal, because they assumed that we knew that. But nobody ever said this is something that is not done.

Left without precise ethical guidance on the issue, some pharmacists assumed that their drug use was acceptable behavior. In explaining this point of view, a 39-year-old female self-medicator stated:

> It's [self-medication]...just part of it [the pharmacy job]. It's just accepted because we know so much. I'm sure it's the same way when the doctors do it. It wasn't a big stretch to start [thinking,] "You know, I got a headache here, maybe I should try one of these Percocets [narcotic analgesic]?"

In fact, many pharmacists spoke about their theft of prescription drugs as if they were a "fringe benefit" that went along with the job. Much like a butcher always eats the best cuts of meat or a car dealer drives a brand-new automobile, pharmacists always will have access to free prescription drugs. This theme is illustrated in the comments of a 45-year-old male pharmacist:

> Why take plain aspirin or plain Tylenol when you've got this [Percocet—narcotic analgesic]? It works better…[so] you don't even have to struggle with it. I really believed that I had license to do that…as a pharmacist. I mean with all that stuff sitting there, you know. Oh, my back was just killing me during that period of time, and this narcotic pain reliever is sitting right there. I thought, "Why should [I] suffer through back pain when I have this bottle of narcotics sitting here?"

III. Out-of-Control Addiction

The abovementioned themes involve cognitive dimensions of the pharmacists' drug abuse in that they speak to common motivational and justification themes that were present in all of the interviews. Perhaps more important is the fact that there was a common behavioral characteristic shared by all 50 pharmacists. In every case, occasional prescription drug abuse eventually gave way to an advanced addictive state that was marked by an enormous intake of drugs, unmistakable habituation, and the constant threat of physical withdrawal. Members of the recreational abuser and therapeutic self-medicator groups alike routinely reported daily use levels exceeding 50 to 100 times the recommended daily dosage. One pharmacist reported that his drug use regimen progressed to 150 Percocets (a strong narcotic analgesic) per day. Another individual reported injecting up to 200 mg of morphine each day. Still another respondent described a daily use pattern that, among other things, included five grams of cocaine.

Invariably, these advanced levels of drug use led to clear signs of habituation and the constant threat of physical withdrawal. At this point, the individuals recall growing increasingly desperate. Consider the following quote from a 44-year-old male pharmacist who was in charge of ordering the narcotics at the independent retail pharmacy where he worked:

> I was ordering excessive quantities and chasing down drug trucks. That's what I used to do. I was really reaching my bottom. I would chase these delivery trucks down in the morning, because I didn't come to my store until mid-afternoon. I was in withdrawal in the morning, and I was without drugs, so I had to have it. I was just going nuts. Many mornings I had gone to work sweating. It would be 30 degrees, it would be January, and the clerk would say, "You look sick," and I would say, "It's the flu." So I would pay the delivery guys extra money to deliver my drugs first, or I would chase the delivery trucks down in the morning. I knew the trucks delivered at six in the morning, they came by my area, and I would get up early and chase the trucks down the highway. I would go in excess of 100 miles an hour trying to catch up with this truck and flag it down.

The advanced stages of addiction almost always produced traumatic physical and psychological events. Take, for example, the following comments that were made by a 39-year-old male pharmacist:

I was out of control for four years. I was just lucky that I never got caught. I don't know how I didn't get caught. I fell asleep twice coming home on Interstate 95. I fell asleep at the wheel doing 70 once and then I scraped up the side of the car and blew out the tires. I also tried to kill myself with a shotgun. She [my wife] was going to leave me. My world was falling apart, but I couldn't do anything about it. I didn't know what to do.

These "out of control" drug use patterns along with the realization of chemical dependency left the pharmacists in a problematic mental state. It was at this point that all of the pharmacists recalled coming to grips with their addiction. This personal realization was accompanied by a shift in the way that they thought about their drug use. They no longer denied the situation by drawing upon recreational or therapeutic explanations. Instead, they finally admitted the dire nature of their situation and became more and more reclusive. In short, all of the respondents grew to realize that they had a drug problem, turning then to fear and ignorance to foster the final weeks or months of their drug addiction.

THEORETICAL IMPLICATIONS—A CONTEXTUALIZED UNDERSTANDING OF DEVIANT CAREERS

Let us now consider how the present research serves to inform the existing literature on deviant and/or criminal careers. We believe that this is best achieved by applying the Best and Luckenbill (1994) conceptual framework to the realities of the 50 drug-using pharmacists that we studied. We chose the Best and Luckenbill (1994) model because (1) it is particularly apropos to the issue of drug use careers, (2) it is positioned at the forefront of the broader literature on criminal careers, and (3) it helps make sense of multiple dimensions and types of social organization. In short, these authors provide a series of valuable conceptual tools that can be used to organize and understand the nature and dynamics of a criminal career, especially one involving drug use. Notwithstanding these merits, there is a paucity of research that attempts to systematically validate these conceptual claims that are inherent in their five-part typology. The present analysis is an attempt to fill this void.

In general, we find strong support for Best and Luckenbill's conceptual claim that there exists patterned organization to both deviants and deviance. Nevertheless, the data expand upon the existing understanding of drug use careers in three very important ways. First, by looking at prescription drug use among pharmacists, we blur the lines between the concepts of crime and deviance, as the individuals are routinely violating both norms and laws. Second, we discovered that a single category of criminal/deviant action (i.e., illicit prescription drug use) within a single category of criminal/deviant actors (practicing pharmacists) could begin and progress under different behavioral and motivational pretenses. Thus, even under the most constrained substantive focus, there can exist variation in the social organization of deviance and deviants.

At the same time, our data suggest that divergent criminal/deviant career trajectories eventually converge to produce very similar behavioral and motivational manifestations in mature offenders. This third observation suggests that there can be a two-way fluidity to the social organization of deviance and deviants, even within the most narrowly defined criminal/deviant phenomena (i.e., illicit prescription drug use among pharmacists). We provide the following discussion to illustrate these assertions.

Therapeutic Self-Medicators—Loners to the End

Best and Luckenbill (1994) identify physician drug addicts as examples of the "loner" category. They contend that the physician's repeated drug thefts and drug usage lead him/her to refine his/her techniques while at the same time solidifying their denial or justifications for on-the-job offending. Given the secretive nature of the loner's crime and deviance, the authors suggest that he/she will become more and more efficient at manipulating and distorting norms and routines within their conventional lifestyles in order to reinforce their unconventional needs. They submit that the techniques and justifications for continued and progressive drug use can be largely traced to the individual's ability to manipulate or exploit their professional standing. These characteristics produce long, drawn-out criminal careers whereby the individual slowly plods along with their wrongdoing.

Drawing also upon earlier work by Winick (1961) to articulate the systematic loner category of deviants, the present analysis offers valuable empirical evidence substantiating the authors' theoretical proposition. Namely, the analysis reveals how some drug-using pharmacists always use prescription drugs in private. They manipulate their access, knowledge, and the messages from other pharmacists to sustain these deviant ways. Moreover, they develop and impose various denial and/or rationalization frameworks to protect them from the shame and hazards of their considerable drug habits. Thus, the effectiveness of these cognitive denial structures is conveniently reinforced by the efficient and secretive nature of their habitual offending.

In summary, we submit that the drug use careers of the 27 therapeutic self-medicators are clearly representative of Best and Luckenbill's (1994) loner category. Specifically, they are secretive deviants with defensive motives who adeptly manipulate and distort aspects of their conformist lives to facilitate their deviance. More importantly, there is a consistency to the social organization of their criminal and deviant acts and interactions throughout the course of their criminal/deviant careers. These individuals never displayed characteristics that would warrant their classification within any of the other four categories of deviant careers, motivations, or transactions.

Recreational Abusers—Peers to Colleagues to Loners

Our discussion of therapeutic self-medicators clearly surpasses what is found in the existing literature. However, we argue that it is our documentation of the recreational abuser category that provides the more exciting findings. Unlike the therapeutic self-medicators, we encountered difficulty when attempting to classify the 23 recreational abusers within Best and Luckenbill's (1994) five-point continuum.

We observe that these pharmacists do not neatly fit within any single category. Instead, the members of the recreational abuser group followed a more dynamic and evolving career path. Over time, this group seemed to move across at least three of Best and Luckenbill's five categories—from peers, to colleagues, and then finally to loners. Corresponding changes are also seen in the nature of their deviant motivations and transactions.

Best and Luckenbill assert that "peers" differ from loners in that there is a collective interaction dimension to their deviance. They use the term "deviant exchanges" to describe the cooperative deviant roles that exist in these relationships. The authors reference recreational drug users as examples of peer-based deviants. Not only are recreational drug users afforded the normative subculture that accompanies a collegial relationship, but also the collective nature of their deviant activities provides them direct and continued social support for their actions and justifications. In other words, shared participation in deviance results in a more stable, closer knit subculture. This yields a more complete socialization process and an even more rapid career trajectory than loners or colleagues.

In the initial days of their illicit prescription drug use, most all of the recreational abusers actively sought out collective opportunities to engage in crime and deviance. Limited access to medications forced drug users to become more reliant on friends or fellow pharmacy students to supply them with prescription drugs. In these earlier stages of the recreational abusers' career, drug-using pharmacists were able to structure deviant acts in the form of "deviant exchanges." That is, while their usage levels were within socially acceptable limits, they knew that they could turn to fellow drug-using peers or colleagues to supply them with drugs and/or the necessary deviant justifications.

The progressive nature of their prescription drug use meant that they came to rely on more experienced users, as well as their newly acquired pharmacological knowledge, to acquire necessary drug use skills and rationalizations. As long as it was done in moderation, they could access other pharmacists' cache of drugs or even use in the presence of others. The key was to disguise their drug use levels as unchanging and occasional in nature. On a cognitive level, exposure to fellow drug users with relatively similar habits afforded these individuals continued normative reinforcement and rationalizations. Clearly, this early drug use served to satisfy a sense of inquisitiveness or adventure that existed in the neophyte pharmacists. In this regard, the recreational abusers started out their deviant careers as a classic example of what Best and Luckenbill would call "peers" who engage in (social) deviant exchanges and are driven by adventurous motives.

As the frequency and intensity of their prescription drug abuse increased, however, these individuals became fearful that their fellow pharmacists might report them to authorities. Drug use that was originally viewed as tolerable among nonusers and normal among fellow users advanced to the level that any rational observer would view as excessive and dangerous. This realization along with a progressive level of habituation resulted in a shift from "peer"-type relations to more "collegial" relations.

"Colleagues" are said to be significantly different from loners and peers. These individuals act principally on their own, but in an environment where there are fellow deviants present. Best and Luckenbill (1994) point to "pool hustlers and computer hackers" as classic examples of this category of deviants. While, like the loners, there is a private quality to their deviant actions (i.e., individual deviance), these individuals are afforded the opportunity to observe or interact with fellow deviants as a way of refining and advancing their deviant techniques and justifications. The authors contend that the loose social organization of their rule-breaking behavior exposes members of the colleague category to a deviant subculture that affords them subtle but important normative direction and reinforcement for their behaviors (i.e., behavioral, cognitive, and ideological guidance). They posit that these individuals are driven by adventurous, reward-based motives.

Best and Luckenbill (1994) contend that colleague-type deviants engage in their aberrant behaviors within a common social environment but do not involve themselves in collective deviant acts. Fearful of detection and the resultant negative stigma, recreational abusers reported that they commonly tried to disguise increased drug theft and usage from their fellow pharmacists. While they curbed their collective crime and deviance, recreational abusers were still aware of drug-using pharmacists who shared their passion for the drugs and relied on this small circle for behavioral and motivational reinforcement. This shift generally occurred late in pharmacy school or during one's earliest work experiences. In other words, we observed a pronounced shift in pharmacists' criminal/deviant careers as they move from experimentation to habituation. Referring to Best and Luckenbill's (1994) model, it can be said that the individual evolves from peer-like conditions to a colleague-based mode of interaction. The scope of deviant exchanges is tightened and a considerable amount of individual offending emerges. Still, the maturing recreational abuser maintains his/her adventurous motives.

All 23 of the recreational abusers described experiencing an epiphany marking the realization that they were no longer in control of their prescription drug use. In short, as their habituation intensified, their denial systems eventually broke down and they had to come to grips with the fact that their benign recreational drug use had now progressed into full-blown addiction. This realization was generally precipitated by serious drug-related physical manifestations (e.g., bleeding ulcers, overdoses, blackouts) or through an embarrassing social incident whereby their pronounced abuse/addiction came to the attention of others.

At this point, the recreational abusers change from acting like deviant "colleagues" to "loners" (Best & Luckenbill, 1994). The distinguishing characteristic between these two categories is that the latter involves more secretive offending that is reinforced internally instead of externally. When these pharmacists began using exorbitant amounts of prescription drugs on a daily basis, they could no longer look to fellow drug-using pharmacists for behavioral or motivational assistance. They regressed into a pronounced routine of private offending. In effect, they were left to fend for themselves. More adventurous motives were replaced by abject fear, while the individuals desperately sought to stay afloat functionally. During this stage of their criminal/deviant careers, the recreational abusers accepted the prob-lematic nature of their heavy drug use and took it underground to avoid detection and stigma. In effect, these individuals were simply trying to postpone the inevi-table crash—desperately trying to escape detection and the loss of their jobs. This survivalist mentality accompanied by secretive drug use behavior was observed in all of the mature therapeutic self-medicators' career trajectories.

CONCLUSIONS

There are several critical points underlying Best and Luckenbill's (1994) depiction of criminal careers. First, the authors stress that we must be aware of structure, process, and social organization when studying deviant behaviors as they emerge and evolve over time. Second, they underscore that we must be sensitive to the interconnections that exist between the deviant actor and the social ecology of the deviant acts. Third, their emphasis on roles, subculture, and the transactional nature of deviant events reinforces the fluid and evolving nature of the cognitive and behavioral aspects of the subject matter. Finally, at the core of their framework is the importance that interactions and the resulting learning play in the social organization of deviants and deviance.

Some of the criminal and deviant behavior that was observed among the respondent pharmacists fits neatly into the Best and Luckenbill (1994) typology. Pharmacists that we classify as therapeutic self-medicators resemble loners with defensive motives who engage in acts of individual offending. However, the crimi-nal/deviant careers of other pharmacists were not so static. Recreational abusers follow an evolving career path whereby they start out as "peers," grow as "col-leagues," and then spend their mature years as "loners." Corresponding changes are also observed in the nature of their criminal/deviant transactions and motives. While ideological issues appeared to remain constant throughout, the longer that the habitual drug use continued, the more similar the traits of the recreational abusers and therapeutic self-medicators became. This leads us to conclude that two criminal/deviant trajectories that started out looking quite dissimilar even-tually became quite similar. While Best and Luckenbill allow for the possibility of intercategory flexibility, this is the first empirical inquiry to provide systematic and detailed documentation of this type of fluidity. We believe that this discovery represents an important finding of this study, as it provides critical evidence that even the most focused forms of crime and deviance are marked by both typo-logical differentiation and commonality, especially if one examines the offender's entire career.

Our findings lead us to endorse a conceptual middle ground. Namely, it seems most advantageous for scholars to seek out a conceptual space that lies between the abstractions of the abstract conceptual models of criminal careers and the prag-matic findings that are generated by the drug ethnographer. While there is much merit in deductive reasoning efforts such as those of Best and Luckenbill (1994) or Tittle and Paternoster (2000), from time to time we must return to the field and undertake inductively based exercises to reevaluate the posited abstractions. In the present case, this allows us to validate many of the claims set forth by Best and Luckenbill while adding important new insights.

Moreover, we submit that our findings have important public policy relevance, especially for those social control entities that deal with drug-addicted pharmacists. These include drug treatment professionals, private security personnel, and members of the criminal justice system.

As mentioned at the outset of this article, drug treatment professionals have long been aware of the propensity for pharmacists to abuse the drugs that they are entrusted to dispense (Hankes & Bissell, 1992). At present, members of the drug treatment community and state licensure agencies alike generally operate under the assumption that there exist two separate, mutually exclusive types of drug-using pharmacists: those who use for therapeutic reasons and those who use for recreational reasons. While we have been able to confirm this general trend, our data suggest that treatment professionals can benefit from taking a fluid approach to the prescription drug user. It appears that considerable time, effort, and money can be saved by evaluation and treatment modalities that are sensitive to the evolving and overlapping qualities of prescription drug use among pharmacists. Most importantly, our research, which targeted individuals with severe histories of drug abuse, provides a glimmer of hope that focused prevention efforts might well stem early drug use behavior from ever maturing into full-blown addiction.

Pharmacists are a highly sought-after commodity in this country. At the same time that we see a new hospital or retail pharmacy popping up on virtually every street corner, the news reports serious shortages of licensed pharmacists. In light of this supply and demand squeeze, employers have been forced to be less selective about who they hire. The authors' personal conversations with corporate executives from major retail drug chains verify that "zero tolerance" policies have been relaxed, and some companies now hire pharmacists who are known to have had a past drug abuse problem. Increased surveillance and social control will undoubtedly be a byproduct of these liberal personnel decisions, and security personnel must be sensitive to the ever-changing nature of these individuals' criminal careers and thus devise intervention and surveillance programs that are duly flexible.

Nationwide data collection efforts have established that illicit prescription drug use levels are on the rise in the United States (Substance Abuse and Mental Health Services Administration, 1999). Of particular concern are the disturbing increases among young people. With increasing regularity, adolescents are turning away from traditional street drugs and coming to rely more heavily on prescription drugs (i.e., narcotics such as OxyContin or stimulants such as Ritalin or Meridia) to satisfy their recreational drug use urges. This situation has produced a coordinated call to arms in which government agencies such as the National Institute on Drug Abuse (NIDA) have begun to direct research dollars toward understanding the trends. In addition, law enforcement agencies from the Drug

Enforcement Administration (DEA) on down to local sheriff's department have begun to simultaneously step up interdiction efforts. Preliminary findings suggest that unethical or incompetent pharmacists play an important role in the proliferation of these drugs into the hands of street users (National Institute on Drug Abuse, 2001). Moreover, the past year alone has seen the flagship trade journal of the pharmacy industry publish several commentaries on the topic of prescription drug abuse amongst their ranks (Baldwin, 2001; Baldwin & Thibault, 2001; Dabney, 2001). Pressure continues to mount at the state and local levels to address levels of prescription-dispensing errors that endanger the patients and customers that entrust our nation's pharmacists. These trends suggest that it is only a matter of time until regulatory, private security, and criminal justice agents launch a concerted effort to more stringently regulate the pharmacy profession. When such an initiative gets underway, it is critical that the powers that be direct considerable attention toward the types of deviant pharmacists that were interviewed in the present study. In doing so, it is critical that the inquiry consider (1) the evolving nature of the drug abuse that impacts some pharmacists, (2) whether the deviant drug use careers documented in this report coincide with or exacerbate additional forms of professional wrongdoing, and (3) whether the career trajectories outlined in the present study are applicable on a larger scale.

REFERENCES

Adler, P. (1993). *Wheeling and dealing: An ethnography of an upper-level drug dealing and smuggling community.* New York: Columbia University Press.

Baldwin, J. N. (2001). Self-medication by pharmacists: Familiarity breeds attempt? *Journal of the American Pharmaceutical Association, 41*(3), 371.

Baldwin, J. N., & Thibault, E. D. (2001). Substance abuse by pharmacists: Stopping the insanity. *Journal of the American Pharmaceutical Association, 41*(3), 373–375.

Becker, H. S. (1953). Becoming a marijuana user. *American Journal of Sociology, 59,* 235–242.

———. (1963). *Outsiders.* New York: Free Press.

Best, J., & Luckenbill, D. F. (1994). *Organizing deviance.* Englewood Cliffs, NJ: Prentice Hall.

Bissell, L., Haberman, P. W., & Williams, R. L. (1989). Pharmacists recovering from alcohol and other drug addictions: An interview study. *American Pharmacy, NS29*(6), 19–30.

Blackwell, J. S. (1983). Drifting, controlling and overcoming: Opiate users who avoid becoming chronically dependent. *Journal of Drug Issues, 13,* 219–235.

Chi, J. (1983).Impaired pharmacists: More programs move to handle the problem. *Drug Topics, 127*(47), 24–29.

Coombs, R. H. (1981). Drug abuse as career. *Journal of Drug Issues, 11,* 369–387.

Dabney, D. A. (1997). A sociological examination of illicit prescription drug use among pharmacists. Unpublished Ph.D. diss., University of Florida, Gainesville, FL.

———. (2001). The onset of prescription drug use among pharmacists. *Journal of the American Pharmaceutical Association, 41*(3), 392–400.

Dabney, D. A., & Hollinger, R. C. (1999). Illicit prescription drug use among pharmacists: Evidence of a paradox of familiarity. *Work & Occupations, 26*(1), 77–106.

Faupel, C. (1987). Heroin use and criminal careers. *Qualitative Sociology, 10*(2), 115–131.

———. (1991). *Shooting dope: Career patterns of hard-core heroin users.* Gainesville: University of Florida Press.

Faupel, C., & Klockars, C. B. (1987). Drug-crime connections: Elaborations from the life histories of hard-core heroin addicts. *Social Problems, 34*(1), 54–68.

Gallegos, K. V., Veit, F. W., Wilson, P. O., Porter, T., & Talbott, G. D. (1988). Substance abuse among health professionals. *Maryland Medical Journal, 37*(3), 191–197.

Greenberg, D. (1996). Criminal Careers, Vol.2. Dartmouth University Press.

Hafley, S. R., & Tewksbury, R. (1996). Reefer madness in bluegrass country: Community structure and roles in the rural Kentucky marijuana industry. *Journal of Crime and Justice, 19*(1), 75–94.

Hankes, L., & Bissell, L. (1992). Health professionals. In J. H. Lowinson, P. Ruiz, R. Millman, & J. G. Langrod (Eds.), *Substance abuse: A comprehensive textbook* (2nd ed., pp. 897–908). Baltimore: Williams & Wilkins.

Martin, S. (1993). Pharmacists number more than 190,000 in United States. *American Pharmacy, NS33*(7), 22–23.

McAuliffe, W. E. (1984). Nontherapeutic opiate addiction in health professionals: A new form of impairment. *American Journal of Drug & Alcohol Abuse, 10*(1), 1–22.

McAuliffe, W. E., Santangelo, S. L., Gingras, J., Rohman, M., Sobol, A., & Magnuson, E. (1987). Use and abuse of controlled substances by pharmacists and pharmacy students. *American Journal of Hospital Pharmacy, 44*(2), 311–317.

National Institute on Drug Abuse. (2001). *Prescription drugs abuse and addiction.* Washington, DC: National Institute on Drug Abuse.

Nettler, G. (1982). "lying, cheating and stealing," Social Forces," 631(1), 283–295.

Normack, J. W., Eckel, F. M., Pfifferling, J-H., & Cocolas, G. (1985). Impairment risk in North Carolina pharmacists. *American Pharmacy, NS25*(6), 45–48.

Penna, R. P., & Williams, R. L. (1985). *Helping the impaired pharmacist: A handbook for planning and implementing state programs.* Washington DC: American Pharmaceutical Association.

Quinney, R. (1963). "Occupational structure and criminal behavior: Prescription violation by retail pharmacists," Social Problems,11.179–185.

Rubington, E. (1967). Drug addiction as a deviant career. *International Journal of the Addictions, 2*(1), 3–21.

Sheffield, J. W. (1988). Establishing a rehabilitation program for impaired pharmacists. *American Journal of Hospital Pharmacy, 45*(10), 2092–2098.

Sheffield, J. W., O'Neill, P., & Fisher, C. (1992). Women in recovery: from pain to progress, parts I & II." *Texas Pharmacy, 8*(1), 29–36 and 8(2), 22–34.

Smith, D. R., & Smith, W. R. (1984). Patterns of delinquent careers: An assessment of three perspectives. *Social Science Research, 13*, 129–158.

Substance Abuse and Mental Health Services Administration. 1999. *National household survey on drug abuse: Population estimates 1999.* Washington, DC: Department of Health and Human Services.

Tittle, C. R., & Paternoster, R. (2000). *Social deviance and crime: An organizational and theoretical approach.* Los Angeles: Roxbury.

Waldorf, D. (1983). Natural recovery from opiate addiction: Some social psychological processes of untreated recovery. *Journal of Drug Issues, 13*, 237–280.

Winick, C. (1961). Physician narcotic addicts. *Social Problems, 9*, 174–186.

✒

CHAPTER 14

Denying the Guilty Mind: Accounting for Involvement in White-Collar Crime

Michael L. Benson

In this classic study, the author examines the excuses and justifications used by white-collar offenders to explain their involvement in criminal activities and deny their criminality. Michael L. Benson's study is based on interviews with 30 convicted white-collar offenders. The interviews were supplemented with an examination of the files maintained by federal law enforcement authorities (prosecutors, probation officer, and judges) concerned with the prosecution of white-collar offenses. The author defines white-collar offenders as "those convicted of economic offenses committed through the use of indirection, fraud, or collusion." The offenses represented in the sample include securities and exchange fraud, antitrust violations, embezzlement, false claims, and tax evasion. All of the offenders were men.

Adjudication as a criminal is, to use Garfinkel's (1956) classic term, degradation ceremony. The focus of this article is on how offenders attempt to defeat the success of this ceremony and deny their own criminality through the use of accounts. However, in the interest of showing in as much detail as possible all sides of the experience undergone by these offenders, it is necessary to treat first the guilt and inner anguish that is felt by many white-collar offenders even though they deny being criminals. This is best accomplished by beginning with a description of a unique feature of the prosecution of white-collar crimes.

In white-collar criminal cases, the issue is likely to be *why* something was done, rather than *who* did it (Edelhertz, 1970, p. 47). There is often relatively little

Source: Benson, M. L. (1985). Denying the guilty mind: Accounting for involvement in white-collar crime. *Criminology, 23*(4), 589–599. Copyright © 1985 by the American Society of Crimonology. Reprinted with permission.

disagreement as to what happened. In the words of one assistant U.S. attorney interviewed for the study:

> If you actually had a movie playing, neither side would dispute that a person moved in this way and handled this piece of paper, etc. What it comes down to is, did they have the criminal intent?

If the prosecution is to proceed past the investigatory stages, the prosecutor must infer from the pattern of events that conscious criminal intent was present and believe that sufficient evidence exists to convince a jury of this interpretation of the situation. As Katz (1979, pp. 445–46) has noted, making this inference can be difficult because of the way in which white-collar illegalities are integrated into ordinary occupational routines. Thus, prosecutors conducting trials, grand jury hearings, or plea negotiations spend a great deal of effort establishing that the defendant did indeed have the necessary criminal intent. By concentrating on the offender's motives, the prosecutor attacks the very essence of the white-collar offender's public and personal image as an upstanding member of the community. The offender is portrayed as someone with a guilty mind.

Not surprisingly, therefore, the most consistent and recurrent pattern in the interviews, though not present in all of them, was denial of criminal intent, as opposed to the outright denial of any criminal behavior whatsoever. Most offenders acknowledged that their behavior probably could be construed as falling within the conduct proscribed by statute, but they uniformly denied that their actions were motivated by a guilty mind. This is not to say, however, that offenders *felt* no guilt or shame as a result of conviction. On the contrary, indictment, prosecution, and conviction provoke a variety of emotions among offenders.

The enormous reality of the offender's lived emotion (Denzin, 1984) in admitting guilt is perhaps best illustrated by one offender's description of his feelings during the hearing at which he pled guilty.

> You know [the plea's] what really hurt. I didn't even know I had feet. I felt numb. My head was just floating. There was no feeling, except a state of suspended animation.... For a brief moment, I almost hesitated. I almost said not guilty. If I had been alone, I would have fought, but my family....

The traumatic nature of this moment lies, in part, in the offender's feeling that only one aspect of his life is being considered. From the offender's point of view his crime represents only one small part of his life. It does not typify his inner self, and to judge him solely on the basis of this one event seems an atrocious injustice to the offender.

For some the memory of the event is so painful that they want to obliterate it entirely, as the two following quotations illustrate.

> I want quiet. I want to forget. I want to cut with the past.
> I've already divorced myself from the problem. I don't even want to hear the names of certain people ever again. It brings me pain.

For others, rage rather than embarrassment seemed to be the dominant emotion.

> I never really felt any embarrassment over the whole thing. I felt rage and it wasn't false or self-serving. It was really (something) to see this thing in action and recognize what the whole legal system has come to through its development, and the abuse of the grand jury system and the abuse of the indictment system.

The role of the news media in the process of punishment and stigmatization should not be overlooked. All offenders whose cases were reported on by the news media were either embarrassed or embittered or both by the public exposure.

> The only one I am bitter at is the newspapers, as many people are. They are unfair because you can't get even. They can say things that are untrue, and let me say this to you. They wrote an article on me that was so blasphemous, that was so horrible. They painted me as an insidious, miserable creature, wringing out the last penny.

Offenders whose cases were not reported on by the news media expressed relief at having avoided that kind of embarrassment, sometimes saying that greater publicity would have been worse than any sentence they could have received.

In court, defense lawyers are fond of presenting white-collar offenders as having suffered enough by virtue of the humiliation of public adjudication as criminals. On the other hand, prosecutors present them as cavalier individuals who arrogantly ignore the law and brush off its weak efforts to stigmatize them as criminals. Neither of these stereotypes is entirely accurate. The subjective effects of conviction on white-collar offenders are varied and complex. One suspects that this is true of all offenders, not only white-collar offenders.

The emotional responses of offenders to conviction have not been the subject of extensive research. However, insofar as an individual's emotional response to adjudication may influence the deterrent or crime-reinforcing impact of punishment on him or her, further study might reveal why some offenders stop their criminal behavior while others go on to careers in crime (Casper, 1978, p. 80).

Although the offenders displayed a variety of different emotions with respect to their experiences, they were nearly unanimous in denying basic criminality. To see how white-collar offenders justify and excuse their crimes, we turn to their accounts. The small number of cases rules out the use of any elaborate classification techniques. Nonetheless, it is useful to group offenders by offense when presenting their interpretations.

ANTITRUST VIOLATORS

Four of the offenders had been convicted of antitrust violations, all in the same case involving the building and contracting industry. Four major themes characterized their accounts. First, antitrust offenders focused on the everyday character and historical continuity of their offenses.

> It was a way of doing business before we even got into the business. So it was like, why do you brush your teeth in the morning or something.... It was a part of the everyday.... It was a method of survival.

The offenders argued that they were merely following established and necessary industry practices. These practices were presented as being necessary for the well-being of the industry as a whole, not to mention their own companies. Furthermore, they argued that cooperation among competitors was either allowed or actively promoted by the government in other industries and professions.

The second theme emphasized by the offenders was the characterization of their actions as blameless. They admitted talking to competitors and admitting submitting intentionally noncompetitive bids. However, they presented these practices as being done not for the purpose of rigging prices nor to make exorbitant profits. Rather, the everyday practices of the industry required them to occasionally submit bids on projects they really did not want to have. To avoid the effort and expense of preparing full-fledged bids, they would call a competitor to get a price to use. Such a situation might arise, for example, when a company already had enough work for the time being, but was asked by a valued customer to submit a bid anyway.

> All you want to do is show a bid, so that in some cases it was for as small a reason as getting your deposit back on the plans and specs. So you just simply have no interest in getting the job and just call to see if you can find someone to give you a price to use, so that you don't have to go through the expense of an entire bid preparation. Now that is looked at very unfavorably, and it is a technical violation, but it was strictly an opportunity to keep your name in front of a desired customer. Or you may find yourself in a situation where somebody is doing work for a customer, has done work for many, many years and is totally acceptable, totally fair. There is no problem. But suddenly they [the customer] get an idea that they ought to have a few tentative figures, and you're called in, and you are in a moral dilemma There's really no reason for you to attempt to compete in that circumstance. And so there was a way to back out.

Managed in this way, an action that appears on the surface to be a straightforward and conscious violation of antitrust regulations becomes merely a harmless business practice that happens to be a "technical violation." The offender can then refer to his personal history to verify his claim that, despite technical violations, he is in reality a law-abiding person. In the words of one offender, "Having been in the business for 33 years, you don't just automatically become a criminal overnight."

Third, offenders were very critical of the motives and tactics of prosecutors. Prosecutors were accused of being motivated solely by the opportunity for personal advancement presented by winning a big case. Furthermore, they were accused of employing prosecution selectively and using tactics that allowed the most culpable offenders to go free. The Department of Justice was painted as using antitrust prosecutions for political purposes.

The fourth theme emphasized by the antitrust offenders involved a comparison between their crimes and the crimes of street criminals. Antitrust offenses differ in their mechanics from street crimes in that they are not committed in one place and at one time. Rather, they are spatially and temporally diffuse and are intermingled with legitimate behavior. In addition, the victims of antitrust offenses tend not to be identifiable individuals, as is the case with most street crimes. These characteristics are used by antitrust violators to contrast their own behavior with that of common stereotypes of criminality. Real crimes are pictured as discrete events that have beginnings and ends and involve individuals who directly and purposely victimize someone else in a particular place and a particular time.

> It certainly wasn't a premeditated type of thing in our cases as far as I can see.... To me it's different than. [name] and I sitting down and we plan, well, we're going to rob this bank tomorrow and premeditatedly go in there.... That wasn't the case at all.... It wasn't like sitting down and planning, I'm going to rob this bank type of thing.... It was just a common everyday way of doing business and surviving.

A consistent thread running through all of the interviews was the necessity for antitrust-like practices, given the realities of the business world. Offenders seemed to define the situation in such a manner that two sets of rules could be seen to apply. On the one hand, there are the legislatively determined rules—laws—which govern how one is to conduct one's business affairs. On the other hand, there is a higher set of rules based on the concepts of profit and survival, which are taken to define what it means to be in business in a capitalistic society. These rules do not just regulate behavior; rather, they constitute or create the behavior in question. If one is not trying to make a profit or trying to keep one's business going, then one is not really "in business." Following Searle (1969, pp. 33–41), the former type of rule can be called a regulative rule and the latter type a constitutive rule. In certain situations, one may have to violate a regulative rule in order to conform to the more basic constitutive rule of the activity in which one is engaged.

This point can best be illustrated through the use of an analogy involving competitive games. Trying to win is a constitutive rule of competitive games in the sense that if one is not trying to win, one is not really playing the game. In competitive games, situations may arise where a player deliberately breaks the rules even though he knows or expects he will be caught. In the game of basketball, for example, a player may deliberately foul an opponent to prevent him from making a sure basket. In this instance, one would understand that the fouler was trying to win by gambling that the opponent would not make the free throws. The player violates the rule against fouling in order to follow the higher rule of trying to win.

Trying to make a profit or survive in business can be thought of as a constitutive rule of capitalist economies. The laws that govern how one is allowed to make a profit are regulative rules, which can understandably be subordinated to the rules of trying to survive and profit. From the offender's point of view, he is doing what businessmen in our society are supposed to do—that is, stay in business and make a profit. Thus, an individual who violates society's laws or regulations in certain situations may actually conceive of himself as thereby acting more in accord with the central ethos of his society than if he had been a strict observer of its law.

One might suggest, following Denzin (1977), that for businessmen in the building and contracting industry, an informal structure exists below the articulated legal structure, one which frequently supersedes the legal structure. The informal structure may define as moral and "legal" certain actions that the formal legal structure defines as immoral and "illegal."

TAX VIOLATORS

Six of the offenders interviewed were convicted of income tax violations. Like antitrust violators, tax violators can rely upon the complexity of the tax laws and an historical tradition in which cheating on taxes is not really criminal. Tax offenders would claim that everybody cheats somehow on their taxes and present themselves as victims of an unlucky break, because they got caught.

> Everybody cheats on their income tax, 95% of the people. Even if it's for $10, it's the same principle. I didn't cheat. I just didn't know how to report it.

The widespread belief that cheating on taxes is endemic helps to lend credence to the offender's claim to have been singled out and to be no more guilty than most people.

Tax offenders were more likely to have acted as individuals rather than as part of a group and, as a result, were more prone to account for their offenses by referring to them as either mistakes or the product of special circumstances. Violations were presented as simple errors which resulted from ignorance and poor record-keeping. Deliberate intention to steal from the government for personal benefit was denied.

> I didn't take the money. I have no bank account to show for all this money, where all this money is at that I was supposed to have. They never found the money, ever. There is no Swiss bank account, believe me. My records were strictly one big mess. That's all it was. If only I had an accountant, this wouldn't even of happened. No way in God's creation would this ever have happened.

Other offenders would justify their actions by admitting that they were wrong while painting their motives as altruistic rather then criminal. Criminality was denied because they did not set out to deliberately cheat the government for their own personal gain. Like the antitrust offenders discussed above, one tax violator distinguished between his own crime and the crimes of real criminals.

> I'm not a criminal. That is, I'm not a criminal from the standpoint of taking a gun and doing this and that. I'm a criminal from the standpoint of making a mistake, a serious mistake.... The thing that really got me involved in it is my feeling for the employees here, certain employees that are my right hand. In order to save them a certain amount of taxes and things like that, I'd extend money to them in cash, and the money came from these sources that I took it from. You know, cash sales and things of that nature, but practically all of it was turned over to the employees, because of my feeling for them.

All of the tax violators pointed out that they had no intention of deliberately victimizing the government. None of them denied the legitimacy of the tax laws, nor did they claim that they cheated because the government is not representative of the people (Conklin, 1977, p.99). Rather, as a result of ignorance or for altruistic reasons, they made decisions which turned out to be criminal when viewed from the perspective of the law. While they acknowledged the technical criminality of their actions, they tried to show that what they did was not criminally motivated.

VIOLATIONS OF FINANCIAL TRUST

Four offenders were involved in violations of financial trust. Three were bank officers who embezzled or misapplied funds, and the fourth was a union official who embezzled from a union pension fund. Perhaps because embezzlement is one crime in this sample that can be considered *mala in se*[1], these offenders were much more forthright about their crimes. Like the other offenders, the embezzlers would not go so far as to say "I am a criminal," but they did say "What I did was wrong, was criminal, and I knew it was." Thus, the embezzlers were unusual in that they explicitly admitted responsibility for their crimes. Two of the offenders clearly fit Cressey's scheme as persons with financial problems who used their positions to convert other people's money to their own use.

Unlike tax evasion, which can be excused by reference to the complex nature of tax regulations, or antitrust violations, which can be justified as for the good of the organization as a whole, embezzlement requires deliberate action on the part of the offender and is almost inevitably committed for personal reasons. The crime of embezzlement, therefore, cannot be accounted for by using the same techniques that tax violators or antitrust violators do. The act itself can only be explained by showing that one was under extraordinary circumstances which explain one's uncharacteristic behavior. Three of the offenders referred explicitly to extraordinary circumstances and presented the offense as an aberration in their life history. For example, one offender described his situation in this manner:

> As a kid, I never even—you know, kids will sometimes shoplift from the dime store—I never even did that. I had never stolen a thing in my life and that was what was so unbelievable about the whole thing, but here were some psychological and personal questions that I wasn't dealing with very well. I wasn't terribly happily married. I was married to a very strong-willed woman and it just wasn't working out.

The offender in this instance goes on to explain how, in an effort to impress his wife, he lived beyond his means and fell into debt.

A structural characteristic of embezzlement also helps the offender demonstrate his essential lack of criminality. Embezzlement is integrated into ordinary occupational routines. The illegal action does not stand out clearly against the surrounding set of legal actions. Rather, there is a high degree of surface correspondence between legal and illegal behavior. To maintain this correspondence, the offender must exercise some restraint when committing his crime. The embezzler must be discreet in his stealing; he cannot take all of the money available to him without at the same time revealing the crime. Once exposed, the offender can point to this restraint on his part as evidence that he is not really a criminal. That is, he can compare what happened with what could have happened in order to show how much more serious the offense could have been if he was really a criminal at heart.

> What I could have done if I had truly had a devious criminal mind and perhaps if I had been a little smarter—and I am not saying that with any degree of pride or any degree of modesty whatever, [as] it's being smarter in a bad, an evil way—I could have pulled this off on a grander scale and I might still be doing it.

Even though the offender is forthright about admitting his guilt, he makes a distinction between himself and someone with a truly "devious criminal mind." Contrary to Cressey's (1953, pp. 57–66) findings, none of the embezzlers claimed that their offenses were justified because they were underpaid or badly treated by their employers. Rather, attention was focused on the unusual circumstances surrounding the offense and its atypical character when compared to the rest of the offender's life. This strategy is for the most part determined by the mechanics and organizational format of the offense itself. Embezzlement occurs within the organization but not for the organization. It cannot be committed accidentally or out of ignorance. It can be accounted for only by showing that the actor "was not himself" at the time of the offense or was under such extraordinary circumstances that embezzlement was an understandable response to an unfortunate situation. This may explain the finding that embezzlers tend to produce accounts that are viewed as more sufficient by the justice system than those produced by other offenders (Rothman & Gandossy, 1982). The only plausible option open to a convicted embezzler to explain his offense is to admit responsibility while justifying the action, an approach that apparently strikes a responsive chord with judges.

FRAUD AND FALSE STATEMENTS

Ten offenders were convicted of some form of fraud or false statements charge. Unlike embezzlers, tax violators, or antitrust violators, these offenders were much more likely to deny committing any crime at all. Seven of the 10 claimed that they, personally, were innocent of any crime, although each admitted that fraud had occurred. Typically, they claimed to have been set up by associates and to have been wrongfully convicted by the U.S. attorney handling the case. One might call this the scapegoat strategy. Rather than admitting technical wrongdoing and then justifying or excusing it, the offender attempts to paint himself as a victim by shifting the blame entirely to another party. Prosecutors were presented as being either ignorant or politically motivated.

The outright denial of any crime whatsoever is unusual compared to the other types of offenders studied here. It may result from the nature of the crime of fraud.

By definition, fraud involves a conscious attempt on the part of one or more persons to mislead others. While it is theoretically possible to accidentally violate the antitrust and tax laws, or to violate them for altruistic reasons, it is difficult to imagine how one could accidentally mislead someone else for his or her own good. Furthermore, in many instances, fraud is an aggressively acquisitive crime. The offender develops a scheme to bilk other people out of money or property, and does this not because of some personal problem but because the scheme is an easy way to get rich. Stock swindles, fraudulent loan scams, and so on, are often so large and complicated that they cannot possibly be excused as foolish and desperate solutions to personal problems. Thus, those involved in large-scale frauds do not have the option open to most embezzlers of presenting themselves as persons responding defensively to difficult personal circumstances.

Furthermore, because fraud involves a deliberate attempt to mislead another, the offender who fails to remove himself from the scheme runs the risk of being show to have a guilty mind. That is, he is shown to possess the most essential element of modern conceptions of criminality: an intent to harm another. His inner self would in this case be exposed as something other than what it has been presented as, and all of his previous actions would be subject to reinterpretation in light of this new perspective. For this reason, defrauders most prone to denying any crime at all. The cooperative and conspiratorial nature of many fraudulent schemes makes it possible to put the blame on someone else and to present oneself as a scapegoat. Typically, this is done by claiming to have been duped by others.

Two illustrations of this strategy are presented here:

> I figured I wasn't guilty, so it wouldn't be that hard to disprove it, until, as I say, I went to court and all of a sudden they start bringing in these guys out of the woodwork implicating me that I never saw. Lot of it could be proved that I never saw.
>
> Inwardly, I personally felt that the only crime that I committed was not telling on these guys. Not that I deliberately, intentionally committed a crime against the system. My only crime was that I should have had the guts to tell on these guys, what they were doing, rather than putting up with it and then trying to gradually get out of the system without hurting them or without them thinking I was going to snitch on them.

Of the three offenders who admitted committing crimes, two acted alone and the third acted with only one other person. Their accounts were similar to others presented earlier and tended to focus on either the harmless nature of their violations or on the unusual circumstances that drove them to commit their crimes. One claimed that his violations were only technical and that no one besides himself had been harmed.

> First of all, no money was stolen or anything of that nature. The bank didn't lose any money.... What I did was a technical violation. I made a mistake. There's no question about that, but the bank lost no money.

Another offender who directly admitted his guilt was involved in a check-kiting scheme. In a manner similar to embezzlers, he argued that his actions were motivated by exceptional circumstances.

> I was faced with the choice of all of a sudden, and I mean now, closing the door or doing something else to keep, that business open.... I'm not going to tell you that this wouldn't have happened if I'd had time to think it over, because I think it probably would have. You're sitting there with a dying patient. You are going to try to keep him alive.

In the other fraud cases more individuals were involved, and it was possible and perhaps necessary for each offender to claim that he was not really the culprit.

DISCUSSION: OFFENSES, ACCOUNTS, AND DEGRADATION CEREMONIES

The investigation, prosecution, and conviction of a white-collar offender involves him in a very undesirable status passage (Glaser & Strauss, 1971). The entire process can be viewed as a long and drawn-out degradation ceremony with the prosecutor as the chief denouncer and the offender's family and friends as the chief witnesses. The offender is moved from the status of law-abiding citizen to that of convicted felon. Accounts are developed to defeat the process of identity transformation that is the object of a degradation ceremony. They represent the offender's attempt to diminish the effect of his legal transformation and to prevent its becoming a publicly validated label. It can be suggested that the accounts developed by white-collar offenders take the forms that they do for two reasons: (1) the forms are required to defeat the success of the degradation ceremony, and (2) the specific forms used are the ones available given the mechanics, history, and organizational context of the offenses.

Three general patterns in accounting strategies stand out in .the data. Each can be characterized by the subject matter on which it focuses: the event (offense), the perpetrator (offender), or the denouncer (prosecutor). These are the natural subjects of accounts in that to be successful, a degradation ceremony requires each of these elements to be presented in a particular manner (Garfinkel, 1956). If an account-giver can undermine the presentation of one or more of the elements, then the effect of the ceremony can be reduced.

Although there are overlaps in the accounting strategies used by the various types of offenders, and while any given offender may use more than one strategy, it appears that accounting strategies and offenses correlate....

NOTES

1. Editor's note: Latin for "evil in itself."

REFERENCES

Casper, J. D. (1978). *Criminal courts: The defendant's perspective.* Washington, DC: U.S. Department of Justice.

Conklin, J. E. (1977). *Illegal but not criminal: Business crime in America.* Englewood Cliffs, NJ: Prentice Hall.

Cressey, D. (1953). *Other people's money.* New York: Free Press.

Denzin, N. K.(1977*).* Notes on the criminogenic hypothesis: A case study of the American liquor industry. *American Sociological Review, 42,* 905–920

——— (1984). *On understanding emotion.* San Francisco: Jossey-Bass.

Edelhertz, H. (1970). *The nature, impact, and prosecution of white collar crime.* Washington, DC: U.S. Government Printing Office.

Garfinkel, H. (1956). Conditions of successful degradation ceremonies. *American Journal of Sociology, 61,* 420–424.

Glaser, B. G., & Strauss, A. L. (1971). *Status passage.* Chicago: Aldine.

Katz, J. (1979). Legality and equality: Plea bargaining in the prosecution of white collar crimes. *Law and Society Review, 13,* 431–460.

Rothman, M., & Gandossy, R F. (1982). Sad tales: The accounts of white collar defendants and the decision to sanction. *Pacific Sociological Review, 4,* 449–473.

Searle, J. R. (1969). *Speech acts.* Cambridge: Cambridge University Press.

꙳

Illegal Occupations

In the previous section, we examined crimes committed by persons in the course of their legal occupations. In this section, we consider offenders whose occupations violate formal law. The central activities of such work are illegal, yet they share many commonalities with legal occupations. Most of those who engage in illegal occupations have regular customers, suppliers, and a formal set of roles and activities that do not substantially differ from those of people who perform legal work.

The chapters in this section take a look at drug dealing, smuggling, and prostitution. What is salient about the chapters presented here is how the authors examine criminal enterprises through an occupational lens. That is, they uniquely analyze how offenders give meaning to their criminal enterprises, as one would with a legitimate occupation. We use the term *occupation* here in the sense that these activities involve some effort or exertion of purpose. The series of articles in this section shed light on criminality as an occupation; the organization, structure, profit, or lack thereof; and hidden markets of crime.

In Chapter 15, "The 'Myth of Organization' of International Drug Smugglers," Scott H. Decker and Jana S. Benson provide a rare look into drug smuggling. Based on interviews with a diverse cross-section of offenders, the authors examine the flow of information, networks, and links of a drug-smuggling operation, along with the various work roles that exist internally within the organization. They discover that high-level international drug-smuggling groups are relatively loosely organized networks containing small groups of people who work together and typically do not have knowledge of what takes place throughout the organization. This paints a far different picture than what many criminologists once believed about these organizations. Drug-smuggling organizations have largely been viewed as being structured much like a "corporate organization." The authors underscore the point that drug-smuggling operations, instead of being rationally focused on maximizing profits, tend to be more focused on minimizing the risk of being detected by law enforcement authorities.

In Chapter 16, "The Second Step in Double Jeopardy: Appropriating the Labor of Female Street Hustlers," Kim Romenesko and Eleanor M. Miller study female street prostitutes and analyze their relationships to the men who control them. They draw parallels between the patriarchal structure of the world of prostitution and that which exists in the noncriminal world. Romenesko and Miller report the existence of a street institution known as a *pseudo-family* that comprises the pimp and the women who work for him. Within this structure, women street hustlers attempt to gain status, but working for men in a secondary role further serves to depress women socially and economically. The pseudo-family is explicitly organized to exploit the female members, who relinquish control of their resources for the affection and recognition of their "man" and the material goods necessary for survival.

In Chapter 17, "Dealing Careers," sociologist Patricia A. Adler provides a rare glimpse into a community of high-level drug dealers. In this classic study, Adler examines recruitment into drug smuggling and dealing, learning the trade, upward mobility, aging in the career, and ultimately phasing out. This chapter, perhaps more than others, draws a parallel between the occupation of drug smuggling/dealing and legitimate occupations.

The studies presented in Section VI illustrate that while the activities of the participants are illegal, they tend to see themselves as "business persons" with a product or a service for sale to the public. They have similar goals and are faced with many of the same problems and goals prevalent in legitimate enterprises. We also learn in this section that previously held beliefs on how some criminal enterprises are organized, such as drug-smuggling rings, are not the case at all. This section is rich with insight into illegal occupations and offers a host of possibilities to inform fundamental criminal justice practice.

꙳

CHAPTER 15

The "Myth of Organization" of International Drug Smugglers

Scott H. Decker and Jana S. Benson

Until recently, most criminologists viewed international drug smuggling as a highly structured and organized operation with vertical lines of responsibility and communication. This view was based on old models of organized crime and romanticized versions of the Medellín cartels that operated in Colombia in the 1980s. The amount of money involved in international drug smuggling is enormous, and it is generally assumed that where large sums of money are present, they will be accompanied by a high level of organization. This view of group offending as highly structured is not confined to international drug smugglers. Criminologists have typically overascribed the levels of structure, organization, and rationality of groups of offenders such as gangs, burglars, robbers, and street-level drug sellers. Often this is the case because information about the organization of offending groups comes from law enforcement, which sees only a small fraction of offenders. In other cases, criminologists' interviews are restricted to "kingpins" or supposed leaders in groups, without external validation of their real role in offending.

This chapter examines the nature and extent of organization in international drug-smuggling groups. Based on interviews with 34 convicted international drug smugglers, we find very little formal organization or vertical structure in drug-smuggling groups. Following a description of these offenders, we discuss the literature on the organization of drug smugglers and other active groups of offenders. This discussion focuses on three major categories of organization: structure, interactions, and rationality. Having established a context for our analysis, we then use the words of convicted drug smugglers to illustrate our findings. Finally, conclusions are drawn about the sources of the "myth of organization" in international drug smuggling.

Source: Written especially for this volume.

THE CURRENT STUDY

The following analysis is based on interviews conducted with 34 individuals held in U.S. federal prisons. A semistructured questionnaire was used to elicit information from individuals who were selected based on their extensive involvement in high-level international drug smuggling. We found 135 of these individuals in federal prisons. Of the 73 individuals approached for participation in the study, 34 agreed. We compared the group who refused participation with the subjects who did take part and found them to be similar in terms of level of involvement in smuggling—specifically, how serious the crime was and their role in the offense. In the end, we assembled a sample of 34 individuals who were heavily involved in drug smuggling. We also gained access to these individuals' federal presentence reports and were able to verify their extensive involvement in drug smuggling.

Table 15.1 presents a summary of key characteristics of the smugglers we interviewed. Of the 34 subjects, the modal category for age at sentencing was 40 to 49 years. Within the sample, 82% reported being between 30 and 59 years old at the time of sentencing. All of the subjects were male. Although almost half of the subjects were U.S. citizens, Cubans and Colombians were also significantly represented in the sample. Twenty-nine individuals, or 85% of the sample, reported being of Hispanic origin. All of the drug smugglers we interviewed operated through the Caribbean, with a majority of the drugs originating in Colombia. Smuggling activity also was described as occurring in the Bahamas, Panama, Cuba, the Dominican Republic, Mexico, Haiti, Peru, Puerto Rico, and Venezuela. The method of smuggling varied, with both private and commercial boats and airplanes being used.

All of the subjects we interviewed were arrested and charged with smuggling large quantities of cocaine. Three individuals also reported smuggling marijuana in connection with the current offense. The mean amount of cocaine with which the subjects were caught was 1,136 kg, or just less than 2,500 pounds. Overall, amounts carried ranged from 15 kg to 5,000 kg. The mean year of arrest was 1993, with reported values ranging from 1988 to 1997. Twenty-two members of the sample were serving a sentence of 20 years or more, with five doing life and six doing a sentence of 30 years or more. Only one subject received a sentence of less than 10 years for his involvement in the smuggling operation.

The individuals interviewed for this study were heavily involved in international drug smuggling. None of the smugglers in the sample were caught on their first act of smuggling. In fact, more than half of the subjects reported having been involved in *at least* 10 prior smuggling operations. These contentions were consistent with the results of their presentence investigations. The smugglers played a variety of roles in the smuggling event for which they were caught, ranging from broker or organizer to transporter or manager. Only one of the individuals could be described as playing a minor role in drug smuggling (offloader), but this individual had an extensive history of involvement in drug smuggling.

Table 15.1 Characteristics of Smuggler Respondents

ROLE	METHOD	REGION	AGE RANGE	WEIGHT OF DRUGS (KG)	SENTENCE LENGTH (Y)
Recruiter	Private vessel	Colombia/Bahamas	40–49	480	30
Organizer	Commercial vessel	Colombia	40–49	1,500	27
Manager	Commercial vessel	Colombia	40–49	630	30
Supervisor	Vessel	Colombia	40–49	165	31
Organizer	Commercial vessel	Colombia	40–49	1,500	8
Organizer	Commercial vessel	Bahamas	40–49	3,345.5	17.5
Leader	Private plane/commercial vessel	Colombia	60–69	500	30.5
Recruiter	Commercial vessel	Colombia	50–59	40	17.5
Broker	Private vessel	Panama	30–39	59	17.5
Leader	Private vessel	Cuba/Dominican Republic	30–39	515	17.5
Leader	Private vessel	Cuba	40–49	2,350.5	19.5
Organizer	Private vessel	Colombia	30–39	728	27.5
Transporter	Private vessel	Mexico	40–49	5,000	
Captain	Private vessel	Colombia/Haiti	30–39	150+	15
Offloader	Private plane	Colombia	40–49	500	16.25
Organizer	Commercial airplane	Peru	50–59	500	20
Leader	Private vessel	Bahamas/Cuba	40–49	50	10
Manager	Commercial airplane	Venezuela	30–39	605.5	27
Leader	Private vessel	Bahamas	50–59	414	15
Recruiter	Commercial airplane	Colombia	50–59	15–50	22
Leader	Private vessel	Caribbean	50–59	1,450	25.5
Manager	Commercial airplane	Haiti	40–49	2,200	15
Captain/Investor	Private vessel	Bahamas	70–79	776.3	27.5
Organizer	Commercial vessel	Panama	30–39	800–1,000	18.5
Organizer	Private airplane/private vessel	Bahamas	50–59	488	

We observed diversity in the methods of smuggling used by members of our sample, which included both commercial and private vessels (boats) and private and commercial airplanes. Combinations of vessels and aircrafts were also reported. The most commonly used transportation was private vessels, with 62% of the individuals reporting experience with this method. In short, this high-level group of drug smugglers with extensive experience in smuggling was in a position to know and understand the structure of drug-smuggling organizations.

LITERATURE ON DRUG SMUGGLERS AND OTHER ACTIVE OFFENDERS

The widely held perception about groups of international drug smugglers is that they are highly structured organizations (i.e., cartels). However, some recent literature on drug smugglers and other active offenders suggests that this is not the case. We here incorporate information on active groups of offenders to discount any possible criticisms that might arise about the inclusion in our sample of only convicted offenders. Recent ethnographic research on active offenders such as burglars, robbers, carjackers, and gang members suggests that offenders do not organize themselves very effectively. Our examination of international drug-smuggling groups will concentrate on the following three features of organization: structure, interactions, and rationality.

Structure

One of the most readily identifiable characteristics of a highly organized group is a hierarchical structure. Formal hierarchies have ranked levels of authority that clearly delineate super- and subordinates, with those in superordinate positions being responsible for overseeing those in the lower offices (Weber, 1946). Highly organized groups have a clear chain of command that signifies the downward movement of decision-making power. Such groups also have functions associated with each level of the structure. The organizational structures of these groups tend to be pyramidal or vertical in nature.

In contrast to hierarchical structures, some groups are organized in a less formal manner. Williams (1998) suggests that some drug-smuggling organizations are more accurately described as networks of connected nodes that are linked across and within organizations. There is no definite vertical chain of command, as individual cells can operate independently from the larger organization because of their individual access to information and technology. To a certain degree, this independence isolates various stages of the drug-smuggling process from others.

Recent research on international drug smuggling suggests that many groups are organized as a series of connected nodes. Zaitch (2002) studied drug importation from Colombia to the Netherlands and found little evidence of vertical hierarchies in drug smuggling. Instead, he perceived smuggling operations as flexible networks comprising dynamic groups that could change tactics quickly and were relatively insulated from other groups found earlier or later in the smuggling transaction chain.

A structure of connected nodes rather than a vertical hierarchy is supported by research on a variety of active offenders. In fact, descriptions of human trafficking and smuggling (Zhang, 2007; Zhang, 2008), terrorist groups (9/11 Commission, 2004; Sageman, 2008), and international trafficking of stolen vehicles (Clarke & Brown, 2003) depict such groups as small networks of individuals who lack much in the way of a formal structure. In addition, research on active burglars (Cromwell, Olson, & Avery, 1994; Shover, 1996), robbers (Wright & Decker, 1997), carjackers (Jacobs, Topali, & Wright, 2003), and gang members (Decker, Katz, & Webb, 2007) also conclude that offenders do not organize themselves in an effective or formal manner.

Interviews with the 34 convicted drug smugglers provided support for the idea that drug-smuggling operations are not well organized. Williams's (1998) concept of connected nodes was illustrated in his interviews with various smugglers, especially those in the role of transporter.

> Transportation is one thing, okay. That office in Colombia is supposed to get the people in Miami to do the smuggling, right? And I was the head, you know, my own group. Got 20 people working for me doing the smuggling, 10 people, whatever, and it was my responsibility. They got nothing to do with that. They just pay me for me to do the job. The other offices, when you get to Miami, I did the smuggling. I brought it already in from the Bahamas, whatever. I get in contact with the people in Miami and give it to them. Then they got it through the names.... Call those people and give it to them. Then those people got their own buyers or whatever they do.... That would be another whole operation. There would be a whole operation to sell it in. There is another office working in Colombia to deal with the money. (2)
>
> The original owner of the load was somebody in Colombia that I don't know. I know the guy who was, that I went to Colombia with, and he make some arrangements in there. The original owner, I don't know the owner. I never knew the original owner. Never. The owner of the merchandise gave the merchandise to a guy that I knew that I went to Colombia with. Well, the guy I went to Colombia with, he was, he was a fugitive from this country, and I was in charge of, in here, to make all of the arrangements and all of the preparations to everyone get his part, and I get mine. I didn't know the people who were going to drive the boat to Fort Lauderdale. No, I only knew one guy—two guys in this, in this enterprise, and there were about 13 or 14 people in the deal, involved there. (4)
>
> Well, I had a connection in New York at the airport. So, basically, [my friend] would package the drugs in '80 and he had a connection at the airport in '80 as well. Well, as far as I know, some of [the drugs] came from Colombia, but that wasn't my connection, you know. That was the person I was dealing with. My part started when it got to Haiti.... I would meet with the guy and we would package everything, do whatever we do so the drugs wouldn't be able to detect by smelling it.... Whenever I come back, my guys would get the drugs, and either he would

arrange it with someone to get it through the airport in Haiti, or if he did come in Haiti, I would arrange it. There's a transaction that takes place between Colombia and Haiti that I don't know about. I don't know the Colombians. The only thing I know is that whatever they would give me, it would have 40%. (11)

In addition to illustrating the concept of nodes, the following quote also exemplifies the independent nature of those nodes, similar to what Williams (1998) describes.

The first load they asked me to bring in, I think it was—the exact amount of 383 keys....I had no idea where it was coming from. I had no idea where it was going other than I would get back, the guy would pick it up. I picked it up in the Bahamas and brought it to Jupiter [Florida]....So they recruited me and asked me to pick up the drugs and set up the operation....I had the boat reconfigured. I engineered all the little particulars like they'd call on the phone, the warehouse, and the codes for the beeper and everything. (21)

The smugglers also explained how a load (or shipment) of cocaine would be organized in Colombia for transportation into the United States. Instead of a single company or group of individuals owning the load, as would be the case with a highly organized operation, various independent parties would contribute to the shipment that would eventually be transported:

The way they do it, you have a collector, and it's—and this was interesting because I learned this myself firsthand at the time. A bunch of people will invest in the load. It's like selling shares of stock. This person will put up this amount of money. Another person will put up another amount of money, and they in effect maybe own two or three keys. Then the collector, or whoever, whatever you want to call him, puts all this together, and this joint venture goes on a plane. So a proprietary interest in this was really shared by many. (30)

Weber (1946) describes formal organizations as having a chain of command; however, the current study found drug smuggling organizations to lack this structural feature. Here, a transporter explains that he did not receive commands from a higher authority about how to operate his stage of the operation:

I'm the transport. I'm the one that tells them this is how we're going to play the game. We're going to do it this way. We're not going to use this. We're going to do this because I'm in charge and I'm aware of surveillance. I know everything—how the government is running things, how things are happening. So I keep constant contact with the office. All the broker does is pick up the drugs and give me the money for my services. And the broker is the one in charge of delivering the money back to Colombia for the load and the profit. (14)

Interviews with the 34 subjects also supported Zaitch's (2002) contention that international drug-smuggling groups have dynamic structures. The adaptable and dynamic nature of these organizations is described by the following individuals as they explain how drug-smuggling groups adapt quickly to changes in personnel or tactics:

When organizing a group of captains and people who could sell these drugs, they were still able to do it once I was caught. They do it with somebody else. They find somebody, they find somebody. (16)

We would constantly change the routes...through the Caribbean. You go around through the Peninsula to the west or you go to the east around the Caribbean Basin.

Interactions

Waring (2002) argues that the way groups of co-offenders are organized rarely corresponds to the structure of formal organizations. Her key focus is on behavior within offending networks, not elements of the structure, as a means to avoid a strict focus on hierarchy or structure. This approach is consistent with that championed by Burt (1992), who argues that all social structure is the product of relations between individuals. Accordingly, we will examine the nature of interactions both within and amongst drug-smuggling groups to better understand their organization.

As a consequence of the vertical hierarchy of authority, highly organized groups are characterized by sustained, formal interactions between members. Interactions typically occur between specific individuals as a result of the vertical nature of the chain of command and the highly structured patterns of communication within such groups. In such groups, direct correspondence commonly occurs only between an individual and one other person, his or her immediate supervisor. Organizational communication in such groups rarely involves personal interaction. Instead, information tends to be exchanged through more formal channels, where correspondence can be more easily documented (e.g., written messages or formal meetings).

In contrast to the concept of highly organized offenders, Best and Luckenbill (1994) suggest that deviance and deviants are generally not well organized. They outline a descriptive typology of co-offending groups using the nature of association among individuals involved in offenses together. In our interviews, we found that the associations between offenders were not formal, had short temporal spans, and were specific to individual offenses. We describe such associations as episodic. More recent research on the interactions between drug smugglers is consistent with these findings. In contrast to interactions based on roles or a chain of command, Zaitch (2002) finds that transactions between smugglers are based on kinship, ethnicity, and language.

Our research on international drug-smuggling groups supports the idea that interactions in these groups are not formal, sustained, or based on hierarchical chains of command. Consistent with Best and Luckenbill's (1994) typology of co-offending groups, the smugglers interviewed described their interactions as more episodic than sustained:

I had very few people working with me. In total, about six or eight people. Some of them were part of my crew, and some of them were what we used to [call] independent contractors. If I needed him, I would hire him. If I didn't need him, he would go to somebody else. (5)

Well, I don't know anything about sale. You know what I mean?...The load come from Haiti, but the cocaine was from Colombia. And my job, to take it from Haiti [to] the U.S. I knew the people in Haiti, but it was the first time I work with them. I knew the people in Colombia. I had not worked with them in the past. They get in touch with me because I know somebody from Haiti. I never work with him before in drugs, you know? I know him because I was there before. So he reached me here in Miami. (6)

In a formally organized group, interactions and communication among members is based on the hierarchy and chain of command. Interviews with the smugglers indicated that this structure was not the way their smuggling activities were organized. In fact, interactions among individuals within and between nodes tended to be based less on hierarchy and structure and more on trust and informal relationships. Consistent with Zaitch (2002), many times this trust was established through nationality or kinship.

You know, they knew that I been in drug smuggling or anything. I never used a weapon in my life. I had no need for it with the people I was dealing with. They were people that would keep their word, and if I see anybody that I didn't like that would create trouble in the future, I would avoid and try not to do business with. (5)

So I called them and I told them I have an importation from Venezuela and the name of the containers, and they go and pick them up and put them in my warehouse. I don't usually bring drugs. It was my first time. I was chosen because I was trusted. They trusted me because they saw my job, my experience. (18)

So, when I was getting a pair of pants made [in South America], some guys comes and talks to me, and he said, "Listen, how's it going? I see you're from Miami." "Yeah, I'm from Miami." He asked me if I wanted to make some money, and I said sure, that's cool. He goes "Well, next time you're in Miami, call some people and see what we can do."...And I said, the hell with it, and I gave him a call. He said, "Well, come on. We're at the club." I come over to a club and he just happened to be in [Miami]. I was in Miami now. I left Colombia and went back to Miami....Three months later, after working for him, he gave me a call and told me to come to Colombia, come back to Colombia and talk to him. I get over there. I see a couple of guys. We talk and hang out, and then they start telling me what's going. (24)

This quotation describes how trust in international drug-smuggling organizations can be established simply through one's nationality. It also illustrates how interactions are less formal and involve more direct communication than in highly organized groups. This latter point is also supported by the account of following smuggler, who describes his contact with the owners of the loads.

I have to meet the people [whose drugs I am delivering]. I have to meet them. Because they give me the contract, you understand me? I mean, the owner of the boat and the merchandise, you know. The owners. All the time, owners, not representatives. (6)

Rationality

In addition to the structure and nature of interactions, we can examine the rationality of offending groups to better understand their organization. We refer to the rationality of an organization as the degree to which the organization is structured to achieve specific goals. In other words, a rationally organized group has a structure and operating procedures that are based on logical reasoning, not chance or other untested criteria.

Cressey (1972) uses the core concept of rationality to describe the extent and nature of organization within offending groups, particularly organized crime. Role specialization and coordination are key concepts by which he describes variation in the degree of organization among offending groups. He notes that well-organized groups are those that are most rationally arranged in the pursuit of efficiency and maximized profits. Therefore, according to Cressey, well-organized groups are very rational because they display high levels of specialization (division of labor based on qualifications) and coordination of activities (interdependence) in an attempt to maximize profits efficiently.

Applying the concept of rationality to offending groups, Donald and Wilson (2000) studied the organization of ram raiders, or individuals who engage in a pattern of smash, grab, and flee at jewelry stores. They found that these groups exhibited generalized roles (no specialization), had low levels of interdependence, and lacked a rational foundation for their structure. Warr (2002) examined active groups of offenders and found them to display little evidence of rational planning or calculation. Some research on gang organization also suggests that these offenders do not organize themselves rationally (Decker & Van Winkle, 1996).

Based on the interviews in the current study, it was clear that drug-smuggling groups foster little specialization or coordination of activities. The following quote shows how the lack of coordination between the nodes of the operation does not cause the entire operation to fail:

> I had a freighter, I knew the owner of the land strip in Guajira. Sometimes they had the loads waiting there for two or three weeks and no one would show up to pick it up. So this guy would call me to ask if I pick it up; I said yes, and the other people would call me. Sometimes they would ask me, for instance, to drop the merchandise in the Bahamas, and I would do it. But I never met those guys. The other guy, the broker, would do everything. He didn't work for anybody. He worked on commission and he trusted me. (17)

Although these groups did not appear to be rationally organized to efficiently maximize profits, reports from the smugglers suggested they might be rationally organized around another goal: managing risk. In his examination of drug-smuggling networks, Williams (1998) notes that while their organization is not highly formal, it does provide the group with various means of self-protection. For example, the lack of a formal structure allows drug-smuggling groups the ability to adapt quickly to changes in law enforcement and therefore minimize the risk of detection. The following subjects describe how smuggling operations in their groups were not based on maximizing profits but instead on minimizing the risk of detection by law enforcement. As such, they were flexible and able to change methods, drugs, and routes.

> Never smuggled heroin, no. I was offered it, but [the boats] weren't ready for the loads at the time, but if we would have, probably I would have done it, because it was a big profit of margin there. There was a big margin there. Smaller amount, and it was about three times the profit that you would get from coke. (5)
>
> We started tightening up right after the war on drugs. Surveillance really picked up. So, I mean, the big plane was out of the question. . . . It was getting more difficult. You know, the boats, my cigarette boats, were like, you know, law enforcement already knew. I mean, a 37-foot Midnight Express with four engines in the back, they knew what the boat was for. So, you know, my operation was getting obsolete already. . . . We did [an air drop] right here in the Bahamas. It was in '89 or '90. I picked up maybe 150 keys and brought it into the Florida Keys, and after that, we waited a while and then we started changing things over here. We started air dropping right in the middle of the Gulf of Mexico. All the way from Colombia to the Gulf of Mexico. . . . [I moved] from marijuana to cocaine, from the late '80s. Right after I moved to Georgia and I came back, I'd say I came back smuggling cocaine because, you know, surveillance was heavier, and I didn't want to work bulky material. I wanted to work something that was, there was plenty of money in it and something that I can get in and out and, you know, do my deliveries fast, didn't have to use a lot of people. You know, a lot more people were cooperating with the government, and you didn't know who was who. So you wanted a small group. You wanted real trusting friends. (14)
>
> A lot of people in smuggling are in more places than one. In other words, they not only do it in boats. They do it—now with Mexico in the business, they're doing vehicles. They're doing airplanes. (29)

As noted earlier, trust and kinship are key characteristics of the interactions between drug smugglers. The previous quote reinforces this point. Many subjects described how a structure of isolated nodes acts to protect individuals from detection when others involved in the operation are apprehended, thus suggesting that the rational foundation of these groups' organization is based on reducing risk.

> Never been stopped by law enforcement. Like I said, you know, they don't catch very much unless somebody tells them, and usually if you find out, when you interview people in prison, most of their cases or their indictments is dry. I mean, what I mean, they didn't catch the drugs. It was just a conspiracy unless somebody talked about. I'm sure you have found that out. They catch very little drugs coming through. I mean, they catch some, but very little overall. It's more dangerous after you have it here in the United States, distribution [more dangerous] than actually bringing it in. (3)
>
> Never been arrested before this. It's been close, but no cigar. The guys who were bringing the marijuana, they were caught, but I wasn't. At the time they didn't talk. When they saw me. . . . Well, they really didn't know me that well. I'm sure that they cooperated right away when they got caught, but they didn't know me that well. And I was, you know, when you work with a lot of people, you got to

protect yourself. You can't, you know, you can't like, "Well, I live here. I live here. This is my last name." So [I gave them] no personal information at all.

We contend that international drug-smuggling groups are rationally organized around reducing risk, *not* increasing profit. This contention is supported when one examines the persistence of these smugglers' offending. Whereas a group that is based on maximizing profit would have high levels of persistence (continued activity over periods of time), the drug smugglers we interviewed reported low levels of persistence in their groups as a result of an effort to reduce risk of detection.

> For a load of marijuana [I would make] $50,000 or $60,000. If I was single at that time, [money would last] about three, four months. Party every day, you know. And that's when I look for another trip that someone needs done. [I would] get the money and party, and when the money starts to run out, I have 20 trips [offered] already. When my money starts to run out, have offers and just take one....I think I had offers from people because of both connections and I was successful. Because everybody knows me, you know? (6)
>
> Well, I knew [how] the government and law enforcement worked and how they set their surveillance, how they would do their interdictions, and I always I'd be a step ahead of them. My technology was always a step ahead of them. So I knew it was impossible for them to catch me....I would have taken more chances because I know I would have kept doing loads, but the more you did it, that would increase your chance of being caught. You typically wait between loads—if I saw things good, it would be two weeks. And if [I] saw things bad, a month or two. (14)

Although Warr (2002) proposes that groups of offenders show little evidence of rational planning, this was not the case with the smugglers we interviewed. Although it is true that little planning or organization was done around the goal of maximizing profits, many subjects described their group taking advanced and deliberate measures to minimize the risk of detection. The following quote from an organizer illustrates how many groups are not searching for the most efficient means of smuggling cocaine into the United States. Instead, they consider techniques that are less likely to be subject to law enforcement detection, not produce the most profit possible.

> I started meeting people, and you know, you learn. When I started doing my own stuff, I would get everybody in a room, the guys that was supposed to be involved in it, and in the planning of the project, how we're going to do it....I always figure that if all of them would come to the same conclusion that this is the best way to do it, then the police and the DEA, too, would think this was the best way to do it. So to me, the best way was to go all different [techniques]. (1)

DISCUSSION AND CONCLUSIONS

Much prior research and many law enforcement descriptions overascribe the level of organization among groups of offenders. One good example is the description of the organizational structure of active gang members. Most gangs appear

to be considerably less well organized than public or law enforcement conceptions of them. Similarly, descriptions of active burglars, armed robbers, and street-
level drug sellers generally depict individuals who live somewhat disorganized,
and even chaotic, lives. Very little structure is found in the offending activities of
these individuals, and their behavior does not reflect a high degree of rationality.
There is reason to suspect, however, that high-level international drug smuggling
groups might have more formal structures, that their interactions would be more
rule directed, and that their behavior—as both individuals and groups—would
be more rational. After all, the large sums of money involved in such activities,
coupled with the apparent sophistication necessary to successfully smuggle drugs
and the age of the individuals involved would lead one to expect that such groups
would be highly organized. Our analysis of interviews with 34 high-level drug
smugglers suggests quite a different picture.

A corporate organizational structure suggests a pyramid with a leader on the
top who passes on orders to a group of subordinates, who in turn pass on orders
to their subordinates. From this perspective, organizational communication is
structured by role and rank within an organization. High-level international drug
smugglers outline a very different picture of their activities. Their drug-smuggling
groups resemble a series of loosely coupled nodes, small groups of individuals who
work together largely unaware of who and what takes place at other steps in their
"organization." Many of the individuals we interviewed did not know anyone outside of their immediate group and were recruited based on informal relationships,
kinship, or ethnicity rather than the possession of a specific skill. Instead of being
rationally focused on maximizing profits, such groups focused on minimizing risk
of detection and apprehension. We believe that this is a key to understanding how
these groups' activities are organized.

It is important to have a fuller understanding of groups of offenders, whether
those offenders are terrorist groups, gangs, burglars, or international drug smugglers. Such an understanding aids our ability to better understand their goals,
structure, interactions, and rationality. Equally important, such an understanding can more fully inform policies designed to minimize the harm caused by
drug importation, gang activity, or burglary. As with many offending groups, the
information provided directly from offenders—in their own words—provides an
important counterbalance to information gleaned from a single source of official
information.

REFERENCES

9/11 Commission. (2004). *Final report of the National Commission on Terrorist Attacks upon
the United States.* New York: Norton.

Best, J., & Luckenbill, D. (1994). *Organizing deviance.* Englewood Cliffs, NJ: Prentice Hall.

Burt, R. (1992). *Structural holes.* Cambridge, MA: Havard University Press.

Clarke, R. V., & Brown, R. (2003). International trafficking in stolen vehicles. In M. Tonry
(Ed.), *Crime and justice: A review of research* (vol. 30, pp. 197–228). Chicago: University
of Chicago Press

Cressey, D. (1972). *Criminal organization: Its elementary forms.* New York: Harper & Row.

Cromwell, P., Olson, J., & Avary, D. (1994). *Breaking and entering.* Thousand Oaks, CA: Sage.

Decker, S. H., Katz, C., & Webb, V. (2007). Understanding the black box of gang organization: Implications for involvement in violent crime, drug sales and violent victimization. *Crime & Delinquency, 54*(1), 153–172.

Decker, S. H., & Van Winkle, B. (1996). *Life in the gang: families, friends, and violence.* Cambridge, UK: Cambridge University Press.

Donald, I., & Wilson, A. (2000). Ram raiding: Criminals working in groups. In D. Canter & L. Alison (Eds.), *The social psychology of crime* (pp. 191–246). Burlington, VT: Ashgate.

Jacobs, B., Topali, V., & Wright, R. (2003). Carjacking, streetlife and offender motivation. *British Journal of Criminology, 43*, 673–688.

Sageman, M. (2008). *Leaderless jihad: Terror networks in the twenty-first century.* Philadelphia: University of Pennsylvania Press.

Shover, N. (1996). *Great pretenders: Pursuits and careers of persistent thieves.* Boulder, CO: Westview Press.

Waring, E. (2002). Co-offending as a network form of social organization. In E. Waring & D. Weisburd (Eds.), *Crime and social organization.* New Brunswick, NJ: Transaction.

Warr, M. (2002). *Companions in crime: The social aspects of criminal conduct.* New York: Cambridge.

Weber, M. (1946). Bureaucracy. In H. H. Gerth & C. W. Mills (Eds.), *Max Weber: Essays in sociology.* New York: Oxford University Press.

Williams, P. (1998). The nature of drug-trafficking networks. *Current History, 97*, 154–159.

Wright, R., & Decker, S. H. (1997). *Armed robbers in action: Stickups and street culture.* Boston: Northeastern University Press.

Zaitch, D. (2002). *Trafficking cocaine: Colombian drug entrepreneurs in the Netherlands.* The Hague, Netherlands: Kluwer.

Zhang, S. X. (2007). *Smuggling and trafficking in human beings: All roads lead to America.* Westport, CT: Praeger.

———. (2008). *Chinese human smuggling organizations.* Stanford, CA: Stanford University Press.

﹏

CHAPTER 16

The Second Step in Double Jeopardy: Appropriating the Labor of Female Street Hustlers

Kim Romenesko and Eleanor M. Miller

Topical life histories were obtained from 14 Milwaukee female street hustlers, aged 18 to 35 years, 11 of whom were members (or former members) of a "street" institution termed the "pseudo-family" (made up of a "man" and the women who work for him). The majority of the women interviewed were institutionalized at the time either at the Milwaukee House of Correction or at a residential drug treatment facility in Milwaukee.

This article is about Milwaukee women who make their living from street hustling. We attempt to document the operation of a patriarchal structure within the world of women's illicit work that parallels that which exists in the licit world of women's work and, ironically, further marginalizes females who hustle the streets of American cities primarily because of preexisting economic marginalization. The socioeconomic status of these women is, as a result of their experiences in this alternative labor market, even further reduced with respect to the licit market because of the criminal involvement, frequent drug and alcohol dependency, psychological and physical abuse, and ill-health connected with the work of street hustling. A particularly tragic element of this process resides in the fact that for many, the world of the streets appears an attractive array of alternative work opportunities when compared to their experience of "straight" work. The impoverishment, dependency, and, ultimately, redundancy of women, particularly women of color, who work in "women's jobs" in the licit world of work and the

Source: Excerpted from Romenesko, K., & Miller, E. M. (1989). The second step in double jeopardy: Appropriating the labor of female street hustlers. *Crime and Delinquency, 35,* 109–35. Reprinted with permission of Sage Publications.

impoverishment, dependency, and redundancy they experience in the illicit work world, we argue, constitute a situation of "double jeopardy."

That there are few viable opportunities for poorly educated, unskilled women like themselves in the licit job market is very clear to women who eventually become female street hustlers. That a parallel situation exists in the illicit job market, however, escapes the view of new female recruits to street hustling because that view is clouded by the appeal of feeling, many for the first time, personally desirable, agentive, and productive as women workers. Furthermore, we will attempt to demonstrate that the central mechanism by which female street hustlers are made dependent, and financially, socially, and physically insecure, the mechanism by which they, themselves, are commodified is the "pseudo-family"—a patriarchal unit made up of a "man" and the women who work for him.

Because nearly all of the literature written about street-level prostitutes (whom we prefer to call female street hustlers because of the clear diversity in their everyday work that includes a broad array of street hustles), indicates that a major reason women enter street life is because of the perceived financial rewards available to them (Brown, 1979; James & Meyerding, 1976; Laner, 1974; Miller, 1986), we became interested in learning how participation in street life in general, and the pseudo-family in particular, actually affects women's financial situation and, more broadly, their life chances. It is the embeddedness of women's hustling work in the social network that is the "pseudo-family," then, that is the focus of this article.

BACKGROUND

Given the inaccessibility of lucrative legal work to most women in our society and the failure of our welfare system to maintain women and their children at a livable standard (Sidel, 1986), participation in the illegal activities of street life is a route that a certain proportion of women see as an occupational alternative. As James and Meyerding (1976, p. 178) say:

> Money-making options are still quite limited for women in this society, especially for unskilled or low-skilled women. Recognition of this basic sex inequality in the economic structure helps us see prostitution as a viable occupational choice, rather than as a symptom of the immorality or "deviance" of individual women.

One of our respondents, Elsie, described how and why she became involved in street life.

> I got married when I was 18. My husband, okay, when I got married, that was my biggest mistake 'cuz he never was around. I had all these little babies. When I was 18 I had two [babies], when I was 19 I had three. He wouldn't work, he wouldn't help support them, and there I'd sit in this little apartment with nothin'—no TV, nothin'—no milk for your babies, and, you know, they gotta have milk and stuff. You know, I was so tired of runnin' to my people askin' 'em for, you know, favors: "Would you go buy the babies some milk?" You know, I was embarrassed doin' that. So then that's when I learned to take a check that wasn't mine and go

cash it. You know that's what really drove me into it. For their sake, not to benefit myself—not at first it wasn't.

The women of this study, we argue, look to street life to obtain the status and economic stability that is largely unachievable for the children of the poor and near poor, be they male or female. The commodification of female sexuality offers them entree to the streets, often initially as prostitutes. As this analysis will show, however, street women are doubly jeopardized: involvement in illicit street life is not a viable avenue to financial stability for women because of the institutionalized obstacles that exist in the underworld—obstacles as difficult to circumvent as those in "straight" society.

Work History

Most of the 14 female street hustlers included in this analysis worked at straight jobs at some point in their lives. (The few that did not became participants in street hustling in their early teens.) Straight work usually took place before the women's entrance into street life; however, in a few cases, women tried straight jobs in an attempt to leave street life. Although some have not given up on the idea that there is some kind of straight work that they could do as the basis of a career, most admitted that they could not go back to boring, low-paying work with inflexible hours. They believe that "the life" (short for street life, also called "the fast life") will pay off sometime in the near future. They think that things will improve, money will be saved, and they will retire from "the life" in comfort. If our analysis is correct, they are probably mistaken.

The types of straight jobs our respondents performed were low-status, low-paying, often part-time jobs that are heavily dominated by females. Examples of the types of jobs the women worked at are fast food attendant or cook, box checker at a department store, housekeeper, dietary aide, beautician, bakery shop clerk, assembly line worker for a manufacturing company, child care aide, hot dog stand attendant, cashier, waitress, hostess, receptionist, go-go dancer, and secretary.

Some women who tried to make it in straight society have been frustrated by their experience and have, essentially, given up. Brandy, a young black woman who participated in the study, had her first straight job when she was 18 years old. She performed clerical duties in Chicago but was eventually laid off. She said:

> BRANDY: I got laid off cuz the plant closed down and opened up in Oak Park and I didn't have a way out to Oak Park from the South Side of Chicago. After that, believe it or not, I was working at [a] hotel on Michigan Avenue in Chicago, Illinois, as a maid. After I took two tests, they gave me a promotion—I was supervisor of house-cleaning....That's why it's weird for me to be goin' through the things I'm goin' through now [Brandy was incarcerated at the Milwaukee House of Correction at the time of the interview]. I'm not a bad person at all.
>
> INTERVIEWER: How long were you supervisor of house-cleaning?

BRANDY: About two and a half years [until she was 21 years old].
INTERVIEWER: What did you do then?
BRANDY: Stayed at home and collect unemployment…and was lookin' for another job, but I never found one.

Other women, although they had no problem finding jobs, were not satisfied with the pay. Once women get a taste for making "fast money" on the street, it is difficult to go back. Tina describes this attraction to the street in the following comments:

INTERVIEWER: What [type of work] were you doing?
TINA: Oh, I did a lot of things.…I was workin' at Marc's Bigboy as a waitress. I've been a waiter, I've been a host, I've been a private secretary, I've been a cashier. I've got a lot of job skills, also.
INTERVIEWER: You've had all these straight jobs and you've got lots of skills. What's the attraction to the streets?
TINA: The money, the fast money. That sums it up.

Elsie, in the passage that follows, relates not only how difficult it is to live on the wages paid by many employers but also how sexism worked (and works) to keep women marginal to the job market. She is describing the first straight job that she had as a dietary aide and why she became disaffected.

ELSIE: I got the job 'cuz I really needed it. In fact, I had just turned 18, so they was payin' me $1.30 an hour. This was like in '67. Yeah, '67, cuz my son was about a year old. They was payin' me $1.30 an hour.…See, I was stayin' at home. My mother, she was keepin' my baby. I'd get my check, I'd give her half, and I'd keep half. Then, the shop was in walkin' distance, you know, from her house where we was stayin', and we'd get our lunch and stuff free cuz I was workin' in the kitchen. But still, that wasn't enough money for that hard work.
INTERVIEWER: How long did you work there?
ELSIE: I worked there nine months.…I would have stayed there but I was pregnant again. I was tryin' to keep it from them, 'cuz back then you could only work 'til you was five or six months pregnant. And so I tried to keep it from 'em. I worked until I was nine months, 'cuz, you know, I never got real big. So I was tellin' 'em I was like four months, and I was really eight—so I could keep my job.

Finally, a few women reported simply being intolerant of supervised nine-to-five work and ending up getting fired from their jobs or quitting. It is interesting to note that the women who fall into this category tended to have the least skills.

INTERVIEWER: What did you do then?
RITA: Worked in a hospital in the laundry department and hated it because it was hot, it was hard work, and I hated my boss.
INTERVIEWER: How much did it pay?

RITA: Minimum wage.

INTERVIEWER: How long did you work there?

RITA: Three months.

INTERVIEWER: Why did you leave?

RITA: I've always gotten fired. But, okay, you could say that I've always gotten fired, but before they could fire me, I know when they're going to fire me, [so] I always quit. Before that "You're fired" comes out, I always quit.

INTERVIEWER: What other kinds of straight jobs have you had?

RITA: Okay, my first job was in the hospital. Nurse's aide was my last—I got fired there. A security guard for the telephone company.

INTERVIEWER: What was the reason behind quitting most of them?

RITA: I just am not a nine-to-five person.... Most of my jobs were during the day. I had to be there in the morning. I didn't have a car; transportation by bus, I didn't like that. So, it was like, I don't like to take buses. I like being my own boss. Work when I want to work, make good money.

For the uneducated and largely unskilled women of this study—whose experience with straight work was unfulfilling or whose jobs were unstable due to a volatile and sexist marketplace—participation in street life, with its promise of money, excitement, and independence, seemed the answer to their problems.

STREET LIFE

According to the women of this study, a prerequisite to working as a street hustler is that a woman must have a male sponsor, a "man," to act as a "keep-away" from other "men" who vie for a living on the street. She must turn her earnings over to this "man" in order to be considered "his woman" and to enjoy the "man's" protection. The "man," besides providing protection from other "men," gives his women material necessities and gifts and, most important, sex and love (Merry, 1980).

The following, from an interview with a respondent whom we have named "Chris," illustrates why street women need "men" to work. When asked why she worked and turned her earnings over to a "man" instead of working for herself and keeping her money, she said:

CHRIS: You can't really work the streets for yourself unless you got a man—not for a long length of time... 'cause the other pimps are not going to like it because you don't have anybody to represent you. They'll rob you, they'll hit you in the head if you don't have nobody to take up for you. Yeah, it happens. They give you a hassle.... [The men] will say, "Hey baby, what's your name? Where your man at? You got a man?"

INTERVIEWER: So you can't hustle on your own?

CHRIS: Not really, no. You can, you know, but not for long.

Women who do hustle on their own are called "outlaw" women, a term that clearly indicates that their solo activities are proscribed. Women who work as outlaws lose any protection that they had formerly been granted under the "law" of the street and are open targets for "men" who wish to harass them, take their money, or exploit them sexually.

Street life is male dominated and so structured that "men" reap the profits of women's labor. A "man" demands from his women not only money but respect as well. Showing respect for "men" means total obedience and complete dedication to them. Mary reports that in the company of "men" she had to "talk mainly to the women—try not to look at the men if possible at all—try not to have conversation with them." Rita, when asked about the rules of the street, said, "Just basic, obey. Do what he wants to do. Don't disrespect him.... I could not disrespect him in any verbal or physical way. I never attempted to hit him back. Never." And, in the same vein, Tina said that when her "man" had others over to socialize, the women of the family were relegated to the role of servant. "We couldn't speak to them when we wasn't spoken to, and we could not foul up on their orders. And you cannot disrespect them."

Clearly, "men" are the rulers of the underworld. Hartmann's (1984, p. 177) definition of patriarchy is particularly apropos of "street-level" male domination.

> We can usefully define patriarchy as a set of social relations between men, which have a material base, and which, though hierarchical, establish or create interde-pendence and solidarity among men that enable them to dominate women. Though patriarchy is hierarchical and men of different classes, races, or ethnic groups have different places in the patriarchy, they also are united in their shared relationship of dominance over their women; they are dependent on each other to maintain that domination.... In the hierarchy of patriarchy, all men, whatever their rank in the patriarchy, are bought off by being able to control at least some women.

"Men," as the quotations that follow illustrate, and as Milner and Milner (1972) have written with regard to pimps, maintain a strong coalition among themselves, allowing them to dominate women. As the number of women a "man" has work-ing for him increases, the time he can spend supervising each female's activities decreases. It becomes very important that "men" be in contact with one another to assure the social and economic control of street women. With watchful "men" keeping tabs on their own and other "men's" women, women know that they must always work hard and follow the rules.

Rose gives an example here of one of the many ways in which "men" pro-tect one another. Rose's sister, who is also involved in street life, was badly beaten by her "man" and decided to press charges against him. She decided to drop the charges because:

> She got scared 'cuz he kept threatening her.... His friends [were] callin' her and tellin' her if she didn't drop the charges they was gonna do somethin' to her. So she dropped the charges.

It is interesting to note that when working women are caught talking with "men" who are not their own, it is considered to be at the women's initiative and they are reprimanded. In other words, "men" can speak with whom they please, when they please, but women are not allowed to speak to or even look at other "men." Ann gives another example of this element of the cohesiveness of "men":

> ANN: If another pimp see you "out of pocket" [breaking a rule] or bent over talkin' to another pimp or somethin' in their car, they will tell your man, "Yea, she was talkin' to some dude in a Cadillac—he try and "knock your bitch." That the word they use.
>
> INTERVIEWER: What does it mean?
>
> ANN: He tryin' to come up with her. He tryin' to have her for himself. That what they mean. That what they be sayin' all the time: "He tryin' to 'knock your bitch,' man. You better put her in check.— In other words, you better, how should I say it? "In check" mean, tell her what's happenin', keep her under control. Or, if you be walkin' around on the stroll and stuff and somebody might see you sittin' down on the bench, and they say, "Man, your ho [whore] is lazy! All the cars were passin' by—that girl didn't even catch none of 'em." 'Cuz they [the "men"] know you and stuff.

The mechanisms that keep women oppressed at the street level are parallel to those of the broader culture. The wage structure in the United States is such that many women cannot financially endure without men. On the street, women also need men to survive, because they are not allowed to earn money in their absence. In addition, women of the street must give all of the money they earn to their "man." A "man," in turn, uses the money to take care of his needs and the needs of his women—although, as we shall see, money is usually not distributed unconditionally but, rather, is based upon a system of rewards and punishments that are dependent upon the behavior of women.

THE PSEUDO-FAMILY

The pseudo-family is a family-like institution made up of a "man" and the women who work for him. Its female members refer to each other as "wives-in-law" and to the man for whom they work as "my man." By focusing on the pseudo-family, we try to isolate and expose a street-level mechanism for female oppression, and to explain why the "wife-in-law" is unlikely to revolt or leave her oppressive situation. Specifically, we attempt to describe how the pseudo-family, while seeming to offer love, money, and stability to the women who participate in it, is structured so that women, in fact, gain little. Our thesis, in other words, is that the security of the pseudo-family for the female street hustler is largely illusory.

The structure of the family is hierarchical and the "man" holds the top position. He collects all of the money that women earn and makes decisions about how it is spent. He is also the disciplinarian of the family: when a rule is broken, he is the person who decides upon and metes out the punishment. The "man" also has the final say about who is recruited into his family. Despite the fact that his women may oppose the idea of additional "wives-in-law," there is typically little they can do about it. If women refuse to accept their "wives-in-law" or try to make life difficult for them, they are likely to be thought "disrespectful" and, as such, will be punished. Next in the hierarchy of the pseudo-family is the position of "bottom woman." When a "man" and woman start out working only as an entrepreneurial couple who, at some later date, recruit another woman into the family to become the first woman's "wife-in-law," the most senior woman is accorded the privileged position of "bottom woman." "Bottom women" help to make sure that the household is in good working order. "Bottom women" are also expected to keep tabs on their "wives-in-law" and to smooth out any differences that may occur between them.

The "man" of the family places a special trust in the woman that occupies the position of "bottom woman." It is, therefore, an enviable position and one to which "wives-in-law" aspire. To safeguard the position, then, and to control the jealousy that her "wives-in-law" may feel toward her because of her higher status, the "bottom woman" must convince her "wives-in-law"—each individually—that they, in fact, are the "man's" favorite.

Dee, a 26-year-old, self-described Puerto Rican/white woman, has been involved in street life since she was 15. She has an extensive background as "bottom woman" and described how she kept her families (of up to six "wives-in-law") together.

INTERVIEWER: Were you always bottom woman?

DEE: Any man I had, yea. Because it was the mind, the mental thing. If you can avoid jealousy and all that and keep a family together, and me being from keepin' families together, it was an easy thing—right up my alley. [You'd have to] make them feel they were number one and you were just a peon. [It] kept them around, kept them bringin' in $400 and $500 dollars a night.

INTERVIEWER: Did you get along with your wives-in-law?

DEE: I would force myself to get along with them.... I would be protection for them so, consequently, they wouldn't really fight with me, per se, but with each other. So that I would say that I'm ... [your] ... friend and her friend and be the mediator between the two. I never really had any problems unless one of them violated some type of code.

To gain the trust of the "bottom woman" and to prove that she is held in high esteem, the "man" often passes on privileged information to the "bottom woman" about her "wives-in-law." Having this information increases the "bottom woman's" feelings of power and prestige and instills confidence in her and her position, motivating the "bottom woman" to do a better job for the "man." Although the information she receives could be used to flaunt the fact that she is her "man's" favorite, the "bottom woman" must remain discreet if she is to retain her position and keep the family together.

A female street hustler can also become a "bottom woman" by working her way up through the ranks of the family. Depending upon the situation, becoming a "bottom woman" in this way can take anywhere from a week to a number of years. Generally, young white women have the best chance of promotion because they make the most money (as a result of the racism of customers and the fact that they can work in more and "better" locations than black women without attracting attention from the police), are without lengthy criminal records when first recruited to the streets, and tend to be more obedient. At least one of our respondents said:

> ["Men"] go for young womens and for the white womens....They figure the young wornens will get out there and maybe catch a case occasionally until she catch on, [but] she won't go to jail...and then they think that white women can work anywhere, make more money...without catching no heat from the police. (Rose)

Although there is limited advancement for women, they can never rise to a status equal to the "man." The rules of "the game" explicitly state that "men" are to dominate women, and women, as subservient creatures, are to respect and appreciate that fact (Milner & Milner, 1972). As there are opportunities for promotions within the family, and into safer and more prestigious hustles outside of the family, women cling to the false hope that "their day will come." In addition, the competition among women for these positions, and for their "man's" affection, creates such divisiveness that it is unlikely that women will conspire to fight for significant changes in the street or pseudo-family structure. Thus "men" are assured that the status quo is maintained.

Male Control

The maintenance of male dominance at the street level is dependent upon "men's" ability to control women. The control of women by "men" is made possible, first of all, by the very fact that women are not allowed involvement in the life without "men" as their sponsors. As "men" are well aware, however, women will not accept them and their rule as against the rule and control of another "man" unless given adequate enticements. These take the form of love, money, and the accompanying sense of security. Once a woman has become attached to the "man," he is then in a position to control her more effectively. Lastly, when all else fails, "men" will resort to physical violence in order to maintain control.

Getting women into positions where they can be dominated begins during the "turning out" process—the process whereby a "man" teaches a woman how to become a street hustler. The "turning out" process, as Miller (1978, p. 142) notes,

> involves a variety of subtle techniques of social control and persuasion on the part of the pimp....[It] involves several steps in which the pimp initially attracts the woman through his sexual and economic appeal and later changes her mind about the propriety of prostitution and the proper relationship between men and women....The critical factor in the beginning of the relationship is the establishment of control over the relationship by the pimp.

Elsie, whom we heard from earlier, is a 38-year-old black woman. She first met her "man" when she was 28 years old; he was 35. Since about the age of 19,

Elsie had been intermittently involved in forgery and other petty street crimes. She was still on the fringe of the life, however, and therefore had never worked with a "man." Elsie described for us how, and under what circumstances, she was turned out by her "man."

> ELSIE: okay, I had met this guy....I knew about stuff like that but I had never indulged in it [prostitution]. I'd done, you know, check forgin' and stealin' but that's it. Me and him was talking—he was dressed up all nice and nice lookin' and he had a big nice Continental outside. So I'm lookin', you know? So I asked him, I said, "What kind of work do you do?" He said, "I sell insurance.... " He said, "You married?" I said, "No, I'm separated but livin' by myself." He said, "Well, could I call you or come by your house, could you give me your number?" I said, "Yeah." So I gave him the number. He called me a couple of times and I said, "Well, come back to my house!" I was all excited—I had the house all spic and span and he came over. Right about that time I was having a few problems 'cuz I owed some back bills and stuff—my phone was gettin' ready to be cut off and stuff. I didn't have no stereo or nothin'. So he come by there that night, looked around. I still didn't really know what was happening, you know. I told him I was in financial trouble, they were gettin' ready to cut my phone off—I need a TV and stereo and stuff. He said, "Well, I'm goin' to pay your phone bill and everything for you." And he did! He paid the phone bill the next day, he brought me a stereo, he did all that. He bought me a new outfit.
>
> One of my girlfriends...she said, "Elsie, you're too naive." She said, "You don't know what he's supposed to be?" I said, "No." She said, "I think he calls himself a pimp." I said, "He's nice, look what he did." She said, "You know, that's the way they do. He trying to set you up." I said, "Girl, go away. I know what I'm doin." I was older than she was, you know, and she's trying to tell me. And sure enough, that's what it was.
>
> INTERVIEWER: How did you find out?
>
> ELSIE: He told me about it, okay. When I found out, I found out on the telephone. I said, "Yea, I heard you was, you know." He said, "No, who told you that?" I said, "I just heard it 'cuz a pimp is noticed on the streets." And he used the name Peachy, that was his street name. So I said, "If that's what you is, stay away from me, 'cuz I don't even want to get involved with nobody like that." He said, "No, it ain't like that with me and you, we can just be friends." I said, "Well, I don't even want nothin' to do with you if it's like that. I got four kids, I ain't got time for nothin' like you." He said, "Elsie, it ain't like that. If you don't wanna do nothin' like that." He said, "I admit, I do do that. I got some ladies that, you know, give me money and stuff, but you ain't gonna have to be like that." He said we could just be friends, that we could have a relationship different from that, you know.
>
> INTERVIEWER: Did you believe him?
>
> ELSIE: Yeah, I did! 'Cuz I liked him! So I fell for it. And then the next thing I knew, he came by and said, "Elsie, I got somethin' set up for you."

After Elsie had serviced her first trick, her "man" came to pick her up. She said:

> I got in the car and I was sittin' up, lookin' all quiet and stuff. He said, "Did you get the money?" I said, "Yeah." He said, "Where is it?" I said, "I got it." He said, "Give it here." I said, "All of it?" He said, "Yeah, and then if you want some, I'll give it to you." That's the part that hurted. I gave it to him. [I thought], "I'll never do that no more." But then, after that, I got smart, not really smart, but I got a little wiser. Okay, when I would do somethin' like that, I would stash me some money.

Rita, a 26-year-old white woman, first met her "man" when she was 18. However, as she describes it, "I was 18 when I met my man, but I was 19 when I first put money in his hand." Rita said that for some months she had had a girl-friend/boyfriend relationship with her "man." He had a 30-year-old white woman working for him, but, according to Rita:

> He wanted a white girl he could turn out himself. Apparently, she [his first woman] had been turned out by somebody else. But I was his turn out completely.

Her "man," like Elsie's, made sure that there was a strong emotional attachment before any money changed hands. Rita said:

> RITA: He made me fall in love with him before I put any type of money in his hand. I was working three months and still dating him and not paying him. But he knew that he was getting me.
>
> INTERVIEWER: So he was turning you out but you weren't giving him any money?
>
> RITA: No, I was not. He knew I was falling in love with him, okay? Finally, that day came where we sat in the car. We had just gone out. I was sitting in the car with him, he had brought me home from going out—we'd gone out drinking. I was sittin' in the car with him and he turns to me and says, "Well, you know, we've been going out…and you know what I'm about, and my lady's getting' kind of mad that ain't nothin' happening and you are working. It's either, you gotta start giving me some money or I can't see you no more." And I did not want that, I fell in love with the man. So it was like, okay, here you go, buddy, am I yours now?

Rita also said that her "man" would not bail her out of jail during that initial period when she was not giving him any money. She said that the reason he wouldn't bail her out was that

> he was just tryin' to show me, "Look, if you go to jail, I'm there and I'm yours and you're mine, I'll get you out. But you're alone and I can't get you out. That's going against what this is all about."

As these excerpts illustrate, the establishment of an emotional tie between the "man" and the woman is an extremely important element of the "turning out" process. Even though a woman discovers relatively early that a "man's" affection is conditional (depending on her payment, respect, and obedience to him), she believes the payoff—being "taken care of" financially, socially, and emotionally— to be worth it. When "wives-in-law" enter the picture, however, and the woman finds that she must "share" her "man" with others, jealousy and conflict arise, creating instability within the family.

GETTING DISENTANGLED FROM
THE PSEUDO-FAMILY

Changes in the composition of the pseudo-family are frequent and occur for various reasons. The intervention of the criminal justice system, the inability of "men" to control adequately the jealously of their women, the heavy drug use of street women and their men, and the decreased marketability of women as they age are all factors that affect family stability.

Criminal Justice System

Because of the highly visible hustles in which street women engage, frequent contact with criminal justice authorities is inevitable. When a woman is arrested and incarcerated, a new woman is often recruited into the pseudo-family to replace the lost earnings of the incarcerated woman. When the incarcerated woman is released and returns to her family, the family must adapt to the new amalgam of personalities. Often, however, the adaptation is unsuccessful and the result is that one of the women may leave the family in search of a better situation. The woman who leaves is replaced by another, creating new stresses within the pseudo-family, and the whole process is repeated.

Also, while incarcerated, women may be recruited into new families. One of the women interviewed—a veteran of the game—chose her new "man" by telephone from the House of Correction. She was recruited by one of his women who was also serving time. Another woman reported that she was considering leaving her "man" of nine years for a new "man" whom she met and corresponded with in the House of Correction via smuggled letters. Women who are unhappy with their current family situation, then, or women who are "between" men, have opportunities while incarcerated to join new families.

Drug Use

Excessive drug use by street hustlers and their "men" also erodes family stability. "Men" have a responsibility to their women to take care of business—to pay bills and post bond, dispense clothing and pocket money, and generally behave as a responsive (if not caring) family member—and women, in return, must provide "men" with money and respect. As Joan says, a real pimp "gonna take care of her 'cuz she's takin' care of him." In other words, there are mutual obligations between "men" and women. When "men" use hard drugs excessively, they are unable to hold up their end of the bargain adequately. Similarly, women who are heavy users are unable to maintain good work habits. Both addicted "men" and women drain the financial resources of the family. In addition, "men" become dependent on their women to support their habits and thereby lose the respect of other "men" and women of the street.

They ["men" in Milwaukee] would take and allow a woman to hold the fact that they're givin' 'em money over their heads. Where, in Chicago or New York, they would get rid of the woman—'cuz women come too easy. The women here are the pimps. And if they're payin' the man they're payin' 'em not because of some strategic level he's at, it's because they want someone to protect them. But he's shootin' so much dope nine times out of 10, that the woman runs it [the family]. She says she's not going to work—he might get down on his hands and knees and beg her 'cuz he's such a punk he needs to go pop from the dopeman....They're shootin' too much dope, they're doin' too much dope. Dope has become a big problem as far as the players and the females. That's taken a lot of good men who have taken the money that women have made 'em, put it in businesses, and smoked up the business. So the drugs alone has killed a lot of the men. It's a vicious circle—it all goes back to the dopeman. (Dee)

Aging Out

As women age, their value as street hustlers declines and they are often discarded by "men" who favor younger, naive women who have yet to establish criminal records. As a woman becomes both increasingly cynical and less attractive (compared to her younger competitors), she is less able to assimilate into the pseudo-family. Jody, for example, said that she and her "man" permitted a "wife-in-law" of two years to remain in jail (pending $500 bail) because "we wanted to leave the state, and she was old, and I had learned everything from her, so she was no longer needed." When Rita, another respondent, entered a family, her "wife-in-law" left, because, as Rita reported, "She knew that I was prettier than her, younger. She was 30 years old. I [was] 19 and freshly turned out."

In addition, older women are more inclined to consider their own needs rather than the needs of their man. Toni, a 29 year old, after working as a street hustler for 11 years, seeks a secure life with a "good" man. As she says:

You become more and more experienced, and you have to do serious time, and you have so much time to think about what you want. If you're going to stay in this life, [you begin to think] about what you want out of it instead of what he wants out of it. It becomes more of a priority. Now, I want someone who does not mess around with drugs....Who has enough money of his own, has enough things going for himself, to where he doesn't need me. That's what I want now.

Because older women hustlers are less financially successful than younger women and often are chary of exploitative "men," they are frequently spurned by "men."

Instability

Though women are not allowed control over their earnings, they often receive costly gifts from their "men." The process of leaving "men," however, is such that women frequently lose the material wealth that they have acquired during the relationship. Since the decision to leave a "man" is usually made in anger—after a beating, or after being left to "sit" in jail, or in a fit of jealousy—women commonly leave their families without their treasured material possessions. As Toni says, "I've had to leave without my stuff a few times. Then you gotta start all over each time. But there's been times when I've got to keep my stuff, too." In addition, women who have accomplished some occupational mobility while with a "man" must start at the bottom of the occupational hierarchy when they choose a new one.

The more frequently women change men, then, the less likely their chance of accumulating any material wealth for themselves.

SUMMARY AND CONCLUSIONS

The pseudo-family, in addition to addressing the emotional and sexual needs of its members, is explicitly organized to realize and exploit the "profitability" that inheres in its female members—that is, their sexuality. But if female street hustlers are both labor and capital "rolled into one," it is difficult to imagine how the "man" can interject himself into the lives of women who, logically, are self-sufficient—in a purely entrepreneurial sense. In fact, the women who join pseudo-families "barter" their way through their family lives, endlessly exchanging their resources as women for, variously, the affections (and recognition) of the "man" and the material goods necessary to survival. There is a twofold answer to the question, therefore, of why women relinquish control of their natural assets in the sexual market of the street. One is that they bring to the street emotional and financial vulnerabilities and so fall prey to "men" prepared to exploit them; the second is that the "sexual" street scene represents a deeply entrenched, patriarchal structure that quickly and effectively punishes independent female hustlers.

REFERENCES

Brown, M. (1979). Teenage prostitution. *Adolescence, 14,* 665–680.

Hartmann, H. I. (1984). The unhappy marriage of Marxism and feminism: Towards a more progressive union. In A. M. Jaggar & P. S. Rothenberg (Eds.), *Feminist frameworks* (pp. 172–189). New York: McGraw-Hill.

James, J., & Meyerding, J. (1976). Motivations for entrance into prostitution. In L. Cites (Ed.), *The female offender* (pp. 177–205). Washington, DC: Heath.

Laner, M. R. (1974). Prostitution as an illegal vocation: A sociological overview. In C. Bryant (Ed.), *Deviant behavior: Occupational and organizational bases* (pp 406–418). Chicago: Rand McNally.

Merry, S. (1980). Manipulating anonymity: Streetwalkers, strategies for safety in the city. *Ethnos, 45,* 157–175.

Miller, G. (1978). *The world of deviant work.* Englewood Cliffs, NJ: Prentice Hall.

———. (1986). *Street woman.* Philadelphia: Temple University Press.

Milner, C., & Milner, R. (1972). *Black players: The secret world of black pimps.* Boston: Little, Brown.

Sidel, R. (1986). *Women and children last.* New York: Penguin.

CHAPTER 17

⚓

Dealing Careers

Patricia A. Adler

In the early 1970s, Patricia Adler and her husband Peter moved to Southwest County (pseudonym) to begin their graduate studies in sociology. There they made friends with "Dave," a neighbor whom they later learned was involved in high-level drug smuggling and dealing. As their friendship with Dave developed, they were introduced to a group of Dave's friends and associates, all of whom were involved in illegal drug dealing. As friendship and trust continued to develop between the Adlers and Dave and his associates, the two were slowly granted access to the world of smuggling, dealing, and drug use. For the next six years, with the knowledge and active assistance of Dave and his friends, the Adlers studied this drug-dealing and smuggling community, conducting interviews and observing their activities. In this selection from her book Wheeling and Dealing: An Ethnography of an Upper-Level Drug Dealing and Smuggling Community, *Patricia Adler explains how thrill seeking, spontaneity, emotionality, and other expressive concerns characterize the lifestyle of these upper-level drug dealers. She follows their careers, first by examining the process of becoming a drug trafficker, then considering the various routes to upward mobility, and finally the experience of aging in the career.*

BECOMING A DRUG TRAFFICKER

Becoming a drug trafficker was a gradual process, where individuals progressively shifted perspective as they became increasingly involved in the social networks of dealers and smugglers (Lieb & Olson, 1976). As Ray (1961) has noted for the careers of heroin addicts, joining these social networks required a commitment to the drug world's norms, values, and lifestyle, and limited the degree of involvement individuals subsequently had with nondeviant groups.

Source: Adler, P. A. (1993). Dealing careers. In *Wheeling and dealing: An ethnography of an upper-level drug dealing and smuggling community* (2nd ed., pp. 123–142). New York: Columbia University Press. Copyright © 1993 by Columbia University Press. Reprinted with permission.

Recruitment

I observed three entry routes to this deviant career. These routes were different for dealing and smuggling, and varied according to the level of trafficking where individuals entered the field.

Dealing

Individuals began dealing drugs through their own initiative, entering the occupation via *self-propulsion*. They fell into two groups, marked by different levels of entry and characterized by significantly varied experiences.

People who began dealing with a low-level entry followed the classic path portrayed in the literature (see Anonymous, 1969; Blum et al., 1968; Carey, 1972; Goode, 1970; Johnson, 1973). These initiates came from among the ranks of regular drug users, since, in practice, using drugs heavily and dealing for "stash" (one's personal supply) were nearly inseparable. Out of this multitude of low-level dealers, however, most abandoned the practice after they encountered their first legal or financial bust, lasting in the business for a fairly short period (see Anonymous, 1969; Carey, 1972; Lieb & Olson, 1976). Those who sought bigger profits gradually drifted into a full-time career in drug trafficking. Their careers as dealers were therefore entwined with their careers as drug users, which usually began by late adolescence (between the ages of 15 and 22). Because of this early recruitment into dealing, low-level entrants generally developed few, if any, occupational skills other than dealing. Although it was difficult to attain the upper level of the drug trade from these humble beginnings, a small but significant percentage of the dealers I observed in Southwest County got their start in this fashion.

A larger percentage of Southwest County dealers made a middle-level entry. Future big dealers usually jumped into transacting in substantial quantities from the outset, buying 50 kilos of commercial marijuana or one to two ounces of cocaine. One dealer explained this phenomenon:

> Someone who thinks of himself as an executive or an entrepreneur is not going to get into the dope business on a small level. The average executive just jumps right into the middle. Or else he's not going to jump.

This was the route taken by Southwest County residents who had little or no previous involvement in drug trafficking. For them, entry into dealing was precipitated by their social relations with local dealers and smugglers (naturally, this implies a self-selecting sample of outsiders who became accepted and trusted by these upper-level traffickers, based on mutual interests, orientation, and values). Through their friendships with dealers, these individuals were introduced to other members of the dealing scene and to their fast life. Individuals who found this lifestyle attractive became increasingly drawn to the subculture, building networks of social associations within it. Eventually, some of these people decided to participate more actively. This step was usually motivated by their attraction to the money and the lifestyle. Dave recounted how he fell in with the drug world set:

I used to be in real estate making good money. Through my property management and investment services I started meeting some rich people. I was the only
person at my firm renting to longhairs and dealing with their money. They all
paid me in cash from a giant wad of bills. They never asked for a receipt and
always had cash, 24 hours a day. I slowly started getting friendly with them,
although I didn't realize how heavy they were. I knew ways of buying real estate
and putting it under fictitious names, laundering money so that it went in as hot
cash and came out as spendable income. I invested their money in gems, metals,
cars. But the whole time I never asked any questions. I just took my commission
and was happy. Then one guy asked me to clear some checks for him through my
bank account—said he was hiding the money from his ex-wife and the Treasury
people. This was the beginning. I slowly got more and more involved with him
until I was neglecting my real estate business and just partying with him all the
time. My spending went up, but my income went down, and suddenly I had to
look around for another way to make money fast. I took the money I was cashing
for him, bought some bricks from another dealer friend of his and sold them out
of state before I gave him back the cash. Eventually I started to deal with him too,
on a front basis. Within six months I was turning 100 bricks at a time.

Once individuals decided to try dealing, they rarely abandoned it after one transaction. Earning money was intoxicatingly alluring, stimulating their greed for
more, while losing money usually necessitated becoming involved in another deal
to recoup what they lost.

People who entered drug dealing at these middle levels were usually between
the ages of 25 and 35, and had worked in some other occupation before dealing
seriously. Many drifted into the lifestyle from jobs already concentrated in the
night hours, such as bartending, waiting tables, and nightclub door bouncing. Still
others came from fields where the working hours were irregular and adaptable
to their special schedules, such as acting, real estate, inventing, graduate school,
construction, and creative "entrepreneurship" (more aptly called hand-to-mouth
survival, for many). The smallest group was tempted into the drug world from
structured occupations and the professions.

Smuggling

Smuggling, in contrast, was rarely entered in this self-directed manner. Only a
small minority of upper-level dealers were able to make the leap into importation
on their own. The rest became involved in smuggling through a form of *solicitation*. The complex task of importing illegal drugs required more knowledge,
experience, equipment, and connections than most people possessed. Those who
got into drug smuggling usually did so at the invitation of an established smuggler. About half of the people smugglers recruited had not dealt before, but came
directly into importation from the drug world's social scene. This implies, like
middle-level entry into dealing, that recruits were attracted to the drug crowd
and its lifestyle, and that they had prior acquaintance with dealers and smugglers.
The other half of the recruits were solicited from among the ranks of middle-level
Southwest County dealers.

Recruits who were solicited were likely to have some skill or asset which the experienced smuggler needed to put his operation together. This included piloting or navigating ability, equipment, money, or simply the willingness to handle drugs while they were being transported. One smuggler described the criteria he used to screen potential recruits for his smuggling crew:

> Pilots are really at a premium. They burn out so fast that I have to replace them every six months to a year. But I'm also looking for people who are cool: people who will carry out their jobs according to the plan, who won't panic if the load arrives late or something goes wrong, 'cause this happens a lot…and I try not to get people who've been to prison before, because if they haven't, they'll be more likely to take foolish risks, the kind that I don't want to have to.

Learning the Trade

Once people experienced some initial success in dealing, their attitude shifted from hesitancy to enthusiasm. Despite the amount of time and effort they invested, most people felt as if they had earned a lot of money for very little work. This was because dealing time and work differed structurally from legitimate work: the latter usually took place within a well-defined physical and temporal framework (the 9-to-5 hours at the office), while dealing was accomplished during discretionary, or recreational, hours and settings.

As business began to go well, the danger translated into excitement, making it seem like fun. Novice drug traffickers felt as if they were earning "gravy" money while simultaneously enjoying themselves. This definition of the situation helped them overcome any remaining reluctance and plunge themselves more deeply into the occupation. They then became eager to learn more about concrete strategies of conducting business safely and successfully.

Learning the trade involved acquiring specific knowledge of potential business connections, ways of organizing transactions profitably, ways of avoiding legal detection and arrest, ways of transporting illegal goods, ways of coordinating participants, types of equipment, and myriad other details. This knowledge was acquired through either *on-the-job training* (Miller & Ritzer 1977, p. 89) or *sponsorship*.

Dealers underwent on-the-job training, refining their knowledge and skills by getting experience and learning from their mistakes. Their early experiences often included getting burned with inferior merchandise, getting "short counted" with low volume, and getting ripped off through carelessness in selecting their dealing associates. While some people abandoned dealing because of these early errors, many returned, better educated, to try again.

Socialization into the technical aspects of smuggling was not as isolated as it was for dealing. Most future smugglers were recruited and trained by a sponsor with whom they had an apprentice/mentor relationship. Those who had been dealers previously knew the rudiments of drug transactions. What they learned from the smuggler was how to fill a particular role in his crew. From there they became familiar with many other roles, learned the scope of the whole operation, and began to meet suppliers and customers. This mentor relationship often led apprentices to form an enduring loyalty to their sponsor....

Identity Shift

Developing a dealing or smuggling self-conception involved more than simply committing illegal acts. A transition in the locus of self was required. Some people assumed the dealing identity immediately and eagerly, having made a conscious decision to pursue dealing as an occupation. Others displayed a more subtle identity shift, as they gradually drifted into membership in the drug world (Matza, 1964). Many individuals, then, became drug dealers by their actions well before they consciously admitted this to themselves. One dealer described his transformation:

> I had a job, school, and I was doing volunteer work, but I was also deviant, and the deviant part was the part I secretly got off on. I was like a Dr. Jekyll with a Mr. Hyde side. When I got into my dealing bag, people would pay homage to me; I'd get respect and recognition.... Eventually the two worlds intermingled and the facade [dealing side] became the reality.

Becker and Carper (1956) have asserted that individuals' identities are based on their degree of commitment to an occupation. Thus, those people who maintained their ties to other occupations took longer to form a dealing identity. They did not become fully committed to dealing until some external event (i.e., an arrest, or the conflicting demands of their legitimate and illegitimate businesses) forced them to make a conscious choice. One dealer related how he faced this decision:

> I had been putting off thinking about it for all those months, but the time squeeze finally became such a thing that I couldn't ignore it any more. I was working at the office all day and staying up dealing and doing drugs all night. My wife was complaining because I'd fall asleep at odd hours, and I never had any time for the kids. I knew I had to choose between my two lives—the straight and the dealing. I hated to give up my job because it had always been my security, and besides, it was a good business cover, but I finally decided I was more attracted to dealing. I was making better money there in fewer hours and this way, I'd have more time to be with my kids during the day.

UPWARD MOBILITY

Once they had gotten in and learned the trade, most dealers and smugglers strove for upward mobility. This advancement took different forms, varying between dealing and smuggling.

Dealers experienced two types of upward mobility: *rising through the ranks* and *stage-jumping*. The gradual rise exemplifies the way upward mobility has historically been portrayed in the sociological literature on dealing (Anonymous, 1969; Carey, 1972; Redlinger, 1975). Individuals from the lowest levels expanded their range of contacts, realized that they could earn greater profits by buying in greater quantities, and began to move up the hierarchy of dealing levels. Rick described his early stage of involvement with dealing:

I had dealt a limited amount of lids and psychedelics in my early college days without hardly taking it seriously. But after a while something changed in me, and I decided to try to work my way up. I probably was a classic case—started out buying a kilo for $150 and selling two pounds for $100 each. I did that twice, then I took the money and bought two bricks, then three, then five, then seven.

This type of upward mobility, though characteristic of low-level dealers, was fairly atypical of the upper-level drug crowd. Two factors combined to make it less likely for low-level entrants to rise through the ranks to the top. The first was psychological. People who started small thought small; most had neither the motivation nor the vision to deal large quantities of drugs. The second and more critical factor was social. People who started at the bottom and tried to work their way up the ladder often had a hard time finding connections at the upper levels. The few people who did rise through the ranks generally began dealing in another part of the country, moving to Southwest County only after they had already progressed to the middle levels. These people were lured to the region by its reputation within drug circles as an importation and wholesale trafficking market.

More commonly, dealers and smugglers stage-jumped to the higher levels of drug trafficking. Beginning at a middle level, and progressing so rapidly that they could hardly acclimate to their increasing involvement and volume, these people moved quickly to the top. Jean described her mode of escalation:

When I started to deal I was mostly looking for a quick buck here or there, something to pay some pressing bill. I was middling 50 or 100 bricks at a time. But then I met a guy who said he would front me half a pound of coke, and if I turned it fast, I could have more, and on a regular basis. Pretty soon I was turning six, seven, eight, nine, 10 pounds a week—they were passing through real fast. I was clearing at least 10 grand a month. It was too much money too fast. I didn't know what to do with it. It got ridiculous, I wasn't relating to anyone anymore. I was never home, always gone.... The biggest ego trip came when all of a sudden I turned around and I was selling to the people I had been buying from. I skipped their level of doing business entirely and stage-jumped straight past them.

Southwest County's social milieu, with its concentration of upper-level dealers and smugglers, thus facilitated forming connections and doing business at the upper levels of the drug world.

Within smuggling, upward mobility took the form of individuals *branching out on their own* (Redlinger, 1975). By working for a smuggler, some crew members developed the expertise and connections to run their own operation. There were several requirements for such a move. They could fairly easily acquire the technical knowledge of equipment, air routes, stopovers, and how to coordinate personnel after working in a smuggling area for six months to a year. It was difficult to put together their own crew, though, because skilled employees, especially pilots, were hard to find. Most new smugglers borrowed people from other crews until they were established enough to recruit and train their own personnel. Finally, they needed connections for buying and selling drugs. Customers were plentiful, but it often required special breaks or networks to serve a foreign supplier.

Another way for employees to head their own smuggling operations was to take over when their boss retired. This had the advantage of keeping the crew and style of operation intact. Various financial arrangements were worked out for such a transfer of authority, from straight cash purchases to deals involving residual payments. One marijuana smuggler described how he acquired his operation:

> I had been Jake's main pilot for about a year, and next after him I knew the most about how his operation was run. We were really tight, and he had taken me all up and down the coast with him, meeting his customers. Naturally I knew the Mexican end of the operation and his supplier, Cesar, since I used to make the runs, flying down the money and picking up the dope. So when he told me he wanted to get out of the business, we made a deal. I took over the set-up and gave him a residual for every run I made. I kept all the drivers, all the dealers, all the connections—everything the guy had—but I found myself a new pilot.

In sum, most dealers and smugglers reached the upper levels of doing business not so much as a result of their individual entrepreneurial initiative but through the social networks they formed in the drug subculture. Their ability to remain in these strata was largely tied to the way they treated these drug world relationships.

AGING IN THE CAREER

Up to this point I have discussed dealers and smugglers separately because they displayed distinctive career patterns. However, once individuals rose to the highest levels, they faced a common set of problems and experiences. I will therefore discuss them together below.

Once they entered the drug world and established themselves at its upper levels, dealers and smugglers were capable of wheeling and dealing on a major scale. Yet this period brought with it a growth of malaise. As they aged in the career, the dark side of their occupation began to surface.

The first part of their disillusionment lay in the fading of glamour and excitement. While participation in the drug world brought thrills and status to novices, the occupation's allure faded over time. Their initial feelings of exhilaration began to dull as they became increasingly jaded by their exorbitant drug consumption. Already inclined toward regular use, upper-level dealers and smugglers set no limits on their drug intake once they began trafficking and could afford all the cocaine they desired. One smuggler described how he eventually came to feel:

> It was fun, those three or four years. I never worried about money or anything. But after a while it got real boring, there was no feeling or emotion or anything about it. I wasn't even hardly relating to my old lady anymore. Everything was just one big rush.

After a year or more of serious drug trafficking, dealers and smugglers became increasingly sensitized to the extreme risks they faced. Cases of friends and associates who were arrested, imprisoned, or killed (because of natural hazards) began to mount. The probability that they were known to the police increased. They gradually realized that the potential legal consequences they faced were less remote than they had earlier imagined. Many individuals became convinced that continued drug trafficking would inevitably lead to arrest ("It's only a matter of time before you get caught").

Dealers and smugglers generally repressed their awareness of danger, treating it as a taken-for-granted part of their daily existence. Periodic crises shattered their casual attitudes, however, evoking strong underlying feelings of fears. One dealer talked about his feelings of paranoia:

> You're always on the line. You don't lead a normal life. You're always looking over your shoulder, wondering who's at the door, having to hide everything. You learn to look behind you so well you could probably bend over and look up your ass. That's paranoia. It's a really scary, hard feeling. That's what makes you get out.

These feelings caused dealers and smugglers to assume greater security precautions. After especially close brushes with danger, they intensified their precautions temporarily, retreating into near isolation until they felt that the heat was off. They also gradually incorporated more precautions into their everyday routines, abandoning their earlier casualness for greater inflexibility and adherence to their rational rules of operating (see Lieb & Olson, 1976). This went against their natural preference, and they found it unspontaneous and cumbersome.

Drug world members also grew progressively weary of their exclusion from the legitimate world and the series of deceptions they had to manage to sustain that separation. Initially, the separation had been surrounded by an alluring mystique. As they aged in the career, however, the mystique was replaced by the hassle of everyday boundary maintenance and their feelings of being expatriated from conventional society. One smuggler described the effects of this separation:

> I'm so sick of looking over my shoulder, having to sit in my house and worry about one of my nondrug world friends stopping in when I'm doing business. Do you know how awful that is? It's like leading a double life. That's what makes it not worth it.

Thus, while the drug world was somewhat restricted, it was not an encapsulated community. As Reuter (1983, p. 174) has noted, criminals maintain an involvement with the legitimate world:

> Criminals do not inhabit a social and physical world that is different from the rest of society. They walk the same streets, dine in the same restaurants, and send their children to the same schools.

This constant contact with the straight world reminded them of the comforts and social ease they had left behind, and tempted them to go straight.

For upper-level dealers and smugglers, then, the process of aging in the career was one of progressive *burnout*. With the novelty worn off, most dealers and smugglers felt that the occupation no longer resembled their earlier impressions of it. Once they had reached the upper levels, their experience began to change and they changed with it. No longer were they the carefree people who lived from day to day without a thought for the future. No longer were they so intoxicated with their glamour that their only care in the world was the search for new heights of pleasure. Elements of this lifestyle remained, but they were tempered with the harsher side of the reality. In between episodes of intensive partying, veteran dealers and smugglers were struck by anxiety. They began to structure their work to encompass greater planning, caution, secrecy, and insulation. They isolated themselves from the straight world for days or weeks at a time, imprisoned and haunted by their own suspicions. They never renounced their hedonism or materialism, but the price they paid increased. Eventually, the rewards of trafficking no longer seemed to justify the strain. It was at this point that the straight world's formerly dull ambience became transformed (at least in theory) into a potential haven.

Shifts and Oscillations

Despite the gratifications dealers and smugglers derived from the easy money, material comfort, freedom, prestige, and power associated with their careers, most of them decided, at some point, to quit the business. This stemmed, in part, from their initial perceptions of the career as temporary ("Hell, nobody wants to be a drug dealer all their life"). Supplementing these early intentions was the process of rapid aging in the career, where dealers and smugglers became increasingly aware of the sacrifices their occupations required and got tired of living the fugitive life. As the dealing life began to look more troubling than rewarding, drug traffickers focused their energies on returning to the straight life. They thought about, talked about, and in many cases, took steps toward getting out of the drug business. But like entering the field, disengaging from drug trafficking was rarely an abrupt act (Lieb & Olson, 1976, p. 364). Instead, it more often resembled a series of transitions, or oscillations out of and back into the business. For once out of the drug world, dealers and smugglers were rarely successful at making it in the legitimate world, because they failed to cut down on their extravagant lifestyle or drug consumption. Many thus abandoned their efforts to reform and returned to deviance, sometimes picking up where they left off and other times shifting to a new mode of operating. For example, some shifted from trafficking in cocaine to trafficking in marijuana, some dropped to a lower level of dealing, and others shifted their role within the same group of traffickers. This series of phase-outs and reentries, combined with career shifts, endured for years, dominating the pattern of their remaining involvement with the business. It also represented the method by which many eventually broke away from drug trafficking, for each phase-out had the potential to be an individual's final departure.

Phasing Out

Making the decision to quit a deviant occupation is difficult. Several factors served to hold dealers and smugglers to the drug world. First, the hedonistic and materialistic satisfactions were primary. Once individuals became accustomed to earning large amounts of easy money, they found it exceedingly difficult to go back to the income scale of the straight world. They were also reluctant to abandon the pleasures of the fast life and its accompanying drugs, sex, and power. Second, dealers and smugglers formed an identification with and commitment to the occupation of drug trafficking. Their self-images were tied to that role and could not be easily disengaged. Their years invested learning the trade, forming connections, and building reputations served as "side-bets" (Becker, 1960), strengthening their involvement with both the deviant occupation and the drug community. And since their relationships were social as well as business-oriented, members' friendship ties bound them to dealing. As one dealer, in the midst of struggling to phase out, explained:

> The biggest threat to me is to get caught up sitting around the house with friends that are into dealing. I'm trying to stay away from them, change my habits.

Third, dealers and smugglers hesitated to voluntarily quit the field because they knew it would be difficult to find another way of earning a living. They feared that they would be unable to account to prospective employers for their years spent in illicit activities. This narrowed their occupational choices considerably, leaving self-employment as one of the few remaining avenues open.

Once dealers and smugglers made the decision to phase out, they generally pursued one of several routes out of dealing. The most frequent pattern involved resolving to quit after they executed one last big deal. While the intention was sincerely uttered, individuals who chose this route rarely succeeded; the big deal too often remained elusive. One marijuana smuggler offered a variation on this theme:

> My plan is to make a quarter of a million dollars in four months during the prime season and get the hell out of the business.

A second pattern involved individuals who planned to get out immediately, but never did. They announced that they were quitting, yet their outward actions never varied. Bruce, with his problems of overconsumption and debt escalation, described his involvement with this syndrome:

> When I wake up I'll say, "Hey, I'm going to quit this cycle and just run my other business." But when you're dealing, you constantly have people dropping by ounces and asking, "Can you move this?" What's your first response? Always, "Sure, for a toot."

In the third pattern of phasing out, individuals actually suspended their dealing or smuggling activities, but did not replace them with an alternative source of income. Such withdrawals were usually spontaneous and prompted by exhaustion, the influence of a person from outside the drug world, or problems with the police or other associates. As one dealer's case illustrated, these phase-outs usually lasted only until their money ran out:

> I got into heavy legal trouble with the FBI a while back and I was forced to quit dealing. Everybody just cut me off completely, and I saw the danger in continuing myself. But my high-class tastes never dwindled. I borrowed money here and

there. Before I knew it, I was in hock over $30,000. Even though I was hot, I was forced to get back into dealing to relieve some of my debts.

In the fourth pattern of phasing out, traffickers attempted a move into another line of work. Alternative occupations they tried included: occupations they had pursued before dealing or smuggling, front businesses maintained on the side while they were trafficking in drugs, and new occupations altogether. While some people successfully accomplished this transition, there were problems in all three alternatives.

Most people who tried to resume their former occupations found that these had changed too much while they were away from the field. In addition, they themselves had changed: they enjoyed the self-directed freedom and spontaneity associated with dealing and smuggling, and were unwilling to relinquish it.

Those who turned to their legitimate front business often found that these businesses were unable to support them. Designed to launder rather than earn money, most of these ventures had become accustomed to operating under a continuous subsidy from illegal funds. Once their drug funding was cut off, they could not survive for long.

Many dealers and smugglers utilized the business skills and connections they had developed in drug trafficking to create a new occupation. For some, the decision to prepare a legitimate career for retirement followed an unsuccessful attempt to phase out into a front business. One husband-and-wife dealing team explained how these legitimate side businesses differed from front businesses:

> We always had a little legitimate scam going, like mail-order shirts, wallets, jewelry, and the kids were always involved in that. We made a little bit of money on them. Their main purpose was for a cover and a legitimate business both. But [this business] was different; right from the start this was going to be a legal thing to push us out of the drug business.

Dealers and smugglers often formed these legitimate side occupations by exchanging their illegal commodity for a legal one, going into import/export, manufacturing, wholesaling, or retailing other merchandise. One former dealer described his current business and how he got into it:

> A friend of mine knew one of the major wholesalers in Tijuana for buying Mexican blankets, ponchos, and sweatshirts. After I helped him out with a favor when he was down, he turned me on to his connections. Now, I've cornered the market on wholesaling them to surf shops and swap meet sellers by undercutting everybody else.

The most future-oriented dealers and smugglers thus began gradually tapering off their drug world involvement, transferring their time and money into a selected legitimate endeavor. They did not try to quit drug trafficking altogether until they felt confident that their legitimate business could support them. But like spontaneous phase-outs, many of these planned withdrawals into legitimate businesses failed to generate enough money to keep individuals from being lured back into the drug world.

In addition to the voluntary phase-outs dealers and smugglers attempted after they became sufficiently burned out, many of them experienced an involuntary "bustout" at some point in their careers. Forced withdrawals from dealing or smuggling were usually sudden and necessitated by external factors, either financial, legal, or reputational. Financial bustouts generally occurred when dealers or smugglers were either burned or ripped off by others, leaving them in too much debt to rebuild their operation. Legal bustouts occurred when individuals got so hot from arrest or incarceration that few of their former associates would deal with them. Reputational bustouts occurred when individuals burned or ripped off others (regardless of whether they intended to do so) and were banned from business by their former associates. One smuggler gave his opinion on the pervasive nature of forced phase-outs:

> Some people are smart enough to get out of it because they realize, physically, they have to. Others realize, monetarily, that they want to get out of this world before this world gets them. Those are the lucky ones. Then there are the ones who have to get out because they're hot or someone else so close to them is hot that they'd better get out. But in the end, when you get out of it, nobody gets out of it out of free choice; you do it because you have to.

Death, of course, was the ultimate bustout. Some pilots met this fate because of the dangerous routes they navigated (hugging mountains, treetops, other aircraft) and because of the sometimes ill-maintained and overloaded planes they flew. However, despite much talk of violence, few Southwest County drug traffickers died at the hands of fellow dealers.

Reentry

Phasing out of the drug world was usually only temporary. For many, it represented merely another stage in their dealing careers (although this may not have been their original intention), to be followed by a period of reinvolvement. Depending on the situation, reentry into the drug world represented either a *comeback* (from a forced withdrawal) or a *relapse* (from a voluntary withdrawal).

Most people forced out of drug trafficking were anxious to return. They had never decided to withdraw, and their desire to get back was based on many of the same reasons which drew them into the field originally. While it was possible to come back from financial, legal, and reputational bustouts, it was difficult and not always successfully accomplished. Dealers and smugglers had to reestablish their contacts, rebuild their organization and fronting arrangements, and raise any necessary operating capital. More important, they had to overcome the circumstances surrounding their departure; once they resumed operating they often found their former colleagues suspicious of them. They were therefore informally subjected to a trial period in which they had to re-prove their reliability before they could once again move easily through the drug world.

Dealers and smugglers usually found that reentering the drug world after they had voluntarily withdrawn from it involved a more difficult decision-making process, but was easier to implement. As I noted earlier, experienced dealers and smugglers often grappled with conflicting reasons for wanting to quit and wanting to stay with the occupation. When the forces propelling them out of the drug world were strongest, they left. But once out, these forces weakened. Their images of and hopes for the straight world often failed to materialize. Many could not make the shift to the norms, values, and lifestyle of the straight society and could not earn a living within it. Yet the factors enticing individuals to resume drug trafficking were not the same as those which motivated their original entry. They were no longer awestruck by the glamorous lifestyle or the thrill of danger. Instead, they got back in to make money both to pay off the debts they had accumulated while "retired" and to build up and save so that their next phase-out would be more successful. Dealers and smugglers made the decision to reenter the drug world, then, for some very basic reasons: the material perquisites, the drugs, the social ties, and the fact that they had nowhere else to go.

Once this decision was made, the actual process of reentry was relatively simple. One dealer described how the door back into dealing remained open for those "who left voluntarily":

> I still see my dealer friends, I can still buy grams from them when I want to. It's the respect they have for me because I stepped out of it without being busted or burning someone. I'm coming out with a good reputation, and even though the scene is a whirlwind—people moving up, moving down, in, out—if I didn't see anybody for a year I could call them up and get right back in that day.

People who relapsed thus had few problems obtaining fronts, reestablishing their reputations, or readjusting to the scene. Yet once back in, they generally were again unsuccessful in accumulating enough of a nest egg to ensure the success of their subsequent phase-outs. Each time they relapsed into drug trafficking they became caught up once again in the drug world's lifestyle of hedonism and consumption. They thus spent the money they were earning almost as fast as they earned it (or in some cases, faster). The fast life, with its irrationality and present orientation, held a grip on them partly because of the drugs they were consuming, but most especially because of the pervasive dominance of the drug subculture. They thus started the treadmill spinning again so that they never got enough ahead; they never amassed the stockpile that they had reentered the drug world to achieve.

Career Shifts

Dealers and smugglers who reentered the drug world, whether from a voluntary or forced phase-out, did not always return to the same activity, level, or commodity which characterized their previous style of operation. Upon returning after a hiatus, many individuals underwent a "career shift" (Luckenbill & Best, 1981) and became involved in some new segment of the drug world. The shifts were sometimes lateral, as when a member of a smuggling crew took on a new specialization, switching from piloting to operating a stash house, for example. One dealer described how he used friendship networks upon his reentry to shift from cocaine to marijuana trafficking:

Before, when I was dealing cocaine, I was too caught up in using the drug, and people around me were starting to go under from getting into base. That's why I got out. But now I think I've got myself together, and even though I'm dealing again, I'm staying away from coke. I've switched over to dealing grass. It's a whole different circle of people. I got into it through a close friend I used to know before, but I never did business with him because he did grass and I did coke.

Vertical shifts moved operators to different levels. For example, one former smuggler returned and took up dealing; another wholesale marijuana dealer came back to find that the smugglers he knew had disappeared and he was forced to buy from other dealers.

A third type of shift relocated drug traffickers in different styles of operation. One dealer described how, after being arrested, he tightened his security measures:

I just had to cut back after I went through those changes. Hell, I'm not getting any younger, and the idea of going to prison bothers me a lot more than it did 10 years ago. The risks are no longer worth it when I can have a comfortable income with less risk. So I only sell to four people now. I don't care if they buy a pound or a gram.

A former smuggler who sold his operation and lost all his money during his phase-out returned as a consultant to the industry, selling his expertise to individuals with new money and fresh manpower:

What I've been doing lately is setting up deals for people. I've got foolproof plans for smuggling cocaine up here from Colombia. I tell them how to modify their airplanes to add on extra fuel tanks and to fit in more weed, coke, or whatever they bring up. Then I set them up with refueling points all up and down Central America, telling them how to bring it up here, what points to come in at, and what kind of receiving unit to use. Then they do it all, and I get 10% of what they make.

Reentry did not always imply a shift to a new niche, however. Some returned to the same circle of associates, trafficking activity, and commodity they worked with before their departure. Thus, drug traffickers' careers often peaked early and then displayed a variety of shifts from lateral mobility, to decline, to holding fairly steady.

A final alternative involved neither completely leaving nor remaining in this deviant occupation. Many individuals straddled the deviant and respectable worlds forever by continuing to dabble in drug trafficking. As a result of their experiences in the drug world they had developed a deviant self-identity and a deviant *modus operandi*. They did not want to bear the social and legal burden of full-time deviant work, but neither were they willing to assume the drudgery of the straight world. They therefore moved into the entrepreneurial realm, where their daily activities involved some sort of hustling in an assortment of legitimate, quasi-legitimate, and deviant ventures, and where they were their own boss. In this way they were able to retain certain elements of the deviant lifestyle and to socialize on the fringes of the drug community. For these individuals, drug dealing shifted from a primary occupation to a sideline, but they never abandoned it altogether.

Leaving Drug Trafficking

This pattern of oscillation into and out of active drug trafficking makes it somewhat problematic to speak of leaving deviance in the sense of a final retirement. Clearly, some people succeeded in voluntarily retiring. Of these, a few managed to prepare a postdeviant career for themselves by transferring their drug money into a legitimate enterprise. A larger group was forced out of dealing and either did not or could not return; their bustouts were sufficiently damaging that either they never attempted reentry or they abandoned their efforts after a series of unsuccessful comeback attempts. But there was no way of determining in advance whether an exit from the business would be temporary or permanent. Here, dealers' and smugglers' vacillating intentions were compounded by the complexity of operating successfully in the drug world. For many, then, no phase-out could ever be definitively assessed as permanent. As long as individuals had the skills, knowledge, and connections to deal, they could potentially reenter the occupation at any time. Leaving drug trafficking was thus a relative phenomenon, characterized by a trailing-off process where spurts of involvement occurred with decreasing frequency and intensity. This disengagement was characterized by a progressive reorientation to the legitimate world, where former drug traffickers once again shifted their social networks and changed their self-conceptions (Lieb & Olson, 1976).

SUMMARY

Dealing and smuggling careers were temporary, fraught with multiple attempts at retirement. Veteran drug traffickers quit their occupation because of the ambivalent feelings they developed toward their deviant life. As they aged in the career, their experience changed, shifting from a work life that was exhilarating and free to one that became increasingly dangerous and confining. Just as their deviant careers were temporary, so too were their retirements. Potential recruits, therefore, were lured into the business by materialism, hedonism, glamour, and excitement. Established dealers were lured away from the deviant life and back into the mainstream by the attractions of security and social ease. But once out, retired dealers and smugglers were lured back in by their expertise, by their ability to make money quickly and easily. People who were exposed to the upper levels of drug trafficking found it extremely difficult to quit permanently. This stemmed, in part, from their difficulty in moving from the illegitimate to the legitimate business sector. Even more significant was the affinity they formed for their deviant values and lifestyle. Thus, few of the people I observed were successful in leaving deviance entirely. What dealers and smugglers intended, at the time, to be a permanent withdrawal from drug trafficking can be seen in retrospect as a pervasive occupational pattern of shifts and oscillations.

REFERENCES

Anonymous. (1969). On selling marijuana. In E. Goode (Ed.), *Marijuana* (pp. 92–202). New York: Atherton.

Becker, H.S. (1960) "Notes on the concept of commitment." American Journal of Sociology, 66,(July).

Becker, H., & Carper, J. (1956). The development of identification with an occupation. *American Journal of Sociology, 66*, 32–42.

Blum, R., & associates. (1968). *The dream sellers*. San Francisco: Jossey-Bass.

Carey, J. T. (1972). *The college drug scene*. Englewood Cliffs, NJ: Prentice-Hall.

Goode, E. (1970). *The marijuana smokers*. New York: Basic.

Johnson, B. D. (1973). *Marijuana users and drug subcultures*. New York: Wiley.

Lieb, J., & Olson, S. (1976). Prestige, paranoia and profit: On becoming a dealer of illicit drugs on a university community. *Journal of Drug Issues, 6*, 356–369.

Luckenbill, D. F., & Best, J. (1981). Careers in deviance and respectability: The analogy's limitations. *Social Problems, 29*, 197–206.

Matza, D. (1964). *Delinquency and drift*. New York: Wiley.

Miller, G., & Ritzer, G. (1977). Informal socialization: Deviant occupations. In G. Ritzer (Ed.), *Working* (2nd ed., pp. 83–94). Englewood Cliffs, NJ: Prentice-Hall.

Ray, M. (1961). The cycle of abstinence and relapse among heroin addicts. *Social Problems, 9*, 132–140.

Redlinger, L. J. (1975). Marketing and distributing heroin. *Journal of Psychedelic Drugs, 7*, 331–353.

Reuter, P. (1983) Disorganized crime: the economics of the visible hand. MIT Press.

ᘏᐧᑊ

Gangs and Crime

This section examines gangs and crime. Gangs are not a new phenomenon in the United States. They have been around since the early 1800s, when gangs such as the Forty Thieves, Bowery Boys, Dead Rabbits, Roach Guards and the like battled to gain control of their territories in New York City (Etter, 2012). In spite of the long prevalence of gangs in the United States, these groups are still not well understood. Gangs are known to use violent tactics in order to intimidate and protect their turf/neighborhoods, to control trade such as illegal drugs, to commit acts as revenge, and to control others. In recent years, the criminal justice system and academic researchers have demonstrated a renewed interest in gangs as these groups have increased sharply in both numbers and violence. The National Youth Gang Center estimates that there are over 700,000 gang members and 27,000 active gangs in the United States today (Anderson et al., 2009). Gangs are dispersed across the United States but tend to be more concentrated in larger cities.

Unlike the turf-oriented gangs of the 1950s and 1960s, the gangs of today are heavily involved in a variety of criminal activities, including drug trafficking. Some experts have described modern street gangs as the new urban tribes because they combine themselves into self-administered structures to help them conduct their criminal enterprises and avoid the police (Etter, 1998). Many gangs have adopted a pseudo-warrior culture in order to more effectively facilitate their criminality. In many cases, gang membership is determined along racial or ethnic lines. Additionally, some gangs operating in the United States view themselves as race warriors, street warriors, or road warriors (Etter, 2012).

This section contributes to our understanding of gangs. In Chapter 18, "Gang-Related Gun Violence: Socialization, Identity, and Self," Paul B. Stretesky and Mark R. Pogrebin examine how gang socialization leads to gun violence, as well as the role that guns play in protection efforts and "impression management"—that is, the ways they serve to project and protect a tough gang reputation. The researchers discover that gangs serve as agents of socialization that assist in shaping their members' sense of self and identity. The authors argue that guns are far more important to the daily lives and identities of gang members than most policymakers might imagine, because they help project a reputation and create respect. The authors argue that if gang culture could be changed through the resocialization of gang members, gun-related gang violence might significantly decrease. These findings suggest strategies for reduction in gun violence.

In recent years, female gang activity has increased considerably. Where women once served primarily in adjunct roles, mixed-gender gangs have become more common. In Chapter 19, "Gender and Victimization Risk among Young Women in Gangs," Jody Miller draws from interviews of 20 female gang members in order to examine gender and victimization in gangs. She discovers that female gang members experience considerable levels of victimization not only at the hands of their gang peers, but also from other gangs. The author points out that joining a gang often involves submission to victimization at the hands of other members, and that gang activities thereafter place female gang members at risk for further victimization.

In Chapter 20, "Voices from the Barrio: Chicano/a Gangs, Families, and Communities," Marjorie S. Zatz and Edwardo L. Portillos take a look at the relationships among gang members, their families, and other residents of poor Chicano and Mexican barrios in Phoenix. The authors interviewed 33 youth gang members and 20 adult neighborhood leaders and youth service providers. Zatz and Portillos conclude that listening to the multiple voices of community members allows for a multifaceted understanding of the complexities and contradictions of gang life, both for the youths and for the larger community. The authors draw on a community ecology approach to help explain the tensions that develop, especially when community members vary in their desires and abilities to control gang-related activities. They discuss ways in which gender, age, education, traditionalism, and level of acculturation can assist in explaining variation in the type and strength of private, parochial, and public social control within a community.

REFERENCES

Anderson, J., Nye, M., Freitas, R., & Wolf, J. (2009). *Gang prosecution manual.* Washington, DC: Office of Juvenile Justice and Delinquency Prevention, U.S. Department of Justice.

Etter, G. (1998). Common characteristics of gangs: Examining the cultures of the new urban tribes. *Journal of Gang Research, 5*(2), 19–33.

———. (2012). Gang investigation. In M. L. Birzer & C. Roberson (Eds.), *Introduction to criminal investigation* (pp. 313–34). Boca Raton, FL: CRC.

⤜

CHAPTER 18

Gang-Related Gun Violence:
Socialization, Identity, and Self

Paul B. Stretesky and Mark R. Pogrebin

The purpose of this study was to examine how violent norms are transmitted in street gangs and examine socialization as a mechanism between gang membership and violence. To explore this issue, the authors draw on in-depth interviews with 22 Colorado inmates convicted of gang-related gun violence. These data are obtained from a subset of respondents in a larger study of gun violence (see Chapter 11 in this volume). The median age of the respondents was 25 years, although their age at the time of the offense for which they were incarcerated was considerably younger. At the time of the interviews, the respondents had been incarcerated an average of 4.7 years. Thirteen of the subjects were African American, five were white, three were Hispanic, and one was Asian. All had been convicted of violent gun-related crimes, including murder, manslaughter, robbery, and kidnapping. All but one was male. The researchers found that gangs are important agents of socialization that help shape a gang member's sense of self and identity. In addition, inmates reported that whereas guns offered them protection, they were also important tools of impression management that helped to project and protect a tough reputation. The findings provide greater insight into the way gang socialization leads to gun-related violence and has implications for policies aimed at reducing that violence.

This study considers how gangs promote violence and gun use. We argue that socialization is important because it helps to shape a gang member's identity and sense of self. Moreover, guns often help gang members project their violent identities. As Kubrin (2005, p. 363) argues, "The gun becomes a symbol of power and a remedy for disputes." We examine the issue of gang socialization, self, and identity formation using data derived from face-to-face qualitative interviews with

Source: Adapted from Stratesky, P. B., & Pogrebin, M. E. (2007) Gang-related gun violence: Socialization, identity and self. *Journal of Contemporary Ethnography, 36*(1), 85–114. © Sage Publications, 2007.

a sample of gang members who have been incarcerated in Colorado prisons for gun-related violent crimes. Our findings, although unique, emphasize what previous studies have found—that most gangs are organized by norms that support the use of violence to settle disputes, achieve group goals, recruit members, and defend identity.

Before our analysis of gang members, we briefly review the literature on the relationship between gangs, crime, guns, and violence. In that review, we emphasize the importance of socialization and the impact of gangs on identity and self. We explain how guns help gang members shape and convey their identity. Finally, in our discussion, we relate our findings to the relative efficacy of different intervention strategies that are focused on reducing gang violence.

GANGS AND VIOLENCE

Research suggests that gang members are more likely than nongang members to engage in crime—especially violent crime (Gordon et al., 2004). According to Thornberry et al. (1993, p. 75), the relationship between gang affiliation and violence "is remarkably robust, being reported in virtually all American studies of gang behavior regardless of when, where, or how the data were collected." Whereas the relationship between gangs and violence is pervasive, "little is known about the causal mechanisms that bring it about" (Thornberry et al., 1993, p. 76). Do gangs attract individuals who are predisposed to violence or do they create violent individuals? The debate in the literature about these explanations of gang violence is rather extensive.

Thornberry et al. (1993) point out that there are three perspectives that inform the debate concerning the relationship between gangs and violence. First, the selection perspective argues that gang members are individuals who are delinquent and violent before joining the gang. Thus, gang members are individuals who are likely to engage in violent and deviant behavior even if they are not gang members (Gerrard, 1964; Yablonsky, 1962). From this perspective, what makes gang members more criminal than nongang members is that criminal individuals have self-selected or been recruited into gangs. The second perspective is known as the social facilitation perspective. This perspective argues that gang members are no different from nongang members until they enter the gang. Therefore, the gang serves a normative function. In short, the gang is the source of delinquent behavior because new gang members are socialized into the norms and values of gang life, which provides the necessary social setting for crime and violence to flourish. The enhancement perspective is the third explanation for the relationship between gang and crime (Thornberry et al., 1993). The enhancement perspective proposes that new gang members are recruited from a pool of individuals who show propensity to engage in crime and violence, but their level of violence intensifies once they enter the gang because the gang provides a structure that encourages crime and violence (see also Decker & Van Winkle, 1996).

According to McCorkle and Miethe (2002, p. 111), the second and third explanations for gang-related crime are the most popular explanations in the literature because both perspectives rely on the assumption that social disorganization increases socialization into the gang subculture, which produces crime. Recent criminological research suggests that the enhancement perspective is the most likely explanation for the association between gang involvement and criminal behavior. For instance, Gordon et al. (2004) discovered that individuals who join gangs are, in general, more delinquent than their peers *before* they join the gang. However, Gordon et al. also found that violent behavior among individuals who join a gang significantly increases *after* they become gang members. Although the work by Gordon et al. provides some answers concerning the potential causal mechanisms of gang violence, it still leaves open the question about why gang members increase their violent behavior after they join a gang. It is for that reason that we focus our research on the concept of socialization as a mechanism that leads to gang-related gun violence.

GANG SOCIALIZATION

Research on gang socialization—the process of learning the appropriate values and norms of the gang culture to which one belongs—suggests that group processes are highly important (Miller & Brunson, 2000; Sirpal, 1997; Vigil, 1988;). In addition, Moore (1991) believes that many city gangs have become quasi-institutionalized. In these cities, gangs have played a major role in ordering individuals' lives at the same time that other important social institutions such as schools and families play less of a normative role (see also Bjerregaard & Lizotte, 1995; Blumstein, 1995; Bowker & Klein, 1983; Vigil 1988). Vigil (1988, p. 63) has found that gangs help to socialize "members to internalize and adhere to alternative norms and modes of behavior and play a significant role in helping…youth acquire a sense of importance, self-esteem, and identity." One way to attain status is to develop a reputation for being violent (Anderson, 1999). This reputation for violence, however, is likely to develop (at least to some degree) after an individual joins a gang.

The reasons individuals join gangs are diverse (Decker & Van Winkle, 1996). According to Decker & Van Winkle (1996), the most important instrumental reason for joining a gang is protection. In addition to instrumental concerns, a large portion of all gang members indicate that their gang fulfills a variety of more typical adolescent needs—especially companionship and support, which tend to be more expressive in nature. That is, the gang is a primary group. The idea that the gang is a primary group into which individuals are socialized is not new. For instance, long ago Thrasher (1927, p. 230) pointed out,

[The gang] offers the underprivileged boy probably his best opportunity to acquire status and hence it plays an essential part in the development of his personality. In striving to realize the role he hopes to take he may assume a tough pose, commit feats of daring or vandalism, or become a criminal.

Thus, gang violence may often be viewed as expressive in nature. The value of masculinity as a form of expression plays an important role in gang socialization (Miller & Decker, 2001). Oliver (1994) argues that gang violence is often a method of expressing one's masculinity when opportunities to pursue conventional roles are denied. Acts of manhood, note Decker and Van Winkle (1996, p. 186), are "important values of [a member's] world and their psyches—to be upheld even at the cost of their own or others' lives." Katz (1988) also believes violence plays an important and acceptable role in the subculture of people living in socially isolated environments and economically deprived areas because violence provides a means for a member to demonstrate his toughness, and displays of violent retaliation establish socialization within the gang.

According to Short and Strodtbeck (1965; see also Howell, 1998), a good portion of all gang violence can be attributed to threats to one's status within the gang. Gang membership, then, helps to create within-group identity that defines how group members perceive people outside their formal organizational structure. By way of altercasting (i.e., the use of tactics to create identities and roles for others), gangs cast nonmembers into situated roles and identities that are to the gang's advantage (Weinstein & Deutschberger, 1963). Altercasting, then, is an aggressive tactic that gangs often use to justify their perception of other gangs as potentially threatening rivals, and it is used to rationalize the use of physical violence against other gangs. If the objective of a gang is to be perceived by the community, rival gangs, law enforcement officials, and others in a particular way, then their collective group and individual identities will be situated in these defining situations. Even though there is a good deal of research examining the important relationship between violence and status within the gang as it relates to socialization, little is known about the specific ways that status impacts gang violence.

Socialization into the gang is bound up in issues of identity and self. Identity, according to Stone (1962), is the perceived social location of the person. Image, status, and a host of other factors that affect identity are mostly created by group perceptions of who we are and how we define ourselves. "People see themselves from the standpoints of their group and appropriate action in relation to those groups becomes a source of pride" (Shibutani, 1961, p. 436). Berger (1963, p. 92) notes that "identities are socially bestowed, socially maintained, and socially transformed."

Moore (1978, p. 60) has suggested that "the gang represents a means to what is an expressive, rather than an instrumental, goal: the acting out of a male role of competence and of 'being in command' of things." The findings of Decker and Van Winkle (1996) and Moore suggest that although instrumental reasons for joining a gang are important, once a member joins a gang they largely see the gang as an important primary group that is central to their lives and heavily influences their identity and personality. Because this is a primary group, the approval of gang peers is highly important. It is this expressive reason for remaining in a gang that may help to explain gang crime and violence, especially as it relates to socialization.

Hughes and Short (2005) provide insight into the area of identity and gang violence. Specifically, they find that when a gang member's identity is challenged, violence is often a result—especially if the challenger is a stranger. If a gang member does not comply with gang role expectations when they are challenged, the result may be a loss of respect. It is important to project a violent reputation to command respect and deter future assaults. Walking away from conflict is risky to one's health (Anderson, 1999). Gang members must by necessity make efforts to show a continued commitment to role expectations to the group (Lindesmith & Strauss, 1968). From this perspective, it appears that character traits that are a consequence of being socialized into street gangs may result in youthful acts of violence through transformations in identity (Vigil, 1996).

Initiation rights are one important aspect of identity formation (Hewitt, 1988; Vigil, 1996). Initiation rights that new gang members are obligated to go through demonstrate commitment to the gang and attest to an individual's desire to gain official membership in the organization. Hewitt (1988) argues that these types of acts help create a "situated self," where a person's self can be defined and shaped by particular situations. Thus, notions of identity formation are highly consistent with notions of gang violence as a function of social facilitation and enhancement perspectives in that they explain why gang members may increase their levels of crime and violence once they join the gang. Moreover, research suggests that the more significant the relationship to a gang is, the more committed an individual is to a gang identity (Callero, 1985; Stryker & Serpe, 1982). In short, gangs provide a reference group for expected role behavior and shape a member's identity and sense of self (Callero, 1985). The greater the commitment a person has to a gang identity, the more frequently that person will perform in ways that enact that identity, ways that include acts of violence (Stryker & Serpe, 1982).

Guns also play an important role in many gangs and are often reported to be owned for instrumental reasons (Decker & Van Winkle, 1996). Gang members who perceive a threat from rival gangs are believed to carry guns to protect themselves and their neighborhoods (Decker & Van Winkle, 1996; Horowitz, 1983; Lizotte et al., 1994; Wright & Rossi, 1986). Gang membership "strongly and significantly increases the likelihood of carrying a gun" (Thornberry et al., 2003, p. 131). However, the reason that gang members carry guns is still unclear. It is likely that in addition to instrumental reasons for carrying a gun, gang members carry guns for expressive reasons (Sheley & Wright, 1995). That is, guns provide gang members with a sense of power, which may be extremely important in identity formation. Guns help gang members project a tough image. Thornberry et al. (2003, p. 125) report that gang members who carry guns may feel "emboldened to initiate criminal acts that they may otherwise avoid."

Sociologists have long recognized that symbols are important indicators of identity. This is especially true of gangs (Decker & Van Winkle, 1996; Vigil, 2003). Gang members often display symbols of gang membership, and this is part of being socialized into the role of a gang member:

Wearing gang clothes, flashing gang signs, and affecting other outward signs of gang behavior are also ways to become encapsulated in the role of gang member, especially through the perceptions of others, who, when they see the external symbols of membership respond as if the person was a member. (Decker & Van Winkle, 1996, p. 75)

Bjerregaard and Lizotte (1995, p. 42) argue that it is plausible that "juveniles are socialized into the gun culture by virtue of their gang membership and activity."

Although there is some indication that gang members are more likely to own guns than nongang members prior to joining a gang, gang membership also clearly appears to increase the prevalence of gun ownership. Bjerregaard and Lizotte (1995) believe that future research needs to focus on why gang membership encourages gun ownership. In this vein, Sanders's (1994) research on drive-by shootings provides some insight into why gang membership may encourage gun ownership. Drawing on Goffman's (1961) notion of realized resources, Sanders argues that gangs are organizations that provide the necessary context for drive-bys. Sanders is clear when he states that guns and cars are the least important resource in producing drive-bys. However, it is also true that guns are necessary for drive-bys to occur and as such are an important part of gang culture to the extent that drive-bys help gang members "build an identity as having heart" (Sanders, 1994, p. 204). Thus, notions of character and identity provide a way to look at drive-by shootings as a product of the gang structure, where guns are important instruments in building identity. Given the importance of guns to a gang member's identity, it is interesting to note that little research exists that examines the relationship between guns and gangs in terms of identity formation.

FINDINGS

We divide our findings into four sections. First, we focus on our subjects' socialization into the gang and the impact that socialization has on their self and identity. Second, we explore the importance of gang commitment as reinforcing a gang member's self and identity. Third, we focus on masculinity as a central value among gang members. During our discussions of masculinity, gang members often referred to notions of respect and reputation. Reputation is a way that gang members can project their image of masculinity to others. Respect was often referenced when their masculine identity was challenged. Finally, we focus on the importance of guns as instruments central to the lives of our gang members in the sense that they help project and protect masculine identities.

Gang Socialization, Self, and Identity

Goffman (1959) argues that as individuals, we are often "taken in by our own act" and therefore begin to feel like the person we are portraying. Baumeister and Tice (1984) describe this process as one where initial behaviors are internalized so that they become part of a person's self-perception. Once initial behaviors are internalized, the individual continues to behave in ways consistent with his or her self-perception. Related to the current study, the socialization process of becoming a gang member required a change in the subject's self-perception. That is, who did our gang members become as compared with who they once were? Social interaction is highly important in the process of socialization because it helps create one's identity and sense of self, as Holstein and Gubrium (2003, p. 119 [emphasis added]) point out:

> As personal as they seem, ourselves and identities are extremely social. They are hallmarks of our inner lives, *yet they take shape in relation to others: We establish who and what we are through social interaction.* In some respects, selves and identities are two sides of the same coin. Selves are the subjects we take ourselves to be; identities are the shared labels we give to these selves. We come to know ourselves in terms of the categories that are socially available to us.

Most inmates we interviewed appeared to indicate that their socialization into the gang began at a relatively young age:

> At about 15, I started getting affiliated with the Crips. I knew all these guys, grew up with them and they were there.... I mean, it was like an influence at that age. I met this dude named Benzo from Los Angeles at that time. He was a Crip, and he showed me a big wad of money. He said, "Hey man, you want some of this?" "Like yeah! Goddamn straight. You know I want some of that." He showed me how to sell crack, and so at 15, I went from being scared of the police and respecting them to hustling and selling crack. Now I'm affiliated with the Crips; I mean it was just unbelievable.

Another inmate tells of his orientation in becoming a member of a gang. He points out the glamour he associated with membership at a very impressionable age:

> I started gangbanging when I was 10. I got into a gang when I was 13. I started just hanging around them, just basically idolizing them. I was basically looking for a role model for my generation and ethnic background; the main focus for us is the popularity that they got. That's who the kids looked up to. They had status, better clothes, better lifestyle.

One of our black study participants residing with his father in a predominantly white, suburban community felt estranged from the minority friends he had in his former neighborhood. He discussed his need to be among his former peers and voluntarily moved back to his old neighborhood:

> A lot of the people that lived where my father was staying were predominantly white. I mean, not to say I didn't get along with white kids, but, you know, it was just two different backgrounds and things of that nature.

His racial and socioeconomic identification in the white community, where he resided with his father, offered little opportunity for him to fit in. When he returned to the city, he became involved with a gang quite rapidly:

> I started getting charged with assaults. Gang rivalry, you know, fighting, just
> being in a gang.

Because he was better educated and did not use street vernacular as his peers did, our participant claims he had to continually prove his racial proclivity to his peers:

> Other kids would call me "whitewash" because I spoke proper English. Basically,
> I wanted to be somebody, so I started hanging around with gang bangers. I was
> planning on being the best gang member I can be or the best kind of criminal I
> can be or something like that.

Consistent with Goffman's (1959) observations, once our subjects became active gang members, their transformation of identity was complete. That is, consistent with the notion of social facilitation and enhancement perspectives (Thornberry et al., 1993), the self-perceptions and identity of the subjects in our study appear to have changed from what they were before joining the gang. Shibutani (1961, p. 523) explains such changes by claiming that a person's self-perception is caused by a psychological reorientation in which an individual visualizes his world and who he thinks he is in a different light. He retains many of his idiosyncrasies, but develops a new set of values and different criteria of judgment.

Violent behavior appeared to play an important role in this transformation of identity and self. Most gang members noted that they engaged in violent behavior more frequently once they joined the gang.

> At an early age, it was encouraged that I showed my loyalty and do a drive by ... any-
> body they [gangster disciples] deemed to be a rival of the gang. I was going on 14.
> At first, I was scared to, and then they sent me out with one person and I seen him
> do it. I saw him shoot the guy.... So, in the middle of a gang fight I get pulled aside
> and get handed a pistol, and he said, "It's your turn to prove yourself." So I turned
> around and shot and hit one of the guys [rival gang members]. After that, it just
> got more easier. I did more and more. I had no concern for anybody.

A further illustration of situated identity and transformation of self is related by another inmate, who expresses the person he became through the use of violence and gun possession. Retrospectively, he indicates disbelief in what he had become.

> As a gang banger, you have no remorse, so basically, they're natural-born killers.
> They are killers from the start. When I first shot my gun for the first time at some-
> body, I felt bad. It was like, I can't believe I did this. But I looked at my friend, and
> he didn't care at all. Most gang bangers can't have a conscience. You can't have
> remorse. You can't have any values. Otherwise, you are gonna end up retiring as
> a gang banger at a young age.

The situations an individual finds oneself in, in this case collective gang violence, together with becoming a person who is willing to use violence to maintain membership in the gang, is indicative of a transformed identity. Strauss (1962) claims that when a person's identity is transformed, they are seen by others as being different than they were before. The individual's prior identity is retrospectively reevaluated in comparison with the present definition of a gang member. Such a transformation was part of the processional change in identity that our prisoners/ gang members experienced.

Commitment to the Gang

> As a creature of ideas, man's main concern is to maintain a tentative hold on these idealized conceptions of himself, to legitimate his role identities.
> —MCCALL & SIMMONS, 1966, p. 71

Commitment to the gang also serves individual needs for its members. We found that gang identification and loyalty to the group was a high priority for our subjects. This loyalty to the gang was extreme. Our subjects reported that they were willing to risk being killed and were committed to taking the life of a rival gang member if the situation called for such action. That is, gang membership helped our subjects nourish their identity and at the same time provided group maintenance (Kanter, 1972). As Kanter (1972) points out, the group is an extension of the individual and the individual is an extension of the group. This notion of sacrifice for the group by proving one's gang identification is expressed by an inmate who perceives his loyalty in the following terms:

> What I might do for my friends [gang peers] you might not do. You've got people out there taking bullets for their friends and killing people. But I'm sure not one of you would be willing to go to that extreme. These are just the thinking patterns we had growing up where I did.

Another inmate tells us about his high degree of identity for his gang:

> If you're not a gang member, you're not on my level....Most of my life revolves around gangs and gang violence. I don't know anything else but gang violence. I was born into it, so it's my life.

The notion of the gang as the most important primary group in a member's life was consistently expressed by our study subjects. Our subjects often stated that they were willing to kill or be killed for the gang in order to sustain their self-perception as a loyal gang member. This extreme degree of group affiliation is similar to that of armed services activities during wartime. The platoon, or in this case, the local gang, is worth dying for. In this sense, the notion of the gang as a protector was an important part of gang life. All members were expected to be committed enough to aid their peers should the need arise. The following gang member points to the important role his gang played for him in providing physical safety as well as an assurance of understanding:

> That's how it is in the hood, selling dope, gangbangin', everybody wants a piece of you. All the rival gang members, all the cops, everybody. The only ones on your side are the gang members you hang with.

For this particular member, his gang peers are the only people he perceives will aid him from threatening others. The world appears full of conflicting situations, and although his gang affiliation is largely responsible for all the groups that are out to harm him in some way, he nevertheless believes his fellow gang members are the only persons on whom he can depend.

Violence against rival gangs was a general subject that the majority of the inmates interviewed discussed freely. However, only a few of our study participants focused on this subject compared with the less violence-prone gang-affiliated inmates. The violent gang members perceived other gangs as ongoing enemies who constantly presented a threat to their safety. As our literature review suggests, there is some debate about whether gang members would be violent without belonging to a gang, or if formal membership in the group provided them with the opportunity to act out this way. However, we find clarity in the inmate accounts that a gang member's identity provided the context necessary to resort to violence when confronted with conflicting events, as the following inmate notes:

> I have hate toward the Crips gang members and have always had hate toward them 'cuz of what they did to my homeboys....I never look back. I do my thing. I always carry a gun no matter what. I am a gang member, man! There are a lot of gang members out to get me for what I done. I shot over 40 people at least. That's what I do.

This perception of being a person who is comfortable with violence and the perception of himself as an enforcer type characterizes the above inmate's role within his gang. Turner (1978) suggests that roles consistent with an individual's self-concept are played more frequently and with a higher degree of participation than roles that are not in keeping with that individual's self-concept. Our study subject in this situation fits Turner's explanation of role identity nicely. His hatred for rival gangs and his willingness to retaliate most likely led to his incarceration for attempted murder.

Masculinity, Reputation, and Respect

For those gang members we interviewed, socialization into the gang and commitment to the gang appear to be central to the notion of masculinity. That is, all gang members we interviewed spoke of the importance of masculinity and how it was projected (though the creation of a reputation) and protected (through demands for respect). The notion of masculinity was constantly invoked in relation to self and identity. In short, masculinity is used to communicate to others what the gang represents, and it is used to send an important signal to others who may wish to challenge a gang's collective identity. A gang member's masculine reputation precedes him or her, so to speak. On an individual level, similar attributes apply as well.

> Whatever an individual does and however he appears, he knowingly and unknowingly makes information available concerning the attributes that might be imputed to him and hence the categories in which he might be placed....The

physical milieu itself conveys implications concerning the identity of those who are in it. (Goffman, 1961, p. 102)

According to Sherif and Wilson (1953), people's ego attitudes define and regulate their behavior toward various other groups and are formed in concert with the values and norms of that person's reference group. They formulate an important part of their self-identity and their sense of group identification. For our gang member study population, the attributes that the gang valued consisted of factors that projected a street image that was necessary to sustain. It was a survival strategy.

Masculinity

"Every man [in a gang] is treated as a man until proven different. We see you as a man before anything." This comment by a gang member infers that masculinity is a highly valued attribute in his gang. The idea of manhood and its personal meanings for each interviewed prisoner was a subject consistently repeated by all participants. It usually was brought up in the context of physical violence, often describing situations where one had to face danger as a result of another's threatening behavior or testing of one's willingness to use physical force when insulted by someone outside of the group.

> Even if you weren't in one [gang], you got people that are going to push the issue. We decide what we want to do; I ain't no punk, I ain't no busta. But it comes down to pride. It's foolish pride, but a man is going to be a man, and a boy knows he's going to come into his manhood by standing his ground.

Establishing a reputation coincides with becoming a man, entering the realm of violence, being a stand-up guy who is willing to prove his courage as a true gang member. This strong association between a willingness to perpetrate violence on a considered rival, or anyone for that matter, was a theme that defined a member's manhood. After eight years in the gang, the following participant was owed money for selling someone dope. After a few weeks of being put off by the debtor, he had to take some action to appease his gang peers who were pressuring him to retaliate.

> I joined the gang when I was 11 years old. So now that I'm in the gang for eight years, people are asking, "What are you going to do? You got to make a name for yourself." So we went over there [victim's residence], and they were all standing outside, and I just shot him. Everybody was happy for me, like "Yeah, you shot him, you're cool," and this and that.

A sense of bravado, when displayed, played a utilitarian role in conflicting situations where a gang member attempts to get others to comply with his demands by instilling fear instead of actually utilizing violent means. Having some prior knowledge of the threatening gang member's reputation is helpful in preventing a physical encounter, which is always risky for both parties involved. Again, the importance of firearms in this situation is critical.

> The intimidation factor with a gun is amazing. Everybody knows what a gun can do. If you have a certain type of personality, that only increases their fear of you. When it came to certain individuals who I felt were a threat, I would lift my shirt up so they would know I had one on me.

In this case, the showing of his firearm served the purpose of avoiding any altercation that could have led to injury or even worse. Carrying a gun and displaying it proved to be an intimidating, preventative factor for this gang member. The opposite behavior is noted in the following example of extreme bravado, where aggressive behavior is desired and a clear distinction (based on bravery) between drive-by shootings and face-to-face shootings is clear.

> If someone is getting shot in a drive-by and someone else gets hit, it is an accident. You know, I never do drive-bys. I walk up to them and shoot. I ain't trying to get anyone else shot to take care of business.

A final example of masculinity and bravado, as perceived by this particular study participant, illustrates his commitment to being a stand-up guy, a person who will face the consequences of gang activity. The situation he discussed had to do with his current incarceration. Here he explains how he adhered to the gang value of not being a snitch and refused to provide information about rival gang members' involvement in two homicides to the police, which could have helped in his prosecution for murder.

> I know what I did [gang war murder], you know what I mean? I'm not gonna take the easy way out [snitch on rival gangs for two homicides]. I know what I did. I'm facing my responsibility.

An interesting note in this scenario has to do with the above inmate's continued loyalty to the values of his gang when he was outside of prison. His information on the rival gang's homicides most likely could have had the criminal charges against him reduced, and subsequently, he would have received a lesser prison sentence. We are taking into consideration that the inmate's cultural code is similar if not the same as the gang code, and our study participant was simply adhering to the same value system.

The image of toughness fits well under masculinity and bravado as an attribute positively perceived by gang members we interviewed. Its importance lies in projecting an image via reputation that conveys a definition of who the collective group is and what physical force they are willing to use when necessary. A clear explanation of this attribute is related by the following subject.

> Everybody wants to fight for the power, for the next man to fear him. It's all about actually killing the motherfuckers and how many motherfuckers you can kill. Drive-by shootings is old school.

The implication here is that having a collective reputation for being powerful motivates this prisoner. He notes that the tough image of shooting someone you are after instead of hiding behind the random shooting characterized by drive-bys projects an image of toughness and power.

There are others who prefer to define their toughness in terms of physical fighting without the use of any weapons—though it was often noted that it was too difficult to maintain a tough reputation under such conditions. For instance, the predicament the following gang member found himself in is one where rival gangs used guns and other lethal instruments, and as a result of this, his reputation as an effective street fighter proved to be of little value. In short, his toughness and fighting skills were obsolete in life-threatening encounters.

> Like my case, I'm a fighter. I don't like using guns. The only reason I bought a gun was because every time I got out of the car to fight, I'd have my ribs broken, the back of my head almost crushed with a baseball bat. I was tired of getting jumped. I couldn't get a fair fight. Nobody wanted to fight me because I had a bad reputation. Then I decided, why even fight? Everybody else was pulling guns. It's either get out of the car and get killed or kill them.

The fact that this prisoner had good fighting skills ironically forced him to carry a gun. The rules of gang fighting found him outnumbered and unarmed, placing him in a very vulnerable position to defend himself. The proliferation of firearms among urban street gangs is well documented by Blumstein (1995) and others. Lethal weapons, mainly firearms, drastically changed the defining characteristics of gang warfare in the late 1980s and 1990s, when most of our study subjects were active gang members in the community.

Reputation

On a collective group level, developing and maintaining the gang's reputation of being a dangerous group to deal with, especially from other groups or individuals who posed a threat to their drug operations, was important. The following inmate points out the necessity of communicating the gang's willingness to use violent retaliation against rivals. Guns often played an important role in the development and maintenance of reputation, though they were rarely utilized in conflicting situations:

> We had guns to fend off jackers, but we never had to use them, 'cause people knew we were straps. People knew our clique, they are not going to be stupid. We've gotten into a few arguments, but it never came to a gun battle. Even when we were gangbangin', we didn't use guns, we only fought off the Bloods.

In addition to a collective reputation, the group serves the identifying needs of its individual members (Kanter, 1972). Our study participants related their need to draw upon the reputation of the gang to help them develop their own reputation, which gave them a sense of fulfillment. People want to present others with cues that will enhance desired typifications of who they are. They desire to present who they are in ways that will cause those they interact with to adhere to their situated claims (Hewitt & Stokes, 1975). The following participant discusses the way gang affiliation enhanced his reputation as a dangerous individual, a person not to be tested by others.

> There are people that know me; even ones that are contemplating robbing me know of me from the gang experience. They know if you try and rob me [of drugs

and money], more than likely you gonna get killed. I was gonna protect what was mine. I'll die trying.

Another study subject perceives gang membership differently. He attained a reputation through gang activity, and guns clearly played an important role in that process.

Fear and desire to have a reputation on the streets made me do it. When I got into the streets, I saw the glamour of it. I wanted a reputation there. What better way to get a reputation than to pick up a pistol? I've shot several people.

Although each prisoner/gang member interviewed expressed a desire to be known in the community for some particular attribute, there were some gang members who simply wanted to be known, sort of achieving celebrity status.

You basically want people to know your name. It's kind of like politicians, like that, you wanna be known. In my generation, you want somebody to say, "I know him, he used to hang around with us."

Respect

One constantly associates the subject of disrespect in gang vernacular with retaliatory violence. Interactions with rivals stemming from an affront to one's self-image often became the excuse to use a gun to redeem one's reputational identity. Strauss (1969) argues that anger and withdrawal occur when a person is confronted with a possible loss of face. For our subjects, this anger was apparent when rivals challenged their self-identity (i.e., when our subjects were disrespected).

According to the gang members we talked to, disrespect, or rejection of self-professed identity claims by others, often was the cause of violence. Violence is even more likely to be the result of disrespect when no retaliatory action may lead to a loss of face. The following inmate relates his view on this subject in general terms.

Violence starts to escalate once you start to disrespect me. Once you start to second guess my manhood, I'll fuck you up. You start coming at me with threats, then I feel offended. Once I feel offended, I react violently. That's how I was taught to react.

The interface of their manhood being threatened seems to be directly associated with Strauss's (1962) concept of identity denial by an accusing other. This threat to one's masculinity by not recognizing another's status claims is apparently an extremely serious breach of gang etiquette.

When someone disrespects me, they are putting my manhood in jeopardy. They are saying my words are shit, or putting my family in danger....Most of the time, I do it [use violence] to make people feel the pain or hurt that I feel. I don't know no other way to do it, as far as expressing myself any other way.

Hickman and Kuhn (1956) point out that the self anchors people in every situation they are involved in. Unlike other objects, they claim that the self is present in all interactions and serves as the basis from which we all make judgments and plans of reaction toward others who are part of a given situation. When being confronted by gang rivals who have been perceived as insulting an opposing gang member, the definition of street norms calls for an exaggerated response. That is, the disrespectful words must be countered with serious physical force to justify the disrespected individual's maintenance of self (or manhood). A prime example of feeling disrespected is discussed in terms of territory and the unwritten rules of the street by one gang member who told us of an encounter with a rival gang who disrespected him to the point that he felt he was left with no other alternative choice of action but to shoot them.

> So, as we were fighting, they started saying that this was their neighborhood and started throwing their gang signs. To me, to let somebody do that to me is disrespect. So I told them where I was from.

A little while later the gang members in question showed up in our study subject's neighborhood and shot at him as he was walking with his two small children to a convenience store to get ice cream. He continues to recite the tale:

> I was just so mad and angry for somebody to disrespect me like that and shoot. We got a rule on the street. There is rules. You don't shoot at anybody if there is kids. That's one of the main rules of the street. They broke the rules. To me that was telling me that they didn't have no respect for me or my kids. So, that's how I lost it and shot them. I was so disrespected that I didn't know how to handle it.

The notion of disrespect is analogous to an attack on the self. Because many of the inmates in our sample reported that masculinity is an important attribute of the self, they believed any disrespect was a direct threat to their masculinity. For those brought up in impoverished high-crime communities, as these study population participants were, there are limited alternatives to such conflicting situations (Anderson, 1999). Retaliation to redeem one's self-identity in terms of his internalized concept of manhood precludes a violent reaction to all actions of insult. To gang members caught in those confrontational encounters, there is a very limited course of action, that of perpetrating violence toward those who would threaten their self-concept of who they believe they are.

Gangs and Guns

The perceived necessity by gang participants to carry handguns became a reality for our study group. They collectively expressed the danger of their life on the street, whether it was selling narcotics, committing a robbery, being a provocateur against rivals, or being the recipient of violent retaliation on the part of perceived enemies. They viewed their world as fraught with potential danger; thus the need for the possession of guns. It is necessary, then, to take the person's definition of the situation into account in explaining their unlawful conduct (Hewitt, 1988). Often, the interviewed prisoners emphasized the importance of the gun as an attribute that communicated their masculinity in some situations but was protection in others. Quite often, both definitions of the situation existed simultaneously.

Our analysis of the interview data dichotomized those gun-using encounters as expressions of either power or protection, based on each participant's perceived definition of the situation.

Carrying a firearm elicits various feelings of power.

> When I have a gun, I feel like I'm on top of it, like I'm Superman or something. You got to let them know.

Another participant explains that the larger the gun, the more powerful he felt:

> I was 15 at that point in time, and I had a fascination with guns. It was like the more powerful impact the gun had, the more fascinated I got and the more I wanted it.

The actual use of a firearm is described in a situation that most lethally expressed the power of guns in an attempt to injure those belonging to rival gangs. In this situation, our subject points out that they were not trying to injure or kill anyone for personal reasons but rather to display a sense of willingness to commit a lethal act for purposes of dominance.

> When I was younger, we used to do drive-bys. It didn't matter who you were. We didn't go after a specific person. We went after a specific group. Whoever is standing at a particular house or wherever you may be, and you're grouped up and have the wrong color on; just because you were in a rival gang. You didn't have to do anything to us to come get you, it was a spontaneous reaction.

When not being involved in collective gang violence, individual members find themselves being involved in gun-use situations as instigators when confronting rivals on one's own.

> My cousin told me if you pull it you better use it. So you gotta boost yourself. When the time came, I was just shooting.

Our findings showed that in the vast majority of gang member–related shootings, most of these violent gun-using situations involved individuals as opposed to large numbers of gangs confronting each other with firearms. Yet, we were told that in gang representation, either on an individual basis or in a small group, whether it be in a protective or retaliatory mode, gang members needed to display a power position to those confronting them to maintain their reputations, and guns were important in that respect.

The issues surrounding gun possession often have to do with interpersonal conflict as opposed to collective gang situations. The fear of being physically harmed within their residential environment, coupled with the relative ease with which a person can attain a firearm, has resulted in a proliferation of weapons in the community. Growing up in such high-crime neighborhoods and then joining a gang can shape a minority teen's perceptions of his or her social world.

> There's a lot of brutality, there is a lot of murder around us. There is a lot of violence, period. There are enemies and all. A lot of pressure, you know. If you're not going to do this, then they're going to do it to you. I'd rather get caught with a gun than without.

The perceived fear for potential harm caused this female gang member to carry a gun with her outside her home. When she expresses the violence that is prevalent in her environment, she is also telling us how random threats can often occur and sees the necessity to harm rivals before they harm her.

Individually or collectively, rival gang members constantly pose a physical threat according to the next inmate. He also discusses the need for protection and how drug sales caused him to be a target for those who would try and rob him.

> I carried a gun because I knew what I was doing, especially since I was in a gang. Other gangs are gonna try and come after us. So I used it [gun] against those gangs and to make sure that my investments in the drugs was protected. I don't want nobody to take money from me.

Finally, one study subject relates the need to carry a gun all the time to protect his jewelry, which he openly displays as a symbol of his monetary success through the use of illegal means.

> I basically carried a gun for protection. Just like you have a best friend. You and your best friend go everywhere. I got over $10,000 of jewelry on me. People see all this jewelry and may try and beat me up. There may be two or three and just myself.

For our prisoner/gang member study population, the descriptive attributes they related all played an important role in shaping their individual gang identity. The roles they learned to play through their processional development into bona fide gang participants were accomplished by group socialization. Their acting upon those perceived valued attributes resulted in their transformed identity. Once the socializing process is complete, the novice gang member has to sustain his reputation and status personally as well as collectively with the formal group.

> An individual who implicitly or explicitly signifies that he has certain social characteristics ought in fact to be what he claims he is. In consequence, when an individual projects a definition of the situation and thereby makes an implicit or explicit claim to be a person of a particular kind, he automatically exerts a moral demand upon others, obliging them to value and treat him in the manner that persons of his kind have a right to expect. (Goffman, 1959, pp. 1–5)

For Goffman, the claims (attributes) our sample of gang members desired to convey to others of just who they perceived themselves to be directly affected their sense of self.

DISCUSSION AND CONCLUSION

Gangs not only fulfill specific needs for individuals that other groups in disadvantaged neighborhoods may fail to provide, but as our interviews suggest, they are also important primary groups into which individuals become socialized. It is not surprising, then, that self-concept and identity are closely tied to gang membership. Guns are also important in this regard. We propose that for the gang members in our sample, gang-related gun violence can be understood in terms of self and identity that are created through the process of socialization and are heavily rooted in notions of masculinity. Thus, our analysis provides insight into the way gang socialization can produce violence—especially gun-related violence.

We find that related to the issue of gun violence, the possession and use of guns among gang members is relatively important because, in addition to protecting gang members, guns are tools that aid in identity formation and impression management. As many of our subject narratives suggest, guns were often connected in some way to masculine attributes. Gang members reported to us that they could often use guns to project their reputation or reclaim respect. We believe that the consequences of our findings regarding gang violence and guns are important for public policy for three reasons.

First, because our sample only consisted of those gang members who committed the most severe forms of violence (i.e., they were incarcerated for relatively long periods of time for their gun-related violence), there may be some interest in targeting individuals like the ones in our sample early in their criminal careers to "diminish the pool of chronic gang offenders" (Piehl, Kennedy, & Braga, 2000, p. 100). We believe this may be one potential method for reducing gang-related violence because the gang members in our sample often had extensive violent histories. Moreover, in studies of gang violence, researchers have generally found that a small number of offenders commit most of the crime. For instance, Kennedy, Piehl, and Braga (1996) found that less than 1% of Boston's youth were responsible for nearly 60% of the city's homicides. Thus, identifying the rather small pool of chronic gang members may be a useful approach to reducing gang violence because they are the ones engaged in most of the violence. This approach, however, is somewhat problematic because identifying chronic offenders is both difficult and controversial (Walker, 1998). Moreover, Spergel and Curry (1990), who studied the effectiveness of various gang-related intervention strategies, argue that law enforcement efforts seem to be one of the least effective methods for reducing gang-related problems.

Second, our research suggests that policies aimed at reducing gang violence should take gang socialization into account. Simply reducing gun availability through law enforcement crackdowns on violent gang members is probably not sufficient (see Piehl, Kennedy, & Braga, 2000). In addition, our interviews suggest that guns are probably far more important to the daily lives and identities of gang members than most policymakers might imagine, precisely because they help project a reputation and create respect. Thus, it might be pointed out that if gang culture could be changed through the resocialization of gang members, gun-related gang violence might significantly decrease. Indeed, studies of gun initiatives such as the Boston Gun Project suggest that gang violence is reduced when gang culture is changed. As Piehl, Kennedy, & Braga (2000, p. 100) point out, one reason homicides in Boston decreased as a result of the Boston Gun Project was because that initiative focused on "establishing and/or reinforcing nonviolent norms by increasing peer support for eschewing violence, by improving young people's handling of potentially violent situations."

Overall, however, the strategy of focusing on gang socialization, however, falls most closely in line with social intervention perspectives that have not proved to be highly successful in various situations (Shelden, Tracy, & Brown, 2001). In short, altering the values of gang members to make gang-related violence less likely may not be the most promising approach to reducing gang violence. As Klein (1995, p. 147) recently noted, "Gangs are by-products of their communities: They cannot long be controlled by attacks on symptoms alone; the community structure and capacity must also be targeted." Whether gang violence can be reduced by the resocialization of gang members appears to remain open to debate, but it is clearly one avenue of intervention that requires further attention in the research.

Third, it is not clear from our research whether simply eliminating or reducing access to guns can reduce gun-related gang violence. For example, studies like the Youth Firearms Violence Initiative conducted by the U.S. Department of Justice's Office of Community Oriented Policing Services does suggest that gun violence can be reduced by focusing, at least in part, on reducing access to guns (Dunworth, 2000). However, that study also indicates that once these projects focusing on access to guns end, gang violence increases to previous levels. Moreover, our interviews suggest that there is little reason to believe that gang members would be any less likely to look to gangs as a source of status and protection and may use other weapons—though arguably less lethal than guns—to aid in transformations of identity and preserve a sense of self. Thus, although reduction strategies may prevent gang-related violence in the short term, there is little evidence that this intervention strategy will have long-term effects because it does not adequately deal with gang culture and processes of gang socialization.

Overall, our findings suggest that gang socialization produces gang-related gun violence through changes to identity and self. Although the problems of gang-related violence appear to play out at the micro level, the solutions to these problems do not appear to be overwhelmingly situated at this level. Instead, we believe that intervention efforts must reside at the macro level and impact socialization processes at the micro level. We agree with Short (1997, p. 181) that "absent change in macro level forces associated with [gang violence], vulnerable individuals will continue to be produced" (see also Shelden, Tracy, & Brown, 2001). Thus, it may be more fruitful to focus on intervention efforts aimed at improving the economic and social environments that create gangs.

REFERENCES

Anderson, E. (1999). *Code of the street: Decency, violence, and the moral life of the inner city.* New York: W. W. Norton.

Baumeister, R., & Tice, D. (1984). Role of self-presentation and choice in cognitive dissonance under forced compliance. *Journal of Personality and Social Psychology, 46,* 5–13.

Berger, P. (1963). *Invitation to sociology: A humanistic perspective.* Garden City, NY: Doubleday.

Bjerregaard, B., & Lizotte, A. (1995). Gun ownership and gang membership. *Journal of Criminal Law and Criminology, 86*, 37–58.

Blumstein, A. (1995). Violence by young people: Why the deadly nexus? *National Institute of Justice Journal, 229*, 2–9.

Bowker, L., & Klein, M. (1983). The etiology of female juvenile delinquency and gang membership: A test of psychological and social structural explanations. *Adolescence, 18*, 739–751.

Callero, P. (1985). Role identity salience. *Social Psychology Quarterly, 48*, 203–215.

Decker, S., & Van Winkle, B. (1996). *Life in the gang: Family, friends, and violence.* New York: Cambridge University Press.

Dunworth, T. (2000). *National evaluation of youth firearms violence initiative. Research in brief.* Washington, DC: U.S. Department of Justice, Office of Justice Programs, National Institute of Justice.

Gerrard, N. (1964). The core member of the gang. *British Journal of Criminology, 4*, 361–371.

Goffman, E. (1959). *The presentation of self in everyday life.* Garden City, NY: Doubleday.

———. (1961). *Encounters: Two studies in the sociology of interaction.* Indianapolis, IN: Bobbs-Merrill.

Gordon, R., Lahey, B., Kawai, K., Loeber, R., Stouthamer-Loeber, M., & Farrington, D. (2004). Antisocial behavior and youth gang membership: Selection and socialization. *Criminology, 42*, 55–88.

Hewitt, J. (1988). *Self and society.* Boston: Allyn & Bacon.

Hewitt, J., & Stokes, R. (1975). Disclaimers. *American Sociological Review, 40*, 1–11.

Hickman, C. A., & Kuhn, M. (1956). *Individuals, groups, and economic behavior.* New York: Dryden.

Holstein, J., & Gubrium, J. (2003). *Inner lives and social worlds.* New York: Oxford University Press.

Horowitz, R. (1983). *Honor and the American dream.* New Brunswick, NJ: Rutgers University Press.

Howell, J. (1998). Youth gangs: An overview. *Juvenile Justice Bulletin,* August. Washington, DC: U.S. Department of Justice, Office of Juvenile Justice and Delinquency Prevention.

Hughes, L., & Short, J. (2005). Disputes involving youth street gang members: Micro-social contexts. *Criminology, 43*, 43–76.

Kanter, R. (1972). *Commitment and community: Communes and utopias in sociological perspective.* Cambridge, MA: Harvard University Press.

Katz, J. (1988). *Seductions of crime: Moral and sensual attractions in doing evil.* New York: Basic.

Kennedy, D., Piehl, A. M., & Braga, A. (1996). *Youth gun violence in Boston: Gun markets, serious youth offenders, and a use-reduction strategy. Research in brief.* Washington, DC: U.S. Department of Justice, Office of Justice Programs, National Institute of Justice.

Klein, M. (1995). *The American street gang.* New York: Oxford University Press.

Kubrin, C. (2005). Gangstas, thugs, and hustlas: Identity and the code of the street in rap music. *Social Problems, 52*, 360–378.

Lindesmith, A., & Strauss, A. (1968). *Social psychology.* New York: Holt, Rinehart and Winston.

Lizotte, A., Tesoriero, J., Thomberry, T., & Krohn, M. (1994). Patterns of adolescent firearms ownership and use. *Justice Quarterly, 11*, 51–74.

McCall, G., & Simmons, J. (1966). *Identities and interactions: An examination of human associations in everyday life.* New York: Free Press.

McCorkle, R., & Miethe, T. (2002). *Panic: The social construction of the street gang problem.* Upper Saddle River, NJ: Prentice Hall.

Miller, J., & Brunson, R. (2000). Gender dynamics in youth gangs: A comparison of males' and females' accounts. *Justice Quarterly, 17*, 419–448.

Miller, J., & Decker, S. (2001). Young women and gang violence: Gender, street offender, and violent victimization in gangs. *Justice Quarterly, 18*, 115–140.

Moore, J. (1978). *Homeboys: Gangs, drugs, and prison in the barrios of Los Angeles.* Philadelphia: Temple University Press.

———. (1991). *Going down to the barrio: Homeboys and homegirls in change.* Philadelphia: Temple University Press.

Oliver, W. (1994). *The violent world of black men.* New York: Lexington.

Piehl, A. M., Kennedy, D., & Braga, A. (2000). Problem solving and youth violence: An evaluation of the Boston gun project. *American Law and Economics Review, 2*, 58–106.

Sanders, W. (1994). *Gang-bangs and drive-bys: Grounded culture and juvenile gang violence.* New York: Walter de Gruyter.

Shelden, R., Tracy, S., & Brown, W. (2001). *Youth gangs in American society.* Belmont, CA: Wadsworth.

Sheley, J., & Wright, J. (1995). *In the line of fire: Youth, guns and violence in America.* New York: Aldine de Gruyter.

Sherif, M., & Wilson, M. (1953). *Group relations at the crossroads.* New York: Harper.

Shibutani, T. (1961). *Society and personality: An interactionist approach to social psychology.* Englewood Cliffs, NJ: Prentice Hall.

Short, J. (1997). *Poverty, ethnicity, and violent crime.* Boulder, CO: Westview.

Short, J., & Strodtbeck, F. (1965). *Group processes and gang delinquency.* Chicago: University of Chicago Press.

Sirpal, S. K. (1997). Causes of gang participation and strategies for prevention in gang members' own words. *Journal of Gang Research, 4*, 13–22.

Spergel, I., & Curry, G. D. (1990). Strategies and perceived agency effectiveness in dealing with the youth gang problem. In C. R. Huff (Ed.), *Gangs in America* (pp. 288–309). Newbury Park, CA: Sage.

Stone, G. (1962). Appearance and self. In A. Rose (Ed.), *Human behavior and social processes* (pp. 86–118). Boston: Houghton Mifflin.

Strauss, A. (1962). Transformations of identity. In A. Rose (Ed.), *Human behavior and social processes: An interactional approach* (pp. 63–85). Boston: Houghton Mifflin.

———. (1969). *Mirrors and masks: The search for identity.* New York: Macmillan.

Stryker, S., & Serpe, R. (1982). Commitment, identity salience and role behavior. In W. Ikes & E. Knowles (Eds.), *Personality, roles and social behavior* (pp. 199–218). New York: Springer-Verlag.

Thornberry, T., Krohn, M., Lizotte, A., & Chard-Wierschem, D. (1993). The role of juvenile gangs in facilitating delinquent behavior. *Journal of Research in Crime and Delinquency, 30*, 75–85.

Thornberry, T., Krohn, M., Lizotte, A., Smith, C., & Tobin, K. (2003). *Gangs and delinquency in developmental perspective.* Cambridge, UK: Cambridge University Press.

Thrasher, F. (1927). *The gang.* Chicago: University of Chicago Press.

Turner, R. (1978). The role and the person. *American Journal of Sociology, 84,* 1–23.

Vigil, J. (1988). *Barrio gangs.* Austin: University of Texas Press.

———. (1996). Street baptism: Chicago gang initiation. *Human Organization, 55,* 149–153.

———. (2003). Urban violence and street gangs. *Annual Review of Anthropology, 32,* 225–242.

Walker, S. (1998). *Sense and nonsense about crime and drugs.* Belmont, CA: Wadsworth.

Weinstein, E., & Deutschberger, P. (1963). Some dimensions of altercasting. *Sociometry, 26,* 454–466.

Wright, J., & Rossi, P. (1986). *Armed and considered dangerous: A survey of felons and their firearms.* New York: Aldine de Gruyter.

Yablonsky, L. (1962). *The violent gang.* New York: Macmillan.

CHAPTER 19

Gender and Victimization Risk among Young Women in Gangs

Jody Miller

This selection examines how gendered situational dynamics shape gang violence, including participation in violent offending and experiences of violent victimization. Although there are numerous studies of gangs and gang-involved individuals, few have explored the concept of victimization of gang members. The author found that young women, even regular offenders, highlight the significance of gender in shaping and limiting their involvement in serious violence. Based on interviews with 20 female gang members in Columbus, Ohio, Miller found that being a member increases one's risk of assaults and other physical victimization, and that these risks are greater for females than for males. She suggests that the act of joining a gang often involves submission to victimization at the hands of other members of the gang, and that gang activities thereafter place these individuals at risk for further victimization.

GIRLS, GANGS, AND CRIME

Until recently . . . little attention was paid to young women's participation in serious and violent gang-related crime. Most traditional gang research emphasized the auxiliary and peripheral nature of girls' gang involvement and often resulted in an almost exclusive emphasis on girls' sexuality and sexual activities with male gang members, downplaying their participation in delinquency (for critiques of gender bias in gender research, see Campbell, 1984; Campbell, 1990; Taylor, 1993).

However, recent estimates of female gang involvement have caused researchers to pay greater attention to gang girls' activities. This evidence suggests that young women approximate anywhere from 10% to 38% of gang members (Campbell,

Source: From Miller, J. (1998). Gender and victimization: Risk among young women in gangs. *Journal of Research in Crime & Delinquency, 35,* 429–453. Copyright © 1998. Reprinted with permission from Sage Publications, Inc.

1984; Chesney-Lind, 1993; Esbensen, 1996; Fagan, 1990; Moore, 1991), that female gang participation may be increasing (Fagan, 1996; Spergel & Curry, 1993; Taylor, 1990), and that in some urban areas, upward of one-fifth of girls report gang affiliations (Bjerregaard & Smith, 1993; Winfree et al., 1992). As female gang members have become recognized as a group worthy of criminologists' attention, we have garnered new information regarding their involvement in delinquency in general, and violence in particular.

Few would dispute that when it comes to serious delinquency, male gang members are involved more frequently than their female counterparts. However, this evidence does suggest that young women in gangs are more involved in serious criminal activities than was previously believed and also tend to be more involved than nongang youths—male or female. As such, they likely are exposed to greater victimization risk than nongang youths as well.

In addition, given the social contexts described above, it is reasonable to assume that young women's victimization risk within gangs is also shaped by gender. Gang activities (such as fighting for status and retaliation) create a particular set of factors that increase gang members' victimization risk and repeat victimization risk. Constructions of gender identity may shape these risks in particular ways for girls. For instance, young women's adoption of masculine attributes may provide a means of participating and gaining status within gangs but may also lead to increased risk of victimization as a result of deeper immersion in delinquent activities. On the other hand, experiences of victimization may contribute to girls' denigration and thus increase their risk for repeat victimization through gendered responses and labeling—for example, when sexual victimization leads to perceptions of sexual availability or when victimization leads an individual to be viewed as weak. In addition, femaleness is an individual attribute that has the capacity to mark young women as "safe" crime victims (e.g., easy targets) or, conversely, to deem them "off limits." My goal here is to examine the gendered nature of violence within gangs, with a specific focus on how gender shapes young women's victimization risk.

METHODOLOGY

Data presented in this article come from survey and semistructured in-depth interviews with 20 female members of mixed-gender gangs in Columbus, Ohio. The interviewees ranged in age from 12 to 17 years; just over three-quarters were African American or multiracial (16 of 20), and the rest (four of 20) were white.

Girls who admitted gang involvement during the survey participated in a follow-up interview to talk in more depth about their gangs and gang activities. The goal of the in-depth interview was to gain a greater understanding of the nature and meanings of gang life from the point of view of its female members.

The in-depth interviews were open-ended and all but one were audio-taped. They were structured around several groupings of questions. We began by discussing girls' entry into their gangs—when and how they became involved, and what other things were going on in their lives at the time. Then we discussed the structure of the gang—its history, size, leadership, and organization, and their place in the group. The next series of questions concerned gender within the gang; for example, how girls get involved, what activities they engage in and whether these are the same as the young men's activities, and what kind of males and females have the most influence in the gang and why. The next series of questions explored gang involvement more generally—what being in the gang means, what kinds of things they do together, and so on. Then, I asked how safe or dangerous they feel gang membership is and how they deal with risk. I concluded by asking them to speculate about why people their age join gangs, what things they like, what they dislike and have learned by being in the gang, and what they like best about themselves. This basic guideline was followed for each interview subject, although when additional topics arose in the context of the interview we often deviated from the interview guide to pursue them. Throughout the interviews, issues related to violence emerged; these issues form the core of the discussion that follows.

SETTING

The young women I interviewed described their gangs in ways that are very much in keeping with these findings. All 20 are members of Folks, Crips, or Bloods sets. All but three described gangs with fewer than 30 members, and most reported relatively narrow age ranges between members. Half were in gangs with members who were 21 or over, but almost without exception, their gangs were made up primarily of teenagers, with either one adult who was considered the OG ("Original Gangster," leader) or just a handful of young adults. The majority (14 of 20) reported that their gangs did not include members under the age of 13.

Although the gangs these young women were members of were composed of both female and male members, they varied in their gender composition, with the vast majority being predominantly male. Six girls reported that girls were one-fifth or fewer of the members of their gang; eight were in gangs in which girls were between a quarter and a third of the overall membership; four said girls were between 44% and 50% of the members; and one girl reported that her gang was two-thirds female and one-third male. Overall, girls were typically a minority within these groups numerically, with 11 girls reporting that there were five or fewer girls in their set.

This structure—male-dominated, integrated, mixed-gender gangs—likely shapes gender dynamics in particular ways. Much past gang research has assumed that female members of gangs are in auxiliary subgroups of male gangs, but there is increasing evidence—including from the young women I spoke with—that many gangs can be characterized as integrated, mixed-gender groups.

GENDER, GANGS, AND VIOLENCE

Gangs as Protection and Risk

An irony of gang involvement is that although many members suggest one thing they get out of the gang is a sense of protection (see Decker, 1996; Joe & Chesney-Lind, 1995; Lauderback, Hansen, & Waldorf, 1992), gang membership itself means exposure to victimization risk and even a willingness to be victimized. These contradictions are apparent when girls talk about what they get out of the gang, and what being in the gang means in terms of other members' expectations of their behavior. In general, a number of girls suggested that being a gang member is a source of protection around the neighborhood. Erica, a 17-year-old African American, explained, "It's like people look at us and that's exactly what they think, there's a gang, and they respect us for that. They won't bother us.... It's like you put that intimidation in somebody." Likewise, Lisa, a 14-year-old white girl, described being in the gang as empowering: "You just feel like, oh my God, you know, they got my back. I don't need to worry about it." Given the violence endemic in many inner-city communities, these beliefs are understandable, and to a certain extent, accurate.

In addition, some young women articulated a specifically gendered sense of protection that they felt as a result of being a member of a group that was predominantly male. Gangs operate within larger social milieus that are characterized by gender inequality and sexual exploitation. Being in a gang with young men means at least the semblance of protection from, and retaliation against, predatory men in the social environment. Heather, a 15-year-old white girl, noted, "You feel more secure when, you know, a guy's around protectin' you, you know, than you would a girl." She explained that as a gang member, because "you get protected by guys...not as many people mess with you." Other young women concurred and also described that male gang members could retaliate against specific acts of violence against girls in the gang. Nikkie, a 13-year-old African American girl, had a friend who was raped by a rival gang member, and she said, "It was a Crab [Crip] that raped my girl in Miller Ales, and um, they was ready to kill him." Keisha, an African American 14-year-old, explained, "If I got beat up by a guy, all I gotta do is go tell one of the niggers, you know what I'm sayin'? Or one of the guys, they'd take care of it."

At the same time, members recognized that they may be targets of rival gang members and were expected to "be down" for their gang at those times even when it meant being physically hurt. In addition, initiation rites and internal rules were structured in ways that required individuals to submit to, and be exposed to, violence. For example, young women's descriptions of the qualities they valued in members revealed the extent to which exposure to violence was an expected element of gang involvement. Potential members, they explained, should be tough, able to fight and to engage in criminal activities, and also should be loyal to the group and willing to put themselves at risk for it. Erica explained that they didn't want "punks" in her gang: "When you join something like that, you might as well expect that there's gonna be fights.... And, if you're a punk, or if you're scared of stuff like that, then don't join." Likewise, the following dialogue with Cathy, a white 16-year-old, reveals similar themes. I asked her what her gang expected out of members, and she responded, "To be true to our gang and to have our backs." When I asked her to elaborate, she explained:

> CATHY: Like, uh, if you say you're a Blood, you be a Blood. You wear your rag even when you're by yourself. You know, don't let anybody intimidate you and be like, "Take that rag off." You know, "You better get with our set." Or something like that.
>
> JM: Ok. Anything else that being true to the set means?
>
> CATHY: Um. Yeah, I mean, just, just, you know, I mean it's, you got a whole bunch of people comin' up in your face, and if you're by yourself they ask you what's your claimin', you tell 'em. Don't say nothin'.
>
> JM: Even if it means getting beat up or something?
>
> CATHY: Mmhmm.

One measure of these qualities came through the initiation process, which involved the individual submitting to victimization at the hands of the gang's members. Typically this entailed either taking a fixed number of "blows" to the head and/or chest or being "beaten in" by members for a given duration (e.g., 60 seconds). Heather described the initiation as an important event for determining whether someone would make a good member:

> When you get beat in, if you don't fight back and if you just, like, stop and you start cryin' or somethin', or beggin' 'em to stop and stuff like that, then they ain't gonna, they'll just stop and they'll say that you're not gang material because you gotta be hard, gotta be able to fight, take punches.

In addition to the initiation and threats from rival gangs, members were expected to adhere to the gang's internal rules (which included such things as not fighting with one another, being "true" to the gang, respecting the leader, not spreading gang business outside the gang, and not dating members of rival gangs). Breaking the rules was grounds for physical punishment, either in the form of a sponta-neous assault or a formal "violation," which involved taking a specified number of blows to the head. For example, Keisha reported that she talked back to the leader of her set and "got slapped pretty hard" for doing so. Likewise, Veronica, an African American 15-year-old, described her leader as "crazy, but we gotta listen to 'im. He's just the type that if you don't listen to 'im, he gonna blow your head off. He's just crazy."

It is clear that regardless of members' perceptions of the gang as a form of "protection," being a gang member also involves a willingness to open oneself up to the possibility of victimization. Gang victimization is governed by rules and expectations, however, and thus does not involve the random vulnerability that being out on the streets without a gang might entail in high-crime neighborhoods. Because of its structured nature, this victimization risk may be perceived as more palatable by gang members. For young women in particular, the gendered nature of the streets may make the empowerment available through gang involvement an appealing alternative to the individualized vulnerability they otherwise would face. However, as the next sections highlight, girls' victimization risks continue to be shaped by gender, even within their gangs, because these groups are structured around gender hierarchies as well.

Gender and Status, Crime and Victimization

Status hierarchies within Columbus gangs, like elsewhere, were male dominated (Bowker, Gross, & Klein, 1980; Campbell, 1990). Again, it is important to highlight that the structure of the gangs these young women belonged to—that is, male-dominated, integrated, mixed-gender gangs—likely shaped the particular ways in which gender dynamics played themselves out. Autonomous female gangs, as well as gangs in which girls are in auxiliary subgroups, may be shaped by different gender relations, as well as differences in orientations toward status and criminal involvement.

All the young women reported having established leaders in their gang, and this leadership was almost exclusively male. Although LaShawna, a 17-year-old African American, reported being the leader of her set (which had a membership that is two-thirds girls, many of whom resided in the same residential facility as her), all the other girls in mixed-gender gangs reported that their OG was male. In fact, a number of young women stated explicitly that only male gang members could be leaders. Leadership qualities, and qualities attributed to high-status members of the gangs—being tough, able to fight, and willing to "do dirt" (e.g., commit crime, engage in violence) for the gang—were perceived as characteristically masculine. Keisha noted, "The guys, they just harder." She explained, "Guys is more rougher. We have our G's back, but it ain't gonna be like the guys, they just don't give a fuck. They gonna shoot you in a minute."

For the most part, status in the gang was related to traits such as the willingness to use serious violence and commit dangerous crimes, and, though not exclusively, these traits were viewed primarily as qualities more likely and more intensely located among male gang members.

Because these respected traits were characterized specifically as masculine, young women actually may have had greater flexibility in their gang involvement than young men. Young women had fewer expectations placed on them—by both their male and female peers—in regard to involvement in criminal activities such as fighting, using weapons, and committing other crimes. This tended to decrease girls' exposure to victimization risk compared to male members, because they were able to avoid activities likely to place them in danger. Girls could gain status in the gang by being particularly hard and true to the set. Heather, for example, described the most influential girl in her set as "the hardest girl, the one that don't take no crap, will stand up to anybody." Likewise, Diane, a white 15-year-old, described a highly respected female member in her set as follows:

People look up to Janeen just 'cause she's so crazy. People just look up to her 'cause she don't care about nothin'. She don't even care about makin' money. Her, her thing is, "Oh, you're a Slob [Blood]? You're a Slob? You talkin' to me? You talkie' shit to me?" Pow, pow! And that's it. That's it.

However, young women also had a second route to status that was less available to young men. This came via their connections—as sisters, girlfriends, cousins—to influential, high-status young men. In Veronica's set, for example, the girl with the most power was the OG's "sister or his cousin, one of 'em." His girlfriend also had status, although Veronica noted that "most of us just look up to our OG." Monica, a 16-year-old African American, and Tamika, a 15-year-old African American, both had older brothers in their gangs, and both reported getting respect, recognition, and protection because of this connection. This route to status and the masculinization of high-status traits functioned to maintain gender inequality within gangs, but they also could put young women at less risk of victimization than young men. This was both because young women were perceived as less threatening and thus were less likely to be targeted by rivals, and because they were not expected to prove themselves in the ways that young men were, thus decreasing their participation in those delinquent activities likely to increase exposure to violence. Thus, gender inequality could have a protective edge for young women.

Young men's perceptions of girls as lesser members typically functioned to keep girls from being targets of serious violence at the hands of rival young men, who instead left routine confrontations with rival female gang members to the girls in their own gang. Diane said that young men in her gang "don't wanna waste their time hittin' on some little girls. They're gonna go get their little cats [females] to go get 'em." Lisa remarked,

Girls don't face as much violence as [guys]. They see a girl, they say, "We'll just smack her and send her on." They see a guy—'cause guys are like a lot more into it than girls are, I've noticed that—and they like, "Well, we'll shoot him."

In addition, the girls I interviewed suggested that, in comparison with young men, young women were less likely to resort to serious violence, such as that involving a weapon, when confronting rivals. Thus, when girls' routine confrontations were more likely to be female on female than male on female, girls' risk of serious victimization was lessened further.

Also, because participation in serious and violent crime was defined primarily as a masculine endeavor, young women could use gender as a means of avoiding participation in those aspects of gang life they found risky, threatening, or morally troubling. Of the young women I interviewed, about one-fifth were involved in serious gang violence: a few had been involved in aggravated assaults on rival gang members, and one admitted to having killed a rival gang member, but they were by far the exception. Most girls tended not to be involved in serious gang crime, and some reported that they chose to exclude themselves because they felt ambivalent about this aspect of gang life. Angie, an African American 15-year-old explained,

I don't get involved like that, be out there goin' and just beat up people like that or go stealin', things like that. That's not me. The boys, mostly the boys do all that, the girls we just sit back and chill, you know.

Likewise, Diane noted,

For maybe a drive-by, they might wanna have a bunch of dudes. They might not put the females in that. Maybe the females might be weak inside, not strong enough to do something like that, just on the insides.... If a female wants to go forward and doin' that, and she wants to risk her whole life for doin' that, then she can. But the majority of the time, that job is given to a man.

Diane was not just alluding to the idea that young men were stronger than young women. She also inferred that young women were able to get out of committing serious crime, more so than young men, because a girl shouldn't have to "risk her whole life" for the gang. In accepting that young men were more central members of the gang, young women could more easily participate in gangs without putting themselves in jeopardy—they could engage in the more routine, everyday activities of the gang, like hanging out, listening to music, and smoking bud (marijuana). These male-dominated, mixed-gender gangs thus appeared to provide young women with flexibility in their involvement in gang activities. As a result, it is likely that their risk of victimization at the hands of rivals was less than that of young men in gangs who were engaged in greater amounts of crime.

Girls' Devaluation and Victimization

In addition to girls choosing not to participate in serious gang crimes, they also faced exclusion at the hands of young men or the gang as a whole (see also Bowker, Gross, & Klein, 1980). In particular, the two types of crime mentioned most frequently as "off-limits" for girls were drug sales and drive-by shootings. LaShawna explained, "We don't really let our females [sell drugs] unless they really wanna and they know how to do it and not to get caught and everything." Veronica described a drive-by that her gang participated in and said, "They wouldn't let us [females] go. But we wanted to go, but they wouldn't let us." Often, the exclusion was couched in terms of protection. When I asked Veronica why the girls couldn't go, she said, "So we won't go to jail if they was to get caught. Or if one of 'em was to get shot, they wouldn't want it to happen to us." Likewise, Sonita, a 13-year-old African American, noted, "If they gonna do somethin' bad and they think one of the females gonna get hurt, they don't let 'em do it with them.... Like if they involved with shooting or whatever, [girls] can't go."

Although girls' exclusion from some gang crime may be framed as protective (and may reduce their victimization risk vis-a-vis rival gangs), it also served to perpetuate the devaluation of female members as less significant to the gang—not as tough, true, or "down" for the gang as male members. When LaShawna said her gang blocked girls' involvement in serious crime, I pointed out that she was actively involved her-self. She explained, "Yeah, I do a lot of stuff 'cause I'm tough.

I likes, I likes messin' with boys. I fight boys. Girls ain't nothin' to me." Similarly, Tamika said, "Girls, they little peons."

Some young women found the perception of them as weak a frustrating one. Brandi, an African American 13-year-old, explained, "Sometimes I dislike that the boys, sometimes, always gotta take charge and they think sometimes, that the girls don't know how to take charge 'cause we're like girls, we're females, and like that." And Chantell, an African American 14-year-old, noted that rival gang members "think that you're more of a punk." Beliefs that girls were weaker than boys meant that young women had a harder time proving that they were serious about their commitment to the gang. Diane explained,

> A female has to show that she's tough. A guy can just, you can just look at him. But a female, she's gotta show. She's gotta go out and do some dirt. She's gotta go whip some girl's ass, shoot somebody, rob somebody or something. To show that she is tough.

In terms of gender-specific victimization risk, the devaluation of young women suggests several things. It could lead to the mistreatment and victimization of girls by members of their own gang when they didn't have specific male protection (i.e., a brother, boyfriend) in the gang or when they weren't able to stand up for themselves to male members. This was exacerbated by activities that led young women to be viewed as sexually available. In addition, because young women typically were not seen as a threat by young men, when they did pose one, they could be punished even more harshly than young men, not only for having challenged a rival gang or gang member, but also for having overstepped "appropriate" gender boundaries.

Monica had status and respect in her gang both because she had proven herself through fights and criminal activities and because her older brothers were members of her set. She contrasted her own treatment with that of other young women in the gang:

> They just be puttin' the other girls off. Like Andrea, man. Oh my God, they dog Andrea so bad. They like, "Bitch, go to the store." She like, "All right, I be right back." She will go to the store and go and get them whatever they want and come back with it. If she don't get it right, they be like, "Why you do that, bitch?" I mean, and one dude even smacked her. And, I mean, and, I don't, I told my brother once. I was like, "Man, it ain't even like that. If you ever see someone tryin' to disrespect me like that or hit me, if you do not hit them or at least say somethin' to them...." So my brothers, they kinda watch out for me.

However, Monica put the responsibility for Andrea's treatment squarely on the young woman: "I put that on her. They ain't gotta do her like that, but she don't gotta let them do her like that either." Andrea was seen as "weak" because she did not stand up to the male members in the gang; thus, her mistreatment was framed as partially deserved because she did not exhibit the valued traits of toughness and willingness to fight that would allow her to defend herself.

An additional but related problem was when the devaluation of young women within gangs was sexual in nature. Girls, but not boys, could be initiated into the gang by being "sexed in"—having sexual relations with multiple male members of the gang. Other members viewed the young women initiated in this way as sexually available and promiscuous, thus increasing their subsequent mistreatment. In addition, the stigma could extend to female members in general, creating a sexual devaluation that all girls had to contend with. The dynamics of "sexing in" as a form of gang initiation placed young women in a position that increased their risk of ongoing mistreatment at the hands of their gang peers. According to Keisha,

> If you get sexed in, you have no respect. That means you gotta go ho'in' for 'em; when they say you give 'em the pussy, you gotta give it to 'em. If you don't, you gonna get your ass beat. I ain't down for that.

One girl in her set was sexed in and Keisha said the girl "just do everything they tell her to do, like a dummy." Nikkie reported that two girls who were sexed into her set eventually quit hanging around with the gang because they were harassed so much. In fact, Veronica said the young men in her set purposely tricked girls into believing they were being sexed into the gang and targeted girls they did not like:

> If some girls wanted to get in, if they don't like the girl, they have sex with 'em. They run trains on 'em or either have the girl suck their thang. And then they used to, the girls used to think they was in. So then the girls used to just come try to hang around us and all this little bull, just 'cause, 'cause they thinkin' they in.

Young women who were sexed into the gang were viewed as sexually promiscuous, weak, and not "true" members. They were subject to revictimization and mistreatment, and were viewed as deserving of abuse by other members, both male and female. Veronica continued, "They [girls who are sexed in] gotta do what-ever, whatever the boys tell 'em to do when they want 'em to do it, right then and there, in front of whoever. And, I think, that's just sick. That's nasty, that's dumb." Keisha concurred, "She brought that on herself, by bein' the fact, bein' sexed in." There was evidence, however, that girls could overcome the stigma of having been sexed in through their subsequent behavior, by challenging members that disrespect them and being willing to fight. Tamika described a girl in her set who was sexed in, and stigmatized as a result, but successfully fought to rebuild her reputation:

> Some people, at first, they call her "little ho" and all that. But then, now she startin' to get bold. . . . Like, like, they be like, "Ooh, look at the little ho. She flicked me and my boy." She be like, "Man, forget y'all. Man, what? What?" She be ready to squat [fight] with 'em. I be like, "Ah, look at her!" Uh huh. . . . At first we looked at her like, "Ooh, man, she a ho, man." But now we look at her like she just our kickin'-it partner. You know, however she got in, that's her business.

The fact that there was such an option as "sexing in" served to keep girls disempowered, because they always faced the question of how they got in and of whether they were "true" members. In addition, it contributed to a milieu in which young women's sexuality was seen as exploitable. This may help explain why young women were so harshly judgmental of those girls who were sexed in. Young women who were privy to male gang members' conversations reported that male members routinely disrespect girls in the gang by disparaging them sexually. Monica explained,

> I mean the guys, they have their little comments about 'em [girls in the gang], because I hear more because my brothers are all up there with the guys and everything, and I hear more just sittin' around, just listenin'. And they'll have their little jokes about "Well, ha, I had her," and then everybody else will jump in and say, "Well, I had her, too." And then they'll laugh about it.

In general, because gender constructions defined young women as weaker than young men, young women were often seen as lesser members of the gang. In addition to the mistreatment these perceptions entailed, young women also faced particularly harsh sanctions for crossing gender boundaries—causing harm to rival male members when they had been viewed as nonthreatening. One young woman participated in the assault of a rival female gang member who had set up a member of the girl's gang. She explained, "The female was supposingly goin' out with one of ours, went back and told a bunch of [rivals] what was goin' on and got the [rivals] to jump my boy. And he ended up in the hospital." The story she told was unique but nonetheless significant for what it indicates about the gendered nature of gang violence and victimization. Several young men in her set saw the girl walking down the street, kidnapped her, then brought her to a member's house. The young woman I interviewed, along with several other girls in her set, viciously beat the girl, and then, to their surprise, the young men took over the beating, ripped off the girl's clothes, brutally gang-raped her, then dumped her in a park. The interviewee noted, "I don't know what happened to her. Maybe she died. Maybe, maybe someone came and helped her. I mean, I don't know." The experience scared the young woman who told me about it. She explained,

> I don't never want anythin' like that to happen to me. And I pray to God that it doesn't. 'Cause God said that whatever you sow you're gonna reap. And like, you know, beatin' a girl up and then sittin' there watchin' somethin' like that happen, well, Jesus that could come back on me. I mean, I felt, I really did feel sorry for her, even though my boy was in the hospital and was really hurt. I mean, we coulda just shot her. You know, and it coulda been just over. We coulda just taken her life. But they went farther than that.

This young woman described the gang rape she witnessed as "the most brutal thing I've ever seen in my life." While the gang rape itself was an unusual event, it remained a specifically gendered act that could take place precisely because young women were not perceived as equals. Had the victim been an "equal," the attack would have remained a physical one. As the interviewee herself noted, "We coulda just shot her." Instead, the young men who gang-raped the girl were not just enacting revenge on a rival but on a young woman who had dared to treat a young man in this way. The issue is not the question of which is worse—to be shot and killed, or gang-raped and left for dead. Rather, this particular act sheds light on how gender may function to structure victimization risk within gangs.

DISCUSSION

Gender dynamics in mixed-gender gangs are complex and thus may have multiple and contradictory effects on young women's risk of victimization and repeat victimization. My findings suggest that participation in the delinquent lifestyles associated with gangs clearly places young women at risk for victimization. The act of joining a gang involves the initiate's submission to victimization at the hands of her gang peers. In addition, the rules governing gang members' activities place them in situations in which they are vulnerable to assaults that are specifically gang-related. Many acts of violence that girls described would not have occurred had they not been in gangs.

It seems, though, that young women in gangs believed they have traded unknown risks for known ones—that victimization at the hands of friends, or at least under specified conditions, was an alternative preferable to the potential of random, unknown victimization by strangers. Moreover, the gang offered both a semblance of protection from others on the streets, especially young men, and a means of achieving retaliation when victimization did occur.

Lauritsen and Davis Quinet (1995) suggest that both individual-specific heterogeneity (unchanging attributes of individuals that contribute to a propensity for victimization, such as physical size or temperament) and state-dependent factors (factors that can alter individuals' victimization risks over time, such as labeling or behavior changes that are a consequence of victimization) are related to youths' victimization and repeat victimization risk. My findings here suggest that, within gangs, gender can function in both capacities to shape girls' risks of victimization.

Girls' gender, as an individual attribute, can function to lessen their exposure to victimization risk by defining them as inappropriate targets of rival male gang members' assaults. The young women I interviewed repeatedly commented that young men were typically not as violent in their routine confrontations with rival young women as with rival young men. On the other hand, when young women are targets of serious assault, they may face brutality that is particularly harsh and sexual in nature because they are female—thus, particular types of assault, such as rape, are deemed more appropriate when young women are the victims.

Gender can also function as a state-dependent factor, because constructions of gender and the enactment of gender identities are fluid. On the one hand, young women can call upon gender as a means of avoiding exposure to activities they find risky, threatening, or morally troubling. Doing so does not expose them to the sanctions likely faced by male gang members who attempt to avoid participation in violence. Although these choices may insulate young women from the risk of assault at the hands of rival gang members, perceptions of female gang members—and of women in general—as weak may contribute to more routinized victimization at the hands of the male members of their gangs. Moreover, sexual exploitation in the form of "sexing in" as an initiation ritual may define young women as sexually available, contributing to a likelihood of repeat victimization unless the young woman can stand up for herself and fight to gain other members' respect.

Finally, given constructions of gender that define young women as nonthreatening, when young women do pose a threat to male gang members, the sanctions they face may be particularly harsh because they not only have caused harm to rival gang members but also have crossed appropriate gender boundaries in doing so. In sum, my findings suggest that gender may function to insulate young women from some types of physical assault and lessen their exposure to risks from rival gang members, but may also make them vulnerable to particular types of violence, including routine victimization by their male peers, sexual exploitation, and sexual assault.

REFERENCES

Bjerregaard, B., & Smith, C. (1993). Gender differences in gang participation, delinquency, and substance use. *Journal of Quantitative Criminology, 4*, 329–355.

Bowker, L. H., Gross, H. S., & Klein, M. W. (1980). Female participation in delinquent gang activities. *Adolescence, 15*, 509–519.

Campbell, A. (1984). *The girls in the gang*. New York: Basil Blackwell.

———. (1990). Female participation in gangs. In C. R. Huff (Ed.), *Gangs in America* (pp. 163–182). Beverly Hills, CA: Sage.

Chesney-Lind, M. (1993). Girls, gangs and violence: Anatomy of a backlash. *Humanity & Society, 17*, 321–344.

Decker, S. H. (1996). Collective and normative features of gang violence. *Justice Quarterly, 13*, 243–264.

Esbensen, F.-A. (1996). Comments presented at the National Institute of Justice/Office of Juvenile Justice and Delinquency Prevention Cluster Meetings, June, Dallas, TX.

Fagan J.E. (1990). "Contributions to delinquency and substance abuse to school dropout among inner-city youth," Youth and Society.

———. (1996). Gangs, drugs, and neighborhood change. In C. R. Hulf (Ed.), *Gangs in America* 2nd ed.). Thousand Oaks, CA: Sage Publications, 39–74.

Joe, K. A., & Chesney-Lind, M. (1995). Just every mother's angel: An analysis of gender and ethnic variations in youth gang membership. *Gender & Society, 9*, 408–430.

Lauderback, D., Hansen, J., & Waldorf, D. (1992). "Sisters are doin' it for themselves": A black female gang in San Francisco. *Gang Journal, 1*(1): 57–70.

Lauritsen, J. L., & Davis Quinet, K. F. (1995). Repeat victimization among adolescents and young adults. *Journal of Quantitative Criminology, 1*, 143–166.

Moore, J. (1991). *Going down to the barrio: Home-boys and homegirls in change*. Philadelphia: Temple University Press.

Spergel, I. A., & Curry, G. D. (1993). The National Youth Gang Survey: A research and development process. In A. P. Goldstein & C. R. Huff (Eds.), *The gang intervention handbook* (pp. 359–400). Champaign, IL: Research Press.

Taylor, C. (1990). *Dangerous society*. East Lansing, MI: Michigan State University Press.

Taylor, R.B. (1993). "Ecological assessments to community disorder; Their relationships to fear of crime and theoretical implications." American Journal of Community Psychology.

Winfree, L. T., Jr., Fuller, K., Vigil, T., & Mays, G. L. (1992). The definition and measurement of "gang status": Policy implications for juvenile justice. *Juvenile and Family Court Journal, 43*, 29–37.

⤳

CHAPTER 20

Voices from the Barrio: Chicano/a Gangs, Families, and Communities

Marjorie S. Zatz & Edwardo L. Portillos

Based on in-depth interviews with 33 youth gang members and 20 adult neigh-borhood leaders and youth service providers, we explore the complicated relation-ships among gang members, their families, and other residents of poor Chicano/a and Mexicano/a barrios in Phoenix. Listening to the multiple voices of community member allows the development of a multifaceted understanding of the complexi-ties and contradictions of gang life, both for the youths and for the larger com-munity. We draw on a community ecology approach help explain the tension that develop, especially when community member vary in their desires and abilities to control gang-related activities. In this exploratory study, we point to some of the ways in which gender, age, education, traditionalism, and level of acculturation may help explain variation in the type and strength of private, parochial, and pub-lic social control within a community.

Criminologists have long been fascinated with the problems posed by youth gangs. In recent years, community ecology approaches to gang-related crime and social control have become popular. One strand of research has focused on macrosocial patterns of crime and inequality among the urban underclass (e.g., Sampson & Laub, 1993; Sampson & Wilson, 1996; Wilson, 1987). A second strand had examined the "dual frustrations" facing inner-city parents who fear both gang- and drug-related crime *and* police harassment of young men of color (Meares, 1997, p. 140; see also Anderson, 1990; Madriz, 1997). These concerns converge in research that examines the connections between and among the structural causes and community-level effects of economic deprivation, institutional and

Source: Adapted from Zatz, M. S., & Portillos, E. L. (2000). Voices from the barrio: Chicano/a gangs, families, and communities. *Criminology 38*(2), 369–402. Used with permission of the authors and the publisher.

personal networks within a community, the capacity of local networks to garner human and economic resources from outside the community, and gang-related crime (Anderson, 1990; Bursik & Grasmick, 1993a; Bursik & Grasmick, 1993b; Hagedorn, 1998; Moore, 19991; Spergel, 1986; Sullivan, 1989). Bursik & Grasmick (1993a) take this approach farthest theoretically, incorporating Hunter's (1985) three tiers of local community social control into reformulation of Shaw and McKay's (1942) social disorganization framework. Their theory of community relations recognizes the relevance of long-term economic deprivation and institutional racism for community-based social control at the private, parochial, and public levels.

Bursik and Grasmick suggest that traditional social disorganization theory, sometimes in combination with subcultural theories, placed an emphasis on the private level of systemic control, as reflected in family and friendship dynamics. In underclass neighborhoods characterized by stable, high levels of delinquency, however, parochial (e.g., churches and schools) and public (eg., police) forms of social control become more apparent. A few researchers, most notably Hagedorn (1998) and Decker and Van Winkle (1996), have applied Bursik and Grasmick's theory to inner-city gang research. Yet, these studies have been limited to midwestern cities. We also draw on this theory of community social control, but focus our research in a Chicano/a and Mexicano/a community in the southwest.[1] As we will demonstrate, our research site reflects a pocket of poverty in the midst of an almost unprecedented economic boom. Also, the community is close to the Mexican border, allowing perhaps for a greater range of traditionalism than might be found in midwestern cities.

Informed by the gang studies noted above and by other scholarship on the urban poor (e.g., Hernández, 1990; Moore & Pinderhughes,1993; Wilson, 1996), we see gang members as integral parts of their communities, engaging in some actions that hurt the community and in some that help it. At the same time, we are particularly attentive to the ways in which gender, age, educational status, and degree of traditionalism differentiate the adults' perceptions of the gangs and choice of private, parochial, or public forms of social control....

THEORETICAL FRAMEWORK: A SYSTEMIC APPROACH TO NEIGHBORHOOD AND GANG DYNAMICS

Most gang research in the United States has been grounded in social disorganization theory, subcultural theories, or, most recently, economic marginalization theories derived from Wilson's (1987) work on the underclass. Bursik and Grasmik (1993a) offer a theoretical framework that combines key elements of Shaw and McKay's (1942) social disorganization theory with resent work on gangs in underclass communities. The central problem with social disorganization theory for gang research, they suggest, is that it overemphasizes family dynamics, focusing on individualized resources and constraints to the exclusion of larger structural concerns. Accordingly, social disorganization approaches cannot adequately account for ongoing patterns of gang behavior in stable neighborhoods where families may live in same house or on the same block for many years, often spanning several generations. The gangs in these neighborhoods are often multigenerational, with several members of the extended family belonging to the gang in each generation.

Although initially subcultural theories became popular because of the inability of traditional social disorganization approaches to explain these multigenerational gangs, Moore (1978; 1985; 1991; 1998), Vigil (1988), Hagedorn (1991; 1998), and Sullivan (1989), among others, have offered an alternative explanation that refocuses attention at structural factors, including, especially, the economic marginalization of underclass communities. These scholars point to the crucial importance of whether, and to what extent, residents of poor but stable neighborhoods have access to public resources. Bursik and Grasmick (1993a) weave these concerns into a larger, more encompassing framework that examines access to private, public, and parochial resources. Drawing from Hunter's (1985) typology of local community social control, they suggest that these three dimensions operate simultaneously and that gang activity is most likely to emerge "in areas in which the networks of parochial and public control cannot effectively provide services to the neighborhood" (Bursik and Grasmick 1993a, p. 141).

Private social control refers to the influences and actions of family and close friends, which could be the nuclear family, the extended family, or the interwoven networks of family and friends that characterize stable barrio communities. Through the family's actions supporting or disdaining particular behaviors, social control is exerted. Parochial social control reflects "the effects of the broader local interpersonal network and the interlocking of local institutions, such as stores, schools, churches and voluntary organizations" (Bursik and Grasmick, 1993a, p. 17). Control is exerted through residents supervising activities within the neighborhood and the integration of local institutions into many aspects of everyday life. Individuals and neighborhoods will vary in the extent to which they can harness parochial forms of social control. For example, monolingual Spanish-speaking parents may encounter difficulties and be easily intimidated when they try to communicate with their children's teachers or school authorities. Public social control, in turn, focuses on the ability of the community to secure public goods and services that are allocated by agencies located outside the neighborhood" (Bursik and Grasmick, 1993a, p. 17). As Moore and Hagedorn have noted most pointedly, poor barrio communities often do not have access to or alliances with key urban institutions. For instance, although many barrio residents must interact regularly with health care, education, welfare, criminal justice, and immigration authorities, they do so from a position of little or no individual or institutional power. The absence of people who might serve as power brokers, interceding between community residents and institutional authorities, means that residents of economically marginal communities cannot effectively use public systemic control. One example that surfaced often in our interviews was access to police. Although many residents perceived the police to be omnipresent, the same residents complained that the police did not respond quickly when they called for help.

Combining these three forms of social control into a fully systemic model enables a more complete understanding of gang–community dynamics. Following Bursik and Grasmick (1993a), we apply this model to Chicano/a and Mexicano/a gangs in Phoenix. We draw from interviews with gang youths and with adults active in the communities to explore how they perceive gang–neighborhood dynamics. One of the unique contributions of our research to this theoretical agenda is our recognition that access to parochial and public resources is very much gendered. Moreover, as we shall show, recent immigrants and parents with more traditional Mexicano beliefs and values may be more intimidated by key societal institutions and by their children. Thus, we suggest that gender and traditionalism cross-cut age, educational level, and income to influence the extent to which individual parents and neighborhoods can draw on private, parochial, and public social control....

ADULT PERSPECTIVES ON GANGS AND THE COMMUNITY

The adults expressed a wide range of views, from seeing gangs as a normal part of adolescence to viewing them as social parasites that must be routed from the neighborhoods. This contrast is not surprising, given the heterogeneity of life experiences among barrio residents. Jankowski (1991), Moore (1991), Hagedorn (1998), Decker and Van Winkle (1996), Sullivan (1989), Padilla (1993), and Venkatesh (1996) also report contradictory or ambivalent stances toward gangs in the communities they studied. In the discussion that follows, we attempt to tease out these different perspectives and to account for some of the divergent opinions.

Gangs, the Neighborhood, and the Local Economy

According to a neighborhood specialist for the city, the major problems that surfaced in a survey of South Phoenix residents were crime, homes and landscaping not being well maintained, graffiti, and a shortage of streetlights, followed by the lack of recreational opportunities for young people. Similarly, community leaders repeatedly voiced the fear that graffiti, combined with the threat of drugs and violence, contributes to urban decay by making the neighborhood less attractive to businesses.[2] Yet, gang activity is only one factor affecting the local economy and can as easily be seen as an outcome of economic dislocation as its cause. The weak linkages to centers of economic and political power, in turn, reduce residents' abilities to exercise public systemic control very effectively (Bursik and Grasmick, 1993a, p. 146; Moore, 1985; Moore & Pinderhughes, 1993). It is in precisely such contexts that Bursik and Grasmick suggest gang activity is most likely to develop.

One of the most important and visible forms of public social control is the police. Although a substantial portion of the community is very willing to work with local police in at least some limited ways to eradicate gangs and crime, another portion sees the police, courts, and similar institutions as unable or unwilling to adequately protect them. Tensions between Latino community members and the police have historically been high, the result of years of institutionalized racism in police and court processing (Escobar, 1999; Mirandé, 1987; National Minority Advisory Council on Criminal Justice, 1980; U.S. Commission on Civil Rights, 1970; Vigil, 1988). Allegations of police use of excessive force often lie at the heart of these strained relations....

Access to public social control goes beyond policing to encompass the range of agencies and actors who can provide public goods and services. The South Phoenix community did not perceive itself as well situated with regard to such access. Respondents criticized state and local politicians and other city officials for reducing the community's resource base and for placing it low on the priority list for revitalization, and businesses for taking money from the community but not investing in it....

Some neighborhood residents work directly with the youths to curtail gang activities. Exercising both private and parochial social control, some residents tutor neighborhood teens with their studies and help them to find jobs; other residents work with voluntary organizations and local churches, organizing block watches to prevent violence, burglaries, graffiti, and drug sales in the neighborhood....

In the past, our respondents noted, "Mexican gangs were tied closely to the community. This has changed." Today, gangs "rob people of their sense of security. They barricade themselves in their homes because they feel so vulnerable." Another adult respondent told us:

> If a gang is neighborhood based, they protect their neighborhoods and one another, and to the extent they can, their families and the families of other gang members. But that doesn't always work.

These quotes reinforce one of the central contradictions inherent in neighborhood gangs. The youths see themselves as protectors of their communities and the police as abusive interlopers, regardless of whether this imagery appears exaggerated to outsiders. The protection gangs offer may be reduced today to simply making sure that competing gangs do not gain a foothold in the neighborhood, but the youths are adamant that protection of the community is still one of their primary responsibilities. In this sense, they are an integral component of parochial social control. Nevertheless, gangs also wreak havoc in their communities, both by their actions and by the lure they present to rival gangs. In particular, neighborhood residents are at greater risk of injury today than they were a generation ago because of the increase in drive-by shootings. A youth service provider expressed the views of many adults:

> A lot of innocent people get hurt in drive-bys. They're just there in the wrong place at the wrong time and get killed or shot when they don't have anything to do with the problem.

Similarly, a Chicano social worker commented:

> Neighbors feel they can't go out at night, can't sit on the porch. There's violence and crime. Many gang members may hang out in the neighborhood and not be involved in violence, but they're targets. Somebody will drive by and verbally abuse them, throw things in their yard, or shoot them.

Thus, two different, though interrelated, perspectives surface within the community. Some residents blame the gangs, seeing "the stigma of having gang problems" as contributing to businesses and middle-class families leaving the neighborhood. Other residents focus on the city's and the media's willingness to ignore economic problems in parts of town where poor people of color live. When city officials and reporters do pay attention to the area, they focus only on the negative aspects of life them, without doing much to improve the infrastructure. To better understand these varied perspectives, we looked for structural patterns in the data. As we will demonstrate, much of the variation can be explained by gender, age, number of generations in the United States, educational level, traditionalism, and the extent to which the person's family is gang identified.

THE MEN'S VOICES

We asked all of the adult respondents to tell us not only their own opinions about the relationships among gang kids, their families, and the community, but also how they thought other adults in the community perceived these issues. We expected men and women to differ somewhat in their views, consistent with the extant literature on fear of crime and neighborhood-based crime control efforts (Bursik & Grasmick, 1993a, p. 91; Madriz, 1997; Skogan & Maxfield, 1981). Considering first how men in South Phoenix viewed gangs, the neighborhood activists and service providers saw men's opinions as determined primarily by whether they are gang identified. For example, one woman observed:

> Fathers don't have a big problem with gangs. They were involved in one way or another when they were younger. They always had a homie-type camaraderie.

Other respondents tied acceptance of gangs to prison life, and pointed to the difficulty of private, familial social control of youths with incarcerated parents. From this perspective,

> [some men] are accepting of [gangs] and are in prison gangs themselves. We have a gang problem because the adult male population is in prison, so the kids are in street gangs.

Regardless of whether they ever formally joined gangs themselves, adults whose families belong to multigenerational gangs appear to be more accepting of their children's involvement in them, may gain prestige from their children's acts, and see the gang as a barrio institution through which cultural norms of personal and family honor are played out. This finding is consistent with similar research in other cities (Harris, 1994; Horowitz, 1983; Horowitz & Schwartz, 1974; Moore, 1978; Moore, 1991; Padilla, 1993; Vigil, 1988). A neighborhood specialist for the city said:

> It's multigenerational. The grandfather may have been in a gang. Grandfathers of 40 could still have ties with the gang. You could have a great-grandfather with ties to old gangs!

As they get older, the men ease out of gang life. Yet, as a Latina director of a youth service center commented:

> The oldsters, old gangsters, sit back and watch what's happening. They are very aware. They are learning they have to pull away if they want to live, but those are strong friendships that last forever.

An African-American male police officer expressed a similar opinion:

> In areas with multi-generational gangs, it is difficult for older males to understand why society comes down so hard on the young ones. The degree of criminal activity has not hit them upside the head until they lose a loved one to a shooting. . . . If the men get a reality slap, they see the differences over time. Or they'll say to the kids, "Why don't you have a gang like we had? We had a good gang."

Yet, some differences of opinion surface among the men. The neighborhood specialist quoted above continued:

> Some men view the gangs with disdain, seeing them as a blight on the community and a threat to community life, and others feel it provides a sense of fraternity, an opportunity to become involved with others who think and act like they'd like to; it provides them with an outlet.

An African-American woman working closely with neighborhood residents drew similar distinctions:

> Some of them are from multigenerational gang families. The parents are hardcore members supportive of the life, and they're raising their kids in it. Others are very hardcore in opposition to it, saying to make prisons tougher. They are harder, more judgmental, saying, "If you do the crime, do the time." . . . They say, "I'm gonna stop it by buying a .45 and blowing away the first motherfucker who comes in my door."

Thus, for some adult men in the community, gangs are perfectly normal, acceptable parts of life. They take pride in their children following in their footsteps. Other adult men abhor today's gangs. Key factors accounting for these differences of opinion include the extent to which the men hold traditional Mexican values, the length of time they have spent in the United States, and educational achievements. . . .

According to the adults we interviewed, men born in Mexico generally hold the most traditional values and tend to disapprove of the gang life. Yet, they are stymied by their inability to control their children or grandchildren, and if public resources exist that they might employ to better control the youths, these immigrant men do not know how to access them. They are also uncomfortable requesting help from parish priests, school teachers, or social workers. The women, as we shall see, are somewhat more willing to reach out for these parochial forms of social control.

A middle-aged woman directing a neighborhood association providing educational and employment-related services and training for youths noted, "Grandfathers disapprove, see them as lazy and shiftless." A Puerto Rican social worker stated similarly:

> A grandfather will say, "I worked in the fields, why can't you?" Kids killing one another is not readily understood by the more traditional older generation.

Yet, another man working closely with boys in the neighborhood said

> For the *abuelos* (grandfathers), they have a firm grasp of life, they've lived through many tragedies, so they appreciate life and the foolish wasting of it in gangs.

Our data indicate that substantial changes have occurred over time in the perceived extent to which gangs protected the larger community, the dangers to gang members and others in the community posed by today's more lethal weapons, and, generally, the respect with which gang members were and are held by others in the community. We were told:

> The general consensus is gangs are negative. This is especially from grandparents who are used to gangs, from the Zoot Suits. They were respected, they were not a danger to the community. They say, 'I don't understand these punks, why are they doing these things, not taking care of us, of the neighbors. They talk all the time about being part of the neighborhood but they don't take care of us.'
>
> INTERVIEWER: What about the fathers?
>
> When I was a kid we had gangs, but we never used guns. We used chains. When we had a problem and fought, it was one-on-one, or a gang an a gang, but never three, five, six to one. That sounds cowardly to them [the fathers]. This generation gap is a problem. The kids say, "Your way wasn't better, it didn't work. I have more money than you, so how am you tell me it's not right, that your way is better?" This is a big issue. They make money! And they [fathers] can't make money in society.

Another local social worker also reminisced about the "old days" when he was involved in gangs:

> In the past, we weren't out to kill each other. Maybe there'd be fist fights or knives, but we weren't out to kill each other. Guns and drugs are the problem, and they're easily bought on the streets.

Thus, educational level, age, and the recency of their family's immigration to the United States structure barrio men's views about gangs and the range of resources they see as available to them. Grandfathers and fathers who immigrated to the

United States may be leery of public forms of social control, such as the police and the juvenile justice system, and more hesitant than their wives to call on the Catholic Church for aid. They rely most heavily on the extended family to control youths, often unsuccessfully. In contrast, men raised in the gang life and still tied to it are more accepting of their children's involvement. Finally, the men raised in the barrio but now successful in local businesses and social services (eg., proba-tion, clinical psychology) have greater access to political and economic brokers in the metropolitan area and, perhaps for this reason, are more willing to rely on public as well as parochial and private forms of social control. Our data suggest that less variation exists within women's perspectives, with the key distinguishing factor being whether they were raised in a traditional Mexican family, either in the United States or in Mexico.

THE WOMEN'S VOICES

The consensus among our adult respondents was that most women disapprove of gangs. A Puerto Rican male working with families of gang members had the impression that "nine out of 10 mothers despise gangs." Some of the women were members themselves when they were younger and may remain at least periph-erally involved, but as they become mothers many grow increasingly fearful that their children could die in a gang-related shooting.

Gendered cultural expectations of child-rearing responsibilities appear to have contributed to mothers becoming more active than fathers in opposing gang activities. Also, many of the barrio's adult men are incarcerated, or for other rea-sons do not interact much with their children. Neighborhood leaders, both male and female, commented that it is primarily the women who come forward to work with them. One neighborhood activist said:

> [The women] are pretty fed up with it....60% of those who come to community meetings are female. They are very vocal, fed up, afraid to lose their children. Some have already lost their children, or their nephews and nieces, at the hands of guns. They want to bring the neighborhood back under control.

Some of these mothers take a very strong line and "won't let daughters date boys who look like cholos." Neighborhood women are also well represented at funerals. A parish priest with the dubious honor of burying the neighborhood's children told us, "At wakes you will see 400 kids, 50 mothers, an maybe 10 fathers." Mothers Against Gangs, a grassroots organization begun by a mother after her 16-year-old son died in a gang shooting, is a prime example of women organiz-ing to reduce gang violence. Again, we see a link between private and parochial forms of social control. When parents and grandparents are not able to control the youths, they often turn to community organization such as Mothers Against Gangs (see, similarly, Fremon, 1995). Moreover, we see that these examples of pri-vate and parochial social control are very much gendered.

Mothers and grandmothers raised with traditional values were less likely to be out on the streets and so did not themselves live the gang life. These traditional women often do not know what to do about their children's involvement with gangs. As an activist knowledgeable about gangs said of the mothers who moved here from Mexico:

> [They] feel helpless. It's something new for them. Many of them have problems with language. The kids speak English better than they [the mothers] do and better than they speak Spanish, so the parents can't communicate with the kids. It's not like in Mexico, where the *abuelos* can say and do things. Here, it depends on the parents.

Similarly, a Chicano social worker stated that for mothers,

> The general feeling is powerlessness. They have to care for them and love them and wish they weren't involved. They may feel guilty. It must be their fault, what did they do wrong.... It is *very* painful if the girls are in the gangs.

The sense of individual, rather than societal, responsibility for gang violence was stressed by many of our respondents. Specifically, they suggested that young mothers often have inadequate parenting skills. A probation officer raised in the barrio commented:

> These kids intimidated their parents way before this. The hardline mothers and grandmothers who really push their kids to stay out [of gangs] are winning the battle. Those who are afraid, and they're mostly the 18–20 year olds, are afraid because they didn't put their foot down enough. It comes down to parenting skills, taking a hard line.

Social workers and neighborhood activists suggest that some mothers are unwilling to believe that their children are involved in gangs, even when signs are all around them. We were told that traditional women, in particular

> [see gangs as] a danger to the family unit. They don't want their kids involved in it, are very protective. But they also may have blinders when it comes to their own kids, saying, "My kid isn't into that" when he is.

A South Phoenix parish priest related a story about a mother who wanted her son to be buried in a red shirt and the pallbearers to wear red, claiming it was always her son's favorite color. Another mother insisted that her son was not involved with gangs, until the priest turned to the young man and asked him to explain the significance of his red shoelaces to his mother.

In conclusion, then, our data suggest that whether and when adults rely on private, parochial, or public forms of social control depends on their access to economic and political resources and their position within the family and neighborhood power structures. One of our contributions to this literature is to show that this access may also be gendered, with women evidencing more indicators of powerlessness, such as not speaking English, and less experience dealing with businesses, courts, and the like. These women are most likely to advocate for a mix of parochial and public social control. They fear for their children's lives, but they tend to be among the most intimidated by their sons and daughters. Many of these women have organized within their communities and work with the police to at least a limited extent, hoping that these efforts will help to keep their children alive. This combination of private, parochial, and public social control is the premise of groups such as Mothers Against Gangs. In contrast, women who were in gangs as teenagers and who maintained that identity are generally the most accepting, and perhaps the least fearful, of gang violence and the least willing to let the police into their communities. Even these women, however, express fears of losing their children to gang violence and may draw on parochial forms of social control within the community.

The perceptions held by adult service providers and residents may be plagued by faulty, perhaps romanticized, recollections of what gangs were like in earlier generations. Also, many of the adults we interviewed had vested interests in the gang problem. Reliance solely on their perceptions ignores how young people see their own lives and the relationship between their gangs and other community members. Consistent with our emphasis on multiple standpoints, we turn now to the thoughts and concerns of the youths.

YOUTH PERSPECTTVES ON GANGS AND THE COMMUNITY

Historically, gangs have been important neighborhood institutions offering disenchanted, disadvantaged youths a means of coping with the isolation, alienation, and poverty they experience every day (Decker & Van Winkle, 1996, Hagedorn, 1991; Hogedorn, 1998; Horowitz, 1983; Jackson, 1991; Joe & Chesney-Lind, 1995; Moore, 1978; Moore, 1985; Moore, 1991; Padilla, 1993; Sullivan, 1989; Vigil, 1988). Yet, gangs are dynamic, responding to transformations in the larger social order. Sometimes, changes in the social and economic structures also cause cracks in what we call the gang–family–barrio equality. It is not so unusual today to find families living in two different neighborhoods and, thus, often participating in two or more gangs. When this situation occurs, fissures appear in the cement bonding the community's social structure together.

Gangs as Neighborhood Institutions

Regardless of what other neighborhood residents may think of them, the youths identify strongly with their neighborhoods, consider themselves to be integral parts of their barrios, and view their gangs as neighborhood institutions. They see themselves as protectors of their neighborhoods, at least against intrusion by rival gangs. A few youths take pride in their care of elderly residents. However, most youths acknowledge that they do not contribute much to their neighborhoods, excluding community service stipulated as part of their probation or parole agreements.[3] For example, one youth stated:

> We spray paint the walls and stuff like that, stealing cars, shooting people when we do drive-bys and stuff like that.

Moreover, some youths recognize that innocent bystanders are occasionally shot in drive-bys or other revenge killings

> People are getting smoked everyday and you don't even hear about it on the news, only if it is crazy and shit.

Chicano/a gangs often take the name of their barrio as their gang name. With few exceptions, the youths must live in the neighborhood and be of Mexican origin to become a member of the neighborhood gang.[4] These membership requirements hold whether the youth is "born into" the gang or "jumped" in. Some, particularly the young women, are simply "born" into the gang because they live in the neighborhood. They do not need any more formal initiation rites: it is their neighborhood, so it is their gang. If they want to be taken seriously as a gang member, though, being "born" in is not enough. The youths—male and female—must endure a serious beating by a group of their homeboys or homegirls (Portillos, 1999).

Beyond feeling ties to the physical boundaries of the barrio, the youths feel strong emotional ties because neighbors are often family members. If we contextualize the term "family" more broadly to include the nuclear family, the extended family, and the fictive family (*compadres* and *comadres*), gang–family ties become even stronger. All of the youths in our sample claimed that at least one other family member was involved in gangs. For example, a youth informed us:

> I got two aunts that were in a gang, my dad was in a gang, my grandpa was in a gang, and I got a lot of cousins in gang. Most of them are in my barrio but some of them aren't.

Siblings, cousins, and family friends so close as to be considered cousins are frequently members of the same gang, resulting in what often appears to be a gang–family–barrio equality. Although these overlapping social relationships have characterized Chicano/a gangs in the past (Moore, 1991; Vigil, 1988; Zatz, 1987), and in large part continue to define them today, we find that geographic dispersion has altered the tight bonds among the gang, the family. and the barrio.

Communities in Turmoil: Family Fighting Family

Family mobility was another issue that came up frequently in our interviews and provides insights into some of the ways in which public social control and, to a lesser extent, parochial control shape and constrain private forms of social control. Sometimes, families moved because of divorce or job opportunities elsewhere in the valley. Other times, they moved because the parents were so fearful of gang activity in the neighborhood. Children also went to live with grandparents or aunts when their parents were incarcerated. Finally, teenagers unable to get along with their parents sometimes moved in with relatives. An unfortunate and ironic side effect of this mobility is that it may lead to gang rivalries cross-cutting families. That is, if gang warfare erupts between these different neighborhoods, families may literally be caught in the cross-fire. This phenomenon of family fighting family is anathema to more traditional Chicanos/as and Mexicanos/as, challenging existing notions of private, familial social control.[5] A 15-year-old female commented that more than 50 members of her extended family are or were in gangs:

> We can't have family reunions or anything because they are always fighting, like my *tíos* (uncles) fight. At the funerals they fight, or at the park, or at a picnic when we get together, they just fight. So sometimes the family don't get together, only for funerals, that's the only time.

Similarly, a 16-year-old male reported that his dad was mad because

> I am from westside; they are from eastside. See, I was supposed to be from eastside, but I didn't want to be from there. He don't want me to be his son because I'm not from eastside.

For the family that is split across two feuding gangs, cycles of revenge killings are particularly devastating. A 17-year-old male described the conflicts within his family:

> And it's crazy because we are like from different gangs, only me and my cousin are from the same gang. Like my brother, I always disrespect him because he's from Camelback and shit, they did a drive-by on my house and shit, and then he called me. I was like, "Fuck you, motherfucker, fuck your barrio and shit," and he was like, "Don't disrespect," and I was like, "Fuck you." That's the only thing bad about it if you decide to join the wrong gang.[6]

Similarly, a young Mexicano-Indian clarified his relationship with his uncles:

> They are from different gangs, though...but I don't care about them because they be trying to shoot at us all the time. My own uncle shot at me, one of them tried to kill me already, but that's alright.

He explained further that although most members of his family, including brothers, sisters, aunts, uncles, his dad, his mom, his grandfather, and numerous cousins were in the same gang, a few claimed different neighborhoods. He noted rather matter-of-factly:

> I got about two uncles in a gang. I had four of them, but one is dead. My uncles killed him for some reason, I don't know, different barrio maybe....

When family feuds become entwined with gang rivalries, it is clear that the private system of social control has broken down. Family and friendship dynamics are no longer able to keep peace within a community. Under these conditions, parochial and public forms of social control typically come into play....

Not to Die For

Gang members are supposed to be willing to do anything for their homeboys and homegirls, even to die for them. The importance of demonstrating one's "heart," or willingness to be "down" for the gang, is the major reason for jumping in new members and the basis for extolling acts of bravery and craziness (*locura*) by gang members (Portillos et al., 1996). To assess the relative importance of gangs and families as predominant institutions in the youths' lives, Decker and Van Winkle (1996) explicitly asked gang members to choose between their family or the gang. The overwhelming majority, 89%, of the youths chose their families. As Decker and Van Winkle explain their finding, "For most gang members, the gang was a place to find protection, companionship and understanding. Their family, however, represented something deeper, a commitment that most saw as transcending life in the gang" (1996, p. 251). As we have shown, often gang members *are* family members.

Given the assumed importance of gangs and historically close ties among the gang, the family, and the barrio, one of our most interesting findings was that more than half of the youths would *not* willingly die for all of their homeboys and homegirls. About a third were willing to die for specific individuals who were in their gang, but not for everyone. Another third straightforwardly stated that they would not willingly die for their gangs. The reason, they said, was "because I know they wouldn't die for me, they ain't that stupid."

In response to the direct query, "For whom would you willingly die?" all of the youths claimed that they would die for their families. When probed, they named their mothers, their children, their siblings, maybe an aunt or grandmother, and specific friends and relatives. Some of these family members belonged to the gang, but others did not. The distinction between someone who is simply a member of one's gang and someone who is family (including fictive kin) was clarified for us by a 16-year-old male who, a few days previously, had been struck by a bullet that, had he not gotten in the way, would have hit a friend's grandmother. He said, "I will die for my *true* homeboy; he would die for me."

We suggest that affirming one's willingness to die for a friend takes on new meaning when easy access to guns makes death a real possibility. When asked about the bad parts of gang life, "death" was typically the first factor named by both the gang members and adults. Probing indicated that the youths have a very real sense that they could die if they remain in *la vida loca*. In earlier generations of gangs, when death was not so common a feature, it may have been far easier to claim, with plenty of bravado, that one would die for one's gang.

The responses to our question reinforce the gendered nature of gang life. Even though female gang members prided themselves on their fighting skills, none of the young women declared a willingness to die for her gang. A few confessed that they might have done so when they were younger, but their tone suggested that this was a phase they had outgrown. These gendered responses are consistent with the general findings in the literature of lower rates of violence and lesser acceptance of violence among females than males (Chesney-Lind & Sheldon, 1998; Curry, 1998; Joe & Chesney-Lind, 1995), but they may also reflect the greater relevance of the family and private social control for young women than for young men.

It is difficult to determine at this point whether we are simply seeing an aging or maturation effect, in which as youths become older and perhaps leave the gang life behind, they see the gang in less romantic terms. They may be maturing into a more adult way of taking care of the barrio, which as we have maintained *is* their extended family, or we may be seeing evidence of a crack in the gang–family–barrio equality.

Of particular interest to our thesis, we suggest that the apparent contradiction between intrafamily fighting and a willingness to die only for one's family may be explained by a more careful analysis of variation in the forms that private social control may take. That is, family fighting family suggests a *reduction* in the amount of private social control, but when youths report that they would die for their families, but not for their gangs (excepting gang members who are family or close family friends), this indicates that the family remains a potent force in their lives. Thus, we do not see a complete breakdown in private social control, but rather what appear to be some changes in the form that private social control takes as we move from more traditional families to more acculturated families. When we add economic stresses and political disenfranchisement, we also see few opportunities for courting public social control on the community's terms. In the section that follows, we return to our earlier theme of economic and political dislocations and what these imply for local youths.

Gangs, Multiple Marginalities, and Urban Dislocations

The final theme that emerged from interviews with the youths brings us back to Vigil's concept of multiple marginalities and urban dislocations. The immediate world within which these youths live is marked by poverty, racial discrimination, cultural misunderstandings, and gendered expectations. As one young man stated, "We are a bunch of project kids, always on the move."

All of the youths in our sample were either kicked out or dropped out of school, and many had not completed ninth grade. This lack of education makes it exceedingly difficult to leave their marginal positions in the inner city and the gang life in their neighborhoods behind (see, similarly, Anderson, 1990; Padilla, 1993; Spergel, 1986). They spoke at length about problems they faced in school. For example:

> I use to go to Lincoln Middle School. The teachers, fuckin' white teachers. The gym teacher, you know just because I was messin' around, threw me up against the locker and I reported him. And nobody said shit about it. I told them, "fuck that, I ain't coming to this school no more," and they didn't even call the damn police. When they did call the police, they said they were going to take me to jail. So I just took off, I was like what the fuck, the motherfucker, he was the one pushing me.

It is interesting to note that the only times when the youths spoke about what we might call parochial and public forms of social control, it was to complain about them. As the above quote indicates, teachers were not viewed as a resource by most of these youths, but rather as authority figures who reinforced their daily experiences of racism, marginality, and alienation. Moreover, their sense was that the police regularly sided with the teachers, rather than protecting the youths against what they perceived to be assaults and other forms of aggression on the part of the teachers.

The teens we interviewed are cognizant of the barriers confronting them. They recognize that their criminal and academic records make it almost impossible for them to move up the socioeconomic ladder. Yet, they still hold very mainstream aspirations. They see themselves as settling down to life with a steady partner or spouse and children, and they hope to be able to find a decent job. They want to become jet pilots, police officers, and firefighters, and they aim someday to purchase their own homes. For example, a young man expressed high hopes for his future but recognized the sad reality of life in the barrio:

> I want to become an Air Force pilot, that wouldn't be a bad thing to be. The only fucked up thing is that I can't become a pilot because I have already been convicted of a felony in adult court.

Thus, although these youths may aspire to very mainstream futures, they recognize that poor schooling, inadequate job training, felony records, and racial/ethnic discrimination limit their potential for success.

CONCLUSIONS

In closing, we must stress that ours is an exploratory study, and our conclusions are based on only 53 interviews. Also, we did not set out to test Bursik and Grasmick's thesis; thus, our study does not constitute a full test of their model. We found, however, that attention to private, parochial, and public social control helped us to better understand the complexities of the relationship between gang members and other community residents.

We urge further research examining the perspectives of adults living and working with the youths. They know a lot about the youths' lives. Some adults are very sad and jaded, having watched their own children die in gang-related incidents. Other adults remain hopeful of making small changes in their worlds, with or without the help of police, business leaders, or politicians. Many adults are themselves former gang members and can shed light on historical shifts in the relationship between the gang, the family, and the neighborhood. Their insights, we suggest, should be incorporated into future studies of neighborhood-based gangs.

In conclusion, our study contributes to the growing body of research on gangs as situated socially and politically within poor urban communities of color. Like many other gang researchers (e.g., Curry & Decker, 1998; Curry & Spergel, 1988; Decker & Van Winkle, 1996; Hagedorn, 1991; Hagedorn, 1998; Horowitz, 1983; Horowitz, 1987; Jankowski, 1991; Joe & Chesney-Lind, 1995; Klein, 1995; Moore, 1978; Moore, 1985; Moore, 1991; Padilla, 1993; Vigil, 1988), we assert that the social, economic, and political contexts within which gang life is set help to explain the complex and often contentious relations among gang members, their families, and the larger communities of which they form a part.

The gang was, and is, composed of brothers, sisters, cousins, and neighbors. The gang gives them a sense of community, a place where they belong. Kicked out of school, assumed to be troublemakers, looking tough and feeling scared, these young people are well aware that their options in life are very much constrained by poverty, racial discrimination, cultural stereotyping, and inadequate education.

Within this context, we suggest that Bursik and Grasmick's (1993a) theory of neighborhood dynamics helps explain the complex and often contradictory relations among the gang, the family, and the barrio. Their attention to private, parochial, and public levels of community-based social control are evident in the barrio we studied, and they point further to the difficulties facing community residents when they try to garner political and economic resources from outside their communities. It is, perhaps, to these political and economic linkages and disconnections that gang researchers and others concerned with crime in poor urban communities should look next.

NOTES

1. For purposes of this paper, Chicano/a refers to men (Chicano) and women (Chicana) of Mexican descent living in the United States. Mexicano/a refers to men (Mexicano) and women (Mexicana) who were born in Mexico. While the Mexicano and Mexicana youths must be living in the United States to become part of our sample, they may not be U.S. citizens or permanent residents.

2. Neighborhood vehemence against gangs defacing the community was highlighted in October of 1995, while we were conducting our field work. More than 40 angry residents appeared at a juvenile court hearing, hoping to convince the judge that two 16-year-olds should be prosecuted in adult court. The youths had gone on a rampage, spraypainting 32 houses and some caw (Whiting, 1995).

3. Members of the gangs we studied sell drugs, steal cars, and commit other crimes as both individual and gang-related activities. Unlike the gangs discussed by Padilla (1993) and Jankowski (1991), however, these gangs are not organized as criminal enterprises.

4. The major exception is a predominantly Mexicano gang that accepts some white youths as members.

5. The theme of intergang conflicts within families arose during the course of our interviews with the youths. Because interviews with adults were taking place at the same time, we were not able to systematically ask the adults for their perceptions of how extensive this problem had become. We did, however, ask samples of probation officers and juvenile court judges whom we later interviewed for a related project to discuss this issue, and we incorporate their views here.

6. Pseudonyms are used in place of individual and gang names throughout this analysts. Street names have also been changed so as not to identify particular neighborhoods.

REFERENCES

Anderson, E. (1990). *Street wise*. Chicago, IL: University of Chicago Press.

Bursik, R. J., Jr., & Grasmick, H. G. (1993a). *Neighborhoods and crime: The dimensions of effective community control*. New York: Lexington.

———. (1993b). Economic deprivation and neighborhood crime rates, 1960–1980. *Law and Society Review, 27*(2), 263–283.

Chesney-Lind, M., & Sheldon, R. G. (1998). *Girls, delinquency, and juvenile justice* (2nd ed.). Belmont, CA: Wadsworth.

Curry, G. D. (1998). Female gang involvement. *Journal of Research in Crime and Delinquency, 35*(1), 100–118.

Curry, G. D., & Decker, S. H. (1998). *Confronting gangs: Crime and community.* Los Angeles: Roxbury.

Curry, G. D., & Spergel, I. A. (1988). Gang homicide, delinquency, and community. *Crimonology, 26,* 381–405.

Decker, S. H., & Van Winkle, B. (1996). *Life in the gang: Family, friends, and violence.* New York: Cambridge University Press.

Escobar, E. J. (1999). *Race, police, and the making of a political identity: Mexican Americans and the Los Angeles Police Department, 1900–1945.* Berkeley: University of California Press.

Fremon, C. (1995). *Father Greg and the homeboys.* New York: Hyperion.

Hagedorn, J. M. (1991). Gangs, neighborhoods, and public policy. *Social Policy, 38*(4), 529–542.

———. (1998). *People and folks: Gangs, crime and the underclass in a Rustbelt city* (2nd ed.). Chicago: Lake View.

Harris, M. G. (1994). Cholas, Mexican-American girls, and gangs. *Sex Roles, 30*(3/4), 289–301.

Hernández, J. (1990). Latino alternatives to the underclass concept. *Latino Studies Journal, 1,* 95–105.

Horowitz, R. (1983). *Honor and the American dream.* New Brunswick, NJ: Rutgers University Press.

———. (1987). Community tolerance of gang violence. *Social Problems, 34,* 437–450.

Horowitz, R., & Schwartz, G. (1974). Honor, normative ambiguity and gang violence. *American Sociological Review, 39,* 238–251.

Hunter, A. J. (1985). Private, parochial and public school orders: The problem of crime and incivility in urban communities. In G. D. Suttles & M. N. Zald (Eds.), *The challenge of social control: Citizenship and institution building in modern society.* Norwood, NJ: Ablex.

Jackson, P. I. (1991). "Crime, youth gangs and urban transition: The social dislocations of postindustrial economic development." Justice Quarterly, 8: 379–398.

Jankowski, M. S. (1991). *Islands in the street: Gangs and American urban society.* Berkeley: University of California Press.

Joe, K., & Chesney-Lind, M. (1995). Just every mother's angel: An analysis of gender and ethnic variation in youth gang membership. *Gender and Society, 9,* 408–40.

Klein, M.W. (1995). The American Street gang: Its nature, Prevalence and Control. Oxford University Press.

Madriz, E. (1997). *Nothing bad happens to good girls: Fear of crime in women's lives.* Berkeley: University of California Press.

Meares, T. L. (1997). Charting race and class differences in attitudes toward drug legalization and law enforcement: Lessons for federal criminal law. *Buffalo Criminal Law Review, 1,* 137–174.

Mirandé, A. (1987). *Gringo justice.* South Bend, IN: Notre Dame Press.

Moore, J. W. (1978). *Homeboys: Gangs, drugs, and prison in the barrios of Los Angeles.* Philadelphia: Temple University Press.

———. (1985). Isolation and stigmatization in the development of an underclass: The case of Chicano gangs in East Los Angeles. *Social Problems, 33,* 1–10.

———. (1991). *Going down to the barrio: Homeboys and homegirls in change.* Philadelphia: Temple University Press.

———. (1998). Gangs and the underclass: A comparative perspective. In J. Hagedorn (Ed.), *People and folks* (2nd ed.). Chicago: Lake View. Introduction.

Moore, J. W., & Pinderhughes, R. (Eds). (1993). *In the barrios: Latinos and the underclass debate.* New York: Russell Sage.

National Minority Advisory Council on Criminal Justice. (1980). *The inequality of justice.* Washington, DC: U.S. Department of Justice.

Padilla, F. (1993). *The gang as an American enterprise.* New Brunswick, NJ: Rutgers University Press.

Portillos, E. L. (1999) Women, men and gangs: The social construction of gender in the barrio. In M. Lind and J. Hagedorn (eds.), Female Gangs in America: Girls, Gangs and Gender. Chicago , Ill. : Lake View Press.

Portillos, E. L.;N. C. Jurik, and M. S. Zatz. (1996). "Machismo and Chicano/a gangs: Symbolic resistance or oppression" Free Inquiry in Creative Sociology 24(2):175–183.

Sampson, R. J., & J. H. Laub. (1993). Structural variations in juvenile court processing: Inequality, the underclass, and social control. *Law and Society Review, 27*(2), 285–311.

Sampson, R. J., & W. J. Wilson. (1996). Toward a theory of race, crime and urban inequality. In J. Hagan & R. D. Peterson (Eds.), *Crime and inequality.* Stanford: Stanford University Press.

Shaw, C. R., & McKay, H. D. (1942). *Juvenile delinquency and urban areas.* Chicago: University of Chicago Press.

Skogan, W. G., & Maxfield, M. G. (1981). *Coping with crime: Individual and neighborhood reactions.* Beverly Hills, CA: Sage.

Spergel, I. A. (1986). The violent gang problem in Chicago: A local community approach. *Social Service Review, 60,* 94–131.

Sullivan, M. (1989). "Getting paid": Youth crime and work in the inner city. Ithaca, NY: Cornell University Press.

U.S. Commission on Civil Rights. (1970). *Mexican Americans and the administration of justice in the Southwest.* Washington, DC: U.S. Government Printing Office.

Venkatesh, S. A. (1996). The gang in the community. In R. C. Huff (Ed.), *Gangs in America* (2nd ed.). Beverly Hills, CA: Sage.

Vigil, J. D. (1988). *Barrio gangs: Street life and identity in southern California.* Austin: University of Texas Press.

Whiting, Brent (1995). Adult justice sought for two teen-age "taggers". *Arizona Republic.* Oct. 19: B1–B6.

Wilson, W. J. (1987). *The truly disadvantaged.* Chicago: University of Chicago Press.

———. (1996). *When work disappears: The world of the new urban poor.* New York: Random House.

Zatz, M. S. (1987). Chicano youth gangs and crime: The creation of a moral people. *Contemporary Crises, 11,* 129–158.

SECTION VIII

⚹

Drugs and Crime

One of the most enduring controversies in criminology is that surrounding the relationship between drugs and crime. Although no one disputes the correlation between drugs and crime, the issue of causation is controversial. Do drugs cause crime, or are they related in some other manner? For some time, the drugs–crime hypothesis has captured the attention of criminologists. There are some data indicating that offenders who commit property crimes (burglary and theft) are more likely to commit these crimes in order to get money to buy drugs. The Bureau of Justice Statistics (BJS) reports that about a quarter of convicted property offenders incarcerated in local jails committed their crimes to get money for drugs, compared to only 5% of violent and public order offenders. The Bureau also reports that the pattern among state prisoners is very similar (Mumola & Karberg, 2004). Drug dependence among offenders is also alarmingly high. One BJS survey found that 53% of federal inmates and 45% of federal inmates met the criteria for, respectively, drug dependence and abuse (Guerino, Harrison, & Sabol, 2011).

The chapters in this section examine the issue from the perspectives of those who use and sell drugs. These articles illuminate how illicit drug offenders construct and give meaning to their involvement with drugs and its accompanying lifestyle.

In Chapter 21, "The Drugs–Crime Connection among Stable Addicts," Charles E. Faupel considers the role that criminal activity plays in facilitating drug use. This classic study uses ethnographic interviews with a population of stable addicts (seasoned, mature heroin users) and argues that the drug–crime connection is much more complex than the "drugs causes crime" hypothesis of popular currency. Instead, he reports that increased heroin consumption is preceded by increased criminal activity. He further debunks the myth of "crazed drug fiends" by examining the rational processes involved in maintaining a drug habit through criminal activity.

In Chapter 22, Wilson R. Palacios and Melissa E. Fenwick provide a vivid narrative of what it's like to participate in the Ecstasy culture. During a 15-month participant observation study, the authors attended dozens of all-night (and sometimes several days in length) "clublike" parties, observing and asking questions of participants. Their article provides a plethora of thick, rich descriptions of how individuals experience Ecstasy, from the method of ingestion and euphoric effects to the eventual coming down. The chapter serves as an introduction to a continuing study, one of the first of its kind examining contemporary Ecstasy culture in America.

In Chapter 23, " 'Cooks Are Like Gods': Hierarchies among Methamphetamine-Producing Groups," Robert Jenkot takes a behind-the-scenes look at female methamphetamine users, dealers, and producers. The author interviewed 31 incarcerated women about their experiences with methamphetamine. He focused on the experiences of methamphetamine producers, or "cooks," as they are referred to in the illicit trade. This study offers insight into the hierarchies of the methamphetamine trade.

In Chapter 24, the final chapter of this section, "Trafficking in Bodily Perfection: Examining the Late-Modern Steroid Marketplace and Its Criminalization," Peter B. Kraska, Charles R. Bussard, and J. John Brent take a provocative look at illicit steroid and human growth hormone culture. Their study fills an important void in the literature. The authors make use of a mixed-methods approach, employing both ethnographic field research and quantitative content analysis of Internet sites that supply material for producing anabolic steroids. Fifteen months of ethnographic field data were gathered in a commercial gym where several nationally known bodybuilders train. These ethnographic data reveal an intricate scheme in which the central informant established an apartment-based manufacturing operation to convert raw steroid chemical compounds ordered off the Internet into injectable solutions. The authors also discovered through content analysis of 186 websites that their ethnographically grounded findings are indicative of a much larger phenomenon. Finally, the authors examine the broader theoretical relevance of the ethnographic findings by contextualizing them within macrostructural (supply) and macrocultural (demand) social forces.

REFERENCES

Guerino, P., Harrison, P. M., & Sabol, W. J. (2011). *Prisoners in 2010* (NCJ 236096). Washington, DC: U.S. Department of Justice, Bureau of Justice Statistics.

Mumola, C. J., & Karberg, J. C. (2004). *Drug use and dependence, state and federal prisoners, 2004* (NCJ 213530). Washington, DC: United States Department of Justice, Bureau of Justice Statistics.

CHAPTER 21

🖈

The Drugs–Crime Connection among Stable Addicts

Charles E. Faupel

In this classic study, Charles E. Faupel examines in detail the lifestyles and career patterns of hard-core heroin addicts and the controversial issue of the relationship between drugs and crime. He also considers the question of whether addict criminals are skilled, rational "professional" criminals or opportunists. This article is drawn from a long-term study of the relationship of drugs to crime. It is based on life history interviews with hard-core heroin addicts in the Wilmington, Delaware, area. Thirty heroin addicts were extensively interviewed for 10 to 25 hours each in sessions lasting from two to four hours. The subjects all had extensive criminal histories and at the time of the interviews, 24 were under correctional supervision (incarcerated, probation, parole, or work release). Women were slightly overrepresented, constituting 12 of the 30 respondents. The sample consisted of 22 blacks and eight whites. Latinos were not represented because there is not a sizeable Latino drug-using population in the area where the research was conducted.

Regarding the drugs–crime nexus, Faupel concludes that drug use does not cause crime, but it may be caused or at least facilitated by crime. His treatment of these issues supports an understanding of the heroin addict as a much more rational being than previously believed.

The complexity of the drugs–crime connection is perhaps most fully apparent during the stable-addict phase. One clear feature is the role that criminal activities play in facilitating drug use. The participants in this study strongly concurred that their level of heroin consumption was a function of their ability to afford it, which was usually enhanced by criminal activity. "The better I got at

Source: Adapted from Faupel, C. E. (1991). *Shooting dope: Career patterns of hard-core heroin users*, pp. 73–86. Gainesville: University of Florida Press. Used with permission of the University of Florida and the author.

crime," remarked Stephanie, "the more money I made; the more money I made, the more drugs I used." She went on to explain,

> I think that most people that get high, the reason it goes to the extent that it goes—that it becomes such a high degree of money—is because they make the money like that. I'm saying if the money wasn't available to them like that, they wouldn't be into drugs as deep as they were.

Contrary to the "drugs cause crime" hypothesis, which suggests that increases in the level of heroin consumption are necessarily followed by stepped-up criminal activity, the dynamics reported by the addicts in this study are quite the opposite: increased heroin consumption is preceded by increased criminal activity as measured by estimated criminal income. This does not necessarily imply a greater frequency of crime, for, as I shall highlight below, stable-addict status usually brings with it greater sophistication in skill and technique, often resulting in higher proceeds per criminal event.

These life history data also reveal, however, that the relationship between drug use and crime is much broader and more complex than simple causality. As I suggested earlier, increased criminal income not only enhances drug availability, but also provides the basis for an expanded life structure, an alternative daily routine. Because these criminal routines usually provide greater flexibility than do most forms of legitimate employment, they free the addict from prohibitive roles and social contacts that may be imposed by more rigid schedules. Drug-using activities are certainly facilitated under these more flexible routines. Nevertheless, criminal routines do impose certain constraints on the addict lifestyle. Moreover, they provide an important structure to one's drug-using activities. It is in this respect that Old Ray likened the routine of dealing drugs to legitimate employment: "When you're working, the world has its rhythm, its time clock. You have your 8-to-5 time clock. Well, it's the same way with dealing drugs." The result is a curious paradox. Criminal activity not only enhances availability, thereby providing for heavier drug consumption, but also places broad limits on the amount of heroin consumed by providing some semblance of structure and routine. There is yet another paradox in the drugs–crime relationship for the stable addict. Although it is true that crime facilitates heroin use, many of the addicts I interviewed indicated that heroin and other drugs played a utilitarian role in their commission of crime as well. Although it is commonly assumed that addicts are most likely to commit crimes when they are sick and desperate for a fix, the addicts in this study reported quite the opposite. The following comments from Joe and Belle highlight the importance of being straight (not experiencing withdrawal) when committing crimes:

> It would be awful hard for me if I was sick to be able to hustle. A lot of times if you're sick you go in and grab stuff. And run without caution. (Joe)
>
> But if I was high it was a different story. I could take my time and get what I wanted. (Joe)
>
> Most people say about drug addicts [that] when they're sick is when they do their most damage. But that's the lying-est thing in the world. When a dope addict is sick, he's sick. He can't raise his hand if he's a drug addict.... They say

when a dope fiend's sick he'll do anything to get money, but how the hell is he going to do it if he can't even go on the street and do it? (Belle)

The prostitutes I interviewed found heroin especially functional in their criminal activities. Never knowing if their next *trick* (client) might be a freak (one who enjoys violence or sadomasochistic acts), carry a disease, or simply have unpleasant body odor, prostitutes understandably approach many of their dates with a good deal of apprehension. They reported that heroin allows them to work under otherwise difficult conditions:

> I think that a woman that tricks has to do something. If they wasn't an alcoholic, they had to be a dope fiend. 'Cause a woman in her right sense, you just can't sit up and do some of the things you do with a trick.
> If I didn't have no heroin in me, I couldn't trick, because it turns my stomach. . . . I didn't feel nothin' then, I just went on and do it. . . . I always was noddin' before I even get to the date. And then when I get to the date, I go to the bathroom and get off again. (Penny)
> I could forget about what I was doing; I didn't give a damn about anything. I just felt good. (Helen)

Heroin is not the only drug that addicts use for functional reasons in their commission of crimes. Amphetamines are also sometimes used to maintain necessary energy levels on particularly busy days. Boss, who was an armed robber among other things, reported that he would frequently use barbiturates before going out on a robbery. He found that they put him in the necessary belligerent mood to play the "tough guy" in order to pull off the robbery successfully. He also reported that he would frequently celebrate a successful robbery with heroin or cocaine or perhaps even a speedball (a heroin and cocaine combination):

> They'd be like a toast. Maybe 9:30 or 10:00 we'd done pulled a good score off and we're sitting there and say, "Hey man, let's go get us some good motherfucking dope." And it would carry you until 2:00. Nodding in the apartment, everybody feeling all right because they got away with the crime, planning what you're gonna do with your half of the money. So it'd be like the cap for you. It'd be like a toast for a job well done.

Finally, the data from these life histories suggest that both drug use and criminal behavior are interrelated elements of a broader subcultural experience that cannot be fully understood in terms of a simple causal relationship. Particularly as stable addicts, these respondents regarded both drug use and crime as important parts of a challenging lifestyle. It is true that drugs provide an important perceptual framework from which addicts interpret their behavior. Boss commented on the importance of drugs in defining the meaning that he attached to his activities:

> The money is good, but I wouldn't want the money if I couldn't have what goes along with selling the money [for heroin]. . . . Like with the whores, I wouldn't want the whores if I couldn't spend the money on dope. . . . It's like a working man. A working man, he wants a home and nice family. Just like in the life of crime you got to have all those essential things that go with it or it's nothing. It would be nothing if I couldn't spend that money the way [I want to].

But while heroin is an important component of the subjective experience of addicts, it is only part of a more general lifestyle, the maintenance of which motivates the addict. Also part of that lifestyle for most addicts is a nice wardrobe, fancy cars (for men), a nice crib (home), and a reputation for generosity with friends. As Boss reflected:

> See, my concern wasn't catching the habit.... My thing was being able to make enough money to supply that habit and make enough money to keep my thing up to par—you know, my clothes, and my living standards...to stay up to par enough so if my mother or sister or brother needed some money, I could loan them some money, plus keep my habit, plus buy some shoes or something, you know, rent a car for the weekend and just hang out like the guy that didn't have the habit. And in the course of that, that called for more crime.

As important as drugs and the fast lifestyle are in motivating addict behavior, one important fact remains: crime is a way of life with stable addicts. These people take pride in their ability to hustle successfully. Criminal success is a mark of stature in the subculture, and the more lucrative or difficult the hustle, the greater the recognition one receives.

> The type of criminal activity he engages in, and his success at it determine, to a large extent, the addict's status among fellow addicts and in the community at large. The appellation of *real hustling dope fiend* (a successful burglar, robber, con man, etc.) is a mark of respect and status. (Preble & Casey, 1969, p. 20; italics in original)

Crime is a challenge that most stable addicts find tremendously appealing. It provides a source of excitement and a sense of accomplishment, similar to the challenge of climbing formidable mountain peaks or rafting turbulent white water. Mario compared the excitement of burglarizing a house with the anticipation experienced by a young child at Christmastime. Each package (house) has its own surprises, its own challenges. Some are located in wealthy sections of the city and have fabulous exteriors (pretty wrappings). Some of these promising houses resulted in a valuable *take* (loot), while others did not. What kept Mario going was the anticipation he experienced with each crime.

Mario's feelings reflect those of many of the addicts who took part in this study. Their perceptions defy any attempt to characterize criminal behavior as somehow being "driven" by an overwhelming need for drugs, even though heroin and other drugs constitute an important feature of a stable addict's motivational structure. For these addicts, drugs and crime are mutually reinforcing elements of a broader lifestyle, both of which play an important role in defining one's position in the criminal-addict subculture. Harry expressed it this way:

> It was never really the drug. It was the lifestyle I was trying to keep going. And the drug was a lot of that lifestyle.... Back then [before becoming a street junkie]...it was just that it was there and I had all this energy and no vent for it. And I had begun to vent it into getting drugs, knocking people in the head, taking their money, going into somebody's house, taking that stuff out, running into the fence,

going to get the drugs—a full-time job. It was more than your basic 40 hours a week. And that's what it was about, sustaining that lifestyle.

By way of summary, in contrast to the occasional-user period of addict careers where drug use and crime are independent, parallel activities, the stable-addict phase is marked by a close interdependence between these two sets of activities. This relationship is more complex than can be captured in the empiricist language of cause and effect, however. The transition to the status of stable addict is a function of increased drug availability and expanded life structure, which, in most instances, result from increased systematic criminal activities. In this respect, we might characterize the stable-addict period as one in which "crime causes drugs" or, at least, crime facilitates drug use. Having attained the status of stable addict, the user has succeeded in jockeying for position in the criminal-addict subculture. The stable addict is, at least by minimal definition, a successful participant in the subculture. Success in the subculture is defined by drug using and criminal activity, both of which are motivating factors in the behavior of stable addicts. In this respect, the drugs–crime relationship is not so much causal as it is reciprocal, itself contributing to one's stature in the subculture.

CRIMINAL SPECIALIZATION AMONG STABLE ADDICTS

The career transition to stable addict usually entails an increasing reliance on a small number of criminal hustles or, in some cases, on a single type of crime. I pointed out [earlier] that early occasional use is a time of experimentation, not only with various types of drugs, but also with a variety of criminal roles. As in other careers, this trial period usually gives way to more focused activity as developing addicts discover what criminal skills and penchants they may have by experimenting with different criminal routines. In short, assumption of the stable-addict role usually implies the development of one or more main hustles.

Developing a main hustle implies not only the achievement of increased specialization but also of increased skill and sophistication as a criminal. Stable addicts go beyond learning the nuts and bolts of their chosen trade(s) to master the subtleties of these criminal enterprises with a finesse more characteristic of a craftsman than of a stereotyped common criminal. Old Ray may have stated it most succinctly when he remarked, "You got to have a Ph.D. in streetology." There are three broad types of skills that the successful criminal addict acquires: technical, social, and intuitive skills (Faupel, 1986).

Technical Skills

This category of criminal skills entails both the knowledge of how to perform the task as well as the physical adeptness for carrying it out successfully. Shoplifters stress the importance of being able to *roll* clothing items tightly with one hand with the clothes still on the hanger. Rolling loosely will not allow as many clothes to be packed in the bag, and keeping clothes on the hanger is important because empty hangers arouse suspicion. This must all be done with one hand because the other hand is used to finger through items on the rack, thereby creating the impression that the shoplifter is a legitimate customer. A slip in any one of the maneuvers involved in the complex process may mean failure to reach a quota for the day or, even more seriously, possible detection and arrest. Moreover, shoplifters must continually keep abreast of technological innovations designed to detect theft, including cameras, one-way mirrors, and alarm devices attached inside expensive clothing items.

Prostitutes also report the importance of developing technical skills, particularly streetwalkers who regularly *beat their johns* (rob their clients) out of credit cards and cash. Belle described her strategy for successfully stealing from her clients:

> The car was sweeter than anything else as far as getting money. Because once you get a dude's pants down, you got him where you want him. He just automatically forgets about he's got money in his pocket.... All she's thinking about is getting him in a position to get his mind off his pocket long enough for her to get in there.... She might take his pants with her and leave him stripped for nothing— 'cause I've done it.

A prostitute must also be able to determine where her trick keeps his wallet, take the wallet from his pocket, and then return it—all in a matter of minutes and without the client's being aware that this activity is taking place. These are skills not readily acquired; developing them takes time and practice, as Penny described:

> When I started off I was scared. It took a little longer.... It might take four or five hours [on an all-night date] to get his wallet.... [Later] it didn't take me but a minute to get it and put it back in.

The acquisition of technical skills is critical to the success of other hustles as well. The technical skills required by burglars have been extensively discussed in the literature on professional crime (Letkemann, 1973; Sutherland, 1937). These same skills were also reported by the burglar-addicts who participated in this study. An intimate knowledge of alarm systems is part of the seasoned burglar's stock-in-trade. Moreover, because most burglars prefer to enter unoccupied homes, they commonly case a residential area for days or even weeks, meticulously noting the mobility patterns of the residents. Burglars working business districts also case their working areas to determine patterns of police surveillance. Paige recalled "staying up all night watching the pattern of the police officers and seeing how regularly he made his rounds of the establishment and charting all that stuff down and trying to get a fix on when's the best time for me to rip that store off."

Stable addicts are also involved in many other types of criminal offenses. The addicts in this study reported engaging in main hustles such as armed robbery, pickpocketing, forgery, fencing stolen goods, pimping, and drug dealing at one time or another during their careers. Each of these criminal enterprises involves its own modus operandi and requires the acquisition of specialized technical skills if one is to be a reasonably successful hustler.

Social Skills

Most criminal hustles require the addict to be verbally and socially skilled as well as technically adept. These social skills involve verbally and nonverbally manipulating the setting to the criminal's advantage such that the offense can be carried out smoothly and without risk of apprehension or arrest.

Social skills, like technical skills, are quite specialized. Shoplifters who work in pairs, for example, frequently find it necessary to engage in small talk with salespersons, thereby diverting attention from the actions of their partners. Moreover, when they are detected, good boosters are often successful in talking their way out of an arrest. Gloria found that she could intimidate lower-level sales personnel from referring her to management by taking on the persona of an indignant, falsely accused customer. Some shoplifters, such as Slick, used a modus operandi that relied primarily on verbal agility. In contrast to the surreptitious strategies employed by many shoplifters, such as hiding stolen goods in garbage bags and false-bottom boxes or underneath one's own clothing, Slick opted for the bold strategy of walking out of the store with his stolen merchandise in full view of store personnel, as if he had paid for it: "I would take McCullough chain saws. . . . I would just pick up the big box, set it up on my shoulders, and even get the store security guard at the door to open the door for me. I just got bold." Then, rather than sell the chain saw to a fence for about one-third the retail value, Slick would rely on his verbal skills once again by returning the item the next day to the very store he had stolen it from (or bring it to another store in the chain) for a full refund.

Needless to say, this sort of strategy requires a unique ability to play the role of a legitimate customer. A shoplifter with highly developed social skills tends to assume this role so completely that he or she takes on the attitudes, feelings, and perspective of the customer. To use Mead's (1934) term, the shoplifter quite literally "takes the role of the other." Socially skilled shoplifters do not take the role of just any customer, however; they assume the role of an assertive customer who takes complete command of the situation. Indeed, they must do so. A legitimate customer can perhaps afford not to be assertive, but a timorous shoplifter may well forfeit his or her career by failing to command credibility as a legitimate customer.

Check forgers make use of some of the same social skills employed by shoplifters. Indeed, social agility can probably be said to constitute the principal stock-in-trade of the check forger. The entire act revolves around successfully convincing a bank employee that the signature on the check is in fact that of the individual whose name it bears, and that the forger is that individual and therefore the rightful recipient of the amount of the check. All of this involves the ability to assume the role of an assertive individual with a legitimate claim, an ability Old Ray cultivated to his advantage:

> I found the hardest teller I could find and she sent me to the manager's office. . . . I went in there telling about this godsent check—a tragedy in my life. It was all acting. . . . You got to story-tell. But it was my check. It became my check the minute I walked into the bank. . . . Once I packed up that type attitude, I became the role.

> And it's easier to go to the top than the bottom. It's easier at the top to get to any-body.... The guy at the bottom, he's gonna give you hell ... but the man at the top, he can afford to be benevolent.

Other criminal hustles require social skills of a slightly different nature. Prostitutes point out the importance of maintaining a position of dominance in the interaction between them and their tricks. Rose advised: "Always try to keep control of the conversation. Never let them see that you're soft.... They see one time that you stutter or aren't in control, they're gonna try to take advantage of you." By maintaining such control, the prostitute is also able to direct and focus her client's attention, which allows her to engage in acts of theft. Penny was so successful at this strategy that she was frequently able to rob her clients without even having to *turn the trick* (engage in sexual acts).

Drug dealing entails social skills with still another focus. Here the primary task is to maintain a relatively stable clientele. This involves advertising one's drugs and establishing a reputation as having "righteous" dope. Harry, who was heavily involved in burglary as well as selling drugs, understood successful dealing to be little more than hype and good salesmanship:

> Conning was part of everything. The whole thing is an image. Believe it or not, it's the American way!...So you learn how to hype....One of my favorite lines was, "You better do only half of one of these." And that just made them get all that much more motivation to do three or four of them. And they'd do three or four, and they'd come back and say, "Hey, that shit was good!" Of course, if they did three or four of them, they did get fucked up.

Inevitably, however, drug dealers are confronted with dissatisfied customers who have reason to believe that they have been ripped off with poor-quality dope. There was no consensus among the dealers I interviewed regarding how they respond to discontented clients. Some would play it tough, on the theory that to give in to a client's demands sets a bad precedent and may serve as a signal to others that here is a dealer who can easily be taken. Others saw themselves as conscientious businesspeople and would quite readily supply dissatisfied customers with more dope, urging them to spread the word that they were treated fairly. In either event, to borrow a phrase from the subculture of pickpockets, dealers must "cool the mark out," employing all of the social skills they have at their disposal to maintain a stable clientele.

Intuitive Skills

This last category of hustling skills entails an acute sensitivity to one's environment. Sutherland (1937) describes this characteristic as *larceny sense*, a term that Dressler also employs to describe the professional criminal: "Larceny sense, it seems, is the ability to smell out good hauls, to sense the exact moment for the kill, and to know when it is wiser to desist" (1951, p. 255). Maurer (1955) applies the term "grift sense" to describe intuitive skills in his classic analysis of the professional pickpocket. But these skills are by no means limited to professional criminals. Gould et al. observe this ability among active heroin users: "Most successful dope fiends show an ability to size up people they meet in terms of trustworthiness and motivation, and have a good memory for people" (1974, pp. 45–46).

The addicts I interviewed also emphasized the importance of intuitive skills. Like technical and social skills, intuitive skills are manifested differently in various criminal contexts, but their general purpose is to help facilitate the commission of a crime or to help the criminal avoid detection and arrest.

Intuitive skills can facilitate the commission of crime by providing the addict with the ability to sense a profitable and reasonably safe opportunity. "I could see money. I could smell money," claimed Old Ray. "I could walk by a store and see if it was vulnerable.... I could sense the whole setup." These are the skills that contribute to larceny (or grift) sense, and many of the participants in this study explicitly acknowledged their importance. Representative observations of a prostitute, a pickpocket, and a shoplifter illustrate how these skills are applied in various hustles:

> Look for the nice dates. When you spot a man with the raggediest car and the oldest clothes, he's probably got the money. Because he's cheap, he don't wanna spend all of that money. It's usually the man that's got all this and that [who] ain't got a dime because he's paying out so many bills. (Rose, a prostitute, who went on to point out that she would probably have to steal his money because he is unlikely to be generous with her either)
>
> As I got better, I could spot people with decent money, and you play them. Whereas in the beginning, on the amateur thing, I might play anywhere from 10 to 15 wallets. But wh en I got professional, I might just play one or two wallets. (Boss, a pickpocket)
>
> All days aren't the same for boosting.... If there's no situation where you can make some money, you just don't go in and make a situation. You understand what I'm saying? The situation has to be laid out for you. And to be really good at it, you got to be the type of person that can recognize a laid-out situation. If you get in there and try to make a situation, then you're rearranging the whole thing and it could be detrimental. (Booter, a shoplifter)

Intuitive skills are also instrumental in avoiding detection and arrest. The addict criminals in this study repeatedly stressed the importance of being able to detect and avoid undercover police officers, floorwalkers, and potential informants. This ability was regarded as absolutely crucial to their success in criminal roles:

> I learned the ropes...how you spot cops. He [a friend] pointed out...those undercover detectives with the bee stingers on their cars, little teeny antennae on top; and how you could pick those cars out; and how two detectives in a car, how there were certain characteristics about them that were always the same. You could smell them a mile away. He really schooled me criminally, you know. (Harry, on drug dealing)
>
> When she [the bank teller] sees the check, if she has to look up [or] if she has to call another teller or something like that, it ain't no good.... If the teller has to pick up the phone, then you tell her, "That's all right, there's something I have to do." (Stephanie, a check forger)

I can tell [who the floorwalkers are]. They constantly keep walking the floor looking at me.... They're still in that same department and ain't bought nothing. (Penny, on shoplifting)

Never take a deal that sounds too good to be true.... This guy came by and wanted to buy 15 bags for $10 apiece—no shorts. Now any kind of a hustler junkie coming off the street and he's got $150, he's not gonna come to you wanting 15 bags. He's gonna come to you wanting 25 or 30. You know what I'm saying? The deal was too good to be true. (Fred, a drug dealer)

These observations illustrate the diffuse qualities characteristic of intuitive skills. It was difficult even for the study respondents to articulate their precise nature. Pagie recalled: "I always had a knack for sensing the police. I don't know why. I don't know if it's an ESP thing or what, but I always could sense when the police was there." It is because of their rather imperceptible quality that I have used the term *intuitive skills* to refer to this important set of abilities. It is important to understand, however, that they are not hereditary talents. These are skills that are acquired through the same process of socialization as are technical and social skills. Together, these three sets of skills distinguish successful stable addicts from beginning occasional users.

I have attempted in this discussion to demonstrate that contrary to stereotyped depictions of addict criminality, stable addicts are skilled criminal entrepreneurs. The level of criminal sophistication required to sustain a livelihood of the magnitude reported by these hard-core addicts is acquired only after spending considerable time in the subculture. Such skills are simply not part of the beginning occasional user's stock-in-trade. In the process of becoming stable addicts, however, most users narrow the range of their criminal activities considerably. I certainly do not wish to represent the stable addict as a professional in the tradition of a Chic Conwell (Sutherland, 1937) or Vincent Swaggi (Klockars, 1974), nor necessarily as specialized as Preble and Casey (1969) imply in their watershed study of addict criminals. The addicts I interviewed, however, do favor a small number of crimes among the vast variety they could be committing. I am suggesting that as stable addicts, these hard-core users are sufficiently successful at their main hustles such that they seldom find it necessary to deviate from their preferred crimes. They attain a level of specialization not characteristic of amateurs nor even of their own criminal patterns during other periods of their careers. Indeed, I contend that it is only by such specialization that these addicts are able to develop the requisite skills for a successful career. There is thus a mutually reinforcing relationship between the development of a main hustle and the acquisition of technical, social, and intuitive skills that correspond to this specialization. The acquisition of these skills is, in the first place, dependent on some level of specialization; at the same time, these skills provide the very foundation for stable addicts to maintain their main hustles.

These main hustles, which constitute more or less full-time criminal roles, also have other important consequences. As I suggested earlier, they provide an alternative basis for life structure that is capable of accommodating higher levels of drug use and consumer activity generally. At the same time, however, the routine nature of the main hustle prevents one's habit from getting out of hand. The stable addict's heroin use still takes place within a rather well-defined, though modified, life structure. Moreover, full-time hustler roles provide addicts with increased dependable income. Unlike the marginal criminality of occasional users, the main hustle is both a primary means of income and a source of identity and prestige in the subculture. The study respondents were quick to distinguish between a main hustle typical of stable addicts and the more amateur or impulsive *flat-footed hustling* style characteristic of less criminally routine lifestyles. Gloria emphasized her distinctive status as a booster: "I'm not a thief—I'm a booster. There's a difference between a thief and a booster. A thief... takes anything and everything from anywhere." Booter understood his role as a pimp in entrepreneurial terms, viewing his prostitutes as an investment:

> You try not to spend too much money unless it's important. You're playing economics here. Like I got some stock.... In order for her to collect the capital, she has to be a product. You have to have something that you can sell. You don't try to give up too much, but say you are into a new girl.... You have to put some clothes on her, put some capital into that to make her look presentable.... You're expecting her to get that money back.

Thus, the stable-addict phase is characterized by a comparatively high degree of criminal specialization, complete with the technical, social, and intuitive skills that contribute to success in the criminal role. As shown by this research and in previous studies, stable addicts are successful and sophisticated criminal entrepreneurs.

REFERENCES

Dressler, D. (1951). *Probation and parole*. New York: Columbia University Press.

Faupel, C. E. (1986). Heroin use, street crime and the main hustle: Implications for the validity of official crime data. *Deviant Behavior, 7*, 31–45.

Gould, L., Walker, A. L., Crane, L. E., & Lidz, C. W. (1974). *Connections: Notes from the heroin world*. New Haven, CT: Yale University Press.

Klockars, C. (1974). *The professional fence*. New York: Free Press.

Letkemann, P. (1973). *Crime as work*. Englewood Cliffs, NJ: Prentice Hall.

Maurer, D. W. (1955). *Whiz mob: A correlation of the technical argot of pickpockets with their behavior patterns*. Gainesville, FL: American Dialect Society.

Mead, G. H. (1934). *Mind, self, and society*, ed. C. W. Morris. Chicago: University of Chicago Press.

Preble, E., & Casey, J. H. (1969). Taking care of business: The heroin user's life on the streets. *International Journal of the Addictions, 4*(1), 1–24.

Sutherland, E. H. (1937). *The professional thief*. Chicago: University of Chicago Press.

CHAPTER 22

"E" Is for Ecstasy: A Participant Observation Study of Ecstasy Use

Wilson R. Palacios and Melissa E. Fenwick

In this selection, Wilson Palacios and Melissa Fenwick offer an insider's view of the Ecstasy culture in south Florida (Tampa). During a 15-month participant-observation study, they attended dozens of all-night (and sometimes several days in length) "clublike" parties, observing and asking questions of participants. Attending the nightclubs and parties where Ecstasy was freely available, the researchers were able to allay suspicion by presenting themselves as a couple interested in the music underground. In some cases, they advised the others that they were researchers; in other cases, they did not, preferring to observe incognito. This chapter is a brief introduction to a continuing study—one of the first of its kind examining contemporary Ecstasy culture in America.

In *Writing on Drugs*, Sadie Plant argues that "every drug has its own character, its own unique claim to fame" (1999, p. 4). This is certainly true in the case of Ecstasy (MDMA). In 1986, Jerome Beck wrote:

> MDMA has been thrust upon the public awareness as a largely unknown drug which to some is a medical miracle and to others a social devil....There have been the born-again protagonists who say that once you have tried it you will see the light and will defend it against any attack, and there have been the staunch antagonists who say this is nothing but LSD revisited and it will certainly destroy our youth. (p. 305)

Beck's statements have proven to be as relevant today as they were 25 years ago, accurately characterizing the current media blitz surrounding the drug MDMA/Ecstasy. On July 1, 1985, at the behest of the U.S. Drug Enforcement Administration, MDMA/Ecstasy was temporarily placed in Schedule I of the Controlled Substance Act (CSA) and permanently placed on November 13, 1986. Although it may seem

Source: Written especially for this volume. This project was supported by funds from USF Research & Creative Scholarship Grant #12–21–926RO.

easy to understand the DEA's objectives in banning MDMA/Ecstasy, their actions inadvertently paved the way for the development of a large, international underground manufacturing and distribution network worth millions of dollars, and, to a greater extent, a larger hidden population of users.

Law enforcement officials and politicians have led this new charge against MDMA/Ecstasy and its users. Newspaper headlines such as "Drug's Night Club Pull Seems Hard to Curb" (*Boston Globe*), "Raving and Behaving: The Reputation of the High-Energy, All Night Dance Parties Outpaces the Reality" (*Buffalo News*), and "Deputies: Ecstasy Overdose Killed Teen" (*St. Petersburg Times*) have been used to usher in a new "war on drugs," which, like our previous efforts with crack cocaine, stands to dramatically increase jail and prison populations and challenge our taken-for-granted notions concerning civil liberties.

Despite attention from the criminal justice system, Ecstasy use and abuse has received minimal coverage from the social scientific community, in particular the field of criminology. Much of what we think we know about patterns of use and abuse concerning this drug stems largely from existing self-report surveys, such as Monitoring the Future (MTF), drug surveillance systems such as Drug Abuse Warning Network (DAWN), and the Arrestee Drug Abuse Monitoring (ADAM) program. Until now, there has been little in the way of active ethnographic field-work in this country concerning MDMA/Ecstasy use and its culture.

This chapter is derived from an ongoing, two-year ethnographic study concerning the use of "club drugs" (i.e., MDMA/Ecstasy, ketamine/Special K, GHB, and nitrates) and club culture in Florida. The research focuses on the emotional state of individuals who ingest MDMA/Ecstasy, the local market for such drugs, and the vernacular of this drug culture.

The drug, formally named 3, 4-methylenedioxymethamphetamine (MDMA), is commonly referred to on the street as Ecstasy (Cohen, 1998). Although other names such as Adam, the Love Drug, Mickey, X, Raven, and M&M's are used to refer to MDMA, the term Ecstasy is the most recognizable. In the Hillsborough and Pinellas County area, the terms *bean*(s) and *rolls* are used interchangeably to refer to Ecstasy. When asked about the origin of these terms, interviewees told us that Ecstasy pills are called *beans* because they "look like little lima beans" and *rolls* because of the way they make you feel.

Ecstasy tablets are sold on the street under names pressed in distinctive designer logos on one side of the pill. For example, in the field we came across Ecstasy pills sold under such names as Mitsubishi, Smurfs, Calvin Kleins, Nikes, Anchors, Rolls Royce (RR), Starburst, Pink Hearts, Double Stack Crowns, Navigator, KnockOuts, Blue Gene, and Red Gene. Many of the Ecstasy pills we encountered in the field were of various colors, although white was the most common. Moreover, we quickly learned that the popularity of these pills was solely dependent on word-of-mouth marketing from the individual consumer level. Ecstasy represents a marketing bonanza because of its ability to induce an intense physiologically and psychologically euphoric state without the stigma associated with drugs like crack cocaine or heroin. In addition, it is a drug that many feel they can realistically walk away from or "schedule" into their lives on an as-needed basis. The following comments typify this attitude:

> It's not like doing crack or smack (heroin)....You don't hit a pipe or needle....I wouldn't do that cause my friends would be like....Hey, crack monster...or crack freak...and that's not cool....Think about it...it's a little pill which takes you for a ride and then it's over....You don't feign (crave) for it....You can do it every weekend or once a month or once or twice a year...just depends on what you've got going in your life and the people around you. (Jason, a single white male, 20 years of age)
>
> When I was in college I would roll [use Ecstasy] every weekend except for midterms and finals...but since I've been out I haven't rolled in the last two years....I'm not saying that I won't...but I've just been busy with work, and since I work for the system [referring to the criminal justice system] I know they drug test....If I will do it again I'll just plan for it....It stays in your system from two to five days. (Mark, a single white male, 29 years of age)

The intense physiological (amphetamine-like) rush from Ecstasy is referred to as *blowing up* or *rolling*. This experience varies across individuals. However, the overwhelming sensation of a heightened emotional and physical state was a commonly reported characteristic. The following comments typify this recurring theme:

> When you're blowing up it is like your fucking skin is going to come undone. Just imagine an orgasm, but 20 or 50 times better and intense. That's the lure of X. (Jerry, a single white male, 25 years of age)
>
> I felt like I was coming undone from the inside. You can feel every inch of your skin, even the tiny little hairs on your arms and legs...feels that good. (Amy, single white female, 19 years of age)

Valter and Arrizabalaga (1998, p. 13) argue that "the world-wide and still increasing use and abuse of MDMA (Ecstasy) is due to its euphoriant properties and capacity to enhance communication and contact with other people." Actually, because of this last property, Ecstasy is really a member of a small class of compounds called *entactogens* or *empathogens* (which means creating contact or empathy) and therefore should not be classified as a "hallucinogenic-amphetamine" drug (see Cohen, 1998). This feeling of connecting with other people is what makes Ecstasy such a psychological draw for most people, including our participants:

> I know I could go to [local nightclub] and after I eat my pill I won't care what people think of me....I won't care if they think I'm fat, too skinny, or if I am wearing the wrong shoes....I just don't care because it becomes about meeting people and just meeting different kinds of people. (Betty, a single white female, 25 years of age, mother of two)
>
> It's about having a good time....I even don't have to worry about guys trying to hook up [reference to sex] with me....If guys are rolling, you know they are not looking at you that way...at least not when they are rolling...maybe later on the comedown [referring to the end of the night], but not during. (Carrie, a white Latina female, 21 years of age)

BLOWING UP

Our participants gauged the strength and purity of a pill according to the intensity of their *blowing up* or *rolling* experience. Some acute reactions experienced by our participants during the blowing up or rolling stage were bruxism (teeth grinding), trismus (jaw clenching), uncontrollable fidgeting of extremities, rapid eye movements, and a heightened sensitivity to all external stimuli (touch, lights, sounds, etc.). To tap into these varied experiences, we asked the following: "How do you know you are/were blowing up?" These are some of the responses we received:

> It usually wouldn't come on until after 30 or 40 minutes, but when it did, you would just feel this overwhelming sensation of all your emotions being flooded [released] throughout your body. I would say after 45 minutes into it I would feel my eyes twitch, and I would have this need to just massage everything and anything around me. One night I was massaging my arms so hard without realizing it or feeling any pain that the next day I woke up and had broken my skin. I was in pain the next morning, but I did not remember feeling any pain when I was doing this.... It just feel so good. (Tim, a white Latino male, 27 years of age, married)
>
> You can't help being or wanting to be touched.... I've seen men touching each other without all the worry about people thinking they were gay or anything.... You know you're rolling when somebody comes up to you and begins massaging your neck, shoulders, or back.... It feels just so good that one time I had my girlfriend massage my lower back so hard that she made me pee in my pants—now that was a good bean.... You can't know what I'm talking about unless you've been there. (Stacie, a white single female, 18 years of age)
>
> The first time I rolled I didn't feel a thing.... I was pissed because I spent some money and everyone around me was rolling their asses off and I was the only one in the group sitting there like a dumbfuck...but the second time I rolled...that's when I can tell you that I honestly blow up.... I first noticed it because of the lights.... Everything was clearer and brighter.... I would see the bright colors from the corner of my eyes and then my feet started swaying to the music.... I looked at my feet and it was like they weren't even mine.... I kept wanting to get up and just walk around and talk to people.... I didn't care what people thought of [me]...I just wanted to be around people. (Lady X, a single white female, 23 years of age)
>
> I really don't like anything speedy.... My father died of a heart attack at a young age.... I don't think I have a heart condition, but I just don't want anything speeding my heart.... I usually like the ones that are not speedy.... I like for it [Ecstasy] to come on slow and gradually over the night.... I want it to last.... I'm not one for dancing or stuff like that, I just want to sit there and take it all in. (Jane, a single white female, 27 years of age)

SIDE EFFECTS

Of all of the possible acute reactions—papillary dilation, headache, hypertension, nausea, tachycardia, blurred vision, hypertonicity, and tremors—that Ecstasy induces, jaw clenching and teeth grinding (trismus and bruxism) were among the side effects most cited by our participants:

> You must always have something to chew on or you'll end up loosening your teeth. (Mary, a single white female, 21 years of age; using Ecstasy for 2 years)
>
> The only thing I hate about rolling is how your jaw feels the next morning. You just can't help chewing gum, but you can chew the same piece of gum all night long and not realize it. . . . You can keep chewing because you need something in your mouth, but you don't realize how much pain your jaw is going to be [in] the next day. There have been times when I couldn't even open my mouth for one or two days after rolling. . . . It's a good thing I didn't want to eat. (Ms. S, a single Latina female, 18 years of age)
>
> The next day I noticed a lot of sores in my mouth . . . probably from my teeth grinding down on my gums. . . . The inside of my mouth hurts for about two or three days after. (Joe, a single white female, 21 years of age)

A number of our participants used candy such as Gummy Bears, Starbursts, Jolly Ranchers, and BlowPops to help mitigate the unpleasantness of their jaw muscles clenching. Actually, any form of hard candy or chewing gum can work as long as it keeps the user from grinding his or her teeth and straining the jaw muscles:

> I've worn away all of my back teeth and I have four sores in my mouth from just grinding the inside of my teeth. I chipped my front teeth one night after dropping [ingesting] five beans. . . . I was blowing up hard. . . . I felt my eyes roll towards the back of my head. I also bit my lip because I didn't realize I was biting down on it until I went to the bathroom at this club and looked in the mirror and noticed a little bit of blood from my upper lip. . . . No biggie, but it scares the shit out of you looking in the mirror and seeing blood. (Ms. G, a single Latina female, 29 years of age)
>
> A Blowpop or a piece of gum never tasted so fucking good as when you are rolling . . . but it helps not lose your teeth, because with a good bean, your teeth will chatter. (Greg, a single white male, 24 years of age)

BUYING ECSTASY

Ecstasy's street price makes it attractive and affordable. Currently, in the Tampa area, the price ranges from $10 to $20 per pill, with an average cost of $15. Factors that determine the price of a pill are market availability and whether or not one is known to the dealers. Market availability is just that—supply and demand. When a large number of pills are on the market, prices are lower. As might be expected, prices are usually higher for strangers than for those people known to the dealer. Prices at nightclubs are also more expensive than prices at other locations. We asked one dealer who we had met during a rolling party whether he overcharged people at nightclubs. He offered the following view:

> If I don't know the person, I will, and definitely if it's in a club. . . . It's the price of doing business in a club. . . . I have to worry about the bouncers [security personnel], off-duty undercover cops, and narcs [people working for the police] . . . just

too much hassle. But I'm going to make my money.... People just have to pay.... If I know you, I'll cut you a break, but not by much.... I really just don't like dealing in clubs.

Our participants preferred to buy and take Ecstasy before arriving at their destinations as a way of minimizing the risk of detection from law enforcement. The following statements are typical:

> I always buy a few days before I know I am going out. That way I don't get caught up with people saying that they can or can't get it [Ecstasy] and then having to go the club and buying something from I don't know who...a narc or undercover, and paying something crazy like $20. (Vanessa, a 20-something Latina female)
>
> We would always drop [take Ecstasy] at our apartment and then go to the clubs.... We knew that we would be at the clubs like in 20 minutes, so we knew that our rolls wouldn't kick in yet or they would start to kick in just as we were in line to get into the clubs.... That's how we'd do it.... We would never have anything on us...just in case they would search you at the door. (Jimmy, a white male, 19 years of age)

ONSET OF EFFECTS

The average user begins to feel the effects from one Ecstasy pill in about 30 to 45 minutes. The overall effects of Ecstasy, or an "E trip," as it is commonly known, can last from four to six hours Time periods are contingent on what and how recently people have eaten, a person's physiology, and whether the pill has adulterants. In recent years, the media and some ill-informed law enforcement officials have alleged that Ecstasy pills contain substances like rat poison and crushed glass, as well as other illegal drugs such as cocaine, heroin, and LSD. However, others have shown (see Beck & Rosenbaum, 1994; Cohen, 1998; Saunders & Doblin, 1996) that these allegations are more myth than reality.

According to DanceSafe, a harm-reduction organization, recent adulterant screening efforts have revealed the presence of such drugs as dextromethorphan, phenylpropanolamine, ephedrine, pseudoephedrine, glyceryl guaiacolate, other amphetamine-like substances (e.g., MDA, MDEA, DOM, 2-CB, and DOT), caffeine, and ketamine, with only trace amounts of such substances as heroin and LSD (DanceSafe, 2001). It is believed that underground manufacturers in clandestine laboratories add many of these substances purely as a cost-saving method, although some of these ingredients do increase the risk for negative reactions, including overdose.

The fact that they could be ingesting a host of other substances in addition to MDMA did not appear to concern our subjects greatly. Our participants took Ecstasy one of three ways: (1) orally, (2) snorting, or (3) "parachuting"/"packing." Some participants elected to use either one or a combination of all three methods during the evening, depending on when they wanted to feel the effects of the pill. With oral ingestion, initial effects were usually felt within 30 to 40 minutes.

Snorting produced effects within 10 to 15 minutes, while parachuting or packing produced effects within 5 minutes.

"Parachuting" Ecstasy involves inserting the pill into the anus, like a suppository. Parachuters believe that this method allows the pill to be absorbed faster and the effects felt in a shorter time. The process of parachuting is described in the following field note excerpt:

> The time was 6:15 a.m. and we had just left an after-hours club where we had spent the last three hours with a group of people we met up with at another club earlier in the evening. In leaving this after-hours club we all got into our cars and headed for a gas station nearby. I asked David, a white male about 29 years of age, what we were looking to get at this gas station. He answered, "I need to refuel. I need to stop and get some Red Bull before we continue or I'm not going to make it." The gas station was less than 10 city blocks from the after-hours club, and we were there within 10 minutes. All three cars pulled into the gas station, and most of the passengers got out of their cars.
>
> In total there were five cars and 10 people all together. One of the drivers, Jake, a Latino male in his early twenties, pulled his red Honda Civic to a gas pump, got out, inserted a credit card, and began to pump gas. I waited outside the car I was riding in for the rest of the group. I noticed that most were in line inside the gas station with items in their hands. Since it was early in the morning on a Sunday and no one was around, I decide to go inside just to be with the folks. In walking into the gas station I noticed that most had either Red Bull, Gatorade, or PowerAde sport drinks in their hands. Two individuals had two bottles of water, Evian, in their hands. I noticed that Fred, a white male in his late twenties was walking towards the back of the gas station.
>
> Soon there was Henry, a white male in his early thirties, following behind him. I think Mary, a Latina female about 20 years of age, noticed I was looking at them, and, in a very low whisper, said, "They going to the bathroom to shoot." I asked, "To shoot what?" She replied, "They still have some beans left," and that's all she said. Now, I knew that shooting beans did not mean using a needle, since I have not seen anyone use this method for taking Ecstasy. So I thought she was referring to "parachuting," but I was not sure. It is a term I had heard before, but I had never seen anyone actually do it. I could not help it, but curiosity got the better of me, and so I headed for the bathroom, and just as I got to the door, Fred looked at me and said, "Hey, professor, do you want to see something?" I replied, "What?" Henry replied, "Come see."
>
> There we were … in the men's bathroom, three males, and I could not help think that under other circumstances, this scene would represent something altogether different. However, there we were. I stood directly in front of the door, and Fred, while reaching for his right pants pocket, said, "I know you've heard about 'parachuting.'" I replied, "Yeah … but I think I know what it is." Fred's reply was, "Well, here you go …" As he said this, he pulled out three beans from a small baggie.… They were white in color, and I knew they were known as RR or Rolls Royce, because that was what the group had been taking for most of the night. As he produced the beans and threw the baggie on the floor, Henry walked over to a bathroom stall and tore off a piece of toilet paper, probably about less than one inch in length. He walks over to the faucet and just wets the piece of paper with

a small amount of water. Fred then walks over and places the three beans into the center of the paper. Henry begins to fold the paper over the pills and forms a nice little wad of paper with its end twisted. He licks the twisted ends and I asked, "Why are you doing that?" His response, "To make sure that it's all nice and tight and that it doesn't come undone when it goes in." As he says this, Fred walks over to a bathroom stall, unzips his pants and lets his pants come down to his thigh area. Henry walks over to him and says, "Are you ready?" Fred's response: "Go ahead." Fred bends only halfway, and Henry takes that wad of paper with the twisted ends and begins to insert it anally into Fred. There I am watching this, and all I could say, "Why can't you do it yourself, Fred?" Fred stands up, and as he zips up his pants he turns around and says, "I just don't like putting anything into me." Henry adds, "I do myself all the time, and I do my girl this way." In almost a comic relief tone, Fred adds, "Now that's 'parachuting,' professor." My only response: "No confusing that one...that's 'parachuting.'"

COMING DOWN

Toward the end of the blowing up stage of an E trip, people respond in many different ways. Some just want to engage in a free-flowing conversation about their lives and their own personal anxieties and fears. Some just want to sit outside to watch the sunrise and feel the cool morning breeze brushing up against their skin. A few have some difficulty accepting that their experience is about to end and therefore consume marijuana as a method for "kicking it back in."

> I always like to have some kind [of] bud [high-quality marijuana] on me to smoke towards the end.... [It] takes the edge off and kicks my roll back in.... It won't be as intense, but you do feel it somewhat.... [It] just relaxes me and give me a smoother roll at the end. (Diego, a white male Latino in his early 20s)

Some also consume drugs like Valium and Xanax as a way of coping with the edginess they felt from Ecstasy:

> The morning after I take a Xane bar [referring to Xanax], then I'm OK...I can go to sleep.... If I don't, my fucking mind is not going to stop talking to me.... It's like you want to go to sleep because you know you're tired but your mind won't let you go.... A Xane bar or some Valium would do the trick. (Keith, a white male in his early 30s)

For some of our participants, the day or days after their use of Ecstasy consisted of moderate to intense fatigue. In communicating the nature of this psychological and physical exhaustion, they used the term *ate-up*. For most, this ate-up feeling was characterized as a loss of appetite, mental exhaustion, some nausea, intense thirst, and body aches. Although these symptoms sound remarkably similar to those experiencd in a hangover, many of our participants did not see such similarities:

> The only thing I hate about E is how I feel the next day.... I just can't do anything.... I mean, I sleep all day, so I waste an entire day and then I get up and just want to lay

in my bed....I can't think, and if I do, I can't get the music or people out of my head. I really don't want to eat anything, but I force myself to eat something....I'm not hungry, but I just force myself. (Christine, a white female in her 20s)

I just can't do anything the next day...all I want to is sleep....I love to take a shower when I get home because it feels good, but then I just head for my bed....I get no headaches or feel like throwing up, but I just don't want anything. (Mike, a white male in his early 20s)

I really don't feel ate-up the next day....I sleep for about six or eight hours and get up....I eat a little something and then I just sit around, turn the TV on, but I really don't watch it....I just want to sit there and think....My legs hurt a bit, but that's from the dancing....If that's ate-up, then maybe, yeah, but nothing like what my friends feel. (Judy, a white female in her late 20s)

For me, the worst is about three days after I rolled. I just feel down...can't start or really finish anything....I just want to lay in my bed and do absolutely nothing....I stop and think that I won't ever do that again [use Ecstasy], but then I remember I had a good time on it, and, well...you know. (Sue, a white female in her late teens)

Such aftereffects are mitigated by the person's physiology, health status prior to use, frequency of use, concurrent drug use (e.g., LSD, cocaine, heroin, or alcohol), and the type and amount of Ecstasy pills consumed. As a result, the ate-up experience is never the same for any one individual.

CONCLUSION

Philippe Bourgois (1999, p. 215) argues, "A major task of participant-observers is to put themselves in the shoes of the people they study in order to see local realities through local eyes." As participant-observers, we have presented a local picture of Ecstasy use among a diverse network of individuals. There is no denying that for our participants, taking Ecstasy—despite all the known risks—is pleasurable. A "local reality" is that Ecstasy is relatively affordable, does not have the same stigma associated with other illegal drugs, and is very much a part of the local youth culture (individuals between the ages of 18 and 35). Because this is an ongoing ethnographic study, there are many areas that we have not yet studied. We wanted to present a "local portrait" of Ecstasy use. We only hope that we remained true to our participants in setting out to accomplish this goal.

REFERENCES

Beck, J. (1986). MDMA: The popularization and resultant implications of a recently controlled psychoactive substance. *Contemporary Drug Problems, 13*, 305–313.

Beck, J., & Rosenbaum, M. (1994). *Pursuit of ecstasy: The MDMA experience*. New York: State University of New York Press.

Boston Globe (n.d.) Drug's Night Club Pull Seems Hard to Curb."

Bourgois, P. (1999). Theory, method, and power in drug and HIV-prevention research: A participant-observer's critique. *Substance Use & Misuse, 34*, 2155–2172.

Buffalo News (n.d.) Raving and Behaving: The Reputation of the High-Energy, All Night Dance Parties Outpaces the Reality."

hen, R. S. (1998). *The love drug: Marching to the beat of ecstasy.* New York: Haworth.

DanceSafe. (2001). Retrieved August 2001 from http://www.dancesafe.org/labtesting/.

Plant, S. (1999). *Writing on drugs.* New York: Farrar, Straus and Giroux.

Saunders, N., & Doblin, R. (1996). *Ecstasy: Dance, trance and transformation.* Oakland, CA: Quick American Achieves.

St. Petersburg Times (n.d.) Deputies: Ecstasy Overdose Killed Teen."

Valter, K., & Arrizabalaga, P. (1998). *Designer drugs directory.* New York: Elsevier.

꒜

CHAPTER 23

"Cooks are Like Gods": Hierarchies in Methamphetamine-Producing Groups

Robert Jenkot

This article uses findings from a qualitative study of female methamphetamine users, dealers, and producers in Missouri and Arkansas. Using in-depth interviews with 31 incarcerated women, the study explores their experiences with methamphetamine, focusing on the experiences of 18 methamphetamine producers, or "cooks." Through their experiences, this study provides an insight into the hierarchies that exist within methamphetamine-producing groups. The hierarchy moves from "simple users" at the bottom, to "dope ho's," "shoppers," "gas men/juicers," and "cooks" at the top of the methamphetamine hierarchy. Understanding the hierarchy within methamphetamine-producing groups can aid us in understanding how new members are added to the group, existing members leave, and new groups form from the existing group. In-group mobility is also examined with regard to group solidarity and reintegration postconfinement. Because all of the participants in this study were women, the interaction between status and gender within the methamphetamine-producing group is also discussed.

In 1965 members of the Hell's Angels Motorcycle Club found that they could produce the synthetic drug methamphetamine; their efforts provide the first documented clandestine methamphetamine production (Lavigne, 1996a; Lavigne, 1996b). The "discovery" of clandestine methamphetamine production roughly coincided with legislation to control its illicit use (Young et al., 1977). Since the 1970s, we have seen an increase in the domestic clandestine production of methamphetamine and a proportionate rise in known methamphetamine use through the 1990s (Drug Enforcement Administration [DEA], 2000). Little is known about

Source: Adapted from Jenkot, R. (2008). "Cooks are like gods": Hierarchies in methamphetamine-producing groups. *Deviant Behavior, 29,* 667–689. Used with permission of the author and publisher.

the social relation within the groups that produce methamphetamine. Even less is known about women's social position within these groups.

The present study, part of a larger study of women involved with methamphetamine use, sales, and production, seeks to inform our understanding of the social relations within these groups. This study in particular uncovers the types of hierarchies present within methamphetamine-producing groups. Understanding the types of hierarchies that exit within these groups can shed light on how members of a methamphetamine-producing group function over time as new members arrive, members leave, or new groups are formed. Further, because the sample is exclusively female, some findings will also illuminate how gendered relations are affected by the hierarchies present in methamphetamine-producing groups.

LITERATURE REVIEW

Studies of domestic methamphetamine use, sales, and production have uncovered four unique characteristics when international smuggling is omitted. First, methamphetamine production is dominated by white Anglo-Americans (Riley, 2000; Pennell et al., 1999). Secondly, white women's use of methamphetamine is often on par with men's use patterns (Riley, 2000). Third, much of the methamphetamine supply is due to domestic production (DEA, 2000). Fourth, small, tight-knit groups of economically marginalized people perform much of the domestic production of methamphetamine (Lavigne, 1996a; Lavigne, 1996b).

Beyond the generalizations noted, determining who is producing methamphetamine is not as clear as who uses the drug. The ADAM (Arrestee Drug Abuse Monitoring) project, as well as associated federally funded projects, have little if any mention of who is involved with methamphetamine production (Meth, Chalmers, & Bossin, 2001; Pennell et al., 1999; Riley, 1999a; Riley, 1999b; Riley, 2000). Research on women involved with methamphetamine production is limited to nonacademic reports (Kurtis, 1997). Although the gendered relationships that exist within these groups has not been explored, it is clear that women are taking part in the production process. The production of illicit drugs goes beyond the expected behavior of women who take part in deviant activities. In effect, women have limitations on their behavior in both licit and illicit groups (Denton & O'Malley, 1999). However, there is a distinct lack of research detailing women's involvement with the production of drugs. It is here that I believe that this research can begin to fill that gap in the literature.

Comparing methamphetamine production to the manufacture of other drugs is troublesome. Although cocaine is a drug with similar psychopharmacological effects, it is usually produced in clandestine laboratories in South America. Crack cocaine is easily produced locally and by a single individual (Bourgois, 1996). The result is that hierarchies have not been explored within crack cocaine manufacturing; the literature on crack cocaine focuses on the sale of the drug and the subsequent hierarchies that exist within the distribution networks (see Schatzberg & Kelley, 1997).

Another drug that is readily "manufactured" domestically is marijuana. Much research exists on the topic but is often relegated to social relations outside of the producing group or apart from the producer. For example, Hafley and Tewksbury (1995; 1996) consider the social relationships between the marijuana growers and the communities in which they exist. Weisheit (1990; 1991) approaches the idea of hierarchies in marijuana cultivation, but his research subjects reflect more on their personal accomplishments and rewards from the behavior. In short, he finds that growers self-rank themselves based on the quality and/or potency of the marijuana they cultivate (Weisheit, 1991). Also, Weisheit's research shows that much marijuana cultivation is performed by individuals and not groups (1990; 1991).

The differences between methamphetamine production compared to crack cocaine and marijuana include: only the production of methamphetamine can result in fire and explosions, the chemicals necessary for methamphetamine production are controlled, and the production of methamphetamine takes greater specialized knowledge than either of the other drugs' production. The production of methamphetamine is a multistage process where specialized knowledge, risky tasks, and time-consuming processes are necessary. In fact, the production of methamphetamine can easily necessitate a division of labor. Unlike the domestic production of crack cocaine and marijuana, methamphetamine production could–and does–benefit from group involvement.

Adding gender into the phenomena of methamphetamine production supports much recent research that illustrates women's involvement in criminal behavior. Until the 1980s, women were often depicted as secondary to males with regard to their criminality. Female offenders have historically been considered status offenders and nonviolent (e.g., runaways) or took part in very gender-specific crimes (e.g., prostitution) (Schur, 1984). Recently we have seen women taking greater part in crimes of all sorts. There are rising numbers of women being arrested and convicted for drug and drug-related offenses as well as violent offenses. Women's prison facilities are getting more crowded. Also we have seen the emergence of "girl gangs" that are involved in violence and drugs. But what are the effects within single- and/or mixed-sex groups taking part in criminal behavior?

Warr (2002) provides a concise means of understanding the interaction between social learning and peer pressure. Using three key issues, solidarity within the peer group can be established and maintained. These three issues are loyalty, status, and fear of ridicule (Warr, 2002). Although maintaining loyalty to fellow group members is clear, Warr provides mechanisms for the establishment of statuses. The more experienced, loyal, and skilled the group member is at either leadership or deviant techniques, the higher the status of that group member. Aiding the division of group members within a hierarchy is the use of ridicule to maintain group cohesion and norms. Using Warr's concepts we can see that within criminal groups hierarchies can be established and maintained.

Through interviews with women who have been charged with drug-related offenses, a recurring theme of status within their peer group was evident. This study seeks to uncover what statuses are present in methamphetamine-producing groups. Further, how do group members maintain these statuses? By identifying what statuses exist within the groups, we can better understand the mechanisms that provide for new members to enter the group and mobility within the group.

METHODS

The data for this study were obtained through in-depth surveys with 31 women incarcerated in county jails in Missouri and Arkansas. Using current lists provided by each facility, every female inmate charged with drug-related offenses (i.e., possession, intent to deliver, maintaining a drug premises) was contacted personally and requested to take part in the study. Two women refused to take part in the study. Each participant selected a pseudonym to allow for confidentiality. Each interview lasted at least one hour, to a maximum of three hours....

DEMOGRAPHICS OF THE SAMPLE

The average age of the sample was 36 years old, with a range of 18 to 48 years old. One woman was 18 years old. Seven women were between 21 and 29 years old, 12 women were between 30 and 39 years old, and 11 women were between 40 and 49 years old. The sample consisted of 28 white women, one African-American woman, and two Hispanic women. The majority of the sample, 19 women, were single at the time of their interview; four women were married, four women were separated, and four women were divorced. Of the 31 women involved in this study, 18 stated that they had "cooked" methamphetamine; the same 18 reported that they had sold or traded methamphetamine for money or other items of value. All 31 women reported that they had used methamphetamine at least one time.

Every woman interviewed was employed prior to incarceration; however, their employment status varied considerably. Fifteen women had regular legitimate occupations (e.g., restaurant mangers, retail clerks, and fast food cooks), 11 women were employed in seasonal or family-operated businesses (e.g., drywall installers, roofing companies, and house painters), and the remaining five women drifted between low-level minimum wage jobs and/or maintained illegitimate occupations (e.g., methamphetamine production, prostitution).

With regard to educational attainment, 26 women had a high school diploma or a GED and the remaining five women possessed an associate's degree, bachelor's degree, or some form of postsecondary education (e.g., med-tech training, paramedic training).

The combination of educational attainment and occupation can be considered hallmarks of class standing. The women in this sample can be considered largely lower- to working-class individuals. Many, if not most, had illegitimate income in addition to income derived from their occupations (e.g., illicit drug sales and /or prostitution). The result is that many reported indicators of wealth (e.g., multiple new automobiles, high-grade stereo equipment, and cash on hand), yet none of the participants reported assets that are normally associated with the wealthy (e.g., real estate, stocks).

The demographic data provided can be used to illustrate that a typical participant in this study would be a single white woman in her mid-30s employed in either a service sector job or manual labor position. She would also hold a high school diploma and live comfortably, but financially would have little to no net worth. She would also be a regular methamphetamine user who occasionally sells the drug, and is capable of producing the drug.

FINDINGS

The hierarchy within methamphetamine-producing groups focuses on maintaining a supply of the drug. From the participants' comments, every action is connected with the production process or used to rank the people present. Of the 18 participants who had experience as a cook, they all related that a similar hierarchy was present in their group. The responses from these women varied in detail. Annie relates the hierarchy present in her group in great detail from highest status to lowest: cook, gas man/juicer, shopper, dope ho, and lastly the "simple user." Because Annie's experiences with a methamphetamine-producing group were related in the greatest detail, her comments comprise the bulk of the narrative regarding statuses within these groups.

The Methamphetamine Cook

Annie (a 32-year-old white woman) is 5′2″ tall, blonde, currently separated from her second husband, and she has three children. She appears to be in good health and claims that the jail food has "bulked" her up. Annie has a long sentence yet appears in good humor. Her good humor was evidenced by the pseudonym she chose. She said that Annie was short for anhydrous ammonia, a key ingredient to the production of methamphetamine. She has earned a college degree and worked as a registered nurse and has had paramedic training. Her second husband began sexually molesting her oldest child from her first marriage; she subsequently separated from him. She stated that the stress of the abuse of her child combined with being alone caused her to gain weight. Her weight ballooned to 285 pounds. Annie stated that her existing stress was compounded by her own self-image as being "fat." It is at this point that she contacted an old friend from high school. The old friend and Annie used to use drugs together during high school. It was this old friend who first offered Annie methamphetamine as a means to control her weight and feel better. She initially began to use methamphetamine to escape from her feelings of powerlessness regarding her second husband's sexual abuse of her oldest daughter. As she said, "I had to just [long pause] get my mind off that shit; meth'll do that for ya for sure." A bounty hunter captured Annie; she had multiple outstanding warrants for drugs. Upon her arrival at the jail, she was in possession of both methamphetamine and marijuana.

All 18 women stated that the cook holds the highest position of privilege and prestige within the group. Annie explains:

> If you are a cook, you are all set. I mean, like, you could have anything you wanted. You want other drugs? You got 'em. You want a stereo? You got it. It might be hot, but you got it. Everyone in every group I saw was, like, tuned-in to the cook. [What do you mean, "tuned-in"?] Well, like the cook is the top dog. Without the cook you'd have to go buy meth on your own—or schmooze [persuade] it outa somebody else.

Reinforcing her experience with methamphetamine-producing groups, Annie clarifies the position of cooks:

> Anyway, at the top of the group was the cook. There might be like two or three cooks in a group—like mine, we had, wait, let's see, five people who could cook decent dope. Cooks are like gods. I mean everyone does whatever they can to keep the cook happy. Food, stereos, supplies, sex, whatever they want they got.

Annie's recollection of methamphetamine cooks as "top dog" constructs the position of methamphetamine cook as a goal for noncooks. Attaining this position includes a constant supply of methamphetamine, deference from others, and the ability to have anything you want. This power can be considered economic in nature, with methamphetamine being the currency.

Group members had to learn that the cook was the most valued member of the group. Although learning this may appear to be simple, learning who holds the greatest power within the group aids in the neophyte understanding the entire structure of the group. As Annie's comments continue, we see how members of the group relegate value and status to its members relative to their behavior within the group.

The Gas Man/Juicer

Annie also provides another position in the hierarchy of methamphetamine-producing groups:

> Above the shoppers were the gas men or juicers. [*What is a juicer or gas man?*] These are the guys—usually guys—that would go get the anhydrous ammonia. It was a real ordeal trying to get anhydrous, if ya fucked up you'd blow up or get burned by the anhydrous. A couple of weeks back I was driving on 55 [Interstate 55] and I saw this car burning on the side of the road and you could smell the, well, it smells special, that smell of anhydrous. They fucked up.

Second only to the cook, whose behavior is very risky and highly valued by the group, being a gas man is much more risky. A shopper (discussed later) can succeed in her or his role by legitimately buying the necessary items, while a gas man can not. Gas men run the risk of arrest but also run the risk of injury and death.

The increased risk gas men face is due to the need for anhydrous ammonia. Anhydrous ammonia (a key precursor chemical in the production of some forms of methamphetamine) is a "dry" form of household ammonia that is in a gaseous state and when it comes into contact with air, it chemically tries to bond with the water molecules present in the air (Falkenthal, 1997; Hargreaves, 2000). If it comes into contact with human skin, it leaches out the water in the skin, resulting in a chemical burn (Falkenthal, 1997; Hargreaves, 2000). If inhaled, the anhydrous ammonia will leach out the water in the mouth, sinuses, throat, and lungs, resulting in internal chemical burns (Falkenthal, 1997; Hargreaves, 2000). Additionally, anhydrous ammonia is explosive (Falkenthal, 1997; Hargreaves, 2000). With this in mind, gas men are at substantially higher risk than any other group member who does not handle the substance. The higher risk accords them more status and privilege within the group.

Whereas 17 women noted the status of gas man or juicer from their experiences, one woman was involved with a group that did not use anhydrous ammonia. Elizabeth detailed her assistance in the production process: "They needed red phosphorus to cook with, so I would get it for 'em." Elizabeth (a 45-year-old white woman) is 5'7" tall, blonde, divorced, and she has two children. She stated that she was bipolar and had only received one of her two daily injections to control her condition. As a result she was pacing in the small interview/visitor's room. Although she was very pleasant and talkative, she was apparently agitated, or on edge. She had a high school diploma and worked (until recently) at her husband's restaurant. Elizabeth claimed that her husband was the son of the local mafia boss. As her marriage began to dissolve, largely due to her husband's use of crack cocaine, she stated that her husband had hired a "hit-man" to kill her and that her husband had tried to kill her with a kitchen knife as well. She began using methamphetamine when friends offered it to her husband; as she said, "When in Rome." She was arrested after a traffic stop resulted in the police finding methamphetamine in her purse. She is unable to pay her bond because none of her friends will accept a collect call from jail, and she is too afraid of her husband to call him. As a result, she is just waiting for her case to come to court.

Regardless of the method of producing methamphetamine used, the person who supplied the integral ingredient held a higher status. Again, status in the group is connected with the risk taken by the group member. With regard to the hierarchy Annie detailed, Elizabeth would hold a status about equal with a shopper and below a gas man. Elizabeth explains:

INTERVIEWER: Did you buy it [red phosphorus], or what?

ELIZABETH: Well, I used to think that you bought like a can of it but all you gotta do is scrape off the striker part of book of matches.

INTERVIEWER: You mean the match heads? The top end that you light with?

ELIZABETH: Oh no! On the actual book, the little strip that you use to light the match. That is where the red phosphorus is. All you gotta do is scrape it away. Takes forever, but you gotta do it just so. I mean if you dig too deep you get paper get paper, but you want all the red phosphorus. So ya gotta do it just so and 1 was good at it. So I'd lend a hand doing it. I'd sit there hours scraping away with a knife. We'd have piles of matchbooks but no way to light them! [laughs]

INTERVIEWER: So you'd watch them cook and just scrape away huh?

ELIZABETH: Yeah, separating those pills takes a while. So we'd bullshit as I would scrape and then by the time they were ready for the red phosphorus, I'd be about done. Course if I wasn't done they'd have to wait for me. Shit, I remember once I showed up and there was this asshole scraping matchbooks; I was kinda pissed cuz he was like taking my job, ya know. Then Joe [a pseudonym] told him to stop and for me to take over.

Elizabeth's status was reaffirmed when the "temp scraper" was pushed aside by the cook so that she could resume her "job." In order for Elizabeth to perform her task within the production process, she had to learn the techniques specific to the task. How did she come to know that the red phosphorus was contained in the striker of the matchbook and not the match head? She learned this from an existing "scraper."

The Shopper

There are other levels of power and status within these groups, as Annie explains:

> Now above the users and dope ho's were the people that would actually help out. First ya got the shoppers. [*What did the shoppers do?*] They would go get anything. I mean anything. They'd get the supplies to cook with: pills, buckets, lithium, tubing, whatever. Shit, I remember this one cook's car broke down and she asked for a Thunderbird. So this shopper I know goes out and steals one—bingo! The cook is happy again. The best shoppers were the ones who would really put their ass on the line. The ones that used like real money to buy pills were still good and all, but the ones that would hold up a store and take all their pills—now that was great. You still had your cash, and the pills. So I guess there is levels within the levels of power there.

The establishment of a specialized role in the methamphetamine-producing group to obtain the goods requested by the cook reaffirms the formal social structure within the group. In their quest to obtain the requested goods any means were acceptable, even theft. In fact, Annie states that the more risk the shopper takes, the greater she or he is valued. What is important to note is that shoppers are integral to the production process within the group.

Brandy (a 42-year-old white woman) is 5'5" tall with dark brown hair; her skin appears to be blotchy, red, and irritated. She is single and has a 19-year-old son. She considers herself to be a functioning addict. She will use a class of drugs (e.g., stimulants or depressants) for a time, then switch to another class of drugs Much of her drug use parallels what she can obtain via theft and fraud. She has an off-putting personality and is not very talkative. When she responds to a question it is usually a one-word response. Further probing gains little additional information. She is currently in jail for cooking methamphetamine in her house.

Brandy could produce methamphetamine on her own, but often chose to be an assistant. As she stated, "I would shop a lot, you know, go get the pills. Truck stops are great for that, plus you get to go on a nice drive!" Additionally, she would "just lend a hand here or there."

Each of the 18 women spoke of their group having at least one shopper; some groups had up to four shoppers. As they described the behaviors of these group members, they echoed Annie's comments. If members of the group wanted anything, especially the cook, the shopper was the person slated to obtain it.

The Dope Ho

Although "simple users" may be at the bottom of the methamphetamine group hierarchy, another status, dope ho, is only slightly above them. Most of the participants knew dope ho's (15 of the 18 participants); the remaining three had heard of men and women trading sex for drugs but had never personally experienced the phenomena. Annie explains the in-group social position of dope ho's:

> Along with users are dope ho's. Now dope ho's are not a problem really. They are around just to trade a blow or a lay for some meth. They are ALWAYS there. Like I said, they are not a problem like the users, but they really don't do anything to help out. Dope ho's are like baggage, they are there taking up space. Now some guy cooking meth would like to have 'em. [*Why would guy cooks like them?*] OH! Well, the dope ho's take care of the cook, with sex. They are not there for everyone to fuck, just the cook. So, like guys are right, they always wanna get laid so the dope ho's handle that. You know, there might be a few dope ho's at a time. It's funny, it's like the cook has a choice who he's gonna bang, "No, not her, not her, yeah I'll bang her today!" That sort of thing.

Positions similar to that of a dope ho are not unique among drug-using groups. We know about people trading sex for crack cocaine, even for a hit of that drug (Ratner, 1993; Maher, 1997). However, with regard to crack cocaine, many, of these women are prostitutes who trade sex with "johns" for the drug that they hold (Ratner, 1993; Maher, 1997). As Annie reports, dope ho's are accepted members of the group unlike the "simple users." Dope ho's function to keep the cook happy (sexually), which aids in the production process. The fascinating thing about the presence of dope ho's is how this (usually) heterosexual relationship interacts with other heterosexual relationships.

> INTERVIEWER: What about a wife or girlfriend? Wouldn't they get mad? Or were the wives and girlfriends of these guys the dope ho's?
>
> ANNIE: Nah, they were nobody's girlfriend or wife, just ho's. Nobody really cared about them either, they were just always there. They were cool and all, just kinda looked down at, 1 mean, shit, you know, they were tradin' a blowjob for a buzz—not a bag of dope, just a buzz. Kinda sad now that I think of it.
>
> INTERVIEWER: Were there guys as dope ho's too?
>
> ANNIE: Yeah, I saw a few and heard of more. But, you know how girls are, they can get laid anytime they want and they don't have to give meth away to get laid! Guys will jump on anything, anytime—"Sex? I'll do it!"—so why have the burden of carrying someone else's habit just to get laid? Still, some chicks would have some around, but it was not like normal to see guy-ho's.

Annie's comments regarding the relationship between dope ho's and men are important. As Annie said, "nobody really cared about them," indicating that dope ho's hold a certain status within the group. The occupy a low status position in which they are marginalized to such a degree that wives and girlfriends apparently do not consider them threats to their monogamous relationship with the male cooks.

To hear Annie talk about dope ho's, her inflection is important; these people are looked down on. However, the status of dope ho can be considered slightly higher than that of the "pain in the ass" user.

The Uses of Methamphetamine

Every women involved in this project agreed that the position that lacks any prestige is that of the simple user. Annie provides a very clear image of the user:

> At the bottom were the users. These were the people that just wanted to buy meth—if ya think of the most strung out, tweeked freaks, that is the user. They are not really in the group. I mean, we all know them, but they are more of a pain in the ass. They always show up at the worst times. They show up when the batch [of methamphetamine] ain't done yet. They show up when you wanna sleep. They show up, well, just like a pain in the ass, there is no good time.

The presence of users in a group creates the issue of risk and trust as being at odds with each other. Members of the group know the users or else they would not be allowed to socialize with the group. However, these people also pose a risk if they are undercover police officers or user-informers. Users are a burden to the group.

Users Versus Simple Users

It is important to differentiate between the types of methamphetamine users: users and "simple users." All of the participants in this study had used methamphetamine at some point in their lives. Most of the methamphetamine cooks (16 of the 18 cooks) were also current methamphetamine users. However, those women who took part, in whatever way, in the production process held a status above the "simple user." The "simple user" only uses the drug. The methamphetamine user is part of the group; the "simple user" is a "pain in the ass," meaning not part of the group.

As Annie (and others) relate, there is a distinct hierarchy within methamphetamine-using groups. Status within these groups is related to the activity regarding the methamphetamine production process. The greater the involvement and/or risk with the production process, the higher the status. Other participants in this study provided information on the process of upward mobility in the group as well as some variations of the statuses in these groups.

In-Group Mobility and Status Variations

There is a process involved in the production of methamphetamine. This process includes multiple people performing specific tasks. The performance of these tasks relates to the performance of social roles in the group. Brandy stated that she was able to cook, purchase the pills used as the base for the drug, and help out where needed. Other tasks that need to be completed in order for the methamphetamine production to be successful include: obtaining key precursor chemicals (P2P, red phosphorus, or anhydrous ammonia), obtaining the other items and compounds used in the production process (containers, lithium, hydrochloric acid, and hot plates), and the actual production of methamphetamine. These associations form a peer group for Brandy where she would "shop a lot." Her performance at this task was positive for the group and she was not stopped from doing it. Because she was able to cook methamphetamine as well, she was able—and allowed—to perform other functions.

The key point to understand is that these groups grow and splinter into networks that maintain some degree of association with each other. In these groups, gender differences fade as the actor rises in status within the group. Once the status of cook has been achieved, the drive for quality drugs equalizes the gender disparity evident lower levels of these methamphetamine production groups.

Annie knew how to cook and did so frequently. However, she would also take part in schemes to obtain anhydrous ammonia, illustrating her mobility within her group. She has earned the highest status, but was able to choose to work at a lower status. For example, Annie stated:

> Me and another girl would get all dolled up and go to farmers' houses. We'd knock on the door, wiggle, wink, giggle and shit. Then just ask if we could have some anhydrous. That always worked. [*So would you be treated as a juicer when you did that?*] Fuck no! [laughs] Shit, once you can cook you are golden, you know. I was just helpin' out. Now the guy we was with, he was the juicer. [*What about the woman you went with?*] Well, actually she was a dope ho. But she was cool.

Status can be earned by working with other members of the group and learning by their example. However, a formal learning process also takes place within methamphetamine-using groups. Cammy (a 42-year-old white woman) is 5'3" tall with brown hair and lives in a suburban area. She is fairly thin, but not as thin as some of the women in this study. Cammy appeared to be depressed and sad about her current situation. She was willing to take part in the interview, yet would often reply with one-word answers and little more when prodded. She did not want to say if she had any children, but she was separated from her husband. Her arrest occurred at a methamphetamine lab raided by the police. She possessed marijuana. Cammy illustrates how she learned to cook within the structure of the methamphetamine producing group when she states:

> I was livin' with this cook right. We was jus' like in the same house, not fuckin' or nothin'. OK, so I know how to cook but not real good. I asks this guy, don't wanna say his name, if he can teach my boyfriend to cook right. So he's like, "Cool," right. OK, so he's showin' my man how to cook and I am learnin' too, right. OK, so like now we both are cooks and we get our own thing goin' and we cook like crazy! It was cool.

Cammy, due to her status with her house-mate and as a cook, was able to bring her non-cooking boyfriend up in status. Once she and her boyfriend were both cooks, their a position within their group was solidified; however, shortly afterward they left this group to form their own group. In their new group they were able to complete all of the functions necessary to produce methamphetamine. Cammy's experiences provide us with a way that methamphetamine group spread. As the unique knowledge is disseminated, so too do the groups that hold this knowledge spread. It should be clear that these groups will be connected in a network of multiple cells of methamphetamine production.

The goal for these groups is the production of methamphetamine, not its sale. The various members of the group operate within a hierarchy where a neophyte can be upwardly mobile within the group, roles are defined, and power and prestige are linked to the status one holds. Interestingly, because the goal is paramount, in these groups they are more willing to dispose of social constructs valid in the dominant culture in order to further their goals. As a result, women who move up in the hierarchy of the production process are not stigmatized for the roles they play. Instead, women appear to become, or perceive themselves to be, the equals of their male counterparts.

Gender and Status in Methamphetamine-Producing Groups

Producing methamphetamine is rather easy even though it involves a number of processes and chemicals that can be hard to obtain. Annie and Brandy illustrated that their ability to change the role they played within the group is tied to their ability to cook methamphetamine themselves. This reflects the status that a methamphetamine cook holds within her group. Brandy can decide to cook one day and go for a drive the next day to obtain other material for the production of methamphetamine. Annie would cook methamphetamine, or choose to assist in obtaining anhydrous ammonia. Holding the status of a cook can be equated with the freedom to play the role of their own choosing. not to be relegated to a subordinate role defined by others within her group.

In every case, the women reported that they were able to complete the entire production process themselves. Their choice to simply "assist" was personal: every woman interviewed stated that she never felt that she was pressured to stand aside. Bea (a 41-year-old Hispanic woman), a homemaker in a suburban community who has a GED, is 5′3″ tall with long blonde hair and she is apparently healthy. Although some people appear to be younger than their actual age, Bea is the opposite; she appears to be much older than she actually is. Bea is married; her husband was also in the jail for unrelated charges. She has no children, but would have liked to have had some. Bea has been a methamphetamine user since the 1970s. She was very willing to discuss every aspect of her involvement with methamphetamine. At times her explanations sounded almost canned, as if she had been telling people about her experiences for years. Bea was arrested for possession of methamphetamine during the course of a traffic stop.

As Bea stated, "Shit, all we wanted was meth. You cook, I cook, who cares so long as it's good! I been cooking for what now [long pause] 20 years? Yeah, been about 20 years of cookin'. I am cool with the guys that cook, and they are cool with me."

Bea's statement identifies that the goal of these groups was methamphetamine, not money, nor material goods, nor quibbling over traditional gender expectations. However, as Bea stated, the higher the quality o the methamphetamine, the more desirable it is. This is an important point as it relates to gendered relationships within the hierarchy of methamphetamine-producing groups. This perceived equality intimates that methamphetamine cooks hold a status that transcends constructed gender statuses evident among female users. The master status for female methamphetamine cooks appears to change from "female" to "methamphetamine cook" due to the group's focus on the production of the drug.

The finding that female cooks can hold power over other group members is contra to traditional gender expectations. Considering this finding we must recall that the goal of the group is acquiring more methamphetamine. The group members are not trying to replicate the dominant cultural view of women, nor are they overtly trying to maintain male dominance in the methamphetamine subculture; all they want is more methamphetamine. Realizing that the groups goal is task-oriented, it makes sense that the group members would not care who produces—so long as the drug is being produced and a supply of methamphetamine is maintained.

These findings support Warr's (2002) research on peer pressure. The presence of a hierarchy (statuses) aids in the maintenance of loyalty and solidarity among group members. Marginal, unneeded, or unwanted persons are derided for their behavior (the '"pain in the ass user"). Importantly, Warr's work is centered on the theoretical premise of social learning and Sutherland's differential association; aspects of such learning can be seen in the methamphetamine-producing group.

Although gendered behavior appears to fade away at the upper levels of methamphetamine-producing groups, female cooks are still willing to use gendered expectations to achieve their ends. For example, Annie relates two other events that occurred with some regularity:

> Well, if you cook in the woods, like way out, we always had a guy and a girl cookin'. That way if ya hear someone walkin' up ya just start rollin' in the leaves kissin'. Shit, we got by a bunch of park rangers that way. They smell the cook, right, they find us makin' out and they freakin' apologize—can ya believe that? We get all huffy, right, then we just leave....Never got busted that way, never.

This recollection is one strategy to disguise their illegal activity. Often methamphetamine production takes place on public lands; the cook[s] will remain nearby, but not necessarily at the production site (Falkenthal, 1997; Hargreaves, 2000). During his investigation, the park ranger comes upon a couple kissing and apologizes for interrupting a behavior that has been constructed as "normal." Interestingly, Annie and her friend the showed that they understood the social construction of gender. They used expected gender roles to hide the fact that they were actually producing methamphetamine. The reaction by the park ranger rein-forced their idea that their use of constructed gender roles was accurate. However, there are other means employed to disguise illegal activities that take place in pub-lic places. Annie continues:

> Another thing we'd do, and it is kinda funny too, while the guys would be gettin' anhydrous I'd hang by the car with the hood up like somethin's wrong. If anybody stop, I just say that my boyfriend would be back soon with a wrecker. Plus that way I was a lookout too. Any cop roll up, I just ask for help, and I'll be damned if the car don't start! [laughs] I drive off and then circle back in a bit and pick up the boys. [laughs] Funny, huh?

In the second instance, Annie used the traditional gendered idea of a "damsel in distress." Relying on widely held constructions of gender Annie had been able to avoid arrest. Throughout these two recollections, Annie and her group know-ingly used gendered behavior to dispel any thoughts that deviant activity was taking place.

CONCLUSION

The roles that the women in this study play within their methamphetamine-pro-ducing groups are varied. The findings show that some statuses are more highly valued by the group, whereas others are not. The value placed on certain statuses indicates the presence of a hierarchy.

It should also be noted that illicit drug sales was not incorporated in the hier-arch of a methamphetamine-producing group Annie (or any other participant) detailed. At no time did Annie or any other participant provide a rank or status for a dealer of methamphetamine or any other drug. However, it is telling that members of these groups did trade and sell methamphetamine yet do not fit the ideal type of drug dealers.

The statuses that these women hold in their methamphetamine-producing groups range from "simple user" to cook. Introduction into the group would begin at the user level. The low status of the neophyte must be negotiated to obtain higher status. The neophyte would not simply obtain high status (e.g., a juicer) until she or he had shed the label of "pain in the ass" user. Group members in the upper echelon could easily take part in behavior that was "below" them without losing status. The rationale for this mobility is that the goal of the group was preeminent: the production of more methamphetamine.

The consensus among the participants is that the status associated with being a methamphetamine cook carries with it power and prestige within the group. It is expected that group members would seek to achieve this status. The data do not provide any intimation regarding persons holding a status that is disagreeable to them (for example, a shopper who disliked holding that position). We can assume that the ready supply of methamphetamine would ameliorate any discontent as the group members could use the drug free of charge.

Central to understanding methamphetamine-producing groups is the realization that they are organized to produce the drug they use. By producing their own supply of methamphetamine, they eliminate the need for a dealer (middle-man), save money, decrease their risk of arrest, and are assured of the quality of the drug they will use. To facilitate that goal, these groups have developed a hierarchy to achieve their aim.

Understanding the statuses and relationships within methamphetamine-producing groups illustrates the difficulties encountered by women as they leave jail or prison. Successful reintegration can be hampered y the ass of power and status they once enjoyed in methamphetamine-producing networks. This loss is exacerbated by the unwelcome realization that they are viewed as just another drug user, Although that label is accurate in societal terms, the women are reduced to what they once despised—"pain in the ass users." Thus, imprisonment results in a crisis of self-identity as well as the loss of power and status in a former social network.

Providing drug treatment, diversionary programs, or other social services to these women should include an acknowledgment of the statuses that these women have held. Beyond a general idea of reintegration, these women will face their crisis of self-identity in any conforming group they would join. Having once been the "top dog," finding themselves as anything less is another hurdle for the recovering drug user to overcome.

REFERENCES

Bourgois, P. (1996). *In search of respect: Selling crack in el barrio.* Cambridge, MA: Cambridge University Press.

Drug Enforcement Administration (DEA). (2000). *United States Drug Enforcement Administration Internet site.* Retrieved June 8, 2012, from http://www.justice.gov/dea/.

Denton, B., & O'Malley, P. (1999). Gender, trust, and business: Women drug dealers in the illicit economy. *British Journal of Criminology, 39,* 513–530.

Falkenthal, G. (1997). Clan labs: A modern problem. *Fire Engineering, 150*(9), 41.

Hafley, S. R., & Tewksbury, R. (1995). The rural Kentucky marijuana industry: Organization and community involvement. *Deviant Behavior, 16*(3), 201–221.

———. (1996). Reefer madness in bluegrass country: Community structure and roles in the rural Kentucky marijuana industry. *Journal of Crime and Justice, 19*(1), 75–94.

Hargreaves, G. (2000). Clandestine drug labs. *FBI Law Enforcement Bulletin, 69*(4), 1–7.

Kurtis, B. (1997). *Investigative reports: Meth's deadly high* [video]. Arts and Entertainment Television Networks.

Lavigne, Y. (1996a). *Hell's angels: "Three can keep a secret if two are dead."* Secaucus, NJ: Carol.

———. (1996b). *Hell's angels: Into the abyss.* New York: HarperCollins.

Maher, L. (1997). *Sexed work: Gender, race, and resistance in a Brooklyn drug market.* New York: Oxford.

Meth, M., Chalmers, R., & Bassin, G. (2001). *Pulse check: Trends in drug abuse mid-year 2001.* Washington, DC: Office of National Drug Control Policy.

Pennell, S., Ellett, J., Rienick, C., & Grimes, J. (1999). *Meth matters: Report on methamphetamine users in five western cities.* Washington, DC: U.S. Government Printing Office.

Ratner, M. S. (1993). Sex, drugs, and public policy: Studying and understanding the sex-for-crack phenomenon. In M. S. Ratner (Ed.), *Crack pipe for pimp: An ethnographic investigation of sex-for-crack exchanges* (pp. 1–36). New York: Lexington.

Riley, J. (1999a). *1998 annual report on drug use among adult and juvenile arrestees.* Washington, DC: U.S. Government Printing Office.

———. (1999b). *Research report: 1998 annual report on methamphetamine use among arrestees.* Washington, DC: National Institute of Justice.

———. (2000). *1999 annual report on drug use among adult and juvenile arrestees.* Washington, DC: U.S. Government Printing Office.

Schatzberg, R., & Kelley, R. J. (1997). *African-American organized crime: A social history.* Piscataway, NJ: Rutgers University Press.

Schur, E. M. (1984). *Labeling women deviant: Gender, stigma, and social control.* New York: McGraw-Hill.

Warr, M. (2002). *Companions in crime: The social aspects of criminal conduct.* New York: Cambridge University Press.

Weisheit, R. A. (1990). Domestic marijuana growers: Mainstreaming deviance. *Deviant Behavior, 11*(2), 107–129.

———. (1991). The intangible rewards from crime: The case of marijuana cultivation. *Crime and Delinquency, 37*(4), 506–527.

Young, L. A., Young, L. G., Klein, M. M., Klein, D. M., & Beyer, D. (1977). *Recreational drugs.* New York: Berkley.

ɬ

Trafficking in Bodily Perfection: Examining the Late-Modern Steroid Marketplace and Its Criminalization

Peter B. Kraska, Charles R. Bussard, and
John J. Brent

Illicit steroid and human growth hormone use by professional athletes has received significant media and political attention in the last five years. The resulting political pressure has compelled federal law enforcement to prosecute serious new control initiatives. To date, no academic research inquiring into the nature of this illicit industry exists. This study fills this void through the mixed methods approach–employing both ethnographic field research and quantitative content analysis. The ethnographic data demonstrate a fascinating late-modern trafficking scheme in which the central informant established an apartment-based manufacturing operation converting raw steroid chemical compounds ordered off the Internet into injectable solutions. Content analysis of 186 websites that supply anabolic androgenic steroids (AAS) demonstrates that these grounded findings are indicative of a much larger phenomenon. Our final analysis examines the broader theoretical relevance of the ethnographic findings through contextualizing them within macrostructural (supply) and macrocultural (demand) social forces.

Source: Adapted from Kraska, P. B., Bussard, C. R., & Brent J. J. (2010). Trafficking in bodily perfection: Examining the late-modern steroid marketplace and its criminalization. *Justice Quarterly, 27*(2), 159–185. Used with permission of the authors and publisher. This research was supported in part by a research grant from the College of Justice and Safety Program of Distinction at Eastern Kentucky University.

Most drug war analysts cite the death of Len Bias in 1986 as the tipping point in the decade-long drug war of the mid-1980s and 1990s (Inciardi, 1992; Trebach, 1987). Bias was a young and highly talented African-American pro-basketball player who overdosed on powder cocaine while partying with friends. His death was the direct catalyst for the U.S. Congress in 1986 to enact the landmark federal drug Legislation known as "mandatory minimums" (Sterling & Stewart, 2006).

Professional sports again take center stage in the emergence of another potential drug war. This time the spotlight is not on people using psychoactive drugs that alter their state of consciousness; rather, the concern is with drugs designed to enhance athletic performance, body aesthetics, life span, and healing after an injury—an entire class of drugs that are referred to by most as "steroids."

Numerous performance-enhancing drug scandals have rocked both professional and Olympic sports. A few examples include Marion Jones (Olympic track star) who has been sentenced to a six-month prison sentence for lying to a steroid investigative body, the constant turmoil surrounding the Tour-de-France cycling race over positive drug tests, and numerous high-profile baseball players being accused of and admitting to using anabolic steroids and human growth hormone (HGH).

The attention on professional sports has also generated a more general concern about the extent to which everyday athletics (both young and old), weightlifters, bodybuilders, and people interested in losing weight or living longer are buying and using these illicit substances (McCallum, 2008). The media (particularly the sports media) has adopted it as a part of their daily news cycle. The U.S. Congress has launched hearings, conducted in-depth investigations, and passed new steroid control legislation (Shipley, 2007; Tucker, 2007). The moralizing about steroids reached the presidential level during a State of the Union Address in 2004:

> The use of performance-enhancing drugs like steroids in baseball, football, and other sports is dangerous, and it sends the wrong message—that there are shortcuts to accomplishment, and that performance is more important than character.

Whether these empirical indicators will materialize into an actual "war on steroids" is unclear. However, several moral panic criteria are evident, including: expert and political outrage and moral condemnation; law enforcement interest in expanding into this arena; new federal and state legislation; a difficult-to-refute trend in an increased use of these substances; and an exaggeration of the likely dangers of these drugs (Cohen, 2002; Goode & Ben-Yehuda, 1994). In short, we may be witness to a significant new development in our society's long history of waging drug wars.

Criminal justice/criminology has yet to provide any research or scholarly discussion about this increasingly important phenomenon and issue.[1] Moreover, while other disciplines have conducted some noteworthy epidemiological studies (particularly on youth steroid use), no research in any field has been published on the illicit steroid marketplace or steroid trafficking. The central purpose of this study, therefore, is to provide some much-needed data, analysis, and theoretical contextualization of the steroid-trafficking industry. The various sports scandals have revealed—at least to the media, politicians, and the government—a potential thriving black market (Cramer, 2005).

Aside from shedding empirical light on an important crime and justice issue, two subobjectives are pursued. First, we demonstrate that the study of the illegal body enhancement drug industry harbors significant theoretical and crime control implications. For example, this research points to a significant shift in the general nature of illicit drug trafficking: a fluid and quite new form of criminality based in a virtually unregulated, Internet-based global marketplace. Second—through a mixed-methods approach that includes both ethnographic field research and quantitative content analysis—we attempt to link the micro-interactive and the macrostructural/cultural dimensions of this phenomenon.

BRIEF CONTEXT: DEFINING AND CRIMINALIZING STEROIDS

Steroids are pharmacologically referred to as "anabolic-androgenic steroids" or AAS. They are manufactured substances related to male sex hormones, and are legally available through a doctor's prescription for the purpose of treating various medical conditions. They are often used to treat individuals with wasting disease, serious illness, and malnutrition. Those suffering from diseases such as HIV/AIDS seem to benefit the most because of the increase in lean muscle mass and the positive effect on the body's immune system (Lenehan, 2003). These same medical benefits make AAS attractive to athletes and nonathletes alike who harbor a desire to gain strength, speed, and lean muscle mass (Hoberman, 2005). The more popular varieties of illicit AAS are Testosterone Enanthate ("Test"), Deca, Sustanon, Dianabol, and Anadrol. The method of application ranges from intramuscular injection, oral administration, and even transdermal application (topical cream form).

However, framing AAS as merely performance-enhancing drugs fails to capture the expanding motivations for using these drugs. While bodybuilders, powerlifters, and athletes attempting to boost their athletic performance likely comprise the core of AAS users, there is strong evidence that their appeal is broadening to include those who want to lose weight, lengthen life span, heal more quickly from injuries, or simply feel and look younger.

The other difficulty with the AAS label is that it excludes numerous other performance and body enhancement substances that are not actually steroids. An example of these is a broader class of drugs called "ergogenic aids" or sometimes "steroid accessory drugs." These substances "enhance energy production, control, and efficiency" and include a large array of substances, both legal and illegal (Silver, 2001). The most well-known include blood-doping drugs (such as EPO [erythropoietin] used by some competitive cyclists to dramatically boost aerobic capacity) and HGH.

HGH received significant media and political attention in 2007–08 —particularly within the aforementioned baseball scandal and with disclosures that some celebrities use the drug for cosmetic reasons (Lyons, 2008). It is not a steroid because it is chemically unrelated to testosterone. Several research studies document its ability to rapidly drop fat deposits, increase muscle mass, bone density, and cognitive ability, as well as make older users feel significantly younger (Mattingly & Estrada, 2008; McCallum, 2008; Peter, 2007). Both EPO and HGH are not currently listed under federal law as controlled substances (Caruso, 2007). For purposes of simplicity, we will be using the labels AAS or steroids, while keeping in mind the caveat that this study includes numerous other ergogenic aids such as HGH.

A Short History of Steroid Criminalization

Until 1990, AAS in the USA were not scheduled as controlled substances and were simply regulated as any other prescription drug by the U.S. Food and Drug Administration. In the mid to late 1980s, during the escalation of the war on drugs, politicians also become increasingly concerned with reports of high school and Olympic athletes using steroids to gain a competitive edge (as in the case of Ben Johnson testing positive for steroid use in 1988 after winning a gold medal in track). Between 1988 and 1990 Congress held hearings to determine if the Controlled Substances Act should be modified to include AAS alongside addictive psychoactive drugs such as heroin and cocaine. Even though the Food and Drug Administration (FDA), Drug Enforcement Administration (DEA), and American Medical Association all argued vehemently against their inclusion, the U.S. Congress passed the Anabolic Steroid Control Act of 1990 (ASCA), which classified AAS as a Schedule III drug (the same category as amphetamines, opium, and morphine). Many states soon followed suit, with New York even classifying steroids as a Schedule II drug—a higher standard than found in federal law. This increased attention was compounded by the media's discussion of "roid rage" in the early 1990s, associating AAS use with "uncontrollable aggressive violence" (Waskul & Vannini, 2006). Steroids were viewed increasingly as a "social problem."

On October 22, 2004, due to a new wave of media/political attention on the use of AAS in sports, the Anabolic Steroids Act of 2004 was signed into federal law (Hoberman, 2005). This act amended the Anabolic Steroid Control Act of 1990, by altering the definition of AAS to include a range of specific chemicals known as "steroid precursor." These chemicals act to boost the production of testosterone by the user (e.g., "Andro" or androstenedione). Additionally, it directed the U.S. Sentencing Commission (USSC) to review the federal sentencing guidelines with respect to anabolic steroid–related offenses, resulting in significantly increased punishments (Hoberman, 2005).

As of this writing, more restrictive legislation is being considered by the U.S. Congress as a reaction to the baseball steroid controversy (McCallum, 2008;

Shipley, 2007). As will be discussed later, it also appears that law enforcement officials have recently gone from taking a very passive role in the enforcement of steroid laws to more aggressive efforts.

The heightened media/political/police attention to this illicit phenomenon has exposed a potentially significant and fascinating new AAS marketplace. While most people envision someone at a gym selling these illegal substances out of the trunk of their car, in actuality the emerging picture of today's AAS marketplace is a decentralized and highly complex mix of local and foreign doctors, Internet prescription sites, Internet supply houses, mid-level distributors, and a vast array of different types of customers. Perhaps the most significant feature of today's AAS marketplace, yet not examined empirically in the academic literature, is the growth in suppliers outside the U.S. borders. These substances are often legal to obtain and unregulated in numerous foreign countries and are readily available for purchase over the counter or Internet.

MIXED METHODS

Two primary research methods were employed to shed empirical light on the AAS marketplace.

Ethnographic Field Research Methods

The first research method used was 15 months of ethnographic field research conducted in 2005 through the first four months of 2006. Fieldwork began at a commercial gym where several nationally recognized bodybuilders trained. Contact was made with numerous bodybuilders, but the closest rapport was established with a bodybuilder, referred to as "Mike," who competed at national events. Mike became the central informant for this research.[2] Research sites included the gym, the primary informant's home, local bars, and numerous strength and bodybuilding competitions. The total geographical area encompassed in this study (including the range of illicit drug distribution associated with this regional operation) was a 60-square-mile radius that included one city of 50,000 people and another almost 300,000.

The central informant's status as a national-level bodybuilder translated into a complex array of contacts within the entire weight-training community in this region—which included collegiate athletes, law enforcement officers and firefighters, recreational weightlifters, amateur power-lifters, and other professional bodybuilders. Even though this study centered on illicit steroid use and trafficking and the participants were made aware of the nature of the research project, all the primary research subjects used in this study (12 in total) were cooperative (due in part to the main informant's high status). These additional contacts were made through snowball sampling, and the study group consisted of 10 men and two women. Fifty-three additional individuals were also included in the study, but our encounters with them were too brief to consider them true informants.

Due to the large size of the community under study, and the extended time length of this ethnography, we decided that the most constructive way to reduce our data into a presentable form was to concentrate our analysis primarily on our central informant, as he was the centerpoint of a large network of AAS distributors and users spread out over a large geographical area....

ETHNOGRAPHIC FIELD RESEARCH: "DUDE, WHERE CAN I GET SOME?"

The central informant for this study was a nationally ranked bodybuilder living in a medium-size mid-western community and married with no children. He had been interested in growing extraordinary amounts of lean muscle on his body since he was 21, and began using an array of illicit ergogenic drugs when he was 22. His reasons for getting involved in bodybuilding were typical among the many weightlifters and bodybuilders we encountered in this study: a "skinny kid" searching for an avenue to obtain a high level of masculine and/or athletic status (Hoberman, 2005; Monaghan, 2002). As demonstrated by Mike's own words, his quest for the "perfect" physique is intense.

> I want to be a freak walking around. I want little children to see me walking down the street and bury their little faces in the shirttails of their parents crying while their parents wonder what in the hell happened to this person! I want them to say, I didn't think a person could actually look like that...like a living and breathing cartoon character that walked right out of a comic book.

The 12 other informants in this study shared Mike's rationale—although most were less extreme in their descriptions. Most framed their desires more in terms of "getting hard," "being ripped/shredded," being massive," "looking scary, " "being scary strong," "wanting the ultimate body," and "wanting to intimidate my opponents at first glance."

The Beginnings of an Internet-Based Growth Industry

The weightlifting subculture studied here is fascinating and rich with theoretical possibilities. However, it became obvious within the first month of this ethnography that the most noteworthy aspect of this fieldwork would be steroid manufacturing and distribution. The long learning process our central informant went through to establish a lucrative steroid-trafficking operation is instructive. We (the authors) were able to observe first-hand some of the latter stages of this operation due to the duration of our study (15 months).

> Of course that was in the beginning...when I was a newbie. You would go and buy some stuff from a buddy of yours that you met in the gym that might have a bottle of this or a bottle of that. Today, though, it is a totally different game. Most people have no clue as to where we get our stuff. They probably think we are traveling to Mexico and filling our bags full of the stuff and crossing the border.

Mike began as an AAS user. He bought his drugs from a fellow weightlifter and friend at his gym (one of the 12 subinformants for this study). He could barely afford the prices he was paying, and started to purchase a surplus of drugs from his dealer so he could make a small amount of money off his friends to offset his expenses. Mike explained, though, how he grew weary of "paying out the ass" for AAS when he knew that the same people he was competing against were getting their drugs for much cheaper. He finally expressed being "fed up" with only being able to afford such small amounts of drugs at a time.

> I basically came to the conclusion that there was no way I was ever going to get to where I wanted to be with the small amount of drugs I could buy. Regardless of whatever genetics I had. It's just that simple. The farther along I wanted to go in bodybuilding, the larger my body had to be and the more drugs I have to take to set there.

Mike surmised that the only way he could compete at a high level in body-building was to purchase a much larger supply at a lower price. Notice that securing a profit was only a means to the end of "getting huge." As found with other types of drug dealing, involvement is often initially motivated by a desire to have someone else offset the costs of their own use (Adler, 1985; Atkyns & Hannenman, 1974; Tunnel, 1993; VanNostrand & Tewksbury, 1999).

He recalled that the guys he originally bought his drugs from referred to "placing an order." He knew these orders were going to people that were connected somehow to foreign pharmacies. He figured his suppliers were probably paying less than half the price he paid, and concluded: "I always sat these after I bought something [more AAS] and thought to myself that if these fucking idiots could do it, so could I." Our central informant explained how he searched the Internet fervently for a long time looking for these overseas pharmacies. "Everywhere I looked it said you could get this or that... but I had to pay some price to get the address of one of these places," he said.

> Then I started paying more attention to these bodybuilding message boards. That is how I found the first overseas place to buy from. It's amazing. These forums have lists of places that include scammers and everything. It just makes it a lot easier to figure out basically who to buy from.

"Scammers" were domestic and foreign businesses that did not deliver on a paid-for AAS order and were then placed on blacklists found on Internet message boards. The researchers for this study visited several of these scammer lists and websites. In some cases jilted customers would post pictures of where the alleged "scammer" lived, worked, the type of car they drove, the name of their spouse, and sometimes even the schedule of the daily routines of the person—a type of informal Ebay-like feedback system. Mike viewed this tactic as an effective deterrent and claimed to have never been the victim of a "scammer."

After several months Mike decided on a website operation based out of Yugoslavia. He expressed a sense of "awe" when viewing the prices. The "Sustenon 250" that he recently purchased from a friend at close to $32 an ampoule was just

$7. "I couldn't believe my eyes and about felt out of my chair when I saw how cheap it was," he exclaimed. It now appeared that our central informant's dream of becoming even bigger and truly competitive was now economically within reach. "I was in heaven," he said. "I found the fucking Holy Grail!"

Mike decided he would only make a $100 order the first time. In order to complete the transaction he had to purchase and send a Western Union money order.

> The cool thing about sending out the Western Union was that I had a friend working at a store that sent them. He told me that if I placed orders under $1,000, that I would not have to provide identification and could just sign a name.

In just a few days the order came wrapped in brown paper with no markings. He had read on some websites that he needed to wait a couple hours before opening it just to make sure that it wasn't being tracked by law enforcement. "Man, I was a nervous wreck. . . . I thought my heart was going to explode sitting there waiting." When he finally opened it up, there was a single VHS tape inside. "I remembered in the email they mentioned that they wouldn't reveal the way they would package it, but I would find it funny when I saw it."

We (the authors) examined numerous websites (as part of the content analysis research) that gave explicit instructions and rationale for their shipping protocols. One read:

- We ship our products world wide and all packages are shipped very discreet.
- Our organization name or anything else that would imply pharmaceutical contents of the package is never used in our shipments.
- The size of our packages are never larger than what would cause unnecessary suspicion. If the order is too large to fit one of these packages, the order will automatically be divided into two or more packages (always included in the S&H charges).
- Shipments are made from various shipping points in different European countries.
- With custom we have 99% success to the USA and Canada, 100% success to any country of EU and 90% success to Australia. Problems with custom are only in New Zealand.

After taking the shrinkwrap off the VHS box, Mike found that all the AAS he ordered were sorted neatly and taped together along with the boxes that the drugs were originally packaged in at the pharmacy and neatly flattened out and placed along the bottom. "I wish I had a picture of me sitting there. . . . I must have looked like a kid on Christmas day. . . . This was it," he said.

Home-Brewed/Globally Obtained: Taking the Next Step

Our central informant immediately made additional orders: "I started making more and more purchases, not really thinking about it at all. But then it hit me what I was getting myself into." He started getting a little worried about the whole idea of buying intact steroids through the Internet, knowing his chances of getting caught were increasing as he became more involved in selling to other people. This pattern of becoming more cautious and even paranoid as the drug-dealing operation grows is noted by Adler (1985) and Desroches (2007). He came across a solution to this dilemma, again through postings on the Internet. He read about a method to convert legal steroids used for cattle into an injectable solution for humans. The specific AAS Mike was referring to is called Trenbolone Acetate, and is commonly known as "Tren" or "Fina." Because it is used to promote rapid muscle growth in cattle, it can be purchased at any farming supply store without a prescription.

The difficulty, though, was the drug came in pellets that were shot into the back of the animal's ear with an implant gun. In order to actually get the drug out of the implant pellet you have to physically break the pellet down. When asked about how he went about this process our central informant said, "Dude they sell all that shit on the Internet also. There are these kits they call 'aromatherapy kits' that contain all the thing you would need in different size kits to make different amounts." With regard to its legality:

> Well, yeah, I guess it is [legal]. The kits can be used to make those aromatherapy products.... You know, all the aromatherapy massage oils and shit, but really you just use all the chemicals to break the pellets down instead.

We (the authors) checked several supply sites and found a ready supply of these kits which came in 2g, 4g, 6g, 8g, and 10g sizes, depending on the amount of animal pellets to be broken down, or the amount of "aromatherapy" product one planned to make.

Converting this product involves adding chemical solutions to the pellets which cause them to separate the active drug from its binders and fillers, yielding multicolored layers that exposed the actual steroid. After the solution was allowed to sit for a while Mike used a syringe, and what is called a syringe filter, to draw the actual drug out of the layered solution and place it into another vial along with a small amount of oil. The vial is then placed into the oven and cooked for a period of time in order to sterilize it. "Of course you do not want to leave it in there too long or else it will oxidize," he said. "And then it is no good at all." After baking the vials are removed, allowed to cool, and then crimped with a rubber stopper.

Besides lowering his risks of arrest, Mike explained that Tren was a superior steroid and very popular. "Man, it [Tren] is like three times as potent as 'test,' with basically none of the side effects. Plus you do not have to use as much... but the downside is that you have to inject it roughly three times a week and you can only use it for short periods of time to minimize any damage done to your body." All seven of the subinformants in this study that sold Mike's home-manufactured drugs cited "Tren" as one of the most popular AAS.

"Home brewing" is the term given to the process of manufacturing AAS and or other illicit performance enhancing drugs. Manufacturing Tren at home in a small desktop operation with few legal risks compelled him to learn more about the possibilities involved in home brewing. He figured out that almost any AAS, or other ergogenic aid, could be purchased very discreetly in its raw, precursor form. All it took was a little home chemistry acumen and some basic pharmaceutical supplies to convert these very cheap precursor chemicals into potent and profitable steroids.

"So I looked around the Internet," he said.

> I must have spent three days or more looking nonstop and BAM…the supplier was right there. It was kind of hard to find at first, the link to the supplier was on a normal business website. I spent roughly around $1,500 myself, which when I made the actual drugs that I would use would have a street value of around $50,000 or so.

Again Mike had purchased these precursor chemicals through the Internet—usually from Chinese-based websites—but this time he would be able to manufacture a much larger amount of AAS himself. "The raw material that came was disguised as plastic chip samples," he said, "and there is no way in hell they are going to seize that!"

In order to home manufacture AAS efficiently and safely, the central informant had to acquire certain lab supplies. "There is nothing illegal about ordering any of these manufacturing supplies, they just tend to add slightly to the cost of everything and, well, other people's money basically covers those costs." The lab supplies included sterile empty vials, crimpers used to seal the bottles, and the solutions to which the raw material would be added. This method was easier than the Tren conversion kits. "You just take the powder and weigh it out and then add it to this, and then add this solution and follow some-what of the same process as the 'Tren,' but without having to separate the pellets, and there you have it." These new opportunities not only allowed Mike to create whatever AAS he could hope for at a greatly reduced price, but at the same time provided a much larger and varied marketplace to the surrounding and growing weightlifting community that used AAS. As a result, his drug-trafficking scheme grew exponentially and he began to incorporate many more subdealers that helped him "move" his product.

This 'home-brewing" drug operation allowed our central informant to manufacture nearly any AAS on the market, and at whatever strength he needed to get impressive results. He routinely bought the necessary supplies for over 20 different types of steroids, fat-cutting compounds, and other drugs that help to mitigate the effects of heavy AAS use. He further explained that by making large purchases of precursor chemicals he could drastically limit the volume of transactions taking place, thereby reducing his risk of "getting busted." It also meant more product for his money. "Why would anyone look at the small tiny silver packages and think…oh, that's steroids. They wouldn't, which is so awesome. Never in a million years would someone think that powder is going to be made into steroids." It is also unclear whether even possessing the precursor chemicals in this particular form is illegal.

Bodily Perfection through Illicit Pharmaceuticals: A Community Service

During the entire 15 months of ethnographic work, our central informant and his drug-dealing associates never even hinted that they viewed themselves as illegal drug dealers: they were merely trying to afford the high costs of being competitive athletes and helping out their friends. "But it's hard not to help friends out here and there, or have somebody else paying for your drugs basically."

What became apparent, however, in interviewing and spending time with the 12 subinformants in this study, and the 53 other contacts, was that Mike was supplying a large number of the individuals in the research area with AAS. This included approximately 25 mid-level dealers (who were also users), and each of these mid-level dealers had anywhere from 5 to 15 customers themselves (approximate customer base of 250 people over a 60-square-mile area). These people included college students that wanted to make faster gains in their weightlifting, numerous police officers using steroids and HGH, firefighters, fellow bodybuilders (both male and female), power-lifters, and collegiate athletes. The network of buyers even included middle-aged men who were using home-brewed HGH for its "health benefits." Despite this, he still perceived his role as fulfilling a need among friends—almost a type of community service.

> I don't really see it that I am a drug dealer. I mean…ok, I sell steroids to people I know and all, but we all help each other out from time to time. So I might have gotten stuff from someone a while back and they are dry now.… Well, I will help them and get them what they need. Hell, it's not like I don't have plenty of it, and since I am making plenty off of it, they are just paying for my next go around is how I see it.

Meeting Demand or Cultivating a Need? The Role of Availability and Price

Given that our central informant was managing to build an underground business, and making available what was previously completely out of reach, he was definitely performing a "service," albeit illicit (see Kelly, Maghan, & Serio, 2005; Stares, 1996; VanNostrand & Tewksbury 1999). What this new marketplace offered most of all was an unprecedented level of availability. All the subinformants in this ethnography agreed that neither themselves nor the many other people Mike sells to could ever afford the quality or wide selection of ergogenic aids to enhance their bodies and performance.

> The biggest thing of using steroids is not actually wanting to use them.… I mean you can see what it does (physical development) and who wouldn't want that? The biggest problem is trying to find what you want to use. Even the basic stuff sometimes was hard to find. And if you are ever going to do a show (competition), unless you have a good source, or stockpile of drugs, it will be even harder to do good without certain ones and those are expensive.

Poor to no supply, limited selection, and high prices kept many of those people who wanted to try AAS from doing so. Our central informant developed a black market business, due to the Internet and a shrinking worldwide market-place; his service provided unprecedented availability and opportunity to those wanting a competitive edge in sports, bodybuilding, a shortcut for the recreational weight-lifter, and in several instances, a perceived method of battling the effects of aging (HGH use). As one female AAS user who routinely bought from Mike said:

> I never questioned it. I knew the guys…. They were the ones helping me with my diet and everything and I just never gave a second thought about getting caught or anything. Sorta just like going to the doctor…. They'd tell me what I needed and what to take as I got closer to my show…and they would have it for a reason-able cost. It's not hard at all.

Low price and top quality was mentioned repeatedly as major motivating fac-tors for both Mike and his customers (also found in Adler, 1985; Pearson & Hobbs, 2001). Buying cheap precursor chemicals from foreign websites and home-brew-ing them into potent AAS was the point at which Mike's drug manufacturing and distribution scheme really took off.

> The price is crazy. What I was getting stuff for before and how much I pay for it now is unreal! [*Chuckling*] While I sit there and make it, sometimes I just keep grinning and thanking the Chinaman.

Moreover, Mike was using the same product he was manufacturing—ensur-ing in the customers' minds that these drug were "clean"—in other words, they were receiving the product they paid for and it was manufactured in a safe manner (i.e., top quality).

The typical black market price for some of the basic AAS used varies from region to region and depends largely on the availability and demand of the drug itself. The following prices are typical. They were derived from field data and cross-validated on several popular steroid-oriented websites (e.g., www.steroid.com) (see table 24.1). In Table 24.2 we see the prices of the same drugs when they are home-brewed using ingredients from foreign Internet businesses.

The chemical compound prices do not of course include the lab supplies needed to manufacture AAS . The operation purchased these in bulk lots in order to cut down on the costs. It routinely converted $15,000 of raw chemical com-pounds into $50,000 of sellable product (a 3,333.00% profit), and its customers were obtaining these drugs for far less than they would from any other source.

Table 24.1 Typical Black Market Steroid Prices

DRUG	DESCRIPTION	BLACK MARKET PRICE
Testosterone enanthate	200 mg 10 cc/ml bottle	$85–120.
Deca-durabolin	200 mg 10 cc/ml bottle	$20–30
Dianabol	5 mg tab	$0.50–1.50
Anadrol	50 mg tab	$3–5
Winstrol tabs	2 mg tab	$1.50–2

Table 24.2 Typical Prices Informant Paid for Chemical Compounds

DRUG	DESCRIPTION	CHEMICAL COMPOUND PRICE
Testosterone enanthate	200 mg 10 cc/ml bottle	$1.70
Deca-durabolin	200 mg 10 cc/ml bottle	$3
Dianabol	5 mg tab	$0.008
Anadrol	50 mg tab	$0.08
Winstrol tabs	2 mg tab	$0.0015–0.003

The final market incentive Mike's operation supplied was a wide selection of products (Monaghan, 2002). While for decades the staple steroids were "test" and "deca," today's AAS marketplace provides a broad assortment of cutting-edge and designer drugs—some of which are formulated so as to not be detectable by drug tests. Typically, the individuals using AAS and/or other drugs switch the specific drug(s) they are using during different time periods. Many of these products are no longer even manufactured by the pharmaceutical companies that originally produced them. As Mike explains:

> Man, five years ago there were a number of drugs that I wanted to do but I couldn't get them when I needed them…either you couldn't get them anymore or you were either getting some other drug or Wesson oil because some idiot didn't want to sell his own stash. Now I never have to worry ever about not having this or that.…Every steroid I could ever hope for I can get the powder to make it. The Last order I made I got 10 different types of steroids…you know…just in case me or anybody else wants to try something different for a change.

So even though pharmaceutical companies have discontinued many of these products, the distributors of the powdered drugs have found outlets through other means and resurrected the market. The AAS market fueled the recreational use of these drug—demonstrating the adaptability and ingenuity of those involved in this global underground marketplace.

ETHNOGRAPHIC CONTRIBUTIONS: LINKING THE MICRO AND MACRO

Microlevel Findings: An Overview

Ethnographic field research is a valuable tool for collecting ground-level qualitative data that help us to develop an empathetic understanding (Weber's Verstehen) of research subjects' behaviors, activities, rationales, and motivations. Several finding are worth highlighting.

Our central informant's development of a drug-trafficking scheme revealed an intriguing process. He went from not being able to afford the drugs he needed to become a competitive bodybuilder, to supplying himself with all the variety and volume of AAS necessary to keep him competitive at a national level. He went from selling his extra supply to a few friends to offset his own drug use, to supplying an entire local community of weightlifters and athletes the same volume and selection he benefited from—as well as making a handsome profit. Mike initially experimented with two avenues to obtain steroids—buying smuggled drugs from a local dealer and remanufacturing cattle steroids from vet supply stores—before settling on his third technique of purchasing raw chemicals from foreign websites and home-brewing them into a useable product.

This informant's ability to progress as a trafficker was made possible in large part by an international underground communication system (found on the Internet) that provided him with the technical knowledge to construct an apartment-based pharmaceutical manufacturing lab. Sutherland's idea of learning from "significant others" takes on an interesting new meaning in this regard; indeed, the extent to which the Internet-based marketplace is impacting the nature of drug dealing has not been explored in criminological studies.

Mike was also able to rationalize his activities in two ways. First, Mike's central goal in life was to be a more competitive bodybuilder. His manufacturing and dealing were all viewed as a means to this end. The profits he incurred were viewed as a nice side-benefit. Second, he saw himself as performing a type of community service—which seems on the surface perhaps a more justifiable position as compared to someone manufacturing and selling methamphetamine from home. Brewing and selling AAS was a way to help out all those people in his local community who shared his same general goal of body and performance enhancement. One can certainly understand how Mike might see a distinction between trafficking in addictive psychoactive drugs such as methamphetamines, and helping his friends become better athletes, get leaner, look more in shape, and get stronger. As explored further in the conclusion, this finding points to the ambiguous ethical foundation for criminalizing AAS use.

This study also suggests that this underground operation was instrumental in cultivating AAS use and helping to construct a drug-using subculture. The data demonstrate that it created a high level of AAS availability—in terms of access, quality, and price. The weightlifting community demonstrated a strong desire to enhance their strength, aesthetics, and athletic ability—even if it meant using home-brewed drugs. This novel operation exploited this desire by providing an unprecedented access to a quality supply of illicit ergogenic aids....

BEYOND BODYBUILDING: HGH AS THE FOUNTAIN OF YOUTH

As mentioned earlier, the drug-trafficking operation uncovered included the drug human growth hormone (HGH). The customer base included mostly middle-aged men attempting to regain their youth (many of whom were police and firefighters). Eighty-one (or 44%) of the web operations specialized in HGH (along with an array of other anti-aging drugs including steroids). These sites were most often referred to as "longevity" or "rejuvenation" clinics. Most characterized the natural decrease in the body's production of HGH as a medical deficiency in need of a pharmaceutical replacement. The following website description was typical.

> Hormone management is replacing the hormones that are no longer being adequately produced by the body. We are genetically programmed to repro- duce and then begin to shut down. The goal of hormone management is to return our hormone levels to that of approximately 30 years of age. This is the age when our immune systems are generally the strongest, our metabo- lism is efficient, and we build muscle rather than fat. Human Growth Hormone (HGH) is thought to be the body's master hormone. Sometime after the age of 30, the pituitary begins to lower the amount of HGH. As the master hor- mone decreases, the other hormones do not get the message to function and the symptoms of aging begin to surface. If Human Growth Hormone, as the keystone is returned to its optimal level, and all the other hormones are brought back to their balanced state, the body is able to regain its vitality. Because hor- mone replacement therapy returns the body to its younger efficiency, with the addition of optimal nutrition and exercise, we are then able to live healthier lives longer. (http://www.napleslongevity.corn/faqs.php)

It is important to note that these claims, although exaggerated, are not with- out some scientific backing (Mayo Clinic Staff, 2008). And the approach taken by medical doctors is to simply return the aging body (anyone over 30) to the "nor- mal" level of a young person—which will require HGH injections. These websites included online prescription services as well as HGH-based clinics throughout the country. The authors, in fact, interviewed a member of just such a facility near West Palm Beach, Florida. The owner is an established medical doctor who has invited federal officials to tour and scrutinize his facility and operations. According to the informant in this interview: "HGH is the new BOTOX of the rich and famous. This doctor's making a killing" (see also Lemendola, 2007).

The HGH research finding documented in both the ethnography and content analysis is significant: it illustrates the enormous growth potential of the illicit AAS marketplace, beyond merely the bodybuilding, weightlifting, or athletic community....

STRUCTURAL CONTEXT: THE GLOBAL MARKETPLACE

We have already discussed how the drug-trafficking operation studied here makes better theoretical sense if we situate it within the larger trend of a late-modern mar- ketplace via the Internet. It is only within the *structural* context of a newly formed, Internet-based, international commerce matrix that a lone person sitting at home in her/his apartment could obtain all the necessary materials (from China) and technical knowledge (from weightlifters around the world) to set up a functional pharmaceutical lab. With a $700 computer and a $29.95-a-month DSL service, this operation had its choice of dozens of websites where the central informant could buy all the chemical compounds needed to produce the most basic and advanced ergogenic drugs available worldwide for remarkably little money. Of course, the online AAS trade is merely an offshoot of a larger online illicit marketplace that peddles numerous prescription drugs such as opioid analgesics, antidepressants ("mood-enhancer"), sedatives, and stimulants (Barboza, 2006; Peter, 2007).

CULTURAL CONTEXT: PURSUING THE PERFECT BODY

In order to better understand this novel drug operation, we must examine them through the lens of larger macrocultural forces. Put differently, situating Mike and his customers' micromotivations and identities within macrocultural forces provides an instructive theoretical framework....

At the root of our analysis is the way in which late-modern society has become preoccupied with the health and aesthetics of the *body*. Recall earlier how the various research subjects characterized their goals: "being ripped/shredded," "being massive," "looking scary," "being scary strong," and "wanting the ultimate body." Clearly these subjects' personal and group identities are constructed in large part around the pursuit of today's hypermasculine norm of bodily perfection—the muscular, low-body fat, well-proportioned physique.

This finding coincides with the work of numerous social theorists who situate the body aesthetic as a central component of identity formation in late-modern society (Baudrillard, 1970; Petersen, 2007). As Petersen (2007, p. 132) in *The Body in Question* summarizes: "It would be no exaggeration to say that contemporary culture has become obsessed with body-related issues, activities, and treatments.... For the individual the body increasingly provides the basis for personal and group identity." The body has emerged, thus, as a "project of the self"—a type of late-modern identity project (Petersen, 2007, p. 132).

Moreover, the body has been converted into an object to be modified, altered, reengineered, and perfected—not just for reasons of health or increased athleticism, but maybe just as important, for visual imagery. This cultural obsession with the body aesthetic is fueled by a pervasive commodification of the ideal body image as found in the health, beauty, fashion, and sports industries (Baudrillard, 1970; Petersen, 2007; Featheestone, Hepworth, & Turner, 1991).

Two important subfactors underlying this fixation include the resurgence of hegemonic masculinity and society's increasing medicalization. The body aesthetic pursued by the subjects in this study is our dominant cultural ideal rooted in traditional notions of masculinity—the lean, highly muscular physique (Wienke, 1998). The criminological literature has documented the significant extent to which mainstream culture is reembracing "hegemonic masculine ideals" (Chesney-Lind, 2006; Connell & Messeschmidt, 2005; Enloe, 2004) Mike and his AAS-using community felt compelled to achieve the ideal image of this masculinist cultural value—even if their chiseled physiques provide no function beyond being a "signifier of social status" (Baudrillard, 1970, p. 131).

Drummond (2006, p. 164), in reviewing Hoberman's (2005) *Testosterone Dreams: Rejuvenation, Aphrodesia, Doping*, highlights another critical cultural factor to consider.

Contemporary western culture has evolved into one in which individuals are open to biomedical interventions where quality of life in relation to aging, sexual activity, and sports are concerned. It appears we are becoming desensitized to the use of supplements to boost various aspects of performance whether it be aesthetics or physical endeavors.

Conrad (2007) sees this greater willingness to use drugs to boost aesthetics or performance as part of the *medicalization of society*—where normal human functioning and appearance are increasingly viewed as difficulties to be overcome with pharmaceuticals and surgery. This medicalization of the populace for purposes of cosmetic and performance enhancements is most evident in the areas of weight control, sexual underperformance, aging, mood management, and undesirable aesthetic features (i.e., cosmetic surgery).

Using HGH or steroids to enhance aesthetics, strength, or muscle mass is consistent, then, with a medicalized culture that has normalized the notion that we can and should improve our bodies, lifestyles, personalities, sexual abilities, and cognitive skills through pharmaceuticals. Add to this a culture obsessed with sports performance, athleticism, and the hypermasculine body aesthetic—along with a widespread consumerist ethic of immediate gratification to fulfill our every perceived need and desire—and it should be easier to understand why Mike's underground business had no problem finding customers.

DISCUSSION AND ANALYSIS: BLACK MARKET GROWTH AND CRIMINALIZATION

The structural and cultural forces detailed above illuminate the huge growth potential of the illicit AAS industry. The structural dimension points to a fascinating late-modem supply apparatus: a globalized yet highly decentralized marketplace that would have been inconceivable only 20 years earlier. It is critical to recognize as well that this research documents a fundamentally different and potentially pathbreaking new model for the manufacturing and distributing of illicit drugs—particularly mind-altering pharmaceutical. The global/local dynamic involved in late-modern trafficking—where the lone individual can order pharmaceuticals in their raw chemical form, convert them though processes learned off the Internet, and then sell them locally for dramatic profits—is unprecedented. It radically alters the availability of not only the drugs themselves, but the ability to set up localized drug operations which originate not in the opium or cocaine fields of the Golden Triangle or Andean nations but in corporate pharmaceutical labs from around the world. This phenomenon is likely indicative, therefore, of a larger online drug-trafficking matrix that markets numerous pharmaceuticals such as synthetic opioid analgesics, antidepressants, sedatives, and stimulants (Barboza, 2006; Peter, 2007).

On the demand side, we find a cultural milieu ideal for cultivating within a large segment of the populace a strong desire to enhance their appearance or performance through the use of pharmaceuticals—whether legitimately obtained or not. Bodybuilders represent only the extreme manifestation of this cultural sentiment—engaged in what we might call a "runaway cultural process" (Vila, 1993). The rest simply yearn to attain today's well-accepted goals—lose weight, live longer, feet better, get ripped, beat the competition, be more beautiful, and/or realize the hypermasculine ideal of a strong, highly muscular body (Connell & Messerschmidt, 2005).

Postscript: Intensifying Criminalization in a Sea of Moral Ambiguity

These structural/cultural forces not only harbor strong potential for expansion, they also point to the distinct possibility of more intense criminal justice scrutiny. Indeed, even though the data for this research were finalized in early 2007, a final postscript series of interviews (completed in February of 2008) reveal that we may be experiencing the beginnings of a "war on steroids."

These postscript interviews found the drug operation under study had changed dramatically. Our central informant had completely given up bodybuilding, he no longer obtained raw AS from foreign websites, his drug-trafficking operation had been reduced by 90%, and he had reverted back to converting cattle steroids (Tren) in order to pursue his new weightlifting endeavor, power-lifting. His explanation for these changes was simple: he was no longer able to maintain his underground business because of a recent federal law enforcement control effort.

Recall Henry Waxman and Torn Davis' investigations into the illicit steroid problem in professional sports that led to the revelation by the GAO that an entirely unregulated AAS market existed on the Internet. One result was an intense federal law enforcement control effort dubbed *Operation Raw Deal*. The effort simultaneously pressured the Chinese government to shut down raw AAS operations shipping to the USA (a request the Chinese did not resist given the upcoming Olympic Games) while launching a nationwide investigation into home-brewing operations. The DEA and FDA discovered 56 such labs and seized $6.5 million dollars (Mike's lab was not one of the 56). The DEA claimed that the customer base associated with these 56 operations was likely 40,000 people (Buser, 2007; Drug Enforcement Administration, 2007; Larson, 2007; Raley, 2007).

As part of this new steroid crackdown, the DEA, in a classic moral entrepreneur strategy, is using sensationalistic anecdotes to construct these activities as highly dangerous for our youth. One of their featured anecdotes highlights the suicide of a high school baseball player. His father believes the son's suicide was caused by depression brought on by steroid use (notice the fallback on the traditional moral theme of the damaging properties of psychoactive drugs). The sensationalistic tone used by the DEA can also be found in the following media release associated with *Operation Raw Deal*.

"DEA successfully attacked the illegal steroid industry at every level of its distribution network—from the manufacturers in China who supply the raw materials, to the trafficker in the United States who market the deadly doses. Operation Raw Deal uncovered a clandestine web of international drug dealers who lurk on the Internet for young adults craving the artificial advantage of anabolic steroids," said DEA Administrator Karen P. Tandy. "Today we reveal the truth behind the underground steroid market: dangerous drugs cooked up all too often in filthy conditions with no regard to safety, giving Americans who purchase them the ultimate raw deal." (www.usdoj.gov/dea/pubs/pressrel/pr092407.html)

Interestingly, Mike and other AAS users on Internet forums are fully confident that once the Olympics are over, and the "hype" about steroids subsides, the AAS-trafficking industry will thrive once again, albeit in modified form. Even Henry Waxman agrees that policing this industry will pose considerable difficulties.

> Law enforcement authorities face significant difficulties in combating the illegal steroid trade. Challenges include little enforcement assistance from legal officers in the drugs' countries of origin, the anonymity of the Intent marketplace, the inability to effectively inspect mail for illegal steroids, and weak federal penalties for steroid trafficking. (Cramer, 2005, p. 1)

Aside from the logistical difficulties in regulating the global AAS market-place, the moral foundation on which these efforts lie may also pose problems. Consider the ethical inconsistency, for example, in defining body and performance enhancement through pharmaceuticals as morally problematic, when cosmetic surgical techniques pursue the same goal but rely on far more invasive medical procedures. Similarly, why would it be immoral for someone to add muscle, lose fat, and increase strength through pharmaceuticals when the exact same approach is used to improve sexual or mood functions? At what point does taking a phar-maceutical drug go from being a legitimate medical "treatment" to an illegitimate medicate "enhancement"? And how do we define what constitutes legitimate med-ical protocols for increasing our life span (e.g., high blood pressure medication) from illegitimate ones (e.g., HGH injections to reset hormone levels)?

More so than even previous drug wars, drawing legal lines around society's pursuit of bodily perfection through drugs will likely result in a mishmash of moral inconsistencies and political hypocrisy.

REFERENCES

Adler, P. A. (1985). *Wheeling and dealing*. New York: Columbia University Press.

Atkyns, R. L., & Hanneman, G. J. (1974). Illicit drug distribution and dealer communica-tion behavior. *Journal of Health and Social Behavior*, 15, 36–43.

Barboza, D. (2006). The wild web of China: Sex and drugs, not reform. *New York Times*, March 8.

Baudrillard, J. (1970). *The consumer society: Myths and structures*. London: Sage.

Buser, L. (2007). Three more caught in steroid sting—Memphis firefighter to answer charges of selling drugs. *Commercial Appeal*, November 14.

Caruso, D. B. (2007). Confusion reigns over U.S. rules on growth hormone even as crack-down is increased. *USA Today: Associated Press*, November 10.

Chesney-Lind, M. (2006). Patriarchy, crime, and justice. *Feminist Criminology*, 1(1), 6–26.

Cohen, S. (2002). *Folk devils and moral panics: The creation of the Mods and Rockers*. New York: Routledge.

Connell, R. W., & Messerschmidt, J. W. (2005). Hegemonic masculinity, rethinking the concept. *Gender and Society*, 19, 829–859.

Conrad, P. (2007).*The medicalization of society: On the transformation of human conditions into treatable disorders*. Baltimore, MD: Johns Hopkins University Press.

Crarner, R. J. (2005). *Anabolic steroids are easily purchased without a prescription and present significant challenges to law enforcement officials*. Washington, DC: U.S. Government Accountability Office.

Desroches, F. (2007). Research on upper level drug trafficking: A review. *Journal of drug Issues*, 22, 827–844.

Drug Enforcement Administration. (2007). *DEA announces largest steroid enforcement action in U.S. history*. Retrieved February 23, 2008, from http://www.usdoj.gov/dea/pubs/pressrel/pr092407. html.

Drummond, M. (2006). Book review, testosterone dreams: Rejuvenation, aphrodisiac, doping. *Journal of Health Psychology*, 11, 163–164.

Enloe, C. (2004). *The curious feminist: Searching for women in a new age of empire*. London: University of California Press.

Featherstone, M., Hepworth, M., & Turner, B. (1991). *The body*. London: Sage.

Fuller, J. R., & LaFountain, M. J. (1987). Performance-enhancing drugs in sport: A different form of drug abuse. *Adolescence*, 12, 969–976.

Goode, E., & Ben-Yehuda, N. (1994). *Moral panics: The social construction of deviance*. Cambridge: Blackwell.

Hoberman, J. (2005). *Testosterone dreams, rejuvenation, aphrodisiac, doping*. Berkeley/Los Angeles: University of California Press.

Inciardi, J. S. (1992). *The war on drugs II*. New York: Mayfield.

Kelly, R. J., Maghan, J., & Serio, J. D. (2005). *Illicit trafficking: A reference handbook*. Santa Barbara. CA: ABC-CLIO.

Larson, T. (2007, October 8). Police arrest alleged myspace steroid dealers in national crackdown. *The Daily Vidette*.

Lenehan, P. (2003). *Anabolic steroids and other performance enhancing drugs* (1st ed.). New York: Taylor & Francis.

Lyons, B. (2008). Steroids beyond sports: Celebrities now among those linked to drug shipments. *Times Union*, January 13.

Mattingly, D., & Estrada, I. (2008). *HGH in forefront to remain young*. Retrieved January 24, 2008, from http: //www.cnn.com/2008/HEALTH/01/24/mattingly.hgh/index .html.

Mayo Clinic Staff. (2008). Human growth hormone: Does it slow aging process? Senior Health, Mayo Clinic.com. Retrieved February 13, 2006, from http://www.mayoclinic .com/health/growth-hormone/HA00030.

McCallum, J. (2008). Steroids in America: The real dope. *Sport Illustrated*. Retrieved from http://sportsillustrated.cnn.com/2008/rnagazine/03/11/steroids1 /index. html.

Monaghan, L. F. (2002). Vocabularies of motive for illicit steroid use among body builders. *Social Science and Medicine*, 5, 695–708.

Pearson, G. and Hobbs, B. (2001). *Middle market drug distribution; home office research study 227,* London: Government Home Office.

Peter, J. (2007). *Much HGH comes from China*. Retrieved February 28, 2008, from http://sports.yahoo.com/top/news?slug=jo-chinesehgh092007&prov=yhooh&type=lgns.

Petersen, A. (2007). *The body in question: A socio-cultural approach*. New York: Routledge.

Raley, D. (2007). How a garage in Aberdeen became a key stop in a global steroid pipeline: Suspects sold pills online and likely met on web, agents say. *Seattle Post–Intelligencer*, October 29.

Shipley, A. (2007). A wider front in doping battle, law enforcement takes the lead in sports probes. *Washington Post*, March 2.

Silver, M. D. (2001). Use of ergogenic aids by athletes. *Journal of the American Academy of Orthopaedic Surgeons, 9*: 61–70.

Stares, P. B. (1996). *Global habit: The drug problem in a borderless world.* Washington, DC: Brookings Institute Press.

Sterling, E. E. and Stewart, J. (2006.) "This legacy of Len Bias's death". In *The Washington Post* June 24.

Trebach, A. S. (1987). *The great drug war.* New York: Collier MacMillan.

Tucker, E. (2007). Feds announce Largest Steroid Crackdown. *Washington Post*, September 24.

Tunnel, K. (1993). Inside the drug trade: Trafficking from the dealer's perspective. *Qualitative Sociology, 16*, 361–381.

VanNostrand, L. M., & Tewksbury, R. (1999). The motives and mechanics of operating an illegal drug enterprise. *Deviant Behavior, 20*, 57–83.

Vila, B. (1993). Is the war on drugs an example of a runaway cultural process? In P. B. Kraska (Ed.), *Altered states of mind: Critical observations of the drug war* (pp. 11–48). New York: Garland.

Waskul, D. D. and Vannini, P. (2006). *Body/embodiment: Symbolic interaction and sociology of the body.* Burlington, VT: Ashgate Publishing

Wienke, C. (1998). Negotiating the male body: Men, masculinity, and cultural ideals. *Journal of Men's Studies, 6*: 255–282.

᭢

Quitting Crime

Section IX examines the issue of desistance from crime. What are the factors that that make them stop? Do criminals continue their careers over a lifetime? Do they desist at some point or begin to engage in less serious offenses? What motivates these changes in criminal activity?

There is a vast literature devoted to attempting to understand why individuals engage in criminality. But there are far fewer studies devoted to investigating the issue of desistance—quitting or reducing involvement in criminal activities. Generally what we do know about desistence is that the majority offenders as they get older will desist from criminality.

The two articles in this section contribute to the body of literature giving attention to criminal desistance. These articles provide rich insights into desistance from the perspective of a group of former offenders. Here we find two excellent articles that provide much rich insight into criminal desistence from a group of former offenders What is unique about these two articles is that they both describe a process that offenders go through leading up to desistance. Whether it is a reexamination or change of the criminal calculus or a process of hitting rock bottom in one's life, there is an inherent process.

In chapter 28, "Aging Criminals: Changes in the Criminal Calculus," Neal Shover provides an insightful analysis of changes in the criminal calculus that help to explain how criminals exit and quit crime. Shover and his colleagues conducted interviews of 50 subjects whose dominant criminal pattern consisted of ordinary property offenses such as grand larceny, burglary, robbery, and auto theft. The research reveals that as offenders get older, two factors have a significant impact on their lives: (1) development of conventional social bonds, and (2) strengthened resolve to abandon crime entirely in order to restrict their criminal activities. Other factors related to desistance identified by Shover include a greater interest in the rewards of a noncriminal lifestyle and a more rational decision making process. The undercurrent running through this article is that the risk-gain calculus employed by criminals tends to shift as they age and mature, thus exhibiting greater concern about the possibility of apprehension and punishment.

In chapter 29, "Getting out of the life: Desistance by Female Street Offenders," Ira Sommers, Deborah Baskin and Jeffrey Fagan examine the role of life events and the relationship of cognitions and life situations to the desistance process. The authors conducted 30 life course interviews with 30 female offenders who had desisted from criminality. The women were selected based on two criteria; they all had at least one past arrest for a violent street crime, and they all had desisted from crime for at least two years prior to the study. Participants decision to desist from crime was a result of hitting bottom, that is, reaching a point to where there criminality seemed senseless. Once they reached this point, they worked to "clarify and strengthen their non-deviate identities. While the authors readily point out, that data findings are the result of retrospective information from offenders who had not offended for two years, and as such, cannot state with certainty whether desistance from crime is permanent. However, is salient in as much that it sheds light on what appears to be a long and painful process that women offenders journey through before they quit crime.

REFERENCES

Akers, R. (1998). *Social learning and social structure: A general theory of crime and delinquency*. Boston: Northeastern Press.

Laub, J.H., & Sampson, R.F. (2001). Understanding desistance from crime. *Crime and Justice: A Review of Research*, 28, 1–68.

Matza, David (1964). *Delinquency and drift*. New York: Wiley.

Wright, K.M., & Wright K.F. (1998). Does getting married reduce the likelihood of criminality: A review of the literature. *Federal Probation, 56*, 50–56.

CHAPTER 25

ル

Aging Criminals: Changes in the Criminal Calculus

Neal Shover

In this selection, Neal Shover compares the decision-making processes of juvenile and young adult offenders to those of older criminals to discover changes in the criminal calculus—the perception of risk and gain associated with a criminal opportunity—as offenders age. "Clearly," he argues in another section of the book, "something about advancing age produces reduced participation in ordinary crime, even by those with extensive criminal records." Shover concludes that aging offenders undergo a number of changes, including the development of new commitments and an increasing fear of incarceration. These shifts cause them to alter their calculus—to evaluate the risks and benefits of crime differently.

Shover's research methodology involved identifying, locating, and interviewing a group of men aged 40 years and over who were involved in ordinary property crime earlier in their careers. Shover and his assistants interviewed 50 subjects whose dominant criminal pattern consisted of ordinary property offenses such as grand larceny, burglary, robbery, and auto theft. All had been convicted of such offenses at least once.

CALCULUS AND OFFENSES OF YOUTH

For many juveniles, involvement in delinquency contains a rich variety of motives and subjective meanings. Juveniles "slide into" their initial delinquent acts for a variety of nonrational, often situationally based reasons (Matza, 1964). Although there is little new in this, it is interesting that the interview subjects recalled their earliest crimes this way. A 45-year-old man said:

Source: Adapted from Shover, N. (1985). *Aging criminals,* pp. 105–126. Beverly Hills, CA: Sage Publications. Copyright by Neal Shover. Reprinted with permission.

I was, like years ago, I was a peeping Tom—when I was a kid, you know....I enjoyed this, you know....But, anyway, then I got married young, and I had two children. And I had bills, you know. I was a kid and I had a man's responsibility....Now, what's the best way to make money? With something you know. I had been peeping in windows when I was a kid. So, I knew, you know, like where the windows would open, where the—you understand what I mean? And then [I] broadened my sense. After awhile I started mixing business with pleasure, you know. I would peep and then later come back and, you know, take this or that.

Another man told of his adolescent fascination with automobiles. As a youth, he often roamed through parking lots, admiring the steering wheels of cars. From there it was a short, tentative step to breaking into the cars and stealing their contents. A great deal of delinquency begins simply as risk-taking behavior and it is only later, with the benefit of accumulated incidents, that it takes on the character and meaning of "crime" (Short & Strodtbeck, 1965). Braley (1976, pp. 11–12) writes,

I began to steal seriously as a member of a small gang of boys. We backed into it, simply enough, by collecting milk and soda bottles to turn in for the deposits, but, after we had exhausted the vacant lots, empty fields, and town dumps, we began to sneak into garages...and, having dared garages and survived, we next began to loot back porches, and, finally, breathlessly, we entered someone's kitchen....Clearly, this was an exercise of real power over the remote adult world and I found it exciting. I liked it....[A]nd it is only now, some 40 years later, that I begin to see how stealing cast me in my first successful role.

Many of the crimes committed by youth are impulsive and poorly planned:

Q: Did you do a lot of stickups [when you were young]?
A: Oh yeah, you know.... [We] stole and shit like that, you know. I didn't give it no thought, no plan, don't know how much money's in it. You know what I mean? Just go in there and say, "We're gonna do it, we're gonna do it."...That was it.

The spontaneous pursuit of fun and excitement provides the impetus for some delinquency:

[When I was a kid] I wasn't a sports enthusiast. I played sports very rarely, but it just wasn't exciting enough....None of [the "normal" adolescent activities] were exciting to me....It's just that we, there was a feeling of participating in something that was daring and dangerous.

To some extent, these collective definitions of misconduct based on expressive vocabularies of motive explain why participants do not always see their activities as criminal. Instead of resulting from a rational decision-making process, they simply "happen," and participants do not appreciate sufficiently the seriousness. A former gang member writes,

It's funny, but we didn't see ourselves as delinquents or young criminal types. Most of what we were into was fighting other gangs....Sure, we got into other kinds of scrapes sometimes, like vandalism and petty larceny from a street vendor or a store. Most of the time we thought of that kind of stuff as "just playing around"— never as crime. (Rettig, Torres, & Garrett, 1977, p. 28)

For other youths, participation in delinquency results from the interactional dynamics of peer groups. Some boys experience a situational need to maintain personal status and face with their peers (Short & Strodtbeck, 1965; Jansyn, 1966). Theft or other acts of delinquency may function to buttress or solidify one's informal ranking within a small group. Youths may occasionally use them as a dramatic, incontrovertible demand for a higher as compared with a lower rank:

> Everybody would look up to me, you know, when I was young.... And seem like every time they wanted something, they'd come to me and say, "Jack, well, come on and do this," or "Help me do this," you know. Fuck it, you know. I had an image I had to live up to, you know. I'd say, "Fuck it, man, come on."

Precisely because many of the criminal incidents of youth are responses to group dynamics or moods, they occasionally "break out" in situationally propitious circumstances. An interview subject related an incident of armed robbery that occurred when he was young. His account illustrates some of the foregoing observations about the impetuous nature of juvenile crime:

> [One day] we were just walking up First Street and [one of my companions] said as we were approaching Rhode Island Avenue, "Let's go in here and rob this drug store," because [another companion] had a gun. We said, "Okay, let's go in here and rob the drug store." Went in there, the soda fountain was filled up...robbed everybody on the stools. Went back in the post office, stole money orders and stamps and stuff, took the cash box. And we turned our backs on everybody in the store, going out! We didn't know whether the proprietor had a gun or what, but it just so happened that he didn't. But, that's just the atmosphere in which, you know, that took place.

Overall, the interview subjects said that as juveniles and young adults they pursued crime with considerable intensity:

> When you're young, or when—the people that I've known who are young, it was nothing to go out and break into two or three places a week just *looking* for money.

Similarly, a retired English thief writes that "when you're young you tend to have a go at anything" (Quick, 1967, p. 142).

Although juvenile crime is impetuous and fun, it is also monetarily rewarding. Indeed, to juveniles from economically deprived backgrounds it may appear more rewarding than any legitimate employment available to them. The sums of money garnered from crime may seem princely indeed. Crime opens up for them new worlds of consumption and leisure activities. The 49 imprisoned armed robbers studied by Petersilia, Greenwood, and Lavin reported that often their youthful crimes were motivated by a desire for and pursuit of "high times" (1978, p. 76).

It seems apparent that many youth become involved in property offenses without having developed an autonomous and rationalized set of criminal motives.

Petersilia, Greenwood, and Lavin discovered a similar pattern in their research on imprisoned armed robbers. Their subjects reported using little or no sophistication in planning the offenses they committed in their youth (1978, pp. 60–65). At the same time, they found that the juvenile offenses committed by men in their sample included "expressive elements" far more than was true of the offenses they committed later (1978, p. 76). (Expressive reasons for committing offenses include such things as hostility, revenge, thrills, or peer influence.)

Juveniles and young adults often have little awareness or appreciation of the legal and personal repercussions of their criminality. This is true especially of their perceptions of time spent in institutions such as training schools and prisons:

> I've seen the time in my life, man, where it might seem foolish, 'cause it seems foolish to me now. When I was in the street, hustling, I'd say, "If I get knocked off and don't get but a nickel"—five years—I said, "Hell with it," you know. The only thing would be in my mind, if I got busted, could I hang around, try to have my lawyer try to get me some kind of plea or something so I wouldn't get but a nickel. 'Cause I knew I could knock five years out.

A 47-year-old man echoed these remarks, saying that when he was young,

> I don't know, man, I just didn't give a fuck, you know. I was young, simple, man. I didn't care, you know. Shit, doing time, you know, I didn't know what doing time was all about. Doing time to me was nothing, you know.

The net result of these youthful meanings and motives is that the potential repercussions of crime to some extent are blunted. Juveniles neither possess nor bring to bear a precise, consistent metric for assessing the potential consequences of delinquent episodes. They fail to "see" or to calculate seriously their potential losses if apprehended. For many youth, crime is a risk-taking activity in which the risks are only dimly appreciated or calculated.

CALCULUS AND OFFENSES OF YOUNG ADULTS

This poorly developed youthful calculus is transformed both by the approach of adulthood and by the experience of arrest and adult felony confinement. Young adults develop the ability to see, to appreciate, and to calculate more precisely some of the potential penalties that flow from criminal involvement. Consequently, by late adolescence to their early 20s men begin to develop a keener awareness of the potential costs of criminal behavior. Gradually supplanting the nonrational motives and calculus of youthful offenders is a more clearly articulated understanding of the price they will pay if convicted of crime. In this sense, aging and its associated experiences are accompanied by an increasing rationalization of ordinary property crime.

Their growing rationalization of crime seems to be a turning point for many ordinary property offenders. As Zimring (1981, p. 880) has noted,

> At some point in adolescence or early adult development, most of those who have committed offenses in groups either cease to be offenders or continue to violate

the law, but for different reasons and in different configurations. Either of these paths is a significant change from prior behavior.

A substantial majority of the uncommitted apparently drop out of crime at this point.

Paradoxically, others—this includes many unsuccessful and most successful offenders—respond to their developing rationalization of crime with a strengthened belief that they can continue committing crime and make it a lucrative enterprise. This is because they convert their developing rationalization of crime into an increased confidence that they can avoid arrest.

For those who continue at crime, theft increasingly springs from a more autonomous set of motives and meanings. The salience of "expressive elements" gradually declines in the process of criminal decision making. Offenders also develop an awareness of the importance of making crime a rational process. They learn the importance of assessing and committing crimes on the basis of an increasingly narrow and precise metric of potential benefits and costs. In this sense as well, their crimes became more calculating and rational. Money increasingly assumes more importance as a criminal objective. After serving a term in the National Training School, one subject and his friends began robbing gamblers and bootleggers. I asked him:

Q: Did the desire for excitement play any part in those crimes?
A: No, I think the desire for excitement had left. It was, we recognized that it was a dangerous mission then, because we knew that gamblers and bootleggers carried guns and things like that. And it was for, you know, just for the money.

Another man made the same point succinctly, saying that "whatever started me in crime is one thing. But at some point I know that I'm in crime for the money. There's no emotional reason for me being into crime." Finally, an ex-thief has written,

When I first began stealing I had but a dim realization of its wrong. I accepted it as the thing to do because it was done by the people I was with; besides, it was adventurous and thrilling. Later it became an everyday, cold-blooded business, and while I went about it methodically...I was fully aware of the gravity of my offenses. (Black, 1926, p. 254)

Interestingly, during their young adult years the 49 California armed robbers expressed a new confidence in their ability to avoid arrest for their crimes (Petersilia, Greenwood, & Lavin, 1978, pp. 69–70). They reported a marked increase in the sophistication of their criminal planning (although the researchers indicate the men never achieved tactical brilliance) (p. 60). Pursuit of "high times" declined in importance as a motive for crime (p. 78) and the need to meet ordinary financial exigencies became more important (p. 76). Concern about arrest declined substantially (p. 70).

Young men, however, tend to exaggerate their ability to rationalize their crimes and to commit them successfully:

Whenever I began to steal it was always with the rationale I wouldn't make the mistakes I had made before....It didn't occur to me there were literally thousands of ways I could get caught. I was sustained by the confidence nothing truly awful could happen to me. (Braley, 1976, p. 65)

Often they confidently assume there are a finite, manageable number of ways that any particular criminal act can fail (Shover, 1971). Consequently, they analyze past offenses for information they believe will lead to ever more perfect criminal techniques and success. Parker's interview (Parker & Allerton, 1962, p. 149) with an English thief reveals this reasoning process:

Q: When you're arrested, what are your reactions at that moment?
A: I think the first thing's annoyance—with myself. How could I be so stupid as to get nicked? What's gone wrong, what have I forgotten, where have I made the mistake?

In most cases, young adult offenders' newly acquired faith in their ability to rationalize theft and thereby make it safer proves to be self-defeating. Few of them are equipped by temperament, intelligence, or social connections to follow through on their plans and dreams. Consequently, subsequent offenses usually only repeat the pattern established in their youthful criminal forays.

CALCULUS AND OFFENSES OF AGING ADULTS

As men age, fail at crime, and experience...[other] contingencies, their rationalization of the criminal calculus changes apace. Now they enter a third and final stage of their criminal careers. Increasingly, they realize that the expected monetary returns from criminal involvement are paltry, both in relative and in absolute terms. "Simultaneously, their estimation of the likelihood of being arrested increases, as do the objective probabilities of arrest" (Petersilia, Greenwood, & Lavin, 1978, pp. 36–39).

Because of the nature and length of their previous criminal record, they generally assume that they will be sentenced to prison again if convicted of another felony. There is evidence to support this assumption (p. 39). Also, older men assume that any prison sentence they receive, given the length of their previous criminal record, will be long. Finally, those who experience an interpersonal contingency are increasingly reluctant to risk losing their newfound social ties. For all these reasons, aging men begin to include factors that previously were absent from their calculus of potential criminal acts. A 46-year-old former addict said,

If I go out there and commit a crime now, I got to think about this: Hey, man, I ain't got to get away. See what I'm saying? I have—man, it would be just my luck that I would get busted. Now I done fucked up everything I done tried to work hard for, man, you know, to get my little family together.

Perhaps it is not surprising that they increasingly begin to see that their potential losses, if imprisoned again, will be immense.

In sum, as offenders age, their expectations of the potential outcome of criminal acts change. Their perception of the odds narrows. Now the perceived risks of criminal behavior loom larger. Note that the Rand Corporation's research on 49 armed robbers found that fear of arrest increases during this age period (Petersilia, Greenwood, & Lavin, 1978, p. 70). Little wonder then that a 56-year-old man said,

> I realized that, even though in crime, even though you might get away, let's say 99 times, the one time eliminates your future. You don't have no future. Regardless of what you have gained, you lost all of that. A rabbit can escape 99 times and it only takes one shot to kill him. So, I was a rabbit....I want to enjoy life. But I know I can't do it successfully by committing crimes.

This does not mean that men cease *thinking* about crime altogether. Rather, they develop a more complex set of reasons for avoiding it in most situations. However, in more advantageous circumstances, some believe they still are capable of resorting to crime:

> A: Now, I'm not going to tell you that if you put $100,000 on that table and I saw an opportunity, that I felt that I could get away with it, that I wouldn't try to move it. But there's no way, even now, there's no way that I would endanger my freedom for a measley four, five, $10,000. I make that much a year now, you know. And I see the time that I wasted—well, I figure I wasted four or five years when I was younger.
>
> Q: What do you mean, you "wasted" it?
>
> A: In and out of jail.

Those men who continue to pursue a criminal career change their approach to crime. Most decide to avoid some of the crimes more characteristic of their youth. They shift to offenses that are less confrontative and, therefore, less *visible*. Armed robbery is the prototypical highly visible and highly confrontative offense. Shoplifting or selling marijuana represents the other extreme. An imprisoned man said,

> When I go out, I'm goin' for the "soft" stuff. I'm going to book the numbers, you know...but *hard* crime...I gave that up a long while ago.

Thus, there is evidence that ordinary property offenders, once their fear of arrest and confinement increases, shift to other types of criminal activities. In doing so, they believe that they simultaneously reduce the chances of arrest and, even if arrested, increase the chances of receiving less severe penalties:

> You know, it's funny, but there's only a few things that a man goes to the penitentiary for: burglary or robbery or something like that. But how many ways of making money are there that you don't have to revert to robbery or burglary? Thousands. I mean [where you're] between being legit and being crooked. You're skating on thin ice and if that ice breaks, it's not going to break bad. You might get your foot wet, you might get a fine or something. What they're [police, prosecutors, courts] really concerned with are these violent cases, man, these people who

are causing these headlines and stuff. . . . If I am going to be a thief, I might as well be the one who is skating on that thin ice. And a person who is skating on thin ice is less likely to go to the penitentiary. . . . 'Cause if you get arrested boosting, shoplifting, it is generally a fine. If worse comes to worst, you're going to have to have to do a year in the county jail—in some places, nine months.

A: I caught one number—that 10 years, all them robberies—and then, you know, everything I did then was more like a finesse thing. . . . I'm not gonna stick no pistol in nobody's face, man, you know. I'm not gonna strong arm nobody, you know. I'm not gonna go in nobody's house. You understand what I'm sayin'? I'm not gonna do that.

Q: You figure as long as you don't do those things you won't go to the penitentiary?

A: Hey, you better believe it. You better believe it.

Along with this reduction in the visibility of their offenses, men try to reduce the *frequency* of their crimes. One subject, who still engages occasionally in nonviolent felonies, told me how he had changed:

I done got a little *softer*, you know. I done got, hey man, to the point, you know, where, like I say, I don't steal, I don't hustle, you know. But I don't pass the opportunity if I can get some free money. I'm not gonna pass. . . . I don't hustle, you know. I don't make it a everyday thing. I don't go out *lookin'* for things, you know.

Another man said,

When you're younger, you can . . . steal to pay the rent, you know. Hell, you can go out and steal seven days a week. And sooner [or later] . . . you learn that—to me, it's exposure time, you know. You don't want to get "exposed" too much.

Petersilia, Greenwood, and Lavin (1978, p. 27) found the same pattern. The average monthly offense rates reported by their subjects decreased from 3.28 when they were juveniles to 0.64 in their adult years. After changing their approach to crime, some men do continue to commit crime for several years, but eventually they desist from crime. Only a handful of ordinary property offenders continue their criminal behavior into old age.

NEGATIVE CASES

Three aspects of the experiences of successful offenders distinguish them from the other types of offenders. First, the former usually develop an autonomous, rationalized calculus of crime at an earlier age, albeit in the same general fashion discussed here. By their late teens, some successful offenders are engaging in carefully planned crimes primarily for the expected monetary gains. Even some successful thieves, however, never entirely slough off all nonmonetary meanings of and motivations for crime:

I know a guy who's relatively well connected, if you know what I mean, with the outfit. [Nevertheless, he would] go on any score! Now he needed money like I need a double hernia. But [he] just loved—don't care if there's any money there or not. "Let's go." [It was] the thrill. I never got any thrills like that myself....The only thrill I got [was] counting the money.

Second, the crimes of successful offenders generally are substantially more rewarding than the crimes committed by other types of offenders. Third, they are more successful than other types of offenders in avoiding incarceration; they spend fewer years in prison. For these reasons, failure at crime does not produce in successful offenders the same impetus to modify their criminal calculus as it does in their unsuccessful peers.

Despite these differences, however, some successful offenders also experience one or more of the contingencies described [earlier]....In such circumstances, they respond in ways similar to unsuccessful offenders (Hohimer, 1975).

Unlike unsuccessful offenders, however, they sometimes make adjustments in their criminal activities without discontinuing them entirely. They can do so, in part, because their theft activities provide them late-career opportunities not available to unsuccessful offenders. For example, because some of them establish extensive social contacts through their work, they can change the nature of their criminal involvement. They are able to shift to other roles in the social organization of theft. Now they eschew the role of *front-line participant* in favor of the role of *background operator* (Mack & Kerner, 1975; Shover, 1983). Still others manage to save enough money from their working years to retire with a degree of material comfort. One man suggested these two strategies account for most late-life patterns of successful offenders like himself. As he put it, "They're either sitting in the rocking chair or out finding something soft for somebody else to pick up."

Nevertheless, a substantial percentage of successful offenders apparently continues "going to the well" despite advancing age. An English thief, who already had served several prison sentences, has written,

> I content myself with the dream—the one that all criminals have—that one day I'll get the really big tickle....That's all I can do now, take my time and wait for the chance to come. I've no intention of going straight, I'm just being more careful, that's all—and I'm getting cagey, I won't take unnecessary risks. It used to be I wanted a 50/50 chance, now I want it better than that, somewhere like 75 to 25. But sooner or later it'll come, the job will be there, I'll do it, get the big tickle, and then I'll retire....This is it, this is the dream, the great rock candy mountain that beckons us all. (Parker & Allerton, 1962, p. 189)

This man subsequently was reimprisoned several times (T. Parker, personal communication, July 10, 1981).

Among the unsuccessful offenders, there are two distinctly different categories of negative cases. Some men simply do not experience the orientational and interpersonal changes described, and so they fail to modify significantly their calculus of ordinary property crime. In assessing their past criminal behavior these men use almost identical verbalizations: "They [police and the courts] could never get even." They use this description to support their contention that they have avoided arrest and prosecution for so many crimes that, even if they were caught in the future, the ledger books still would show an advantage for them. A man who shoplifts almost daily as a means of support had this to say:

Q: Have you ever thought that you were a good thief, or a good hustler?
A: Yeah, I am....
Q: What makes you think you're a good hustler?
A: 'Cause I *produce*.
Q: Yeah, but you've done a lot of time, too, haven't you?
A: Yeah, but considering, you know, in comparison, I ain't did that much. I think, if they gave me 199 years they couldn't get even.... They couldn't get even.

REFERENCES

Black, J. (1926). *You can't win*. New York: A. L. Burt.

Braley, M. (1976). *False starts*. New York: Penguin.

Hohimer, F. (1975). *The home invaders*. Chicago: Chicago Review Books.

Jansyn, L. R., Jr. (1966). Solidarity and delinquency in a street corner group. *American Sociological Review, 31*, 600–614.

Mack, J., & Kerner, H.-J. (1975). *The crime industry*. Lexington, MA: D. C. Heath.

Matza, D. (1964). *Delinquency and drift*. New York: John Wiley.

Parker, T., & Allerton, R. (1962). *The courage of his conviction*. London: Hutchinson.

Petersilia, J., Greenwood, P. W., & Lavin, M. (1978). *Criminal careers of habitual felons*. Washington, DC: National Institute of Justice.

Rettig, M., Torres, J., & Garrett, G. R. (1977). *Manny: A criminal addict's story*. Boston: Houghton Mifflin.

Quick, H. (1967). *Villain*. London: Jonathan Cape.

Short, J. F., & Strodtbeck, F. L. (1965). *Group processes and gang delinquency*. Chicago: University of Chicago Press.

Shover, N. (1971). *Burglary as an occupation*. Unpublished Ph.D. diss., University of Illinois, Urbana.

———. (1983). "The later stages of ordinary property offenders careers." Social Problems, 208–218.

Zimring, F. (1981). Kids, groups, and crime: Some implications of a well-known secret. *Journal of Criminal Law and Criminology, 72*, 867–885.

꙳

CHAPTER 26

Getting Out of the Life: Crime Desistance by Female Street Offenders

Ira Sommers, Deborah R. Baskin, and Jeffrey Fagan

This selection considers the role of life events and the relationship of cognitions and life situations to the desistance process. The authors are concerned with whether the social and psychological processes and the events leading up to their desistance from crime vary by gender. In other words, do men and women differ in the processes and events that lead to their decision to give up crime?

The authors constructed a sample of 30 women. To be included in the sample, a woman had to have had at least one official arrest for a violent street crime and have desisted from crime for at least two years prior to the study. Life history interviews were conducted by the first two authors. Each interview lasted approximately two hours.

The subjects had engaged in a wide range of criminal activities. Within the sample, 87% were addicted to crack, 63% had been involved in robberies, 60% had committed burglaries, 94% had sold drugs, and 47% had at some time been involved in prostitution. The authors found that the reasons for desistance from crime were remarkably similar to those found for men. The women in this study had begun to take the threat of incarceration seriously and attempted to reestablish links with conventional society while severing relationships in the deviant subculture.

Studies over the past decade have provided a great deal of information about the criminal careers of male offenders (see Blumstein et al., 1986, and Weiner & Wolfgang, 1989, for reviews). Unfortunately, much less is known about the initiation, escalation, and termination of criminal careers by female offenders. The general tendency to exclude female offenders from research on crime and delinquency may be due, at least in part, to the lower frequency and comparatively less

Source: Sommers, I., Baskin, D. R., & Fagan, J. (1994). Getting out of the life: Desistance by female street offenders. *Deviant Behavior, 15*(2), 125–149. Reprinted with permission.

serious nature of offending among women. Recent trends and studies, however, suggest that the omission of women may seriously bias both research and theory on crime.

Although a growing body of work on female crime has emerged within the last few years, much of this research continues to focus on what Daly and Chesney-Lind (1988) called generalizability and gender-ratio problems. The former concerns the degree to which traditional (i.e., male) theories of deviance and crime apply to women, and the latter focuses on what explains gender differences in rates and types of criminal activity. Although this article also examines women in crime, questions of inter- and intragender variability in crime are not specifically addressed. Instead, the aim of the paper is to describe the pathways out of deviance for a sample of women who have significantly invested themselves in criminal social worlds. To what extent are the social and psychological processes of stopping criminal behavior similar for men and women? Do the behavioral antecedents of such processes vary by gender? These questions remained unexplored.

Specifically, two main issues are addressed in this paper: (1) the role of life events in triggering the cessation process, and (2) the relationship between cognitive and life situation changes in the desistance process. First, the crime desistance literature is reviewed briefly. Second, the broader deviance literature is drawn upon to construct a social-psychological model of cessation. Then the model is evaluated using life history data from a sample of female offenders convicted of serious street crimes.

THE DESISTANCE PROCESS

The common themes in the literature on exiting deviant careers offer useful perspectives for developing a theory of cessation. The decision to stop deviant behavior appears to be preceded by a variety of factors, most of which are negative social sanctions or consequences. Health problems, difficulties with the law or with maintaining a current lifestyle, threats of other social sanctions from family or close relations, and a general rejection of the social world in which the behaviors thrive are often antecedents of the decision to quit. For some, religious conversions or immersion into alternative sociocultural settings with powerful norms (e.g., treatment ideology) provide paths for cessation (Mulvey & LaRosa, 1986; Stall & Biernacki, 1986)....

A model for understanding desistance from crime is presented below. Three stages characterize the cessation process: building resolve or discovering motivation to stop (i.e., socially disjunctive experiences), making and publicly disclosing the decision to stop, and maintaining the new behaviors and integrating into new social networks (Stall & Biernacki, 1986; Mulvey & Aber, 1988). These phases...describe three ideal-typical phases of desistance: "turning points" where offenders begin consciously to experience negative effects (socially disjunctive experiences); "active quitting," where they take steps to exit crime (public pronouncement); and "maintaining cessation" (identity transformation).

Stage 1: Catalysts for Change

Socially Disjunctive Experiences

- Hitting rock bottom
- Fear of death
- Tiredness
- Illness

Delayed Deterrence
- Increased probability of punishment
- Increased difficulty in doing time
- Increased severity of sanctions
- Increasing fear

Assessment
- Reappraisal of life and goals
- Psychic change

Decision
- Decision to quit and/or initial attempts at desistance
- Continuing possibility of criminal participation

Stage 2: Discontinuance
- Public pronouncement of decision to end criminal participation
- Claim to a new social identity

Stage 3: Maintenance of the Decision to Stop
- Ability to successfully renegotiate identity
- Support of significant others
- Integration into new social networks
- Ties to conventional roles
- Stabilization of new social identity

Stage 1: Catalysts for Change

When external conditions change and reduce the rewards of deviant behavior, motivation may build to end criminal involvement. That process, and the resulting decision, seem to be associated with two related conditions: a series of negative, aversive, unpleasant experiences with criminal behavior, or corollary situations where the positive rewards, status, or gratification from crime are reduced. Shover and Thompson's (1992) research suggests that the probability of desistance from criminal participation increases as expectations for achieving rewards (e.g., friends, money, autonomy) via crime decrease and that changes in expectations are age-related. Shover (1983) contended that the daily routines of managing criminal involvement become tiring and burdensome to aging offenders. Consequently, the allure of crime diminishes as offenders get older. Aging may also increase the perceived formal risk of criminal participation. Cusson and

Pinsonneault (1986, 76) posited that "with age, criminals raise their estimates of the certainty of punishment." Fear of reimprisonment, fear of longer sentences, and the increasing difficulty of "doing time" have often been reported by investigators who have explored desistance.

Stage 2: Discontinuance

The second stage of the model begins with the public announcement that the offender has decided to end her criminal participation. Such an announcement forces the start of a process of renegotiation of the offender's social identity (Stall & Biernacki, 1986). After this announcement, the offender must not only cope with the instrumental aspects (e.g., financial) of her life but must also begin to redefine important emotional and social relationships that are influenced by or predicated upon criminal behavior.

Leaving a deviant subculture is difficult. Biernacki (1986) noted the exclusiveness of the social involvements maintained by former addicts during initial stages of abstinence. With social embedment comes the gratification of social acceptance and identity. The decision to end a behavior that is socially determined and supported implies withdrawal of the social gratification it brings. Thus, the more deeply embedded in a criminal social context, the more dependent the offender is on that social world for her primary sources of approval and social definition.

The responses by social control agents, family members, and peer supporters to further criminal participation are critical to shaping the outcome of discontinuance. New social and emotional worlds to replace the old ones may strengthen the decision to stop. Adler (1992) found that outside associations and involvements provide a critical bridge back into society for dealers who have decided to leave the drug subculture. With discontinuance comes the difficult work of identity transformations (Biernacki, 1986) and establishing new social definitions of behavior and relationships to reinforce them.

Stage 3: Maintenance

Following the initial stages of discontinuance, strategies to avoid a return to crime build on the strategies first used to break from a lengthy pattern of criminal participation: further integration into a noncriminal identity and social world and maintenance of this new identity. Maintenance depends in part on replacing deviant networks of peers and associates with supports that both censure criminal participation and approve of new nondeviant beliefs. Treatment interventions (e.g., drug treatment, social service programs) are important sources of alternative social supports to maintain a noncriminal lifestyle. In other words, maintenance depends on immersion into a social world where criminal behavior meets immediately with strong formal and informal sanctions.

Despite efforts to maintain noncriminal involvement, desistance is likely to be episodic, with occasional relapses interspersed with lengthening of lulls in criminal activity. Le Blanc and Frechette (1989) proposed the possibility that criminal activity slows down before coming to an end and that this slowing-down process becomes apparent in three ways: deceleration, specialization, and reaching a ceiling. Thus, before stopping criminal activity, the offender gradually acts out less frequently, limits the variety of crimes more and more, and ceases increasing the seriousness of criminal involvement.

Age is a critical variable in desistance research, regardless of whether it is associated with maturation or similar developmental concepts. Cessation is part of a social-psychological transformation for the offender. A strategy to stabilize the transition to a noncriminal lifestyle requires active use of supports to maintain the norms that have been substituted for the forces that supported criminal behavior in the past.

FINDINGS

Resolving to Stop

Despite its initial excitement and allure, the life of a street criminal is a hard one. A host of severe personal problems plague most street offenders and normally become progressively worse as their careers continue. In the present study, the women's lives were dominated by a powerful, often incapacitating, need for drugs. Consequently, economic problems were the most frequent complaint voiced by the respondents. Savings were quickly exhausted, and the culture of addiction justified virtually any means to get money to support their habits. For the majority of the women, the problem of maintaining an addiction took precedence over other interests and participation in other social worlds.

People the respondents associated with, their primary reference group, were involved in illicit behaviors. Over time, the women in the study became further enmeshed in deviance and further alienated, both socially and psychologically, from conventional life. The women's lives became bereft of conventional involvements, obligations, and responsibilities. The excitement at the lifestyle that may have characterized their early criminal career phase gave way to a much more grave daily existence.

Thus, the women in our study could not and did not simply cease their deviant acts by "drifting" (Matza, 1964) back toward conventional norms, values, and lifestyles. Unlike many of Waldorf's (1983) heroin addicts who drifted away from heroin without conscious effort, all of the women in our study made a conscious decision to stop. In short, Matza's (1964) concept of drift did not provide a useful framework for understanding our respondents' exit from crime.

The following accounts illustrate the uncertainty and vulnerability of street life for the women in our sample. Denise, a 33-year-old black woman, has participated in a wide range of street crimes including burglary, robbery, assault, and drug dealing. She began dealing drugs when she was 14 and was herself using cocaine on a regular basis by age 19.

> I was in a lot of fights: So I had fights over, uh, drugs, or, you know, just manipulation. There's a lot of manipulation in that life. Everybody's tryin' to get over.

Everybody will stab you in your back, you know. Nobody gives a fuck about the next person, you know. It's just when you want it, you want it. You know, when you want that drug, you know, you want that drug. There's a lot of lyin', a lot of manipulation. It's, it's, it's crazy!

Gazella, a 38-year-old Hispanic woman, had been involved in crime for 22 years when we interviewed her.

I'm 38 years old. I ain't no young woman no more, man. Drugs have changed, lifestyles have changed. Kids are killing you now for turf. Yeah, turf, and I was destroyin' myself. I was miserable. I was…I was gettin' high all the time to stay up to keep the business going, and it was really nobody I could trust.

Additional illustrations of the exigencies of street life are provided by April and Stephanie. April is a 25-year-old black woman who had been involved in crime since she was 11.

I wasn't eating. Sometimes I wouldn't eat for two or three days. And I would…a lot of times I wouldn't have the time, or I wouldn't want to spend the money to eat—I've got to use it to get high.

Stephanie, a 27-year-old black woman, had used and sold crack for five years when we interviewed her.

I knew that, uh, I was gonna get killed out here. I wasn't havin' no respect for myself. No one else was respecting me. Every relationship I got into, as long as I did drugs, it was gonna be constant disrespect involved, and it come…to the point of me gettin' killed.

When the spiral down finally reached its lowest point, the women were over-whelmed by a sense of personal despair. In reporting the early stages of this period of despair, the respondents consistently voiced two themes: the futility of their lives and their isolation.

Barbara, a 31-year-old black woman, began using crack when she was 23. By age 25, Barbara had lost her job at the Board of Education and was involved in bur-glary and robbery. Her account is typical of the despair the women in our sample eventually experienced.

The fact that my family didn't trust me anymore, and the way that my daughter was looking at me, and, uh, my mother wouldn't let me in her house any more, and I was sleepin' on the trains. And I was sleepin' on the beaches in the summer-time. And I was really frightened. I was real scared of the fact that I had to sleep on the train. And, uh, I had to wash up in the Port Authority.

The spiral down for Gazella also resulted in her living on the streets.

I didn't have a place to live. My kids had been taken away from me. You know, constantly being harassed like three days out of the week by the Tactical Narcotics Team [police]. I didn't want to be bothered with people. I was gettin' tired of the lyin', schemin', you know, stayin' in abandoned buildings.

Alicia, a 29-year-old Hispanic woman, became involved in street violence at age 12. She commented on the personal isolation that was a consequence of her involvement in crime:

> When I started getting involved in crime, you know, and drugs, the friends that I had, even my family, I stayed away from them, you know. You know how you look bad and you feel bad, and you just don't want those people to see you like you are. So I avoided seeing them.

For some, the emotional depth of the rock-bottom crisis was felt as a sense of mortification. The women felt as if they had nowhere to turn to salvage a sense of well-being or self-worth. Suicide was considered a better alternative than remaining in such an undesirable social and psychological state. Denise is one example:

> I ran into a girl who I went to school with that works on Wall Street. And I compared her life to mine and it was, like, miserable. And I just wanted out. I wanted a new life. I was tired, I was run down, looking bad. I got out by smashing myself through a sixth-floor window. Then I went to the psychiatric ward and I met this real nice doctor, and we talked every day. She fought to keep me in the hospital because she felt I wouldn't survive. She believed in me. And she talked me into going into a drug program.

Marginalization from family, friends, children, and work—in short, the loss of traditional life structures—left the women vulnerable to chaotic street conditions. After initially being overwhelmed by despair, the women began to question and reevaluate basic assumptions about their identities and their social construction of the world. Like Shover's (1983) male property offenders, the women also began to view the criminal justice system as "an imposing accumulation of aggravations and deprivations" (p. 212). They grew tired of the street experiences and the problems and consequences of criminal involvement.

Many of the women acknowledged that, with age, it is more difficult to do time and that the fear of incurring a long prison sentence the next time influenced their decision to stop.

Cusson and Pinsonneault (1986) made the same observation with male robbers. Gazella, April, and Denise, quoted earlier, recall:

> First of all, when I was in prison I was, like, I was so humiliated. At my age [38] I was really kind of embarrassed, but I knew that was the lifestyle that I was leadin'. And people I used to talk to would tell me, well, you could do this, and you don't have to get busted. But then I started thinking, why are all these people here? So it doesn't, you know, really work. So I came home, and I did go back to selling again, but, you know, I knew I was on probation. And I didn't want to do no more time. (Gazella)
>
> Jail, being in jail. The environment, having my freedom taken away. I saw myself keep repeating the same pattern, and I didn't want to do that. Uh, I had missed my daughter. See, being in jail that long period of time, I was able to detox. And when I detoxed, I kind of like had a clear sense of thinking, and that's when I came to the realization that, uh, this is not working for me. (April)

> I saw the person that I was dealing with—my partner—I saw her go upstate to Bedford for two to four years. I didn't want to deal with it. I didn't want to go. Bedford is a prison, women's prison. And I couldn't see myself givin' up two years of my life for something that I knew I could change in another way. (Denise)

As can be seen from the above, the influence of punishment on these women was due to their belief that if they continued to be involved in crime, they would be apprehended, convicted, and incarcerated.

For many of the women, it was the stresses of street life and the fear of dying on the streets that motivated their decision to quit the criminal life. Darlene, a 25-year-old black woman, recalled the stress associated with the latter stage of her career selling drugs:

> The simple fact is that I really, I thought that I would die out there. I thought that someone would kill me out there and I would be killed; I had a fear of being on the front page one day and being in the newspaper dying. I wanted to live, and I didn't just want to exist.

Sonya, a 27-year-old Hispanic woman, provided an account of what daily life was like on the streets:

> You get tired of bein' tired, you know. I got tired of hustlin', you know. I got tired of livin' the way I was livin', you know. Due to your body, your body, mentally, emotionally, you know. Everybody's tryin' to get over. Everybody will stab you in your back. Nobody gives a fuck about the next person. And I used to have people talkin' to me, "You know, you're not a bad-lookin' girl. You know, why you don't get yourself together."

Perhaps even more important, the women felt that they had wasted time. They became acutely aware of time as a diminishing resource (Shover, 1983). They reported that they saw themselves going nowhere. They had arrived at a point where crime seemed senseless, and their lives had reached a dead end. Implicit in this assessment was the belief that gaining a longer-range perspective on one's life was a first step in changing. Such deliberations develop as a result of "socially disjunctive experiences" that cause the offender to experience social stress, feelings of alienation, and dissatisfaction with her present identity (Ray, 1961).

Breaking Away from the Life

Forming a commitment to change is only the first step toward the termination of a criminal career. The offender enters a period that has been characterized as a "running struggle" with problems of social identity (Ray, 1961, p. 136). Successful desisters must work to clarify and strengthen their nondeviant identity and redefine their street experience in terms more compatible with a conventional lifestyle. The second stage of the desistance process begins with the public announcement or "certification" (Meisenhelder, 1977, p. 329) that the offender has decided to end her deviant behavior. After this announcement, the offender must begin to redefine economic, social, and emotional relationships that were based on a deviant street subculture.

The time following the announcement was generally a period of ambivalence and crisis for the study participants, because so much of their lives revolved around street life and because they had, at best, weak associations with the conventional world. Many of the women remembered the uncertainty they felt and the social dilemmas they faced after they decided to stop their involvement in crime.

> I went and looked up my friends and to see what was doing, and my girlfriend Mia was like, she was gettin' paid. And I was livin' on a $60 stipend. And I wasn't with it. Mia was good to me, she always kept money in my pocket when I came home. I would walk into her closet and change into clothes that I'm more accustomed to. She started calling me Pen again. She stopped calling me Denise. And I would ride with her knowing that she had a gun or a package in the car. But I wouldn't touch nothin'. But that was my rationale. As long as I don't fuck with nothin'. Yeah, she was like, I can give you a grand and get you started. I said, I know you can, but I can't. She said, I can give you a grand, and she kept telling me that over and over; and I wasn't that far from taking the grand and getting started again. (Denise)

> After I decided to change, I went to a party with my friend. And people was around me, and they was drinkin' and stuff, and I didn't want to drink. I don't have the urge of drinking. If anything, it would be smokin' crack. And when I left the party, I felt like I was missing something—like something was missing. And it was the fact that I wasn't gettin' high. But I know the consequences of it. If I take a drink, I'm gonna smoke crack. If I, uh, sniff some blow, I'm gonna smoke crack. I might do some things like rob a store or something stupid and go to jail. So I don't want to put myself in that position. (Barbara)

At this stage of their transition, the women had to decide how to establish and maintain conventional relationships and what to do with themselves and their lives. Few of the women had maintained good relationships with people who were not involved in crime and drugs. Given this situation, the women had to seek alternatives to their present situation.

The large majority of study participants were aided in their social reintegration by outside help. These respondents sought formal treatment of some kind, typically residential drug treatment, to provide structure, social support, and a pathway to behavioral change. The women perceived clearly the need to remove themselves from the "scene" to meet new friends, and to begin the process of identity reformation. The following account by Alicia typifies the importance of a "geographic" cure:

> I love to get high, you know, and I love the way crack makes me feel. I knew that I needed long-term, I knew that I needed to go somewhere. All away from everything, and I just needed to away get from everything. And I couldn't deal with responsibility at all. And, uh, I was just so ashamed of the way that I had, you know, became and the person that I became that I just wanted to start over again.

Social avoidance strategies were common to all attempts at stopping. When the women removed themselves from their old world and old locations, involvement in crime and drugs was more difficult.

> Yeah, I go home, but I don't, I don't socialize with the people. I don't even speak to anybody really. I go and I come. I don't go to the areas that I used to be in. I don't go there anymore. I don't walk down the same blocks I used to walk down. I always take different locations. (April)
>
> I miss the fast money; otherwise, I don't miss my old life. I get support from my positive friends, and in the program. I talk about how I felt being around my old associates, seeing them, you know, going back to my old neighborhood. It's hard to deal with, I have to push away. (Denise)

Maintaining a Conventional Life

Desisters have little chance of staying out of the life for an extended period of time if they stay in the social world of crime and addiction. They must rebuild and maintain a network of primary relations who accept and support their nondeviant identity if they are to be successful (the third stage of this model). This is no easy task, since in most cases the desisters have alienated their old nondeviant primary relations.

To a great extent, the women in this study most resemble religious converts in their attempts to establish and maintain support networks that validate their new sense of self. Treatment programs not only provide a ready-made primary group for desisters, but also a well-established pervasive identity (Travisano, 1970), that of ex-con and/or ex-addict, that informs the women's view of themselves in a variety of interactions. Reminders of "spoiled identities" (Goffman, 1963) such as criminal, "con," and "junkie" serve as a constant reference point for new experiences and keep salient the ideology of conventional living (Faupel, 1991). Perhaps most important, these programs provide the women with an alternative basis for life structure—one that is devoid of crime, drugs, and other subcultural elements.

The successful treatment program, however, is one that ultimately facilitates dissociation from the program and promotes independent living. Dissociation from programs to participate in conventional living requires association, or reintegration, with conventional society. Friends and educational and occupational roles helped study participants reaffirm their noncriminal identities and bond themselves to conventional lifestyles. Barbara described the assistance she receives from friends and treatment groups:

> A bunch of friends that always confronts me on what I'm doin' and where I'm goin', and they just want the best for me. And none of them use drugs. I go to a lot, like, outside support groups, you know. They help me have more confidence in myself. I have new friends now. Some of them are in treatment. Some have always been straight. They know. You know, they glad, you know, when I see them.

In the course of experiencing relationships with conventional others and participating in conventional roles, the women developed a strong social-psychological commitment not to return to crime and drug use. These commitments most often revolved around renewed affiliations with their children, relationships with new friends, and the acquisition of educational and vocational skills. The social relationships, interests, and investments that develop in the course of desistance reflect the gradual emergence of new identities. Such stakes in conventional identity form the social-psychological context within which control and desistance are possible (Waldorf, Reinerman, & Murphy, 1991).

In short, the women in the study developed a stake in their new lives that was incompatible with street life. This new stake served as a wedge to help maintain the separation of the women from the world of the streets (Biernacki, 1986). The desire to maintain one's sense of self was an important incentive for avoiding return to crime.

> I like the fact that I have my respect back. I like the fact that, uh, my daughter trusts me again. And my mother don't mind leavin' me in the house, and she don't have to worry that when she come in, her TV might be gone. (Alicia)
>
> I have new friends. I have my children back in my life. I have my education. It keeps me straight. I can't forget where I came from because I get scared to go back. I don't want to hurt nobody. I just want to live a normal life. (Barbara)

Janelle, a 22-year-old black woman, started dealing drugs and carrying a .38-caliber gun when she was 15. She described the ongoing tension between staying straight and returning to her old social world:

> It's hard, it's hard stayin' on the right track. But letting myself know that I'm worth more. I don't have to go in a store today and steal anything. I don't deserve that. I don't deserve to make myself feel really bad. Then, once again, I would be steppin' back and feel that this is all I can do.

Overall, the success of identity transformations hinges on the women's abilities to establish and maintain commitments and involvements in conventional aspects of life. As the women began to feel accepted and trusted within some conventional social circles, their determination to exit from crime was strengthened, as were their social and personal identities as noncriminals.

DISCUSSION

The primary purpose of this study was to describe—from the offenders' perspective—how women embedded in criminal street subcultures could end their deviance. Desistance appears to be a process as complex and lengthy as that of initial involvement. It was interesting to find that some of the key concepts in initiation of deviance—social bond, differential association, deterrence, age—were important in our analysis. We saw the aging offender take the threat of punishment seriously, reestablish links with conventional society, and sever association with subcultural street elements.

Our research supports Adler's (1992) finding that shame plays a limited role in the decision to return to conventional life for individuals who are entrenched in deviant subcultures. Rather, they exit deviance because they have evolved through the typical phases of their deviant careers.

In the present study, we found that the decision to give up crime was triggered by a shock of some sort (i.e., a socially disjunctive experience), by a delayed deterrence process, or both. The women then entered a period of crisis. Anxious and dissatisfied, they took stock of their lives and criminal activity. They arrived at a point where their way of life seemed senseless. Having made this assessment, the women then worked to clarify and strengthen their nondeviant identities. This phase began with the reevaluation of life goals and the public announcement of their decision to end involvement in crime. Once the decision to quit was made, the women turned to relationships that had not been ruined by their deviance, or they created new relationships. The final stage, maintaining cessation, involved integration into a nondeviant lifestyle. This meant restructuring the entire pattern of their lives (i.e., primary relationships, daily routines, social situations). For most women, treatment groups provided the continuing support needed to maintain a nondeviant status.

The change processes and turning points described by the women in the present research were quite similar to those reported by men in previous studies (Shover, 1983; Shover, 1985; Cusson & Pinsonneault, 1986). Collectively, these findings suggest that desistance is a pragmatically constructed project of action created by the individual within a given social context. Turning points occur as "part of a process over time and not as a dramatic lasting change that takes place at any one time" (Pickles & Rutter, 1991, p. 134). Thus, the return to conventional life occurs more because of "push" than "pull" factors (Adler, 1992), because the career of involvement in crime moves offenders beyond the point at which they find it enjoyable to the point at which it is debilitating and anxiety provoking.

Considering the narrow confines of our empirical data, it is hardly necessary to point out the limits of generalizability. Our analysis refers to the woman deeply involved in crime and immersed in a street subculture who finds the strength and resources to change her way of life. The fact that all the women in this study experienced a long period of personal deterioration and a "rock-bottom" experience before they were able to exit crime does not justify a conclusion that this process occurs with all offenders. Undoubtedly, there are other scenarios (e.g., the occasional offender who drifts in and out of crime, the offender who stops when criminal involvement conflicts with commitments to conventional life, the battered woman who kills) in which the question of desistance does not arise. Hence, there is a need to conceptualize and measure the objective and subjective elements of change among various male and female offender subgroups. Furthermore, the evidence presented here does not warrant the conclusion that none of the women ever renewed their involvement in crime. Because the study materials consist of retrospective information, with all its attendant problems, we cannot state with certainty whether desistance from crime is permanent. Still, it is also clear that these women broke their pattern of involvement in crime for substantial lengths of time and have substantially changed their lives.

REFERENCES

Adler, P. (1992). The "post" phase of deviant careers: Reintegrating traffickers. *Deviant Behavior, 13,* 103–126.

Biernacki, P. A. (1986). *Pathways from heroin addiction: Recovery without treatment.* Philadelphia: Temple University Press.

Blumstein, A., Cohen, J., Roth, J. A., & Visher, C. A. (1986). *Careers and career criminals.* Washington, DC: National Academy Press.

Cusson, M., & Pinsonneault, P. (1986). The decision to give up crime. In D. Cornish & R. Clarke (Eds.), *The reasoning criminal: Rational choice perspectives on offending.* New York: Springer-Verlag, 72–82.

Daly, K., & Chesney-Lind, M. (1988). Feminism and criminology. *Justice Quarterly, 5,* 101–143.

Faupel, C. (1991). *Shooting dope: Career patterns of hard-core heroin users.* Gainesville: University of Florida Press.

Goffman, E. (1963). *Stigma: Notes on the management of spoiled identity.* Englewood Cliffs, NJ: Prentice-Hall.

Le Blanc, M., & Frechette, M. (1989). *Male criminal activity from childhood through youth: Multilevel and developmental perspective.* New York: Springer-Verlag.

Matza, D. (1964). *Delinquency and drift.* New York: Wiley.

Meisenhelder, T. (1977). An exploratory study of exiting from criminal careers. *Criminology, 15,* 319–334.

Mulvey, E., & Aber, M. (1988). "Growing out" of delinquency: Development and desistance.In R. L. Jenkins & W. Brown (Eds.), *The abandonment of delinquent behavior: Promotingthe turnaround.* New York: Prager.

Mulvey, E. P., & LaRosa, J. F. (1986). Delinquency cessation and adolescent development: Preliminary data. *American Journal of Orthopsychiatry, 56,* 212–224.

Pickles, A., & Rutter, M. (1991). Statistical and conceptual models of "turning points" in developmental processes. In D. Magnusson, L. Bergman, G. Rudinger, & B. Torestad (Eds.), *Problems and methods in longitudinal research: Stability and change* (pp. 110–136). New York: Cambridge University Press.

Ray, M. (1961). The cycle of abstinence and relapse among heroin addicts. *Social Problems, 9,* 132–140.

Shover, N. (1983). The latter stages of ordinary property offenders' careers. *Social Problems, 31,* 208–218.

———. (1985). *Aging criminals.* Newbury Park, CA: Sage.

Shover, N., & Thompson, C. (1992). Age, differential expectations, and crime desistance. *Criminology, 30,* 89–104.

Stall, R., & Biernacki, P. (1986). Spontaneous remission from the problematic use of substances: An inductive model derived from a comparative analysis of the alcohol, opiate, tobacco, and food/obesity literatures. *International Journal of the Addictions, 2,* 1–23.

Travisano, R. (1970). Alteration and conversion as qualitatively different transformations." In G. Stone & H. Farberman (Eds.), *Social psychology through symbolic interaction* (pp. 594–605). Boston: Ginn-Blaisdell.

Waldorf, D. (1983). Natural recovery from opiate addiction: Some social psychological processes of untreated recovery. *Journal of Drug Issues, 13*, 237–280.

Waldorf, D., Reinerman, C., & Murphy, S. (1991). *Cocaine changes*. Philadelphia: Temple University Press.

Weiner, N., & Wolfgang, M. E. (1989). *Violent crime, violent criminals*. Newbury Park, CA: Sage.